Susan La Rue

Alvira L. Irby

Summer - 1961

HCJ

5 25

A

History

OF

THE South

Francis Butler Simkins

A
History
OF
THE South

NEW YORK: ALFRED A. KNOPF

1 9 5 9

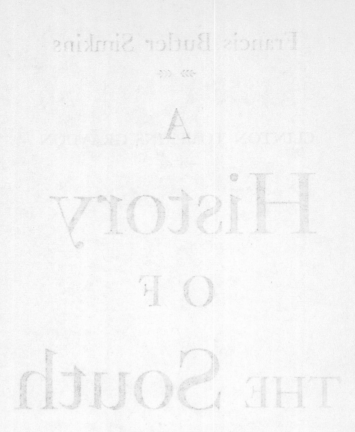

L. C. Catalog Card Number: 52–8516

THIS IS A BORZOI BOOK
PUBLISHED BY ALFRED A. KNOPF, INC.

Originally published in 1947 as THE SOUTH OLD AND NEW: A HISTORY 1820–1947. Reprinted three times.
Second edition, revised, enlarged, reset, and printed from new plates, 1953.
Second printing of Second Edition, April 1956.
Reprinted 1958, 1959

TO

CLINTON TOMPKINS GRAYDON

≫ ≪

Preface

⇒⇒⇒-⇒⇒⇒-⇒⇒⇒-⇒⇒⇒-⇒⇒⇒-⇒⇒⇒-⇒⇒⇒-⇒⇒⇒-⇒⇒⇒-⇒⇒⇒-⇒⇒⇒-⇒⇒⇒-⇒⇒⇒-⇒⇒⇒-⇒⇒⇒-⇒⇒⇒-⇒⇒⇒-⇒⇒⇒-⇒⇒⇒-⇒⇒⇒

I DO NOT ATTEMPT to emphasize here the contributions of the South to the history of the United States. I propose instead to stress those political and social traits that make the region between the Potomac and the Rio Grande a cultural province conscious of its identity. For this reason my narrative gives more space to the 132 years since 1820 than to the 213 years between the settlement at Jamestown and the events of 1820. It was in 1820 that the Negro question, in the form of the slavery controversy, first appeared as a political issue in the full-dress Congressional debate that resulted in the Missouri Compromise. The projection of the race issue into a forum to which Americans always listen created instant and lasting sectional awareness. The South was made to realize that it had practices and ambitions that set it apart from the other sections of the country.

"To write of the South when there was no South is a task not without difficulties," says a historian of the section's Colonial period.[1] This author demonstrates that the first settlers along the Southern Atlantic coast thought of themselves as Englishmen and not as Southerners or even as Americans. It was not until the fifty years after the American Revolution had made them conscious of their Americanism that they became conscious of their Southernism. The struggles in which Southerners participated before 1820, with transitory exceptions, did not involve the defense of institutions peculiarly Southern. Statesmen of the Southern Atlantic area of that period who contributed immeasurably to the building of the nation—Nathaniel Bacon, George

[1] Wesley Frank Craven, *The Southern Colonies in the Seventeenth Century*, p. xiii.

((vii))

Washington, Thomas Jefferson, James Madison, and John Marshall—
were more Virginian or American than Southern.

Nevertheless a narrative that attempts to explain the full background of the region cannot ignore the years before 1820. Factors in
the structure of Southern society before that date made the later regional consciousness possible. It was in the Colonial period that slavery
took root. It was then that plantation life with its ideals of social stability, aristocratic distinctions, and rural worth had its origin. The
Southern talent for politics had its beginning among the Colonial vestrymen and assemblymen. The Southern common man with his pride
of caste and possessions is a descendant of the Colonial yeoman farmer.
The religious inclinations of most Southerners today have Colonial
origins. It was then that the Episcopal and Presbyterian churches won
their upper-class status and that the Baptist and Methodist churches
began their successful efforts to make Christians out of middle-class
Southerners.

Moreover, in the Colonial and Revolutionary periods ideals were
established through which Southerners of the post-Civil War period
could aspire to make their region no longer the South in the perverse
sense of slavery, race prejudice, and sectional animosities. They could
regard the South of the Cotton Kingdom and the proslavery argument
as an unhappy interlude that hindered but did not stifle the promises
of an earlier South of small farms, diversified occupations, nationalism,
religious freedom, and other achievements dear to present-day progressives. Despite the shadow of the ante-bellum past, today they accept
with pride aspects of the American creed of liberty and equality
enunciated by their Colonial and Revolutionary fathers.

More than half of this book is given to the years since the Civil War.
The New South is emphasized because for the most part it has been
neglected by the historians. Another reason for concentration on the
more recent period is to show that, despite its assimilation of national
ideals and techniques, it survives as a regional entity as distinct in many
respects as the Old South.

It is of course difficult to establish this regional entity distinctly
enough to satisfy those who wish a precise correlation of the statistics
presented in a book of this type. Usually the South is considered the
region between the Potomac and the Ohio on one side and the Rio
Grande and the plains of the Southwest on the other. Actually it has
been a region of fluctuating borders. Fifteen states had slavery, but only
eleven joined in the Confederacy, and in these eleven there were important non-Confederate elements. Today seventeen states and the
District of Columbia have race segregation in schools, twenty-nine
prohibit the intermarriage of the races, cotton is grown in California,

the Southern Baptists are active in states as far north as Washington and Oregon, and in Chicago and New York there are so many Southerners of both races that these cities have many of the characteristics of Richmond and Memphis. At the same time the West has imposed itself to such a degree upon Texas, Arkansas, and Oklahoma, and the North has imposed itself to such a degree upon Kentucky, Maryland, and Florida, that there are doubts about the true Southern character of those states.

The South is an attitude of mind and a way of behavior just as much as it is a territory. This book is an account of the development of that attitude of mind as well as a history of the territory in which it had its greatest fulfillment.

FRANCIS BUTLER SIMKINS

Farmville, Virginia

Contents

Exam. *pp. 1 - 152.*

((xi))

CONTENTS

Illustrations

((xiii))

A
History
OF
THE South

CHAPTER I

The Land and the Tradition

∙⇒⇒⇒⇒⇒⇒⇒⇒⇒⇒⇒⇒⇒⇒⇒⇒⇒⇒⇒⇒⇒⇒⇒⇒⇒⇒⇐⇐⇐⇐⇐⇐⇐⇐⇐⇐⇐⇐⇐⇐⇐⇐⇐⇐⇐⇐⇐⇐∙

FOR SEVERAL hundred years there has been a section of the United States known as the South. This section has never lacked a culture as distinctive as its area or its climate. Political, social, and even psychological variations have marked it off from other sections of the country almost as sharply as one European nation is distinguished from another.

How can we explain the common features of the states extending from Maryland south and west to Texas and Arkansas? Climate is one explanation. In the South, winter is neither long nor very cold; in summer for fifty afternoons the temperature climbs to ninety degrees in the shade; throughout the year there is great humidity, more sunshine, and less wind than elsewhere in the United States. At certain seasons there are torrential rains, and along the Gulf of Mexico the growing season lasts nine months. These "imprints from sun, rain and wind" have exerted gross as well as subtle influences. Long, hot seasons favored the creation of kingdoms of tobacco, cotton, rice, and sugar, slowed the tempo of living and of speech, promoted outdoor life, modified architecture to make indoor living cooler, and encouraged the employment of Negroes on the land. The poorer soils, when eroded and leached by heavy rains, gave white and black alike excuse for poverty.

Yet the South is so varied in topography and soil that one can well say, "History, not geography made the solid South." [1] The section is not separated from the rest of the United States by mountain barriers. Instead it is itself cut up into parts by mountain ranges and rivers which divide the land into plains and valleys that unite with similar areas in the North. Thus the South is composed of many re-

[1] Rupert B. Vance, *Human Geography of the South*, pp. 22, 351.

gions: coastal plains facing the Atlantic Ocean and the Gulf of Mexico; the red-soiled Piedmont; highlands of ridges, valleys, and a veritable chaos of high mountains in North Carolina and Tennessee; areas of bluegrass, black prairies, and clay hills beyond these mountains; bluffs, flood plains, bayous, and delta lands along the Mississippi River; and beyond the great river—in Louisiana, Arkansas, and Texas—plains, black waxy soils, the Ozark Mountains, and stretches of land almost as arid as a desert.[2] So much variety of terrain makes the South a section of many regions.

To explain the solidarity of the South in terms of economic or social forces likewise presents many difficulties. The section has never possessed any commercial, political, industrial, or intellectual capitals of its own, but has followed the leadership of New York and other cities outside its borders. Moreover, nothing in the racial composition of its first white settlers distinguished them from Colonial Americans who settled elsewhere. English, Scotch-Irish, German, and other nationalities were represented among the people of the Southern colonies in about the same proportions as in all parts of English America.

Noting these facts, Ulrich B. Phillips reached the conclusion that white supremacy was "the central theme" of Southern history. In the presence of large masses of Negroes, the white people developed a superior and unique attitude toward the other race "in the interest of orderly government and the maintenance of Caucasian civilization." Their attitude, according to Phillips, is the essence of Southernism; abolish it and the South would be only a geographical part of the United States.[3]

The most remarkable manifestation of white supremacy is that the Southern white race has been able to keep itself free of any recognizable degree of Negro blood during the 333 years in which the African has lived in its midst. Miscegenation has been frequent, but the offspring of such union has almost invariably been classed as Negro.

To white supremacy Avery O. Craven has added another explanation of Southernism—the prevalence of the country-gentleman ideal, a pattern of society borrowed from the English, justified by the physiocratic philosophy of the French, and taking root naturally in the agricultural South.[4] Southernism has also been explained in more exalted terms. John Crowe Ransom regards it as the creation, by men of the Old South, of the ideal of a conservative civilization which they wished to preserve. Rather than adopt the progressive culture of the North,

[2] Avery O. Craven, *The Coming of the Civil War*, p. 19.
[3] "The Central Theme of Southern History," *The Course of the South to Secession*, p. 152.
[4] *The Repressible Conflict*, pp. 14–15.

Haiti, Brazil and W.I. islands - their
inhabitants have intermingled with Negro.
. THE LAND AND THE TRADITION . . 5
Spanish and Portuguese don't mind mixing because
they've
been in
contact
....

these Southerners desired to "put the surplus of energy in the free life
of the mind," giving scope to the refinements of a settled life in rural
comfort.[5]

By others, Southernism has been variously attributed to the fundamental piety of the people, their emphasis on home life, the peculiarities
of their food, the survival of rural ways even in growing cities, and a
powerful nativism largely untouched by the stream of foreign immigration that has influenced the remainder of the United States during the past hundred years. All would probably agree with James G.
Randall,[6] who suggests that Southernism is a reality too elusive to be
explained completely in terms of historical origins and cultural conditions. It is something like a song or an emotion. "Poets have done
better," remarks Randall, "in expressing the oneness of the South than
historians in explaining it."

A wealth of factual and interpretative scholarship has described the
Old South as it contrasted with the Old North. There was the difference between the lands of Cavalier and Puritan, of slavery and freedom,
of agriculture and industry, of planter and small farmer, of static contentment and progressive aspirations. To all these differences the Civil
War has been ascribed. Contemporaries were aware of sectional diver-
gences. In 1856 one Southerner stated: "The North and the South are
two nations, made by their institutions, customs and habits of thought,
as distinct as the English and the French; and our annual meetings at
Washington are not Congresses to discuss the common interests, but
conventions, to contest antagonistic opinions and to proclaim mutual
grievances and utter hostile threats." [7]

The Old South of differences and contrasts was defeated at Appomattox. In its place was created the New South in which human
freedom and political unification were achieved and industrialization
and sectional reconciliation became aspirations. The South's central
problem since 1865 has been to adjust Southern standards, whether
political, industrial, or social, to those of the victorious North. The
most worth-while events in the annals of the section during that time
have been concerned with adjustments to the demands of Northern
progress. These adjustments have been happy experiences out of which
Southern leaders and people have gained much. The truth of these
contentions will be attested by the evidence presented in many chapters of this book.

It will be shown that during Reconstruction the South recognized

[5] John C. Ransom, "The South Defends Its Heritage," *Harpers Magazine*, CLIX,
108–18 (June, 1929).

[6] *The Civil War and Reconstruction*, pp. 3–4.

[7] *Charleston Mercury*, cited in Avery O. Craven, *The Repressible Conflict*, p. 28.

the supremacy of the Union, free labor, equality of all men before the law, and representation in legislative bodies according to population; as the result of Bourbon rule and agrarian revolt, national ideals of business success, industrial advance, and political democracy won victories over the heritage of the Old South; and the New South demonstrated in practice the New England-inspired concept of universal education. It will be shown, too, how imported liberal views of religion and science were accepted by college-bred leaders; how imported class alignments and recreational activities altered social life; how, in deference to the critical standards of metropolitan areas, the South created a literature that affronted its romantic pride; how, despite a painful sensitivity, it allowed the Negro to progress along lines consistent with Northern concepts of uplift; and how, with unreserved patriotism, Southerners fought in the battles of three national wars and their statesmen joined the councils of four national administrations. Because of these concessions to Northern standards, there is indeed some basis for the conclusion that by the 1930's the states of the former Confederacy had so far receded from the agrarianism and the sectionalism of 1861 that they were about to become a mere segment of a unified republic.

To justify this progression out of an unhappy past two groups of publicists arose. First were the champions of the New South movement of the 1880's and 1890's, led by Henry W. Grady, Walter Hines Page, and Jabez L. M. Curry. Without repudiating the heritage of the past, they demanded progress along lines of industrial development and liberal thinking. The second group were Southern liberals who made their views known in the 1920's and 1930's. Like Grady and his coadjutors, they drew from the South's past. In the name of a liberal tradition said to be inherently Southern, they assaulted religious orthodoxy, puritanism, demagoguery, rural conservatism, and other undesirable aspects of the contemporary scene. Edwin Mims, in *The Advancing South,* introduced the anticlerical tradition of the American Revolution as a defense against church authority that would stay the teaching of Darwin. In their studies of Andrew Johnson, George Fort Milton and Robert W. Winston found much that was genuinely Southern in a leader who opposed the Confederacy. Broadus Mitchell strengthened the advocacy of industrialism by praising William Gregg, an ante-bellum cotton manufacturer. Virginius Dabney traced Southern liberalism to antecedents reaching back to the eighteenth century, emphasizing Jefferson's fight against the Established Church, his antislavery principles, and his plans for public education. Clement Eaton found the roots of Southern liberalism in the post-Revolution planters, contrasting their deism and devotion to other aspects of eighteenth-century enlightenment with the Presbyterian orthodoxy and the proslavery agrar-

Virginians descended from the Cavaliers — this is a legend, really ((7. much the same as the average Mass. settler

ianism that have been accused of putting out the lights of progress in the 1830's.

Despite their professed fealty to the past, Southern liberals were modern enough to advocate state action in social and economic fields quite beyond the Jeffersonian concept of an agrarian society in which governmental action was reduced to the minimum. They believed in good roads, libraries, hospitals, school expansion, social legislation, and such material comforts as the common people in all progressive societies demand of their governments. Some of them—for example Thomas S. Stribling and Ellen Glasgow—frankly satirized and condemned the Southern tradition.

Advocates of the New South movement were not adequately answered by contemporaries. Little attention was paid to the protests of the anti-Yankee extremists Albert Taylor Bledsoe and Robert Lewis Dabney, who protested in the name of the old chivalry and religious conservatism. Responsible conservatives did not care to breast the liberal tide; more often than not they rendered lip service to it while violating in practice as much of it as suited their convenience. The liberalism of the next generation, however, was not received with such evasiveness.

In 1930 a group of twelve Southern Agrarians wrote *I'll Take My Stand: The South and the Agrarian Tradition,* a manifesto against Southern liberals. Under the more attractive name of regionalism, these writers attempted to reconcile the sectionalism of unhappy memory with the needs of their own time. Granting that the past was unrecoverable in its old forms, they disavowed the progressive outlook as unfit for Southern needs and as a betrayal of a worthy and congenial heritage. The true South they characterized as rural, conservative, stable, and religious. Inherited prejudices against Northerners and Negro equality were as warmly advocated as the modern school and religion —turned into sociology—were denounced. They believed that the South should revive its agrarian tradition and repudiate the industrial invasion as unsound economically and as deceptive in its humanitarian motivation. Like their opponents, they drew upon the past for precedents. In Thomas Jefferson they found justification of agrarianism and condemnation of the social welfare state. John C. Calhoun provided arguments for the protection of the minority states against a numerical majority. Like their opponents, however, Southern Agrarians recognized the need for contemporary adjustments. As they learned from Sinclair Lewis and others of the standardization that machinery forced upon regions adopting it, they were thankful that this development had been retarded in the South. They shared the disillusion of thoughtful people throughout the world following World War I, and saw no

The Plantation Tradition by Page.

~~Page~~ now the "keeper of the tomb" at W and L (former President of W and L)

good reason why they should favor a spirit of liberalism and progress that had failed to solve the problems of other regions. In returning to a conservative past they saw a means of escaping these difficulties.

Southern Agrarians attracted less attention than had the Southern liberals of the decade before. Many regarded them as harmless literary eccentrics who, indeed, found but a small audience in the Southern reading public, which was unwilling to depart from the habit of getting its literary pabulum from New York. Not to be read was the logical fate of intellectuals who extolled the unintellectual ruralism of the Southern tradition. Yet these writers regarded the conservative South as nearer realization than that progressive South praised by liberals. They understood that national standardization had not annihilated the fundamental differences of their beloved section. They knew that even though the modern Southerner joined Westerner and Northerner in adopting a common type of automobile, house, and clothes, he had not necessarily surrendered his distinctions of thought and emotions; that reading the same book and attending the same school did not necessarily eliminate provincial thinking. They understood that the conversion of many educated Southerners to the logic of liberalism did not mean that many converts were willing to put aside inherited habits in order to live according to the new logic. They knew, for example, that few of the many who wrote and talked against race prejudice were willing to suffer the inconvenience of violating customary racial barriers; that few of those who believed that the cause of liberalism would be promoted by having two political parties were willing to incur the displeasure of their conservative neighbors by joining on a local level any political party other than the Democratic.

The facts do not justify the claim that the history of North-South relations since 1865 has been a record of steady decline in intersectional asperities. There has been a series of ups and downs in a continuing battle between the forces making for sectional reconciliation and those making for sectional estrangement.

The let-us-have-peace sentiments at Appomattox were followed by the hates of Reconstruction. Indeed, the bitterness created by the Reconstruction attempt to give the Negro some share of the American dream of equality was more lasting than the bitterness created by the previous bloodshed. The good will created by the surrender of the North in 1877 on the Reconstruction issue was matched by the ill will created by the so-called Force bill of Congressman Henry C. Lodge in 1890 and by the disfranchising amendments to the Southern state constitutions. The intersectional and interracial friendship created by Booker T. Washington was dimmed by affronts to Southern standards of caste committed by Theodore Roosevelt and the muckrakers.

"hands across the bloody chasm

Jim Crow laws

Aristocrat well educated + etc. Mother from South – he a genuine Northerner

1884 Grover Cleveland, a Democrat, elected President.

Muckrakers – political writers who painted out the corruptness of American way of life.

THE LAND AND THE TRADITION

a Virginian and a Presbyterian

The sense of national pride engendered in Southern hearts by the election of Woodrow Wilson and the victories of World War I was followed by attacks on the South that have been characterized as "more abusive and unrelenting than anything the Southern states have experienced since the last Federal troops were withdrawn from their soil."[8] These were the Ku-Klux exposures, ridicule of Southern political and religious attitudes, and the uncovering of abuses of interracial justice. The good will between Franklin D. Roosevelt and the South was marred by legislative proposals that overrode the traditions of the section. The willingness of the South to bear its share of the crusade to impose American ideals of equality upon Japan and Germany was followed by the demand that the South apply these ideals to the Negro. An atmosphere of suspicion and alarm was created over Northern intentions as strong in 1952 as any time in the twentieth century.

Examination of various phases of the institutional life of the New South reveals a constantly recurring condition: despite changes which the catastrophe of 1865 made inevitable the distinctive culture of the section was never destroyed. In politics, to cite the most obvious example, to the suggestion that the Negro be given the equalities mentioned in the Declaration of Independence the South responded by reducing the race to political impotence. The opening since 1937 of the Democratic primaries to the Negroes by the federal courts effected a change more technical than actual. While there was a considerable increase in colored voters, the new voters merely won the privilege of ratifying procedures already determined by white majorities. An unchanging caste system generally prevented the Negro from becoming a candidate for office or from advocating policies contrary to the will of the whites.

Forces worked against the apparent progress made from rural stagnation to industrialization. People who moved from country to city or from farm to factory frequently did not surrender their rural ideals. In the South the country conquered the city as effectively as elsewhere the city had conquered the country. Invading Northern industrialism so adjusted itself to Southern traditions that it fastened on the section a new feudalism resembling that which had existed under slavery. Southern people as a whole kept their old-time religious beliefs despite the conversion of many among the more educated to an alien liberalism. The average Southerner remained orthodox, went to church more often, and showed little inclination to abate the religious separatism based on distinctions of race and of class that are characteristically Southern.

Although important concessions were made to the liberal spirit in

[8] Donald Davidson, *The Attack on Leviathan*, p. 315.

regard to the Negro, the South remained adamant in the matter of greatest importance. The bonds of caste by which the Negro was kept subordinate and underprivileged were weakened in few respects. Although universal education in the Northern sense was applied to both races, it was not used to mix or equalize the races. Textbooks written in the North gave an anti-Southern bias to instruction in history, literature, and speech; but this bias was offset by less formal and perhaps more effective indoctrination in local prejudices and ideals which survived the regimentation of the schools.

The South accepted Northern dictation in literary matters more completely than in other fields. A book, even one about the South and by a Southerner, won little attention from Southerners unless it was published in New York. No magazine of Southern origin was widely read. There is danger, however, of overemphasizing literary materials in measuring the outlook of a people, especially a people so nonliterary as those of the South. The section had a way of ignoring its critics and taking to heart only those writings that conformed to its conceits.

The modern Southerner shared the patriotic emotions which have gripped Americans from time to time. He accepted without reluctance material benefits offered by the federal government and northern industrialists, and he was as willing as other Americans to make sacrifices for his country. Yet he also cherished sectional prejudices and loyalties. A Southerner with traditional anti-Yankee feelings could yet be a complete jingoist. He could, with equal fervor and in almost the same breath, vilify his country's enemies and fellow Americans who were not Southerners. In his unguarded moments it was possible for him to confuse the much-belabored Yankee with Spaniard, German, Japanese, or other victims of national wrath. Yet he could, as he did during the Presidential canvass of 1928, reconcile sectional and national prejudices, using, for example, the Southern predilection against Negroes, the city-bred, the liquor-drinkers, and the non-Protestants, to support nationalistic feelings against the alien morals and customs of immigrant-influenced Northern cities.

For all his vehemence, however, the Southerner's paradoxical emotional state is more apparent than real. He has often been able to identify sectional with national feelings. Moreover, despite his self-conscious provincialism, he possessed more cultural traits in common with the Northerner than with any other inhabitant of the earth. The South since the fall of the Confederacy has in no sense been a nation. It has lacked independence in origin, language, industrial life, and culture; factors which render a people willing and able to stand alone. It is only a section, neither willing nor able to support a recurrence of the separatism which brought on the tragedy of 1861. Realizing that the sur-

In reality, many Southern ideas have triumphed over the North. Southerners love Lincoln just as Northerners love Lee. (works both ways)

render of Lee irreparably destroyed its national ambitions, the South has wisely distinguished patriotic and sectional emotions. Thus it has developed a practical harmony between two loyalties not unlike that which Americans as a whole have formulated between church and state.

Even as the South accepted many ideas of the victors it was imposing upon the North some of its own beliefs, in a manner suggestive of the Greek triumph over the Roman conquerors. The failure of Reconstruction proved the inviolability of the states and spread throughout the entire nation various aspects of the Southern attitude toward the Negro. No small part of the reactionary nationalism of the twentieth-century United States can be directly attributed to the South's pronounced conservatism and its comparative isolation from contact with foreigners and foreign ideas. Its native prejudices gave strength to restrictive immigration laws; its Anglo-Saxon racial and political ideals were rallying points for the unification of a nation of diverse origins; its Protestantism and its Puritanism gave shape and strength to the peculiarities of the national religion and morals. One expression of this strident nationalism was the Ku Klux Klan, an organization Southern in origin and ideals but national in influence. A more reputable group was the Robert E. Lee cult, the embodiment of the best in the sectional tradition.

Literature of the twentieth century reflected an increasing tolerance of Southern viewpoints in Northern thinking. Charles A. Beard, spokesman for historians, saw in the war between the states a conflict primarily motivated, not by moralistic conceits about slavery and secession, but by economic factors concerned as much with the overweening ambitions of Yankee plutocrats as with those of Southern planters. William A. Dunning and James G. Randall gave coldly convincing justifications of the section's contentions concerning war and Reconstruction. Novels such as Margaret Mitchell's *Gone With the Wind* (1936) vividly portrayed for the masses of the North the Old South of romance and emotion. Visits to the monuments of the Old South further enriched the Northerners' picture of the area. The mellow beauty of old Charleston, New Orleans, Natchez, Richmond, and rural Virginia was called to the attention of visitors by native guides with an effectiveness far greater than that of Yankee schoolma'ams who came South to praise Northern institutions.

Indeed, it is interesting to speculate whether the victory will ultimately rest with the South or with the North. One may recall the prediction made by Count Hermann Keyserling, who in 1929 asserted that when the American nation finds itself culturally, "the hegemony will inevitably pass over to the South. There alone can there be a question of enduring culture." The region below the Potomac possesses the type which "was truly responsible for America's true greatness in the past. That is the type of the Southern gentleman, with the corresponding type of woman. For these are the only types of 'complete souls' that the United States has as yet produced." [9]

[9] "The South—America's Hope," *The Atlantic Monthly*, CXLIV, 607–8 (November, 1929).

CHAPTER II

The English Pattern

1607 - 1733 -- Colonization period
↠↠↠↠↠↠↠↠↠↠↠↠↠↠↠↠↠↠↠↠↠↠↠↠↠↠↠↠↠↠↠↠↠↠↠↠
triumph of English tradition - religion,
government, books & clothes.

THE ENGLISH colonists who established themselves in Virginia in 1607, in Maryland in 1634, in the Albemarle region by 1653, in South Carolina in 1670, and in Georgia in 1733 possessed one common purpose. They wanted to live as Englishmen. In this ambition they succeeded in great measure. They established the Anglican church by law and at the same time tolerated other forms of Christianity congenial to English customs. The Southern county and parish governments reproduced English concepts of local administration, and the Southern provincial governments of charter, governor, and representative assembly were reproductions, on a smaller scale, of the English system. Education and architecture followed English patterns. English books were read, English clothes worn, English tools and furniture used, and English holidays celebrated. For generations correspondence was maintained with English relatives.

The English settlers of the South suffered grievously at times because of an unimaginativeness which prevented the adaptation of English ways to non-English conditions. In the end statesmanlike compromises resulted in a civilization that long retained more English characteristics than any migration of Anglo-Saxons since the original members of the race colonized Britain. English observers have been critical of the fact that adaptation to the demands of the Southern environment has caused variations from the English norm of excellence. But the South acquired a civilization that compares favorably with that of English settlements in other regions of the earth. It is a civilization that produced such noble types of Anglo-Saxon manhood as George Washington, Thomas Jefferson, Robert E. Lee, and Woodrow Wilson.

((13))

② on other page.
Virginia has a continental climate -- not modified by the Gulf stream, etc.
Hot in summer -- very cold in winter
(torrid) - Randolph -- (arctic)

1493 - Pope Alexander VI gave ½ of US to Spain, ½ to Portugal (line of Demarcation) Treaty of Tordesillas

1496 - Santa Domingo City founded by Columbus -- 1st permanent established in America.

Spanish also settled in Mexico, Central and South America

Spanish
1) greedy
2) pious
3) religious
4) adventure
Reasons for settling

Five barriers had to be surmounted in order that the colonizers of the South might carry out their resolution to create an England in America. These barriers were the threats of Spanish and French imperialism, the perils of a semitropical climate, the menace of treacherous natives, and the presence of large numbers of African Negroes who could not be completely assimilated. All of these barriers were overcome, not, however, without beneficial effects from the forces behind them. Spanish, French, Indian, Negro, and climatic influences helped create a civilization American and Southern and therefore not entirely English.

In 1493 Pope Alexander VI divided the world outside Europe in two halves as though the earth were an apple. He gave Africa, Asia, and Brazil to Portugal, and the rest of the Americas and the Philippines to Spain. England, Protestant and possessing a stable government and an ambitious merchant class, refused to abide by this arrangement. John Hawkins, an English sea captain, in the 1560's defied the Spanish and Portuguese monopolies by procuring slaves in Africa and selling them in the Spanish West Indies. Others, notably Sir Francis Drake and Thomas Cavendish, plundered Spanish treasure ships and cities and brought rich booty home to England. Virginia, the first of the English settlements, was a thorn in the side of the Spanish empire; Georgia, the last of the English colonies in the South, was a buffer state designed to contain Spanish territorial ambitions.

Within the hundred years preceding the Virginia settlement, Spanish conquerors traversed the vast wilderness between northern Mexico and southern South America. They looted the treasures of Montezuma and Atahualpa, opened mountains of gold and silver in Mexico and Peru, killed or subdued and Christianized millions of Indians, founded cities and universities, built monasteries and churches, and, through cultural and commercial restrictions, isolated themselves and their Indian wards from contact with other Europeans.

The Spanish believed that under the privileges given them by Pope Alexander VI they had the same rights to what is now the Southern United States as they had to Mexico and South America. The motives of adventure, piety, lust, and greed that led them into tropical lands lured them into the regions north of their West Indian and Mexican bases. While the English were having their first dream of empire, the banner of Spain was planted in the area between the swamps of Florida and the plateaus of Texas. The Spanish explorers who threaded their way through the Southern wilderness were armored knights mounted on horses floundering in swamps and briar thickets. They were luridly superstitious, seeking wonders with the zeal of Don Quixote. They wished to possess both the heathen's gold and the heathen's soul. They

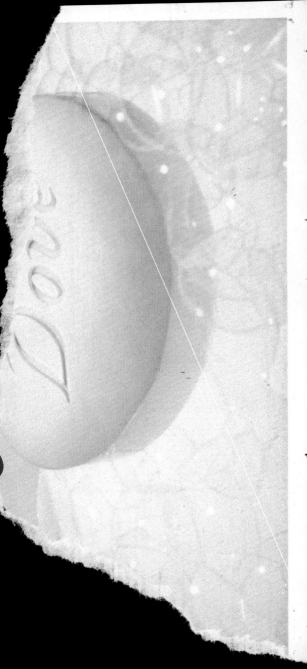

were as pitiless toward themselves as they were toward others, never giving up their quarries short of death or triumph.[1]

Between 1512 and 1600 a procession of Spanish explorers revealed the nature of the country between the Potomac and the Rio Grande. The first of these was Juan Ponce de León, governor of Puerto Rico, *first explorer* who in 1513 explored the entire coast of Florida seeking a place for colonization and a fo____ d a river in which old men could bathe themselves into ____nk in the splendid tale of the cacique Carlos wh____ ____over a realm abounding in gold. Ponce de Le____ ____e Carlos' land; there he met his death

____ez de Ayllón, an official of Santo ____ land that he called Chicora, which ____arolina. He was accompanied by a ____na who told tales of pearls, giant ____h inflexible tails which they used ____h what Chicorana said that he ____er force than that with which ____ a colony at the mouth of a ____pe Fear. Dissatisfied with this ____Pee Dee River. Here he died; ____ Indians, returned to Santo

____ in the conquest of Mexico, ____ged into the interior seek- ____ this place proved to be a ____ to return to their ships. ____ a thousand miles away, ____ After discovering the ____ Galveston Bay. One of ____ medicine man among ____ hardships he appeared ____ge Indian following. ____re Gulf coast and a

More ____ ____ome the Southern region of ____ ____y Hernando de Soto and *greatest g* Francisco ____ ____. Stimulated rather than discouraged *explorers* by Cabeza ____ ____erul odyssey, de Soto in 1539 entered Florida at the head ____ ooo gentlemen elaborately equipped with armor for themselves and for their horses, with materials for the celebration of the Roman mass, and with iron collars and chains for prospective slaves.

[1] Herbert L. Bolton, *Spanish Borderlands*, pp. 2–3.

WIVES FOR JAMESTOWN, 1619. *The shipment of English women to be wives of the Virginia settlers made practical the imposition of bans on interracial marriages.*

SETTLERS IN GEORGIA, 1733. *This scene of the building of Savannah is a vigorous demonstration of the intention of the Anglo-Saxon settlers of the South to occupy territory claimed by the Spanish.*

The wild Indians were a menace to the Spanish -- very uncivilized

Angered by this intrusion of foreign heretics in his domains, Philip II of Spain sent his great naval commander Pedro Menéndez against Fort Caroline. In 1565 Menéndez mercilessly slew most of its defenders and founded St. Augustine. This was the first permanent settlement by Europeans within the present limits of the South. Menéndez next established a series of posts from Tampa Bay on the west coast of Florida to Santa Elena in South Carolina. He even planned a settlement on the Chesapeake Bay.

Climate ① malarial summers, ② pneumonial winters Also, great storms.

Menéndez' efforts were supplemented by those of Jesuits and Franciscan missionaries. The Jesuits may have extended their activities as far north as the Rappahannock River in Virginia. By 1615 the Franciscans had erected more than twenty missions in Florida, Georgia, and South Carolina. These northward thrusts of Spanish soldiers and priests were halted by the hostility of the Indians.

The Spanish supplemented military and missionary expansion by intrigue against the English invaders of the territory they claimed for themselves. The Spanish ambassadors to the English court early in the seventeenth century tried to convince King James I that he should order the Virginia colony abandoned, and they urged King Philip III of Spain to uproot that infant settlement before it grew strong. A Spanish spy at Jamestown wondered why this "hydra" had not been strangled, and two reconnoitering expeditions were sent into the Virginia capes. But in the end Spain did not act. This was because her imperial interests lay to the south, because of her habit of procrastination, and because she cherished the fatuous notion that Virginia was a wasteland where the English were dissipating their men and money.

Spanish missions here (Jesuits) great heathens.

Spanish colonial efforts had constructive influences on the English colonies. Spanish ships coming to America were veritable Noah's arks, loaded with all manner of animals, seeds, and plants. Spanish domestic animals ran wild in the Southern wilderness and were later appropriated by Anglo-Saxon frontiersmen. Spanish achievements in adjusting European plants to the New World were largely responsible for the extensive experiments of the English colonists in the production of sugar, wine, olive oil, silk, rice, and indigo. Spanish West Indian experience in the production of great staples by the use of African slaves was a model for the system of agricultural economy destined to differentiate the Southern colonies from the other English settlements. A considerable number of Negroes imported in the seventeenth century came from the nearby Spanish islands and bore Spanish and Portuguese names.

Less menacing than Spain to the success of English colonizing experiments in the South were the ambitions of French imperialists. Catholic France was no more inclined than Protestant England to accept the papal line of demarcation. France told Spain that she "much desired to see Adam's will to learn how he had partitioned the world." As already noted, the French made unsuccessful attempts to colonize Florida and the South Carolina coast forty years before the establishment of Jamestown. Beginning at Quebec in 1608 they spread over the interior of North America in a great crescent, the southern prong of which rested east of the mouth of the Mississippi. With an audacity comparable to that of the Spanish conquerors, the Frenchman Robert Cavelier de La Salle would open for France a new empire in the Mississippi Valley far more fertile, he said, than Canada with "its forests, its barren soil, its harsh climate." He passed through the Great Lakes and down the Mississippi to the Gulf of Mexico. Here in 1682 he ceremoniously set up a post with the arms of France upon it, declared the entire region the possession of France, and named it Louisiana after King Louis XIV.

Another expedition under Pierre Le Moyne d'Iberville effected at Biloxi in 1699 the first permanent French settlement on the Gulf of Mexico. Iberville explored the Louisiana interior as far north as Baton Rouge. Other penetrations were effected by missionaries and fur hunters. In 1713 the first permanent settlement within the limits of modern Louisiana was made at Natchitoches on the Red River. Three years later Natchez was occupied. In 1718 New Orleans was founded near the mouth of the Mississippi. In 1722 New Orleans succeeded Biloxi as the capital of Louisiana.

The colonization of Louisiana by the French was intensive enough to impress that province indelibly with the civilization of the mother country. The French government turned over the promotion of settlements to John Law, a speculator. He attracted immigrants by picturing Louisiana as a veritable paradise. Among those attracted were Germans who occupied a strip of territory along the Mississippi known as the German Coast. By 1724 Negro slaves had become numerous enough to require the passage of the *Code Noir* to protect whites against them. Other settlers came from Santo Domingo and the Canary Islands. An interesting group was some two thousand French-speaking Acadians who settled in south Louisiana following their expulsion from Nova Scotia by the British in 1755. These Acadians (later called Cajuns) were a prolific but unaggressive folk given to cattle-raising and peasant handicrafts.

The Louisiana French lacked the qualities necessary to outdo the English in the task of conquering and populating the American South. They showed less aptitude in dealing with the Indians than did the Canadian French. The incentive to rival their northern kinsmen by traversing wide areas in search of furs was largely absent. This was because pelts shipped down the Mississippi spoiled in the warm climate of New

Orleans and because the Louisianans could not secure manufactured
goods for the Indian trade as cheaply as did the English. _ _ *not energetic*

France failed to develop a wise colonial policy. That country was
more interested in European wars than in overseas expansion; by policy
it restricted immigration and trade, and through autocratic rule it stifled
initiative. The result was that the French in Louisiana had less influence
upon the Anglo-Saxon South than did the Spanish in Florida and Texas.
By the end of the eighteenth century the French had effectively peopled
only a limited area. New Orleans, the largest city of the Mississippi
Valley, had less than 10,000 inhabitants. Population centered along the
Mississippi and the Red rivers and the bayous to the southward. The remainder of the modern state of Louisiana had scarcely been penetrated
except by hunters and trappers.

Inevitably English people who had heard of the treasures the Spanish
found in regions to the south were moved by hopes of untold wealth   *greedy.*
in Virginia. Explorers for Sir Walter Raleigh reported seeing Indians
wearing ornaments of gold and copper. In a play partly written by Ben
Jonson Virginia was described as a place "where gold and silver is more
plentiful than copper is with us" and where prisoners' fetters were made
of fine gold. The ships of the early settlers at Jamestown carried back to
England particles which glistened in the sands. When these particles
turned out to be pyrites or fool's gold the explorers were not discouraged. They moved toward the mountains searching for the precious
stuff. *James River mud*

When such searches proved vain, the hope was cherished that products of Spanish and Portuguese soils might be grown in comparable
American latitudes. Virginia was expected to produce grapes and hops   *"olives"*
for wines and brews; olives for oils; hemp, flax, and silk for textiles and   *turned out*
cordage; saffron and madder for dyes; and a great variety of fruits in-   *to be*
cluding such exotics as oranges, lemons, figs, and pomegranates as well as   *persimmons!*
such common products of England as apples, plums, and apricots.
Thereby it was believed that England would be relieved of dependence   *never learned*
for many of its needs on "infidels or our doubtful friends."   *wanted to
grow grapes*

The first settlers of Virginia were filled with notions about the Indi-   *so they wouldn't*
ans as exalted as their notions about the land. They assumed that the   *need to buy*
aborigines were like themselves. They made treaties with them as   *Spanish wine.*
though the Indians understood international obligations as European
nations understood them. They dressed the savages in the social and   *wanted to*
cultural habiliments of ladies and gentlemen of the Elizabethan age.   *make silk*
Pocahontas was called a princess and the chieftain Powhatan was called   *so as not*
an emperor and a crown of copper placed on his head. Idealists declared   *to rely on*
that the purpose of the English was not to dispossess the Indians but to   *France*

grew a little

*really non-
comprehensive savages*

share with them the riches of a boundless land and to impose upon them the benefits of a better life. If the English did not occupy the country, these idealists argued, the Spanish would do so and thereby subject the natives to the horrors of Catholicism and the cruelties Spain had visited upon the people of the West Indies.

The literature promoting the colonization of Virginia was permeated with a fervent desire to "propagate the Christian religion to such people as yet live in darkness and miserable ignorance of the true nature and worship of God." A first settler enthusiastically exclaimed: "What is more excellent, more precious, more glorious than to convert a heathen nation from worshipping the devill to the saving knowledge and true worship of God in Jesus Christ." Before the English obtained an adequate insight into the native character, the opinion prevailed that the Indians' ferocity might be softened by their listening to the reading of the English prayer book. That the English did not initially provide a missionary establishment so impressive as that of the Spanish was due as much to wise precautions as to the hypocritical indifference of Anglo-Saxons toward the welfare of inferior people. It was thought that actual colonization should precede missionary efforts. Through the example of civilized living the natives might be made amenable to Christian influences.

The problem of adjustment to the Virginia environment and native people which confronted the English settlers was more difficult than had been imagined. Encouraged by reports that the northeastern coast of what is now North Carolina was a region "the most plentiful, sweete, fruitful and wholesome of all the worlde," inhabited by a people who were the "most gentle, loving, and faithful, void of all guile and treason, and such as live after the manner of the golden age," the romantically inclined Sir Walter Raleigh in 1587 sent colonists to Roanoke Island under the leadership of John White. White returned to England to get supplies, leaving behind his newly born granddaughter Virginia Dare. When he returned to Roanoke Island in 1591 he found deserted houses and the single word "Croatoan" carved on a tree. What became of the Lost Colony has ever since been the subject of conjecture. Perhaps its members succumbed to the hardships of a strange environment, were massacred by the Indians, or were absorbed by friendly Croatoan Indians. From the viewpoint of the ideals of civilization and race destined to be established in the South the latter fate was just as disastrous as either of the other two.

The failure of the Roanoke Island adventure was ascribed to the fact that "it is a difficult thing to carry over colonies into remote countries upon private men's purses." The British crown was too much involved in domestic difficulties to afford the necessary resources. But England at the beginning of the seventeenth century was moved by a powerful drive for empire which, despite initial discouragements, was bound to find expression. When peace with Spain in 1604 released the necessary energies, a successful agency of colonization was hit upon—the joint-stock method of financing. This device of pooling the interests of the rich and ambitious members of the English merchant class had been tried successfully outside America. It was destined to be the means of securing enough capital to make the planting of a colony like Virginia a success.

It was the London or Virginia Company which in 1607 sent three ships with more than a hundred men to Virginia to establish a colony. The grandiose purpose of the Virginia Company was to convert the Indians, to discover gold, to find the Northwest Passage to India, and to produce the commodities England imported.

The first Englishmen in Virginia were charmed with the sights and scents of the new land: the jewel-green marshes, the wide waters of the estuaries, the safe harbors, the bright sun, the rich flora and fauna, and above all the great forests lit by Virginia sunsets. "We found nothing worth speaking of," wrote George Percy, "but faire meadows and goodly tall Trees, with such Fresh waters running through woods as I was almost ravished at the first sight thereof." There were "many squirrels, conies, Black Birds with crimson wings, and divers other Fowls and Birds of divers and sundrie colours." "We passed," he added, "through excellent ground full of Flowers of divers kinds and colours, and as goodly trees as I have seene, as cedar, cipresse and other kindes; . . . fine and beautiful strawberries, foure times bigger and better than ours in England."

The first colonists were men more interested in searching for gold than in tilling the soil. For some years the only riches Virginia exported were forest products. Jamestown, the place of first settlement, was so malarial that it was ultimately abandoned. *Tried to grow English products — not prosperous*

So frightful was the toll of disease, starvation, and Indian massacres that in 1624 only 1,275 of the 6,000 colonists of Virginia survived. In the summer a heavy breath rose from the marshes and the floor of the forests. In the winter the houses were too flimsy for adequate protection against the weather; for the tight log cabin, a creation of the Swedes, had not yet been introduced among the English. Half the newcomers promptly died of pneumonia or of malaria, as the season of their arrival dictated. Had this not happened, all, both old and late arrivals, might have died of starvation.

In England there were no storehouses of food from which supplies could be drawn; had such supplies existed, the ships of the day did not have space enough to carry them to Virginia. Oysters and fish were plentiful, but the white man had not yet learned how to catch them. The land was capable of a bounteous harvest, but the trees had first to be felled or girdled. The Indians themselves were only possessed of enough food to keep them above the level of starvation. From time immemorial they had been engaged in a savage struggle with each other over this scant supply; to protect it they were willing to turn on the invading whites.

The attempt of the white settlers to come to terms with the natives proved a failure. Indians seemingly lurked behind every bush and guarded every shore on which the whites attempted to land. It seemed as though they instinctively understood that they were engaged in an epic struggle with an aggressor bent on taking their lands from them. Not one word of the English prayer book or other Christian pronouncements were intelligible to the aboriginal brain. Highly exceptional was the case of the Indian maid Pocahontas, who was converted to English and Christian ways and who, through her marriage to John Rolfe, became the honored ancestor of many of the first families of Virginia.

The red men of the South Atlantic coast, unlike those of Mexico and Peru, were so backward culturally that they could not be tamed into effective slaves. Imprudently employing them as huntsmen, the white man provided them with guns and ammunition. At the same time the whites spread over the open country in the rush for tobacco fields, leaving several miles between plantations and in many cases absorbing the corn fields of the Indians. This impelled the Indians to execute the bloody massacre of 1622, in which a quarter of the population of the colony was killed. Among those who perished by the blows of the tomahawk was George Thorpe, an Englishman whose zeal for the spiritual welfare of the aborigines had prompted him to manage an Indian college. The colonists after 1622 adopted a policy of "perpetual enmity" toward the natives, destroying Indian towns and crops year after year.

The experiences of the English with the Indians were not without advantages to the Virginia colonists. Foodstuffs wheedled from the natives played a crucial part in the battle against starvation. From them the whites learned to use Indian corn, melons, squash, gourds, sweet potatoes, and pumpkins; how to make canoes, how to hunt, how to girdle trees, and the intricate strategems of forest warfare.

At first wheat could not easily be grown on the Southern coastal plain due to the presence of too much nitrogen in forest soils and the difficulty of plowing amid tree stumps. This led to the most important dietary discovery in the history of the South, the use of Indian corn. This grain could be grown with little or no plowing. The settlers learned from the natives to eat it as grits, as hominy, as roasting ears, and as corn pones. Ultimately they learned to make from it a substance strange to the Indians—corn whisky.

Tobacco growing, which became the basis of Virginia's prosperity, was a joint contribution of the Indians and the Spanish. The North American variety of this famous plant was smoked by the aborigines in long-stemmed pipes with stone bowls. Because of its bitter taste it was less popular among white persons than the Spanish variety. But after John Rolfe taught the Virginians to grow the sweet-scented type which the Spanish had developed [2] a prosperous future was assured for Virginia tobacco. By 1624 Virginia was exporting 60,000 pounds of the golden leaf. It became a source of revenue to Virginia and her neighbors more substantial than that which came to Spain through the real gold of Mexico and Peru.

The Virginia Company refused to give up its Virginia enterprise despite the discouragements of disease, starvation, and massacre. During the eighteen years of its existence the company spent the huge sum of £100,000 on Virginia without any profit to itself. In 1608 and 1609 it sent out relief expeditions which prevented the colony from expiring. Although it regarded Virginia as a commercial undertaking, hope of profit was not its only motive. Such company stockholders as Sir Edwin Sandys and the Earl of Southampton thought of Virginia as a national enterprise designed for the extension of English civilization and English practices of self-government. Governors of heroic resolution like Sir Thomas Gates, Sir Thomas Dale, and Lord Thomas de la Ware were put in immediate charge of affairs. Population growth was assured by liberal immigration policies. "Sturdy beggars" and condemned criminals were encouraged to go to Virginia, as well as skilled artisans and men of higher estate. Communal farming was abandoned in favor of private ownership. The hired servants of the company became sharecroppers when their indentures expired. Men of substance who paid the passage money of immigrants were granted large tracts of land known as hundreds.

The problem of labor on the expanding tobacco farms of Virginia was met in a variety of ways. The first was the importation of persons obligated to work out the cost of their transportation. The fate of the average indentured servant of this type was not entirely unhappy. He was better fed, better lodged, and better clothed than the English farm laborer. At the end of his period of service he was given a bonus of food and clothing, with the opportunity through industry to acquire land and social position. In 1629, seven of these former servants were members of the House of Burgesses. Some, perhaps only one in ten, acquired land. The majority died in bondage, became hired laborers, small rent-

[2] See below, p. 59.

Hog thrived — could defend itself and also live in swamps. Came from Bermuda

"Enclosure Movement" stopped farming for pasture — didn't have work, so they come here

Much land — few people

ers, or dropped into the class of ne'er-do-wells and thereby became in part the ancestors of the Southern whites of the lower classes. This was not due as much to lack of opportunity as to the worthless character of many of the indentured servants.[3]

A class as important but less numerous than the indentured servants were the freemen who came to Virginia at their own expense. They joined those who had served out periods of indenture to make up the great body of small landowners. The small landowners became the backbone of the community. Collectively they were the largest group of tobacco producers, and as a consequence were the most substantial source of the colony's wealth. With little opportunity or desire for political preferment, they exercised their suffrage privileges in favor of their social betters. This behavior was not a sign of their acceptance of social degradation but merely an application to Virginia of English social values. Their numerical strength and their pride of race and nationality gave a secure basis for a doctrine that since the middle of the seventeenth century has been written into the laws of the Southern communities. This is the doctrine of white supremacy, the belief that the excellences of Southern society are dependent upon the maintenance of Anglo-Saxon power and racial continuity.

White supremacy was threatened by the fact that among the early settlers the men greatly outnumbered the women. And men, even Englishmen with extreme pride of race, must have wives, even if their wives are no better than the brown women of the forests. The Spanish solved this problem by marrying brown women, thereby creating a numerous mestizo race. According to Captain John Smith, Indian girls emerged naked from the woods to torment the early Virginians with lascivious antics. One of the duties of Indian hospitality was to furnish one's guests with women for the night. With the exception of John Rolfe, however, white Virginians did not marry Indian women. There were two reasons for this. One was the great difference in the cultural levels of the English and the Indians. "Pocahontas," Governor Thomas Dale warned Rolfe, "is of a different and despised color; of different manners and uneducated; of a hated race, not one of whom has ever looked above the meanest of the Colonists." The other reason was that the lure of Indian women was checkmated by the importation of English women. Some of these women were criminals, others were kidnapped girls. The most famous importation was that of one hundred carefully selected "maids for wives" sent over in 1619. Their importance in the destiny of the white race is made clear by Mary Johnston in her popular romance *To Have and to Hold*.

The fact that land ownership was the prerogative of all white men

[3] Abbot E. Smith, *Colonists in Bondage*, pp. 296–306.

Pocahontas died in England of TB --
some say due to alcoholism.

THE ENGLISH PATTERN   ((25

stimulated the importation of Negro slaves to meet the labor needs of the large tobacco planters. Industrious white servants when they became free of indentures were not inclined to become tenants; they were more likely to become landowners. Because of the presence of the blacks, the social position of this class improved over what it had been in the mother country. They joined other white men in lording over the subordinate race and they looked forward to the time when they might own Negroes.

The Negroes were a greater menace to the biological integrity of the white race than the Indians. They adjusted themselves easily to the ways of the white man. They were introduced into white homes as servants. They were physically competent, and ever increasing in number. Their women, as is usual with slave women, appreciated the disadvantages of refusing the sexual advances of members of the master race. White women also, as sporadic records reveal, mated with Negro men. great mulatto race - but classed as Negro.

As soon as the Negroes became numerous a wall of caste was erected against them. "While the individual lot of the Negro might vary according to the attitude of the master in whose hands it was his lot to fall," writes a historian of early Virginia,[4] "the trend from the first was toward a sharp distinction between him and the white servant." In 1630, at a time when the Negro population did not exceed 300, a Virginia court decreed that Hugh Davis, a white man, "be soundly whipped, before an assembly of Negroes and others for abusing himself to the dishonor of God and shame of Christians, by defiling his body in lying with a negro." Soon the developing distinctions of race were reflected in the exclusion of Negroes from the militia and by their separate classification in census and tax returns. A law of 1662 settled the question of whether a child got by an Englishman upon a Negro woman should be slave or free. It declared that the child should take the status of the mother. This law imposed double penalties upon "any christian" guilty of cohabitation "with a negro man or woman." By a law of 1682 the distinction between freeman and slave was shifted from a difference in religion to a difference in race. It declared that conversion to Christianity could not be used as a basis for claiming freedom.

The making of the Negro into an inferior caste was duplicated by the English in all the Southern colonies. This was also true of the French in Louisiana. The *Code Noir* of Louisiana was more lenient than the black codes of the English colonies, but it did not tolerate interracial marriages. The Creole aristocracy and the Cajun country folk of the French colony were as proud of their freedom from Negro blood as were the gentry and yeomanry of Virginia and the Carolinas. The

[4] Wesley F. Craven, *The Southern Colonies in the Seventeenth Century*, p. 219.

Reasons for English prejudices as compared to Span Port.
1) farther North
2) Came into contact latter (Portugese -- 1441)
3) 1st came " " with barbarians (more cultured
4) Spanish and Portuguese had a church and a crown

system of concubinage symbolized by the Quadroon Balls of New Orleans did not possess the degree of social approval ascribed to them by legend. The alliances were between white men and colored girls, never between colored men and white girls; they were therefore no greater threat to the integrity of white families than were the numerous but unritualized unions between white men and colored girls of the English colonies.

The insistence of the English and the Louisiana French on racial purity contrasted sharply with the behavior of other European peoples in contact with the Negro in America. The Spanish and the Portuguese in those areas where Negroes were numerous mixed so freely with the darker race that whole populations tended to become mulatto. The fact that the Iberian people made interracial contacts early in their history with North African people not very different from them in culture and physical appearance militated against initial development of race prejudice. This experience softened potential aversions for colored persons when later the Spanish and the Portuguese, by a gradual process extending as far back as 1441, came in contact with the genuine Negro.

The English and the French, on the other hand, had had little contact with darker peoples when in the seventeenth century they began meeting Negroes. The disparity was among the sharpest in history: that between a fair race of the highest civilization and a black race of barbarous culture. A feeling of revulsion for the Negro was thereby created among the French and the English, a feeling that soon hardened into a lasting caste consciousness.

Early in their history the English in Virginia established the basic ideal of Southern civilization. This was and is today the Anglo-Saxon pattern of culture. This pattern had to be consciously fostered because of the presence of forces in the Virginia environment that worked against the continuation of the English way of life. There was the threat of the envelopment of the Virginia colony by the Spanish or the French. There had to be a hard fight against the savage Indians and a strange climate. The threat to the continuity and integrity of the white race offered by a rising Negro population had to be overcome by stern laws and social customs. The English way of life triumphed over these difficulties. At the same time, wise compromises with the environment, with the Indians, the French, the Spanish, and the Negro, gave a predominantly English colony an American and Southern flavor.

also;
Church
and
crown

English Triumphed over
1) Spanish
2) French
3) Climate
4) Negro
and the colonies became predominately English

CHAPTER III

Here 6 March —

Colonial Expansion

➤➤➤-➤➤

As SIGNIFICANT as the ability of the English settlers of the South to establish and maintain Anglo-Saxon institutions was their ability to extend their area of occupation, first along the Atlantic coast with England and Virginia as bases, then westward over the mountains with Virginia and other coastal colonies as bases. This expansion up to the time of the American Revolution was slow and unsensational. Long after the Spanish and the French had spread over vast areas, the English were confined to a narrow string of settlements east of the Alleghenies.

The failure of the early English settlers to extend their operations was offset by their ability to make compact settlements. In restricted areas they established themselves in large numbers on a secure agricultural basis. The large numbers were caused by high birth rates and liberal immigration policies. North Europeans were allowed to settle alongside the English primarily because these north Europeans possessed physical characteristics and cultures not greatly different from those of the English. The foundation was laid for a great westward movement which eventually swept the more tenuous French and Spanish settlements before it. The aggressiveness of the Southerners was not checked until the appearance in the West of rivals with English backgrounds. These rivals were colonists out of New England and New York whose talents for western expansion were in many respects superior to those of Southerners.

The first settlement of Englishmen outside Virginia was in Maryland. In 1632 King Charles I granted proprietary rights in that territory to Cecilius Calvert, second Lord Baltimore. Lord Baltimore was given title to more than 10 million acres and the right to appoint all officials,

in the South

((27))

make ordinances, and administer justice to the extent of inflicting the death penalty within his grant.

In March, 1634, under Lord Baltimore's authority two vessels, the *Ark* and the *Dove*, with more than 200 immigrants aboard, entered the Potomac, an estuary so majestic that the Thames seemed "but a little finger to it." The colonists established themselves some seventy miles north of Jamestown at St. Mary's, on a high bank overlooking a good anchorage. It was, says a historian, "one of the most attractive places selected by our forefathers."

The first Marylanders established good relations with the Indians by furnishing them with hatchets, axes, and cloth, in exchange for village huts and planted fields. The newcomers thereby secured enough of the necessities of life to meet their immediate needs. No time was lost in searches for gold or the Northwest Passage. Advantage was taken of the proximity of other English colonies. Salt fish was imported from New England, and swine and cattle from Virginia. The Indians of the St. Mary's area were a dying race who welcomed the English in hopes of receiving protection from other Indians. There were in early Maryland no horrid massacres or starving times.

Reasons did exist for possible discord between the two Chesapeake Bay colonies, however. The Maryland land grant infringed upon Virginia claims. The Maryland charter was granted to one man with feudal powers as extensive as those of a lord of border counties in the Middle Ages. Such autocracy created fears in the minds of liberty-loving Virginians. The Protestant suspicions of Virginians were aroused by the fact that Maryland was a refuge for Catholics and that Jesuits were among the first settlers. These suspicions had been demonstrated when, five years before the founding of St. Mary's, the first Lord Baltimore was ordered out of Virginia because as a Catholic he had refused to take the Oath of Supremacy to the English crown. It was, said a Jamestown resident, "accounted a crime almost as heinous as treason, nay to speak well of that colony [Maryland]."

William Claiborne, a Puritan trader who had colonized Kent Island within the Maryland grant, was a source of almost endless trouble to the Maryland proprietor. This pugnacious interloper, with the legislature at Jamestown secretly on his side, refused to accept Lord Baltimore's authority. He was suspected of stirring up the Indians against the settlers. A petty war broke out which ended in the taking of Kent Island by the Marylanders in 1638 and the recognition by the English government of Lord Baltimore's title to the island.

Evidence of discord between Maryland and Virginia was more than neutralized, however, by forces working in the opposite direction. Both colonies were English, and both were becoming more American and more Southern. In both, religious ideals were subordinated to material development. This meant that the Catholic founders of Maryland, like the Anglican directors of Virginia, did not restrict immigration to their own faith. Maryland wanted more settlers than the Catholics of England were willing or able to supply. As in Virginia, the main inducement to settle in Maryland was nothing less material than a land grant. As a consequence of this practical liberalism, the majority of Maryland settlers from the beginning were Protestants. Catholics were ordered to maintain silence "upon all occasions of discourse concerning matters of religion." The third Lord Baltimore believed that without the concession of religious freedom it was doubtful that the Maryland project would have been successful.

The fierce suspicions of Catholics by Virginians were further allayed by other concessions by the Lord Baltimores to the secular or nonsectarian spirit. The most famous of these was the Toleration Act of 1649 protecting the "conscience in matters of religion" of all persons who believed in Christ. It enjoined the colonists against the use of such recriminating terms as heretic, papist, anabaptist, schismatic, and idolater. Another step in this direction was the halt put upon the development by the Jesuits of a spiritual empire like that which the Spanish and the Portuguese members of that famous order effected in South America. In 1641 Lord Baltimore put an end to such ambitions by prohibiting the Jesuits from acquiring land from the Indians and by applying the statute of mortmain against gifts of land to churchmen. This was followed by the appointment of a Protestant governor and by permission to the Virginia Puritans to settle in the colony. When these aggressive people deprived Lord Baltimore of his authority, he proved to be such a good diplomat that he was able to recover his position by appealing to Oliver Cromwell, the Puritan ruler of England.

In the meantime Maryland was approximating the Virginia norm in its social and economic behavior. Father Andrew White and his fellow Jesuits sought out the Indians and preached to them with a zeal like that of the Protestant missionaries of early Virginia. But these missionary efforts failed for the same reason that those of Virginia failed. The Maryland Indians could not understand Christian doctrines. No interracial brotherhood was formed. Instead there developed a brotherhood of white men devoted to the grim business of defense against the savages.

Maryland's reactions to the problems of land and labor were the same as those of Virginia. An agrarian aristocracy grew out of liberal land grants and the profitable cultivation of tobacco. A broad foundation was given to white supremacy by the coming of Puritan, Quaker, Dutch, Swedish, and French settlers, and by the sale to the planters by

shipmasters of white indentured servants. After 1677 Negroes were imported in such large numbers that they soon outnumbered the white
indentured servants. But the Negroes were relegated to a separate caste.
By 1715 it was decreed that Negroes and their children should be slaves
for life, that baptism could not be used as a plea for freedom, and that a
white man or woman who was the parent of a child of mixed race
should be condemned to seven years of servitude.

The two Chesapeake Bay colonies early discovered that their mutual
interests were greater than their rivalries. Both benefited by the exchange of goods and by the mutual return of fugitive servants. Agreements were made over the rights of trade, and each colony gave faith
and credit to documents executed in the other. Thus precedents were
established for the development of a Southern consciousness which,
under the leadership of Virginia, was later to include Maryland and
many states to the south and the west of the Chesapeake Bay. Because
of its northern location and colder climate, Maryland had much in common with the colonies of the North; but the commonwealth became so
truly Southern that 250 years after its foundation an invasion of Northern soldiers was necessary to shatter the resolution of many of its people
to join in the struggle of the South to become an independent nation.

The settlement of North and South Carolina accentuated the distinction of the South from the English colonies north of Maryland. The
directors of English imperial policy wished to find a climate free from
Virginia's "nipping frosts" where commodities unsuccessfully experi-
mented with in that colony might be produced. The grand objective
still was to create a self-contained empire. Hopes were cherished for the
production in Carolina of silk, olives, coffee, rice, and other products of
warm climates.

Initiative in the settlement of Carolina was taken by Francis Yeard-
ley, Roger Green, and other Virginians who in the years following 1654
occupied the Albemarle region of northeastern North Carolina. About
the same time New Englanders, seeking lands close to deep water,
established themselves near the mouth of the Cape Fear River. This
project was soon abandoned in apparent disgust over the poor quality
of the soil. Significant for the peopling of the region south of Cape Fear
was the exploration of the South Carolina coast by William Hilton.
Hilton was a prospector for Barbadian planters who were seeking space
outside the narrow confines of their West Indian island to cultivate
staple commodities with slave labor. Hilton's activities opened prospects
of recruits for the settlement of Carolina who were in many respects
more experienced in the agricultural methods destined to prevail there
than prospective immigrants from England or Virginia.

Into the atmosphere of promise which these explorations created eight English noblemen projected themselves. In 1663 and 1665 they obtained from King Charles II appointments as Lords Proprietor of Carolina, with jurisdiction over the region extending southward from the southern border of Virginia to well within the present borders of Florida and westward from the sea to the region of the setting sun. They were given rights comparable to those of the Calverts in Maryland. This meant the management of the affairs of the province as they chose, with certain practical limitations. Laws must not be repugnant to those of England and must be enacted with the consent of the resident freemen. Provision was made for exemptions from oaths of religious conformity. One of the proprietors, Sir Anthony Ashley Cooper, better known by his later title of Lord Shaftesbury, in collaboration with the philosopher John Locke, wrote the Fundamental Constitutions of Carolina. This organic act for the new colony reads like the dream of a romantic feudal domain. There were to be five "estates;" eight supreme courts; a chamberlain; a lord high admiral; a nobility of barons, caciques, and landgraves possessed of manorial estates; and a common people with more modest holdings.

There is a tendency among historians to regard the Lords Proprietor of Carolina as parasitical court favorites whose ignorance of colonial conditions was exceeded only by their desire to make profits without exertions. The Carolina grantees were politicians of influence at the royal court who skillfully organized themselves into a lobby too weighty for the king to resist in their desire to secure authority over a large domain. But as a whole they were experienced leaders closely identified with the framing of imperial policies. Because of their favored position in English public life they were able to give their nascent colony the unity of command which made possible its orderly occupation. They wisely encouraged seasoned immigrants from Virginia and the Barbadoes. Three of the Lords Proprietor possessed backgrounds which especially fitted them to direct the Carolina enterprise. Sir William Berkeley, the veteran governor of Virginia, possessed long experience in exploratory enterprises extending southward from his colony. Sir John Colleton, a sugar planter of Barbados, was thoroughly acquainted with his fellow planters' necessity of finding broader fields for their agricultural ambitions. Sir Anthony Ashley Cooper was a hardheaded politician who was experienced in plantation affairs through investments in a Barbadian plantation and in the African slave trade.

The Fundamental Constitutions contained more than impractical survivals from the feudal age. The elaborate political and social structure described therein was intended for ultimate rather than immediate application. Although the settlers of Carolina dropped their grandiloquent titles as inappropriate to nonfeudal America, many of the conventions of landed aristocracy took root. The plan of awarding large acreages to men of means was a promotional device which proved as effective in Carolina as in other new countries.

Evidence of a practical knowledge of the special needs of the colony was shown in the document's inclusion of one principle of extreme tyranny and another principle of extreme liberalism. The principle of extreme tyranny was in the encouragement of Negro slavery because of what were felt to be the necessities of agrarian economy in a semi-tropical climate. Masters were given absolute authority over their bondsmen; it was boldly proclaimed that conversion of the slaves to Christianity did not alter their servile status. The principle of extreme liberalism was in a broad religious tolerance which included Jews and Quakers. This, together with a tolerance of aliens, was wisely designed to encourage immigrants.

The practical wisdom of the Lords Proprietor was expressed in two policies. One was the adoption of the headright system as a basic land policy. Under this policy immigrants came in growing numbers to choose lands for themselves, to secure titles, and to begin farming. The other policy was the exemption from custom duties of a list of non-English commodities which the proprietors hoped could be grown in the colony. Experiments were made in the production of silk, olives, wine, indigo, and cotton. Success with rice and naval stores was among the most significant achievements in the history of experiments in agriculture and the extractive industries.

The settlement of Carolina made steady progress under the Lords Proprietor. Following instructions from his seven associates, Sir William Berkeley started North Carolina on the road to autonomous existence by giving the already-settled Albemarle region a governor and a legislative assembly. Settlers were given land without much concern over their religious or national origin. Quakers early got a foothold, and one of their number became governor. French Huguenots founded the town of Bath and settled along the Neuse and Trent rivers. Swiss and Germans founded the town of New Bern. With the founding of Wilmington and the pushing of settlements to the mouth of the Cape Fear, the colony acquired anchorages for ocean-going vessels. Tobacco and cattle from North Carolina's open lands, and lumber, tar, pitch, and turpentine from its forests, became the basis of a thriving overseas trade.

Much was said in contemporary reports about the backwardness of North Carolina as compared with Virginia and South Carolina. It was isolated from the centers of civilization by sand bars, shallow harbors and great stretches of pine barrens. So desert-like seemed the landscape that Governor Arthur Dobbs suggested the introduction of camels. It was called Rogues' Harbor because of the supposed thriftlessness of its

Germans from Penn. settled in back country.

inhabitants. These landlubbers, that is, dwellers away from navigable
waters, in the opinion of the scornful William Byrd II of Virginia, *isolated from culture*
"loiter away their lives, like Solomon's sluggard, with their arms across,
and at the end of the year scarcely have bread to eat."

Despite these real or imaginary handicaps, North Carolina early
manifested traits characteristically Southern. Oak-covered acres were *TOBACCO*
cleared for the establishment of prosperous farms. Tobacco became the *Cotton,*
most important staple. About New Bern and Edenton and along the *Lumber,*
Cape Fear River arose mansions in which lived a cultured gentry own- *pitch and*
ing household slaves, silver plate, and libraries. By 1754 the province had *tar*
15,000 slaves restricted to a caste status like that in Virginia. The white
population dominated numerically; and the white man in North Carolina, whether planter, yeoman, or poor white, was controlled by the
Southern concept of race. The presence of a Negro minority made that
attitude inevitable.

The Lords Proprietor paid more attention to South Carolina than
they did to the northern portion of their grant. In 1670 they sent there
colonists from England and Barbadoes who settled on the Ashley River
a few miles above its mouth. Finding this place unhealthful, the settlers
moved to the point where the Ashley and the Coopers rivers meet,
which was later called Charleston. In 1680 this town became the seat of
government.

South Carolina grew rapidly in population. The political and religious liberties allowed by the Lords Proprietor caused the coming of
English dissenters, of Huguenots fleeing from the persecutions of a
French king, and of Scotchmen willing to risk the wrath of the Spanish
by settling at Stewart's Town near the Savannah River. This outpost
was destroyed by a Spanish expedition from Florida.

The attempt of England and Spain in 1676 to come to an understanding by recognizing the rights of each other to territory already
settled ended in failure. Frontier controversies continued. The South
Carolinians developed an acute sense of insecurity because the Spanish
were exciting the Indians against them. Thereby were fostered anti-
Catholic and anti-Indian prejudices as intense as those prevailing in
Virginia. These prejudices made it possible for South Carolina to play
an important part in the development of the Protestant and pro-English
patriotism that became an earmark of the regional patriotism.

The development of slavery and the plantation system in South
Carolina was facilitated by the coming of settlers from Barbadoes. In
South Carolina, as in Barbadoes, the slaves outnumbered the whites, and
a slave code more stringent than that in Virginia was considered neces-
sary. Rice became the plantation crop to take the place of sugar in
Barbadoes. By 1694 rice proved to be peculiarly suited to the South

Irrigated the land with fresh water

Carolina swamps. By 1742 indigo *aye* became a supplementary plantation crop. Typical of the enthusiasm with which the settlers accepted the newly created industrial order of plantations and slavery was the conduct of the Huguenots. They came to South Carolina to produce silk, *French Protestants* olives, and grapes, and they ended by producing rice, race horses, and indigo. In 1749 the province had 29,000 whites and 39,000 blacks.

Georgia was founded by twenty trustees who secured a charter from King George II in 1732. They hoped to establish in the wilderness *Last of the British North Am. colonies* between the Savannah River and Florida a Southern Arcadia removed from both the slums of Europe and certain unapproved characteristics of the South. Philanthropy was uppermost in the minds of the Georgia trustees. Exalted sentiments were supplemented by the long-established imperial policy of pursuing the fur trade and extending the frontier at the expense of the Indians and the Spanish.

General James Oglethorpe and Lord John Percival, the principal promoters of the project, wanted a haven for inmates of English debtor prisons and for persecuted German Protestants. No self-government was to be allowed the colonists. This was not for selfish reasons but because the colonists were poor persons too inexperienced in politics to protect themselves. The trustees were forbidden to secure any pecuniary profits for themselves either through officeholding or through land grants. At the end of twenty-one years they were obligated to turn the colony over to the crown. Trade in rum and the owning of slaves was prohibited. To prevent the growth of a plantation aristocracy and to foster a yeoman class the size of landholdings was limited. The Georgia idea caught the imagination of the English people, and gifts of money poured into the trustees' treasury.

Under the personal direction of Oglethorpe, 130 immigrants arrived in Georgia in 1733 and founded the town of Savannah. For some time there was a steady stream of new arrivals attracted by the recruiting policies of the colony's sponsors. Among those who came were New Englanders, Scotch Highlanders, and German Salzburgers. The latter were Lutheran refugees from Catholic persecutions. In thanks for the freedom of their Georgia home they called their settlement Ebenezer.

Georgia did not continue to grow, having in 1760 not more than 6,000 inhabitants. The principal reason for this was the restrictions which prevented the colony from developing along the lines of the other Southern colonies. The benevolent despotism of Oglethorpe frustrated the desire of the more influential members of the colony to conduct the government in their own interest. The prohibition of rum was burdensome upon a people living in a malarial climate. The Georgians wished to exchange their lumber for West Indian rum; they needed the fiery liquid for exchange with the Indians for furs. Bootleggers, in the manner of their Georgia descendants two hundred years later, plied their trade with the connivance of the officers of the law. Georgians were compelled to cultivate their narrow lands with their own hands while South Carolinians became rich through slave labor in their broad fields. Many ambitious Georgians crossed into South Carolina, while South Carolinians crossed into Georgia defiantly bringing their slaves with them.

Admitting the impractical character of their regulations, the trustees gradually abandoned the restrictions on landholding, rum, and slavery. In 1751 a legislative assembly was permitted. In 1752, a year before their charter privileges expired, the trustees voluntarily relinquished their rights to the king. By 1755 the English government was in full control. Georgia became a typical Southern colony, happy to be free of the meddlesome idealists who had founded it. The economy of slaves and plantations was assimilated, and about all that remained of the trustees' regulations was the prohibition of interracial marriages.

The westward advance of Southerners into the forests and hills that lay beyond the lower courses of the Atlantic rivers began in 1671. It was then that a party under Thomas Batts and Robert Fallam was sent out from Petersburg on the edge of the Virginia tidewater. These explorers went as far west as the New River and thereby made the first contact of Englishmen with waters flowing into the Ohio. This expedition was followed by the establishment above the falls of the James and the Appomattox of cabins and blockhouses in which dwelt a handful of pioneer folk, with small companies of rangers for protection against Indian forays. Governor Alexander Spotswood in 1714 planted a colony of Germans on the Rapidan River to work iron deposits. He also established a fort on the Meherrin River, a tributary of the Roanoke, for the promotion of Indian trade.

Moved by the desire to mend his personal fortunes and to keep the French from hemming in the English, Spotswood in 1716 led a party of adventurous gentlemen to the westward. This expedition climbed to the crest of the Blue Ridge and, amid copious toasts in fine wine, looked down upon the Valley of Virginia. This gallant accomplishment was commemorated by the creation of the Knights of the Golden Horseshoe. Spotswood's success pointed to two events of the future: the occupation of the Virginia back country by migrants from the tidewater extending beyond the first mountain barrier, and the transmontane region attracting gentlemen as well as commoners.

The great planters of the tidewater were as active in western pioneering as were lesser men. They sought new grounds to take the place of old fields exhausted by failure to rotate crops and to use fertilizer; they wanted the profits of land speculation. Governor Spotswood, for example, deeded to himself 60,000 acres of undeveloped land.[1] Room was left, however, for many small farmers seeking virgin soil for tobacco. Where rivers were not available for the transportation of this product, the farmers rolled it to the water's edge in hogsheads drawn by oxen. In the Valley of Virginia, where transportation was difficult, subsistence farming developed.

The North Carolina back country was opened for settlement by the driving out of the Tuscarora Indians in 1713. There the Virginia custom of granting land in large tracts was duplicated.[2] But the poor of North Carolina did not allow themselves to be left out of the division. Indentured servants and other lesser folk secured land titles, and what Virginians called bad citizens became squatters and rioted when the agents of the big landowners tried to collect rents.

By 1750 the colonization of South Carolina had been pushed up the Savannah and its tributaries as far as Ninety Six; up the Pee Dee almost to Cheraw; up the Wateree as far as the Catawba Nation; and along the branches of the Santee. Welshmen came from Delaware to establish the Welsh Neck settlement on the Pee Dee, and Scotch-Irish came directly from Belfast to establish Williamsburg north of Charleston.

The South Carolina authorities made concerted efforts to attract Protestant settlers from central Europe. Emigrant agents were appointed, and the transportation costs of settlers were paid by the colonial government. The desire was to increase the white population as a security against the Negro majority and to create a more diversified economy. In response to this desire Swiss settlers founded Purrysburg on the Savannah and German settlers occupied Orangeburg District and the Dutch Fork region in the center of the province. Governor James Glen was able to declare in 1749 that beer was the only article of consumption which had to be imported.

As Virginians moved west across the Appalachian Mountains, South Carolinians moved southwest around those mountains. The lure was Indian slaves and deer and buffalo skins. Slaves were purchased from Yamasee Indian allies and sold to good advantage in the West Indies. By 1700 South Carolinians were trading in skins with Indians from across the Mississippi, and by 1748, 160,000 deerskins were sent annually from Charleston to England.

The influence of the South Carolinians had become paramount among the Indians of the Gulf region east of the Mississippi. The South Carolinians had, with the aid of the Creek Indians, invaded northern Florida in 1704, destroyed Apalachee and other Indian towns and Spanish missions, and reduced Spanish authority in Florida to near impo-

[1] See below, p. 61.
[2] See below, p. 62.

tence. English goods—guns, ammunition, knives, vermilion paint, mirrors, and cloth—which the South Carolinians used to barter with the Indians, were so superior to anything the Spanish had to offer that the South Carolinians did not find it necessary to follow the Spanish example of attracting the Indians with Christian missions. It was the traders, of whom James Adair and Louchlan McGillivray were outstanding, who frustrated the desire of the French and the Spanish to unite with the Indians and thereby bring about the extinction of the English influence on the frontier. There the Indians outnumbered the English ten to one.

The whole Gulf region as far as Louisiana might have been annexed to South Carolina before the American Revolution but for shifts of Indian alliances. With the aid of the Creeks, the South Carolinians had a fair chance of visiting upon the French settlement at Mobile the fate of the Apalachees. But the Creeks became disgruntled and withdrew from the English frontier to the Chattahoochee region and allowed the French to establish a fort at the juncture of the Coosa and the Tallapoosa rivers. Mobile was protected by the Choctaw allies of the French. As a result of these events, the English had to content themselves with the consolidation of their power in the region east of the Chattahoochee River. The French were able to establish a line of communication between New Orleans and their older settlements in Canada. They did this by building forts at Natchez and at Memphis and on the banks of the Tombigbee River. A stalemate in the South resulted. It was finally broken by decisive events in Canada that led to the cession of the Gulf region east of the Mississippi to the English under the Treaty of Paris of 1763.

The South's habit of receiving immigrants from the North began during the Colonial period, as did its habit of bending these invaders to its way of life. The Northern invasion began early in the eighteenth century when the Scotch-Irish and Germans of Pennsylvania moved into the Valley of Virginia and later spilled into the Yadkin Valley and other sections of the Southern Piedmont. There they were joined by Scotch Highlanders and Scotch-Irish who entered the country by way of Charleston and Wilmington.

The Scotch-Irish were Presbyterians of the Lowlands of Scotland who at the time Jamestown was being founded had been settled in northern Ireland by English sovereigns as a means of promoting loyalty in a rebellious land. Within less than a hundred years they began leaving Ireland for Pennsylvania and other parts of America because of high taxes and onerous religious and commercial restrictions at home. From the Pennsylvania frontier they moved southward during the three decades before the American Revolution. They were seeking lands on which to practice their thrifty type of agriculture. Accustomed to border warfare in Ireland and in Pennsylvania, they made excellent frontier fighters. They were practical, self reliant, and devoted to an austere Presbyterianism which did not, however, prohibit the manufacture and drinking of whisky. They were scornful of landlords and tax collectors and often squatted on unoccupied lands. Their capacity for politics expressed itself in the production of Southern statesmen and in the zeal with which at the time of the American Revolution they became "phanatical and hungry Republicans."

The second largest group to move southward into Virginia and North Carolina were the Pennsylvania Germans. They were Protestants from Austria and the Rhine region to whom Queen Anne gave haven from the persecutions of their rulers. They moved into the South a little earlier than the Scotch-Irish, establishing colonies in the Valley of Virginia as early as 1727. There they founded the towns of Winchester, Woodstock, Strasburg, and Harrisonburg. Many moved into North Carolina, occupying the counties of Rowan, Guilford, Forsyth, and Davidson. In 1753 Moravians of Bethlehem and Nazareth in Pennsylvania sent some of their group to build houses in Forsyth County on lands purchased from Lord Granville. Here were founded the villages of Bethabara, Bethania, and Salem. At Salem a beautiful Easter sunrise service was observed, a southern counterpart of that held at Bethlehem in Pennsylvania.

The German colonists of the South had many sterling qualities. They were devout Lutherans, Mennonites, Moravians, or Dunkards, who brought with them their massive Bibles, quaint dress, fine music, and habit of building substantial houses. Their foresighted methods of farming contrasted with the wasteful methods of the Anglo-Saxons. They were skilled in choosing good soils and in practicing crop rotation, deep plowing, and the preservation of woodlands and meadows. Yet they exercised little influence upon the development of the dominant ways of the South. They did not enter politics, promote wars or give up their independent yeoman ways in favor of slavery, plantations, and other extravagances which Southern expansiveness induced among less thrifty and more imaginative peoples. It was not until they gave up the German language and some of them anglicized their names in the middle of the nineteenth century that they entered the main stream of Southern life.

The Scotch-Irish early became Southerners. They were of the same Anglo-Saxon stock as the people of the coast regions. They were as land-greedy as any of the great families of the lowlands and just as ready to fight against the Indians, the French, and the English, whenever what they considered their God-given right to inherit the lands of the West was challenged. They accepted with alacrity the system of indentured servants and slaves. Their genius for the Southern brand of politics is attested by the fact that they produced Andrew Jackson, John C. Calhoun, George McDuffie, James K. Polk, and Andrew Johnson. Stonewall Jackson, a Scotch-Irishman of the Valley of Virginia, was as true a symbol of devotion to the ways of the South as was Robert E. Lee, the tidewater aristocrat.

The conquest and colonization of the region between the Atlantic and the Appalachians was a prelude to occupation of the great expanse beyond the mountains. Wars were won to make that region safe for the Anglo-Saxons, wars in which the English and the Scotch-Irish of all classes joined. First were the wars against the French and the Indians, ending in the surrender by the French in 1763 of the lands east of the Mississippi. Second was the American Revolution, which ended the British government's efforts to reserve the western lands for the Indians. Third was the War of 1812, in which the Southern War Hawks, Henry Clay, John C. Calhoun, and Felix Grundy, demanded that the British be driven north into Canada, and in which the Tennessean Andrew Jackson won a victory assuring that New Orleans and the lower Mississippi country should be American.

The first act in the drama of Southern occupation of the region beyond the mountains was the settling of Kentucky. This was "the dark and bloody ground" on which Northern and Southern Indians carried on a struggle comparable to that of Northern and Southern white men a hundred years later in the same region. It was the Great Meadow, with "soil as rich as cream," with a lush sod, the wild plum in bloom, and many game animals at its salt licks, into which Virginia and Carolina homeseekers moved.

The outstanding pioneer of this land was the semi-legendary Daniel Boone, the son of a Pennsylvanian who had settled in North Carolina to escape the restraints of Quakerism. Guided by John Finley, one of the numerous group of hunters who had explored the region beyond the mountains, Boone began his romantic career in Kentucky by leading a group of settlers into Powell's Valley beyond the Cumberland Gap. The group returned home after an Indian attack. This failure was followed by the first permanent settlement in Kentucky, which was made at Harrodsburg in central Kentucky in 1774, under the guidance of James Harrow of Pennsylvania.

The next developer of the region was Richard Henderson of North Carolina who in 1775, as head of the Transylvania Company, an organization of land speculators, purchased from the Cherokee Indians for a few thousand pounds their shadowy claims to the lands lying between the Kentucky, Ohio, and Cumberland rivers. In the same year

Boone, as an employee of the Transylvania Company, blazed Boone's Trace, leading to the Bluegrass region of Kentucky, and founded Boonesborough on the Kentucky River. To buttress his dubious title to the region Henderson on May 23, 1775, under a great elm at Boonesborough, organized the Transylvania colony with all the constitutional paraphernalia traditionally associated with such enterprises. Henderson and his associates conceived of Transylvania as a proprietorship comparable to that of the Lords Baltimore, in which the substance of power was in the company's hands. Their hopes for profits through the collection of quitrents and the sale of land were frustrated by protests from Kentuckians to the Virginia legislature. Kentucky was recognized as a county of Virginia, and the Transylvania state collapsed. By an act of the Virginia legislature of 1779 old settlers were confirmed in their possessions and new settlers were offered land titles. Henderson had failed because he was out of touch with the spirit of self-assertion which had prompted the Kentucky colonists to leave Virginia and North Carolina. These were men who had had enough of feudal restraints.

With the coming of the American Revolution the Indians, inspired by the British governor of Detroit, fell upon the Kentucky settlers. These settlers had to look for defense of a type the Transylvania Company had not been able to give. They found this defense in intrepid leaders like Boone, George Rogers Clark, and Simon Kenton, and in the lively interest in their protection manifested by the Virginia authorities. While the safety of the settlers was being secured, other colonists found their way over the mountains and moved into Kentucky by way of the Wilderness Road. This was a trail which stretched from the Cumberland Gap, in the extreme southwest of Virginia, to the Ohio River. By the end of the American Revolution 12,000 persons had taken this route.

These immigrants coming from the Valley of Virginia and from the Virginia and North Carolina Piedmont formed a cross section of Southern society. The largest element, as elsewhere in the South, were "cabin and corn patch men," that is, small farmers. Others were Virginians to the manner born who, with the aid of their slaves, established plantations of tobacco, hemp, and race horses, and gave the Bluegrass region the legendary splendors associated with Virginia and South Carolina. Laws favoring slavery were enacted, and the spirit of gentility and pride associated with the beneficiaries of that institution were manifest.[3]

Before the settlement of Kentucky, groups of Virginians and North Carolinians moved southwestward from the Cumberland Gap to make

[3] Clement Eaton, *A History of the Old South*, pp. 121–32.

Tennessee into a Southern province. The spearhead of this movement was the Watauga settlement of 1769 in the northeastern corner of Tennessee. It was made by a people whose experiences in the Southern Piedmont had taught them how to survive on the frontier. They met the problems of remoteness from other settlements of whites, of the want of law and justice, and of defense against the Indians, by organizing in 1772 the first autonomous government west of the Appalachians. A written constitution was made providing for a legislature of thirteen members. This state lasted until 1777, when Watauga became part of a North Carolina county that included the whole of the future state of Tennessee.

The pioneer of middle Tennessee was James Robertson, who in 1779 founded Nashville at the French Lick in the Valley of the Cumberland. The palisaded forts of the Southerners then appeared in middle Tennessee. At the end of the American Revolution ex-soldiers expecting land bounties and frontiersmen seeking relief from debts followed the trail James Robertson had blazed. Further colonization was promoted by William Blount and other land speculators. In hopes of securing protection from the Indians they persuaded the North Carolina legislature to cede Tennessee to the Congress of the Confederation.

When this device did not prevent raids by the Cherokees, the people of East Tennessee, in convention at Jonesboro in 1784, organized the state of Franklin with John Sevier as governor. John Sevier, a cultivated Virginia gentleman, was an outstanding figure in the colonization of Tennessee. The Franklin experiment was in part an expression of frontier democracy; it was also motivated by land speculation. It survived for only a few years. Internal dissension brought a threat of civil war, Congress refused to recognize the new state, and North Carolina reasserted its authority over the region. Franklin ceased to exist when North Carolina completed the cession of her western territory to the national government. It was included in Tennessee when that area achieved statehood in 1796.

The Southern pattern of colonization was reproduced in Tennessee to as great a degree as in Kentucky. The fertile mountain valleys of the east afforded homes for small farmers who did not adopt the plantation system. East Tennesseans were a distinctive type who nevertheless in their prejudices and ideals carried many of the earmarks of genuine Southerners. The Valley of the Cumberland drew planters of both tobacco and cotton, while the settlers on the western and southern borders of the state made cotton their single staple and acquired the plantation psychology as completely as the people of other regions of the South. In the Tennessee atmosphere it was easy for roughnecks of the type of Andrew Jackson to be changed into aristocrats. No compromise with habit or tradition was necessary for successful frontiersmen to assume the habit of command that came with land, slaves, money, horsemanship, the deference of the community, and the other attributes of aristocratic privilege.

In the 1790's there already existed in Tennessee the same regard for social superiors long characteristic of tidewater society. "No strong and universal antagonism existed . . . between the rich and the poor," asserts the historian of the period.[4] "In fact, political office was rarely sought even in the frontier but by the natural leaders of society, and they secured the suffrage of their neighbors by reason of their prestige, without resort to electioneering methods."

Tennesseans and Kentuckians pioneered in the extension of Anglo-American institutions into the Gulf region. Their immediate motive was to gain access to the sea by way of the Mississippi and other rivers. By the treaties which ended the American Revolution Spain acquired control of these outlets. Her statesmen saw the necessity of damming up the expansive energies of the Anglo-Saxons who threatened to plunge down the rivers to the west in order to take undeveloped lands and perhaps to deprive Spain of its empire. To accomplish its purpose Spain retained Natchez and other posts within American territory, used the Indians in a barbarous border warfare, closed ports to American commerce, and corrupted prominent Kentuckians and Tennesseans.

The United States government was slow to heed the needs of its western citizens and foolishly sanctioned the Jay-Gardoqui treaty under which Americans would have surrendered the right to navigate the Mississippi for twenty-five years. There was a movement under James Wilkinson to organize a separate western nation. William Blount and John Sevier engaged in dubious negotiations with the Spanish in an effort to open the Tombigbee River to western traffic. But most Kentuckians and Tennesseans did not wish to come under Spanish influence. Chances of a separatist movement were destroyed by the Treaty of 1795, which gave the westerners the right of transshipment of their products at New Orleans, and by the cession of the vast Louisiana territory to the United States in 1803. The way was cleared for the taking of Florida in 1819 and of Texas in 1845 as means of giving further extension to the South.

[4] Thomas P. Abernethy, *From Frontier to Plantation in Tennessee*, p. 149.

CHAPTER IV

Colonial Self-Government

━━━━━━━━━━━━━━━━━━━━━━━━━━━━━━━━━━━━━━━

SIR HUMPHREY GILBERT, a promoter of American colonization, thought of the establishment in the overseas wilderness of a state based on the most exalted ideals of which a people as practical as the English were capable. He was inspired by Sir Thomas More's *Utopia*, a book suggesting escape from the injustices and bad living conditions of England into a co-operative dreamland which might have been placed in the semitropical South. Gilbert's dream was never realized because this gallant adventurer was drowned on his way home from a fruitless colonial expedition. His last words were, "We are as near Heaven by sea as by land."

The ideas of Gilbert and More were supplemented by the desires of those who wished to extend overseas the heritage of Elizabethan England. There must be constitutional government as expressed in jury trials, local self-government, legislative assemblies, and other free institutions destined to form a precious heritage to future generations of Southerners. Outstanding among the promoters of such practices was Sir Edwin Sandys, treasurer of the Virginia Company. This philanthropic radical while serving in Parliament advocated religious toleration, the election of the king, and even republicanism. He wished Virginia to have schools, a legislative assembly, a new system of land tenure, political freedoms, and material prosperity based on industrial variety. Except for the legislative assembly, Sandys' plans failed. But they were not without significance for the future.

Others who cherished the Elizabethan heritage wished to project in the South the landholding and social practices of feudal England. This was attempted by the proprietors of Maryland and Carolina. It

((43))

was a form of idealism as important in the destinies of the Southern colonies as more democratic reforms. The trustees of Georgia attempted to establish a wilderness Arcadia by combining authoritarian methods with radical reforms. Autocratic procedures were designed to forestall injustices inherent in colonial adventures.

The idealism of the English sponsors of colonization was best expressed in plans for the projection of the English form of Christianity in the Southern colonies. As has been explained,[1] the failure in early Virginia and Maryland of Indian missions was caused by the natural resistance of the natives rather than lack of zeal on the part of the English. Such missionaries as George Thorpe and Andrew White tried to make relations between the white men and the red men co-operative and friendly.

Exalted motives as well as custom prompted the colonial authorities to make the Church of England a state-supported institution in all the Southern colonies. Englishmen in the eighteenth century were as sincere in believing that the public welfare was promoted by taxing the people for the support of a particular form of Christianity as are twentieth-century legislators in taxing for the support of public schools. Compulsory church attendance in Colonial Virginia was prompted by the same convictions of community good as is compulsory school attendance in the present-day South.

Motives of self-interest were not absent from those who promoted the colonization of the South. Such motives were necessary to sustain interest in projects which had many practical angles. Richard Hakluyt, in his writings promoting overseas expansion, put a premium upon southern soil and climate where English products might be supplemented by the production of commodities which were coming from hostile Latin lands. This idea fitted in with the mercantilist philosophy of national self-sufficiency of the merchant oligarchy of England. The Maryland and Carolina proprietors wanted to have feudal estates from which they could draw rents. The founders of Virginia were businessmen organized in a stock company with dividends as a primary expectation.

Out of this combination of unselfish and selfish motives grew the type of control the English government imposed upon its Southern colonies. This control was exercised by the crown. In theory the crown meant the king. But as a result of the English Revolution it became little more than a conglomeration of powers exercised by a corps of officials headed by the Board of Trade under the supervision of Parliament. Because Parliament for the greater part of the colonial period was dominated by a merchant oligarchy, its laws were in the interest of this

[1] See above, pp. 22, 29.

class. Thus one series of statutes protected the Colonial investment of the English merchants. The land and slaves of the planters were made liable for debts, the use of commodities as money was controlled, and the lowering of the value of Colonial currency was prohibited.

Another series of statutes was designed to prevent the production in the colonies of commodities which the English wished to sell. Such restrictions had little effect upon the South except to hamper iron manufacture in Virginia. The region was devoted to the production of forest and field commodities that could not be produced in the mother country.

A third series of statutes restricted colonial trade to British ships. Against these regulations the Southern colonies had reason to complain. They had to pay high rates on tobacco exports through English shipping interests because of the exclusion of Dutch competition. On the list of "enumerated goods" that had to be shipped through English ports even if destined for other countries were such Southern exports as rice, tobacco, naval stores, and lumber. Thereby Southerners were forced to pay English merchants additional freight, insurance, and handling charges. Southerners were forced to buy salt for the curing of beef and pork from New England although in a free market it could have been purchased more cheaply in Spain and the Cape Verde Islands.

Due to their warmer climate the Southern colonies fitted better than the colonies of the North into the English plan of using overseas dependencies as sources of commodities which could not be produced at home. Consequently they were favored by imperial policy. Southern tobacco planters were given a monopoly of the English market through the prohibition of tobacco growing in the mother country and through the exclusion of Spanish tobacco from the English market. South Carolina indigo enjoyed a bounty of sixpence a pound and was admitted to the English market free of duty. Carolina producers of naval stores were able to capture the English market from Swedish rivals because of the high bounties Parliament paid the Southerners. In the middle of the eighteenth century rice was admitted into England free of duty and was taken off the enumerated list to the extent of being allowed to be exported directly to Spain and the Mediterranean countries.

The English government exercised its authority in the colonies through a group of officials with extensive executive and judicial functions. The chief of these officials was the royal governor. He arrived in his domain with elaborate instructions to implement his prerogatives. He had power to summon and dissolve the legislature, to appoint officials, to grant land patents, to control the military forces, and to issue proclamations.

Some of the Southern governors, like Seth Sothel of the Carolinas and Sir John Harvey and Sir Henry Chicheley of Virginia, were weak, tactless, or mercenary. Others, like Gabriel Johnson of North Carolina, were unpopular because they struggled to maintain the authority of the crown against greed and disorder among the colonists. The most famous Southern colonial official was Sir William Berkeley, who in 1642 gave up a career as playwright and courtier to become governor of Virginia. He held this office except during the period of Puritan ascendancy until his removal in 1677. The evil reputation he gained by strictures against public education and by his ruthless punishment of participants in Bacon's Rebellion has overshadowed the accomplishments of this unwearied promoter of Virginian interests. He quieted political factionalism, encouraged new crops and industries, and courageously defended his colony against the Indians and the Dutch. His persecutions of the Quakers and the Puritans were based on a sincere and perhaps sound conviction that these sectarians were politically subversive.

Virginia for a third of the eighteenth century had as governors three enlighted Scotchmen. They were Alexander Spotswood, William Gooch, and Robert Dinwiddie. Spotswood demonstrated his largeness of view by encouraging German immigrants, by opening iron mines, and by leading the way to western expansion.

Gooch was a gentleman of much piety and love of the colony he governed. He protected local interests against the greed of the English merchants, carefully supervised church affairs, and tolerated dissenters.

In his first address to the House of Burgesses Dinwiddie said, "It is with great Joy I landed here, invested with the Power of doing Good to a people, among whom I have formerly mingled in Scenes of domestic Felicity, and experienced the endearing Reciprocation of Friendship." He implemented his words by defending the frontiers of Virginia against the menaces of the French and Indians, and by asking the co-operation of the other colonies in what should have been a common duty.

The great powers with which the crown endowed the governors brought them in conflict with the Colonial assemblies. Many causes of disagreement arose: Who should own the land? Who should pay the taxes? Who should provide for defense? How should debts and currency be regulated? In the struggle over these and kindred interests, the Southern assemblies had by 1700 won two privileges: the right to assent to laws and taxes, and the right to initiate legislation. Using these powers as a fulcrum, the assemblies usurped many of the legislative and judicial functions of the governors. This was possible because except in Georgia these officials had to depend on colonial sources for their incomes. In Virginia this salary came from a fixed tax on tobacco exports, in North Carolina it depended on uncertain quitrents, and in South Carolina it came from temporary grants by the assembly.

Parliament after 1689 tried to extend the prerogatives it had wrested from the crown by taking unto itself the authority the king was supposed to exercise over the colonies. The colonies resisted this attempt to transfer imperial authority. They claimed that their legislative assemblies should be co-ordinate with Parliament; that each within its own sphere should exercise sovereign authority, with king and governors in Virginia and the Carolinas being mere symbols of imperial unity in the same manner in which the king and his agents had already become mere symbols of national unity in England. Parliament accepted compromise, contenting itself with the regulation of such "external affairs" as trade and currency. In internal affairs the Southern colonies were allowed to move so far toward the status of unacknowledged republics that Governor James Glen of South Carolina remarked in 1748: "The people have the whole of the administration in their hands."

Attempts were made to strenghten British authority over the Southern colonies through the Anglican church. A successful movement in this direction was the establishment in 1701 of the Society for the Propagation of the Gospel in Foreign Parts, under the sponsorship of the Archbishop of Canterbury. This organization sent religious literature and missionaries to meet the needs of the Indians, the Negroes, and neglected communities of whites. Its most significant accomplishment was to convince the planters that no harm would come to the institution of slavery by the conversion of the blacks to Christianity.

Protracted attempts were made to have Colonial bishops as a means of providing supervision of the clergy and of making possible the exercise in America of the episcopal functions of ordination and confirmation. When these attempts failed, clerical supervisors called commissaries were allowed as disappointing substitutes. The commissaries did not have the power to confirm or ordain.

Three of these officials performed their functions with idealism and practical sagacity. Commissary Thomas Bray of Maryland recruited missionaries, established libraries for clergy and laity, undertook the discipline of derelict clergymen, and persuaded the legislature to make the Anglican the state church of the colony. Commissary James Blair of Virginia beat down the opposition of self-seeking politicians to secure in England the charter and the money necessary for the establishment of the College of William and Mary. Commissary Alexander Garden of South Carolina sustained English notions of religious propriety by instituting annual meetings of the clergy, by refuting what he considered the unorthodox preaching of the evangelist George Whitefield, and by establishing in Charleston a school for Negro youth.

Despite the conviction that the Anglican way was the best way to salvation, the rulers of the Southern colonies adjusted their religious standards to practical exigencies. As indicated elsewhere,[2] in the whole South except in seventeenth-century Virginia a variety of non-Anglican faiths was tolerated. Virginia in the eighteenth century tolerated Quakers, Presbyterians, Lutherans, German pietists, and Baptists.

Religious freedom in the colonial South was motivated in part by John Locke's philosophy of common sense which, in the eighteenth century, convinced the gentlemen of England, Virginia, and the Carolinas that in matters of faith there should be no state censorship. Thereby was laid the foundation of one of the regions's most honored heritages: a strong faith in God without dictation by law of the form that faith should take.

"No inferiority complex," remarks a historian of the region,[3] "was included in the luggage of the English immigrant to the South." This immigrant was not, like the settlers of Pennsylvania and New England, fleeing from unfavorable economic, religious, or political conditions. He was pulled rather than pushed into a new land by hopes of acquiring more privileges than he had at home. Maryland was only in part a refuge for oppressed Catholics. The Catholics of England were not persecuted severely enough to prompt them to leave home in sufficient numbers to form a majority of the population of their overseas haven. The Huguenots of South Carolina gave up their Calvinist ways so readily in favor of those of the Anglican church that it is easy to believe that social and economic opportunity was a more compelling motive in bringing them to America than the push of religious persecution.

A people so opportunistic as the Southern colonists were inevitably prone to set aside idealistic professions to attain their real objectives. The early Virginians opposed co-operative landowning and a planned system of diversified crops in order that they might exploit the land for individual profit. The early Georgians struggled successfully against the creation of a society in which exploitation was prohibited. They had come to the New World to turn the tables, to exploit rather than to be exploited. Everywhere in the Colonial South men moved ruthlessly forward to gain personal fortune by using the land. They sought land grants, imported white bondsmen from Europe, and black slaves from Africa; they destroyed the Indians or forced them farther into the wilderness.

[2] See above, pp. 29, 32, 34.
[3] Robert S. Cotterill, *The Old South*, p. 68.

BACON'S CASTLE, VIRGINIA, *ca. 1650. One of the earliest surviving great mansions of Virginia, built in the Jacobean style. This house was seized by participants in Bacon's Rebellion in 1676.*

WESTOVER, VIRGINIA, 1726. *Home of William Byrd II, author of the Westover Mss. and possessor of one of the finest libraries of Colonial Virginia. This classic example of early eighteenth-century architecture still stands on the James River.*

BELMONT, TENNESSEE, 1850. *Designed by the famous William Strickland, this great ante-bellum mansion shows the splendor of Southern
neoclassicism.*

GREENWOOD, LOUISIANA, 1830. *A flamboyant Greek Revival mansion of
the type built by the great planters of the lower Mississippi.*

The more fortunate colonists became rich. They did this by securing large land grants, by land speculation, by wrenching the substance from the soil through wasteful methods of farming, and by monopolizing the trading posts along navigable rivers. By these means they created an oligarchy as far removed from modern concepts of democracy as the feudalism of the Old World. Colonial self-government meant giving power to the landed and slaveholding aristocracy for the same reason that the decentralization of government in medieval Europe put power in the hands of the landed nobility.

In the South the tradition of social distinctions was too deeply engrained to allow the development of class conflict. The granting of suffrage to the small farmers did not bring about demands for social and economic changes. There were few complaints from immediate neighbors when the Virginia planters or the Charleston planter-merchants monopolized public office. Protests were of a territorial rather than a class character. Men of all classes protested against acts of the imperial government in London, as men of all classes of the back country protested against the privileges and exactions of the coastal oligarchies.

The combination of intelligent selfishness with more exalted motives was expressed in the development of the institutions of early Virginia. The Virginia Company was as interested in planting a nation where none was before as it was in money-making. When hopes of easy wealth resulted in poverty, sickness, and idleness among the colonists, the company would not accept failure. New colonists were sent, and the land was worked in corporate form under heroic taskmasters. The settlers were marched twice a day into field and forest and twice a day they were marched back to Jamestown to eat and pray.

This arrangement, though immediately successful, did not attract immigrants. Englishmen did not like a planned society. They were willing to come to Virginia if they could improve upon the liberties they enjoyed at home. Reforms were necessary. These reforms came in three ways. One was through the cultivation of tobacco, a commodity which yielded steady but not demoralizing profits. Another was the right to win a stake in the community through land ownership. The third was the establishment of institutions of self-government.

In 1618 the Virginia Company surrendered its monopoly of Virginia lands in favor of the hundreds and headright systems. Under the first plan a man of means who brought into the colony a group of settlers was granted a tract of land. Under the second plan individuals who paid their own transportation costs were given fifty acres for themselves and fifty acres for anyone whose passage they had paid. Thus private gain was enlisted as a means of building up the colony's population, and a mass of independent farmers came into being. These farmers were, under the English system, entitled to the privileges of officeholding and voting.

In England this coupling of land ownership with political rights was a means of perpetuating aristocracy, because of the excess of population over acreage. In Virginia and the other Southern colonies, however, it was a means of furthering political democracy, because of the excess of acreage over population. Land could be had by almost all freemen. The perpetuation of the monopolies of officeholding and social privilege among the large landholders was carried on only with the consent of the small landholders.

The most momentous step toward the achievement of self-government was the convening of the first legislative assembly in the history of the New World. This took place at Jamestown on July 30, 1619. The assembly consisted of two representatives from each of eleven boroughs of Virginia. This was a fulfillment of the guarantee of the Virginia charter that the colonists should live according to the laws of England. It was a means of balancing the demands of local interests with the necessities of closer union within the colony. Out of this first assembly developed the bicameral legislature. The governor and the council constituted the upper house; the representatives of the boroughs constituted the lower house, which was known as the House of Burgesses.

Another fulfillment of the promised liberties of Englishmen was the establishment of local self-government through counties. Throughout the colonial period counties were freely created to meet the demands of settlements at a distance from the center of authority at Jamestown or Williamsburg. A board of commissioners known as the county court possessed functions covering the fields of local justice and administration. Among these functions were the keeping and interpretation of land titles, the maintenance of highways, and the regulation of the tobacco market. In the settlement of disputes the county court acted as a board of arbitration which dispensed justice without the formality of jury trial. In their individual capacities as justices of the peace, the members of the county court were the men to whom neighbors naturally turned for the settlement of differences. So powerful was the county court that membership in it was sought and secured by the most important persons of the colony.

The county justices extended their influence into provincial politics through their control of the election machinery, through their knowledge of local conditions, and through their positions as the social leaders of the counties. The House of Burgesses was a body speaking for the county courts or for those closely allied with them in station and interest. Thus came about the practice of expressing local interests through an oligarchy of leading citizens. This condition was so satisfying to all classes that the practice was followed everywhere in the South and up to the present has been modified in no important particular.

The unit of local church administration was the parish. The parishes were ruled by the vestries, self-perpetuating bodies composed largely of the same groups as the county courts. The vestries selected the clergymen, administered the glebe or church lands, regulated church taxes, cared for the poor, and presented lawbreakers to the county courts. In the interest of local self-expression, the vestries denied parish ministers certain privileges enjoyed by English clergymen. The vestries refused to give the ministers security of tenure or income; they opposed the appointment of bishops under whom ecclesiastical authority could have been centralized and native Virginians conveniently ordained for the ministry. This created a condition which has since been a feature of Southern life: churches in which lay control is so dominant that the authority of the clergymen is insignificant.

The development of political institutions in the other Southern colonies followed the Virginia model. Under instructions from the Lords Proprietor, the first general assembly of North Carolina met in 1665, a few years after the settlement of the Albemarle region. The vigor of this body is attested by its protests against the attempt to make the people settle in towns and against a less liberal land policy than that prevailing in Virginia. Shut off from ready communication with the outside world, the North Carolinians asserted themselves in the manner of Kentucky and Tennessee frontiersmen a hundred years later. They refused to pay duties when levied; they protested against foolish laws and the demand that the colony be subordinated to Charleston; they drove out two governors and demanded for themselves a "free parliament."

The Lords Proprietor and the London authorities, more interested in a colony of greater promise, allowed North Carolina to go its own way. By 1689 the precinct courts were assuming functions which were held in the eighteenth century by justices of the peace and county courts. In 1712 the colony got a governor independent of the governor of South Carolina, and in 1729 it became a royal possession independent of the Lords Proprietor.

These changes did not end North Carolina's struggle for a greater degree of self-government. So assertive were its people that William Byrd II of Virginia said that they were "accustomed to live without law or gospel." Royal governors strove to bring "the chaos into form" and to reduce "Anarchy into regular Government." These officials complained of desertions from the militia, of insecure jails, of the scattering of public records, and of tax collectors absconding with the public funds. Into this situation came the autocratic Governor William Tryon who, after suppressing the revolt of the Regulators and thereby winning popularity in the eastern counties, gladly retired in 1771 from the thankless task of imposing the discipline demanded by his commission as chief agent of the crown.

The Lords Proprietor made more strenuous efforts to enforce their authority in South Carolina than in North Carolina. This was because South Carolina showed greater promise of material prosperity. A South Carolina legislature met for the first time in 1671. It consisted of the governor as deputy of the chief of the Lords Proprietor, a council composed of the deputies of the other proprietors, and delegates elected by the freeholders of the province. At first the Commons House of Assembly, as the house of representatives was called, was not allowed to initiate legislation, and its acts were subject to the veto of both the council and the proprietors. Despite these restrictions, South Carolina moved in the direction of self-government. Its inhabitants were determined to tolerate no government or forms of land tenure which did not satisfy their needs. These needs were interpreted by a small ruling clique of council members. The council members were rich men whose local interests took precedence over obligations to the absentee proprietors. They combined with the popular party in opposition to the enforcement of the Fundamental Constitutions of Carolina.

Neither the aristocratic nor the democratic party was satisfied with the concessions won from the overlords. Both parties complained against the neglect of religion, education, and frontier defense, and against the refusal of the proprietors to confer titles of nobility for other than mercenary considerations. The demand of the legislature for the holding of elections in different precincts instead of only in Charleston was rejected by the proprietors. The rich men of the province wanted effective defense of their expanding rice plantations. They were menaced by the Spanish and their Indian allies who were harboring runaway slaves. The small farmers wanted new lands. The fur traders wanted the defense of a strong government against the Louisiana French.

The answer to these demands was a niggardly policy of land allotments, the continued imposition of quitrents, and notice that the colonists were to provide for their own defense. The murderous assault of the Yamasee Indians in 1715 was met by little aid from the proprietors, and the South Carolinians got no help when the French interrupted their westward movement by the seizure of forts. Revolt came when the proprietors tried to frustrate the plan of the colonial assembly to give to white settlers lands taken from the Yamasees. The provincial militia seized Charleston in 1719, and a petition was sent to the English authorities asking that the colony be made a royal province. This request was willingly granted.

The church problem in South Carolina was solved in accordance with local wishes. A legislative act of 1697 gave religious freedom to all Christians except Roman Catholics. This made possible the growth of the Baptist, Huguenot, and Presbyterian denominations. In 1704 an overzealous governor attempted to make the Church of England the church of the state, to tax dissenters for its support, and to require the legislators to be members of it. Protests brought about the repeal of this law and the creation of a more liberal Anglican establishment. The state church was supported by all taxpayers, but membership in it was not required for officeholding. Laymen of each parish were allowed to select the vestrymen, the church wardens, and the minister. Ecclesiastical authority passed into local hands to as great a degree as in Virginia.

A despised feature of the early constitution of Georgia was the absence of self-government. A legislative assembly was created in 1751. When the trustees relinquished their authority to the crown in the following year, Georgia acquired a government like other colonies. It had an assembly, a governor, and a council. This meant a high degree of self-government and greater freedom for ambitious leaders. A plan of absentee absolutism for the promotion of economic and political equality had given way to the freedom and inequality which was the norm of Southern life.

The Maryland charter provided for the enactment of laws and the levying of taxes by the consent of the freemen. This necessitated a legislative assembly. Early in the history of the colony the governor called primary assemblies of landowners to enact laws, with the proviso that those unable to attend should assign proxies. Because this practice put voting in the hands of a few, the landowners were in 1659 given an elective house of delegates with the right to sit as a body separate from the governor and council. This body could prevent the imposition of laws and taxes without its consent; it wrung from the proprietor the right to initiate bills and the promise not to exercise his veto more than eighteen months after a bill was passed. Yet Maryland, with some breaks, remained an oligarchy governed in the interest of the Calverts until the American Revolution. Only landowners could vote for membership in its house of delegates; acts of that body could be overridden by vetoes of the council, the governor, or the proprietor. The Anglican

church was officially established in 1702, but the vestries never acquired powers of control over the clergy as great as in Virginia and
South Carolina.

The failure of the Marylanders to attain powers of self-government
comparable to those of the other Southern colonies was not caused by
inertia. They constantly resented the presence of a Roman Catholic
minority, the payment of quitrents, and the restrictions imposed on land
grants and fee simple ownership. Between 1650 and 1689 there were
five popular revolts. In 1654-5 the Puritans deposed the governor and
erected an independent government. A revolt in 1660 threatened the
destruction of proprietary rights and the establishment of a republic.
Malcontents inspired by Bacon's Rebellion revolted in 1676, but they
were suppressed by an energetic governor. Another revolt in 1681 required another energetic suppression. When in 1689 the news of the
expulsion of King James II came to the colony, a Protestant party composed of planters and small farmers seized the government from agents
of the proprietor. This caused Maryland to be made into a royal
province in 1691. It was not until 1716 that the authority of the
Calverts was restored. They were able to allay discontent only by
tactful exercise of their autocratic powers, and by abandoning Catholicism for Protestantism.

The political disturbances of the South during the colonial period
were of a sectional rather than a class character. Resistance to governors
and councils was not primarily against those officials as representatives
of the upper classes but against them as representatives of an authority
three thousand miles away. Gains in self-government did not generally
mean gains in power by the lower classes, but often rather of the tidewater oligarchies.

The men of the back country had more reason to hate these
oligarchies than they did the London bureaucrats. The coastal cliques
had the support of their immediate constituencies whether the suffrage
was extended to the many or reserved for the few. "Instead of voting
for the demagogues who tried to lure them with liquor and barbecues,"
a historian observes,[4] "the voters elected aristocrats, possessing learning
and character." The secret of aristocratic power was not to be generous
in extending legislative representation to the back-country counties.
The men of the back country resented the concentration of power in
the hands of the gentlemen of the coast.

The men of the back country were different from the men of the
lowlands in origin and institutions. They were in part distinguished by
their German or Scotch blood, by membership in German, Presbyterian, or Baptist churches, and by the absence among them of large

[4] Clement Eaton, The Old South, p. 58.

estates, many slaves, or much culture and refinement. Their society was more democratic.

It would be a misunderstanding of the whole course of Southern history, however, to assume that the dissatisfaction of the hinterlanders was caused by a desire to revolt against the social values of the coastal region. The men of the back country were not opposed to slavery, plantation leisure, hedonistic living, and other aristocratic practices. They wished to be rid of the oppressions of the tidewater oligarchs so that they too might move forward in keeping with Southern standards already established on the eastern seaboard. To the degree to which they were able to remove these oppressions they were able to practice the coastal ideals.

The men of the back country wanted cheap paper money as an easy means of paying their debts to the coastal merchants. They wanted roads and bridges so that they could grow staples and transport them to markets as did the planters of the tidewater. They were as anxious as the men of the coast to possess broad acres. For this reason they wanted government aid in pushing back the Indians; as land speculators and squatters, they were bitter when they ran afoul of the land claims of seaboard magnates. As dissenters they objected to paying parish taxes for the support of the Anglican church.

These grievances could not be easily removed because of the refusal of the legislatures to grant back-country representation in proportion to the population. In South Carolina under the so-called parish system each county of the coastal region was given six or eight representatives, whereas the interior counties were each allowed only one or two. In Virginia the small eastern counties were given the same number of representatives as the large piedmont counties. As late as 1780 Thomas Jefferson was able to write that "19,000 men below the falls give the law to 30,000 living in other parts of the state."

That this disparity in representation was tolerated was due largely to the recognition that the tidewater rulers of the colonies gave to the rising upper class of the back country. From this rising upper class of surveyors, lawyers, debt collectors, merchants, and land speculators came those to whom the governors and the councils gave local public offices. First came the justices of the peace who composed the county courts. These courts decided disputes, levied the taxes, and nominated the sheriffs and other county officers. The authority exercised by these local representatives of tidewater interests was in general resisted to no greater degree than the local representatives of Northern capital in the South of the twentieth century. In both cases the agents of the outsiders were well-integrated citizens of their communities who gave valued services in return for the tributes they collected. The twentieth-century agents of Northern capital gave Northern mechanical devices and Northern ideals of civilization; the eighteenth-century agents of coastal governments gave the people of the back country the standards of refinement and social distinctions that were the Southern ideal.

The fact that the back country was not profoundly dissatisfied with tidewater dominance was demonstrated by the failure of the only two important insurrections in the history of intraprovincial sectionalism. These outbreaks were separated by almost a century; one was in Virginia in the last quarter of the seventeenth century, the other in North Carolina near the end of the colonial period.

The first of these insurrections was Bacon's Rebellion of 1676 in Virginia. It was caused primarily by the high-handed conduct of the irascible old Sir William Berkeley, who had returned to the governorship after the restoration of the Stuart king in 1660. Berkeley took advantage of royalist enthusiasms and his ability to control the governor's council and the House of Burgesses to effect his reactionary intentions. He strengthened the power of the prevailing oligarchy by restricting the suffrage to the freeholders and by refusing for fifteen years to call an election for a new assembly. The greatest resentment was caused by sectional rather than class grievances. The governor refused to heed the demands of the frontiersmen that the Indians be pushed off the lands to which the Indians had been assigned. After the savages had killed many of the settlers on remote farms, the frontiersmen chose as their spokesman a passionate young planter named Nathaniel Bacon who was high enough in the governing oligarchy to be a member of the governor's council. When Berkeley refused the request for protection, Bacon marched against the Indians without the governor's authorization. When Berkeley declared him a rebel, Bacon is said to have exclaimed, "Damn my blood, I'll kill Governor, Council, Assembly and all." He marched on Jamestown and burned it.

Bacon died in the midst of his triumphs, and his movement collapsed. How far he intended to go is not clear. Some historians think he wished to lead a liberal revolt in the manner of Patrick Henry a hundred years later. Most probably he was moved by the popular desire to protect and extend the frontier. This was certainly true of his followers, who, in the words of a contemporary, "do not think themselves engaged against the king's authority, but merely against the Indians."

There were no other major sectional disorders in colonial Virginia. This was true despite the fact that the commonwealth was divided by geographical and social differences: the separations of rivers and mountains, and a growing diversity of race and religion.

The holding of the colony together was a major triumph of statesmanship. After Bacon's Rebellion royal commissioners arrived to stay Berkeley's vengeful hand, and a newly elected assembly instituted reforms and decreed a general amnesty. As we have seen, earlier religious restrictions gave way in the eighteenth century to a tolerance of invading Presbyterians and Baptists. It was discovered that the members of these churches differed from other Virginians only in religious matters. They accepted the Virginian standards of race and class distinctions and Virginian notions of correct behavior toward the issues of war and government. Tolerance of them extended to the point of allowing vestrymen of some parishes to be Presbyterians. In the crisis of the American Revolution the Presbyterians and the Baptists joined with the tidewater Episcopalians to make Virginia as united as any other colony against the crown.

The people of the Old Dominion were bound together by compromises in religion, by resistance to restrictions on the occupation of western lands, and by the proud tradition that Virginia was a coordinate dominion of the crown and not a mere colony of the English nation.

In the 1760's North Carolina had in Governor William Tryon and the Regulators the counterparts of Governor Berkeley and Bacon's militia. The men of the North Carolina back country asserted, "We have long yielded ourselves slaves to remorseless oppression." They complained against venal lawyers and officials, disproportionate taxation, the withdrawal of paper money from circulation, and unfair land laws. In 1768 the formed the Regulator Associations to halt the exactions of the tax collectors. They elected a majority of the provincial assembly, but hopes of legal redress were frustrated by Governor Tryon's dissolution of this body and by the packing of the courts with his partisans. When the Regulators tried direct action the governor moved against them with decision and defeated them in the Battle of the Alamance in May, 1771. The revolt collapsed, since the Regulators were not willing to continue the fight. Some of them migrated to Tennessee. Others remained behind to fight on the British side in the American Revolution against the hated tidewater oligarchy.

Out of the exchange of ideas and experiences between imperial policymakers and influential elements in the Southern colonies there developed a political system which worked successfully. This system was the adaptation of elements of the rich English heritage to the needs and lively ambitions of men of English descent living in the Southern wilderness. The compromise resulting was so satisfactory that the Southern states today retain many features of their Colonial governments. The War of American Independence in the South has been seen by some as more a secession than a revolution. Secession in this case was caused by the refusal of both sides to make ultimate concessions: the refusal of the mother country to make the colonies her equals, and the refusal of the colonies to check their overweening ambition to govern themselves.

The compromises that were successful are impressive. The attempt to import English feudal customs was only in part a failure. Proprietary government survived to the end of the colonial period in Maryland. Land monopoly and serfdom could not survive in a region where land was almost free. Yet the feudal concept of aristocracy was expressed in the development of slavery and great estates, and in the growing belief that the slavemasters were the descendants of the Cavaliers. English idealism signally failed in Indian missions and in the Georgian Arcadia. Yet the hope of maintaining the English form of Christianity through state churches was realized with one notable variation. The Southern passion for local self-government led to the control of church affairs by laymen. The practice of religious toleration appealed to the idealism and self-interest of both the Southerners and their English sponsors.

The projection of the proprietary or royal will through governors with extensive powers took root; but the governors were handicapped in the exercise of their powers by claims of local magnates, who justified themselves by customs inherited from England. These local magnates made good their claims through the provincial assemblies and the counties. Out of conflicts between the governors and the provincial assemblies came a high degree of self-government. Out of the conflicts between local communities and those who held power in the tidewater capitals grew strong counties. Out of a general desire for autonomy grew a spirit of rebellion which was twice expressed: in the demand in the late eighteenth century to be free from central authority in London, and in the demand in the middle of the nineteenth century to be free from central authority in Washington. The Southern feeling for states' rights has a Colonial background.

CHAPTER V

Handwritten annotations: "abol 1889" · "Also slavery in [not] Brazil ⟩ but not as extensively developed" · "Fr. Haiti" · "BWI"

Colonial Labor and Life

Handwritten: "abol 1833"

>>>->>>

Handwritten: "plantation agriculture motivated by slavery"

A DISTINCTIVE quality was given the Southern colonies through the development of an agricultural system different from that of Europe and the Northern colonies in America. This was the plantation system of producing great staples with slave labor. That the owners of plantations and slaves were outnumbered by small farmers who tilled the soil with their own hands was of no great moment. The planters gave tone to Southern life. To equal them in wealth and prestige was the ambition of lesser men. *Handwritten: "set the standard"*

John Rolfe in 1612 introduced into Virginia a West Indian type of *Handwritten: "Trinidad"* tobacco which was without the bitter taste of the variety used by the Virginia Indians. This innovation opened the European market to Virginia and thereby laid the foundation of the Southern plantation system. King James I said that the smokers of the new weed were "guilty of sinful and shameful lust." King Charles I and English officials wished to divert Virginians to the growing of commodities which created more than unsubstantial smoke. Their protests were in vain. Before Rolfe made his discovery Sir Walter Raleigh had made smoking a diversion of the English gentry; it became such a social craze on the continent of Europe that the expansion of the tobacco market was almost unlimited. Its production fitted into the prevailing mercantilist theory of national *Handwritten: "Advantages of cd"* self-containment. Instead of exporting precious specie to buy foreign varieties, tobacco produced in territory under English control could be paid for in English goods and handled by English traders. Because of its small bulk and high value it surmounted the barriers of high freight rates and the difficult Atlantic passage better than any other Southern product.

The virgin soil beneath the girdled trees of Virginia was perfectly suited for tobacco. The high price of five shillings a pound which prevailed at first made it possible for farmers to make five times as much from tobacco as from other crops. By 1627 Virginia's annual exports amounted to 500,000 pounds. By the 1630's the industry spread to Maryland, and the Virginians who settled in the Albemarle region in the 1660's made tobacco the principal crop of North Carolina.

Tobacco determined to so great a degree the unique economic and social characteristics of Virginia, North Carolina, and Maryland that they were called the Tobacco Colonies. It was their money crop, the means through which necessary European imports could be had. Because of the scarcity of gold and silver coins tobacco became a legal medium of exchange. Salaries of clergymen were paid in tobacco, and for leaf of high quality deposited in warehouses receipts were exchanged that were accepted as legal tender in the payment of debts and taxes. When overproduction eventually caused low prices, both the English and colonial governments attempted remedies. The growing of tobacco was prohibited in England, and the Spanish variety was excluded from English markets. In 1629 and 1630 the Virginia assembly resorted to a system of crop control similar to that of the Franklin D. Roosevelt administration three hundred years later. Each planter was limited by law to the cultivation of two or three thousand plants. In 1670 Virginia selfishly imposed an embargo on the importation of North Carolina tobacco and its shipment through Virginia ports. When these remedies did not work, the small planters took the law in their hands, going through the fields and cutting down plants.

South Carolina found in rice a staple as reliable as its neighbors found in tobacco. Before 1700 it was discovered that the moist lowlands of the province's coast was ideal for the production of this grain. Soon rice planters were making 40 per cent on their investments. Its cultivation and export became the basis of a wealthy aristocracy of a few hundred planters operating within the narrow range of the tidal flow near Georgetown, Charleston, and Beaufort and in adjoining areas of North Carolina and Georgia. At first the inundations necessary for the cultivation of rice were achieved by impounding streams above inland swamps. The scarcity of water of this origin led to the employment after 1758 of the system of tidal-flowing. Lands lying within the range of fresh-water tides were equipped with banks, ditches, and sluices which were used for the flooding and draining of the rice fields thrice a year. At the time the tidal-flowing system was adopted, drills and harrows were substituted for hand labor, and water-driven threshing machines replaced sticks and windfans.

The staple crop of the dry lands of South Carolina and Georgia im-

Buck

mediately above the rice fields was indigo. In 1744 Eliza Lucas, the planter-daughter of the governor of a West Indian island, demonstrated that the production of this dye-stuff was practical in South Carolina. Neighboring planters promptly adopted Miss Lucas' idea as a supplement to the cultivation of rice. Stability was given to the industry by a parliamentary bounty in 1748 and by the coming to South Carolina in 1756 of Moses Lindo, an experienced indigo-sorter. The plant was cut in full bloom, placed in vats of water, beaten while in ferment, dried, and finally cut in cubes for the market.

Reason no rice in SC now -- Negroes refused to work after civil War.

The acquisition of great tracts of land was an almost unlimited source of wealth in the Southern colonies. These holdings were acquired in various ways. Energetic planters received many fifty-acre headrights through the importation of indentured servants. Shrewd planters frequently increased their holdings by exaggerating the number of servants imported, by adding zeroes to the records of their land patents, or by receiving blank patents signed by governors in advance of surveys. Outright grants of huge estates were made by proprietors or kings. Such, for example, was the Thomas Lord Fairfax holdings of 6 million acres in the Northern Neck of Virginia, the Lord Granville tract along the northern border of North Carolina, and the Henry McCulloh "principality" in western North Carolina. Among the great land monopolists were the Carroll and Dulany families of Maryland, "King" Robert Carter of Virginia who possessed 333,000 acres, the Beverley family who possessed 100,000 acres in the Valley of Virginia, the Byrds of Westover with plantations in central Virginia, and Sir James Wright with extensive holdings in Georgia.

Vast concentrations of land existed nowhere in English North America outside the South except among the patroons of the Hudson River Valley and a few other Northerners. Southern grants were perpetuated through the partial operation of the laws of primogeniture and entail. Under the former, entire estates were inherited by eldest sons if fathers left no wills. Under the latter, estates were made permanent by requiring that they be passed intact from father to son generation after generation.

The great estates of the Colonial South were sources of wealth through the cultivation of rice, indigo, and tobacco. They were still greater sources of wealth through their use for speculative purposes. Land speculation, say historians,[1] was in Virginia "the most socially respectable way of growing wealthy." Members of families noted for their revolutionary liberalism and aristocratic virtues were not too good to be land speculators. Among such persons were Thomas Lee, Peter

[1] Samuel E. Morison and Henry S. Commager, *The Growth of the American Republic*, I, 169.

Jefferson the father of Thomas, George Mason, and George Washington. Such activities helped make George Washington the first American millionaire.

Early settlers became the beneficiaries of that greatest of American marvels, the miracle of real estate. They bought undeveloped lands and sold them later to incoming immigrants. The holding of unused lands was facilitated by tax evasions. The Lords Baltimore allowed their friends to take out land warrants and to postpone the payment of fees and the fullfillment of the legal requirements of cultivation until these friends could make profits out of sales. Vainly did Governors Francis Nicholson and Alexander Spotswood of Virginia try to encourage the growth of small proprietorships and to discourage holdings of unused lands by demanding payments of quitrents. Landed magnates were too influential with the colonial government to be so disciplined.

An adequate labor force was needed to establish the value of the many estates into which Virginia, Maryland, the Carolinas and Georgia were divided. Small farmers, who were to be found in prevailing numbers in all colonies, carried on their regular work with the aid of their families. Large tasks—logrolling, house-raising, and corn shucking— were summarily disposed of by community working parties. Such a limited source of labor, however, could not meet the needs of those desiring to exploit the unlimited lands available almost for the taking or as generous favors from public authorities. Voluntary labor for this purpose did not exist, since free men could obtain their own land. Some form of involuntary labor had to be devised if the great estates were to be worked, for serfdom of the European type was impossible. As the Spanish had done in Mexico and Peru, landowners practiced Indian servitude to a limited degree, especially in South Carolina; but the Southern aborigines were too few, too vengeful, and too unaccustomed to hard work to adapt themselves to the exhausting routine of civilized farming.

More practical was the use of white indentured servants who were by law bound to work for Southern masters for specified periods, sometimes as long as fourteen years. One authority says 12,000 such persons resided in Virginia in 1683. They were made up from two classes of British: those who were willing to sell themselves into temporary servitude to pay for their passage to America, and paupers, criminals, and kidnapped persons transported by public authorities. Despite severe laws devised for their control, indentured servants realized greater advantages from their contracts than the masters whom they were obligated to serve, for by the time they had become accustomed to the Southern climate and way of farming they were free to shift for themselves. Many became owners and renters, and a few ascended to the ranks of the landed gentry. They and their descendants made a constructive if indirect contribution to a society dominated by the planter aristocracy. They formed the nucleus of a white caste too numerous and too vigorous in every Southern colony to suffer absorption or extinction by the black tide that lay beneath it.

Large landowners of the Southern colonies found a more satisfactory solution to their labor problem in the use of Negro slaves. The selective nature of immigration from Africa guaranteed slaves possessing physical hardihood sufficient to withstand the shock of transfer to a new climate and society. Indeed, their coming inaugurated the growing of rice and indigo on lands which because of their malarial character were considered too unhealthy for the survival of white laborers. The long cultural development of the Negroes made possible their relatively rapid acquisition of the habits of ordered labor necessary for usefulness in civilized society. The Negroes in their African environment, contrary to popular belief, were not savages but a high order of barbarians with an extensive agricultural system.

The circumstances under which they were brought to America made their cultural assimilation easier. They did not come voluntarily in groups but were individually snatched from tribal moorings and thrown into the company of strange Negroes of diverse languages and customs. With a genius for imitation, they inevitably adopted the culture of their white captors as a common basis of social intercourse. Their masters, having an intimate interest in their Negroes, so successfully introduced them to Anglo-Saxon customs that few African traits survived. This not only made the Negroes good laborers, but it also cast such a spell over them that they were willing to act as the white man directed. In their new environment, they were probably more loyal and contented than they would have been if they had remained as slaves in the African homeland.

The slave ship that visited Jamestown in 1619 was a forerunner of thousands that were to come to America on the same mission. Although the Royal African Company, an English concern, was given the monopoly of the African slave trade in 1672, before the end of the century individual traders were permitted to enter the business. They came first from London, Liverpool, and Bristol, and later from New England, notably from Newport in Rhode Island. The trade reached its peak in 1734 when 70,000 slaves were imported into North America. In later years annual importations exceeded 50,000. Ulrich B. Phillips, the historian of slavery, estimated that 5,000,000 were imported to America during the entire period of the African slave trade; however, only one tenth of these were brought to the North American continent.

The slave trade was a brutal business. Traders established themselves on the African coast, where native slave hunters exchanged their unfortunate captives for rum, bright clothes, and gewgaws. Then came the horrors of the "middle passage" to America. The hapless passengers were herded like cattle in unsanitary ships where many perished because of inadequate ventilation, food, and water. High profits of the trade blinded captains of the slave ships to mortality rates. Even though the onus of this nefarious traffic must rest primarily upon Englishmen and New Englanders, Southern merchants who profited by the exchange of the human cargoes to planters eager to make purchases were not without blame. The name of practically every pre-Revolution Charleston merchant was at some time affixed to notices of Negro sales. Condemnation of this trade was deleted from the Declaration of Independence, says Thomas Jefferson, "in compliance to South Carolina and Georgia, who have never attempted to restrain the importation of slaves and who on the contrary wished to continue it."

Returns from capital invested in slavery of the Colonial South frequently reached 20 per cent. As a consequence society was revolutionized. In the eighteenth century slave labor supplanted indentured servitude, as the small farms of the previous century were replaced by large plantations. In Virginia slave-owning planters acquired vast estates, built manor houses along navigable rivers, and protected their inheritances through entail and primogeniture. These families—the Carters, Lees, Beverleys, Ludlows, Tayloes, Blairs, and Pages—comprised the first families of Virginia. Coastal planters of North Carolina controlled four fifths of the seats in the colonial assembly. South Carolina, where property qualifications for officeholding were the highest in America, was ruled by a small group of rice and indigo planters who were allied with the merchants of Charleston to form a landed-commercial aristocracy. In Charleston the Rutledges, Pinckneys, Draytons, Hugers, Pringles, and others formed what Northern historians have called "the most exclusive and delightful society in the American colonies." [2]

Slave labor met perfectly the needs of tobacco cultivation. The teaching of its numerous but easily defined processes was the first step in the making of a barbarous and alien race into the genuine Southerners the Negroes ultimately became. The newly arrived bondsmen learned how to sow the seeds in the forest soil, how to make ready the hills while the seed were germinating, and how to transport the shoots after the spring rains. Later there must be hoeing, the removal of the hornworms, and the cutting of excessive leaves so that those remaining might be large and heavy. When the leaves turned yellow in autumn the slaves cut them and hung them from rafters in barns. With the coming of the next spring it was the duty of the slaves to strip the leaves

[2] *Ibid.,* I, 53.

from the stalks, to pack them in hogsheads, and to roll them to nearby wharves for export.

Indigo was the answer to the problem of employing slaves during the seasons of the year they were not needed in the rice fields. The production of these two commodities involved so many disagreeable tasks that free labor probably could not have been induced to perform them. In this connection it is significant that few non-slaveholding whites lived near the malaria-infested rice lands and that the planters and their families left for the towns or the pine lands during the sickly seasons. The whip of the overseer was necessary to induce blacks to wade into malarial bogs to cultivate the rice. The fermentation and pressing of indigo involved onerous and repulsive labor disagreeable to free men.

The southern planters supplemented the production of the great staples by the production of food for their families and slaves. They raised Indian corn, other grains, hogs, vegetables, and fruits. Virginia's stock of cattle increased from 20,000 in 1649 to 100,000 in 1665.

But from tobacco, rice, and indigo came the material basis for the life of elegance and ease which became the ideal of aspiring Southerners. Thereby the planters were able to supply themselves with the hardware, tools, sugar, tea, wines, silks and other fine fabrics, and with the light but elegantly designed furniture in the Chippendale, Hepplewhite and Sheraton styles. To secure these articles they fell into chronic debt to the British merchants. The merchants controlled the prices both of what the planters bought and what they sold, and the planters were so fully absorbed in agriculture and other outdoor activities that they were little inclined to save money by making articles for themselves. Unlike the New Englanders, they did not take to the sea and thereby retained the profits of the carrying trade. They did not indulge in the making of fine cloth because of the failure of silk culture and because the presence of hunting dogs and a moist climate prevented sheep raising from being profitable.

The outward sign of aristocracy was the colonial mansion through which the owner demonstrated his social superiority and perpetuated his status among his descendants. Its seventeenth-century expression was the Tudor house with its steep and gabled roof, its casement windows, and its long rectangular plan of only one room in depth. To meet the needs of the Southern climate this structure acquired high ceilings and a wide reception hall running through its center, with doors at each end. Famous among extinct residences of this type was "Green Spring," the manor house of Sir William Berkeley. Bacon's Castle in Surry County, Virginia, survives today, a cumbersome affair of brick with clustered chimney stacks, curved and stepped gables, and a closed porch on one side and a stair tower on the other.

A more elaborate expression of aristocratic pretensions was the Georgian house, which was introduced from England in the eighteenth century. Examples of this style still exist in the Miles Bruton House in Charleston, the Hammond House in Annapolis, "Gunston Hall" on the Potomac, and "Shirley" and "Westover" on the James River. The Georgian house differed from its Tudor predecessor in having a hipped roof and a square floor plan of two rooms on each side of a central hall. Externally it was adorned with classic doorways, sash instead of casement windows, pilasters, and balustrades. Interior elegance and beauty were achieved by means of high ceilings, spacious chambers, graceful stairs, delicately carved doorways, and furniture of shining mahogany.

In the meantime many Southerners were building less ostentatious houses which were better adapted to the climate and the materials at hand. The English custom of using stone was abandoned in favor of timber because of the absence of stone and because of the presence of wood on the Southern coastal plain. Shingles replaced the English thatched roof, and the fence of hickory rails replaced the English hedge. The native cabinetmakers liked to work in walnut, which was not to be had in England. To dissipate the heat of the cook's fire chimneys were placed at each end of the house rather than in the center as was the custom in colder climates.

The first durable houses were palisades of slabs against a framework built around four posts. The roofed pen of logs known as the log cabin should have been one of the first inventions of a forest people; but it had no English precedent and was not built until contacts were established with the Swedes of Delaware. It became the typical domicile of the poorer frontiersmen. More prosperous persons built houses of hewn logs covered with weatherboarding. To allow the circulation of cool air houses were set high off the ground and divided into two parts by a passageway known as halls in mansions and as "dog runs" in cabins. The need of shade in a sunny climate was supplied by the erection of porches. In the designing and ornamentation of these accretions the Southern architect displayed his most original talents.

Rich Southerners of the colonial period had a natural desire to walk in formal gardens like those of the mother country. This ideal could be approximated in Virginia and in Maryland, as evidenced by what is found today in Williamsburg and Annapolis. The climate and landscape of coastal Carolina forced English-planned gardens to grow into yard displays unlike any other in the whole world. They were open spaces rescued from semitropical forests of live oaks, cypresses, and Spanish moss. In these spaces bright and fragrant flowers bordered lagoons that reflected the beauties of their shores. This type of landscaping reached its ultimate perfection in Middleton Gardens, which were designed in 1740 on the banks of the Ashley River near Charleston.

Before the days of Jeffersonian simplicity in dress the Southern gentleman was privileged to adopt the latest modes of English society. This meant garments so fancy and so nonutilitarian that they seemingly proved that their wearers did not engage in physical toil. This meant bright colors, short breeches, silk stockings, lace ruffles at necks and wrists, low shoes of black kid with silver buckles, powdered wigs, and ornamental swords. The Southern lady wore full skirts of rich cloth billowing from tight waists, lace caps, stays, and elaborate coiffeurs ornamented with jewels. Thereby did this lady demonstrate her dignity and her self-restraint and seemingly make herself so helpless that she was incapable of any activity less refined than the Virginia reel. The aristocratic child was dressed like an adult as a means of preparing him for the rigid discipline of the position of wealth and distinction he would inherit.

Of course there was much make-believe in these aristocratic habiliments. The gentleman was more than a man of leisure; actually he was also a business man and a farmer. His lady had other things to do than to dress for ceremonious frolics; she was often busy with the management of her household, her slaves, and her own numerous brood. For out-of-door activities and indoor chores the gentleman and the lady had clothes less costly than those worn at parties. But even their plainest apparel was sufficiently different from that of the masses to establish their social superiority. The poorer classes wore homespun or osnaburg, a coarse cloth of German origin. The women of the lower classes spun and wove shapeless dresses out of linen and wool.

The distinguishing mark of Virginia and Maryland life was its rural character. Almost everywhere in these two colonies the people dwelt in the open country. Most of the great mansions were so located. Even the dead were not concentrated in churchyards; each family had a separate burying ground. Baltimore and Richmond, established respectively as towns in 1729 and 1742, were in the eighteenth century mere villages. The forty-five so-called towns of Virginia created by acts of the legislature before 1759 were inconsiderable places, half with no more than five houses each. The crown in the eighteenth century discouraged the growth of towns, fearing that they might become centers of competition with English industrial places. There was little need of market centers in the tidewater areas because the planters could conveniently market their tobacco at private wharves. The custom of rural separateness was so well established that towns grew slowly even in settlements not within easy reach of the estuaries of the Chesapeake Bay.

The nearest approach to urban life in the Chesapeake colonies were the provincial capitals, each of which had less than a thousand inhabitants. There life was festive, and planters had houses which they occupied at least during sessions of the legislatures. The elegance of Annapolis, the Maryland capital, is attested by the survival today of its substantial Georgian houses with gardens surrounded by brick walls. The splendor of the Virginia capital is today evident in the restoration of Williamsburg. There can be seen the Governor's Palace, the Capitol, the Christopher Wren Building, the Raleigh Tavern, and numerous private homes. These buildings are proof to modern observers of the varied activities of the old Virginia gentry.

South Carolina was unique among the Southern colonies in possessing an important city. "Charleston," says an eminent historian,[3] "was in fact so complete a focus of commerce, politics, and society that South Carolina was in a sense a city-state." In 1790 Charleston was the fourth city of the United States with a population of 8,089 whites, 7,865 slaves, and 586 free Negroes. The fact that the creeks of the adjoining coastal plain were too shallow for ocean-going vessels attracted the export trade to the wharves of the city's fine harbor. Because the city enjoyed relative immunity from malaria it attracted during the hot months planters from the mosquito-infested rice swamps. The city was a center of a fashionable society: a swarming of coaches, chariots, and chaises in front of churches; household slaves in livery; men and women in the latest Europeans creations. The Charlestonians were accused in 1749 of importing goods "too fine and ill-calculated for the circumstances of an infant colony:" Dutch linens, French cambrics and chintzes, and gold and silver fabrics.[4]

In Southern homes was established the cult of Southern hospitality. It was an extravagance or a virtue of all classes: rich and poor, patrician and plebeian. It was a means of relieving the loneliness of those living far from each other. It demonstrated the affections which the Southerner bestowed upon his cousins near and remote, whom he regarded as members of his clan. Providing for one's guests entailed no acute problems of supply. The forests, the fields, and the streams gave abundantly of their products. Every plantation and farm possessed a kitchen garden which produced nearly all the vegetables known to the American housekeeper of the twentieth century. Sweet potatoes, watermelons, and muskmelons were the South's special contribution to the table. Those of select tastes supplemented home-produced foods by cheeses, spices, gingers, lemons, teas, and coffees imported from distant places. Liquor of many varieties was consumed in large quantities on most occasions. The decorous George Washington lingered long over the table in order to drink five or six glasses of wine. Rum was popular. The presence

---

[3] Ulrich B. Phillips, *American Negro Slavery,* p. 96.
[4] Lawrence H. Gipson, *The Southern Plantations,* p. 187.

of stills on many plantations made possible large quantities of peach and *Plenty of* apple brandy, cherry fling, and rum. Corn whisky, a favorite drink of *liquor* all classes at a later date, had not become popular. The preferred wine of the Southern gentleman was madeira. *(Portuguese Island) — 24% al.*

During the seventeenth century the pleasure-loving inclinations of Virginians were handicapped by puritanical restrictions such as the laws requiring church attendance and prohibiting profanity and Sabbath-breaking. With the increase of wealth in the eighteenth century, re- *Change —* straints on gay diversions were removed. Gambling became universal, as evidenced by the many packs of cards imported. George Washington kept a record of his gains and losses in gaming and would not waste his time on small stakes. Horse racing, declared by a Virginia court to be "a sport only for gentlemen," became a regular practice after 1730. It was then that the first blooded stallion was imported into the Old Dominion. Racing prizes in the form of purses, punch bowls, tankards, and saddles and boots were given. There were race courses at Annapolis, Alexandria, Fredericksburg, Charleston Neck, and on numerous private estates. Horse races were often supplemented by fairs, where puppet shows, ropewalking and fortune telling were enjoyed. In Virginia fairs *Ring* were occasions for the paying of debts, the buying of land, and other business transactions.

Fox hunting was the sport of gentlemen. The red fox was imported so that the Virginia aristocrat could imitate a distinctive sport of English squires. Other types of hunting, however, were not so artificial or so exclusive. They were pursued by all classes with enthusiasm because of either the sporting instinct or the desire for food. The woods were full of bears, deer, panthers, otters, foxes, beavers, and raccoons. Buffaloes in upper South Carolina were so plentiful that a few men with dogs could kill twenty in a day. Guns were perfected, and the use of the rifle became a widespread and highly esteemed skill. Animals were killed without regard for the future of the species. Sometimes circles of flames were built around forests as a trapping device. This and other un- *No game* sportsmanlike practices made game less plentiful in the eighteenth cen- *laws.* tury than in the seventeenth. Large animals disappeared from the coastal areas.

Southern gentlemen had a fondness for cockfighting. There was no attempt, as in later times, to hide this brutal sport from public notice, as evidenced by the emphasis given it in newspapers scattered from Annapolis to Charleston. Champion cocks, like champion horses, were known by name. The stakes were high, and as many as twenty pairs of roosters were pitted against each other at one meet.

The social arts of music and drama were given polite attention. Southerners played such musical instruments as the spinet, the harpsichord, the violin, the guitar, the flute, and the French horn. Benjamin Carter, the son of the master of Nomini Hall in Virginia, was tireless in his practice on a variety of instruments, and Josiah Quincy, Jr., of Massachusetts, attended a meeting of the St. Cecilia Society of Charleston where he thought the music was for the most part "good," "grand," or "incomparable." In the half century before the American Revolution theater-going became a habit among the better classes. The first playhouse in America was erected at Williamsburg in 1716; it was later turned into a town hall. The Dock Street Theater was opened in Charleston in 1736, the first building in the English colonies devoted wholly to the drama.

The first players in the Southern theaters were of a nondescript character. But in 1752 Williamsburg acquired the services of the first well-trained company of actors to reach America. They were Lewis Hallam, his wife, his two children, and a supporting company. In 1773 Charleston opened a new theater. One hundred and eighteen performances were crowded into its first season, including eleven Shakespearean plays and all the popular operas of the day. The South Carolina and Virginia capitals enjoyed what were perhaps the gayest and most popular dramatic seasons in the history of the English colonies. Certainly they were the gayest and most popular dramatic seasons in the whole history of the South except in New Orleans in the 1850's.

The theater of the Colonial South was an imported affair with no local contributions in the way of successful playwriting. This was almost as true of the books that were read. Yet Southern gentlemen were extensive readers. In the seventeenth century the library of Ralph Wormeley of "Rosegill" in Virginia consisted of 385 volumes. William Fitzhugh in the same colony in the same century included in his collection books on law, history, medicine, physics, and morals. The emphasis then was on theological works with a sprinkling of classical titles and treatises on mathematics and geography. In the eighteenth century libraries became larger. That of the Byrds of "Westover" was probably the largest private collection in the English colonies at the time. The books of the Carters of Nomini Hall numbered 1,503; Grey Elliot of Savannah possessed 200 volumes, and George Washington of "Mount Vernon" had 903 volumes. To the older books on religion and practical subjects had been added histories, biographies, essays, novels, and books of poetry.

That these books did not lie idle on the shelves of rich men is proved by the records of such persons as Godfrey Pole of Virginia and a Dr. Farquharson of Charleston in which are noted the lending of books to friends. From the lending of books as a favor to the establishment of circulating libraries was but a step. Commissary Thomas Bray estab-

Judge people by what they eat, not by what they head — FBS. Fish not popular — couldn't get it.

COLONIAL LABOR AND LIFE   ((71

lished a series of "lending libraries" for the use of the clergy of Maryland and other colonies. Socially minded citizens, like Edward Moseley of Edenton, North Carolina, put their personal libraries at the disposal of the public without charge. The Charleston Library Society was founded in 1748 and soon had many books in circulation. Georgia had a library association as early as 1763.

Portrait painting became so widely appreciated in the Southern colonies that no one with family pride failed to adorn his walls with likenesses of his family and ancestors. Most of the artists who did this work were not natives. Henrietta Johnson of England and Jeremiah Theus of Switzerland worked among the South Carolina magnates. John Singleton Copley of Boston painted portraits of many important persons in both the Carolinas. Charles Willson Peale, a Marylander of many trades, won fame as the producer of scores of pleasing and highly decorated canvases which preserve the dignity of colonial life. Peale is most famous for his realistic likenesses of Washington.

R P I an accomplished creative school

The most popular publications of local origin were almanacs. They circulated from the coast to the backwoods and furnished the common people with their main source of information on science, religion, and politics. The best known was Tabler's *South Carolina and Georgia Almanac*.

The first Southern newspapers were the *South Carolina Gazette*, founded at Charleston in 1732, and the *Virginia Gazette*, founded at Williamsburg four years later. These weeklies were lively chronicles of the political and social life of their communities.

good deal of news. —

The nearest approach to a literary production of formal design was William Byrd II's *History of the Dividing Line*. Byrd was an aristocrat who did not let his wide acquaintance with European life and literature destroy his interest in the vulgar realities near at hand. With a mordant wit he describes the people who lived south of the line that he had been commissioned to survey between Virginia and North Carolina. His narrative is prejudiced but vivid and convincing. It is the first and the most effective of the many quips that snobbish Virginians have made at the expense of what they considered the less cultured North Carolinians. *His diaries have been published — filthy*

he got to draw the line —

Another book which grapples with the local scene is Robert Beverley's *History and Present State of Virginia*. It was published in London in 1705 in answer to a jejune account of the American colonies which Beverley had read. In this book a shrewd description of the Indians and the laws and government of Virginia is flavored with humorous comments on the foibles of the planters and the admonitions of a patriot wishing Virginia to become economically more independent of the mother country.

Hampton –
"1st free public
school in
America"

"Thank God!"
– no schools!

Sir William Berkeley's boast to the Commissioners of Plantations in 1671 that Virginia had no free schools to cause "disobedience, heresy and sects" was inaccurate. At that time the province had two free schools, the Syms and the Eaton schools. The *South Carolina Gazette* between 1733 and 1774 contained 412 advertisements relating to schools and schoolmasters. Maryland under its Free School Act of 1694 made an ineffective attempt to have education supported out of general taxation. The Society for the Propagation of the Gospel in Foreign Parts scattered its instruction free over the South.

The accomplishments of the region in public education were so meager in comparison with those of New England that it is just to conclude that Governor Berkeley's statement was relatively if not literally true. The more judicious Governor William Bull wrote from Charleston in 1770:

We have not one good grammar school, though foundations for several in our neighboring parishes. All gentlemen who have anything of a learned education, have acquired it in England. . . . We have a provincial free school, the master and usher whereof are paid by the public, but their salaries being established at the early age of the province, are insufficient to engage and retain fit men. The masters when tolerably well qualified have frequently quitted the laborious task of teaching boys, for the more easy office of preaching in some country parish.

The South inherited the English conception of education as a private or church responsibility. Wealthy people preferred to educate their children at home. Free education lost caste because it was identified with poverty. The concentration of effort necessary for effective schools was hindered also by religious differences and by the scattered character of a rural population.

It should not be forgotten that the masses of Southerners of both races received a basic education in the school of experience which taught them how to live and how to make a living in a strange environment. They learned to farm, to hunt, to fight, to make simple tools, and generally to protect themselves against an environment that might have destroyed less enterprising people. Perhaps this practical training was all that was needed for the opportunities of humble folk in a frontier society. It inculcated enough of the heritage of European civilization to prevent a relapse into barbarism.

Perhaps the greatest triumph in the whole history of American education was the application of this strategy to the Negro. In the industrial and cultural school of the plantation the Negro learned the white man's handicrafts, his language, his social habits, and his ideals of religion and ethics. This meant the eradication of almost all vestiges of

African culture and its replacement by a thoroughgoing Americanism.

Formal education in the Southern colonies was for the purpose of endowing the children of the leisure class with the adornments of mind and the habits of application and restraint which set them apart from the poor and the less fortunate. The aristocratic child was taught the proper accent, the correct style of writing, the use of Greek and Latin phrases, and studies such as law that fitted him for the exercise of political power. Planters employed tutors to train their children and those of their neighbors. These teachers were of varying degrees of proficiency, some highly educated and some poor in intellectual and social experiences. Those with the necessary graces were treated as equals by the planters' families. Such a person was Philip Fithian, who has left a sprightly account of his career as teacher of the Carter children at Nomini Hall. He taught them Latin, Greek, mathematics, English, and the history of England. Such a course of study was not always successful, for Southern youths tended to be lazy and to put the love of horses, outdoor life, dancing, and fine clothes above the storing of the intellect.

dancing? today comes from negroes

Only one of the nine colleges established in Colonial America was in the South. That this was not caused altogether by the paucity of the Southern intellect is attested by the fact that four Southerners—John Mitchell, John Tennent, Alexander Garden, and William Byrd II— were accorded the highest honor in the English scientific world, fellowships in the Royal Society of London. It was caused in part by the fact that the wealthy planters, notably those of South Carolina, preferred to send their sons to Oxford and Cambridge and occasionally to colleges in the North. Especially popular for the reading of law were the several Inns of Court in London. At a time when all colleges were founded on sectarian bases it was difficult for any one of the several denominations in which the people of the South were divided to accumulate sufficient resources for the establishment of a college. This explains in part at least why in the whole region south of Virginia not even so energetic a person as George Whitefield was able to launch a college. That famous divine tried unsuccessfully in 1764 to turn his orphan house in Savannah into a center of higher learning. Several academies, however, were established in the lower South which were destined after the Revolution to become colleges.

The religious unity which prevailed in Virginia in the seventeenth century made possible the foundation by the energetic Commissary James Blair in 1693 of the College of William and Mary at Williamsburg. There students, after studying Latin and Greek in a preparatory division, put on the cap and gown of collegians in order to study rhetoric, logic, ethics, mathematics, and the classics. At first the college did not prosper. In 1705 its buildings were burned. In 1712 William Byrd II recorded that it had only twenty-two students and that the headmaster had been dismissed for drunkenness. In 1724 one of the professors asserted that it was "a college without a chapel, without a scholarship, and without a statute, having a library without books, comparatively speaking, and a president without a fixed salary of late."

But by the end of the colonial period William and Mary had become a distinguished college. It had trained such eminent statesmen of the future republic as Thomas Jefferson, John Marshall, Edmund Randolph, and James Monroe. Its buildings were among the finest academic structures in America. Here in 1776 was founded the Phi Beta Kappa Society. Here Jefferson while governor of Virginia in 1779 allowed the students latitude in the choice of their studies and partly secularized the curriculum by turning chairs of divinity and Hebrew into professorships of law and modern languages. Here Jefferson also started the system under which American institutions of higher education have since been governed. Ruling authority was taken away from the professors of William and Mary and given to nonresident trustees who dispensed the revenues. Thereby did the great Virginian in a very true sense preside over the grave of academic freedom, while at the same time he provided colleges and universities with the means of securing adequate material resources.

The piety of the early settlers of the South gave way in the eighteenth century to a decline in religious interest. The ruling classes were more interested in peopling their lands than they were in excluding the religiously undesirable. Although the coastal gentry believed that for them the Anglican church was the only way to heaven, they admitted that there were other roads to salvation for lesser folk. Such aristocratic snobbishness led to a cold tolerance; the impulse to persecute in order to save the persecuted from the evil of their ways was absent. Indeed the Anglican gentry harassed the pastors of their own churches to a greater degree than they did the pastors of other churches. They filled the *Virginia Gazette* with unflattering articles about the Anglican clergy. Through the parish vestries they tightened their control of ecclesiastical affairs. They successfully opposed the appointment of Colonial bishops for fear of being deprived of their power to appoint and dismiss parish ministers at will. Had Virginia or South Carolina secured a bishop, he probably would have been forced to confine his activities to preaching in Bruton Parish Church at Williamsburg or in St. Philip's Church at Charleston; the vestries would not have allowed him to exercise supervisory functions.

State churches were fostered not as agencies of priestly power but as a means of giving government officials, planters, and merchants the control of ecclesiastical affairs. In Virginia the same gentlemen who composed the county courts composed the parish vestries. In South Carolina the parishes were units of representation in the provincial assembly; in the parishes lay commissioners supervised church affairs. These laymen were worldly enough to deny religious instruction to their slaves until the churchmen proved that such instruction was an effective force in making Negroes better bondsmen. The South Carolina authorities prohibited clergymen from going among the Indians. Missionaries were considered a disturbing factor in the commercial concord resulting in the exchange of hides for English cloth, trinkets, liquors, and weapons.

Only a fraction of the people of the colonial South—perhaps not more than 20 per cent—were church members. Ministers were scarce because of low salaries, insecurity of tenure, and the necessity of going to England to receive ordination. They could not conduct services at frequent intervals because of the great distances between churches.

18th "deists"

There were outcries against the paucity of religious influences. Travelers in Maryland spoke of that province's religious life as stagnant and of its people as godless and profane. Governor James Glen of South Carolina in 1750 spoke of "old settled townships" of his province's back country which "yet have never had any Minister or School Master among them." [5] Not until 1700 was there a resident clergyman in North Carolina, and there churches were few in number fifty years later. William Byrd II in 1729 wrote of Edenton, a town far removed from the frontier, as follows: "I believe this is the only metropolis in the Christian or Mohammedan world where there is neither Church, Chapel, Mosque, Synagogue, or any place of public worship, or any sect or religion whatever."

3 new churches

"The work of the church in colonial Georgia," asserts the historian of that colony,[6] "was little less than a failure." A missionary declared in 1753 that the whites of Georgia were "as great Heathen as their Slaves," using "many sophistical arguments to obstruct ye Instruction of the Servants." The clergymen dispatched from England to minister to these heathenish people behaved badly. One was the notorious Thomas Bosomworth who turned from his holy mission to marry Mary Musgrove, the queen of the Cherokee Indians, and to menace Savannah by descending upon the town at the head of a band of savages. Another was the subsequently famous John Wesley, who came to the colony in 1736 with impractical plans for the conversion of the Indians. He departed from Georgia suddenly after giving offense because of his High Church proclivities and because of his refusal to give the Holy Communion to a lady who had refused to marry him.

[5] *Ibid.*, p. 175 n.
[6] E. Merton Coulter, *A Short History of Georgia*, p. 69.

Unfortunate religious conditions in the Southern colonies were in part remedied by the activities of non-Anglican Protestants. The dissenters, as they were called, were attracted by the practical religious tolerance which prevailed in all the Southern colonies by the middle of the eighteenth century. Earliest among them were the Quakers, who for a time were the most numerous sect in North Carolina. They filtered into Virginia, South Carolina, and Georgia; but they became extinct or declined into an inconsequential minority after 1790. The type of religious tolerance which the men of the American Revolution created was not broad enough to cover the Quakers. They were despised because of their pacifism, their hatred of slavery, and their austere way of life. Specifically they were the victims of the aggressiveness of the Presbyterians, the Baptists, and the Methodists.

These three denominations derived their strength from the revival of religion that originated in 1734 under the inspiration of Jonathan Edwards. This is known as the Great Awakening. It spread into the South under the guidance of George Whitefield, whose spectacular preaching attracted large audiences as far south as Georgia. "Enthusiasm" was the designation Anglican adversaries gave Whitefield's demand that the soul "feel" the Spirit working within if it were to be saved.

The instrument of regeneration among the Southern Presbyterians was Samuel Davies of Delaware. He was in 1748 invited to Hanover County, Virginia, by a group of laymen whose religious interests had been aroused by serious conversations and the reading of holy books. Under the spell of Davies' magic preaching, Presbyterianism became a dynamic force in the Southern Piedmont; it brought within its fold many of the unchurched and many who had been members of the Established Church.

The Great Awakening entered a more expansive phase with the spread of the Baptists. Members of that denomination had entered South Carolina before 1700, and by 1751 they had become numerous enough to establish the Charleston Baptist Association. But it was not until the following two decades that the Baptist church grew into a body of great promise in the religious development of the South, when missionaries from New England and Pennsylvania moved into the region. Pre-eminent among them were Shubal Stearns, Daniel Marshall, and Oliver Hart. By the time of the American Revolution Virginia alone had 10,000 Baptists.

The Baptist church appealed to a lower and more numerous segment of society than did the Presbyterian. This was because of its democratic congregationalism, its formless creed, its distinctive symbol of baptism by immersion, its animated and sometimes unlettered preachers, and its opposition to all forms of union of church and state. Here was the perfect adaptation of a historic form of European Protestantism to the consistencies of the Southern back country. This tolerance of conditions in a new country paved the way for the Baptists to become the most numerous of Southern religious groups. This sort of compromise did not, however, involve the sacrifice of the orthodox core of traditional Christianity. Doctrinally the Baptists remained the least liberal of the larger religious bodies of the South.

The early Baptist ministers in Virginia were called Anabaptists and thrown in jail because they refused to seek licenses to preach. But as soon as the governing cliques of Virginia's religious liberals discovered that these dissenters from the Established Church had no revolutionary ambitions of a political or social character, the way was cleared for the complete religious freedom which came to the Baptists with the American Revolution.

The Methodists followed in the wake of the Presbyterians and the Baptists in spreading the principles of the Great Awakening. Under the inspiration of Devereaux Jarratt, an Anglican clergyman turned enthusiast, Methodist revivals were held in Virginia in the years immediately preceding the Revolution. By 1776 there were 3,449 Methodists in Virginia, with lesser numbers in the Carolinas. The strength of the Methodist movement lay in its centralized organization, its traveling preachers, its persuasive hymns, its democratic theory of salvation, and its vigorous use of the press and the school. The Methodists organized themselves into an independent church in 1784 and were to be the greatest rival of the Baptists in winning souls to Christ.

The frontier enthusiasm manifested in the Great Awakening did not destroy the Southern branch of the Anglican church. If its clergy had cause to mourn the loss of members to the more emotional denominations, it had in its favor a factor which gave it a place of lasting importance in Southern life. It remained the church of the tidewater aristocracy and was destined to be the church of those who were aspiring after social distinction.

The Episcopal church possessed other sources of strength. If the Baptist church offered a statesmanlike compromise between European tradition and Southern actuality, the Episcopal church offered a statesmanlike compromise between Protestant zeal and the good life. The typical Anglican gentlemen of the South did not follow the example of Thomas Jefferson and Willie Jones of North Carolina in seeking happiness by substituting reason and common sense for divine Revelation and divine Providence. He was more like George Washington, who went to church from force of habit and as an example to lesser folk, while depending for personal guidance more on self-interest and practical ethics than on God. The classical virtues of fortitude, prudence, temperance, and courtesy were the ideals of the Christian gentleman of the South. His "sin" was not moral laxity, but a secularization of outlook which tolerated the life that wealth and position made possible. He was quick to defend his church when it was challenged by a Whitefield or a Davies; yet he was tolerant not only of religious indifference but also of faiths different from his own.

As detailed in this chapter, the distinctive features of Southern economic and social life were created during the Colonial period. An aristocratic society based on slavery and the plantation economy then became fixed as the Southern ideal. This ideal had its faults. It was in part a denial of the democratic philosophy which Southerners at the end of the Colonial period joined other Americans in extolling. But it was able in a great measure to withstand the disrupting influences of both the American Revolution and the American Civil War. It has always appealed to Southerners. Their ambition has never been to pull down their betters but to climb into their circles. They admire the good life of big houses, fine dress, and pliant Negroes; and on the whole they are as willing as the Virginians of the eighteenth century to speculate in lands and use the toil of others as means of attaining the life of the privileged.

CHAPTER VI

The Revolution:
Liberalism and Reaction

-->>>

AT THE TIME of the American Revolution the statesmen of the South took a leading part in writing into the Declaration of Independence, into state constitutions, and into the Constitution of the United States the principles of equality and freedom that the Swedish scholar Gunnar Myrdal calls the American Creed. Southern liberals believed that government should be by the consent of the governed, that class distinctions should be eradicated, and that certain privileges should not be taken from the individual by the state.

Southern liberals were sometimes embarrassed by the discrepancy between this refulgent radicalism and their actual practice of aristocratic privileges. Realistic historians have since discovered that behind their idealism was much selfish design. Yet this criticism is not entirely fair, for the leaders of the Revolutionary generation did inaugurate concrete reforms. Because of their accomplishments in this respect, forward-looking men of later generations were able to bestow unreserved admiration upon Thomas Jefferson and his Southern coadjutors. When necessary for their purposes, Northern reformers have been able to take the principles of the Revolutionary leaders of the South out of their proper contexts and thereby create the Jeffersonian legend. It is a noble faith by which Northerners justify universal freedom, universal suffrage, universal education, and the other means by which the American people have applied their concept of democracy.

Southerners behaved in about the same manner. As is asserted often

((79))

in this book, the main justification for regarding the section below the Potomac as a distinctive province was its refusal to accept the freedom and the equality of the Negro. Yet Southerners, even during the 1830–65 period in which they proclaimed the proslavery argument, were generally not conscious of violating the equalitarian ideals of the Revolutionary Fathers except in regard to the Negro. The white race was the only element of the South's population which the section's theologians and scientists thought innately capable of exercising the full prerogatives of man. During this period the region accepted the Jacksonian faith in the common man by demanding universal education and universal manhood suffrage to the white race. It provided the economic atmosphere in which common men were able to become rich planters and merchants.

The great Virginians of the Revolutionary generation were moved by philosophical dreams which presaged a democracy of a type the world had not known before. One of these dreams was John Locke's idea that civil institutions had evolved out of a contract between the people and their rulers for the purpose of preserving the people's rights to life, liberty, and property; therefore if the rulers should deny these rights to the people, it was the people's duty to depose them and choose new rulers. That the exercise of this right of revolution would be pursued benevolently was believed to be assured by the acceptance by the Virginia theorists of Jean Jacques Rousseau's assertion that mankind is innately good.

Such fanciful conceptions of political history and human nature might have led to wild experiments had not the Southerners of the Revolutionary period been practical statesmen as well as dreamers. They tied their dreams to traditional experiences and existing realities. These experiences and realities were the many privileges that Southerners possessed as heirs of the English way of life or that they had won in constitutional struggles with the imperial authorities. Through their legislatures and county governments Southerners possessed many rights of self-government. "The Virginians," said a British traveler in 1760,[1] "are haughty and jealous of their liberties, impatient of restraint, and can scarcely bear the thought of being controlled by any superior power. Many of them consider the colonies as independent states, not connected with Great Britain, otherwise than by having the same common King, and being bound to her [Great Britain] by natural affection."

The leaders of the American Revolution in the South enjoyed many aristocratic privileges. It was therefore natural for these leaders to use

[1] Andrew Barnaby, *Travels through the Middle Settlements in North America in the Years 1759 and 1760*, p. 24.

the teachings of Locke more as justifications of their own practices and ambitions than as justifications of a reordering of society along democratic lines. They were not in practical matters unaware of the interests of the dominant classes of their community. They did not effect internal revolution in favor of the lower white classes or in favor of the Negroes they held in bondage. The British tyrannies against which they applied the right of revolution for the most part ran counter to the ambitions of the Colonial upper classes.

The most concrete grievance of the Southern revolutionists was against the restraints that the British government imposed on the acquisition of frontier lands. A baffling imperial problem had been created by the French cession of the lands west of the Alleghenies to the English in 1763, and by the Indian revolt of the same year known as the Pontiac Conspiracy. The Indians were brought to terms, but the question was, how should they be treated? Should their hunting grounds be preserved for their use against the greed of land-hungry frontiersmen? The British answer to this question was the creation of the Proclamation Line of 1763, reserving all western territory between Quebec and Florida for the Indians. After Governor John Murray Dunmore gained the favor of the Virginians by forcing the Indians to renounce their hunting rights in the region south of the Ohio River, the British government tried to stop so obvious a threat to the maintenance of the Proclamation Line. Royal governors were ordered to grant no lands and to permit no settlements in the west except after surveys and allotments had been made.

This order prompted Thomas Jefferson's *Summary View of the Rights of British America,* in which this great Virginia liberal denied the right of the crown to dispose of western lands. The exercise of such a prerogative ran counter to the speculating ambitions of Southern planters organized in such real estate adventures as the Greenbrier Company and the Ohio Company. It also ran counter to one of the strongest urges in Southern history: the desire of the common man to use western lands as a means of making himself into a great planter. More than any other reason it accounts for the fact that Virginians, despite the cleavage between tidewater and back country, entered the American Revolution with as great a unanimity as any other American colony. Of a people supposedly under his authority, Governor Dunmore wrote in 1772:

Wandering about Seems engrafted in their Nature; and it is a weakness incident to it, that they Should for ever immagine that the Lands further off, are Still better than those upon which they are already Settled. . . . They do not conceive that Government has right to forbid their taking possession of a Vast Tract of Country, either uninhabited, or which Serves only as a Shelter to a few Scattered Tribes of Indians.[2]

Equally radical was the desire of the Southern leaders to supplement their existing liberties by endowing their legislatures with authority co-ordinate with that of the British Parliament. In other words, these leaders claimed that the British government had no more right to legislate for Virginia and South Carolina than the Virginia and South Carolina legislatures had to legislate for the British Isles.

This revolutionary concept was given dramatic expression by Patrick Henry, a young Virginian from the frontier possessed of greater oratorical ability than formal schooling. In his argument over the Parson's Cause, Henry struck death blows at both the royal prerogative and the Established Church. Under the Twopenny Act of 1758 the Virginia House of Burgesses had allowed the vestries to pay the clergy in money instead of in the accustomed tobacco. Thereby was established the rule of scaling down salaries when tobacco was dear without providing any compensation when the commodity fell below the normal price. When so unjust a plan was vetoed by the Privy Council, the clergy sued the vestries in Virginia courts for the difference between their money commutations and what their salaries would have been in tobacco. In one of these cases Henry represented the defense, skillfully turning the unjust cause of a ruling clique into a general appeal for religious liberty. He won the applause of the Southern populace by proclaiming that the king, in vetoing a supposedly beneficial measure, had lost the right to his subjects' obedience. The jury returned the nominal verdict of one penny in favor of the aggrieved clergyman. The great body of Virginians had been enlisted in the Revolutionary cause.

During the excitement in 1765 over the act of the British Parliament imposing revenue stamps upon a variety of American printed matter, Henry precipitated a crisis by suddenly introducing in the House of Burgesses a resolution which denied the right of Parliament to tax the colonies. Identifying the power of British imperialism with the person of the king, the Virginia orator exclaimed: "Caesar had his Brutus—Charles the first, his Cromwell—and George the third—may he profit by the example." Henry's resolution became the basis of violent agitation in all the colonies from Boston to Charleston.

The best cause of complaint by the Southern ruling class was the English merchants' practice of extorting from the planters an unfair share of the returns from the great Southern staples. Thus at the time of the Revolution the Southern planters owed British merchants £2,-000,000, despite the fact that exports from Virginia, Maryland, and

[2] Cited in Morison and Commager, *Growth of the American Republic*, I, 144.

South Carolina to England exceeded imports from the mother country by an annual average of £91,000. The merchants created an invisible balance of trade in their favor by setting the prices of both what they sold to the planters and what the planters sold to them, and by charging generous interest, insurance, shipping, and commission rates. As early as 1706 Governor John Seymour of Maryland observed "how much the country is indebted" to the London merchants, "very many plantations being mortgaged to them, of which there seems to be little probability of redemption considering the growing interest." The planters, so the merchants claimed, conspired to free themselves of their debts by picking a quarrel with their creditors. Tom Moore gibed:

> "Those vaunted demagogues, who nobly rose
> From England's debtors to be England's foes
> Who could their monarch in their purse forget
> And break allegiance but to cancel debt."

Because the balance of trade was against them the Southern colonies were constantly drained of their specie. They attempted to remove this difficulty by importing foreign coins and resorting to paper money. Such practices were frowned upon by the British government as obviously injurious to the British creditors. In 1764 Parliament forbade the Colonial legislatures to make bills of credit legal tender. Thereby a severe money shortage was created, which in turn created a deep sense of grievance against the imperial authorities.

The Revolution in the South was almost exclusively under aristocratic leadership. But there was popular participation. Patrick Henry, although not himself of the aristocracy, aroused the masses by the magic of his rustic antics. Admiring plebeians roared liberty songs over tavern tables in response to the boisterous oratory of gentlemen. Outstanding among these gentlemen was Christopher Gadsden, who found an enthusiastic following among Charleston mechanics. He organized the Liberty Tree party, effected boycotts against British goods, and forced the Charleston merchants to co-operate with him.

In Virginia Governor Dunmore answered the agitations of the patriots by garrisoning his palace with marines, by threatening "to proclaim liberty to the slaves and to reduce Williamsburg to ashes," and by declaring Patrick Henry an outlaw under much the same circumstances that Governor William Berkeley had outlawed Nathaniel Bacon a hundred years earlier. Under the direction of their traditional leaders, Virginians took effective countermeasures. They cowed loyalists into silence or portrayed them as "monsters of ingratitude." Merchants who had long endured the snubs of the planters now felt "lashed with a rod of iron," glad to fly to "any corner on the face of the earth." Dunmore was chased into Norfolk by the militia, and after he had burned the water front of the town the patriots retaliated by reducing the whole place to ashes. The governor was forced to flee the colony. The patriots, tyrannical but seldom cruel, extirpated loyalism from Virginia through test oaths, confiscations, and exilings.

North Carolina, South Carolina, and Georgia followed the same pattern of revolt as Virginia. In these colonies the patriot leaders quarreled with the governors through the elected assemblies. The governors dismissed the assemblies and attempted to rule without them. The people retaliated by electing provincial congresses which acted as legislatures and set up executive bodies known as councils of safety. Open conflict developed between the governors and these revolutionary agencies. Because they had no support among the people of the coastal region, the governors were forced to retire to British warships stationed off the coast for their protection.

Within two months after Governor Dunmore escaped from Williamsburg in June, 1775, Governor Josiah Martin of North Carolina fled from New Bern and Governor William Campbell of South Carolina fled from Charleston. Governor James Wright of Georgia escaped from Savannah early in 1776. Governor Martin, writing at New Bern before his flight, explained that "the people of this town and county have formed themselves in companies and taken up arms, watching most narrowly every movement about my house, both day and night, while I am not supported by a single man."

Not all Southerners championed the patriot cause, however. In Virginia and Maryland the loyalist party was weak, but in the Carolinas and Georgia it was strong. Officials close to the governors, some merchants, and a few Anglican clergymen were loyal because of connections with the mother country. A few of the great planters, men like Daniel Dulany of Maryland and William Byrd III and Lord Fairfax of Virginia took the king's side. Many men of the back country, like the Regulators of North Carolina, remained loyal because they had greater grievances against the tidewater oligarchies than against the imperial government. The strong loyalist party in Georgia stemmed from the popularity of Governor Wright, the subsidies Parliament gave the province, and the need of imperial protection against the Indians.

The British government in 1776 vainly tried to come to the rescue of Southern loyalists. The attempt of an expedition under Sir Peter Parker to effect a juncture in North Carolina with Scotch royalists ended in an overwhelming victory for the patriots at Moore's Creek Bridge on February 27. Parker later was driven from Charleston when his cannon balls sank harmlessly in the spongy palmetto logs of Fort Moultrie. In the meantime the Georgians, aided by a sizeable patriot force from

South Carolina, put an end to British power in their colony by destroying English vessels in Savannah Harbor. The Carolinas and Georgia had for the time being been saved from a reassertion of British authority in the same manner that New England had already been saved by the battles of Lexington and Concord and the maneuvering around Boston.

The British during the last half of the Revolution made a second attempt to subdue the South. In December, 1778, they seized Savannah and overran Georgia. In May, 1780, they captured Charleston, and the following August they put South Carolina at their mercy by roundly defeating General Horatio Gates at Camden. Two months later an army composed of patriots from the western settlements fell upon a British force consisting almost entirely of loyalists at Kings Mountain and won a decisive victory. This good fortune restored the morale of the Southern patriots and enabled General Nathaniel Greene, the new patriot commander, to force Lord Charles Cornwallis out of the interior of the Carolinas. After an unsuccessful attempt to reckon with the Marquis de Lafayette in central Virginia, Cornwallis allowed himself to be bottled up at Yorktown by American and French forces under Washington. There the entire British command was surrendered on October 19, 1781. The American Revolution had ended with the independence of the American colonies.

In the meantime the checks imposed upon the reassertion of British authority enabled the Southern colonies to play prominent roles in the proclamation of American independence. North Carolina was able to take the first step in this direction because the nature of its coast protected it against raids from British warships. At Halifax, a little town near the Virginia border, a North Carolina convention on April 12, 1776, adopted the first resolution instructing a delegation to the Continental Congress to vote for American independence. Ten days later Richard Henry Drayton, the spokesman of South Carolina, said that the law of the land "authorized him to declare . . . that George the Third . . . had abdicated the government; and that the throne was thereby vacant: that he had no authority over us, and that we owe no allegiance to him." Already on April 5, the provincial congress of Georgia had empowered its delegates to the Continental Congress to vote for independence. "We therefore, gentlemen," declared the instructions of the delegates, "shall rely upon your patriotism, abilities, firmness and integrity, to propose, join, and concur in all such measures as you think calculated for the common good."

Thus was Virginia encouraged by her Southern neighbors to sponsor two of the great landmarks in the American struggle for human equality and liberty. One was the Declaration of Rights which, on

June 12, 1776, was adopted by the Virginia House of Burgesses at the suggestion of George Mason. A restatement of English principles as embodied in the Magna Carta, the Petition of Right, and the Bill of Rights, this famous document is the source from which sprang most American and foreign laws protecting the individual against the overweening power of the state. The second document was the Declaration of Independence, written by Thomas Jefferson and proposed before the Continental Congress by Richard Henry Lee on instructions from a Virginia convention. It was adopted by the Continental Congress on July 4, 1776.

Borrowing the philosophy of natural rights from English thinkers of the seventeenth century, the author of the Declaration of Independence believed that nature had yielded to inquiring minds the laws of man's conduct with the generosity with which it had yielded the laws of physics to the scientist of the seventeenth century. Jefferson felt that "these truths" were "self-evident": that "all men are created equal"; that all men are endowed "with certain unalienable Rights"; that governments derive "their just powers from the consent of the governed"; and that when a government becomes destructive of these ends, the people have the right "to alter or to abolish it." Hostile critics were quick to point out that these assertions did not square with the actual experiences of man; how, for example, did Jefferson and the other signers of the famous document justify depriving their African slaves of liberty and pursuit of happiness if these rights were unalienable? But, as sagacious students remark,[3] Jefferson was making history, not writing it. He was laying down principles that were to be expanded in justification of all democratic reforms. The doctrine that all men are created equal has come to mean that all men are equal, or that if this is not true, they ought to be equal. The great Virginia liberal did not wish to include slaves as men, but subsequent generations adjudged Negro bondage inconsistent with the Declaration of Independence, and Virginia and the other Southern states developed uneasy consciences over their denial of the equalities to the descendants of the slaves.

Concessions were made to the principles of the Declaration of Independence when, in the months before and after the adoption of that famous document, the Southern colonies made state constitutions. In protest against the tyrannies of monarchy and aristocracy, the people were declared to be the source of political power, and sharp restrictions were imposed upon the powers of government. The traditional English guarantees of religious freedom, moderate bail, humane punishment, and speedy trial by means of juries were supplemented by guarantees of the equal operation of the laws, of freedom of speech, freedom of assembly,

[3] Ibid., I, 196.

the right of the citizen to bear arms, and the right of the majority to reform the government.

Colonial experience and the teachings of Montesquieu led Southern statesmen to write into their state constitutions the principle of the separation of powers. Provisions were made for chief executives, independent judiciaries, and bicameral legislatures (except in Georgia). Actually, however, the legislatures were made supreme by making the governors into figureheads. Most of them were elected by legislatures for short terms and deprived of the powers of veto, appointment, and the summoning and the dissolving of the legislatures. A disgusted North Carolina conservative remarked that the only power given the governor was the right "to sign a receipt for his salary."

The new Southern constitutions were not in any realistic sense revolutionary documents. In fundamentals they drew upon the solid foundation of English and Colonial experience, resembling to a much greater degree the Colonial charters than the idealistic statements of the leaders of the Revolution. Restraints were imposed upon the possible desire of the mob to override settled practices and vested interests. Despite what was said in the preambles of the constitutions about the sovereignty of the people, these documents were actually written by college-bred gentlemen—moderate democrats like Jefferson, George Mason, and Richard Henry Lee, and conservatives like Edmund Randolph and John Rutledge. The liberties allowed by the Bill of Rights were in practical application for the benefit of the aristocrats, those few among the Southerners of that day with enough education and independent thought to exercise mental and social freedom. The enhancement of the powers of the legislatures meant greater freedom for native oligarchies now free of the restraints of imperial authority. Jefferson warned that the Virginia legislators might become 173 despots, and Madison said that the concentration of power in their hands "may justly be pronounced the very definition of tyranny."

That the American Revolution did not basically disturb the power of the Colonial aristocracy is indicated by the fact that no Southern state at that time granted universal white manhood suffrage, removed property qualifications for officeholding, or altered the arrangements by which tidewater areas were allowed a disproportionate share of the seats in the legislatures. The Georgia and North Carolina constitutions were the most democratic, but in both of these states a voter was required to be a taxpayer. In Virginia, Maryland, and South Carolina the individual voter was required to possess twenty-five or more acres of land. Property qualifications for officeholding were high. In Georgia an assemblyman had to be worth £250, and in Maryland £500. In South Carolina a state senator had to be worth £2,000 if a resident of the senatorial district from which he was elected; if a nonresident, £7,000. The governor of North Carolina had to possess £1,000; the governor of South Carolina, £10,000. In the latter state the seaboard area, with only one fourth of the white population, possessed 144 of the 209 seats in the legislature. In Virginia a like arrangement secured the supremacy of the tidewater.

Had the suffrage been placed on a broader basis there would probably have been no shift of power. The lower classes of the South, whether enfranchised or disfranchised, generally accepted the leadership of their social and economic superiors. Paradoxically they were flattered by the assertion of their aristocratic leaders that all men are equal; the lower classes were, therefore, less inclined to question their actual social and political status than the common people of societies in which distinctions between patrician and plebeian are acknowledged. The South was no place for a class-conscious type of radicalism.

It is significant in this connection that the most radical reforms of the Revolutionary era of an economic character were at the expense of the British and the loyalists rather than at the expense of the land magnates among the patriots. The estates of Lord Baltimore, Lord Granville, Lord Fairfax, and Sir James Wright were seized and broken into small holdings. Tory property was confiscated. A South Carolina law of 1782 took the property and banished all who had supported the British or who had proved to be "inveterate enemies of the state." Ungranted lands belonging to the king were seized, quitrents abolished, and the obstacles to western aggressions imposed by the Proclamation Line of 1763 were removed. At the same time the large landholdings of the patriots were protected by constitutional guarantees against leveling tendencies. Thus did the American Revolution make more sacred the right of property in land without attempting in any general way to equalize the holdings.

As will be made clear,[4] the Southern states during and immediately after the Revolution curbed the African slave trade, and their representatives in Congress consented to the exclusion of slavery from the Northwest Territory. Under the leadership of Thomas Jefferson much was said about the inconsistency between the continued existence of slavery and the liberal proclamations of the Revolution. Certain philanthropic individuals freed their bondsmen, but little concrete was accomplished toward the extinction of the slave system. The clause in the Northwest Ordinance respecting slavery, wrote an informed contemporary[5] "was agreed to by the southern members for the purpose of

---

[4] See below, p. 117.
[5] William Grayson of Virginia, cited in Andrew C. McLaughlin, *The Confederation and the Constitution, 1783–1789*, pp. 123–4.

preventing tobacco and indigo being made on the northwest side of the Ohio, as well as for several political reasons." The fear of slave insurrections and the fear of depressing the prices of slaves and of the commodities they produced were the main reasons Southern legislators put curbs on the African slave trade. Jefferson drafted a law for gradual emancipation, but failed to introduce it in the Virginia legislature because, as he explained, "the public mind would not bear the proposition." He accompanied his attack on slavery with an impractical notion that the Negroes should be deported. "This unfortunate difference of colour, and perhaps of faculty," he explained,[6] "is a powerful obstacle to the emancipation of these people. . . . Among the Romans emancipation required but one effort. The slave when made a free man might mix without staining the blood of his master. But with us a second is necessary unknown to history. When freed, he is to be removed beyond the reach of mixture."

A much-emphasized reform of the Revolutionary era was the abolition of the laws of entail and of primogeniture by all the Southern states within the fifteen years following 1774. Jefferson led the assault, hoping to establish "an aristocracy of virtue and talent" in place of an aristocracy of inheritance. The French observer de Tocqueville thought that the democratic trend in America was due in part to the practice of equal inheritance. Certainly the removal of restraints upon the disposal of property facilitated the breakup of the great hereditary families of the Colonial South. This explains in part why the region below the Potomac in the nineteenth and the twentieth centuries, unlike New England, New York, and Pennsylvania, possessed few families who retained wealth and power for many generations. Free play was given to certain destructive traits in a people as careless and as liberty-loving as those of the South. Frequently the right of untrammeled ownership made it easy for them to neglect their lands or to lose them through mortgages or speculations.

The most radical break that the South made with the English pattern of life at the time of the Revolution was the separation of church and state. The North Carolina constitution of 1776 forthrightly declared: "There shall be no Establishment of any one Religious Church in this State in Preference to any other." This same action was taken by Maryland, Virginia, Georgia, and South Carolina within the following three years. This achievement in Virginia, said Jefferson, its chief promoter, gave rise to "'the severest contests in which I have ever engaged." The growing number of dissenters—Baptist, Methodist, and Presbyterian— were freed of disagreeable tests and taxes and won complete religious freedom in theory as well as in fact. The Statute of Religious Liberty,

[6] *Notes on Virginia*, Query 14.

which Jefferson wrote into the laws of Virginia in 1786, has been widely copied by civilized governments; it has been grafted into the actual behavior of the American government and people to a greater degree than any other civil liberty. It declared that no man could be compelled to attend or support any religious group; it went far enough to protect the atheist in his constitutional rights that no religious test whatsoever could "diminish, enlarge or affect" a person's "civil capacities."

The abolition of the Anglican establishments in the Southern states was not a deep uprooting in either a material or spiritual sense. It did not involve the destruction of a great vested interest; for the Colonial church, as we have indicated,[7] was a weak and harassed institution whose employees were hired aliens. The disestablishment did not destroy the Anglican church or result in the confiscation of its places of worship. That body, though weakened by the withdrawal of state subsidies and the confiscation of some of its lands, continued to exist as an institution of the coastal aristocracy. Religious freedom meant increasing strength for the Baptist, Methodist, and Presbyterian churches, sects more powerful and more intolerant than the Anglican establishments had been since 1700. These churches championed slavery and a belated puritanism, and, through popular pressure, imposed an orthodox religiosity. Jefferson in his old age thought that these communions were being supplemented by Unitarianism. But this New England form of religious liberalism sent only feeble rays south of the Mason and Dixon Line.

Southern leaders, as we have seen, were able to temper or emasculate revolutionary enthusiasms when they were confronted by such inherited realities as slavery and landed aristocracy. This made it possible for them to play leading roles in the reaction against the liberal rhetoric, the paper money craze, and the mob violence of the Revolutionary period. They helped create the Constitution of the United States in order that liberty might be tempered by order; that checks might be put upon the popular will; that the freedom-loving inclinations of the states might not stifle the necessity of national unity. Leadership in the convention that framed the new instrument of government was in the hands of George Washington and James Madison of Virginia, with Edmund Randolph of Virginia, Charles Pinckney, Charles Cotesworth Pinckney, and John Rutledge of South Carolina playing secondary roles. The reluctance of the liberal revolutionists to accept the great document was placated by writing into it parts of George Mason's Bill of Rights.

In launching the strong national government for which the Constitution called, George Washington and other Southern members of the

[7] See above, p. 75.

Federalist party played conspicuous parts. When Federalist policies fell into disfavor, it was Chief Justice John Marshall, another Virginian, who stepped into the breach, and in a series of lasting decisions established the supremacy of the federal government and of the rights of property against the threats of provincial agrarians.

Southerners became alarmed when Washington allowed his faction to fall under the domination of Alexander Hamilton and the plutocratic interests of the Northeast. A majority of Southerners promptly became champions of states' rights in face of the aggressions of a national government expressing the superior economic and numerical power of the North. They observed that currency deflation was enriching Northern money-changers at the expense of Southern agricultural interests. Uneasiness over the future of slavery was expressed as Southerners saw that institution abolished in all states north of Delaware.

In protest against these trends a Southern political party was organized by Jefferson, the most masterful of American politicians. This party was a deft combination of agrarian toryism and democratic liberalism, of unity between the rich and the poor. Within it were many of the characteristics which ultimately gave the South a lasting regional consciousness.

A decade before the new party was started a New Englander [8] predicted that in any close union the North and the South would continually be at variance because, this Yankee explained, "our manners are widely different from the southern states." Already while the two areas needed unity to repel the British invader, there were sectional clashes in the debates of the Continental Congress. The Flour Colonies manifested jealousy of the Rice Colonies when question of commercial restrictions arose. The use of Negroes in the war effort caused sectional recriminations, as did the fixing of blame for the failures of military campaigns. Before the War for American Independence was over there began the absurd sectional argument over whether the original proponent of national liberty was Samuel Adams of Massachusetts or Patrick Henry of Virginia.

The Declaration of Independence, greatest of all American manifestos of brotherhood, was not allowed to encroach on sectional interests. We remember that criticism of the slave trade, according to Jefferson, had been deleted from the great document in compliance with the wishes of South Carolinians, Georgians, and the New England slave traders. So deeply engrained did the sectional differences seem to a British observer that he said that he would just as soon expect the wolf

[8] Benjamin Randall, cited in Clement Eaton, *A History of the Old South*, p. 145.

and the lamb to feed together, as for Virginians to form a cordial union with the saints of New England.[9]

The making of the United States Constitution was the greatest blow delivered against untrammeled sectional self-expression until Abraham Lincoln, seventy-odd years later, crushed the movement for Southern independence. The South, it is true, accepted the Constitution, but it did not do so without a partial awareness of the perils to sectional interests this acceptance involved. It might not have ratified the document had not the proponents of the Constitution compromised with sectional feelings, or had political democracy really prevailed. They made concessions in favor of self-government by limiting federal authority to those powers delegated to it by the Constitution. They made concessions to the slaveholders by leaving the regulation of slavery to the individual states and by making provisions for the return of fugitive slaves, for the counting of the slaves as three fifths in the apportionment of Congressional representation, and for the continuation of the foreign slave trade for twenty years.

Southern opponents of the ratification of the Constitution were not satisfied by these compromises; in strident tones they laid the foundation for lasting suspicions of the new government. "There is," said Patrick Henry, "a striking difference and great contrariety of interest, between the states." This difference would make the South the victim of the tyranny of the Northern majority. "Is there not, then," explained the Virginia orator, "a settled purpose to check the Southern interest? . . . How can the Southern members prevent the adoption of the most oppressive mode of taxation in the Southern States, as there is a majority in favor of the Northern States?"

The Tenth Amendment, which says that "the powers not delegated to the United States by the Constitution, nor prohibited by it to the States, are reserved to the States respectively or to the people," did not satisfy the minority consciousness of thoughtful Southerners. There were objections to the so-called sweeping clauses of the Constitution; the right of the national government "to . . . promote the welfare," to do what was "necessary and proper" to put into effect the national powers; and the power given the Congress to institute a hierarchy of federal courts. "But when I find that the Constitution is expressed in indefinite terms . . . ," wrote John Tyler, Sr., "I find no rest in my mind. Those clauses which answer different constructions will be used to serve particular purposes." George Mason saw in the power to create federal courts "as numerous as Congress may think proper" the es-

---

[9] Jonathan Boucher, cited in Claude H. Van Tyne, *The War of Independence, American Phase*, pp. 308–09.

tablishment of "one great, national, consolidated government." [10]

When in the 1790's Alexander Hamilton, with the co-operation of Washington, proved that the Constitution was being used to serve the "particular purposes" and the "consolidated government" of which Tyler and Mason spoke, there were protesting howls. The federal tariff was said to be a means for "the advancement of commerce and manufacturing in preference to agriculture" and for the making of the South into "the milch cow out of whom the substance would be extracted." James Madison in 1789 warned that out of the doctrines of implied powers used to justify the creation of the First Bank of the United States, "a chain may be formed that will reach every object of legislation, every object within the whole compass of political economy." The Virginia legislature the next year saw in the assumption by the national government of state debts "the prostration of agriculture at the feet of commerce, or a change of the present form of foederal government, fatal to the existence of American liberty." [11] Georgia in refusing to appear as a defendant before the Supreme Court in the case of Chisholm versus Georgia declared that acquiescence in this suit "would effectively destroy the retained sovereignty of the States" and "render them but tributory corporations to the government of the United States."

Such fears were proclaimed in a radical form after Congress enacted the Alien and Sedition Laws of 1798. Resolutions written by Jefferson and Madison and passed by the Virginia and Kentucky legislatures declared these laws null and void and called on the states to remonstrate in order to secure their repeal. The resolutions were based on the belief that each state had the right to act as umpire when the constitutionality of acts of Congress was under question. This was the beginning of nullification, a doctrine destined for a time to be the South's defense against the aggressions of the Northern majority acting through Congress and the Supreme Court.

The revolt of the 1790's had a tentative character. This was because Jefferson despite the clarity of his theories was a politician willing to compromise. When he saw the opportunity for the agrarian party to gain power through alliance with commercial and industrial interests he abandoned in part at least his agrarian and states' rights principles. Yet the social and economic factors responsible for his initial grievances against Northern interests smoldered among a firm minority of Jeffersonians. They were ready to act when more compelling causes were

[10] Cited in Jesse T. Carpenter, *The South as a Conscious Minority*, pp. 8, 26, 42 n., 63.

[11] *Ibid.*, pp. 29–30, 50–1, 55.

added to the Southern sense of dissatisfaction. This, as we shall see, happened in 1820.

The American Revolution gave opportunity for the expression of much political liberalism by Southern leaders. This liberalism had found expression in significant reforms. But the new doctrines in many instances proved so unreal that they were often followed by reaction in favor of traditional interests. The conservative trend, however, could not remove the impress of equality and liberty from the minds of Southerners. Slavery was never again, as during the Colonial period, accepted as a matter of course; it had in the future to be moralized over, pro and con. The slave trade until its abolition bore a stigma comparable to that of bootlegging in the twentieth century. Jefferson's Declaration of Independence was timeless; it was destined to haunt the good Southerner during his deeds of darkest reaction and to inspire him with ideals of greater democracy in his hopeful moments.

CHAPTER VII

1820 — Beginning [handwritten]

Development of Sectional Consciousness

⋙-⋙

It has been made clear that many elements necessary for defining the region below the Potomac as a distinct cultural unit of the United States had roots far back in the Colonial period. Such, for example, was Negro slavery, out of which grew Ulrich B. Phillips' "central theme" of Southern history; such also was plantation life that produced distinct ideals of social stability, rural worth, and home life. Not until some four decades after the American Revolution, however, did leaders of the Southern states become acutely and permanently aware that their people possessed peculiar virtues and ambitions that needed defense from Northern interference. Before 1820, with the important exceptions which have been noted, struggles in which Southerners participated did not involve defense of slavery or other institutions especially Southern. During the colonial and early national periods the geographical cleavage was generally between the coastal and interior regions within each state, rather than between Northern and Southern states. The American Revolution was a civil war between Whigs and Tories, but in this war there was no division between North and South. There were loyalists in every colony. They were more numerous in the Southern colonies of Georgia and the Carolinas and in the Northern colonies of New York and Pennsylvania; smaller numbers were found in Virginia and Massachusetts. Although abolition of slavery in Northern states during the American Revolution created potentialities of conflict, these potentialities did not become sharply manifest for several decades. Southern leaders of the

[right margin handwritten notes: *Reasons:* ① *slavery* ② *plantation system* — ⅓ *Patriots* / ⅓ *Tories* / ⅓ *didn't give a* —]

((95))

Revolutionary generation were not enthusiastic over slavery and apparently looked forward to its gradual extinction. Before 1820 there was little difference between the North and the South in the volume and vigor of antislavery expressions. In that year Governor Thomas M. Randolph of Virginia spoke of "the deplorable error of our ancestors" in fixing slavery upon posterity by "copying a civil institution from savage Africa."

Thomas Jefferson and James Madison in the 1790's anticipated, as we have seen, the agrarian and states' rights principles which in the 1820's became the lasting bases of Southern sectionalism. When federal tyranny seemed to threaten the liberty of the states they suggested nullification as a remedy. The two Virginia statesmen, nevertheless, were more interested in using this belief as a means of winning the election of 1800 than they were in proclaiming an unchanging principle. By winning the election of 1800 and establishing themselves in national power, they lost their minority consciousness and became practical nationalists. President Jefferson violated his doctrine of strict construction of the Constitution by accepting the annexation of Louisiana. President Madison sponsored a war of aggression, not merely to add to the territory of slavery but also to annex Canadian lands in which slavery would not have been introduced.

When New Englanders invoked nullification doctrines as a means of opposing this war, friends of Jefferson and Madison called them unpatriotic and treasonable. Jefferson, outgrowing earlier prejudices against industry, wrote in favor of the protective tariff of 1816: "We must now place the manufacturer by the side of the agriculturist." People of Virginia and other Southern states acquiesced in the nationalistic enthusiasms of their leaders. Only John Randolph of Roanoke, John Taylor of Caroline County, Virginia, and Nathaniel Macon of North Carolina dissented from the prevailing trend, foreseeing with prophetic insight that the South would have to become sectionally minded to preserve its regional interests.

The sporadic nature of sectional consciousness before 1820 cannot be more convincingly demonstrated than by the fact that before that date the man who later would make its classical defense was an unalloyed nationalist. John C. Calhoun entered Congress in 1811 as the representative of a district of upper South Carolina in which the system of plantation slavery had not become firmly rooted. Early in his Congressional career he won distinction as a leader of those who precipitated and supported the War of 1812. After the war he continued his nationalist enthusiasms, advocating increased armaments, internal taxation, national banks, and the construction of means of communication at federal expense. He joined Henry Clay in inducing Congress to extend the

Cumberland Road westward; the protective tariff of 1816 was largely his work; and he introduced the bill chartering the Second Bank of the United States. He deprecated sectionalism and "refined arguments on the constitution." He spoke of the protective tariff as "a new and more powerful cement," and in 1817 declared exultantly of the nation as a whole: "We are greatly and rapidly—I was about to say fearfully— growing." Even in 1821 John Quincy Adams, the New England nationalist, wrote of the South Carolinian in his diary: "He is above all sectional and factious prejudices, more than any other statesman of this Union with whom I have ever acted."

Two events caused Southern leaders to reconsider their nationalist enthusiasms and return to the suspicions that Virginians before 1800 had voiced against federal authority. One of these events was the business panic of 1819 which followed on the heels of the prosperous years that followed the end of the war in 1815. The South was hit hard. Its overexpanded debts caused the Bank of the United States and other financial institutions of the North to call in their loans. Its overexpanded fields caused the price of cotton to fall from 33 to 15 cents a pound, and the price of tobacco to fall from 25 to 5 cents a pound. Property values fell sensationally; cities decreased in population; there were many bank and business failures. There was a great outcry against the Northern centers of financial power. The banks were described as "horse-leeches" which "drained every drop of blood they could suck from a suffering community." Yankee peddlers were described as a "worthless set of beings and generally rogues, too lazy to get a living honestly." Unless the dissatisfaction existing in the South and the West was assuaged, a Kentuckian predicted, it would lead "with a steady pace, to civil war and dissolution of the union."

In 1820 another issue arose that alarmed the most distinguished Virginian. "This momentous question, like a fire bell in the night, awakened and filled me with terror," wrote Jefferson. "I considered it at once the knell of the Union." "A geographical line, coinciding with marked principle," he explained, had been held up to the angry passions of men and would never be obliterated. An acrimonious debate had taken place *Missouri* in Congress demonstrating a sharp difference of opinion between representatives of free and slave states. Henry Clay declared the words "civil war" and "disunion" were uttered "almost without emotion." Thomas W. Cobb of Georgia warned the Northern congressman who had evoked the issue, "We have kindled a fire . . . which seas of blood can only extinguish." John Quincy Adams reported that when Senator Rufus King spoke against the South's ambitions, "the great slave-holders in the House gnawed their lips and clinched their fists." Representatives of the free states had asserted that slavery was wrong according to the dictates of humanity, the teachings of the Scripture, and the principles of democracy.

The issue was precipitated by the attempt of Representative James Tallmadge of New York in 1819 to attach to Missouri's petition for admission into the Union an amendment prohibiting further extension of slavery into that territory and requiring the freeing there of all slave children born after the admission of the state when they should attain the age of twenty-five. The reason that this proposal created such a disturbance is not difficult to understand. Clearly the real issue was whether slavery should be confined within the eleven states east of the Mississippi and south of the Ohio where it already existed, or whether it should be extended to regions west of the Mississippi.

The North was opposed to opening the western country to slavery. Accustomed to free labor and small farms, it feared that its westward-moving population would be excluded by the competition of the plantation system of slave labor and that its influence in national affairs would be diminished by the appearance in Washington of representatives from slaveholding states that would be carved out of the West. The South, on the other hand, had reasons equally fundamental in demanding Missouri for slavery. As the next chapter will indicate,[1] the expanding kingdom of slavery needed new lands. Before 1820 settlers from Tennessee and Kentucky had brought 10,000 slaves into Missouri and had discovered that its southern section was suitable for cotton and was healthier than malarial regions to the south. Moreover, a free Missouri would destroy the equality with the North which the South possessed in the Senate. Already the population balance between slave states and free states had been broken. In 1820 the free states had 667,000 more people, which gave them, under the system of apportionment by which only three fifths of the slave population was counted, 105 members of the lower house of Congress to the slave states' 81. The balance, however, was maintained in the Senate, where the 22 representatives of the eleven free states were matched by representatives from the eleven slave states. Naturally the South was alarmed when the Tallmadge measure passed the House by a sectional vote and was blocked in the Senate only by a combination of Southerners with Northern moderates.

Politicians, ever mindful of the advantages of party harmony, stepped into the sectional chasm with the famous Missouri Compromise. It provided that Missouri as a slave state should be balanced by Maine as a free state, and that in the remainder of the Louisiana Purchase the dividing line between slavery and freedom should be 36° 30', an extension of the southern border of Missouri. The South was satisfied, and

Balance kept for a long time

didn't settle a thing.

[1] See below, pp. 120–1.

politics resumed a delusive tranquillity with twelve free states offsetting twelve slave states.

John Randolph of Roanoke, a sharp-tongued Virginia freelance, first taught the South the lesson of the Missouri Compromise: that the section should abandon the pursuit of nationalist policies in order to preserve its peculiar interests against majority aggression. Although his appeal lacked the dignity it needed to become the formal creed of a fateful cause, it was sufficiently vivid and realistic to arrest attention and to revive for its author the popularity he had lost by opposing the policies of the Virginia dynasty.

Opposed War of 1812 -- said it was to capture Canada.

His campaign began in 1823 when Daniel Webster sentimentally proposed resolutions condemning the Turks for slavery and other abuses against the Greeks. Turning to his Southern colleagues, the Virginia congressman shouted: Were they who had "the misfortune to reside on the wrong side of a certain mysterious line" prepared to endorse action by the United States saying "that the act of holding human beings as property is sufficient to place the party so offending under the ban of its high and mighty displeasure?" The next year he ran counter to nationalist sentiments by opposing a survey for the possible construction of a grand system of canals and roads. When George McDuffie, the protégé of Calhoun, spoke to the contrary, the wary Virginian proclaimed that if Congress possessed this power it might logically assume the power of emancipating every slave in the country. He threatened resistance by "every other means short of actual insurrection." "We shall keep on the windward side of treason," he said.

↓ Madison said to vindicate our rights at se

During congressional consideration of the tariff of 1824 he supplemented the moderate antiprotectionist arguments of McDuffie by claiming that the North was using the tariff and other federal policies to impoverish the agricultural South. "We are the eel," he said, "that is being flayed while the cook-maid pats us on the head and cries with the clown in *King Lear*, 'Down, wantons, down.' . . . A fig for the Constitution! When the scorpion's sting is probing us to the quick, shall we stop to chop logic. . . . There is no magic in the word *union*." "His acts," Henry Clay ruefully confessed, "came near shaking the Union in the center and desolating this fair land." [2]

Randolph's strident words were symptomatic of a shift of Southern interests which the compromisers of 1820 could not halt. South Carolina, where Southern sentiments were most pronounced, became convinced that it had made a mistake in hoping the South could win industrial diversity through the aid of the protective tariff and internal improvements. In 1825 the cotton-growing states of North Carolina,

[2] Cited in William C. Bruce, *John Randolph of Roanoke*, I, 476–7, 449, 490–4.

Mobile & New Orleans now more imp't then Ches w Norfolk

South Carolina, Georgia, Alabama, Mississippi, and Tennessee possessed only a small fraction of American capital and labor employed in manufacturing. The great industrial development was in New England and the Middle states. As will presently be explained,[3] surplus capital and labor of the South was being absorbed by agriculture; as cotton growing spread westward, prices fell below the cost of production on Carolina and Georgia lands worn out by the one-crop system. The benefits of protection were going to Northern manufacturers while Southern planters bore the burden of higher prices for manufactured goods.

The legislatures of South Carolina, Georgia, and Alabama passed resolutions denying the constitutionality of the protective tariff. Dr. Thomas Cooper, president of South Carolina College, at a gathering of planters declared: "We shall ere long be forced to calculate the value of our Union, to ask of what use is an unequal alliance by which the South has always been the loser and the North always the winner." Despite these protests, greedy manufacturers joined with those who wished to put Jackson in the White House to induce Congress in 1828 to enact the so-called Tariff of Abominations.

Calhoun was faced with a dilemma. If he recanted his protectionist views he might lose his distinguished position as a national leader. If he did not recant, he might be repudiated by South Carolina and other cotton states. Naturally he hesitated, joining in 1828 in an attempt to divide Eastern and Western protectionists as a means of defeating the ambitions of both. When this jockeying failed and was followed by the Tariff of Abominations, the South Carolina statesman prepared anonymously the "South Carolina Exposition," embodying the doctrine that was to become famous as nullification.

Still he jockeyed, pinning his faith on Andrew Jackson, the native Carolinian who became President in 1829, and nursing a plan of intersectional accord under which the West was to be placated by internal improvements, the South by a general tariff reduction, and the North by specific tariff concessions. Then came the enactment by Congress of the systematically protective tariff of 1832, which was signed by Jackson. Disillusioned, Calhoun aligned himself with the people of his state, returning home to write other defenses of their position. Unlike the violent and unsystematic Randolph, he was capable of sustained and rigorous reasoning, and soon he had formulated "The Address to the People of South Carolina" and "The Fort Hill Letter," embodying the principle of nullification.

The Union, said Calhoun, was an agreement among states, legalized in the Constitution, under which powers were divided between the states and the national government. Supreme power, however, was not

[3] See below, p. 130.

divided, for sovereignty is indivisible and must rest with either the states or the nation. Unquestionably the states possessed it before the Union was created and, in the opinion of Calhoun, did not surrender it when the Union was formed. The Union was subordinate to the states, he said. Therefore, when a dispute arose between the two concerning the constitutionality of an act of Congress, the Supreme Court or other federal agency could not sit in judgment, but this judgment must be pronounced by a state agency competent to exercise its sovereignty. The only competent agency was a convention of the people of the state, called for the specific purpose of expressing the will of its people in the matter under dispute. If the convention declared an act of Congress null and void, operation of this act would be suspended within the limits of the state. The only recourse of Congress in this contingency would be the setting aside of the judgment of the state through the difficult process of constitutional amendment. If this expedient proved successful, the state would still have the last move. It could secede from the Union.

Nullification was brought to the front of the national scene in January, 1830, when Senator Robert Y. Hayne of South Carolina engaged Daniel Webster of Massachusetts in one of the most significant constitutional debates ever held in the United States Senate. Webster, of noble countenance, flashing eyes, and almost unlimited vocabulary, was an able constitutional lawyer and the country's most prominent orator. He had a worthy opponent in Hayne, who typified the best in Southern aristocracy and was second only to Webster in grace of person, eloquence of phrase, and knowledge of the Constitution. The joust between these two giants attracted the widest attention in an age which held oratory in high esteem.

Hayne, seeking Western support in the South's fight against the tariff, opposed a resolution of Senator Samuel A. Foot of Connecticut that would have restricted the sale of public lands. When Webster countered Hayne's denunciation of the "selfish and unprincipled" attitude of the East, the South Carolinian abandoned discussion of the Foot resolution to champion nullification and denounce the consolidation of national power. The Massachusetts senator vindicated his reputation as an orator by a glowing defense of a strong union, but in sustained arguments Hayne was his match, advancing proof of the economic injustice of the protective tariff toward agricultural areas. Hayne brought clearly to the attention of the country the necessity for a system of checks and balances to prevent majority tyranny. To guarantee full sectional liberty he believed that a state might lawfully apply the doctrine of nullification. The Hayne-Webster debate cleared the issue between states' rights and nationalism, and provided for both sides a multitude of arguments as bases for action.

In 1832 Congress enacted a tariff which gave to the principle of protection an air of permanency. Hayne's suggestion to the western states that they join the South in opposing predatory eastern interests went unheeded. South Carolina members of Congress, under Calhoun's leadership, advised their people that "all hope of relief from Congress is irrevocably gone" and that the proper remedy was nullification.

Nullifiers and antinullifiers within South Carolina fought for control of the convention of the people. George McDuffie, an ardent nullifier, declared that the North would not dare push the cotton states to the extremity of secession because of the devastating effects upon the national economy of the elimination of cotton exports. The South Carolinians were impressed, and their convention on November 24, 1832, passed an ordinance nullifying the tariffs of 1828 and 1832. No enforcement of these laws was to be allowed in South Carolina, and the federal government was warned that if it attempted to enforce them South Carolina would withdraw from the United States. President Andrew Jackson, who two years earlier had supported Georgia in the nullification of a decision of the Supreme Court concerning the land rights of the Cherokee Indians, declared the act of South Carolina treason and, with characteristic vigor, sent ships and soldiers to Charleston with orders to be ready for instant action.

Congress sustained the President by passing the Force Bill, under which he was authorized to employ armed forces to carry out the law. Although South Carolinians called this measure the Bloody Bill, Calhoun did not oppose its passage, because Jackson and Henry Clay demonstrated a desire to come to terms with the intransigent South Carolinians. They did this through the Compromise Tariff of 1833, which provided for a gradual reduction of duties by 1842; after this time rates were not to exceed 20 per cent on any article.

In response, the South Carolina convention rescinded its Ordinance of Nullification, with, however, a face-saving device by which the Force Bill was declared null and void. Nullification, the South Carolinians contended, had proved effective because it had forced the hated national majority to redress their grievances. Nationalists, on the other hand, asserted that the venturesome little commonwealth was saved from humiliation and tragic defeat by a government which had both the will and the means to bring it to terms.

Other Southern states were unwilling to support South Carolina in its formal defiance of federal authority. The legislature of Georgia expressed their attitude when it bluntly declared: "We abhor the doctrine of nullification as neither a peaceful, nor a constitutional remedy, but, on the contrary, as tending to civil commotion and disunion." Kentucky wanted tariff protection for hemp and Louisiana wanted it for sugar. Although various Southern states were using their dislike of the tariff to promote sectional consciousness, their immediate individual interests in 1832 made them reluctant to push states' rights doctrines to extremes. Georgia, Alabama, and Mississippi were enjoying the aid of President Jackson in effecting the removal of the Indians. While South Carolina was loudly proclaiming its theory of nullification, Alabama was applying this doctrine with complete success. That state in 1833 forced the federal government to set aside its treaty against white squatters in territory of the Creek Indians. Disapproval of nullification in Virginia and Maryland was perhaps identified with their desire for federal aid in the development of internal transportation. Virginia sent an agent to South Carolina to counsel moderation, and the legislatures of Alabama and Georgia asked for a convention of the cotton states to settle the tariff controversy. It is significant that a Southern state never again declared itself formally for nullification.

In 1833, as in 1820, statesmen of the country succeeded in staying the threats of sectional breaks. Yet by 1833 sectionalism had reappeared in a different and more menacing manner. Previously, dissension had occurred over two questions: whether planters should carry their slaves into territories desired by men of the free states, and whether inhabitants of the agricultural states should pay more for their manufactured products in order to increase the profits of the manufacturing states.

These issues were important, but they were not so serious as a supplementary issue which struck at the very roots of sectional interests and distinctions: was slavery as an institution morally worthy of the legal support of a nation that was boasting more and more of its faith in liberty and equality? The slave states took the offensive, advancing in the 1820's the "positive good" theory of slavery as a substitute for the Jeffersonian belief that slavery was an evil necessary only until some practical means of ending it could be devised.

The policy of reticence concerning the merits of the institution gave way to open advocacy. This new attitude was first manifest when William Smith of South Carolina in the Senate on January 26, 1820, "justified slavery on the broadest principles, without qualification or reserve." Three years later Richard Furman, a prominent Baptist divine, declared that the South should justify slavery on moral grounds and not merely on the plea of necessity. Thomas Cooper in 1826 advanced the argument that the Bible nowhere forbade slavery and that slavery had existed in some form or another throughout history. Governor Stephen D. Miller struck the keynote for the next thirty years when, in a message to the South Carolina legislature in 1829, he declared: "Slavery

is not a national evil; on the contrary, it is a national benefit . . . upon
this subject it does not become us to speak in a whisper, betray fear, or
feign philanthropy." [4]

This change of attitude had been induced by the antislavery aggressiveness of Northern spokesmen in the Missouri Compromise debate
and thereafter, by the Denmark Vesey Plot,[5] and by the desire of some
members of the American Colonization Society to seek an African
homeland for slaves as well as for free Negroes. This organization was
called "a society reprobated in the South, and justly regarded as murderous in its principles." [6]

Two years after Governor Miller spoke the sectional consciousness
of the South was further accentuated. In Boston on January 1, 1831,
William Lloyd Garrison, the most fanatical of the antislavery agitators,
brought out the first number of *The Liberator*. This journal was to keep
up a relentless bombardment of the South until slavery was abolished
Garrison called the attention of the public to the most repulsive aspects
of the South's peculiar institution, castigating slave masters as the vilest
of criminals, acknowledging no color problem, and tolerating no delay
in the coming of emancipation day. The Constitution of the United
States, because it sanctioned slavery, was declared to be "a covenant
with death and an agreement with hell." A copy of it was burned while
the fiery editor cried: "So perish all compromisers with tyranny!"

His complaint of the apathy of the North certainly was not applicable to the South. There his incendiary words evoked such fear and anger
that a peaceful attainment of his aims was made impossible. When the
Nat Turner Insurrection [7] occurred within eight months of the first
appearance of *The Liberator*, angry and alarmed Southerners accused
Garrison of attempting to accomplish his purpose by inciting slave revolt.

Study has since proved that the South was unduly alarmed by *The
Liberator*. With the exception of the lonely fanatic John Brown, no
Abolitionist attempted to organize slave rebellion through direct invasion of the slave states or through an underground conspiracy. Garrison's newspaper never had more than three thousand subscribers, and
was largely ignored by Northern newspapers and other periodicals. A
mob of Boston business men handled Garrison so roughly in 1835 that
he had to seek safety in a jail. "It was, indeed," says a sober historian,[8]
"the Southern opponents of Garrison, rather than his Northern supporters, that gave him notoriety."

[4] William S. Jenkins, *Pro-Slavery Thought in the Old South*, pp. 71-7.
[5] See below, p. 128.
[6] *Charleston Mercury*, cited in Jenkins, *ibid.*, p. 76.
[7] See below, p. 129.
[8] James G. Randall, *The Civil War and Reconstruction*, p. 102.

Other antislavery leaders with greater popularity and organizing ability than Garrison, however, agreed with his fundamental thesis. Mildest of these were the Free-Soilers, who used the controlling influence which they had over Northern public opinion after 1820 to check the spread of slavery in the territories. The philosophical abolitionists —New England's Emerson, Whittier, and Lowell, for example—opposed slavery on very much the same grounds as Jefferson and an earlier generation of Virginians. Garrison and his New England associates were unpopular largely because they eschewed political methods, were antagonistic in their manners, and cherished unorthodox opinions on a variety of subjects including religion. This, however, was not true of others who shared Garrison's views on the slavery question. Such, for example, were the western leaders Theodore D. Weld, Charles G. Finney, and James G. Birney, who were politically active.

At first Northern churches were hostile to the abolitionists, but after 1836 an antislavery movement among church people swept through sections of New York, Ohio, Pennsylvania, and Michigan, and soon antislavery views became dominant among the Northern Methodists and Baptists. By 1840 more than 150,000 members had joined some two thousand local abolitionist societies.

Those interested in the maintenance of slavery had reasons to fear the societies. These organizations represented "the bitter zeal of righteous men" who, in keeping with the Puritan heritage, could identify goodness with their own ideas and practices and evil with the ideas and practices of strangers. Assailing distant slaveholders provided a definite and convenient exaltation. Having lost faith in a heaven beyond the sky, they hoped to make a heaven—or at least a New England—of that section of the country cursed with slavery. The South's unique institution seemed the one great evil. They failed to realize that the faults of that section might have a more complex origin or "that the method of destroying what they assume to be bad may have more badness in it than the thing destroyed." [9] They indulged in slanderous propaganda against the slaveholders, calling them robbers, manstealers, and thieves who worked the slaves to death in seven years, beat them with many lashes, cropped their ears for purposes of identification, threw them to bloodhounds to be chewed, put red pepper, turpentine, and vinegar in their wounds, and failed to give them enough clothes to protect them from the weather.

Despite the tactlessness and arrogance of the abolitionists, their agitations were to bring about the greatest reform that ever captured the imagination of Americans. All men, the reformers asserted, are brothers in the sight of God and by the implications of the Declaration of Inde-

[9] Wirt Borden, cited in Randall, *ibid.*, p. 147.

American creed

Moral law higher

Grimké's turned Quaker.

pendence, and, therefore, should be free and equal. This idea had been used to further religious liberty and universal white manhood suffrage. Why should it not be used to give the Negro freedom and equality, the divine or natural heritage of all men? In the name of this "higher law" of God or nature, all man-made laws and constitutions of state and federal governments sanctioning slavery should be rejected by good Americans.

The South, as self-righteous and as Biblical as New England, matched the vehemence of the abolitionists. As will be explained later,[10] after 1831 the slave codes were made more severe. Georgia offered a reward for Garrison's arrest and conviction. The abolitionists James G. Birney, Cassius M. Clay, and Angelina and Sarah Grimké were exiled from the South. Had they continued their agitations in the South, they might have been lynched. Petitions were presented to Congress by Whig members in 1835 asking the abolition of slavery and the slave trade in the District of Columbia. Although those who presented these documents were more interested in creating dissension between the Northern and Southern Democrats than in advancing the antislavery cause, the friends of slavery in 1836 pushed through the House of Representatives a resolution banning consideration of these documents. The Gag Rule, as this action was called by its opponents, led to the accusation that the South was upholding the cause of slavery by sacrificing the constitutional right of petition.

Abolitionists collected $30,000 to flood the states below the Potomac with magazines and tracts denouncing slaveholders, using the mails to distribute their literature. The South was alarmed and feared dissatisfaction among the slaves and even insurrection. On a midsummer night of 1835 a Charleston mob extracted bundles of the objectionable literature from the local post office and burned them. When the Charleston postmaster begged the national authorities not to allow the forwarding of such documents, President Jackson was sympathetic, calling the mailing of the odious papers a "wicked plan of exciting the negroes to insurrection and to massacre."

The expressed conviction of Southern leaders in the 1820's that slavery was "a positive good" grew into a systematic philosophy after 1831 and was later embodied in a voluminous treatise known as *The Pro-Slavery Argument* (1852). One of its earliest proponents was Thomas R. Dew, a young professor at the College of William and Mary, who had learned while studying in Germany that the inequality of man was fundamental to all social organization. In 1832 his *Review of the Debate in the Virginia Legislature of 1831 and 1832* boldly repudiated the antislavery views of George Wythe and St. George Tucker, his predeces-

[10] See below, p. 125.

sors on the William and Mary faculty. This essay, says William E. Dodd,[11] was the "ablest of all the works treating slavery from historical and social points of view." His arguments were supplemented by almost everyone of importance in both the upper and lower South, including members of the clergy.

Outstanding among proslavery advocates were the South Carolinians Chancellor William Harper, Senator James H. Hammond and William Gilmore Simms, James D. B. De Bow of Louisiana, Josiah C. Nott of Alabama, and George Fitzhugh and Edmund Ruffin of Virginia. Calhoun lent the prestige of his name to the argument, cunningly combining the repudiation of the belief in the equality of man with the American faith in democracy and republicanism. He declared as early as 1837: "Many in the South once believed that it [slavery] was a moral and political evil. That folly and delusion are gone. We see it now in its true light, and regard it as the most safe and stable basis for free institutions in the world." Calhoun and other proslavery advocates revealed their faith so keenly and comprehensively that most Southerners were convinced, forgetting the contrary views of their post-Revolutionary leaders.

Slavery, it was contended, was "a good—a positive good" for reasons economic, Biblical, social, and ethnological. Its abolition would bring destitution to those who were deprived of their human property, thriftlessness and poverty to the Negroes, and the extermination of the whites as had occurred in Haiti. The Biblical argument was impressive to an age that accepted the Scriptures literally. Had not the Jews practiced slavery under the watchful care of Jehovah? Did not the Ten Commandments mention "servants" thrice? Did not Christ's silence upon the subject carry by implication His approval? Did not the Apostle Paul urge the fugitive Onesimus to return to his master? Was not the Ethiopian as the descendant of Ham fated to be the hewer of wood and the drawer of water?

Slavery was historically justified as part of the normal order of society. It had been practiced by the Greeks and Romans and approved by such philosophers as Aristotle and John Locke. The equalitarian teachings of the Declaration of Independence were boldly rejected in favor of a society in which the slave was "the mudsill." "It is the order of nature and of God," said Dew, "that the being of superior faculties and knowledge and therefore of superior power should control and dispose of those who are inferior." Such a society was peaceful and calm with none of the poverty, insecurity, discord, and prostitution of free society. At its top was leisure for the development of the higher arts of civilization; at its bottom were the slaves who had been trans-

[11] *The Cotton Kingdom*, p. 149.

formed from African savagery into a civilization that gave them Christianity and social and economic security. Both science and the Bible were invoked to prove that Negroes were so innately inferior to white men "that any attempt to improve their condition is warring against an immutable law of nature." Profits of the slave trade and of investments in slaves were cited to prove that the institution was economically desirable. For those not satisfied by material justifications, there was the social argument: slavery created a society so happy and so excellent in morals and manners that it should be maintained at all costs.

The triumph of the "positive good" theory of slavery was accompanied by an intensification of political democracy, as that term was defined by contemporary Americans. This assertion is contrary to the opinion of eminent historians, including James Ford Rhodes. "The political system of the South," Rhodes bluntly declares,[12] "was an oligarchy under the republican form." Such an opinion, however, was based, says one who has carefully studied the evidence,[13] "on moral hatred of Negro slavery, rather than a true knowledge of Southern state governments or a philosophical or realistic understanding of democracy." It was naïvely maintained that, because government by popular consent was assumed to be good, a government that sanctioned an alleged evil institution like slavery could not be democratic. It was forgotten that the common people of the South, through the agency of democratic political institutions, might have supported the economic and political institutions of their upper class of slaveholders as easily as common people of other countries supported their upper classes of financial and industrial magnates.

Facts prove that the states of the Old South, through a series of progressive reforms, conformed to the contemporary definition of democracy as "an equal division of political rights, not of property." They cast aside the Colonial heritage of suffrage restrictions, property qualifications for officeholding, and unequal apportionment of legislative representation. Kentucky, Maryland, and South Carolina established universal white manhood suffrage by 1810. Popular dissatisfaction with aristocratic privilege caused six Southern states in the 1830's to hold constitutional conventions dedicated to democratic reform. Consequently, property qualifications for voting were abolished in all Southern states except Virginia, North Carolina, and Louisiana, and for officeholding in all except South Carolina and Louisiana. Progress was also made in the reapportionment of legislative representation to give a

[12] *History of the United States from the Compromise of 1850*, I, 345.
[13] Fletcher M. Green, "Democracy in the Old South," *The Journal of Southern History*, XII, 5 (February, 1946).

more accurate proportion of the seats to the interior counties. In the 1850's constitutional reforms in seven states abolished almost all the remaining aristocratic privileges except in South Carolina. Until after the Civil War that state continued to have governors and Presidential electors chosen by the legislature, and to apportion legislative representation through a combination of property and white population.

These restrictions, however, were not more comprehensive than those prevailing in Massachusetts until 1853 and in Rhode Island until 1888. Broadening of white suffrage was accompanied by eliminating free Negroes from voting in Virginia, Kentucky, North Carolina, and Maryland, which were among the states of the Old South that had granted them that privilege. This action was paralleled in the North where, by 1821, all but five states had denied the free Negro suffrage. Regardless of whatever Jefferson and other proponents of the natural rights philosophy might have thought about the matter, Americans, both North and South, did not consider Negroes in their application of the "inalienable rights" with which "all men" were supposed to be endowed.

Paradoxically, democratization of Southern politics gave proslavery advocates a stronger hold upon the Southern consciousness. The upper classes, often Whigs in political affiliation, inherited in some measure the liberal views of the eighteenth-century aristocracy. They opposed extreme sectional agitations and the insidious efforts of popular politicians to stir the masses against the antislavery men. As persons who were already on the top, they were naturally eager to prevent eruptions that might alter the *status quo*.

The leaders of humble folk, on the other hand, were often Democrats "on the make"; they hoped to acquire slaves themselves, and they appealed to the race prejudices of constituencies that feared the effects of the agitations of those who wished to elevate the Negroes. Andrew Johnson spoke for this group when he said: "If you liberate the Negro, what will be the next step? . . . Blood, rape and rapine will be our portion. You can't get rid of the Negro except by holding him in slavery." [14] Indeed, Calhoun so cunningly combined the proslavery argument with American ideals that servitude appeared to be the very condition of democracy.

The notion of a free society, in which the virtuous and the capable entered into partnership for the good of the commonwealth and for the wardship of those capable only of simple toil, was accepted. The white race, of course, constituted the virtuous and capable, and the black race comprised those capable of simple toil. Since the Negro was made for manual labor, white skin protected the white man against

[14] Cited in Clement Eaton, *Freedom of Thought in the Old South*, p. 251.

social degradation and formed the basis of a brotherhood of race. This was an idea of democracy borrowed from the Greeks, but it made possible that pride and fellowship of race which have been considered by white Southerners as a vital part of free government.

Sectional dissension in politics was accompanied by similar disagreements in the field of religion. As another chapter of this book will reveal,[15] the acceptance by the Southern political leaders of the "positive good" theory of slavery was followed by a sweeping espousal of this philosophy by Southern churchmen. The general officers of the great national churches, fearing for the unity of these bodies, tried to pursue a moderate policy with respect to slavery by condemning the extreme abolitionists. For this reason William Lloyd Garrison developed an anticlerical obsession, even charging that the churches were the chief support of the slave system. After 1840, however, the great body of evangelical Christians of the North could no longer remain indifferent to an institution that was regarded as the acme of unrighteousness, and were converted to the antislavery cause. Under these circumstances controversy and schism were inevitable.

Despite the efforts of governing bishops, the slavery issue could not be excluded from Methodist assemblies. In 1844, the general conference of the church by a vote of 111 to 61 asked Bishop James O. Andrew of Georgia to desist from his episcopal labors until he should dispose of the slaves he had acquired by a second marriage. Andrew refused to comply. Had he done so, he would have destroyed his usefulness as a Southern pastor. The Southern delegates withdrew from the general conference, and, at Louisville in 1845, organized a separate church known as the Methodist Episcopal Church, South. The bitterness which for many decades dominated the relations of the two principal branches of American Methodism was begun in 1848 when the Northern church repudiated the generous plan of separation previously granted the Southern church.

Southern Baptists, resenting the refusal of the national mission boards of their church to take slaveholders in their service, withdrew from their Northern connections in 1845 and organized the Southern Baptist Convention at Augusta. The conduct of Baptist abolitionists was declared "censurable and meddlesome." Episcopalians successfully kept the slavery issue out of their convocations and were therefore able to maintain national unity until 1861.

Religious dissension was supplemented by the revival of controversy over slavery in the western territories. Soon after the Missouri Compromise, Southern migration to the Mexican province of Texas was encouraged by the Mexican government, then eager to populate its

[15] See below, p. 165.

[handwritten marginalia at top: 1787 – Northwest Ordinance prohibited slavery west of Ohio River. 1804 – No slaves in North. 1833 – slavery abolished in BWI. South only English-speaking people still having slavery (Brazil, Cuba and P. Rico still had slavery)]

northern regions. By 1835, after 20,000 Anglo-Americans had joined 3,000 Mexicans living in Texas, Mexican authorities, fearing their disruptive influence, prohibited slavery and additional immigration. In the struggle which followed, Anglo-Americans, led by Sam Houston, won independence for Texas in 1836 and established the Lone Star Republic. A protracted agitation led to the incorporation of Texas into the United States as a slave state, and finally to war with Mexico. Victory brought to the United States not only confirmation of its annexation of Texas but the acquisition of the vast westerly region known as New Mexico and California.

This acquisition of territory was but another manifestation of the great westward movement by which Anglo-Americans peopled the continent. Motivated by a general land hunger, this movement would have come had there been no Southern planters to covet cotton lands. Alike it drew contemporary Northerners into Oregon, and Southerners into the cotton-growing areas of Texas. Wage labor was virtually nonexistent in Texas, since land was free to all white settlers. Stephen F. Austin, the leader of colonization, saw the necessity of slave labor and fostered its importation. The South as a whole quite naturally welcomed Texas as an addition to the body of slave states and looked forward to the creation of others from the Mexican cession. Confusing association with cause, enemies of the South saw in the Texas phase of the westward movement a conspiracy on the part of slaveholders to stake off new lands for their despised institution, and large segments of Northern public opinion opposed the annexation of Texas and the war with Mexico. When the forces of expansion proved more compelling than opposition to slavery, a principle most irritating to the South was advanced. It was embodied in the Wilmot Proviso.

In 1846 David Wilmot, a congressman from Pennsylvania, attempted to attach to the appropriations for the negotiation of the treaty of annexation a proviso prohibiting slavery in the territory about to be acquired to the west of Texas. The Northern majority in the lower house of Congress carried the measure, but the slave states' thirty Senators prevented its passage. The South regarded the proposal as a diabolical conspiracy to overturn the balance between their states and the fifteen free states which would exist after Wisconsin would be admitted in 1848 as a free state. Had the proviso been adopted, new area below the Missouri Compromise line would have become free territory. California and New Mexico might then be admitted as the sixteenth and seventeenth nonslaveholding states while there remained no additional territory for the expansion of slavery.

Resenting this and other interferences with the progress of slavery, in 1849 a caucus of Southern congressmen asked the people of their section to unite in one party. At the suggestion of Calhoun, a Mississippi assembly requested a convention of the slaveholding states to meet at Nashville in June 1850, "to devise some mode of resistance" to Northern aggression. Nine states attended, with Robert Barnwell Rhett, fiery editor of the *Charleston Mercury*, among the delegates. Resolutions were adopted asserting that citizens of the several states had equal rights to migrate to the territories and that Congress had no power to exclude them. The convention expressed willingness to settle the slavery controversy by extending the Missouri Compromise line to the Pacific. It then adjourned with plans to meet again after Congress had taken action.

After the Compromise of 1850 the Nashville body reassembled with a changed and more radical membership. It rejected the Compromise of 1850 without calling on the Southern states to secede. Its injunctions went unheeded by the people of the South because, for the moment at least, they were tired of sectional strife and wished to abide by the congressional settlement. Yet the Nashville Convention had not been without results. It increased the feeling of sectional nationalism, the belief that, if action must come, it must be that of all the Southern states.

Despite the bitterness of the sectional controversies of the preceding thirty years, the South in 1850 was willing to accept the olive branch for several reasons. One was the realization of a common nationality with Northerners, based on the Anglo-Saxon heritage of language, religion, customs, patriotic experiences, and ideals. The economic systems of the two sections were in many respects complementary: the South furnished cotton and other raw materials for the Northern mills and received manufactured articles and the use of the transportation and trade facilities of the Northern cities in return. "Those who demanded separation for economic reasons," says a thoughtful historian,[16] "were not thinking sufficiently in terms of mutual dependence." If Abraham Lincoln was not a prophet when he said that the two sections could not separate, it was certainly true that they could not do so conveniently. Southerners of the upper classes frequently came into contact with Northerners—at trading, watering, political, and educational centers— and found themselves to be more like the men beyond the line of slavery than they had thought.

The numerical inferiority of which the South was conscious was counteracted by the strategy of its statesmen. Through the Democratic party they consummated an alliance with both the conservative North and the agricultural West. The Northern alliance, which stemmed from the days of Jefferson, was based on foundations of patriotism and mutual interests. The alliance with the West was derived from the desire of farmers for monetary inflation, the market that Western farm-

[16] Randall, *op. cit.*, pp. 113–14.

ers found on the plantations for their pork and grain, and the control which the Mississippi River and New Orleans exercised on Western access to the sea. The Democratic party was strong in every state and was, therefore, an effective force for national unity. It dominated the national government except for two short intervals from 1829 until 1861. Southern leaders had sound reasons to cherish this dominance, for they largely controlled the party policies. They dedicated the Democratic party to territorial expansion of slavery and they tolerated the elevation of non-Southerners to high office only because Southerners were usually the power behind the throne. By 1850 they had succeeded in creating the Solid South by forcing the aristocratic leaders of the once powerful Southern branch of the Whig party into their organization. Before the bar of public opinion the Whigs were convicted of protariff leanings and of failure to be definitely proslavery.

That the dominant element in Southern politics was not eager to sacrifice its position in national affairs is proved by the conduct of the man most prominently associated with sectionalism. This man was John C. Calhoun. He was motivated by a sincere love of the Union as well as by a haunting fear that the peculiar institutions of the South might be overwhelmed by the growing numerical majority of the free states. To reconcile these divergent views he proposed a compromise both constructive and ingenious, which became known as the theory of the Concurrent Majority. By this plan, Calhoun suggested the imposition upon the whole national majority of the will of a geographical majority in order "to give to the weaker section, in some form or another, a negative on the action of the government." There should be, said Calhoun, two executives instead of one, each representing a section and each having the power of veto over acts of Congress. A measure should be required to pass that body, not by the members voting as one body, but by the representatives of the two sections voting separately. By one or the other of these devices, the Southern minority could protect itself from invidious measures. Calhoun, says Vernon L. Parrington, was a realist because he rejected as naïve the rule of the people in favor of functional or economic representation. A numerical majority unrestrained by effective constitutional limitations on its will was no friend of justice. It established "the tyranny of the majority," which was as great a menace to liberty as the tyranny of the despot or of the oligarchy.

On March 4, 1850, Calhoun, his tall frame emaciated by illness, his piercing eyes still bright, was brought into the Senate Chamber to hear the last address of his career read by a colleague. It was a gloomy occasion for Calhoun. His territorial theorizing had been put to scorn by a demand that had to be granted. Big, booming California, clamoring for admission to the Union as the sixteenth free state, was menacing the fifteen-fifteen balance between free and slave states. Apparently no territory was available out of which a sixteenth slave state could be carved. Calhoun could do nothing but lament what he regarded as the deplorable change of the general government from a federal republic into a consolidated democracy, a change that was making the Union intolerable to the minority section. Plaintively he called attention to the growing economic and political preponderance of the North, attributing it to the tariff, internal improvements, and other oppressive acts on the part of the majority section. He demanded the cessation of abolitionist agitations and the granting to the South of equal rights in the territories.

The Union was saved—temporarily at least—by its statesmen. Daniel Webster, speaking three days after Calhoun, recognized the justice of the South Carolinian's complaint, even asking for the adoption of a stricter fugitive slave law and the elimination of the "taunt or reproach" of the Wilmot Proviso. Henry Clay, the peacemaker, sought to reconcile the two viewpoints by the Compromise of 1850, formulated on a give-and-take basis. To compensate for the admission of California as a free state, the South's desire for a more effective fugitive slave law was fulfilled. The territories of Utah and New Mexico were organized with the understanding that when they submitted constitutions on applying for statehood they could decide the slavery issue themselves. Slavery was continued in the District of Columbia as a concession to the South, but the slave trade there was prohibited. Calhoun, partly satisfied with this measure, magnanimously praised Webster's Seventh of March speech. North and South alike welcomed the truce as a basis of permanent accord between the sections.

South Carolina leaders were unsuccessful in their attempt to call another Southern convention to continue the agitations broken off at the Nashville Convention. A Georgia convention, called to discuss current issues, was thoroughly unionist in sentiment; it accepted the compromise and begged the North to be faithful to its provisions. In the state election which followed, those who favored compromise triumphed. In Mississippi, Henry S. Foote, who favored compromise, defeated Jefferson Davis, who was opposed, for the governorship. The other Southern states generally accepted the position of Georgia and Mississippi; they were glad to be free of strife.

Yet the Compromise of 1850 proved to be not only temporary but from the Southern viewpoint a tragic mistake. Southern leaders were to learn that by waiting eleven years after 1850 to push the sectional issues to an ultimate decision they lessened their chances of success. When the decision came in 1861, the disparity of resources between the North and the South had grown so great that no amount of valor and sacrifice could prevent the failure of the South. Foreseeing this tragedy, the dying Calhoun less than a month after his Fourth of March speech lamented: "The South, the poor South."

CHAPTER VIII

The Slave System

The Slave System

By THE Northwest Ordinance of 1787 slavery was excluded from the territory north of the Ohio River; all states north of Maryland and Delaware had abolished it by 1804, and by 1833, the British West Indies. Southerners thus remained the only English-speaking Americans who held slaves. If sectional differences characteristic of the South could be attributed to slavery alone, it can be said that out of the black soil of human bondage sprang those institutions peculiarly Southern. The section's friends called the products of this soil white flowers: gentlemen with chivalric manners, ladies of high virtue, a satisfying social system, and superb political and social leadership. To the area's enemies its harvest was but noxious weeds: overseer's lashes, a hectoring and callous master class, scandals of the domestic slave trade, and the poverty and ignorance of the poor whites.

In the period of the American Revolution the interest of the South in slavery declined. Thoughtful persons saw a glaring inconsistency in demanding life, liberty, and happiness for themselves, while denying these reputed natural rights to their Negroes. Patrick Henry presented this confession of guilt: "Would any one believe that I am Master of Slaves of my own purchase! I am drawn along by the general Inconvenience of living without them; I will not, I cannot justify it." Henry Laurens of the South Carolina rice country wrote bitterly when he declared, "I abhor slavery." But "great powers oppose me, the laws and customs of my country, my own and the avarice of my countrymen." The slaveholding author of the Declaration of Independence revealed his impatience with his situation when he said: "I tremble for my country when I reflect that God is just; that his justice cannot sleep forever." George Washington, less idealistic than some of his contemporaries, wrote in 1794 of his desire to be rid of his slaves: "I shall be happily mistaken if they are not found to be a very troublesome species of property ere many years have passed over our heads."

The decade following 1783 brought depression to the entire Southern plantation area. Tobacco prices and exports were low, and the new lands made available for cultivation were offset by the abandonment of old tracts. Rice culture was experiencing the inconvenience of transfer to the low-tide system, and indigo culture was becoming extinct. As slave prices declined, Southern representatives transmitted into legislation their lack of confidence in the system. The Ordinance of 1787 prohibiting slavery in the Ohio country was not opposed by a single Southern congressman. By 1807 African slave trade had been permanently prohibited by all states except South Carolina, which had reopened it in 1803. Federal legislation outlawing this much-criticized traffic in 1808 received the wholehearted support of Southern members of Congress.

The freeing of slaves by the wills of planters of the post-Revolutionary generation was so common that the number of free Negroes in the South nearly doubled in each of the two decades following 1790. Several Southern states repealed their laws against freeing slaves and permitted manumission provided the owners could guarantee that the freedmen would not become community liabilities. Robert Carter of Nomini Hall set an example by freeing more than 500 Negroes in 1791. George Washington freed his by will; Jefferson was prevented from adopting a similar course by bankruptcy. John Randolph of Roanoke freed approximately 400 slaves in 1833, and George W. P. Curtis of Virginia liberated two or three hundred in 1857. Tolerance was shown toward abolitionist agitations in Virginia and the back country, especially in the conventions of the Methodist, Presbyterian, and Baptist churches. The Virginia legislature in 1831 and 1832 seriously debated the question of abolition; no action was taken primarily because of the expense of compensating slaveowners and transporting the freed Negroes out of the country.

By 1817 the American Colonization Society had been organized with the support of slaveholders in Virginia, Maryland, and Kentucky. In 1822 this group established the Republic of Liberia on the west coast of Africa and transported more than a thousand blacks, in pursuit of its purpose of returning free Negroes to Africa. The hardships of the African environment and the limited scope of the society presented practical difficulties which the organization could not overcome. Nevertheless, it represented a sincere attempt to meet the objections of many who believed that the free Negro was a menace to Southern society.

As cotton culture assumed a dominant position in the economy of the Old South, the section entered a new period, the most significant of its entire history. The languishing institution of slavery was revitalized and the scope and influence of the plantation spread to extents hitherto unthought of. Before the American Revolution cotton had been cultivated on a petty scale from New Jersey to Georgia. In England spinning and weaving machines had created an insatiable demand for materials to be made into fabrics. The hand process of separating cotton fibers from their seeds could not match the speed of these machines. Until a cotton gin for this purpose could be devised, this foreign market would remain closed.

Along the coasts of Georgia and South Carolina successful experiments were made with the long staple or sea-island variety of cotton. Its fibers were easily detached from the seeds, but this advantage was offset by the small yield per acre and the restricted area—the coastal region—which could produce it. So little cotton was exported in the years after the Revolution that in 1784 eight bags of the fleecy staple were said to have been seized by the customs officers of Liverpool "on the ground that since America could not produce so great a quantity the invoice must be fraudulent." In 1791 total American production was only 400 bales.

Two years later, however, Eli Whitney, a Yankee living on a Georgia plantation, made his revolutionary invention of the cotton gin. It was a simple machine consisting of rollers equipped with wire teeth which tore the cotton from the seed, depositing the seed in a hopper constructed of slats. Operated by hand, this mechanism could do the work of ten men; by horsepower, the work of fifty men. Surprisingly, Southerners were slow to adopt the new device. By 1810 cotton production had reached only 177,824 bales of 500 pounds each. Yet by 1830 it had leaped to 732,218 bales, by 1850 to 2,136,003, and by 1860 to 3,841,416 bales. This latter figure represented two thirds of the world's production of cotton.

The vast region from Georgia to the Rio Grande was occupied during the years between the American Revolution and the annexation of Texas in 1845. By 1812 the population of Louisiana was sufficient to form a new state, and five years later Missouri was demanding admission into the Union. After the extinction of Indian claims in the area west of Georgia, two new states were created: Mississippi in 1817 and Alabama in 1819. The pressure of Georgia and Alabama frontiersmen upon Florida effected its incorporation in the Union in 1845. By 1830 the frontier had advanced to the western border of Arkansas; six years later that area became a state. That same year, as noted earlier, Texans

22 May, 1961 --

won their independence from Mexico, and in 1845 they joined the Union.

The South contributed generously to the settlement of the Southwest. It has been estimated that South Carolina gave two fifths, North Carolina and Virginia one third, and Georgia one fourth of their total population. This movement to the West was not wholly caused by slaves and cotton, for, inaugurated as it was by typical pioneer farmers before the cotton plantation became a significant part of the national agriculture, it was rather a manifestation of the spirit of the times. Nevertheless, master, slave, plantation, and cotton soon followed the pioneer farmer.

The first regions to feel their influence were the uplands of South Carolina and Georgia, where pioneer grain and dairy farmers were forced to surrender economic and social supremacy to the cotton planters. The planters then advanced across the rich Black Belt of Alabama and Mississippi to occupy the great valleys of the Mississippi and Red rivers as far north and west as Memphis and the Indian Territory. The historian of the American frontier pictures "the southern planter crossing through the forests of western Georgia, Alabama, and Mississippi, or passing over the free state of Illinois to the Missouri Valley, in his family carriage, with servants, packs of hunting-dogs, and a train of slaves." [1] Many of the earlier settlers, unable to compete with slave labor or with the higher prices the planters could pay for lands, surrendered the best lands and moved northward or westward, or remained behind to become "crackers" or poor whites in less fertile regions. By the 1830's the center of cotton culture had shifted west of the mountains, taking with it the center of Southern wealth. The richness of virgin soil had forced this change. To the plantation-dominated commonwealths of Virginia, the Carolinas, and Georgia had been annexed Alabama, Florida, Mississippi, Tennessee, Texas, and Arkansas. Thus was created the Cotton Kingdom.

Simultaneously with the rise of the Cotton Kingdom sugar plantations were replacing the diversified agriculture of the delta region of southeastern Louisiana. The Eli Whitney of the sugar region was Jean Étienne Boré, a Creole who in 1794–5 demonstrated on his plantation that the staple could be produced with profit. This development was facilitated by the arrival of immigrants from the sugar island of Santo Domingo and the liberal introduction of slaves from the United States after the acquisition of Louisiana. In 1802 sugar estates numbered 81; thirty years later the area had 691 such estates worked by some 36,000 slaves.

[1] Frederick J. Turner, *The Rise of the New West*, p. 92.

The center of tobacco cultivation moved westward from tidewater Virginia and Maryland to the piedmont of Virginia and North Carolina. During the American Revolution emigrants from Virginia crossed the mountains with their slaves and established tobacco plantations in middle Tennessee, central and western Kentucky, and in the Missouri Valley. Cultivation of hemp in Kentucky led to the establishment of plantations in that area. Thus to the four plantation-dominated commonwealths of colonial origin and their six cotton satellites were added Louisiana, Kentucky, and parts of Missouri, to make up the thirteen slave states of the Old South.

The high price of slaves and low price of land tempted cotton and tobacco planters to skim the fertility from the soil and pass on to new lands "somewhat as a Tartar horde moved across Asia, eating the fat of the land and leaving devastation behind." The custom of paying the overseer in proportion to his production had the same effect. Resulting rural devastation stretched from Virginia to Texas. Frederick Law Olmsted, one of the best-known ante-bellum travelers, described Madison County, Alabama, in 1855: "One will discover numerous farm houses, once the abode of industrious and intelligent freemen, now occupied by slaves, or tenantless, deserted, and delapidated; he will observe fields, once fertile, now unfenced, abandoned, and covered with those evil harbingers—fox-tail and broomsedge; he will see moss growing on the mouldering walls of once thrifty villages." [2]

The one-crop, slave-plantation system was not, however, the sole cause of soil exhaustion. Americans in areas outside the South, notably in New England and the Middle West, exhausted not only the soil, but timber and mining resources with a hasty extravagance. This was caused there, as in the South, by the migratory habits of Americans, high cost of labor, desire for quick wealth, ignorance of the principles of soil conservation, and above all, the prevalence of rich new grounds to the westward. As James G. Randall sapiently observes,[3] Southern lands were abandoned as "exhausted," not because of absolute infertility, but because of their inferiority to other lands. The failure of Southern planters to conserve their soil resources was not without compensations. It made possible the rapid conquest by Cotton Kingdom slaveholders before equally avaricious settlers from other sections of the country could take over the black lands of the Southwest; it was an easy road to wealth which created a sense of sectional pride that those who grow rich in the plunder of a new land often feel.

Conquerors of the American South, like other conquerors of history, were not unaware of the devastation they had wrought, and intelligent

[2] *A Journey in the Seaboard Slave States,* p. 577.
[3] *Civil War and Reconstruction,* p. 22.

planters turned to diversified agriculture, deep plowing, and the use of fertilizers to rebuild worn-out soil. In *The Arator,* a pioneer book on agricultural improvement which was published in 1813, John Taylor of Caroline County, Virginia, advocated the use of vegetable material for manures and the planting of leguminous plants which would draw fertility from the atmosphere. The greatest agricultural reformer of the Old South was Edmund Ruffin, who expounded his doctrines in his *Essay on Calcareous Manures,* published in 1833, and in the columns of his magazine the *Farmers' Register.* He was a soil chemist who wanted to rejuvenate the soil of eastern Virginia by neutralizing its acid condition by the application of marl, a fine shell deposit. He proved the values of his ideas by great increases in the production of wheat and corn on his experimental farms. His fame spread, and he was invited to North Carolina, South Carolina, and Georgia to give advice on soil improvement.

A successful group of agricultural reformers were the planters of Hancock County, Georgia, who, under the leadership of David Dickson, checked erosion, developed improved strains of cotton seed, introduced such new crops as strawberries and peaches, and bred quality livestock. Thomas Spalding of Sapelo Island in Georgia was a tireless experimenter who believed in the proper balance of one crop against another.

The ideas of these and numerous other agricultural reformers were popularized through a great increase in agricultural societies and farm journals and the beginning of agricultural fairs. Between 1837 and 1841 state agricultural societies became active in Maryland, South Carolina, Kentucky, Tennessee, Alabama, Mississippi, and Louisiana. Pre-eminent among the agricultural periodicals was the *Southern Cultivator,* founded in Augusta in 1843, which attained a circulation of 10,-000 copies. An agricultural fair was held at Macon in 1831. Ten years later this institution had become popular in many sections of the South. Through its exhibition of the latest improvements in farming and stock raising the ordinary farmer learned much.

The application of science to the problems of the farm caused an agricultural renaissance in the seaboard South in the two decades before the Civil War. Wheat became the major crop on lands once exhausted by tobacco. In reaping the cradle took the place of the scythe. The mule was gradually introduced as the major draft animal. This tough creature was fast at the plow and able to withstand the abuses of the Negroes. Worn-out lands, especially those of Maryland and Virginia, were returned to production.

The opening of new cotton lands created a great demand for slave labor, which, after the outlawing of the African trade in 1808, had in part to be met illegally. During each of the next eight years more than 15,000 slaves were smuggled into the country. Although in 1820 foreign slave trade was held to be piracy and antismuggling laws were more stringently enforced, when the price of slaves increased in the 1850's there was a revival of smuggling. Phillips estimates that 15,000 were imported in 1858. Even so, he believes that after 1808 "these importations were never great enough to affect the labor supply in appreciable degree." [4]

The major source of supply was domestic. Many migrating planters took their slaves to the Southwest. An elaborate traffic sprang up between Virginia and the Carolinas, where the plantation system was in decline, and Alabama, Florida, and Mississippi, where transported slaves were used to work new lands. Protected by laws that permitted a ruthless separation of families, the domestic slave trader carried on his business for decades. Frederic Bancroft [5] estimates that 180,000 Negroes were involved in this traffic between 1840 and 1850, and some 230,000 in the following decade.

Slave markets were established in the chief towns of the Old South; Alexandria, Richmond, and Charleston were the principal centers in the East, and Natchez, New Orleans, Mobile, and Memphis in the West. The slaves were shipped "down the river" by boat or transported overland in coffles, but, unlike their African forebears, they received humane treatment in transit, for good business necessitated their arrival at places of sale in sound condition. The differential between prices paid for slaves in the old and new states allowed ample profits after transportation costs were paid. For five decades a prime field hand brought about $300 more in the New Orleans markets than in those of Virginia. A single trader, Isaac Franklin of Natchez and New Orleans is said to have made half a million dollars. Nathan B. Forrest, who was to win fame as a Confederate cavalry general, made $50,000 annually as a slave trader of Memphis.

John Randolph of Roanoke once named as the greatest orator he had ever heard "A slave, Sir. She was a mother, and her rostrum was the auction block." The motif of Mark Twain's *Pudd'nhead Wilson* was the fear of a border state slave that her child might be "sold down the river" to a plantation of the lower South. [6] This theme of the slave trade dominated antislavery literature. Attention was directed to the anachronism of Virginia, whose Revolutionary fathers had proclaimed liberty and democracy and denounced slavery, once again promoting

[4] *American Negro Slavery*, p. 147.
[5] *Slave-Trading in the Old South*, pp. 393-5.
[6] See below, p. 437.

slavery because the excess of her brood of bondsmen could be sold at constantly rising prices.

The slave trade gave new life to a declining institution by taking Negroes from areas where they were not needed into regions where the bonds of servitude were more permanent and the planters less patriarchal. One authority believes that free Negroes kidnapped for the trade were as numerous as the slaves who escaped bondage by flight. Slaves were torn from their families, marched along the highways in chains, and sold at New Orleans or Memphis like cattle.

A part of the uneasiness which Southerners felt from this evil found expression in their general contempt for the slave trader. He was regarded as a necessary evil. A Mississippi lawyer declared: ". . . I can imagine a man . . . who would think it . . . right to own [slaves] . . . , and yet . . . abhor . . . the speculator and the dealer, and . . . shun his society. And I can imagine a community of such men." [7] State laws prohibiting the export or import of slaves and the sale of young children from their mothers likewise gave an indication of Southern feeling regarding the traffic. Such laws, however, were mere sops to the consciences of Christian people; they became tangled in practical or legal difficulties and were ineffective. The sheriff sales of the property of bankrupts and divisions of property by wills were constant threats to the integrity of Negro family life. There was no prohibition of the separation of husband and wife by sale.

It was not true, as the literature of denunciation alleged, that "slave breeding" was deliberately practiced to meet the demands of southern markets. Fecundity was highly esteemed in slave society, but this was also true of contemporary free society; it was more an incident of the good treatment of Negro women than the result of encouragement for mercenary reasons. Avery O. Craven has demonstrated with comparative statistics,[8] that the birth rate among slaves was no higher than among either Northern or Southern whites. A study of wills and advertisements shows that many masters in stipulating the disposal of their slave property provided that individuals were not to be sold away from their families or transported out of the state. Inevitable economic law rather than fiendish conspiracy prompted the movement of slaves from the agriculturally stagnant regions. Perhaps as many or more slaves moved into the Southwest with their masters as were sold into that region. Among whites this economic movement was voluntary; had Negroes been free, they, too, would have migrated of their own accord.

As the Cotton Kingdom expanded the value and number of slaves

[7] Randall, op. cit., pp. 56–7.
[8] The Coming of the Civil War, pp. 83–6.

increased. Able-bodied males between eighteen and thirty years of age brought $500 in 1800, $900 in 1810, $1,000 in 1820, $1,300 in 1834. After a drop to $790 in 1837 the price reached $1,800 in 1860. Women usually sold for three fourths the price of men and boys of corresponding ages, and both males and females declined in value after they had reached 30 years; at 65 they were considered commercially valueless.

Relative Negro population in the South as a whole did not increase in direct proportion to the expansion of the Cotton Kingdom; between 1820 and 1860 the Negro population per 1,000 whites declined from 592 to 582. The preponderance of white immigration and the development of hill areas not suited for plantation economy accounted for this ratio. There was a great absolute increase of Negroes: from 1,643,000 in 1820 to 4,097,000 in 1860, and in a vast crescent stretching from southeast Virginia through the rich midlands of the South into southeast Texas slaves outnumbered whites.

Plantations varied in size, with some as large as 5,000 acres. In 1860 Alabama had nearly 700 estates of 1,000 or more acres, Virginia more than 600, and Georgia more than 900. In that year 1,733 great planters owned 100 or more slaves each, and middle-class planters owning between 50 and 100 slaves each numbered almost 10,000. Some 90,000 small planters who had between 10 and 50 slaves each and a few hundred acres practiced plantation methods and considered themselves members of the governing class.

Around the big house or mansion were grouped kitchen, office, stables, ginhouse, and smokehouse, and a short distance away was the communal village of Negroes, known as the slave quarters or "the street." The success of the larger plantation depended upon the much-abused overseer who handled the routine of management and production. He was master of the intricate processes of tobacco, rice, sugar, or cotton culture, and in addition maintained a constant check on the slaves. He was assisted in their management by the "slave driver," an individual chosen from the slaves for his resourcefulness. The plantation was worked as a unit by gangs who were assigned daily tasks of plowing, hoeing, picking, or ginning; the slavedriver was held responsible for the execution of these duties. The work day lasted from sun to sun, with liberal midday rest periods.

To insure plantation discipline Southern legislatures set up slave codes even more rigid than those prevailing in Portuguese-, Spanish-, and French-speaking areas of the Western hemisphere. South Carolina initiated the move by adopting the slave laws of Barbadoes; following the Stono River slave revolt of 1739 these regulations were further extended. Legislators responded promptly to the pressure of their electorate when real or imaginary threats to the slave system arose.

Laws for the control of slaves in no way reflected the liberal philosophy of the late eighteenth century. Actually, the trend was in the opposite direction. Free of imperial restraints exercised in London and elsewhere, the legislatures of self-governing American communities were able to be repressive whenever dominant groups felt that the slave system was endangered. From the slave revolt of 1791 in Haiti to John Brown's raid of 1859 every attack upon the integrity of the system brought denials of liberties to blacks. For example, the relatively liberal *Code Noir* which Louisiana inherited from its French rulers assumed a stern American character. Such enactments "as thorough and stringent as their framers could make them," Phillips believed, "left an almost irreducible minimum of rights and privileges to those whose function and place were declared to be service and subordination." [9]

Humane considerations—on the statute books, at least—were almost entirely subordinated to the protection of property rights in slaves and of white society against possible Negro violence. Slaves were permitted to testify in courts only in cases involving other slaves. Certain crimes committed by whites were punished less severely than those committed by slaves. The violation of slave women was without legal penalty. Assembly and travel were rigidly controlled, and the possession of firearms and the formation of secret societies were prohibited. Not only were no provisions made for the education of the blacks, but so great was the fear that they would be contaminated by abolitionist propaganda that such instruction was positively prohibited. Slaves as the personal property of their masters were denied the right to own property except with their masters' consent. Since the main purpose of slave codes was to secure maximum labor, executions and long imprisonments as punishments for crimes were less favored than were penalties that were sharp and informal. This meant flogging summarily imposed at the discretion of the master. Attacking a white man was punishable by lashes on the bare back. All persons with noticeable strains of African blood were presumed to be slaves unless they could prove the contrary. Marriages among slaves were not matters of legal record and could be effected merely by the masters' approval.

In actual practice restrictions upon Negroes were not so severe as the laws provided. "It would have required a European bureaucracy to keep such laws fully effective; the individualistic South was incapable of the task." The marching of patrols charged with enforcement "were almost as futile and farcical as the musters of the militia." [10] Southern forests were too deep and nights too dark to prevent the slaves' moving about. They congregated despite prohibitive laws, and

[9] *Op. cit.*, p. 501.
[10] *Ibid.*, p. 501.

some of them learned to read and write. They frequently worked at forbidden employment. They married and maintained family life.

Sheer difficulty of enforcement was not wholly responsible for this relaxing of laws. Masters, resenting the interference of public authorities or neighbors, with apparent deliberation often directed their slaves to perform unlawful tasks or errands. In practice humane considerations actually helped to qualify the laws. Christian consciences were salved by permitting Negroes to marry, to learn to read the Bible, and to be treated with a kindness that fostered a relationship almost parental between master and slave.

Proscription of public schools for Negroes resulted in an illiteracy rate of more than 90 per cent. The average slave was proverbially ignorant of even the rudiments of formal education. But he was not unlearned. Slavery was in itself an educational process which transformed the black man from a primitive to a civilized person endowed with conceits, customs, industrial skills, Christian beliefs, and ideals of the Anglo-Saxon of North America. His jungle lore was supplanted by folklore and his sacred songs and beliefs of English and Hebraic origins were modified by the Methodist and Baptist churches and plantation life. With the exception of some few words in the Gullah dialect of the South Carolina coast his language became completely English. "A Negro understands a white man better than a white man understands the Negro," said a sagacious observer.[11] The slave was accepted as an intimate part of Southern society. White children were suckled by black mammies and played indiscriminately with pickaninnies; the two races attended the same churches; and white girls of plantation households sometimes supervised the weddings of their maids. Frederick L. Olmsted was struck by what he called "the close cohabitation and association of black and white." "Negro women," he recorded in 1855, "are carrying black and white babies together in their arms; black and white children are playing together (not going to school together); black and white faces are constantly thrust together out of doors, to see the train go by." [12]

Every slaveholder found it advantageous to encourage skills among his bondsmen. They were taught the processes of tobacco, rice, sugar, and cotton growing. They became domestic servants, carpenters, blacksmiths, brickmasons, coopers, sailors, coachmen, bakers, cabinetmakers, and seamstresses; only the intellectual and elevating occupations were closed to them. After the Nat Turner Insurrection of 1831 independent Negro preachers were not tolerated. Talented men were subject to the

[11] Captain L. V. Cooley, in *ibid.*, p. 327.
[12] *Op. cit.*, p. 17.

caprice of their white owners, who had no regard for intellectual abilities and considered them merely their possessions.

Evidence can be presented to support almost any generalization—favorable or unfavorable—concerning the treatment of slaves. Cruelty was often encouraged by circumstances—the almost complete authority which law and custom gave master or overseer, the ever-present temptation to achieve maximal production of staples. Slaves were expected to work from sun to sun on a sustenance of food and clothing which averaged no more than forty dollars annually.[13] Like cattle and horses, their primary function was to make profits for their masters, and when the tempo of their work slowed or infractions of rules occurred, the whip meted on-the-spot punishment. On the Rice Coast and in the lower South slave discipline was harsher than in the upper South. Although many accounts have pictured the relatively easy life of house servants, there is no trustworthy comprehensive record of the treatment of the masses of field laborers.

Often kindly masters were unaware of the cruelty and neglect existing on their holdings. Fanny Kemble was shocked by conditions in the infirmary of her wealthy husband's Georgia plantation—sick slaves lying on the floor without mattress or pillow, on filthy ragged blankets. "Take note," she wrote, "that this is the hospital of an estate where the owners are supposed to be humane, the overseers efficient and kind, the Negroes well cared for."

Slavery had another side. Abolitionist assertions that the bondsmen were frequently inadequately clothed, underfed, and driven to death are economically unreasonable. Masters wished to preserve the health and life of their slaves because a sick Negro was a liability and a dead Negro was worth nothing. A rude plenty prevailed on the average plantation. "The best preventive of theft is plenty of pork," was the advice of a Virginian.[14] Kindliness and patience, frequently extended even to a tolerance of slackness in every concern not vital to routine, created a degree of contentment among the slaves sufficient to keep them docile. Although Jefferson had declared, "The whole commerce between master and slave is a perpetual exercise of the most boisterous passions," Harriet Martineau sympathized with the masters. She wrote: "Nothing struck me more than the patience of the slave-owners . . . with their slaves." Travelers wondered who were the actual victims of the slave system. The best of masters were forced to tolerate tasks undone, orders

[13] Thomas Cooper in Phillips, *op. cit.*, p. 348. Estimates varied from $17.50 to $44. Robert W. Smith, "Was Slavery Unprofitable in the Ante-Bellum South?" *Agricultural History*, XX, 62–3 (January, 1946).

[14] Cited in Phillips, *op. cit.*, p. 276.

forgotten, and lying and thievery. Of a Virginia planter, Olmsted wrote: "During three hours or more I was in company with the proprietor I do not think there were ten consecutive minutes uninterrupted by some of the slaves requiring his personal direction or assistance. He was even obligated three times to leave the dinner table."

Despite abolitionist allegations to the contrary, flights and mass revolts were infrequent. Fear that they should become general led the South to introduce ruthless laws for the apprehension of the absconders and to demand federal legislation to protect their institution. Actually, however, the thousands of slaves who ran away formed but a slight portion of the millions comprising the total slave population. During the several decades of its existence only some 75,000 Negroes used the Underground Railroad, which was organized to aid them in their attempt to reach Canada.

Flights were prompted by various causes. Some slaves undoubtedly ran away because they were talented or sensitive persons who desired freedom. Others wished to escape from barbarous punishments peculiar to the slave system. Many fled from slave traders or new masters, not to escape bondage but to return to their families and former homes. Some strayed away for reasons not especially associated with slavery; they became tramps or vagabonds or fugitives from deserved punishments for crimes. Most slaves, unlike migratory free Negroes of a later generation, did not move from their original homes.

Rumors of the Northern press, successful revolts in Santo Domingo and Haiti, and a general Southern fear of slave insurrections combined to create a fairly constant tone of uneasiness. Of course, "Rumors were not revolts, and revolts seldom materialized, just as rumored conspiracies, more often than not, had no reality." [15] Actually few revolts took place. In the eighteenth century Virginia and South Carolina were often threatened with violence by uncivilized Negroes newly arrived from Africa. On Stono River in South Carolina in 1739 a large number of Negroes broke open a store, seized arms, and before they were suppressed killed twenty-one persons and burned several houses. Forty-four of the insurrectionists were killed or executed.

Near Richmond at the opening of the nineteenth century Gabriel Prosser's Insurrection, a well organized plan, was frustrated before it reached fruition. Similarly, in 1822 the attempts of Denmark Vesey, a talented and successful mulatto preacher of Charleston, were thwarted. He was betrayed by a confederate and hanged, along with thirty-four followers. Nine years later, in August, 1831, Nat Turner, a fanatical lay preacher who believed himself divinely selected to lead the blacks out

[15] J. G. de Roulhac Hamilton in *American Historical Review*, XLIX, 505 (April, 1944).

of bondage, led 60 Negroes in the only revolt after 1739 from which
mass killings resulted. Fifty-five persons were murdered before the
whites could mobilize their forces. Turner's movement collapsed, and
there is no evidence to support the contemporary belief that the insurrection had widespread effect in the South. This was the last organized
effort of slaves to revolt, although individual crimes often occurred.
Negroes remained generally submissive, and when in 1859 John Brown
attempted to arouse them to armed revolt their response was a bewildered inaction.

Whether American Negro slavery was a profitable method of agricultural production has long been questioned. Most contemporary and
modern students of the slave problem, including Phillips, believe it was
not. They have generally agreed with Thomas Cooper, who wrote in
1826 that slave laborers were barely two thirds as efficient as free workers. Slave labor, explained President Cooper, "is all forced, and forced
too from a class of human beings who have the least propensity to voluntary labour even when it is to benefit themselves alone." Likewise,
study has confirmed James H. Hammond's assertion that "as a general
rule . . . free labor is cheaper than slave labor." Against the income
accruing to a master for a slave's labor during his thirty or forty years
of effective work was set a variety of expenses that were said by older
writers on the slave system to encroach dangerously upon his margin
of profit. These included the cost of buying or rearing the slave; amor-
tization of the capital investment; insurance against flight, premature
death, and the disabilities of illness and age; and the maintenance of
health during productive years. A master could not hope to reduce the
initial cost of his bondsmen by deliberate breeding, for the heavy expenses of childbirth and of maintenance during the unproductive years
of childhood sometimes equaled the purchase price of a mature worker.

Until the Civil War "the remorseless advance of slave prices" dis-
rupted value standards. Proprietors, attempting to reduce their over-
all cost of operation by achieving a maximum efficiency, bought additional slaves at prices above their actual per capita earnings. Slave
prices were further inflated by the speculative spirit prevailing in the
new and richer agricultural areas of the South. Virginia tobacco planters and rice planters of South Carolina, forced to stand aside in the
bidding for slave labor, suffered crippling labor shortages. Although
immigrants who were more efficient than Negroes lived in these areas,
they were unwilling to accept black labor standards. Manual labor was
generally stigmatized by the presence of slaves. Southern whites of every social level developed aristocratic prejudices against hard work, and
"Northern thrift" was disdainfully rejected for "Southern gentility."
Lower-class whites, unable to meet the competition of slave labor, were

driven from the better lands. Middle-class whites in emulation of big planters bought slaves even though their needs might have been better served by free labor.

A diversified agricultural and industrial economy might have been created in the South. Capital which could have been used for this purpose instead was absorbed by slave purchases. Virginia, despite its coastal location, did not develop a merchant marine; the Carolinas and Georgia failed to build up a textile industry which would utilize their cotton fields and water power. Even though mill managers and railroad builders found the use of hired labor more profitable than ownership of slaves, slaveowners, fearing the effect upon health and discipline, were reluctant to permit their slaves to be hired. Agricultural concentration of the South led to the production of a greater supply of her staples than the world markets could absorb at sufficiently remunerative prices. Travelers on the Ohio observed the greater prosperity of the northern, non-slaveholding, bank of the river. Compared with the North, the South as a whole was a poor and shabby land. This difference the travelers ascribed to slavery alone.

Slavery was introduced in the South in response to a definite economic need for an effective labor supply for the growing of three or four staples. Planters could feel that their objectives had been attained; in 1850 two thirds of the nation's exports came from the South. They questioned the validity of moral and economic complaints against slavery raised by those in the North and England who made profits from Southern trade and raw materials. On the other hand, the planters could not claim sole credit; as a colored speaker reminded his audience of post-bellum Southerners: "It was the brawny arm of the Negro that has cared for you in your cradle, made your harvests, protected you in your home." These achievements were possible because the slave system "kept the main body of labor controlled, provisioned and mobile. Above all, it maintained order and a notable degree of harmony in a community where confusion worse confounded would not have been far to seek." [16]

A system that could drive a competing system of free labor from the best cotton lands undoubtedly had a degree of efficiency. Indeed, the views of Phillips and others that the incomes of planters hardly amounted to fair rates of interest on the money invested in slaves has been challenged by those who believe that slavery operated on an economically efficient basis. These writers assert that slaves produced more than they consumed because their owners depressed their consumption near the minimum of sustenance and compelled them to produce the maximum consistent with health and contentment. The $30 or $40 an-

[16] Phillips, *op. cit.*, p. 401.

Agricultural Renaissance -- led in Va. by Edward Ruffin -- introd. Soil Chemistry.

nual cost of maintaining a slave was amply compensated by the $100 or more realized from three or four bales of cotton which the average slave produced annually. In answer to those who claim that the money invested in Negroes was the principal cause of the alleged unprofitable character of slavery, it is contended that the assessed valuation of slaves should not be considered the capital upon which slaveholders were entitled to receive interest, since the money actually invested was seldom as high as the inflated prices of slaves prevailing in the lower South after 1845. Many slaves were acquired through inheritance or through natural increase; others were purchased by planters in the cheaper markets of the East. The amazing productivity of Western soil justified the higher prices which planters had to pay for slaves there, and brought a return for capital invested as great, if not far greater, than in the East.[17]

RR helped to make transportation of Cotton possible.

Commercial fertilizer also helped.

It is an error, moreover, to ascribe the economic weaknesses and relative poverty of the Old South entirely to slavery. Weakness and poverty characterized Southern life eighty years after the extinction of slavery.[18] This suggests supplementary explanations: the tendency under a capitalistic economy for an agricultural section to be drained of its wealth by commercial and industrial sections; the South's lack of attractiveness to European immigrants because of prejudices against a warm climate; the lack of industrial diversity caused by habit and the lure of money crops; the neglect of the lower classes of the whites because of the monopolistic greed of the fortunate and wealthy; the exhaustion of the soil.

Negro slavery was finally destroyed by armed invasion of the South. Had this not occurred, would not the whole slave system have collapsed or gradually disappeared under the weight of its own internal weaknesses? Those who answer the question in the affirmative believe that final catastrophe would have overtaken the Cotton Kingdom when its Western expansion left no new lands to exploit. The belief is that this limit was nearly reached in 1860. But the dominant elements of the white South, persons well informed and in a position to take action, did not think so. They expressed an unalloyed confidence in the institution of slavery until the end of the Civil War. A concrete expression of this belief was their willingness to pay higher and higher prices for slaves. Some Southerners, including the governor of South Carolina in 1856, advocated the reopening of the African slave trade. Lewis C. Gray believes that in 1860 "the plantation system was not limited by the scarcity

[17] Smith, *op. cit.,* pp. 62–4. Cf. Lewis C. Gray, *History of Agriculture in the Southern States to 1860,* I, 462–81, and Thomas P. Govan, "Was Plantation Slavery Profitable?" *The Journal of Southern History,* VIII, 513–35 (November, 1942).

[18] See below, p. 487.

Not slave system that made the South poor — South didn't have good rich soil.

North had foreign immigrants

of land" because the railroads and other agencies were making new areas accessible.[19]

It must be remembered that an agricultural system is often more than a mere economic pursuit, to be abandoned as soon as losses become obvious. It may be a way of life, a social system surrounded by so much tradition that it would not be abandoned except in the face of a superior outside force. This was emphatically true of the agricultural system of the South before 1865. Slavery was close to the heart of the peculiar social practices of the Old South. The relation between master and slave had the sanction of habit and custom; it was invested by religion with a sanctity similar to that bestowed upon the relation between parent and child. Material adversities short of catastrophe probably would have strengthened rather than weakened the resolution to hold onto slavery. In 1860 there was no possibility of its destruction by such internal weaknesses as slave insurrections or flights. The many Southerners who had no direct material interest in its continuation and the few Southerners who, like Robert E. Lee, continued to disapprove of it, dared offer no alternative, for slavery was believed to be a social necessity for keeping the Negro "in his place." Southern thinkers saw no reason to capitulate to forces of the outside world which, in the name of the progressive liberalism of the nineteenth century, were demanding the eradication of human bondage. The South only tightened the logic of the proslavery argument and prepared, if necessary, to engage in physical combat for the vindication of this institution.

[19] *Op. cit.*, I, 476.

CHAPTER IX

Classes in this
I upper class -- Slave owner (1,250,000
non-owners; 250,000 did own them

Eng. Comparison of Eng. and Am. aristocrats
Titles / No titles Am.

Ante-Bellum Society

II Yeoman farmer -- few slaves and contempt
of learning; courtesy

>>>-

III Crackers, Sand-hillers +-- lived in poor, sandy
lands   IV 250,000 free Persons of color -- free due
to acts of
heroism,
special favors,
voluntary
freeing by
owners, etc.

THE OLD SOUTH was dominated socially by the comparatively small
group of Southern planters. Of approximately 1.25 million white families living in the slaveholding states in 1850 only 347,000 heads of
families owned slaves. Thus, no more than one fourth of Southern white
society was directly involved in slavery. Five sevenths of these slaveholders were but yeoman farmers, since each owned less than 10 slaves.
To be of consequence a planter had to be the master of 50 or more
slaves; in this class were less than 8,000 persons. The holders of more
than 100 slaves numbered less than 1,800. Only eleven persons owned
500 or more slaves. The largest slaveholder in the whole South was
Nathaniel Heyward of South Carolina. When he died in 1851 he possessed 1,843 slaves.

Didn't prosper
-- discriminated
against and
not thrifty
(John Randolph
didn't free
his own --
sent them to
Mercer Co., Ohio
-- they sent
them back
didn't want
labor competition

Ownership of most of the better lands, just as of the larger percentage of slaves, was concentrated in the hands of a small group of
slave magnates. Like Northern millionaires of a later generation, they
controlled a disproportionate share of the income of their region. The
annual income of 1,000 families of the Cotton Kingdom has been estimated at $50,000,000; the remaining 666,000 families received only
about $60,000,000.[1] Here was a sound economic basis for the legend of
a glamorous aristocracy.

Few gained
position --
Dabney, Evans
and Willis,
Lafoon.

The Southern planter often lived in feudal splendor. The "big
house" or the plantation mansion generally stood on an elevation near
the main road, flanked by slave cabins, kitchen, office, stables, smokehouse, and other outbuildings. It was usually a wooden structure of not
more than fifteen rooms, but it was made imposing by a row of white

[1] William E. Dodd, The Cotton Kingdom, p. 24.

(133)

lived in a community -- together
V Slaves. (3, 954000) -- according
to law, supposed to be forcefully treated
-- weren't tho!
Hunted, killed hogs, etc. Dressed gaily
had no promise of a better future

Generally no
higher than Negro
of today. Rigid
laws against --
they were loyal
to the slave
system and South

columns as tall as the house itself and by a lavish garden. There was a
screen of spreading trees, borders of the odorous boxwood, and a tangled mass of flowering and sweet-smelling shrubs. Ample use was made
of such semitropical plants as Cherokee rose, live oak, crepe myrtle,
magnolia, and the pride of India. The interior of the house was dominated by huge halls with an impressive stairway. On the first floor were
the parlors, dining room, and library; on the second floor were bed-
rooms for family and guests. High ceilings, heavily shaded porches, and
drafty passageways gave comfort in summer, but little comfort in the
sharp Southern winters. Fireplaces were large, however, and wood was
plentiful. Floors were rather sparsely covered by thin carpets, and the
furniture was of a plain but massive elegance. A tall clock in the hall
was the family's pride, even though its warnings concerning the passing
of time failed to disturb the lazy tempo of plantation life. On the walls
were family portraits and steel engravings of battle scenes or of George
Washington. Sometimes the dining room was separated from the main
body of the house by a porch, and usually the kitchen was well apart
so that its odors, heat, and clatter might not contaminate the main
house.

The master of this establishment was neither the tyrant pictured in
abolitionist fiction nor the improvident and sacrificial gentleman of
romance. He was usually a successful business man who depended upon
slave labor to produce with substantial profits one of the great Southern
staples. The plantation was primarily a business enterprise and second-
arily a country seat given over to gentlemanly indulgences. That the
planter got his power and prestige from Cavalier forebears of Old
World origin is entirely unfounded. Only a few of the planters of 1850
inherited their positions from the eighteenth-century aristocracy of
coastal Virginia, Maryland, and the Carolinas. The mass were self-made
men, like Gerald O'Hara in Margaret Mitchell's *Gone With the Wind*,
who carved fortunes for themselves from a new country. It was possible, says a historian,[2] for men to mount "from log cabin to plantation
mansion on a stairway of cotton bales, accumulating slaves as they
climbed." Such men, for example, were Elisha King of Alabama, a poor
man who accumulated 8,000 acres and 186 slaves, and Joseph Davis, the
brother of Jefferson Davis, who carved out of the Mississippi wilderness enough land to produce 3,000 bales of cotton annually. Theirs was
an aristocracy with a yeoman background and without heraldic devices.
Such men had little time to be ostentatious, leaving to descendants the
creation of the Southern myth, and to the merchants of Charleston,
Mobile, and New Orleans the privilege of dressing like the Prince of
Wales. These planters were as truly lords of their surroundings as their

[2] Charles S. Sydnor, *The Development of Southern Sectionalism, 1819–1848*, p. 14.

prototypes of the Middle Ages, and were so accepted by non-slavehold-ing whites.

The planter who ruled his slaves successfully did so by a mixture of self-control, firmness, and passion. The kindly virtues won the co-operation of a race of warm emotions and infinite loyalty. Yet unlim-ited power over a race that possessed exasperating habits provided a constant temptation to bluster and use violence, to impose sudden if not ruthless punishment. An anonymous writer of 1827 presented this problem of the planter:

With his disdain of all that is coarse and little and mean, there often mingle the failings of a too sensitive pride, jealousy of all superiority, im-patience of contradiction, quick and violent resentment. His liability to these vices is so obvious that it is often an especial purpose of early instruction to guard against them; and thus is formed in happy natures such a habit of self-command and virtuous discipline as to make them remarkable for their mildness and moderation.[3]

Scholars have proved that the plantation and the planter were not so charming as pictured in books of reminiscences. Some plantation structures on close inspection turned out to be cottages with ridiculous false fronts. Some were log houses without structural pretensions. Trav-elers were often struck by the lack of domestic conveniences, by the shabbiness resulting from the lackadaisical habits of both master and slave, by a soil prolific in weeds, briers, and bushes. Saddles, whips, guns, shoes, clothing, and farm tools were often awkwardly displayed on front porches and in halls, and the most conspicuous piece of furni-ture that attracted the eye of the casual visitor might be a washstand. Olmsted wrote: "On their plantations, generally, the Virginia gentle-men seem to drop their full-dress and constrained town-habits, and live a free, rustic, shooting-jacket life." Dodd remarks, "It had long been a mark of distinction in a gentleman of Virginia to dress in shabby or last year's suits." [4] If this were true of Virginia planters, what of those of Texas? The ubiquitous Olmsted discovered opulent barbarism: a rich planter who lived in a large house with more than half of its eighty panes broken and no latches on its doors, who ate "the eternal fry, pone and coffee," and whose water was transported in tubs from a creek by Negro girls.

Of more compelling importance than such awkward realities, how-ever, was a persistent belief about plantation life—the assumption that every planter who had acquired rich lands and Negroes was a gentle-man in the formal sense of that word. He was endowed with generosity,

[3] *American Quarterly Review*, II, 251-2, cited in Ulrich B. Phillips, *Life and Labor in the Old South*, p. 363.
[4] *Op. cit.*, p. 76.

elegance, tact, and the other aristocratic virtues. As an explanation of these virtues, he was said to be a descendant of the great plantation aristocrats of Virginia and the Carolina coast and knightly forebears who had ridden with Prince Rupert at Naseby and with William the Conqueror at Senlac. Genealogists looked among the ancestors of many a planter and found lords and ladies, kings and queens of the Middle Ages. In the novels of Sir Walter Scott and his imitators the planter and his lady found a mirror of their life and ideals. Thus was established the concept of the Virginia cavalier and Southern chivalry.

Naturally, planters and those Southerners who wished to be planters accepted this legend of the South. It gave them a satisfying sense of superiority to the low-bred traders and artisans of the North. Yet what was more remarkable, it was accepted as true by the enemies of the plantation system. The awesome Southern aristocrat was a target for the democratic hate of the abolitionists. Novelists demonstrated an odd reluctance to disturb the plantation tradition. Even Harriet Beecher Stowe made her chief villain, not a planter, but a Yankee gone South to be an overseer.

This ideal of the Old South was as near the truth as was the ideal of medieval chivalry on which it was so largely modeled. The Old South had its Galahads and its Parsifals. There was, to give one example, Joseph Bryan of Georgia, whose nobility moved John Randolph of Roanoke to eulogy. "Educated in Europe . . . ," said the Virginian of Bryan,

he was utterly free from taint of foreign manner. . . . He possessed wonderful activity and strength of body, united to undaunted resolution; but he was not more terrible as an enemy than as a friend he was above all price. His mind was of the first order, and stored with various and desultory reading. His honor [was] unsullied. Quick in his resentment but easily appeased when injured, and equally ready to acknowledge an error when wrong, provided the appeal was made to his sense of justice, for he knew not fear. He was brave even to rashness, and his generosity bordered on profusion.[5]

Some planters, like Thomas S. G. Dabney of Mississippi, were Virginia gentlemen by birth. Dabney's daughter writes: "Everyone knew when he was awake by the merry sounds preceding from his chamber. He did not go into breakfast till he had danced the Fisher's Hornpipe for the baby, singing along with the steps and drawing an imaginary bow across imaginary strings. All the nursery flocked about him, one or two of the little tots joining in the capering." [6] Another Virginia gentleman was John Hampden Randolph, who was able to express the tradition of aristocratic living on the rich sugar lands of Louisiana on a scale

[5] Cited in Phillips, *Life and Labor in the Old South*, p. 363.
[6] Susan D. Smedes, *Memorials of a Southern Planter*, pp. 115–16.

more extravagant than ever dreamed of by his Virginia kinsmen. He employed tutors to teach literature, dancing, and music to his children and later sent them to Eastern schools. He enjoyed hunting and pleasure trips and purchased books and newspapers. "Nottaway," his plantation house on the banks of the Mississippi, was bigger than any mansion on the James or the Potomac. It contained fifty rooms, many of which were decorated with intricate plaster mouldings, marble mantels, and bronze and crystal chandeliers. All this magnificence culminated in a glittering ballroom decorated in white from enameled floor to plastered ceiling.

Others who could not claim Virginia lineage captured "much of the beautiful courtesy and dignity and gesturing grace" of the true Virginian. This was even true of Andrew Jackson, the former border ruffian who gave the United States a democracy more real than that of Thomas Jefferson. Jackson's Tennessee establishment at "The Hermitage" was as elaborate and in as good taste as Jefferson's establishment at "Monticello."

Although few Southern planters were descendants of Cavaliers, many of them developed into knightly heroes. Their Civil War experiences were an adventure as chivalric as anything that engaged the attention of Arthur and his knights or of Charlemagne and his Roland.

The most prosperous yeoman farmers lived in the series of valleys stretching from the Shenandoah to northeastern Alabama. They were largely without the aid or the competition of slave labor. Possessed of rich lands, strong fences, frugal ways, and snug houses, they were handicapped by inadequate market facilities. They lived on what they made and developed no fine manners.

More numerous than these men of the valleys were the yeomen who lived near the great plantations. They worked with their few slaves, or alone with their families if they owned no slaves. They did not know that white people could not endure the Southern sun and that the slave system had placed a stigma upon manual labor. They lived in almost unbelievable disorder. "Nearly all of them," says Cash, "enjoyed some measure of a kind of curious half-thrifty, half-shiftless prosperity—a thing of sagging rail fences, unpainted houses, and crazy barns which yet bulged with corn." The average yeoman professed contempt for many of the domestic conveniences and comforts cherished by Northern farmers. He read little beyond the almanac and was often given to hard drinking, hard swearing, and to acts of violence. His social diversions were few—hunting the 'coon, the 'possum, and the rabbit, and attending court and political rallies. Nevertheless, he adopted from the plantation aristocracy certain traits that fit his homespun character. "The result was a kindly courtesy, a level-eyed pride, an easy quietness, a barely perceptible flourish of bearing, which for all its obvious angularity and fundamental plainness, was one of the finest things the Old South produced." [7]

Although the yeomen suffered much from the competition of slave labor, from the tendency of the plantations to swallow up the best lands, and from inability to secure markets for surplus products, the evidence is overwhelming that except in some of the hill regions they were enthusiastic champions of slavery whether they owned Negroes or not. They wished to climb to the level of the planter. They often succeeded in this ambition, for the Old South was far more fluid socially than many historians are willing to admit. The poor man did not always lose in competition for the possession of the fertile cotton lands of the frontier, and in settled regions frequent bankruptcies made it possible for yeomen to build up estates of slaves and broad acres.

A characteristically American lack of class consciousness was fostered by actual or assumed kinship between planter and yeoman, by intermarriage between the two classes, by the tendency of the grand gentleman to lay a familiar hand on the shoulders of poor neighbors at political gatherings, and by the inviting of farmer neighbors and cousins to the festive board of big houses. Moreover, one of the most remarkable facts about the Southern plantation was that it existed without exploiting the labor of the free whites. The average white man, because of the abundance of land, was able to become a proud landowner, as independent of the great planter as the great planter was of him. A student of the land problem estimates that at least 60 per cent of the non-slaveholders outside the upper seaboard states were landowners.[8] The relation of master and servant arose in connection with an alien group, the Negro slave.

The exploitative attitude which both rich and poor whites developed toward the slave created a solidarity of interests which was readily rationalized into a solidarity of class. A contempt for the black man made all white men brothers in a sense and elevated the common white man to membership in a superior caste. When criticisms of the master-and-slave relationship arose from the outside, the common white man joined the master class in hating "the nigger-loving scoundrels" called abolitionists. He gave no voice to Hinton R. Helper's plea that his best interests could be served by his abandoning both master and slave.

Almost as socially degraded as the slaves were the million or more Southerners who in 1850 composed the class known as the poor whites. More than a hundred years earlier, in 1730, William Byrd had described

[7] Wilbur J. Cash, *The Mind of the South*, pp. 22, 70. Cf. Frank L. Owsley, *Plain Folk of the Old South*, pp. 1–22.
[8] Owsley, *op. cit.*, p. 8.

these "slothful inhabitants of Lubberland," and in the twentieth century they would be personified by Jeeter Lester and the Okies. Seldom did they have the ambition or opportunity to rise above their class. Most so-called poor whites who rose to higher social or public positions were in reality members of the yeoman class. "There is no . . . method," said a Southern sociologist of these people,[9] "by which they can be weaned from leading the lives of vagrom-men, idlers, and squatters, useless to themselves and the rest of mankind."

As "crackers" and "hillbillies" in Georgia, "sand-hillers" in South Carolina, "rag, tag, and bobtail" in Virginia, "squatters" in Alabama and Mississippi, "people of the barren" in Tennessee, and "po' white trash" and "po' buckra" to the Negroes, they have filled many pages of the accounts of travelers and storytellers. Descriptions of their ignorance, poverty, filth, lack of ambition, and misshapen forms would hardly be believed were the evidence not confirmed by reliable observers from Frederick L. Olmsted and Mark Twain to the proslavery apologists. Although families were large, they cooked, ate, slept, and died in a miserable hut of one room. The earth served as a floor; roofs were leaky and shutters took the place of windowpanes. The principal articles of furniture were a homemade table, a few rickety stools, a dirty bed or two, a spinning wheel, and an inherited frying pan. There was no china, no knives and forks. Physically these people were characterized by "a striking lankness of frame and slackness of muscle in association with a shambling gait, a boniness and misshapeliness of head and feature, a peculiar sallow swartness, or alternatively a not less peculiar and a not less sallow faded-out colorlessness of skin and hair." The men when not hunting and fishing lolled away their time in the company of hounds and jugs of moonshine whisky. Vegetable patches and a few acres of corn were planted conscientiously but were later abandoned to the weeds.

Some writers ingeniously explain these peculiar people as descendants of the convict, indentured servant, and debtor classes of the colonial period. Their large numbers and wide distribution from the Dismal Swamp to the Everglades and from the Atlantic Ocean to Arkansas and Oklahoma argue against the acceptance of this as more than a partial explanation. For the most part they were merely the weakest elements of the frontier population who were driven into the mountains, the red hills, the sand lands, the swamps, and the pine barrens by the advance of planters and yeomen farmers. Their isolation contributed much to their general ignorance. Their lack of ambition was promoted by their inability to obtain adequate returns for labor on submarginal soils and by the prevalence of enervating diseases such as hookworm and malaria. Nu-

[9] David R. Hundley, *Social Relations in Our Southern States*, p. 119.

tritional deficiencies, rather than moral degradation which some writers have asserted, at times forced them to eat clay.

They were genuine white Southerners, as blond and sharp-featured as other Anglo-Saxons. Some of them, indeed, had been the least competent members of middle- or even upper-class families who allowed themselves to be edged back to the poorer lands, where they joined the ranks of the "crackers" and were forgotten by their more fortunate relatives. There were only a few Jukes and Kallikaks among them, with the characteristics of genuine degenerates. They were energetic, at least when drunk; theirs was a coarse and pungent humor; and the mountaineers among them improvised or repeated lively ballads. For all their ignorance, sloth, and barbarous poverty, they possessed some aristocratic attitudes, hating manual toil and taking on "a sort of unkempt politeness and ease of port, which rendered them definitely superior, in respect of manner, to their peers in the rest of the country." [10] Many were proud of their barren acres. Neither exploited nor mistreated by the governing classes, they were simply ignored because they were useless in the slave economy. Since they were not oppressed, they were free to share the lordly contempt of other whites toward the Negroes. This made them loyal Southerners who were willing, when the tragic days arrived, to demonstrate latent virtues on many battlefields.

In 1860 there were 250,000 Negroes in the South who were not slaves; 58,000 were concentrated in Virginia and 85,000 in Maryland. Throughout the period of slavery Negroes had either bought their freedom or gained it by the performance of special service that won the gratitude of masters. During each of the two decades following 1790 masters by deed or will freed so many slaves that the number of free Negroes more than doubled. White fathers, particularly in Louisiana, freed many mulatto or quadroon children and often endowed them with money and property. Naturally, slaves who proved their talents for self-direction by buying their own liberty made better members of the community than those who were freed for sentimental reasons. The manumitted slaves who were established in Virginia as petty landowners under Richard Randolph's will proved thriftless, and Olmsted believed that the poverty of free Negroes was not due to lack of opportunities.

So fair in general was the treatment of free Negroes in the South before 1830 that some of them became eminent in their communities. Such, for example, was Austin Dabney, a veteran of the American Revolution, who was given a farm by the Georgia legislature and was entertained in the home of the governor of the state. Such, also, was

[10] Cash, *op. cit.*, pp. 24 n., 70.

Henry Evans, whose fervent preaching won him a Methodist congregation of both races at Fayetteville, North Carolina. There was John Chavis, a dark brown man who distinguished himself as a Presbyterian minister in Virginia and North Carolina and as a teacher who prepared well-born North Carolinians for college. There was Joseph Willis whom we have mentioned as the pioneer Baptist missionary of Louisiana. There was Jehu Jones, the proprietor of one of Charleston's most popular hotels, who accumulated a small fortune, and Thomy Lafon, merchant and moneylender of New Orleans, who possessed a half million dollars. Some colored freemen themselves owned numerous slaves. A Negro planter of the South Carolina lowlands was reported to have 200 slaves in 1799 and Martin Donato of St. Landry Parish, Louisiana, in 1848 left an estate which included 89 slaves. In 1860 the tax returns of Charleston listed 130 colored persons as possessing 390 slaves.

The barriers of race and social distinction prevented free colored men from attaining widespread distinctions, however. After the Nat Turner scare of 1831 Southern legislatures imposed severe restrictions upon them. They could not testify in court in their own behalf or serve on juries; they were deprived of the right to vote and to serve in the militia. Some states would not permit free Negroes within their borders, and others required them to register and to post bonds for their good behavior. Assemblage was made unlawful, and it was a crime to teach them to read and write. Often they were forced back into slavery by kidnapping or legal tricks. They were truly the pariahs of Southern society. Masters, fearing their influence over the slaves, would not accord them the protection they were willing to give the slaves against penalties imposed by race-prejudiced mobs and courts. In Mississippi, the number of free Negroes declined from 1,366 in 1840 to half that number in 1860, and in that state a slave could not be freed except by special act of the legislature. A Louisiana law of 1859 encouraged free Negroes to select a master and return to slavery.

Yet, as was true of slaves, the laws against free Negroes were more severe in the letter than in practice. A general sympathy of the whites for the free Negroes was partially responsible for this lessening of actual restrictions; further, experience had failed to justify any suspicion of the loyalty of free colored persons. They had submitted readily to the proscriptions of Southern society because of habit, because resistance would have brought on greater restrictions, and because they enjoyed at least the privilege of freedom. In the secession crisis colored leaders of Louisiana proclaimed the loyalty of their followers: "They are dearly attached to their native land, . . . and are ready to shed their blood for her defense. They have no sympathy for abolitionism; no love for the North, but they have plenty for Louisiana." Even though the free Negroes were given no promise of a better future, like other under-privileged classes they supported the Southern system.

The 3,951,000 Negroes who were held in slavery in 1860 comprised the "mudsill" of Southern society. Rigid living standards were pre-scribed for them. The plantation force has been aptly described as "a conscript army, living in barracks . . . under an authority as complete as the commanding personnel could wish." [11] There were captains, quar-termasters, and sergeants under the names of masters, overseers, and foremen who issued orders, distributed rations, and saw that the tasks were executed by obedient slaves.

The basic weekly food allowance was standardized at a peck of meal, four pounds of meat, and a quart of molasses, with something less for the children. Clothes were of the coarsest quality. Adults received each year a new dress or a new suit of clothes, two pairs of shoes, and a cheap hat, and at Christmas time small portions of whisky, a little spend-ing money, and some trinkets for the women. The pickaninnies were provided with a simple shirt that reached to the knees, and were re-quired at all seasons to go without shoes and hats. Each family was al-lowed a cabin usually built of logs with crevices effectively daubed with clay. There was a broad and plentifully fueled fireplace at which the food was cooked and the family gathered in cool weather. Variety in diet was achieved by leaks and gifts from the planter's table, by the hunting of 'possums by night and of squirrels and rabbits by day, by the gathering of plums, blackberries, and persimmons from abandoned fields, and of hickory nuts, walnuts, and muscadines from the forests, by the cultivation of vegetables in garden plots allowed by the masters, and by participation in the autumn festival of hog-killing. Hams, shoul-ders, sides, and lard were saved for the plantation smokehouse, but other parts of the hog were enjoyed by every mouth on the plantation. These were the spareribs, feet, souse, liver, chitterlings, and "crack-lings" taken from the boiling lard.

Despite legislative acts the slaves managed to dress gaily on holidays. Some travelers even asserted that for these occasions they often dressed better than the whites. One described the Sunday attire of slaves in Richmond in 1833: "The females wear white muslin and light silk gowns, with caps, bonnets, ribbons and feathers; some carry reticules on the arm and many are seen with parasols, while nearly all of them carry a white pocket-handkerchief before them in the most fashionable style. The young men among the slaves wear white trousers, black socks, broad-brimmed hats, and carry walking-sticks."

The social and economic security that slavery engendered created

[11] Phillips, *Life and Labor in the Old South,* p. 196.

among the Negroes a spirit of abandon which burst into gaiety during the evening rest periods, on Sundays, and during the week's holiday which prevailed at Christmas. "The plantation," says Phillips, "was a pageant and a variety show in alternation." There was the pursuit by torchlight of the 'possum and the 'coon to the music of the hounds, the joining of the planters and their guests on fox hunts, and rabbit hunting, fishing, and trapping during hours stolen from the routine of field work. At the horse races the jockeys and many of the spectators were Negroes. Marriage festivals in the big house were echoed in the slave quarters; and sometimes the wedding of a favorite housemaid was held in the hall of the mansion. The evening frolics in the slave quarters gave material for the American institution called the minstrel show. The fiddle and the banjo and the clapping of hands and bones created lively rhythms, and there were jigs, clogs, and cakewalks, interlarded with humorous musings. The slave knew how to dance spontaneously and how to laugh at himself.

He learned to escape from the fun-killing preachments of the puritanical religion his master tried to impose upon him. One device was to turn the supposedly austere ceremonies of the Protestant church into occasions of joy. The ecstasy of the revivals frequently led to holy dances called "shouts." At the camp meetings of the Methodists, the Negro readily mixed the festive with the spiritual. Baptisms in creeks and mill ponds of the Baptists were occasions of lively demonstrations. The Negro, to a greater degree than other persons, succumbed to the human inclination not to practice what he preached. Converted from sin by an emotional experience, this mercurial individual often fell back into sin. Sometimes he donned the garments of piety on Sunday and conveniently took them off on weekdays. By an overwhelming logic sanctity was sometimes reconciled with sin, as illustrated by a certain Brudder Brown's petition for divine approval of a Christmas dance in Irwin Russell's poem "Christmas Night in the Quarters."

The Negroes doubtless were impressed with the injunctions of white preachers concerning the wisdom of chastity and monogamous marriages. Yet the communal nature of the slave quarters facilitated sexual familiarities offensive to the family standards of free Americans. The conception of each slave as a separate piece of property prevented slave marriages from having the character of legal contracts and often led to their dissolution on the initiative or by the consent of masters. Divorces and remarriages were frequent, for the masters' consent was easy to secure and the slaves themselves were often eager to change wives. Negro men could afford to be polygamous because the support of wives and children devolved upon the slave system, rather than upon the individual husband or father. Children were perhaps more wel-

3 Standards of morality
1) for white men
2) " " women
3) " negro

come to slave mothers than to free mothers, for pregnancy and mother-hood brought a lightening of work and created no economic anxieties. Masters were generally indifferent to slave morals, however censorious they may have been concerning other aspects of Negro behavior. "Their morals and their manners," a planter told an English traveler,[12] "are in their own keeping. The men may have, for instance, as many wives as they please, so long as they do not quarrel about such matters." "Bad books," said Mary B. Chesnut of the planter class, "are not al-lowed house room . . . ; but bad women, if they are not white, and serve in a menial capacity, may swarm the house unmolested. The ostrich game is thought a Christian act."

Not all slaves were engaged in the dull routine of field work. Grada-tions in slave society were almost as pronounced as those that developed after the race became free. There was the distinction between common blacks and quadroons and mulattoes, who enjoyed special favors be-cause they were descended from the master class. There was the distinc-tion between town slave and country slave, between the Negroes of old American stock and those who had been recently brought from Africa, and above all between the house servant and the plantation laborer. House servants were frequently well fed, well mannered, and well dressed, and most conceited in their attitude toward the less privileged slaves and "po' white trash." They adorned themselves in the castoff garments of their masters and mistresses and imitated their behavior. They failed to develop an aristocratic psychology only because of the necessity of fawning before white superiors.

The separation of the races into two distinct castes was the most important reality of Southern society. There was no escape for the tal-ented or intellectual slave, no understanding by the ruling element that the proscriptions of race were annihilating the budding talents of a Booker T. Washington or a Frederick Douglass. Interracial marriages were not approved, and had been forbidden in Maryland as early as 1663.

Yet, despite this basic race stratification, the conditions of slavery fostered a degree of interracial intimacy that would shock Southerners accustomed to twentieth-century distinctions. The two races led es-sentially the same life, if on different levels. Thus, says William Faulk-ner, the planters were

only in the surface matter of food and clothing and daily occupation any different from the Negro slaves who supported them—the same sweat, the only difference being that on one hand it went for labor in the fields where on the other it went as the price of the spartan and meager pleasures which

[12] Basil Hall, cited in Phillips, *Life and Labor in the Old South*, p. 204.

were available to them because they did not have to sweat in the fields: the hard violent hunting and riding; the same pleasures: the one, gambling for worn knives and brass jewelry and twists of tobacco and buttons and garments because they happened to be easiest and quickest at hand; on the other for money and horses, the guns and watches, and for the same reason; the same parties: the identical music from identical instruments, crude fiddles and guitars, now in the big house with candles and silk dresses and champagne, now in dirt-floored cabins with smoking pine knots and calico and water sweetened with molasses.

The plantation population was a large family in whose affairs master, mistress, and overseer had a compelling interest. They wished to control the lives of the slaves so that the maximum labor might be achieved. The lash played its role, but of greater significance was the inculcation of contentment and good will which came through nursing the sick, feeding the hungry, teaching the manual arts, and displaying an honest concern in personal and domestic affairs. Discipline, whether harsh or paternal, was always intimate.

Social intimacy between the children of the two races was unimpaired by race consciousness. They played together in woods, kitchen, and slave quarters; together they listened to folklore in the slave quarters and to Bible and fairy tales in the big house. The white children scarcely knew the difference between their mammies and "uncles" by courtesy and their mothers and uncles by blood. With adulthood race consciousness became definite, but the genuine Southerner felt no physical repulsion for colored persons. His aversion to manual labor was indulged by surrounding himself and his family with a bevy of servants. Negro women did the cooking and the cleaning, and Negro boys and girls waited on the table. Fires were made, horses were harnessed, and cows milked by black hands. Ideally, a servant would be available for every personal service—to bring a glass of fresh water or brush the flies away.

Slavery stimulated the concubinage of slave women to planters, their sons, and overseers. It promoted social intimacy, made Negro women subject to white men and prompted them to offer bodily favors as a certain means of winning social and material advantages. The taboo against miscegenation did not overcome the lure of the uninhibited passions of colored women, and more than one white man left his Victorian wife for the fellowship of dusky women. William Gilmore Simms acknowledged that there were great abuses in the easy gratification of white men's lust with black women—"illicit and foul conduct of many among us, who make their slaves the victims and the instruments alike of the most licentious passions." James Madison's sister may have exaggerated when she complained that the planter's wife was but the mistress of a seraglio,[13] but miscegenation under slavery was far from uncommon. The 1860 census reported 518,000 persons of mixed blood. This represented one seventh of the Negro population.

If defense of their actions were needed, Southern white men might have justified the liberties they took with colored women on the basis of the purported stifling of their desires to take such liberties with the ladies of their own race. A vital part of the Southern legend was the cult of Southern womanhood, the belief that it was the duty of the gentlemen to cherish and protect the virtue of their women. The strain of violence that ran through Southern life—the shooting affrays and duels—was largely prompted by the extreme sensitiveness which Southern men felt toward the character of their women. The women were the keepers of the standards of the Christian home and of the purity of the race. Chancellor William Harper in 1837 spoke of only one known instance of an unfaithful South Carolina wife of the upper class. Olmsted in 1854 asserted, "The women of the South are unexcelled in the world for every quality which commands admiration, love and respect." Perhaps Southern ladies practiced the Victorian virtues to a greater degree than other women; certainly they seldom shamed Southern society by sexual intimacy with Negroes.

The younger members of the planter's family were proud of their soft hands and their ignorance of the vocabulary of labor and trade. The responsibilities of adulthood, however, forced an awakening from this reverie. The successful master had to know how to supervise the work of overseer and slave; the successful mistress had to cope with her own spoiled children and the prevarication, forgetfulness, and immorality of her slaves. Her patience and watchfulness had to be endless. At home she had no time to be fastidious in dress.

The hospitality of the master and the industry of the mistress and the slave culminated in the glory of the Southern table. Frugality was a vice which was justly shunned because vegetables and eggs were perishable, everything was plentiful and inexpensive, and willing consumers for the surplus waited in the kitchen and slave quarters. The gardens provided lettuce, cucumbers, several varieties of greens, beans, squash, Irish potatoes, turnips, okra, asparagus, artichokes, and beets. The field added green corn, pumpkins, sweet potatoes, and rice. From the orchards came figs, apples, pears, quinces, and peaches, and the hedgerows and forests furnished blackberries, plums, muscadines, and walnuts. Many forms of edible game were to be had, but chicken and pork were the meats most widely used. Beef and mutton were scarce

[13] Cited in James F. Rhodes, *History of the United States*, I, 336.

because pastures were poor. "If ever tables were in the habit of groaning it was those of the planters," says Phillips.[14]

When the visitor entered the dining room, he found the table, according to Southern "country style," already crowded with several varieties of meats, vegetables, pickles, preserves and jellies; to it were added relays of breads hot enough to melt butter. The chicken was served fried, roasted, and in dumplings; and pork appeared as ham, bacon, and sausage. From wheat flour were made the biscuits and the waffles; white corn yielded grits, muffins, spoon bread, hoe cake, and pone. Sweet potatoes were served roasted, fried, and candied. The dessert was peach, blackberry, or sweet potato pie, or apple dumpling.

The plenitude of servants, food, and space characterizing the Southern rural establishment found expression in the cult of Southern hospitality, the part of the Southern legend that was nearest reality. Uncles, aunts, old-maid cousins, friends, and even occupationless gentlemen who drifted in from a distance were welcomed at the plantation house. The genteel stranger was met at the plantation gate with an extended hand and with a cordial invitation to partake of whatever beverage was being consumed by those gathered on the porch; as a matter of course he was asked to share any meal in prospect and to spend a night, which might easily be extended into weeks or even months. There were no charges for such services and some planters had the roads patrolled by slaves to inveigle strangers within their gates. Although they sought seclusion from village life, they did not wish to be lonesome.

Edmund Ruffin believed that the famed "hospitality of Oid Virginia" was the main cause of the economic adversities of the lowlands of that state. "Such effects," he explained, "are certainly not produced merely by the meat and liquor consumed by friends and visitors; but it is our custom to give up to all our visitors not only the best entertainment but also the time, the employments and the habits of the host—and this not only to friends and visitors . . . but for every individual of the despicable race of loungers and spongers which our custom of universal hospitality has created." George Washington, although an efficient and successful businessman and farmer, discovered that most of the profits of his Mount Vernon estate not consumed by his slaves were eaten up by the stream of relatives, friends, and distinguished travelers who passed his way.

Aside from the hospitality of the home and the table, recreational activities of the planters were not extensive. There were, of course, dances to the tunes of Negro fiddlers and wedding feasts proclaimed afar by bonfires along the avenues. Every planter possessed hounds,

[14] *American Negro Slavery*, p. 312.

horns, horses, and guns—and neighbors ever ready to accept invitations to the chase. Wandering for a day or a night through the expansive wilderness of field and forest was profitable, for squirrel, wild turkey, dove and quail, and even bear and deer were plentiful. The supreme sport was the fox hunt; all the countryside "loved the yelp of the pack and the excitement of the galloping group of horsemen, and the hard ride . . . 'across a country that was only for those who dared.' " [15] Horsemanship was the natural prerogative of those who regarded themselves descendants of the Cavaliers. Trained from infancy to ride, the planters were like centaurs. "The Mississippian," said an observer,[16] "never seems to think of himself or the position of his limbs. They yield, as does his whole body, pliantly and naturally to the motions of the animal beneath him, with which his own harmonizes so perfectly and with such flexibility that there seems to be but one principle actuating both."

All classes gathered to hear ambitious planters advance their candidacies for public office or to hear the younger sons of the planters argue cases in court. The whole plantation family turned out on Sundays for church. On the Atlantic seaboard, they attended the formal services of the Episcopal church, pausing after the sermon to allow families isolated from their neighbors for six days an opportunity for an hour of animated exchange of gossip. In the back country, church-going had more elaborate social features. All-day services of singing and preaching were held among the dominant Methodists and Baptists, with picnic dinners in church yards. In the late summer these occasions expanded into week-long affairs known as camp meetings among the Methodists and as protracted meetings among the Baptists. Religious objectives did not mar the festive nature of these gatherings. In many rural communities they were the chief social events of the year.

The great planter, unlike the lesser planter and the general run of plain people, could leave the somewhat listless life of the plantation to visit the city and resorts. To be able to do this, one had to possess an appreciation of sophisticated life, a plantation large enough to support an overseer, and ample means to maintain a coach and horses. Before the extension of the railroads the carriage was a necessary means of travel; in the sharp competitions of high society it was an obvious way of proclaiming wealth and social position. The antebellum carriage was a large and cumbersome vehicle, swung high on suspension springs, that rocked and rolled along the rough highways. Often it was trimmed in brass and gold and adorned with the family

[15] Paul Wilstach, *Mount Vernon*, pp. 97–8.
[16] Joseph H. Ingraham, cited in Phillips, *Life and Labor in the Old South*, pp. 361–2.

coat of arms. The horses were carefully groomed and well harnessed; and high above, liveried and proud, sat the coachman, the most privileged of the slaves.

Where were these planters traveling in such lordly estate? Perhaps they were Georgians traveling to nearby Athens or Washington to be guests in the colonnaded mansions of local magnates. They might have been Alabamians on their way to Tuscaloosa to enjoy entertainments in impressive homes built on cotton profits, Mississippians on their way to the Gulf beaches, or South Carolinians seeking the nonmalarial sand lands or the cool airs of mountain retreats. They might even have been rich gentlemen of the Black Belt making a tour of the mineral springs of Virginia. A few among the sophisticated and the very rich were perhaps on their way to Saratoga or Newport to add the legendary charms of the Southern gentleman, his lady, and his daughter to the luxurious splendors of watering places in distant Yankeeland. Regardless of their destination, the planters generally stayed away from their homes for weeks or even months, for these long excursions were too tiresome to justify early returns.

The choicest society of the Old South was found in Charleston. In 1860 it was a city of 40,522 inhabitants with traditions in architecture, literature, the theater, horse racing, gentlemen's clubs, dancing assemblies, and Paris fashions. It possessed the oldest museum and the third oldest subscription library. Its St. Cecilia Society, founded in 1762 for musical concerts, had been transformed into an exclusive social organization that featured balls. The planters of the South Carolina low country continued to visit Charleston during the warm months to avoid the malaria of the rice swamps; they sometimes returned in winter to enjoy the balls, the races, and the dinners and private parties that wealth and culture made possible. They contributed a dignity to the city's society which could not have been created by a commercial aristocracy. Cultural tone was given to the place by an aristocracy of the mind, forming, some thought, an aggregate of talent not equaled in any other state. The Charleston elite built dwellings near the Battery, a park on the point of the peninsula on which Charleston is located. The palmettoes and live oaks of the Battery, and its broad view of bay and islands, overshadowed the ugliness and clutter of docks and mercantile streets.

Charleston's domestic architecture was a subtle adaptation of English models to the conditions of a semitropical climate. Houses were constructed of two or three stories with galleries and single-depth rooms that invited the breezes in three directions. Their gables, turned sideways, assured the occupants of privacy. Wrought-iron gateways gave only glimpses of the flowery shade within. Almost the year around

Charleston was a city of flowers: daffodil, camellia, and the sweet olive in winter, a riot of wisteria and azalea in spring, and oleander and althea in summer.

In 1860 New Orleans was four times larger than Charleston and far more varied in the composition of its population and the character of its architecture. Here French and Spanish influences met the newer influences of the expanding Cotton Kingdom of the Anglo-Saxon South. Here sugar and cotton planters with town mansions met Yankees, Jews, Germans, and Irishmen who came down the Mississippi to capture the trade of the Southern metropolis. It was the mart of the pioneer West and a center of Southern leisure. Within New Orleans were two cities. One was the Vieux Carré, or the French Quarter, with its two- or three-story buildings, galleries adorned with wrought-iron railings, and patio gardens bright with oleander, wisteria, camellia, and banana and yucca plants. Among the public buildings were the Cathedral, the Cabildo, the Hotel Royal with its auction block for slaves, and the Opera House where the masked balls of the Mardi Gras were held. Beyond the French Quarter lay the expanding "American" city with its warehouses, cotton compresses, wharves, shops, banks, and counting-houses. In its Garden District, Southerners with plantation ideals built houses with broad verandas and large white columns, and deep gardens. New Orleans was a city of contrast: Methodists and Presbyterians with their Puritan heritage and Anglo-Saxon domestic exclusiveness; Catholic Creoles with their colorful night life strange to the South; slaves at the auction block; colored concubines honored by gentlemen friends at the Quadroon Ball. It was a city of carnivals and duels, a haven of drama, opera, gambling, and a multitude of abandoned women. It was a place "where tragedy and gaiety walked side by side in chivalrous converse."

Those who set the standards of Southern society congregated in many cities other than Charleston and New Orleans. There were Savannah, Wilmington, Mobile, and the lesser towns of the coast where spacious houses still give evidence of an earlier gentry resembling that of Charleston. Likewise, there were similar towns in the interior, Tuscaloosa in Alabama, Athens and Washington in Georgia, Hillsboro in North Carolina, Edgefield in South Carolina, and Columbia in Tennessee. There was Lexington in the Bluegrass region of Kentucky where race horses of Virginia lineage brought together an aristocracy of prosperous farmers. There were state capitals such as Milledgeville in Georgia, Nashville in Tennessee, and Montgomery in Alabama where planters turned politicians gathered for public affairs. In the Virginia towns of Richmond, Fredericksburg, and Petersburg, mansions of the great statesmen of the Revolutionary and early national periods were gathering places of the South's aristocracy. Memphis was the center of the developing cotton trade of west Tennessee, Mississippi, and Arkansas. Its population came largely from the eastern South and its dominant class of merchants and traders displayed much of the polish of the country aristocracy of which they considered themselves a part. They patronized the theater and the concert hall, dueled beneath the oaks on Hernando Road, and gathered for the races at Montgomery Park.

The Old South had no city that furnished social and cultural leadership for the whole region. Despite its size, wealth, and fabulous activities, New Orleans was unable to fill this role for several reasons. Its population was too polyglot and too commercial to appeal to the imagination of a rural people with puritanical and chivalric ideals of Anglo-Saxon origin. Its Creole aristocracy accepted Southern standards of slavery, but it was too easygoing and too confirmed in its French customs to secure the leadership of the surrounding world. Its main cultural interest was the promotion of a brilliant cuisine of crayfish bisque, gumbo filé, pompano, and other delicacies. Charleston was nearer the Southern ideal of a city, but it, too, failed to become the capital of the South. Separated from other sections by swamps and rivers, it was avoided by railroads seeking the commerce of the west-ward-moving Cotton Kingdom. By 1850 it had even lost the leadership of South Carolina politics to the men of the cotton-growing upcountry. Its aristocracy was too Brahmanic in its urban exclusiveness to suit the men of the red hills; its confinement to a narrow peninsula did not attract the rich from the backcountry who wanted a rural expansiveness in town houses and gardens. Despite its western location, Memphis was even less successful in gaining Southern leadership. The plantation aristocracy shunned it because it never learned to segregate its "flatboat folk" and its numerous gambling dens and bawdy houses from more respectable districts. The observant Olmsted was displeased by the meal of grimy bacon and greasy cabbage he was expected to consume in Western-like haste at the city's leading hotel.

The genius of the Old South was rural. Its elite, even when they dwelt in cities and towns, retained or assumed the manners of country gentlemen. Virginia was their model, the focal point on which they patterned their houses and their manner of life. It was not the Virginia of Richmond and other towns, but the Virginia of plantations, of manor houses, of a simple home life, of courteous squires, and of the Washingtons, Jeffersons, Randolphs, and Lees. It was the Virginia that was to assume unmistakable leadership in the crisis of the Confederacy.

But long before this crisis arose Virginia was a leader of society. In the eighteenth century visitors had sought the salubrious waters of her mountain mineral springs—Hot, Warm, Sweet, Red Sulphur, Green-brier, and White Sulphur. In the nineteenth century plantation families came to these resorts for a cool climate and restrained social pleasures. These plantation families could feel at home, for the areas were as rural as those from which they had come, and the individuality of home life was maintained by cottage dormitories. Gay social life provided a welcomed change from their home routine. In the course of a summer each family would make the rounds of all the springs. Planters were probably undisturbed by the observation of a mordant Englishman that accommodations were often expensive and uncomfortable and that the subjects of conversation among the gentlemen were the relative merits of hams and oysters instead of the relative merits of artistic productions.[17] Visits to the Virginia springs afforded opportunities for girls from the deep isolation of the plantations to make advantageous matches under proper chaperonage. For this purpose definite ritual was followed. In the afternoons girls and beaus walked in front of the cottages. Before the evening balls the girls attracted the attention of masculine bystanders by promenading through the parlors, with the elders watching from the sidelines.

[17] George M. Featherstonhaugh, cited in Percival Reniers, *The Springs of Virginia*, pp. 3–24.

CHAPTER X

The Old South Turns Orthodox

>>>->>>

THE MOST significant development in the thinking of the Old South through the early decades of the nineteenth century was the establishment of orthodoxy and conservatism. Jeffersonian liberalism gave way to reaction. The deism and skepticism of the older generation yielded to the orthodoxy of new theologians and to waves of evangelism which swept outward from the back country. Respect for such natural rights as freedom of religion and of speech was supplanted by the theory that rights were nothing more than the sanctions of society. The tidewater aristocrats who had learned by experience on exhausted lands that slavery was unprofitable and even morally wrong were succeeded by slaveholders of the back country whose experience on the black lands of Alabama and Mississippi had convinced them that slavery was profitable and right. The liberal heritage was doomed by the South sinking into what a Virginia gentleman called "the slough of democracy." [1] All over the United States the common man came into power with the election of Andrew Jackson to the presidency in 1828. In the South he demanded adherence to majority opinion in matters religious, social, and racial. He was persuaded by religious revivals to accept the evangelical faith; he rejected equalitarian ideals and practices of the frontier for his desire to join the advancing plantation society with its class distinctions based on quick wealth and contempt for the Negro in any but a menial role. The South had found a new basis for existence.

[1] Beverley Tucker, cited in William P. Trent, *William Gilmore Simms*, p. 186.

This was a reactionary philosophy; it was, in a sense, a repudiation of the principles of the eighteenth-century enlightenment embodied in the Declaration of Independence. Unwillingness to compromise with these principles was to cause the downfall of the Old South. Yet the new reactionary philosophy was more in harmony with contemporary realities and aspirations than the ideals that had been imported from England and France by Revolutionary intellectuals. Indeed, there was an element of unreasoning sentimentality in slaveholders like Patrick Henry and Thomas Jefferson who denounced slavery; in Willie Jones of North Carolina, "a wealthy planter who lived like a prince but who talked and voted like a Jacobin"; and in George Mason, author of the famous Virginia Bill of Rights, who owned more than 300 slaves and regarded George Washington as an upstart. The ideals of such men were ignored or forgotten in the advancing world of slavery and religious conformity. Deists like Edmund Randolph and John Randolph of Roanoke were reconciled to orthodox Christianity; Jefferson concealed his religious views from the public in his old age; Senator James M. Mason refused to allow the historian George Bancroft to quote derogatory remarks made about slavery by his grandfather, George Mason.

The recession of liberalism in the region below the Potomac did not plunge the South into utter intellectual darkness. Some wealthy Whig planters kept alive the Jeffersonian tradition of tolerance and free inquiry. Even though criticism of slavery and religious orthodoxy was not tolerated, there was opportunity for scientific research, educational advancement, and the creation of private libraries. An awareness of the need of progressive reforms was suggestive of the contemporary humanitarianism which stirred New England. The Bill of Rights, which remained a much-emphasized part of the Southern creed, was given reality by the independence of rural life and the freedom of all classes of whites from oppression by those above them. Aristocratic notions fostered by slavery gave rise to a strong sense of personal dignity. In response to the movement for democratic reform all the slave states adopted white manhood suffrage. Moreover, the South did not feel that it was sacrificing right and justice by preferring religious orthodoxy to free thought, and "Southern womanhood" to equality of the sexes. Southerners were proud of their chivalric manners, the freedom of their plantation life, and they enjoyed an attitude of mind that fostered easy contentment rather than pursuit of progress.

The mode of life of the Cotton Kingdom ran counter to the progressive thinking of the age. Its rulers had no time to develop the liberality of spirit and culture which for two centuries had characterized the slaveholding aristocracy of the Atlantic seaboard. Throughout its short existence of scarcely four decades, the Cotton Kingdom was fundamentally marked by the isolation and rawness of the frontier. Its planters were primarily concerned with the culturally uninspiring tasks of clearing fields and setting up houses and all the other material appurtenances of civilization. They talked of guns, powderhorns, saddles, bridles, and whips; and their homes lacked reading lamps, pianos, books, and the cultural refinements of the better homes of tidewater Virginia and the North. Abolitionist criticism made them aware of the fact that they were an isolated, almost beleaguered people who could avoid surrender only by narrowing their intellectual and social ideas. Some individuals among them escaped from current problems by romantically comparing their civilization based on black slaves, with that of medieval manors based in part on white serfs.

The Cotton Kingdom had no great cities to encourage the growth of education, literature, science, and the arts. Promoters and traders— the successful businessmen—were more highly regarded in the Old South than those who perpetuate the plantation legend are willing to admit, but since they were not so rich as the corresponding classes of the North, they were unable to support the arts as well. A rural dullness ruled the land. The isolation of the plantation establishments was increased by difficulties of communication caused by rough roads and poor railroad connections. Plantation life, dominated by Negro labor, created an indolence which left many people oblivious to the passing of time. The front porch and everlasting rocking chair were notable Southern institutions.

Religion in the Old South illustrates most concretely the triumph of reactionary conservatism over eighteenth-century tolerance and skepticism. First came the conversion of many common people by waves of evangelism which swept the back country in 1796 and afterwards. Then a new generation of orthodox theologians and intellectuals took over education, influenced all Southern thinking, and finally transformed religion to fit the uses of slavery.

Religious conditions following the American Revolution alarmed those who cherished the traditions which had brought their forefathers to the Colonial wilderness. The Episcopal church, described as "an exotic in America which established itself only under royal patronage," [2] more than perhaps any other religious institution in the United States felt the impact of the eighteenth-century enlightenment. Its lack of vivid affirmations and its preference for common sense and formal ritual, instead of unconventional emotionalism, kept it from satisfying the needs of the common people. In 1860 it had only 60,000 Southern

[2] Wilbur J. Cash, *The Mind of the South*, p. 55.

members, mostly in the tidewater region and in cities such as Savannah and Charleston, with outposts in the back country among planters attempting to imitate the ways of South Carolina and Virginia.

Easterners were shocked by the religious indifference of the frontiersman, who might forget the Bible or hoot at the agents of ecclesiastical authority. Profanity, shooting, drunkenness, Sabbathbreaking, and lawlessness were natural to life on the frontier. Logan County, Kentucky, soon to become the center of a great religious revival, was known as Rogues' Harbor, a haven for counterfeiters, robbers, and murderers. As late as 1820 only one person in twelve in Kentucky was a church member.

Yet a sense of sin and of piety, deeply embedded in people whose ancestors had been devout British Protestants, was not to be uprooted by the liberating circumstances of a new environment. Between 1797 and 1805 the frontier was swept by a religious revival whose effects were so widespread that the movement has been called the Second Awakening. It began in Logan County under the leadership of James McGready, an uncouth but earnest Presbyterian minister who had been accused in South Carolina of "running people distracted." His persuasive preaching attracted Presbyterian, Methodist, and Baptist ministers—including John McGee, a Methodist, who was overcome by his feelings and "shouted and exhorted with all possible energy." From the whole Western or Cumberland country the movement spread into Virginia and the Carolinas. Meetings were attended by thousands of intent listeners. From among the ten to twenty-five thousand attending, the number "brought to the ground" by conviction of sin was estimated at one thousand.

Converts were seized with the "jerks," running, dancing, and barking, and, most commonly, with attacks in which "with piercing screams they fall like a log on the floor or ground" seemingly dead. During August, families gathered for camp meetings with provisions and tents, prepared to stay for days. These were impressive occasions, especially at night, with camp fires and torches shining on hundreds of ecstatic faces, with the swelling and falling of the chants, the impassioned exhortations and prayers, "the sobs, shrieks, or shouts, bursting from persons under intense agitation of mind; the sudden spasms which seized upon scores, and unexpectedly dashed them to the ground." [3]

Weaknesses in the revival movement were apparent. Adverse critics maintained that encouragement of emotionalism increased prejudice and violence among country people. Often the ease and suddenness of the process of conversion were followed by relapses into sin as sudden

[3] Unidentified quotation in William W. Sweet, *The Story of Religion in America,* p. 331.

and as easy. Sectarianism was accentuated. Opposition to the "fervor, noise and disorder" of the poorly educated exhorters led to schism in the Presbyterian church and the formation of the warmly evangelical Cumberland Presbyterian church. In 1832 dissenting Presbyterians and Baptists, led by Barton W. Stone and Alexander Campbell, formed the Disciples of Christ or the Campbellites.

Yet the revival movement was not without commendable features. It promoted sobriety, increased respect for law, and improved speech. Church trials were frequently held, and the penalty of excommunication was imposed for a variety of offenses. They included drunkenness, sexual immorality, gambling, cursing, fighting, dancing, and abusing one's parents, husband, wife or child. To combat relapses into sin evangelistic campaigns were conducted annually in almost every Southern community.

The religious movement promoted education. Bibles and tracts were distributed by such traveling ministers as George Washington's biographer, Parson Mason L. Weems. Between 1802 and 1830 twenty-seven religious periodicals were founded in the South Atlantic states. They were potent factors in shaping public opinion on political and social questions as well as on moral and religious issues. Missions and Sunday schools were organized despite the opposition of persons who feared bias more than ignorance in the interpretation of the Bible. Religions chiefly inspired by Bible-reading could not logically oppose schools. Frontier Protestants established academies and colleges almost as soon as they built churches. The comment of John Randolph—that when the Methodists became educated they would no longer be Methodists —was unjustified, for the support this denomination came to give education equaled that of any other sect.

These activities swelled the membership of the evangelical bodies. Between 1820 and 1850 the number of Methodists in the South Atlantic states increased from 93,000 to 223,713 and the number of Baptists from 99,000 to 246,000, while the whole population of these states increased only one third. Comparable gains were made in the states west of the mountains.[4]

Scotch-Irish Presbyterians had settled the frontiers long before the American Revolution. Although their clergymen played a prominent part in the Second Awakening, their church did not become popular in the back country. In the 1820's, for example, only 2,700 of Kentucky's 46,000 Protestants were Presbyterians. Their creed was too rigid and too exclusive in form and doctrine to appeal to the common people; their educational standards were too high to attract many ministerial

[4] Charles S. Sydnor, *The Development of Southern Sectionalism, 1819–1848*, pp. 54, 294.

candidates. Most Presbyterians came from the educated and wealthy classes.

The Roman Catholic church profited from the religious freedom that resulted from the American Revolution. Its greatest strength was in Kentucky, eastern Maryland, and southern Louisiana. It established Spring Hill College in Alabama and St. Mary's College in Kentucky in the 1830's. Due partly to the coming of Irish immigrants every Southern city by 1860 had an active Catholic congregation. That church produced its share of prominent Southerners. Among them were Father John Carroll, Revolutionary leader; Père Antoine, famous cathedral preacher of New Orleans and stormy enemy of episcopal authority; and Bishop Patrick N. Lynch, civic leader of Charleston. The activities of the Know-Nothing party resulted in anti-Catholic violence in Kentucky and Maryland; but these disturbances were not so extensive in the South as elsewhere. Henry A. Wise in Virginia and Andrew Johnson in Tennessee, advocates of religious toleration, won resounding victories at the polls.

The Catholic church accepted easily the Southern attitude toward slavery and the Negro; but it took no forward steps in the development of the regional consciousness. It remained urban and foreign in a rural and nativist area. It allowed itself to be dominated by its Irish element and thereby lost the social prestige it had enjoyed when under the control of the Colonial aristocracies of Louisiana and Maryland.

The Baptist church had the most extensive following among Southerners because it adjusted itself to their needs to even a greater degree than the Methodists. Its simple system of government, through which all members had an equal voice in the business of the congregation, suited the democratic sentiments of the back country. The ministers were generally farmers elected to preach by their congregations, and they supported themselves with their own hands. These farmer-ministers had little formal education, but their sermons were phrased in a language intelligible to their neighbors. Their conservatism made them deaf to any doctrines not found in the Bible. The authoritarian principles of the Old Testament were respected, even in this republican land, and they adopted no ritual foreign to their people. Their most impressive ceremony was baptism: the immersion of converts in creeks and millponds while witnesses looked on. The influence of the Baptist church extended to the community relationships of its members. At the monthly congregational meetings disciplinary measures were imposed for shady business deals as well as for religious and moral lapses.

The ante-bellum Baptists were so successful in winning Negroes to their church that the foundation was laid for a future in which a majority of Southern Negro Christians would be members of that church.

The Baptists did this less by deliberate missionary efforts than by accepting Negro members on a basis of Christian brotherhood that seems strange in the twentieth-century South. There were many instances in which gifted Negroes were allowed to preach to congregations of both races. The first Baptist church west of the Mississippi was established on Bayou Chicot in Louisiana in 1812 by Joseph Willis, a mulatto from South Carolina.

The Methodists were almost as successful as Baptists in converting the westward-moving Southern people. Methodism was well adapted to sparsely settled communities. John Wesley's system of circuit riding made it possible for an individual minister to call on many settlements each month, establishing "classes" and "class leaders" to carry on his work after he left. These ministers on horseback worked every day of the week, preaching in log cabins, in taverns, and in the open, and visiting new communities not only to find Methodists but to make Methodists out of the unconverted. The founder of the circuit riding system in the United States—and its greatest disciple—was Bishop Francis Asbury, who frequently crossed the Alleghenies between 1788 and 1800 preaching and organizing churches.

Bishop Asbury also created a centralized church government; as its head, he assumed supreme appointive power. Dissatisfied with this undemocratic system, James O'Kelly, a prominent Virginia preacher, led a withdrawal of Republican Methodists. Asbury's church continued, although it gradually modified its autocratic controls.

In contrast to the Calvinist doctrines of limited grace and predestination, Methodists taught that man was master of his destiny. They exercised less care than Presbyterian and Episcopal congregations in selecting preachers, but supplemented their clergy with lay or "local" preachers. These amateur exhorters, like the Baptist farmer-preachers, were often uneducated young men with a natural eloquence, full of a zeal that moved the most obdurate souls.

The revivalists, together with orthodox theologians, created a religiously solid South long before a politically solid South existed. They were determined to preserve the body of religious knowledge which would guide Christians to the means of grace leading to eternal salvation. This was "the old-time religion," to which the thinking of the rationalists, the facts of science, and the allurements of earthly progress were either subordinate or irrelevant. Its proponents held that religious truth should not be altered every time new scientific knowledge or social enthusiasms widened the field of induction or offered empirical disproofs of accepted dogmas. Although this attitude was not uniquely Southern, it was maintained in the region below the Potomac with such intensity that one historian has asserted that "the Southern people reached the eve of the Civil War one of the few religious peoples left in the Western world." [5]

The Presbyterians, the intellectual elite among Southern churchmen, took the lead in the defense of religion. Throughout the region they established colleges and theological seminaries to counteract the deistic and secular spirit prevailing in Southern state universities and the social radicalism found in the schools of New England. The Union Theological Seminary, founded by Moses Hoge at Hampden-Sydney College in Virginia, became the center of a conservatism best expressed in the lectures of Robert L. Dabney. He asserted that virtue had its origin in divine fiat and was therefore immutable. James H. Thornwell of the Columbia Theological Seminary in South Carolina fervently gave voice to the wish of many a Southern theologian: "God forbid that I should falter in maintaining the faith once delivered to the saints. I look upon the tenets of modern Unitarianism as little better than downright infidelity."

Christian conservatism completely engulfed the unorthodox who had been imported by liberal aristocrats of the post-Revolutionary period. Horace Holley, a brilliant young Unitarian who had made Transylvania University in Kentucky the focus of intellectual life in the West, was driven from his post in 1827, a martyr to the growing intolerance of churchgoers. He had opposed the doctrine of the depravity of human nature, preached a religion of love and tolerance, and adopted a genial manner of living which included card playing and the exhibition of a nude female statue.

When Jefferson invited Thomas Cooper, a refugee from Northern anti-Jacobin sentiments, to become professor of chemistry in the newly founded University of Virginia, the vehement objections of the people of Virginia forced Cooper to decline the offer. Despite Jefferson's hopes, religious instruction was added to the curriculum; chaplains from different Christian sects lectured on the evidences of Christianity. Cooper became president of the South Carolina College. After fourteen years in this capacity he was forced to resign. He had affronted the beliefs of the clergy and as a consequence caused a great decline in the enrollment of the college. This tactless old man had declared that the book of Genesis was a collection of "absurd and frivolous tales," that greedy priests had ordained the Sabbath, and that Christ had prohibited public prayer. After Cooper's resignation a professorship of Christian ethics was established; and James H. Thornwell became president of the college.

Freedom of religion at the University of North Carolina was ef-

[5] Richard M. Weaver, "The Older Religiousness of the South," *Sewanee Review*, LI, 248 (Spring, 1944).

fectively blocked by the despotism of its Presbyterian president, Joseph Caldwell, and by an act of the legislature declaring: "If any student shall deny the being of a God, or the divine authority of the Holy Scriptures, or shall assert, and endeavor to propagate among the students any principle subversive of the Christian religion, he shall be dismissed."

By 1860 religious liberalism was virtually extinct in the South. Only 20 of the 634 Universalist churches in the United States and 3 of the 257 Unitarian societies were to be found in the area. Unitarianism, which John C. Calhoun had supported financially in 1832, was hard pressed to prove that it was neither atheistic nor agnostic. Unitarian churches that had been established at Augusta, Savannah, Mobile, and Richmond died out, leaving only small and isolated groups at Charleston, Louisville, and New Orleans. Thomas Cooper was the last of the skeptics to arouse a widespread public antagonism; after his retirement so few skeptics remained in the South that controversy seldom occurred.

The Old South accepted science as a fascinating and useful technology, and tolerated many of its practioneers. Yet this interest did not create a skepticism or a tendency to make of scientific postulates a religion. When it attempted to deflect the Southerner from the view that man holds a central position in the universe under divine direction, the Southerner for the most part was unconcerned. The storm created in contemporary England by the discoveries of geology, for example, was not even approximated in the South. Instead, eminent scientists tried to reconcile orthodox religion with science. Henry W. Ravenel of South Carolina claimed that the antiquity of the earth established by geology did not conflict with the Mosaic account of creation, and Matthew F. Maury of Virginia, quoting the Bible to confirm the teachings of physical geography, maintained that the Mosaic account of creation was correct. The less learned were less conciliatory. Should science disagree with divine revelation, said a student of the University of Virginia in 1860, "away with science and cling to our Bible." [6] In an address at the University of North Carolina in 1853 J. H. Dickinson asserted that geology furnished no clue to the mysteries of creation and that speculation concerning the origin of the world provided only negative results and fostered infidelity.

Intellectual radicalism and humanitarian reform swept New England in the 1830's and 1840's. Men searched for the meaning of the new day that seemed to be dawning and turned with enthusiasm to the betterment of conditions on earth. There were transcendentalists, Unitarians, spiritualists, experimenters in utopias, feminists, free lovers,

[6] Clement Eaton, *Freedom of Thought in the Old South*, pp. 288, 311 n.

prohibitionists, abolitionists, and advocates of reforms in the treatment of the blind, the insane, the uneducated, and the criminal. Perfection on earth seemed to have replaced perfection in heaven as the ideal of the Yankee world.

Nearly all the reform movements,[7] derisively called "isms," filled the South with cold disdain. The South, said Henry W. Ravenel in 1857, was "the breakwater which is to stay that furious tide of social and political heresies now setting toward us from the shores of the old world."[8] The spiritualists in Fayette County, Virginia, the Icarians in Fannin County, Texas, the revolutionary Free German societies of Richmond and Louisville, and the experimenters in Frances Wright's interracial communism at Nashoba Farm in Tennessee, were regarded with suspicion and hostility by Southerners. These experimental communities soon failed.

Southern women enjoyed many privileges. Mississippi in 1839 was the first American state to grant married women equal rights to property. But generally the woman's rights movement won few supporters south of the Potomac. Most southern women lacked education in public questions. The injunctions of St. Paul prevented their seeking equal rights with men, and the prevailing cult of chivalry furthered the double standard. The women were shielded from lewd or profane words and were expected to stay within the sphere of the home and to uphold the religious tradition. It was the custom at social gatherings for the two sexes to segregate themselves. An exasperate foreigner commented: "There appears to be no sympathy between the sexes. They have no subjects of conversation in common."[9]

The women were willing perpetuators of this system. They had no particular desire to speak in public. Nor were they attracted by the ugly if practical clothes designed by Amelia Jenks Bloomer. To the Southerner—devoted to home life and jealous of the reputations of his women folk—the free love or "complex marriages" of the Oneida Community in New York were simply unthinkable. Even such a mild aspect of perfectionism as organizations for universal peace made little progress in the South. Angelina and Sarah Grimké, members of the aristocratic and wealthy family of Charleston, were unique among the women of the Old South. After becoming Quakers, they left South Carolina for the North, where they could advance their antislavery and feminist views more freely and could give social recognition to a mulatto kinsman. They were regarded as outcasts in Charleston; there one

[7] For exceptions see below, p. 164.
[8] Cited in Eaton, *op. cit.*, p. 330.
[9] Una P. Hennessy, ed., *An Aristocratic Journey; Being the Outspoken Letters of Mrs. Basil Hall*, pp. 212–30.

of their abolitionist pamphlets was publicly burned, and its authors threatened with imprisonment if they returned home.

One of the basic objectives of the New England awakening was the abolition of slavery. The reason for its ban in the South is obvious. Southerners were quick to see the relationship of the antislavery crusade to other reforms. They saw William Lloyd Garrison supplement abolitionism with advocacy of woman's rights, peace, and the abolition of Sabbathkeeping. They saw Horace Mann, the educational reformer, load the copybooks with antislavery mottoes. They cited Harriet Beecher Stowe as an example of the union of abolitionism and feminism. Southern thinkers knew that faith in the ability of man to create perfection in one respect led logically to a general applicability. Therefore, not believing in the possibility of general perfection, they would have none of it—or only so much of the reform movement as could be fitted comfortably into the needs of the conservative South.

Moreover, in the opinion of thoughtful Southerners, the New England reform movements were a capital offense against traditional religion. They assumed that man was capable of perfection on earth, with the supreme aim of bringing heaven to earth. This repudiated the traditional assumption that since perfection could exist only in heaven, man should strive to attain salvation in the next world. Southern thinkers believed that it was no mere accident that the triumph of the "isms" in New England was accompanied by a breakdown of orthodox faith and the emergence of transcendentalists, Unitarians, agnostics, atheists, and other "Northern fanatics" and freethinkers.

As has been said, Southerners accepted the elements of nineteenth century progress that did not disturb their dedication to orthodox religion and social conservatism. The South's adoptions of universal white manhood suffrage carried with it a conviction comforting to conservatives. This conviction was that the common man was no revolutionist but as stalwart a supporter of the Southern heritage as the most privileged aristocrat. At the suggestion of Dorothea L. Dix and Samuel G. Howe, both Bostonians, the South instituted reforms in the treatment of the insane and the blind, but these innovations were not of general social significance.

The most notable reform movement of the Old South was the temperance movement. It originated in New England and was furthered by the same faith in the possibilities of earthly perfection that led Southerners to condemn other reform agitations. The editors of Northern temperance journals, however, were careful to disassociate themselves from those who wanted to change the peculiar institutions of the South. Temperance reform was in harmony with the puritanical feelings of many Southerners. John B. O'Neall and Robert B. Rhett of

South Carolina and Governor Henry A. Wise and General John H. Cocke of Virginia were prominent antiliquor crusaders. On his plantation Cocke erected a temple with the inscription: "Dedicated to the Sons of Temperance." In 1839, Josiah Flournoy, a rich planter and Methodist lay reader, led petitioners to demand that the Georgia legislature outlaw the retailing of liquors. The proposal was defeated by a vote of 98 to 54. The Washingtonian movement for total abstinence had many aggressive local units in Southern colleges in 1842, notably at the University of Virginia. In 1851 the Sons of Temperance had more than 13,000 members in Georgia, and the agitations of Father Theobald Mathew in New Orleans brought forth 12,000 abstinence pledges. By 1860 Puritanism was as deeply embedded in the Southern consciousness as was the legend of the gay Cavalier. In fact, it was more prevalent in Alabama and Mississippi than in Massachusetts and Connecticut. Dancing, card playing, and Sunday pleasures were widely condemned.

The most startling contribution of the Old South to religion was the reconciliation of Christianity with slavery. During the early years of the Republic, Southern churches condemned slavery for very much the same reasons that Jefferson had. A typical expression of the opinion of the times was the resolution of the General Committee of the Virginia Baptists in 1789, declaring that "slavery is a violent deprivation of the rights of nature and inconsistent with the republican government and therefore recommend it to our brethren to make use of every legal means to extirpate this horrid evil from the land."

The mood of the Southern churches, however, was reversed after cotton growing became profitable and after abolitionists started their agitations. The interference by the state in the relations between master and servant was declared unwarranted scripturally, and the failure of Christ and His apostles to interfere with the slavery of their day was cited to sustain this position. "The right of holding slaves," declared a distinguished Baptist clergyman of South Carolina, "is clearly established in the Holy Scriptures both by precept and example." [10] James H. Thornwell defined slavery as an obligation to labor for another determined by the providence of God. Though founded on a curse, it was not inconsistent with the spirit of the Gospel, as that spirit operates among "rebels and sinners" in a degraded world, he added. President William A. Smith of Randolph-Macon College offered a less complex argument, declaring that slavery was divinely established and that it was the duty of all good men to defend it.

The proslavery churchmen of the South used the bondage of the

[10] Dr. James C. Furman, cited in William W. Sweet, *The Story of Religion in America*, p. 427.

soul to make more secure the bondage of the body. After the Denmark Vesey threat, slaveholders suppressed the independent African Methodist church, and such believers in religious freedom as the Reverend Morris Brown of Charleston were forced to move out of the South. Negro religious activities were placed directly under white control and it became the habit of white clergymen to give a generous portion of their services to the slaves. Orthodox planters felt that a minister who was not good enough for their slaves was not good enough for them; hence, such eminent divines as the Methodist Bishops William Capers and Holland N. McTyeire, Baptist James C. Furman and Basil Manly, and Presbyterian Thornwell and Benjamin M. Palmer, willingly assumed the obligation of preaching to the slaves. Negroes were especially welcomed at camp meetings and other revivals since they were likely to respond most promptly to the challenges of the pulpit. In those communities in which whites were numerous and Negroes few, the blacks were segregated in the galleries. If Negroes predominated they usually worshipped in separate buildings.

The slaves were taught such scriptural injunctions as "Servant obey thy masters"; "Render therefore unto Caesar the things which are Caesar's"; and "Well done, thou good and faithful servant." They were also taught that it was the duty of the Christian to endure the tribulations and trials of this world in order to gain blessings in the world to come. These teachings helped to keep the Negroes satisfied with their earthly position. As a reward they were allowed to hold religious assemblies independent of those held under direct white supervision. In these independent meetings carefully selected Negro exhorters were allowed to speak. Although these congregations were highly emotional, they gathered for the same purpose as whites: to return to the Bible to discover salvation. There was no acceptance of New England heresies or retrogression to African paganism. The Negroes had been well indoctrinated by their masters.

White pastors and masters had reasons to be proud of their aggressive interest in the religious life of the slaves. They despised abolitionists for saying that Negroes were not the sons of Ham. But they felt an almost equal contempt for the disreputable minority of Southerners who would not regard the Negro as a human who possessed a soul worthy of salvation. The slave, said Thornwell, was neither a tool, a chattel, nor a brute, but an immortal spirit assigned to a peculiar position in this world of sin. Such men as Thornwell gave as much energy and zeal to the religious welfare of the Negroes as they did to refuting arguments of the abolitionists. Bishop Leonidas Polk, who was ardent in his proslavery views, joined hundreds of other planters and their wives in establishing slave Sunday schools. Although oral instruction was the safest way to teach the Negro the Bible, a few slaves were taught to read and write.

Slaves, as well as their masters, benefitted from their conversion to Christianity. Millions of Negroes found comfort and hope in the belief that a life of labor and privation would be followed by the glorious rewards of heaven. Christianity softened the impact of master on slave, an influence wholly lacking in ancient Rome. Southern masters and mistresses supplemented scriptural teachings against freedom by a liberal practice of the scriptural injunctions in favor of charity, compassion, and mercy toward the meek and lowly.

CHAPTER XI

Education in the Old South

THE CULTURAL background of the Old South favored the development of a distinguished system of higher education. Thomas Jefferson and other leaders of the Revolutionary period were trained in the only college existing in the area, the College of William and Mary, but a majority of them were educated in Europe and the colleges of the North. Rich planters, especially those of South Carolina, sent their sons to Eton, Oxford, and the Middle Temple. Of the 350 Americans admitted to the Inns of Court in London before 1860, nearly two thirds were from the South or were closely identified with it. Harvard, Yale, and Princeton were so intimately concerned with Southern education that Jefferson complained in 1821 that "Harvard will still prime it over us with her twenty professors." [1] Nearly half the students of Princeton in 1850 came from the South. Among the eminent Southern statesmen educated in the North were John C. Calhoun, William L. Yancey, Robert Toombs, Joseph E. Brown, Henry A. Wise, and Judah P. Benjamin.

The college-bred statesmen of the South promoted the establishment of state institutions in their own section of the nation. In 1785 Georgia issued the first charter for a state university in the United States, but the first state university actually to begin instruction was North Carolina, ten years later. The University of Georgia and the South Carolina College started operation in 1801 and 1804 respectively. The University of Virginia opened its doors in 1825, Alabama and Tennessee in 1831 and 1832 respectively, and Mississippi and Louisiana sixteen years later. Kentucky had no state university, but Transylvania

[1] Cited in Albert B. Hart, *Slavery and Abolition*, p. 24.

University for a time was partially state supported. The Civil War frustrated the Texan plan of 1858 for the establishment of a state institution.

Religious denominations vied with the states in the promotion of higher education. The Presbyterians, inspired by the example of Princeton and frightened by the secular spirit of state education, established Hampden-Sydney College in Virginia in 1776 and Washington College (now Washington and Lee University) in the same state in 1782. Davidson in North Carolina, Oglethorpe in Georgia, Erskine in South Carolina, and Centre in Kentucky were also founded by Presbyterians. The Methodists set up Randolph-Macon in Virginia in 1832, Emory in Georgia, Emory and Henry in Virginia, Wofford in South Carolina, and Trinity in North Carolina. Early prejudices against formal education, especially against the education of ministers, delayed the establishment of Baptist colleges. Mercer in Georgia led the way for this denomination in 1833, followed by Wake Forest in North Carolina in 1834, Richmond in Virginia in 1840, Furman in South Carolina in 1850, and Carson-Newman in Tennessee in 1851. Other denominational colleges were Bethany in Virginia (now West Virginia), established in 1840 by the Disciples of Christ, and Roanoke, founded by Lutherans in Virginia in 1853. Although denominational colleges were most numerous in Tennessee and Kentucky, those of Virginia were stronger.

No Southern college followed the example of Oberlin in admitting women students, but there is no truth to the charge that Southern distinctions of sex prohibited women from enjoying educational facilities comparable to those of men. Elizabeth Female Academy, a Methodist school at Old Washington in Mississippi, was chartered as a college in 1819, and in 1836 the Georgia Female College (now Wesleyan College) was authorized to give degrees. Although Vassar in New York, which did not open its doors until 1865, is generally accepted as the first institution for women in the United States that actually adopted college standards, these institutions of the lower South made strong efforts in that direction. La Grange Female College in Georgia, Warrenton Female College in North Carolina, Science Hill in Kentucky, and Hollins and Mary Baldwin colleges in Virginia were other early schools for women.

"If college attendance is any test of an educated people," says the historian Frank L. Owsley, "the South had more educated men and women in proportion to [white] population than the North, or any other part of the world." According to the census of 1860, out of a white population of 7,400,000 there were 25,882 students enrolled in Southern colleges; whereas in the North, with a white population of

19,000,000, there were only 27,408 students enrolled in college. There was one student for each 247 white inhabitants in the South and one in 703 in the North. The South's 260 colleges represented half the total of the United States. Although the enrollments of most Southern colleges was small, William E. Dodd shows that in the decade between 1850 and 1860 "practically every college and university doubled in attendance." A few institutions, like the University of Virginia, had over five hundred students. The annual outlay of the southern states for higher education in 1860 was $708,000, while the wealthier New England states spent only one half this amount.[2]

The quality of Southern higher education was not inferior to that of the North. Emphasis was placed on Greek and Latin; their most scholarly exponent was Professor Basil L. Gildersleeve of the University of Virginia. The devotion of Southern students to the classics and their participation in recitations and debates of the literary societies accounts to a large degree for the grace of manner, classical allusions, and flowing melody of the Old South's numerous orators.

Although historical and literary scholarship was neglected in Southern academic circles, this was not true of the natural and social sciences. Robert Dale Owen was disappointed when he failed to obtain a professorship at the University of Alabama in 1847; there Frederick A. P. Barnard, Michael Tuomey, and John W. Mallet made notable scientific studies. John and Joseph LeConte were brilliant teachers of science at the South Carolina College and the University of Georgia, and Louis Agassiz did some of his greatest work at the Medical College of Charleston. The first systematic observations of the stars to be made in the United States utilized the astronomical observatory of the University of North Carolina for which President Joseph Caldwell had been responsible. William B. Rogers, who later founded the Massachusetts Institute of Technology, lectured at the University of Virginia. Francis Lieber of the South Carolina College was the foremost teacher of political science in the United States, and at the University of Louisiana James D. B. De Bow introduced modern methods of teaching the commercial subjects. Josiah C. Nott of the University of New Orleans was a scientist who attempted to prove that all men did not come from a common ancestor.

A number of Southern physicians made contributions to the advance of medical science. Ephraim McDowell of Kentucky was a pioneer in abdominal surgery. Marion Sims of Alabama has been adjudged "the father of modern gynecology" because in the 1840's he

[2] Frank L. Owsley, *Plain Folk of the Old South*, pp. 147–148; William E. Dodd, *The Cotton Kingdom*, pp. 111, 112 n.; Clement Eaton, *Freedom of Thought in the Old South*, p. 196.

operated on three slave women afflicted with fistula. Crawford W. Long of Georgia in 1842 discovered the use of ether as an anesthetic.

The South had distinguished college presidents: Basil Manly of the University of Alabama; Frederick A. P. Barnard of the University of Mississippi; the inimitable Thomas Cooper, whom South Carolina College tolerated for years; Augustus B. Longstreet, the humorist, who served as president of Emory College, the University of Mississippi, and the South Carolina College; and William A. Smith, preacher and proslavery moralist, of Randolph-Macon College.

The University of Virginia was the South's most original contribution to education. Its foundation was a landmark in the history of higher education in the United States, and Thomas Jefferson, the university's father, regarded it as one of his three greatest accomplishments. For its use he designed what is called "the only perfect college quadrangle in America." Unlike most designers of educational buildings who have come after him, Jefferson made his architectural plans conform to the design of his school rather than to those of a book of architecture. "This institution," said the great Virginian, "will be based on the illimitable freedom of the human mind. For here we are not afraid to follow the truth wherever it may lead, nor to tolerate any error, so long as reason is left free to combat it." It was perhaps the most liberal educational project of its time. There were to be no religious tests for professors or students, but students of theological schools were invited to attend. The modern languages and the sciences were given equal importance with the classics and mathematics. Agriculture and political science for the first time found places in the curriculum of an American university. Students were allowed to choose their own studies from a wide list of subjects provided by the eight vertical "schools" into which the university was divided. Provision was made for student self-government and for the honor system under which the students themselves supervised examinations. The American method of control by a president chosen by a nonresident board of trustees was rejected in favor of faculty government under the chairmanship of one of its own members. To promote liberalizing influences from aboard professors were brought from Europe. After initial setbacks caused by inadequate financial support, the University of Virginia prospered materially, attracting many students from the leading families of the cotton states and earning fame for its courses in the liberal arts and law.

It did not, however, attain the Jeffersonian ideals. Southern public opinion was hostile to the deistic atmosphere, and the students took advantage of the mild discipline to live riotously and to commit acts of lawlessness. They were not sufficiently trained to accept the European standards that foreign professors imposed. Jefferson's university did not become a second Harvard, a means by which the South might have become acquainted with other regions of the world. It schooled its sons well for American politics, but not for the necessities of diplomacy created by the Civil War crisis.

Basic to the success of the colleges of the Old South were the secondary schools known as academies. They prepared students for college and often were themselves the nuclei from which colleges developed. The University of Virginia grew from Albemarle Academy; Hampden-Sydney from Prince Edward Academy; Washington (now Washington and Lee University) from Liberty Hall Academy; and the University of Nashville from Davidson Academy. In 1850 there were 3,000 academies in the South; a state as new as Arkansas had 90 such institutions.

The academy was an institution of English origin adapted to the needs of the Southern frontier, and it was found in greatest number in the piedmont regions. Planters who wished their sons to acquire the training of gentlemen banded together to establish academies. These schools operated under state charters, were endowed by private subscription, and governed by self-perpetuating boards of trustees drawn from the public-spirited men of the community. Although they occasionally received state or denominational aid, they always depended primarily on student fees for current expenses. Generally religious in tone, they avoided the narrow sectarianism which divided the people of the South; this was a necessary precaution to win the allegiance of whole communities. They had few books and no expensive equipment, and their buildings varied from a single log house to several well-built structures.

Their teachers, whoever could be found, taught only subjects which they had themselves mastered and could convey to their pupils, solving the problem, as John Gould Fletcher notes,[3] between the mere acquisition of knowledge and the "acquisition of power for independent work."

Since most of the teachers were college trained, the instruction was classical: Latin and Greek, elementary mathematics, English grammar, and metaphysics. Some academies offered training in the natural sciences and manual arts. Virginia Military Institute and The Citadel in Charleston were noted for their training of officers who later distinguished themselves in the cause of the Confederacy. But the main purpose of the academies was the education of young men in law and politics, virtually the only professions open to gentlemen. Most successful in this respect was the Reverend Moses Waddel's school which flourished at Willington in South Carolina between 1804 and 1819. Its

[3] In Twelve Southerners, *I'll Take My Stand*, p. 103.

pupils included John C. Calhoun, William H. Crawford, Hugh S. Legaré, George McDuffie, Augustus B. Longstreet, and James L. Petigru.

The academy system had two great defects. One was the indulgence in "an almost undisciplined orgy of political oratory and civic patriotism" to the neglect of modern literature and philosophic criticism which might have given the South a better understanding of itself and its potential enemies. Its other great fault was its complete neglect of children whose parents were unable or unwilling to pay tuition fees. Yet this limitation had the advantage of eliminating the unfit of the type who encumber the modern high school. The tuition, board, and lodging charges were exceedingly small. For less than $150 a year a boy or a girl could attend an academy in the Old South.[4]

The Old South was slow in supplementing its generous provisions for higher education with provisions equally generous for the common people on the elementary level. Survivals out of the Colonial past were the "old field schools" and the private tutors. The old field school was a one-teacher affair maintained by private subscription. Tutors were usually young Northerners who were eagerly received in plantation households. "Every man brought his son or his daughter," wrote a tutor of his experiences in Virginia, "and rejoiced that the day was arrived when their little ones could light their tapers at the torch of knowledge." Both the old field schools and tutorial systems were designed for the upper classes and did not meet the needs of the masses.

A dark cloud of illiteracy hung over the slave states far into the nineteenth century. As is explained elsewhere,[5] the Negroes were prohibited from going to school and were therefore largely illiterate. Conditions among the lower-class whites were almost as bad. During the 1830's various observers estimated that about a third of the adult white population was illiterate. Of the 4,682 men who applied for marriage licenses in Virginia in 1818, 1,127 could not write their names. Governor David Campbell pointed out twenty years later that there had been no significant improvement in this record and that he feared it would have been worse had the women been required to sign their marriage licenses. Twenty-eight of the 111 North Carolinians who testified before a Congressional committee investigating an election in 1831 made their marks, being unable to write their names. The South Carolina legislature was informed in 1847 that the state was paying for the education of less than 9,000 children and that there were eight times this many South Carolina children who were not attending school. According to the census of 1850, 8.27 per cent of the adult white population of the slave states were illiterate as compared with

[4] Owsley, op. cit., p. 148.
[5] See below, p. 260.

3.36 per cent in the non-slaveholding states. Of the various elements of the American white population, only certain European immigrant groups were more illiterate than the Southern whites.[6]

The neglect of public education was traceable to the circumstances of Southern life rather than to deliberate conspiracy against the enlightenment of the masses. Schools flourish where large groups of people are conveniently brought together; the Old South had a scattered rural population and bad roads. Southerners did not inherit from English ancestors any belief that it was the duty of the state to furnish schools for all children. Many Southerners preferred private to public education, believing that an education for which the individual paid was superior to one that the state furnished. Governor George R. Gilmer of Georgia expressed this attitude when he declared in 1830: "The policy of making appropriations by the Government to effect objects which are within the means of individuals has always appeared to me to be extremely questionable."

Many common people in the South were unwilling to take advantage of such schools as the states provided. President Joseph Caldwell of the University of North Carolina remarked that great numbers of the illiterate or semi-illiterate people were proud of their ignorance of "book learning" and were contemptuous of the profession of teaching. William Gregg could get only 60 children from 800 people in his cotton factory at Graniteville, South Carolina, to go to school. Moncure D. Conway reported conditions in Virginia in 1850: "There was little or no longing for education among the poor whites—probably more among the Negroes." Many were too proud of their liberties to allow their children to be herded into classrooms, and were opposed to the financial burdens of education. President Caldwell predicted in 1832 that any proposal to establish a school system supported solely by taxation was doomed to failure at the hands of public opinion. This attitude was to some degree justified by the realization that the education available was of little practical use.

Despite these obstacles, the Old South made definite progress in establishing a system of universal education for white children at public expense similar to that of Prussia or New England. Thomas Jefferson furnished the leadership. In Virginia and throughout the South he spread the conviction that if government were to be based on the consent of the governed, the state should provide schools for the training of the people. He introduced in the Virginia legislature of 1779 the Bill for the More General Diffusion of Knowledge, whose purpose was "to illuminate, as far as practical, the minds of the people at large" in

[6] Charles S. Sydnor, *Development of Southern Sectionalism, 1819–1848*, pp. 59, 305; Eaton, *op. cit.*, pp. 64–67. Cf. Owsley, *op. cit.*, p. 146.

order that popular government might not be "perverted by tyranny."
He believed "that those persons, whom nature hath endowed with
genius and virtue" should be "educated at the common expence . . .
without regard to wealth, birth or other accidental condition or circumstance." Although Jefferson did not demand education for everyone regardless of his talents, he felt that the worthy among the poor
and the obscure should not be denied opportunities. His ideas were
embodied into a law in 1796, but were never actually carried out, for
local authorities failed to implement it.

The Jeffersonian idea of popular education did not die. North Carolina and Georgia were, respectively, the second and third states of the
Union to make constitutional provisions for schools. Their example
was followed by Tennessee in 1835, Virginia in 1851, and by all the
states of the Southwest, with the exception of Louisiana, on their admission into the Union. Louisiana joined the others in 1845; South
Carolina was thus the only state of the Old South that did not assume
the educational burden by constitutional declaration.

Individual states financed their public education in different ways.
In spite of her neglect of Jefferson's law Virginia gave some support
to public education. A long line of governors endorsed it; in 1810 a
Literary Fund was established, and eight years later a law was enacted
providing that portions of this fund be distributed among the counties
and towns for the education of children of the poor. In 1811 South
Carolina, to compensate for her lack of permanent endowments for
school purposes, established by direct appropriations to each county
as many schools as there were members of the legislature and granted
to each $300 annually. These institutions were free to all whites, but,
since the wealthy were reluctant to use them, they were generally regarded as charitable agencies. After toying unsuccessfully with a grand
plan of popular education under the control of the state legislature,
Georgia, by legislative acts of 1817, 1821, and 1822, created endowments for the support of poor children in schools that would receive
them. Although, as in other states, invidious distinctions were drawn
between rich and poor, the Georgia laws placed elementary instruction
within reach of many children to whom it would otherwise have been
denied. Tennessee owed the origin of its public schools to an act of
Congress in 1806 which set aside public lands for educational purposes.
The funds arising from the sale of these lands were not sufficient to
set up a school system until 1830. The "pauper school" stigma was imposed upon Tennessee children by the law authorizing free textbooks
for poor children. North Carolina was slow to carry out the educational
mandates of its constitution, enacting no legislation in behalf of public
education until 1826, when its Literary Fund was established. North

Carolinians were aware of the benefits of public schools, but were confused about the forms their schools should take, and were especially adverse to paying the necessary taxes. Archibald D. Murphey's report of 1817, providing for the education of the white people without distinction of class, was rejected, but the idea was to bear fruit later.

Thus, by 1830 the older states of the South had made definite beginnings in public education. Unfortunately, the state-supported schools were considered pauper institutions, designed primarily for those who could not pay for their education. It is questionable whether the training children received in these schools counterbalanced the stigma of their attendance. The South was slow to adopt the American ideal that education is a civil right that should be extended to all children regardless of their social or economic status.

Gradually, however, a favorable atmosphere for the fruition of this idea developed in the 1830's. Every Southern state except South Carolina set up literary funds, educational endowments similar to those created in Tennessee in 1806 and Virginia in 1810. These eliminated the need of direct taxation for educational purposes. In Virginia this fund was derived from escheats, fines, forfeitures, and other properties accruing to the commonwealth, but in other states it was derived from the sale of public lands. The endowments were often mismanaged; in Tennessee, for example, it was discovered in 1837 that the state treasurer had robbed the school fund of more than $120,000. Nevertheless, the literary funds grew. Texas set aside 50 million acres for schools, giving that state the largest permanent endowment for education in the United States.

When in 1837 the federal government distributed its surplus revenue among the states, the South received some 8.5 million dollars; much of this money was allocated to the public school reserves. Grants from the literary funds were often made contingent upon local levies in order to surmount opposition to local taxation. In North Carolina, where this strategy was most successful, $193,000 was collected in 1860. The adoption of universal white manhood suffrage by the Southern states in the 1830's and 1840's increased the obligation for universal education.

The centrally administered educational systems inaugurated by Horace Mann, Henry Barnard, and Thaddeus Stevens in Massachusetts, Connecticut, and Pennsylvania challenged leaders of the South. Educational reformers appeared in the land of slavery. Plantation aristocrats fell in line with the liberal trend of the nation in this respect. Men of humble origin advocated reform: Governor Joseph E. Brown of Georgia, Christopher G. Memminger of South Carolina, Albert G. Brown of Mississippi, and Andrew Johnson of Tennessee. They were joined by representatives of the upper class: Archibald D. Murphey of North Carolina, Governor Henry A. Wise of Virginia, and Robert J. Breckinridge of Kentucky. Plebeian and patrician alike desired to bring schools to the white masses and use them as agencies for eliminating class distinctions. "Let the children of the richest and the poorest parents in the State," said Governor Brown, "meet in the schoolroom on terms of perfect equality of right. Let there be no aristocracy there but an aristocracy of color and conduct." Governor Wise struck at the "pauper school" idea, declaring that poor children should have the right "to taste of the more delicate food of the mind" rather than merely the coarser husks provided by the charity schools.

In the two decades preceding the Civil War the Southern states made notable achievements toward realizing their ideals. North Carolina in 1839 adopted a state-controlled system of free education modeled largely on that of Massachusetts. Tennessee and Alabama followed her example in 1845, Louisiana in 1847. In Mississippi, Florida, Arkansas, and Texas state funds were created for this purpose, but they were not applied. Georgia, South Carolina, and Virginia retained the decentralized systems they had adopted early in the century.

Kentucky's and North Carolina's educational progress was greater than that of other states in the Old South. Robert J. Breckinridge, state superintendent of education in Kentucky, in the 1840's assured his state a progressive school system by protecting the school fund and by inducing the legislature to impose a two cent educational tax on all property. Calvin J. Wiley, elected first superintendent of public education for North Carolina in 1852, adopted measures which led to the establishment of 3,000 schools enjoying an annual revenue of $279,000; this law showed "a grasp of educational problems, a comprehension of school difficulties and school needs and a modernity of methods and aims that are truly astonishing." [7] Alabama, under William B. Perry as state superintendent, emulated North Carolina, spending $474,000 in 1856 for the education of 90,000 children. By 1860 the larger cities of the South had school systems as good as those of Northern cities. De Bow described education in New Orleans as "one of the most perfect systems of public schools in America." Charleston's educational program was headed by a normal school and a distinguished city college, and in Memphis more than 1,600 pupils attended 21 schools. In the rural areas almost as much had been accomplished.

Dodd has shown that the cotton states were spending $2,432,000 for the education of 425,600 children in 1860. This meant that one child in every seven members of the white race was in school as compared

[7] Stephen B. Weeks, cited in Edgar W. Knight, *Public Education in the South,* p. 252.

with one child for every five or five and one half persons in the remainder of the United States. This also meant the reduction of the high illiteracy rate of 1850 to figures not much greater than those of the states of the Middle West.[8]

At the end of the ante-bellum period rural isolation and popular inflexibility were still handicaps to educational progress, and a major revolution was needed to force the land of slavery from its dark resolve not to transmit the light of learning to its Negro minority. Yet for its white majority public schools of the South were establishing a creditable record. Then came the destruction of the Civil War. While this catastrophe was approaching, Wiley, the North Carolina apostle of free education, wrote with poignant apprehension: "A great and glorious revolution seemed to be rapidly going on, and in ten years if we had been permitted to pursue our career every citizen could have lifted up his head as a member of a rich, happy and powerful Commonwealth."

[8] William E. Dodd, *op. cit.*, p. 115.

CHAPTER XII

Ante-Bellum Literature

>➤➤➤-➤➤➤-➤➤➤-➤➤➤-➤➤➤-➤➤➤-➤➤➤-➤➤➤-➤➤➤-➤➤➤-➤➤➤-➤➤➤-➤➤➤-➤➤➤-➤➤➤-➤➤➤-➤➤➤-➤➤➤-➤➤

THE MOST flourishing literary art of the Old South was public speech. Fostered by the study of Demosthenes and Cicero in the classical curriculum of colleges and academies, oratory was the only extracurricular activity for most students. As Herbert M. McLuhan remarks, this forensic education "was no mere archaelogical revival;" it carried with it "the full gentlemanly code of honor, dignity, and courtesy." It was the main weapon of defense in the controversies over Southern institutions and aroused widespread popular interest in political contests. Until the rise of the military leader in 1861, the orator-politician was almost the sole hero of the South. He appealed to an unsophisticated rural folk by his florid language, his rhetorical circumlocutions, and his picturesque appearance. The Southerner qualified easily in an art that required colorful personality and extravagant speech rather than sensitive imagination and disciplined expression.

A thousand and one orators flourished south of the Potomac between 1820 and 1860. At the top of the list were Seargent S. Prentiss of Mississippi and William L. Yancey of Alabama. Prentiss won the admiration of the South by a magnetic personality, a voice of silver, and the ability to marshal a wide range of materials in orderly form with little preparation. Yancey was a duelist and a fiery advocate of secession principles who scorned patronizing acclaim and recognized only the dictates of his own judgment. The eloquence with which he expressed his convictions moved his audiences as effectively as the persuasive oratory of a camp-meeting speaker.

Not all rhetoricians, however, were of the Prentiss-Yancey types. There was John Randolph of Roanoke who in neither personal appearance nor manners resembled the prototype. Yet he won fame by his brilliant invective, criticism, and taunts of those who sacrificed principles for expediency. There was the whole school of the defenders of Southern rights who placed logic above literary resplendence. They were classicists rather than romanticists. Their chief was John C. Calhoun, who shares a place in history with Edmund Burke as one of the few original thinkers among orators. Without resorting to the flowery brilliance so popular in his section, Calhoun devised a logical and elaborate means to preserve central authority without infringing upon the liberties of local minorities. Removed from its slavery context, his doctrine of states' rights is the classic defense of regional self-expression against the tyranny of nationalistic standardization.

Ante-bellum journalism in the South was as exuberant as its oratory. The 15 Southern newspapers of 1784 increased to 601 by 1850; 67 of these were dailies. Their columns were loaded with dull poetry and lugubrious essays; even after the telegraph was extended to the South in the 1840's they failed to give major attention to "news." Yet they were fairly popular and a few of them, because of the vehemence of their editor-politicians, exerted a section-wide influence.

The Old South was dominated by "personal journalism." "Every Southern political editorial," writes Robert S. Cotterill,[1] "contained the ingredients of a duel; many of them were potential invitations to homicide." "The cartoon of a Southern editor with a quill in one hand and a dueling pistol in the other was not entirely out of line with reality," says another historian.[2] The best-known newspaper was the Richmond *Enquirer,* which owed its popularity to the passion with which its editor, Thomas Ritchie, proclaimed his Democratic principles. Its rival was the Richmond *Whig,* as vigorously edited by John Hampden Pleasants. The deadly earnestness of the rivalry between the two newspapers was revealed when Ritchie's son killed Pleasants in a duel. In Charleston Richard Yeadon's *Courier* and Robert Barnwell Rhett's *Mercury* carried on a similar warfare. The *Courier* represented at first Jacksonian nationalism and later the conservatism of the Whig party; the *Mercury* advocated nullification and secession as uncompromisingly as William Lloyd Garrison's *Liberator* promoted the antislavery cause. The *Mercury* strove to "fire the Southern heart" to rid itself of the "subserviency to the North" which it accused the conservative press of furthering. In Louisville, George D. Prentice, the Whig editor of the *Journal,* contended with Walter N. Haldeman, the secessionist editor of the *Courier.* Prentice's vitriolic paragraphs made his newspaper the most influential Whig organ in the South. The most

[1] Robert S. Cotterill, *The Old South,* p. 299.
[2] Clement Eaton, *A History of the Old South,* p. 483.

vivid personality in Southern journalism was Parson William G. Brownlow, editor of the nationalistic and proslavery Knoxville *Whig*. He lived a life of continued tumult amid neighbors exasperated by his vituperative attacks on every doctrine that hinted at Southern independence. Public opinion demanded that the newspapers support the institution of slavery. When this rule was violated, as in the case of Cassius M. Clay's *The True American* of Lexington, Kentucky, the journal was suppressed and the editor deported.

The newspaper conforming nearest to twentieth-century standards was the New Orleans *Picayune* which was founded in 1837 by George W. Kendall. It expressed the conservative opinions of merchants, sold for a penny a copy, and was exceptionally alert in gathering news.

"The Old South," says Cotterill, "was a fertile field for newspapers but it was a graveyard for magazines." Between 1790 and 1850 more than a hundred magazines were founded, but only nine survived. Almost every town in the section at some time in its history fostered at least one of these purported evidences of literary culture. Charleston brought out no less than thirty-four magazines. Although some of them were extremely sentimental—*The Floral Wreath and Ladies Bower*, *The Magnolia*, *The Southern Rose*—many were projected by a serious literary group. Under the leadership of William Gilmore Simms, Hugh S. Legaré, James L. Petigru, and Robert Y. Hayne this group hoped to make their city the cultural capital of the South. The most pretentious of the early Charleston periodicals were the *Southern Review* (1828–32) and the *Southern Literary Gazette* (1828–29). In 1844 the two-year-old *Southern Quarterly Review* was moved from New Orleans to Charleston, where Simms kept it going until 1857. Simms then associated himself with Paul Hamilton Hayne in *Russell's Magazine*, which lasted until the year of secession.

The most successful of the Southern magazines, the *Southern Literary Messenger*, was founded in Richmond in 1834 and lasted until the firing around the city became intense thirty years later. It reflected adequately and even brilliantly the views of the slaveholding aristocracy, whose best writers contributed to its pages. The original and trenchant criticisms of its editor, Edgar Allan Poe, made it perhaps the outstanding literary medium of the United States from 1835 to 1837. Benjamin B. Minor and John R. Thompson successfully edited the magazine at other periods. Of a different nature was *De Bow's Review*, founded in New Orleans in 1846 and published, with interruptions, until fifteen years after Appomattox. It was primarily devoted to the commercial interests of the section, but the broad vision of its editor, James D. B. De Bow, made it a comprehensive explanation and defense of the economic and social life of the South. The majority of Southern magazines were so earnestly devoted to the dull purpose of proclaiming Victorian virtue in general and Southern virtue in particular that they looked upon sprightliness with horror. "To the contributors to Southern magazines," concludes Cotterill, "life was real and desperately earnest, and their mission on earth was to elevate, if it cost the life of the last subscriber." [3]

Southern magazines were but an evidence of the general failure of the Old South to produce an imaginative and critical literature commensurate with the richness and individuality of its experiences. Southerners for the most part were a new and rural people no more interested in polite letters than were frontiersmen the world over. Despite their denials, the minority who read books were not interested in a free delineation of themselves. Imaginative literature provided for them an escape into a romantic or classical past. In their colleges and academies they labored over Greek and Latin classics "from sun to sun, like the slaves in the fields," gaining inspiration for nothing more creative than oratory. In their mature years their literary taste was colonial, as they turned to the great books of the mother country— Shakespeare's oratory, the common sense of Pope and Johnson, Lord Byron's reckless adventure, Carlyle's defense of social subordination and class distinctions, and above all, Sir Walter Scott's championship of aristocracy and feudal caste. Nevertheless, Southerners were Americans, needing literary inspiration on this side of the Atlantic to supplement the stream of thought they received from England. They grudgingly turned to the North for books and magazines as frequently as for other articles of commerce.

Charleston, Richmond, and New Orleans could not compete with Boston and New York as literary centers. The Southern author, both before the Civil War and after, tried to attune his literary output to Northern sympathies. Writers of the New South were able to do this,[4] but the sectional differences of the ante-bellum period were too great to be overcome. Writers of the Old South were hostile to the humanitarian sympathies of New England and largely indifferent to the rich vein of Southern song and folklore that Northern critics encouraged their successors to exploit after the Civil War. "The suggestion," says a student of Southern letters,[5] "that the source of literature existed here, too, in these towns, on these plantations, would have been regarded as a subtle impropriety." Perhaps it was no accident that a Pennsylvanian, Stephen C. Foster, "attuned the beauty and pathos of

[3] Cotterill, *op. cit.*, pp. 299, 303.
[4] See below, pp. 427 ff.
[5] Ludwig Lewisohn, *Expression in America*, p. 79.

the Old South to the human heart in 'Uncle Ned,' 'Old Black Joe,' and 'My Old Kentucky Home.' " Southern writers loyally turned to sectional ideals and prejudices for inspiration, expecting to obtain from their proclamation of proslavery and anti-Northern sentiments a share of the applause given Southern orators and politicians. But their efforts were unrewarded. "The models before him," says William P. Trent of the author of the Old South,[6] "were those of statesmen and men of action, and he lost his chances for distinction if he proposed for himself any others. Besides, he had no critics, no audience whose applause was worth having. His easy verses were received with a smile by his friends or with extravagant praise by an editor only too glad to fill his columns."

William Gilmore Simms best illustrates the thankless role of the ante-bellum Southern author. By remaining steadfast to the ideals and prejudices of his people he failed to develop his natural talent, yet he was ignored by the people of whom he wrote. The consistency of purpose throughout his long literary career is matched in the annals of the South only by that of Ellen Glasgow.

He was born in Charleston in 1806, the son of an Irish immigrant who neither by birth nor by fortune could win a position for himself in the South Carolina ruling class. Although democratic by nature and impressed by the rough humors of the frontier, young Simms refused to migrate with his father to Mississippi. Instead, he established himself in his native city as a poet, journalist, and miscellaneous writer, and married into a family no more distinguished than his own. After the death of his wife and financial reverses, he moved North where he won the friendship of William Cullen Bryant, and gained recognition through the publication of *Martin Faber* (1833), *Guy Rivers* (1834), and *The Yemassee* (1835). However, Simms did not feel at home in the North, and returned to Charleston to devote himself to the defense of the aristocratic tradition. In 1836 he married into the landed aristocracy and established himself in rural dignity at "Woodlands," the Barnwell District estate of his father-in-law. For the next six or seven years he was a romantic writer, producing ten novels, among them the South Carolina tales, *Mellichampe* (1836) and *The Scout* (1841). As a member of the lesser gentry, he devoted the decade following 1842 to a passionate defense of South Carolina against its maligners. He wrote history, biography, essays, and oratory, edited magazines, and did whatever a literary man of industry could do to bring culture to South Carolina. In the decade before the Civil War, he turned again to romances, adding *Katherine Walton* (1851), *The Sword and the Distaff* (1853), *The Forayers* (1855), *Eutaw* (1856), and *The Cassique of*

[6] William P. Trent, *William Gilmore Simms*, p. 148.

Kiawah (1859) to his chronicle of South Carolina. Financially ruined by the Civil War, he could do little to recoup his fortunes during the five remaining years of his life. He edited *War Poetry of the South* (1867) and busied himself with journalism and serials for cheap magazines.

The tragedy of Simms's life was not the Civil War but the manner in which Charleston and the South in the days of their prosperity received his loyalty to their principles. His writings were ignored by the people of his city even after he had become known in London and New York. Although Charlestonians organized clubs for the promotion of local literature, they did not recognize the merits of their own author. Simms wrote in 1858: "All that I have [done] has been poured to waste in Charleston, . . . which has steadily ignored my claims, which had disparaged me to the last, has been the last place to give me its adhesion, to which I owe no favor, having never received an office, or a compliment, or a dollar at her hands." [7] The encouragement and the critical discipline he might have received in the North, and his natural talent for realism which might have found expression in the West were subordinated to his efforts to cajole an indifferent city.

Unlike James Fenimore Cooper, with whom Simms has often been compared, his novels lack unity of theme. His ladies and gentlemen are too fine to be convincing; his realistic characters are from the non-aristocratic class. His novels of the frontier are full of rogues, magnificent in their vulgarity and swaggering ruthlessness. Lieutenant Porgy, a huge and rowdy gourmand who prances through the pages of the Revolutionary romances, Parrington calls "the most amusing and substantial character in our early fiction." [8]

More fortunate in worldly circumstances than Simms but far less aware of the robust confusions of life was John Pendleton Kennedy, son of a Baltimore merchant and a Virginia aristocrat. His *Swallow Barn* (1832), sketches of plantation life in the days before the slavery controversy, helped to establish the plantation legend of Ole Virginia: "the mellow, bland, and sunny luxuriance of her old-time society—its good fellowship, its hearty and constitutional *companionableness,* the thriftless gaiety of the people, their dogged but amiable invincibility of opinion, and that overflowing hospitality that knows no ebb." [9] Kennedy's *Horseshoe Robinson* (1835) was an unrealistic tale, equally divided between the gentry and the common folk; *Rob of the Bowl* (1838) pictured Maryland in the days of Charles II. *Quodlibet,* a sparkling satire on Jacksonian democracy, was the last of his literary

[7] Cited *ibid.,* p. 239.
[8] Vernon C. Parrington, *The Romantic Revolution in America,* p. 131.
[9] Kennedy in *Swallow Barn* (2nd ed., New York, 1851), p. 8.

efforts, for he devoted the remainder of his life to politics. He had created flattering pictures of Southern life which, because of their simplicity, won more applause than the weightier portraits by Simms.

"The primary fact in Southern literary taste and writing before the Civil War," declares Shields McIlwaine,[10] "is its divorcement from the soil; it was an air-plant." In *Swallow Barn*, he observes, Kennedy "did not allow a playful notice of one lone poor-white to blur the genteel pattern of Squire Meriwether's estate." Yet all Southern writers were not so fastidious. Some portrayed the life of frontiersmen, yeoman farmers, and poor whites. A pioneer was William A. Caruthers, who set down in *The Kentuckian in New York* (1834) a sketch of a poor white comparable to William Byrd's comic masterpiece of a century earlier.

In 1834 was published a more notable work, *Georgia Scenes*, a book of local genre. The author was Augustus Baldwin Longstreet. After studying at Moses Waddel's academy, at Yale, and the law school in Litchfield, Connecticut, he became a jack-of-all-trades, passing from one profession to another—lawyer, newspaper editor, story writer, Methodist minister, politician, and president of four colleges. A champion of nullification and secession, he was also an active leader in establishing an independent Methodist church. He justified the writing of *Georgia Scenes* by giving these tales a moral and making them, for all their humor and crude realism, illustrative of the history of his state. By these pretentious devices Longstreet could reveal his own robust nature, free of the romantic inhibitions of other respectable Southerners. Through the interplay of practical jokes, repartee, boyish pranks, and humorous dodges, he threw authentic light upon the ways of the Georgia cracker. His favorite character, Ransy Sniffle, was a grotesque poor white.

The boisterous society that lay beyond the genteel circles of the romancers was given further literary dignity by the publication in 1834 of the purported autobiography of David Crockett. He was a mighty hunter but a shiftless farmer whose tall tales led the Tennessee voters to send him to Congress despite the opposition of Andrew Jackson. The frontier humor of this coonskin hero was recorded in a book by an anonymous writer so that Crockett might be presented as proof of the democratic spirit of the Whig party. By this partisan trick an authentic folk character was created. With a gift of speech as vivid as that of Longstreet, this frontier wastrel traveled the length of Tennessee, drinking, dancing, bragging, scratching a few acres of land, and killing enough bears in a single season to feed the dogs, hogs, and buz-

[10] *The Southern Poor-White*, p. 17.

zards as well as his own family. Parrington [11] calls him "first among the Smart Alecks of the canebrakes."

Another master of the art of boisterous realism was Joseph G. Baldwin, who recorded in *Flush Times of Alabama and Mississippi* (1853) the confusion and speculative mania of a raw and turbulent frontier society. His book is faithful in its study of character, brilliant in its description of ludicrous situations, and frank in its exposure of shams and follies. A writer in the same vein was Johnson Jones Hooper, an Alabama newspaperman, who put into his *Adventures of Captain Simon Suggs* (1846) strong doses of humor and local color.

There were many poets in the Old South but most of them were amateurs, divorced from life and tied to outworn sentiments. Hence they failed to depict the beauty and human realities which surrounded them. "The author is not a poet by profession or ambition," confessed one in a volume of his verses.[12] "He has written only at long intervals or at the instigation of trivial or transient causes." John P. Kennedy's characterization of a pamphlet of verses as "a delicate effusion of superfine sentiment woven into a plaintive tale," may pass as a description of this poetry.[13]

Three poets, however, made lasting contributions to the literature of the Old South. One was Richard Henry Wilde, a Georgia congressman, whose "My Life Is Like the Summer Rose" (1819) was set to music by Sidney Lanier. Another was Theodore O'Hara, Kentucky soldier and journalist, who is remembered for "The Bivouac of the Dead" (1847), a sonorous dirge written as a memorial to Kentuckians who fell in the Mexican War. It is still as popular with Americans as Gray's *Elegy*, and lines from it have been carved on many soldiers' monuments.

The third poet was Edgar Allan Poe, whose greatness was established beyond dispute by a score of poems, among which are *To Helen, Israfel, The City by the Sea, The Raven,* and *Annabel Lee.* Whether Poe can be called a Southerner, actually or in spirit, is not beyond dispute. Born in Boston in 1809 of actor parents, as a child he became a member of the household of John Allan, a Richmond merchant who gave him a thorough education in England and at the University of Virginia. Poe forsook Richmond at the age of eighteen but returned in 1835 to edit in brilliant fashion *The Southern Literary Messenger.* Dismissed from the editorship in 1836 because of his irascible dispo-

[11] *Op. cit.,* p. 179.
[12] Albert B. Meek, cited by Edwin Mims in *Cambridge History of American Literature,* II, 288.
[13] Cited in McIlwaine, *op. cit.,* p. 18.

sition, he soon became dissipated and irresponsible, incapable of supporting himself. He returned again to Richmond to renew a youthful
love affair shortly before his death. He died in Baltimore in 1849, as the
result of a drunken spree. From these facts it is clear that Poe was a
Southerner, in the circumstances of his life. In spirit he was certainly
not identified with New England, with its moral idealism and democratic optimism. As a literary critic he penetrated the hollowness of
New England's much-praised Henry Wadsworth Longfellow. His
stories are dominated by terror or the ingenious, not by social purpose.
As an artist, however, he always lived aloof from the Virginia world, a
romanticist, but with a romanticism completely divorced from the
school that justified plantation society. He was, in fact, a man working
out of time and place, with no relation to his environment or to his age.
Lacking human sympathy, he created a world of beauty and ghostly
fancy.

It took the emotions of the Civil War to arouse the South deeply
enough to write poetry nearer greatness than any verse the section had
created before. It was war poetry, expressing without reservation the
emotions of men in sympathy with the moral purpose and high resolve
of the Confederacy. The poets fought in battle or knew those who had.

Most popular were war songs. Soldiers adopted Daniel D. Emmett's
plantation melody, *Dixie*, and made it the favorite tune of the Confederacy. *The Bonnie Blue Flag*, an old Hibernian melody to which
Harry Macarthy, an Arkansas soldier, wrote words, was wafted from
a New Orleans theater in 1861 to take possession of the whole South.
Music and verse were best united when James R. Randall, a Marylander living in Louisiana, wrote *Maryland, My Maryland* after he
heard of the Federal invasion of his native state. The Cary sisters of
Baltimore sang these words to the tune of the German song, *Tannenbaum, O Tannenbaum* before a regiment of New Orleans soldiers, and
the song was taken up by hundreds of rebel throats to become the
Marseillaise of the Confederacy.

Every emotion of the Southern army and almost every event in its
history was expressed in verse. The gauntlet was thrown down in such
verses as Randall's *Battle Cry of the South*, Ernest Halphin's *God Save
the South*, James Barron Hope's *Oath of Freedom*, and St. George
Tucker's *The Southern Cross*. John R. Thompson supplemented dirges
for Captain William Latané and Turner Ashby with verses in a lighter
vein ridiculing the Yankees for their military failures in Virginia. The
personality of a hero was revealed in John W. Palmer's *Stonewall Jackson's Way*, and Jackson's dramatic death was memorialized in *Under
the Shade of the Trees* by Margaret J. Preston. The common soldiers
felt moved to chronicle their history in song as they marched by day

and bivouacked around camp fires at night. Their rough minstrelsy was full of harsh realism and disillusioning satire. Francis O. Ticknor, a Georgia surgeon with the Western armies, caught the heroism and pathos of the youthful soldier in *Little Giffen of Tennessee*, based on his experience of hospital life. The most popular poet of the Confederacy was Father Abram J. Ryan, a Catholic chaplain who attended sick and dying soldiers. His *Sword of Robert E. Lee* and *The Conquered Banner* were the requiem songs of the Confederacy, and pathetic verses of the latter will be remembered as long as the Stars and Bars are cherished.

It is appropriate to close this discussion of literary expression in the Old South with Henry Timrod and Paul Hamilton Hayne, leaders of the coterie who gathered around William Gilmore Simms. They served the cause of Southern independence with their patriotic verse. Timrod was born in Charleston in 1828, son of a bookbinder of uncommon intellect from whom he inherited his lyrical temperament. A close and sensitive student of poetic tradition, he became one of the most correct of poets, sonorous, firm, devoid of slackness in taste or in execution. On the eve of the Civil War, he produced a memorable nature lyric, *The Cotton Bowl*. Through the symbolism of the section's most famous plant, the whole Southern landscape is surveyed with a lofty imagination. The war gave him a more stirring subject. He ushered in the Confederacy with an elaborate ode, *Ethnogenesis*, in which the human and natural virtues of the South are arrayed against the crass materialism and fanaticism of the North. This was followed by *A Cry to Arms, Carolina, Carmen Triumphale, Charleston*, and other poems which won for him the title of the laureate of the Confederacy. Broken in health and fortune by the war, he wrote, shortly before his death in 1867, *The Magnolia Cemetery Ode* in honor of the Confederate dead. It possesses "the carved and cool completeness of Latin verse." [14]

Hayne was born in Charleston in 1830 of a distinguished family. He abandoned law to devote himself to literature. Before the War he edited *Russell's Magazine* and wrote three volumes of verse which won recognition for their idyllic delicacy and appreciation of nature. The war gave Hayne an outlet in patriotic verse. He wrote of Vicksburg and other battlegrounds, but Charleston aroused his tenderest affections. His best war poem is *The Battle of Charleston Harbor*. After the war, he turned from the wreckage of his city to dwell for the rest of his life, a poor poet, in the pine barrens near Augusta. Like Simms, he wrote too much—biographies, essays, and many poems that simply echoed the Victorian masters. He was offended by the fact that writers of no greater talents than his enjoyed greater popularity because they

[14] Ludwig Lewisohn, *op. cit.*, p. 80.

were not wedded to Southern traditions. He was poet of the pines as truly as Sidney Lanier was poet of the marshes.

The conditions of life in the Old South had a more restrictive influence upon literature than upon education. Writers elaborated the plantation ideal with myths derived from the Old World, omitting the quickening impulse of New England humanitarianism and the common realities of the local scene except in their comic aspects. The Old South's ideal of excellence was the scholar-statesman of encyclopedic knowledge, practical experience, and public eloquence. Literary ability was drained off into political and legal channels. Since it is anarchy and not tyranny which is the death of art, as an English critic wisely says, literature under the plantation order of society might have flowered had there not been other enemies of the creative impulse. These enemies were the lack of an audience because of rural indifference, and the habit of the educated to look beyond the South for what they read. The result was that Simms, the only writer of sufficient talent and energy to represent the South creatively, wasted his words in a wilderness.

CHAPTER XIII

The Road to Secession

JOHN C. CALHOUN had foretold the tragic future in his Fourth of March words: unless the majority section were willing to give constitutional protection to the rights and interests of the minority section the South would be forced to seek security in independence. He asked the North to cease the agitation of the slave question, to grant the South equal rights in the territories, and to enforce the fugitive slave laws. He had little hope that his request would be fulfilled, observing at the close of his life that it was "difficult to see how two people so different and hostile can exist together in one common Union." After the compromise of 1850 the South assumed a conciliatory attitude, but when this was met by what the South considered Northern aggression, it retaliated. Southern aggression took the form of attempted expansion of slavery in the territories and elsewhere as a means of re-establishing the balance in the United States Senate. The reaction of the North was inevitable; in 1858 Abraham Lincoln asserted that the nation could not endure half slave and half free. The South tried to slip out of the Union peacefully, but Lincoln adopted military measures to arrest the secession movement. It was war to the death, with the national aims of the minority section doomed to extinction.

Historians in recent years have analyzed the controversy which led to secession and Civil War as a clash of economic interests. Slavery, they affirm, was merely a blind to cover the conflict between the Southern system of plantations with slave labor and the Northern system of small farms with free labor; between Southern planters seeking cheap goods through free trade and Northern industrialists seeking high profits through protective tariffs and other governmental aids to industry; between New Orleans and the cities of the East for the control of the trade of the West. Sectional interests other than slavery, historians assert, caused the nullification movements of 1798, 1814, and 1833. After the latter date the "peculiar institution" of the South was merely the outward manifestation of sectional bitterness; the real cause lay perhaps behind the scenes, in the rivalry between agricultural expansionists of the two sections for possession of the Western lands.

Scholars claim that Northerners invoked the moral law against human bondage to deprive the Southerner of the means by which he was accustomed to exploit virgin soils. Had their Southern rival not possessed slavery, some other Southern sin could have been shrewdly conjured up for moralizing purposes—for example, the Southern one-crop practice or the fondness of Southerners for the rural way of life. Northern industrial and financial leaders wished to destroy the influence of the agrarian South in Washington in order to use the powers of the federal government to their own advantage. Northern common people wished slavery restricted or abolished because they objected to the competition of cheap labor, not because they wished to make the bondsmen their equals. Both of these groups revealed their intentions when the Southern influence was removed from the federal capital and when the Negro was free. The business leaders imposed high tariffs, constitutional protection to corporations, monetary deflation, and centralized banking. The common people denied the free Negro access to Western lands and imposed upon him caste restrictions in some respects sharper than those of the South. "It is not humanity," said Jefferson Davis to the North in 1861, "that influences you in the position that you now occupy before the country. . . . It is that you may have a majority in the Congress of the United States and convert the government into an engine of Northern aggrandizement. It is that your section may grow in power and prosperity upon treasures unjustly taken from the South."

Whatever the origin of Northern wealth, its growth between 1850 and 1860 was so great that thoughtful Southerners grew bitterly apprehensive. They feared that a North grown arrogant on wealth would overwhelm the poorer section before the South could gain protection by withdrawal from the Union. The most disconcerting manifestations of Northern power were the destruction of the unity of interest between the farmer of the Northwest and the plantation South, and the weaving of North and West into a single economic and social pattern. Railroads connected New York and Philadephia with the West, thus displacing New Orleans as the principal outlet for Western trade.

Almost as disconcerting to the South was the behavior of the 2 million foreigners who settled in the United States between 1850 and

1850. Landing usually in Northern ports, the immigrants did not move from north to south, but from east to west along the newly-established railroads. They generally avoided the South because of its climate and labor standards. Their settlement in the West helped to bring three new free states into the Union; nineteen free states could then easily outvote the fifteen slave states. In the decade of the 1850's, six of the 8.5 million people who constituted the population increase of the country lived in the free states. Immigration, cheap transportation, cheap land, and the invention of the reaper by the Virginian, Cyrus McCormick, furthered the development in the West of a wheat kingdom that was to prove more powerful than the Cotton Kingdom.

The industrial advance of the North was even more significant than its agricultural growth. During this period the sewing machine, Bessemer steel process, Goodyear rubber developments, and the Colt revolver were perfected. A mighty industrial empire was spreading from Massachusetts west to Chicago and St. Louis. Pittsburgh became a center of coal and iron, and Massachusetts became so rich in textiles that the real estate values of one of its counties exceeded those of the entire state of South Carolina. This was the age of the Astors, Belmonts, Vanderbilts, and other magnates who were creating social distinctions based on wealth and destined to outlast those of the South.

Although many of the Northern rulers preferred a businessman's peace to an abolitionist war on the Southern system, it apparently did not occur to them that some of the arguments used against the Southern slave system might be applied to their own wage slavery. The fundamental tenets of the prevailing capitalism were scarcely questioned, except by a few reformers. Indeed, Northern capitalism was eagerly imperialistic, spreading west through the encouragement of liberal land grants to railroad corporations and to immigrants and other settlers, and sending forth ships to open the markets of distant countries. Its success was creating a nation of dollar-worshippers, optimists, and boosters who regarded themselves as the lords of creation. They tore down in order that they might rebuild. To tear down the civilization that lay to their south was but a chapter in their history.

The moral and political indictment of the South by an earlier generation of abolitionists was supplemented in the 1840's and 1850's by an indictment of the plantation system on economic grounds. Daniel R. Goodloe, a North Carolinian who edited an antislavery newspaper in Washington, explained in 1846 the comparative economic backwardness of the South in terms of its degraded labor and the absorption by slavery of capital which otherwise might have been employed in the development of industry. Henry Ruffner, president of Washington College in Virginia, published in 1847 a pamphlet attacking slavery as a wasteful system which caused many Virginians to emigrate into the Northwest.

More sensational was *The Impending Crisis of the South* (1857), a book by Hinton R. Helper, another North Carolinian. By using citations from the census of 1850, Helper made invidious comparisons between the wealth of the sections. The backwardness of the South he attributed to the impoverishment of free labor by the competition of slave labor. Although he hated the Negroes to the extent of wishing them expelled from the country, he attacked the slaveholders violently and suggested servile insurrection as a means of ridding the white masses of their degradation. He has been called the Karl Marx of the non-slaveholding whites because he urged them to struggle against the slavemasters. His book was banned from Southern markets, and its author was exiled from the South, hated as much by the non-slaveholders as by the slave masters. On the other hand, he became a hero to Northern opponents of the Southern system, and a fund was raised to print 100,000 copies of his book as a Republican campaign document in 1860.

In 1862 appeared *The Slave Power* by John E. Cairnes, a distinguished British economist, whose sweeping indictments of the economy of slavery made a great impression both in England and the United States. The Southern institution, said Cairnes (on the basis of evidence gathered from inaccurate and prejudiced sources) inculcated such thriftless habits that the masters could accumulate no surplus funds and were prompted to degrade both the slaves and the non-slaveholding whites into barbarians.

A people who, as one writer asserts,[1] "had always been singularly lacking in meekness and timidity" did not accept the accomplishments and the criticism of their Northern rivals with resignation. The South, too, had its material triumphs and patriotic writers who hurled maledictions at its enemies with a zeal matching that of Helper and Cairnes.

The decade of the 1850's brought unexampled prosperity to the South. The railroad mileage of the section grew from 2,068 to 10,386, stimulating the expansion of agriculture and industry. The lumber industry, concentrated in the pine lands of Georgia, Alabama, and Mississippi, doubled. Flour production, especially in the coastal regions of Virginia and North Carolina, increased decidedly. Cumberland in Maryland, and Wheeling and Richmond in Virginia produced railroad iron, and locomotives were built at the Tredegar factory at Richmond. The agitations of a series of Southern commercial conventions which met between 1852 and 1859 resulted in the establishment of a line of ships between Virginia and Europe. Efforts to expand cotton manufacturing

[1] Robert S. Cotterill, *The Old South*, p. 233.

did not produce sensational results. The value of cotton manufacturing increased $2,000,000 in the fifties as compared with an increase nearly three times that amount during the forties. Southern manufacturers complained that Northerners were "dumping" goods on the Southern market to crush their rising industry.

Southern cotton manufacturing was not more successful mainly because of the great prosperity of cotton growing. Prices for the raw cotton were high; as a result slaves and capital were diverted from the cotton mills to the cotton fields. The combination of good prices and bumper crops increased the cotton growers' income from $100,000,000 in 1850 to two and one half times this amount ten years later. Of the 3,841,416 bales which were produced in 1860, two thirds were exported to form the major portion of the world's supply.

Observing how inextricably this huge crop was tied up with the commerce of the world, Southern economists believed that the South held the key to universal prosperity. "Cotton is king," they exclaimed exultantly, and David Christy wrote a book in 1855 with that title. Cotton was king of England, it was argued, because normally that country depended on the South for five sixths of the raw material that made possible one of its basic industries. The English cotton textile industry employed more than a million laborers, brought prosperity to Liverpool and Manchester and six nearby shires, and furnished more than one half of the total exports of England. Cotton was king of the western United States because cotton producers consumed annually $30,000,000 worth of western foodstuffs. It was king of the North because it formed the basis of a textile industry which produced $100,-000,000 worth of goods each year, because cotton export employed Northern shipping, and because the supplying of cotton growers with manufactured goods gave the North annually a $150,000,000 business.

In reply to William H. Seward's boast of Northern prowess, Senator James H. Hammond said in 1855: "Without the firing of a gun, without drawing a sword, should they [the Northerners] make war upon us, we could bring the whole world to our feet. What would happen if no cotton was furnished for three years? . . . England would topple headlong and carry the whole civilized world with her. No, you dare not make war on cotton. No power on earth dares make war on it. Cotton is King." [2]

De Bow's Review and Thomas P. Kettell, in a book called Southern Wealth and Northern Profits, massed data to refute those who asserted that the weaknesses of Southern economy were attributable to slavery. The South, they said, created the major portion of the national wealth by furnishing the bulk of the exports. The North, like a leech, sucked

[2] Congressional Globe, 35th Cong., 1 Sess., p. 961.

up through an unjust monopoly of the processes of trade the wealth created by the South. The money-changers of New York, it was asserted, held the rich cotton trade in bondage, creating panics and other market tricks by which the South lost enough money to establish marketing facilities of its own. Earlier attacks on the comparative cruelties of the English and New England industrial systems were supplemented by the assertion that the Southern industrial system was so superior that the systems of free economy must fall before it.

George Fitzhugh, a Virginia lawyer, in *Sociology for the South* (1854), changed the proslavery argument from a mere rebuttal to a statement of positive benefits. He believed that free capitalist society was a failure, deserving the denunciations that Thomas Carlyle and other reformers heaped upon it. To forestall chaos and destitution, he believed the members of society must be subjected to discipline and assigned to useful tasks according to their several abilities. In other words, society, to save itself, must conform to the Southern model. "Slavery," cried Fitzhugh in anticipation of Lincoln's well-known remarks about the "house divided," [3] "will everywhere be abolished, or everywhere be reinstated." Because of the assumed superiority of Southern economy, he predicted that the slavery half would become the national whole. If the owners of Northern industry would make slaves of their workingmen, strife and poverty would disappear. Fitzhugh and other Southern enthusiasts felt that their arguments were bolstered by the course of the financial panic of 1857. While Northern industry was paralyzed, the cotton crop was large and prices and exports were sustained. "The wealth of the South," said De Bow, "is permanent and rich; that of the North is fugitive and fictitious."

The nationalistic tradition of 1812 died with Calhoun in 1850 and Clay and Webster in 1852. A new generation of national compromisers took their places—men like Stephen A. Douglas of Illinois, John Bell of Tennessee, and John J. Crittenden of Kentucky—but the initiative was held largely by men who would not compromise on sectional issues. In the North were the ardent antislavery leaders—Charles Sumner of Massachusetts, William H. Seward of New York, and Salmon P. Chase of Ohio. In the South the Fire-Eaters—Robert Barnwell Rhett of South Carolina, William L. Yancey of Alabama, Albert G. Brown of Mississippi, and Edmund Ruffin of Virginia—kept up a ceaseless agitation for secession by appealing to the fears and ambitions of the enfranchised white masses.

Rhett accepted Calhoun as his mentor without sharing the famous South Carolinian's hope of satisfactory compromise within the Union. After the introduction of the Wilmot Proviso, Rhett favored the im-

[3] Cited in Harvey Wish, *George Fitzhugh*, p. 104.

mediate secession of South Carolina, believing that other Southern states would follow its example. Over him hovered the alarming thought of the North growing stronger and the South weaker with the passage of time.

Yancey changed from an ardent unionist into an agitator who believed that there could be no security for the Southern way of life in a union with a Northern majority. He demanded that slavery not only should be permitted to expand in the federal territories but should also be protected by Congressional legislation. If these demands were not granted, Yancey favored the formation of a separate Southern republic.

The Fire-Eaters of the South were checked by the more calculating leaders of Southern opinion such as Jefferson Davis of Mississippi and Robert Toombs of Georgia, who argued against precipitate action. They were able to dominate because Southern statesmen held the national government in an unbroken political grip until 1860. Over the ruins of the Southern branch of the Whig party, they helped elect Franklin Pierce President in 1852 by giving him the vote of every Southern state except Kentucky and Tennessee. Pierce appointed a cabinet largely proslavery; Jefferson Davis became his Secretary of War. In 1856 every Southern state except Kentucky gave its presidential vote to James Buchanan. Buchanan favored slavery even more than Pierce. He appointed Howell Cobb of Georgia Secretary of the Treasury and John B. Floyd of Virginia Secretary of War. These Southern leaders used their positions to advance the interests of their section.

Gratified by President Pierce's assertion that his administration would "not be controlled by any timid forebodings of evil from expansion," Southern leaders cast covetous eyes on non-American territory that might be used to re-establish the balance between free and slave states. To promote the construction of a railroad connecting Memphis and the Pacific coast, Secretary of War Davis secured the Gadsden Purchase from Mexico in 1853. Between 1856 and 1859 Southerners tried to extract concessions from Mexico as opening wedges for possible annexation of territory.

Far more promising was the Spanish island of Cuba, a rich area given to plantations and slavery. The South hoped to convert this territory into five slave states with ten proslavery United States senators. After Spain refused President Polk's offer to purchase Cuba, an illegal filibustering expedition was attempted. Narciso Lopez, a Venezuelan adventurer who had lived in Havana, conceived the idea of liberating Cuba by organizing an invasion from the United States. His project excited so much popular enthusiasm in the South that the federal government seemed powerless to enforce the neutrality laws. After his first descent upon the island failed, Lopez found his way back to New Orleans, where he was acquitted of violating the neutrality laws. In 1851 he gathered a new group of 450 men, many from the best families of the South. The nephew of Attorney General Crittenden was second in command. This attempt failed, and its members were imprisoned or executed by the Spanish authorities.

In 1854 the Ostend Manifesto was made public. James Buchanan, American minister to Great Britain, John Y. Mason, minister to France, and the ardent French Louisianian Pierre Soulé, minister to Spain, declared that the United States would not rest until Cuba was within her boundaries; that an effort should be made to purchase the island; and that if Spanish possession of it "endangered the peace and existence of our Union," the United States would be justified "by every law human and divine" in taking it from Spain. Such a frank confession of predatory intent was not consistent with the traditions of American diplomacy. The Ostend Manifesto was repudiated by the State Department, and Cuba was not again to be molested by Americans until long after the destruction of the power of the slaveholders.

The last imperial gesture of the South was directed against the Central American republic of Nicaragua. William Walker, a native of Tennessee, had made himself master of that country in 1856. Under what was perhaps the mistaken conviction that Walker's hope was to bring his domain into the Union as a slave state, Southerners enlisted in his cause. When he was brought home to be tried for violation of the neutrality laws, no New Orleans jury could be found to convict him.

While these abortive attempts to expand the slave empire into foreign lands were being made, Southerners were seeking means of repealing the Missouri Compromise, thereby extending slavery into lands north of the 36°30' line. Their opportunity came when Stephen A. Douglas, senator from Illinois, introduced in Congress a bill proposing to organize Kansas and Nebraska into territories of the United States. Douglas realized that his bill had to have Southern support. Since he was under pressure from his constituents for the construction of a transcontinental railroad by the central route, he bargained with Jefferson Davis, who was planning a railroad by the Southern route. In return for Southern support, the Kansas-Nebraska Bill was revised to contain the provision that the people living in these territories could decide through their legislatures whether or not they would have slavery. By this principle of "popular sovereignty," Douglas hoped to transfer the controversial issue of slavery from Congress to the local governments.

The measure became law on May 30, 1854. Although only two Southern senators and nine Southern representatives voted against it, the South did not accept it with enthusiasm. Despite Douglas' explicit statement to the contrary, Southern leaders interpreted the "nonintervention" of the federal government to mean protection of slavery during the territorial stage. People of territories could reject or affirm slavery only when they sought admission as states. After a long and bitter controversy with Douglas, Davis was successful in obtaining a declaration by the Senate in February, 1860, that the territories were the "common possession" of all the states, from which neither Congress nor the territorial legislatures could exclude slavery.

In the meantime, the United States Supreme Court, which, since the discrediting of nullification, had been generally accepted as the final arbiter of the Constitution, sustained the Southern position. In the Dred Scott decision (1857), Chief Justice Roger B. Taney and four Southern associates rejected a Negro's claim for freedom based on his residence in free territory. The court held that Dred Scott could not be a citizen of the United States and therefore had no right to sue in a federal court. But, more significantly, in an *obiter dictum*, it ruled that a slave residing north of the 36°30' line had no right to freedom, since the slave was undeniably property. The court decided that when Congress, in the Missouri Compromise, had prohibited slavery in that area, it had denied to slave property the "due process of law" guarantee of the Constitution.

Slaveholders sought to lift the ban on the African slave trade. Rising prices of slaves during the prosperous 1850's was evidence that the demand exceeded the supply. This deficiency they hoped to relieve by reopening the slave trade. Northerners were peopling the West with immigrants from Europe; why should not Southerners obtain immigrants from Africa? Illicit importations grew rapidly. Stephen A. Douglas stated that 15,000 slaves were brought into the country in 1859. Juries refused to condemn the captains or owners of slavers who entered Southern ports. A Southern commercial convention meeting at Vicksburg in 1859 agreed, by vote of 49 to 19, that "all laws, state and national, forbidding the African slave trade, ought to be repealed." A Georgia delegate to the Democratic national convention of 1860 declared that the only realistic way to implement the desire for slavery in the territories was to import Negroes to people these regions. Otherwise, affirmed William L. Yancey, the Kansas-Nebraska Act and the Dred Scott decision were empty victories. If slavery were the boon to civilization that Southerners maintained, why not, asked the Alabama leader, increase its benefits by extending the area of its beneficence?

The Southern leaders, however, placed tact above such reasoning and continued, as in the past, to approve the practice of slavery without openly sanctioning the African trade.

Southern aggression was met by Northern counteraggression. William H. Seward, leader of New York politics, supplemented his "higher law" assertion of 1850 by a declaration in 1858 that the slavery struggle was "an irrepressible conflict" between enduring forces. The Kansas-Nebraska Act was regarded by the North as an "enormous crime." As a result of its enactment diverse elements opposing the extension of slavery formed the Republican party. Unlike the Democratic and the dying Whig party, this new party was outlawed in the South. The Dred Scott decision, to quote only a few contemporary statements, was denounced as a "new and atrocious doctrine," a "deliberate iniquity," and "the greatest crime in the judicial annals of the Republic."

More threatening than such sweeping rhetoric was the refusal of the North to enforce the laws guaranteeing the return of fugitive slaves. Seward and Chase, leaders of the rising Republican party, won fame as court defenders of runaway slaves. Fearless abolitionists like the Reverend Samuel J. May of Syracuse led righteous mobs in rescuing fugitives from federal marshals. When Anthony Burns, an escaped slave, was returned from Boston to his Virginia master, a thousand soldiers were needed to protect his captors from a mob. The Underground Railroad intensified its hiding of Negroes by day in barns and closets; at night they could follow the north star into Canada where, under British law, they were safe from extradition.

Northern states passed statutes known as Personal Liberty Laws which the South, with reason, denounced as a kind of nullification. These laws denied the use of local jails for the detention of fugitives held under federal law, forbade state judges to assist in the execution of this law, and authorized jury trials and writs of *habeas corpus* in cases involving Negroes claimed as slaves. A Wisconsin court, under a writ of *habeas corpus,* discharged an abolitionist arrested by a federal marshal for rescuing a fugitive slave. This assumption by a state court of the authority to release a prisoner held under federal judicial authority for violating United States law aroused Chief Justice Taney to assert that federal jurisdiction in federal matters was vital to the operation of the national government. That the abolitionists accused the Supreme Court of "usurpation" was proof that the enemies of slavery were willing to put their concept of the "higher law" above laws which Congress had made to promote peace between the sections.

Douglas predicted that the application of the principle of popular sovereignty would end the painful forensic battle over slavery in the territories, which had been going on for decades. In placing his faith in the American manner of resolving controversy by the ballot box, he apparently forgot that neither Northerner nor Southerner was above using fraud and violence to settle controversies involving vital moral or material interests. This was especially true in new communities where residential and other qualifications necessary for orderly balloting were not established by earlier law. Thus Kansas exploded while Senator Douglas was still proclaiming the merits of his doctrine.

Southerners, with a continued balance between slave and free state as their standard of justice, conceded Nebraska as a free state because it was a colony of the free state of Iowa to the east. At the same time they assumed that Kansas would be a slave state because it was a colony of its eastward neighbor, Missouri. With this principle in mind, they tolerated the organization of Nebraska as a free territory and endeavored to occupy Kansas. Immigrants from Missouri won control of the territorial legislature in the election of 1855. They adopted a drastic slave code under which imprisonment was prescribed for those claiming that slavery did not legally exist in Kansas. The antislavery party denied the legality of this code, claiming that it had been brought into being by border ruffians imported for the purpose. Reinforced by various emigrant aid societies, the antislavery party organized a rival government at Topeka. For this government they asked admission to the Union. Thus early in 1856, Kansas had two governments hopelessly at odds over the question of slavery.

While the American people looked on, Kansas gave a preview of the civil strife in which the whole country was soon to participate. Southerners took the offensive. In May, 1856, a posse of 800 men under the leadership of a United States marshal and a county sheriff descended upon the antislavery town of Lawrence to execute warrants for "treason." The posse became a mob which burned a hotel and private residences, smashed newspaper offices, and terrorized helpless citizens. Although the raid was almost bloodless, lurid descriptions of events in Lawrence were published in the Northern press, and Northern public opinion was outraged.

Southern public opinion was, in turn, outraged by an act of bloody retaliation. John Brown, who was inspired by a wild desire to translate New England idealism into deeds, swept down upon the cabins of proslavery settlers on Pottawatomie Creek and murdered five men in cold blood. It was "a Free State warning to the proslavery forces that it was to be a tooth for a tooth, an eye for an eye."

Some scholars assert that events in Kansas were but manifestations of lawless pioneering in the Wild West, or struggles between rival emigrant bands for the possession of land in which the institution of slavery actually played little part. To contemporaries the slavery issue was a vital one. For Democrats Kansas symbolized Southern rights; the Republicans utilized "bleeding Kansas" as a valuable campaign cry for their ambitious young party. The North, because of its superior propaganda facilities, dramatized the situation more effectively.

The way in which events in Kansas poisoned the atmosphere is vividly illustrated by the Brooks-Sumner affair in the halls of Congress. A few days before John Brown's attack at Pottawatomie, Senator Charles Sumner of Massachusetts delivered his "Crime against Kansas" speech in which he accepted without question the authenticity of every charge against the proslavery element in Kansas, and heaped personal abuse upon the unoffending and aged Senator Andrew P. Butler of South Carolina. "It is his object," commented Douglas on the effort of the Massachusetts senator, "to provoke some one of us to kick him as one would a dog in the street, that he may get sympathy upon the just chastisement." [4] Two days after Sumner had spoken, Douglas' suggestion was carried out. Preston S. Brooks, a representative from South Carolina and a kinsman of Butler, got the satisfaction of a Southern gentleman by beating the vituperative New Englander into insensibility with a gutta-percha walking stick while Sumner was sitting at his desk in the Senate.

This act of violence served to intensify the sectional hatred. The *New York Tribune* interpreted it as the normal expression of Southern character by "that almost sainted champion of slaveholding dominance" who would not hesitate "at an assault or a murder." [5] Although it is probable that Sumner's illness was not sufficient to justify a protracted invalidism, he remained out of public life for three years, leaving his seat in the Senate eloquently vacant.

Many Southerners believed that Brooks's act was unwise because it played into the hands of the abolitionists, although there were few who felt that it was not justified. His Southern colleagues prevented his expulsion from Congress by refusing the necessary two-thirds majority, and when he resigned voluntarily he was re-elected with only six votes cast against him. Enthusiastic friends presented him with suitably inscribed canes and wrote exultant editorials. Brooks did not like these vulgar manifestations of approval. He was a courtly gentleman far removed from the ruffian depicted in the abolitionist propaganda. To him the chastisement of Sumner was an unpleasant duty under a code of honor which required that the slanderer of a helpless kinsman should not go unpunished. He died within a short time, his last months perhaps troubled by the fear that he had hurt rather than helped his section. Over his grave at Edgefield was placed a splendid

---

[4] Cited in Avery O. Craven, *The Coming of the Civil War*, p. 367.
[5] Cited *ibid.*, p. 369.

tomb bearing inscriptions which prove that his people did not regret his deed.

After the antislavery government organized at Topeka had failed to gain admission into the Union, an attempt was made by proslavery forces. The constitution that they adopted at Lecompton declared slave property inviolable and denied to the legislature the power to prohibit immigrants from bringing in slaves. This document was submitted for popular ratification in such a manner that a vote against slavery was impossible. President Buchanan recommended the speedy admission of the state under this constitution, stating that its rejection would be "keenly felt by the people of the fourteen states of the Union, where slavery is recognized under the Constitution of the United States."

When it was evident that the Lecompton constitution could not pass the House of Representatives, a compromise was effected through which it was submitted to a genuine popular referendum. It was rejected by such a decisive majority that all chances of making Kansas a slave state vanished. In fact, because of the territory's remoteness from the plantation area and because of its disturbed social conditions, it had never been an area in which the prudent planter cared to risk his slaves. Kansas was admitted into the Union as a free state in January, 1861.

Another wedge of separation between the sections was the publication in 1852 of Harriet Beecher Stowe's *Uncle Tom's Cabin or Life Among the Lowly*. In its immediate effect upon the minds and emotions of men it ranks as the greatest American book ever written. Three hundred thousand copies were sold within a year of publication; it was translated into twenty languages, and as a drama it reached millions who did not read books. It was an important influence in dedicating a whole generation to a militant hatred of slavery and it fixed for the world a stereotype of the South. Its intimate and vivid detail supplanted the vague generalizations of past decades of antislavery literature. Uncle Tom became a living person, a beloved symbol who took his place with the pitied heroes of Charles Dickens. The most famous character in American fiction had been created.

Yet *Uncle Tom's Cabin* is not a great novel, nor even a novel at all. Its author was artistically dishonest, lacking a firsthand acquaintance with materials about which she claimed authority. She looked upon slavery from the distance of her Cincinnati home. The chief factual bases of her narrative were the declarations of refugees from the South which Theodore D. Weld compiled in 1839 under the title of *The Testimony of a Thousand Witnesses*. In her pages scenes of culture, refinement, and peace are sensationally mingled with scenes of murder, cruelty, and violence. Her Uncle Tom was a man of unctuous piety subjected to painful servitude; how the supposedly vile slave system could produce such a spotless character did not trouble Mrs. Stowe's sentimental readers. The answer is obvious; Uncle Tom is untrue to Negro character and environment. That he has long since been supplanted by Uncle Remus, Nigger Jim, Scarlet Sister Mary, and other more accurate portrayals of the Negro would seem adequate proof of her misconception.

The South considered the book a slander, knowing that the American and foreign public would neglect the passages revealing the kinder side of slavery for parts emphasizing the murderous brutality of the overseer Simon Legree. An intelligent Southern woman found the book "too sickening" to read. "Flesh and blood revolt," said Mary B. Chesnut, at such details as a "man sending his little son to beat a human being tied to a tree." But the indignation of the civilized world had been so skillfully aroused that reasoned protests went unheeded. More than a dozen Southern authors wrote novels to correct the false impression created by the book, but no one read their works. State authorities tried to stop its circulation, but thousands of Southerners read it surreptitiously. The South's only effective answer to its slanders was to tighten the region's internal defenses.

While proslavery forces were carrying on their fight for the domination of the territories, the Northern imagination was captured by a leader who predicted that slavery was on the road to ultimate extinction. This man was Abraham Lincoln, who by a subtle mixture of political trimming with moralizing in favor of national unity and freedom rose from an obscure lawyer to become one of America's truly great statesmen. He was no mere abolitionist with a forthright program which might frighten away those who knew how to win political power. As a casuist of skill, he modestly denied what he seemed to have said, repeatedly declaring against interference with slavery in the states. Yet he could not erase his words. In accepting the nomination of the Illinois Republicans for the United States Senate in 1858, he said:

A house divided against itself cannot stand. I believe this government cannot endure permanently half slave and half free. I do not expect the Union to be dissolved; I do not expect the house to fall; but I do expect it will cease to be divided.

The South felt these words were cause for alarm. It saw in them a premonition of the destruction of slavery as a necessary means of preserving the national unity. Lincoln it regarded as a Black Republican who would invoke the dreaded weapon of the numerical majority to make his principles effective. It is not clear from his explanations that he had such plans, although future events proved that Southern apprehensions were well founded. The Illinois leader was to abandon the ambiguous words of the politician to become the righteous prophet who, with eloquent benignities on his lips, forced the South back into the Union without slavery.

A year and a half after Lincoln's "house divided" speech, Southerners were aroused to fever heat by the attempts of abolitionists to implement their violent words with violent deeds. On the night of October 16, 1859, a band of thirteen white men and five Negroes under the leadership of John Brown, the avenger of Kansas, crossed the Potomac at Harpers Ferry to start a slave rebellion in Virginia. The men carried arms for themselves and also for expected confederates among the slaves. The town of Harpers Ferry was seized, and unsuccessful attempts were made to induce captured slaves to join the attackers. Most of the invaders were killed or captured. Brown himself was taken in custody by Colonel Robert E. Lee, adjudged sane, and after a fair trial executed for treason against the Commonwealth of Virginia. While in prison Brown was metamorphosed into a martyr in the eyes of Northerners because of his noble letters and heroic attitude toward death. The purposes of the South would have been better served had the Virginia authorities committed this inspired maniac to an insane asylum.

Although the slaves were apparently unmoved by the raid, whites in both North and South showed great concern. Southerners expected Brown's act to initiate a second Santo Domingo. The deeds of this maniac were considered but one manifestation of a general conspiracy against Southern society. They were reluctant to accept as typical the great mass of conservative Northern opinion which condemned the outrage and, instead, called attention to the few who openly approved. The *Richmond Enquirer* charged that while only the blatant few openly expressed sentiments of approval, thousands of other Northerners silently supported John Brown. There was a growing conviction that the safety of the South demanded withdrawal from the Union and the establishment of military forces.

Secession became the non-slaveholder's cause, too. Should emancipation occur, said a spokesman of the common white men of Mississippi, "The rich will flee the country. . . . The poor will have to bear its fury." [6]

Initial Northern disapproval of Brown's raid soon gave way to acceptance of his motives and purpose; a distinction was made between what Brown tried to do and his means of doing it. Hatred of the slaveholders had subtly effected this change of opinion. Ralph Waldo Emerson referred to him as a "new saint awaiting his martyrdom, and

[6] Albert G. Brown, cited *ibid.*, pp. 411–12.

who, if he shall suffer, will make the gallows glorious like the cross."
"Saint John the Just," Louisa M. Alcott called him, and Henry D.
Thoreau saw in him "an angel of light." [7] Brown had had the courage
to do what weaker men wished to do. In death he became greater than
in life. John Brown's Body was a standard under which a million men
marched to destroy slavery.

Before the bitterness engendered by the Harpers Ferry raid had
abated, the presidential campaign of 1860 brought the sectional conflict to a final crisis. In this canvass the usual claptrap of contending
politicians gave way to vital issues. The program adopted by the Republicans was designed for Northern and Western interests. Although
it recognized "the right of each state to order and control its own
domestic institutions," it denied "the authority of Congress, or of a
territorial legislature, or any individual, to give legal existence to slavery
in any territory of the United States." This cry for freedom was supplemented by a bid for the support of business and finance. Relief was
promised vested interests suffering from the low tariffs enacted by the
Democrats. Seward, the party's best-known member, was rejected as
the presidential candidate because he had talked about "the higher law"
and an "irrepressible conflict." Instead, the nomination went to Lincoln, whose "house divided" speech was given two interpretations.
Abolitionists contended that his prophecy that the country would become all free or all slave promised the complete destruction of slavery;
to those who did not wish to disturb existing arrangements it could be
explained as a gradual process to be accomplished only in the remote
future. This double explanation was an effective vote-catcher in the
regions of the country uncertain about methods of meeting the sectional crisis, but it gave no comfort to Southerners fearful for the
security of their social system.

"The South seceded in 1861," remarks a historian,[8] "because it had
lost faith in the willingness of the Democratic party to fight for Southern interests." Many Southerners believed that the Northern wing of
the party was compelled to reflect the opinions of constituencies almost
as antislavery as those of the Republican party. This loss of faith in their
political brethren found expression in the repudiation of Stephen A.
Douglas, the leading Democrat of the North, who, in his debates with
Lincoln in 1858, had interpreted the Dred Scott decision and the repeal of the Missouri Compromise as barren victories for slavery. One
group of influential Southerners, however, regarded Douglas as the
symbol of the coalition through which Southern statesmen had helped
rule the country.

[7] Cited *ibid.*, p. 408.
[8] Cotterill, *op. cit.*, p. 245.

As the Democratic convention of 1860 approached, the initiative was taken by those who feared the Northern Democrats. Their leader was William L. Yancey, whose radical views had been held in check for almost a decade by those who wished to maintain the Compromise of 1850. This fiery orator of the lower South induced the Alabama legislature on February 24, 1860, to declare that the state would not submit to a "foul sectional party" and to promise the calling of a convention if a Black Republican were elected President. When the Democratic national convention met at Charleston in the following April, he presented the Alabama declaration as an ultimatum: it must be accepted or the delegates of the lower South would bolt the party. He and his followers insisted on a forthright assertion that slavery should be protected in the territories by the federal government. The convention, dominated by a Northern majority, refused to accept a platform inconsistent with self-government in the territories. Yancey left the hall and was followed by the delegates from Alabama, Mississippi, Texas, and Florida and by a majority of those from several other states. Thus, on Southern initiative came a rift which made inevitable the most momentous political defeat the South and the Democratic party have ever suffered.

Foreseeing disaster, party strategists tried to re-establish harmony at a second convention held at Baltimore a few weeks later, but a renewal of strife caused a second division. The majority, or Northern wing, nominated Douglas for President and Herschel V. Johnson of Georgia for Vice-President; those who bolted the convention named John C. Breckinridge of Kentucky for President and Joseph Lane of Oregon for Vice-President. Still another manifestation of the confusion of the times was the emergence of a fourth pair of candidates, John Bell of Tennessee for President and Edward Everett of Massachusetts for Vice-President, representing the Constitutional Union party.

In the South the campaign of 1860 was fought between secessionist and unionist Democrats, with the Republican candidate standing as the great external menace for whom no Southerner could or would vote. The secessionist Democrats determined to make 1860 the turning point of their political history. The North, they asserted, was self-righteous and materialistic and therefore bent on destroying slavery and plundering the South for selfish gain. Race feeling was aroused by a reiteration of the social evils of emancipation. Sectional material ambitions were appealed to by an emphasis on the plenty which would result from freedom from the North. Like their Revolutionary ancestors, many Southerners saw obvious advantages in picking a quarrel with their creditors, favoring a general smashup that would wipe out a debt of between two and three hundred millions which Northerners held against them.[9]

Southern unionists, on the other hand, had equally effective appeals to Southern sentiment. Although they opposed Lincoln, they asked, "Why the hot haste, excitement, and precipitation?" When had the South suffered any "real detriment, loss or humiliation from the fanatical doctrines" of the North? Had not the South triumphed in "nine cases out of ten in all the geographical and sectional conflicts" which had arisen? Was the right of secession "worth a fig, as long as others choose to test that right by force?" Would not the severance of the Union spell disaster to rich planting and commercial interests dependent upon Northern trade? [10]

In the meantime, the Republicans shrewdly ignored Southern complaints and concentrated on the majority section. Their tenets were basically anti-Southern. To conservative business interests they talked of the potentialities of the West as a market to replace the South, of Southern extravagance, of the economic weaknesses of slavery, and of the profits to be gained by Republican tariff and internal improvement policies. The prejudices of the common man were aroused by attacks on the Southern concept of a stratified society and an inferior laboring class. The Democratic party was described as "the true 'nigger party' " which, through the competition of slave labor, hoped to degrade free white labor. The threat of secession was pictured as a "humbug" because Southern leadership was said to be dominated by swagger and "windy bombast." Although the Republican platform disclaimed any intention of interfering with slavery in the states, antislavery oratory was rampant. Abolitionists like George W. Julian believed that the Republican program contemplated the extinction of slavery; Charles Sumner said that the Constitution gave no protection to that hated institution; and William H. Seward told a Boston audience that Lincoln "confesses the obligation to the higher law . . . and avows himself . . . a soldier on the side of freedom in the irrepressible conflict between freedom and slavery." [11] The Presidential candidate himself refused to reassure the South in the face of the accusation that he was a Black Republican who was an enemy of Southern institutions. Privately he justified his silence by saying that "bad men . . . North and South" would subject his pronouncements to further misrepresentation. He allowed friends to conduct his campaign with parades and roaring demonstrations and with a diversity of promises designed to please every opinion except that of the South.

[9] See quotation in Arthur C. Cole, *The Irrepressible Conflict*, pp. 282–3.
[10] Quotations in Craven, *op. cit.*, pp. 245–6.
[11] *Ibid.*, pp. 419–21.

This appeal to sectional prejudice won the election for Lincoln. He received 180 electoral votes while his three opponents combined received only 123. He carried every Northern free state except New Jersey but did not receive a single electoral vote in slave states. He has been called a minority victor, since his three opponents together received almost a million more popular votes than he. But further analysis proves that this assertion is unjustified. He won, not because of division among his opponents, but because he possessed small majorities in populous states which a union among the opposition would not have disturbed. Had there been such a union, it is statistically demonstrable that he would have won by a majority of 35 electoral votes. Moreover, it is almost a certainty that had the only candidates been Lincoln and Breckinridge the superior voting power of the North would have given the Republican candidate a clear popular majority and a still greater majority in the electoral college.

The stark reality of 1860 was a tragic sectionalism that could not be erased by political diplomacy. The Republicans capitalized upon this sectionalism with such consummate ruthlessness that no room was left for compromise. Yancey could not have saved the election for the South by accepting Douglas as the Democratic candidate. The Illinois compromiser was a Northerner and a politician who would have been forced to heed the wishes of his people. He stood by Lincoln during the latter's inaugural address; and before Douglas' death a few months later, he bluntly declared: "There can be no neutrals in this war; only patriots—or traitors." [12]

[12] Cited in Nathaniel W. Stephenson, *Lincoln and the Union*, p. 121.

CHAPTER XIV

Secession and War

-⫸

IMMEDIATELY after Lincoln's election, while the South as a whole hesitated, South Carolina decided upon secession. Its newly elected governor, Francis W. Pickens, spoke for its people when he declared that Lincoln had been elected "upon issues of malignant hostility and uncompromising war to be waged upon the rights, the interests, and the peace of half the States of the Union." The streets of Charleston were thronged with enraged people determined that the Union should be ended once and forever, and when on November 13, the legislature unanimously called a convention of the people to "consider the dangers incident upon the position of the State in the Federal Union," there was such great popular rejoicing that secession seemed a *fait accompli*.

On December 20, 1860, the convention, by unanimous vote of its 169 delegates, passed the Ordinance of Secession declaring that "the union now subsisting between South Carolina and the other States . . . is hereby dissolved." To prove that this was not an act of illegitimate revolution, a Declaration of the Immediate Causes of Secession was issued. The United States Constitution, it was asserted, was a "compact" which "free, sovereign, and independent" states had joined of their own free will and could dissolve in the same manner. The free states, it was explained, "have assumed the right of deciding upon the propriety of our domestic institutions"; a "sectional party" had achieved the election as President of a man "whose opinions and purposes are hostile to slavery," and who had declared that the "government cannot endure permanently half slave, half free." Commissioners were dispatched to effect understandings concerning the disposal of federal properties in

JOHN C. CALHOUN. *This is taken from an unheroic daguerreotype of the man who struggled most heroically to find a comfortable place for the South in the Federal Union without a sacrifice of its peculiar ambitions and way of life.*

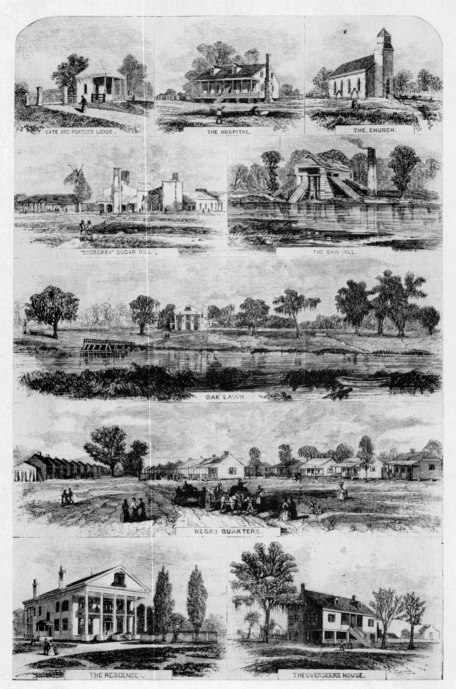

AN ANTE-BELLUM LOUISIANA PLANTATION. *This drawing from* Frank Leslie's Illustrated Newspaper *reveals the full structure of the plantation life typical of the Deep South.*

South Carolina, and urgent messages were sent other Southern states asking them to follow South Carolina's example.

South Carolina moved with confidence because it was assured that other states would follow its example. The governors of Alabama and Mississippi were represented at the secession convention, and on December 13, seven days before South Carolina acted, a group of Southern congressmen addressed their constituents: "The argument is exhausted. All hope of relief in the Union . . . is extinguished, and we trust the South will not be deceived by appearances or the pretense of new guarantees."

Events seemed to justify this viewpoint. On December 26 the federal government, apparently beginning a policy of aggression, concentrated its Charleston garrison in the more easily defended island fortress of Sumter. South Carolina retaliated by occupying the other Charleston forts and by seizing the customhouse, post office, and arsenal in Charleston. At the same time all federal officers in South Carolina resigned. Hopes for compromise were abandoned when the Senate committee of thirteen failed to accept the proposal of Crittenden of Kentucky. He suggested that the Constitution be amended to permit the restoration of the Missouri Compromise line; masters would be federally reimbursed for fugitive slaves; no future constitutional amendment should ever be made to interfere with slavery in any state. This attempt to give sectionalism permanent status was acceptable to Robert Toombs and Jefferson Davis of the committee. Indeed, if the Republicans had accepted the measure the problem at hand might have been solved and war prevented. Appeal was made to President-elect Lincoln, but he refused to alter his position. "Entertain," he wrote a congressman on December 11, "no proposition for a compromise in regard to the extension of slavery. The instant you do they have us under again: all our labor is lost, and sooner or later must be done over. . . . The tug has to come, and better now than later."

South Carolina's example was followed by six other states of the South in the first months of 1861: Mississippi, January 9; Florida, January 10; Alabama, January 11; Georgia, January 19; Louisiana, January 26; and Texas, February 1. This result was not achieved without considerable efforts. In Alabama the opposition of the men of the hill counties was so great that the secession ordinance passed by only a vote of 61 to 39. In Louisiana secessionist sentiments ran counter to the material interests of the sugar planters and the commercial interests of New Orleans. The former feared the disruption of the protective tariff policies of the United States; the latter feared the disruption of their trade with the Northwest. In the election for delegates to a convention, 17,296 Louisianians voted against the secessionist delegates out of a total vote of 37,744. In Texas the secessionists had difficulty in overcoming the strong unionist sentiments of Governor Sam Houston.

The battle for Georgia, the "empire state of the South," was a crucial one; without this state an independent government would have been as impractical as the Federal Union of 1789 without New York or Virginia. Governor Joseph E. Brown, Robert Toombs, and Howell Cobb favored immediate action; Alexander H. Stephens, Benjamin H. Hill, and Herschel V. Johnson argued for "sober deliberation." "I tell you upon the faith of a true man," said Toombs to the people of the state, "that all further looking to the North . . . ought to be instantly abandoned. . . . Secession by the 4th of March next should be thundered from the ballot box by the unanimous voice of Georgia." Although the secessionists won by the narrow margin of 164 to 133, nearly all their opponents signed the Ordinance of Secession. "My allegiance," Stephens afterwards explained, "was . . . not due to the United States, or to the people of the United States, but to Georgia in her sovereign capacity."

On the invitation of Alabama, representatives of the seceding states assembled at Montgomery on February 4, 1861, to organize a provisional government for the Confederate States of America. Statesmen who had gained their political experience in Washington could be expected to model the constitution of the new nation after that of the United States. There were, however, certain significant exceptions. The new document was ordained, not by a united people, but by "the people of the Confederate States, each acting in its sovereign and independent capacity." In vindication of the Southern position in congressional debates, prohibitions were incorporated against the payment of bounties, against protective tariffs, and against appropriations for internal improvements. No federal law "denying . . . the right of property in slaves" was admissible, and, in all territory belonging to the Confederate States, slavery was "recognized and protected by Congress and by the territorial government." The foreign slave trade, however, was prohibited.

Other variations were written into their fundamental organ. A pious people invoked the "favor and guidance of Almighty God" in the preamble. The President was to be elected for a term of six years and was not eligible for re-election. To prevent padding by Congress, the President was empowered to veto items on appropriation bills without disapproving entire measures. A step toward cabinet government was taken by providing that heads of executive departments might be granted seats in either house of Congress.[1]

Jefferson Davis was unanimously elected President of the Confed-

[1] William M. Robinson, Jr., *Justice in Gray*, pp. 620–7.

eracy and Alexander H. Stephens Vice-President. Provisions were made for recruiting an army, and commissioners were dispatched to Washington to negotiate a treaty with the United States, and to Virginia to induce the mother commonwealth to secede and join the new government.

A curious omission from the Confederate Constitution was an explicit affirmation of the right of secession, the legality of which was the basic justification of the whole Montgomery procedure. Perhaps the constitutional theorists took this right for granted as a condition inherent in their union of states. It is more probable that they were replacing the minority role they had assumed in Washington with an integrated nationalism. The needs of the hour demanded strengthened bonds of union, not the diffusion of power inherent in the doctrine of states' rights. The new constitution was declared "permanent." Restrictions were imposed on the states in very much the manner of the United States Constitution; the Constitution, laws, and treaties of the central government were proclaimed the "supreme law of the land"; and provision was made for a Supreme Court, despite Southern experience with that agency of the central government which had curbed the powers of the states. Requirements similar to those in the United States Constitution allowed a majority of two thirds of the states the privilege of imposing constitutional amendments upon the minority.

That the Montgomery statesmen were interested in creating a central government stronger than the logic of secession seemed to justify is further illustrated by the men chosen to lead the new government. William L. Yancey and Robert Barnwell Rhett were not given important positions in this government created by their agitations: Yancey was sent on a bootless mission to England and Rhett was allowed to cool his heels in disgruntled desuetude. Vice-President Stephens was a conservative; Robert Toombs, the Secretary of State, was a moderate secessionist compared with Yancey and Rhett; and Judah P. Benjamin was a foreign-born Jew without fixed dogma. President Davis had written Rhett in 1860 discouraging secession. He placed Southern nationalism above the interests of a particular state. Davis came from Mississippi, a new community of the Southwest inhabited by men who were born in many Southern states and who were bound together by a common Southernism as strong as the state patriotism of the men of the eastern seaboard.

Foreseeing the course of the South with prophetic clarity, Davis realized that a close integration of Southern energies was necessary if the anticipated war was to be won; this synchronization he was unable to create. Internal forces of disintegration, in some respects more deadly than the external assault from the North, destroyed the President's nationalist program. He lived to realize that the philosophy of secession—individual or local self-expression—could be turned against a capital south of the Potomac as readily as against one north of that river.

Foreign observers have often said that American professions of pacifism are a cloak to hide the real intent of a truly warlike people. This generalization could not be applied to Arkansas, Tennessee, North Carolina, and Virginia, the four states of the upper South that were confronted with secession in 1861. They were torn between unionist sentiment and a profound Southernism based on the ideals of the plantation and white supremacy; troublemaking Northerners were resented no more than troublemaking secessionists.

The Virginia convention which met on February 13, instead of promptly passing an ordinance of secession, exploited the opportunities for compromise, disapproving a secession proposal by vote of 88 to 45 as late as April 4. The people of Arkansas and Tennessee voted decisively against leaving the Union, and North Carolina voted the same way by a small majority. Thus did the states of the upper South assume an attitude of waiting as unheroic as it was sensible and kindly. They wanted peace, reconciliation, and respect for Southern rights within the United States.

At a peace conference which met at Washington on February 4, with the venerable former President John Tyler presiding, Virginia made a desperate effort to preserve the Union. This gathering, composed of distinguished leaders representing twenty-one states, presented a plan of conciliation not unlike the rejected Crittenden compromise of a few weeks earlier. "Virginia steps in," said an optimistic citizen of that state,[2] "to arrest the progress of the country on its road to ruin." The suggested peace, however, received little support in Congress. The seven seceded states were unrepresented in the deliberations, and the radical Republicans rejoiced over the failure. "No Republican State," wrote Zachariah Chandler of Michigan, "should have sent delegates. . . . Without a little blood-letting this Union will not, in my estimation, be worth a rush."

In the interval between the secession of South Carolina and the inauguration of Lincoln, the bone of contention between the federal government and the South Carolina authorities was the possession of the Charleston forts. As vindication of its proclaimed sovereignty, South Carolina demanded all federal property within its borders. It implemented this demand by seizing all such property that was not

[2] William C. Rives, cited in James G. Randall, *Civil War and Reconstruction*, pp. 205–06.

defended by military force, and bottled up Major Robert Anderson and his little garrison of United States troops within the defenses of Charleston Harbor. It energetically negotiated with Washington for the surrender of these establishments, hoping to avoid bloodshed.

Although President Buchanan ardently desired peace, he denied the constitutionality of secession and signified his intention of retaining the Federal position in Charleston Harbor by sanctioning Anderson's concentration of his forces in Fort Sumter. Early in January, 1861, he attempted to send an unarmed merchant vessel, *Star of the West*, to relieve the fort. When it was repelled by the fire of the South Carolinians, the President refused to interpret the incident as a cause of war. He had strong constitutional scruples against the coercion of a state; the Union, he believed, could not be cemented with blood. In this attitude he had the support of important elements of Northern public opinion.

By the time Lincoln took office Confederate authorities, fearing hasty action from South Carolina, had assumed control of the delicate Fort Sumter negotiations. As responsible leaders of a government which claimed to be sovereign and independent, they could not win world respect if they permitted a foreign government to hold a fortress within the harbor of one of their principal cities. The guns of Sumter dominated not only every point in Charleston Harbor but the city itself. To the Washington government, on the other hand, Sumter was more than property; it was a symbol of federal integrity. War was imminent. The only question was which government would commit the aggression necessary to solve the Sumter problem and thereby provoke actual conflict. Would Lincoln pursue the dilatory course of Buchanan or would he be aggressive and forthright as the leader of the party which had condemned the Buchanan policy? He did neither. Instead, he carried out a plan of his own which was so devious, so subtle, and perhaps so confused that it is almost as difficult for the historian to understand as it was for the men of the times. Some scholars believe that he blundered into war, overestimating the strength of the Union party in the South. It is more likely that, with a subtlety approaching the diabolical, he provoked the Confederates into firing upon Fort Sumter in order to solidify Northern public opinion.

President Lincoln's inaugural address was filled with double talk. He promised that "the power confided in me will be used to hold, occupy, and possess the property and places belonging to the Government"; yet he added that "no bloodshed or violence" would be involved in this process. There "will be no invasion, no using of force against or among the people anywhere." "He was going," comments one historian,[3] "both to coerce and to conciliate!" He was, another suspects, all things to all men. To aggressive Republicans his address indicated determination to exact submission; to Northern moderates and men of the border states it promised conciliation; to the seceded states it threatened coercion and civil war.

On the very day of his inauguration Lincoln was confronted with the necessity for action, for he was informed by Major Anderson, who commanded Fort Sumter, that he would be forced to give up Sumter unless he received relief. Then ensued a period of indecision. A majority of the President's cabinet advised against a relief expedition. Secretary of State Seward, who was regarded as the spokesman of the administration, gave the Confederate commissioners in Washington the "promise" that the Sumter garrison would be withdrawn. When unionist members of the Virginia secession convention approached Lincoln on the subject, the President is reported to have said: "A state for a fort is not a bad business." Ward H. Lamon, Lincoln's special observer at Charleston, gave both Governor Pickens and Major Anderson the impression that the Washington government intended to withdraw.

Yet as early as April 4 the President had decided upon a definite plan for relieving Sumter. Perhaps he was induced to change his mind by the pressure of an aggressive group of Republican governors who visited him on that day; perhaps he was moved by the growing depletion of Anderson's supplies. He acted despite the fact that Governor Pickens had told Lamon that only the President's "unalterable resolve *not* to attempt any reinforcement" could prevent war. Lincoln was, in fact, making one of the most momentous decisions in American history, a decision between possible peace and bloody tragedy.

It was "reasonably certain," say his official biographers,[4] "that he expected hostilities to ensue."

His announcement to the governor of South Carolina was couched in the pacific language the circumstances warranted. Pickens was told that an attempt would be made to supply the fort with provisions only, and that "without further notice," no reinforcements would be landed except in case of attack. Was this skillfully worded message just another example of Lincoln's ability to make a sentence say one thing to one group and something entirely different to another group? To Northerners it meant that their government was taking food to hungry men to whom it was obligated. To them it was not a threat, merely a promise to use force only if it could not be avoided. To Southerners Lincoln's message conveyed the information that Anderson would be

[3] Avery O. Craven, *The Coming of the Civil War*, p. 480.
[4] John G. Nicolay and John Hay in Kenneth M. Stampp, *And War Came*, p. 284.

provisioned, and also that force would be used if the provisioning were interrupted.[5]

Whatever were Lincoln's intentions, his message to Governor Pickens precipitated a resort to force. The onus of taking the initiative had been deftly thrown upon the Confederates. They were forced to reckon with Fort Sumter by violence or to yield on the matter of provisions pending "further notice" from Lincoln concerning reinforcements. The Confederate Cabinet chose to attack. From this decision Secretary of State Robert Toombs dissented. "This will inaugurate a civil war," he predicted, "greater than any which the world has ever seen. It will lose us every friend in the North. It puts us in the wrong. It is fatal."

When news came that a relief expedition was under way, General Pierre G. T. Beauregard, the Confederate commander at Charleston, was ordered on April 11 to "reduce the fort." At the break of dawn on April 12 the bombardment began. It continued for forty hours while the inhabitants of Charleston looked on in excitement, and while the Federal relief squadron lay beyond the bar unable to come to the aid of Anderson and his garrison. After the fort had been reduced to ruins Anderson put up a white flag and was allowed to depart with the honors of war. Two hours later the flag of the Confederacy was raised above the battered walls of Fort Sumter.

Although there had been no casualties at Fort Sumter, the attack aroused the anger of almost every Northerner. The secessionists were adjudged the offenders. "It was," ran a typical editorial, "an audacious and insulting aggression upon the authority of the Republic, without provocation or excuse." Another newspaper piously interpreted the event as "precisely the stimulus which . . . a good Providence sends to arouse the latent patriotism of a people." Conservative business, caught in the quiet before the storm, joined the war Democrats.

Taking advantage of the psychology of the moment, Lincoln cast aside his defensive garments to appear fully arrayed in the habiliments of war. The day after the fall of Sumter he called upon the militia to suppress an insurrection, "to cause the laws to be duly executed," to preserve the Union, and "to redress wrongs already long endured." A few days later he was justifying bloodshed to prevent the Union from being broken into fragments.[6] Although Lincoln did not confess

---

[5] The facts and interpretations in this paragraph are based largely on Charles W. Ramsdell, "Lincoln and Fort Sumter," *The Journal of Southern History*, III, 259–88 (August, 1937). See also Kenneth M. Stampp, "Lincoln and the Strategy of Defense in the Crisis of 1861," *ibid.*, XI, 297–323 (August, 1945), and *And War Came*, pp. 263–86; and Craven, *op. cit.*, pp. 436–9, 480.

[6] Stampp, *loc. cit.*, pp. 319–21.

his part in provoking the Civil War with the cynical honesty of a
Bismarck, he did speak certain revealing words. He consoled the commander of the Fort Sumter relief expedition for that officer's failure:
"You and I both anticipated that the cause of the country would be
advanced by making the attempt to provision Fort Sumter, even if it
should fail, and it is no small consolation now to feel that our anticipation is justified by the result." Shortly after the fall of the fort he was
quoted by a close personal friend: "The plan succeeded. They attacked
Sumter—it fell, and thus, did more service than it otherwise could." [7]
A few of his party friends congratulated him upon his masterful stroke.
The *New York Times* believed that "the attempt at reinforcement was
a *feint*,—that its object was to put upon rebels the full and clear responsibility of commencing the war. . . ." Jefferson Davis, others
exulted, "ran blindly into the trap." [8]

Lincoln's call for troops was followed by the secession of the four
states of the upper South that had so anxiously and so helplessly
awaited the course of events. In Virginia the question was whether
the state should respond to Lincoln's call or whether it should resist
the invasion of its territory and the South. The mother commonwealth
gave her answer on April 17, 1861, approving by vote of 88 to 55 an
Ordinance of Secession. Sacrificially she assumed the main burden of
the defense of the Confederacy which her exposed position made
necessary.

Antisecessionists rallied to the cause of the commonwealth. "Since
Mr. Lincoln's proclamation," wrote one,[9] "I have no sympathy with
the U. S. Government—no respect for its rulers—very little regard
for the Northern people." Another antisecessionist whose name was
to be written highest on the honor roll of the Confederacy made what
Thomas Nelson Page calls the choice of Hercules. Robert E. Lee resigned his commission in the United States Army to join his native
state.

Arkansas and North Carolina heeded the example of Virginia. The
former state passed its Ordinance of Secession on May 6 by vote of
65 to 5; the latter followed the same course fourteen days later without
a dissenting vote. In Tennessee the situation was more complicated
because no definite provision had been made for a secession convention
at the time of Lincoln's call for troops. Governor Isham G. Harris and
the legislature took the matter in their own hands. The legislature arranged a popular vote on the issue of secession, but before the people

---

[7] Orville H. Browning, cited in Randall, *op. cit.*, p. 238 n.

[8] Cited in Stampp, *And War Came*, p. 281.

[9] Bishop James H. Otey, cited by James Elliott Walmsley in *American Historical Review*, XXXI, pp. 82–101 (October, 1925).

could make a decision, the governor decided for them. He formed a military alliance with the Confederacy and implemented it by organizing an army of 55,000. On June 8 the people recognized the *fait accompli* by endorsing secession by vote of 104,913 to 47,238. Unionist sentiments were so strong in East Tennessee that this region threatened to secede from the seceding state and rejoin the United States. This movement, however, was frustrated by the timely arrival of Confederate troops.

The Lincoln government found a certain compensation for the secession of the four upper South states in the retention for the Union of the three slave states of Missouri, Kentucky, and Maryland, and the withdrawal of the western counties of Virginia to form the state of West Virginia. This border region was vast in area and contained almost as many white people as the Confederate South. Its people were divided in sentiment. They were drawn to the North by economic ties and nationalist sentiments and to the South by slavery and the social attitudes that grew from that institution. They did not wish to take sides in the great sectional controversy, hoping for compromise. That they adhered to the Union was traceable more to the forceful aggression of the Washington government than to their freely expressed will.

In Missouri genuine civil war broke out between unionists under Nathaniel Lyon and secessionists under Sterling Price. The unionists were victorious and their victory was stabilized by the presence of Federal troops and by the firm but tactful policies of President Lincoln. A small section of the state remained in secessionist hands, and the fact that 30,000 Missourians fought for the Confederacy is proof of continued division in the state. Kentucky, native state of the great compromisers Clay and Crittenden, avoided expressing its pronounced Southernism by secession. To stay the forces of war, the state tried to remain neutral, declaring on May 20, 1861, that it would "take no part in the civil war now being waged, except as mediators and friends to the belligerent parties." Events soon forced Kentucky from this role.

Kentuckians enlisted on both sides before the First Battle of Bull Run. Both Confederate and Union forces invaded the state. In September the legislature openly abandoned its neutrality policy by organizing a military force to repel the Confederates. Yet the state was by no means united in its adherence to the Union, and contained a strong minority so Southern in sentiment that the Lincoln government was forced to adopt repressive military measures.

Military power and arbitrary government blatantly forced Maryland's adherence to the Union. The people of the eastern half of the commonwealth demonstrated their pro-Southern sentiments by mobbing a Massachusetts regiment when it passed through Baltimore, on April 19. Although they did not wish to secede, a majority of the eastern Marylanders opposed the war of invasion. On May 10 the state legislature implored President Lincoln "to cease this unholy war," recognized the independence of the Confederate States, and declared the occupation of the state by Federal troops unconstitutional. When secession was threatened, the occupying forces arrested political and civil leaders. The Merryman case intensified feelings even more. General George Cadwalader, the Federal commander at Fort McHenry, refused to honor a writ of habeas corpus issued by the Chief Justice. The military leader declined to bring his prisoner, who had been charged with drilling a secessionist military company, before the court. "The despot's heel is on thy shore!" cried James Ryder Randall in the song.

When Virginia seceded, representatives of its northwestern counties gathered in convention at Wheeling in the summer of 1861 to organize a separate state by irregular methods that did not involve the consent of the parent state. The new commonwealth was admitted to the Union on June 20, 1863, as the state of West Virginia. Delaware, the fifteenth slave state, was too near the center of Northern power for its pro-Southern minority to take effective action. It remained in the Union without a struggle.

In this and the preceding chapter the steps have been traced that led from the Compromise of 1850 to the outbreak of war in April, 1861. The industrial causes of sectional conflict, regarded by some historians as basic to the much-publicized slave controversy, have been appraised. A description of the aggressive expansiveness of Northern industry, commerce, and population has been supplemented by an account of the renewed Northern attack on slavery—particularly its economic efficacy. An irritated South retaliated, boasting of the expanding power of King Cotton, making gestures toward economic independence through the development of a more diversified economy, and evolving plans for the addition of other slave states to the existing fifteen.

The conflict between Southern and Northern agricultural systems came to a head in the Kansas controversy. The dispute over this western area was the occasion for the renewal of the feud between the sections, with the Harpers Ferry raid as the most dramatic incident. As late as 1860 the South could feel itself safe within the Union because, with the aid of Northern Democrats, it controlled the Washington government. This security vanished with the election of 1860. The sequel was secession, Fort Sumter, and war.

Both sides were moved by a tense earnestness. When President Jefferson Davis set aside June 13, 1861, as a day of prayer, an overseer on a Louisiana plantation petitioned his God "that every black Republican" opposed to slavery "shal be trubled with pestilents and calamtys of all Kinds and Drag out the Balance of their existance in Misray and Degradation." In behalf of humanity the leading Northern newspaper called for a terrible retribution against the Southerners: "We mean to *conquer* them, to Subjugate them . . ." Never would traitors be permitted to "return to peaceful and contented homes"; instead they "must find poverty at their firesides, and see privation in the anxious eyes of mothers and the rags of children." A correspondent of the *New York Herald* told his readers of the alleged barbarities practiced by Southerners after the First Battle of Bull Run. He asserted that a Northern soldier carried a wounded Southerner to the shade and gave him a drink of water. Revived by the drink, the ingrate drew his pistol and shot his benefactor through the heart. "Rebel fiends in human shape" were accused of taking "the bayonets and knives of our wounded and dying soldiers and thrusting them into their hearts and leaving them sticking there." Others supposedly severed the heads of the dead and amused themselves by "kicking them about as footballs." [10] It was a people's war of hate and lies.

[10] Quotations in Stampp, *And War Came*, p. 297, and in Craven, *op. cit.*, p. 439.

CHAPTER XV

The Beleaguered Land

⋙⋙⋙⋙⋙⋙⋙⋙⋙⋙⋙⋙⋙⋙⋙⋙⋙⋙⋙⋙⋙⋙⋙⋙⋙⋙⋙⋙⋙⋙⋙⋙⋙⋙⋙⋙⋙⋙⋙⋘

"AT A DISTANCE of sixty years," say historians writing in 1924,[1] "men wonder at the rash and hopeless gallantry of the Southern war for independence." The disparity of resources in the two sections was striking. The population of the twenty-three states that adhered to the Union was 22,700,000; that of the eleven of the Confederacy was 9,000,000. The odds against the South were, therefore, 5 to 2, and 4 to 1 if the 3,500,000 slaves of the South are not considered. This omission is justified, for, while the Negroes furnished no soldiers to the Confederate army, they contributed 93,000 enlistments to the Union army. The odds against the South climb still higher if the Southern mountain regions, which gave thousands of recruits to the Federal army, are counted on the Northern side.

On the basis of the foregoing analysis, one authority believes that the Confederacy could count on the support of a white population of only 6,000,000 while the Union armies could draw on nearly four times that number. Another authority, however, puts the fighting odds at only 3 to 1, assuming that the disaffected or indifferent elements of the North were proportionally much greater than those of the South.[2] Experts estimate the total enrollment of the Confederate armies at about 850,000; that of the Union armies reached twice as many.

The North demonstrated greater superiority in material resources than in manpower. Although Southern farm acreage exceeded that of

[1] Samuel E. Morison and Henry S. Commager, *The Growth of the American Republic*, I, 549.
[2] Oliver P. Chitwood and Frank L. Owsley, *A Short History of the American People*, I, 696; and William Wood, *Captains of the Civil War*, p. 61.

the North, Northern farms possessed a greater gross value. Moreover, the number of workingmen in Northern manufacturing firms was 6 times as many as that of the South, and the value of what they produced was 5⅕ times as great. In addition, the banking capital of the North was 7 times as great, and the railroad system of the North twice as extensive. The South was almost entirely dependent on other regions for the tools and machines needed to maintain industrial production. There were in the South few shipyards, few locally owned ships, and no munitions works or manufactories easily transformed into munitions works, apart from the Tredegar Iron Works in Richmond and a few smaller establishments. These deficiencies meant that the Confederacy was seriously lacking in the industrial and technological equipment necessary to wage modern warfare—a situation only partly remedied by the seizure of Federal arsenals and the purchase of 10,000 rifles in Europe before the blockade was enforced. Throughout the war the Confederate soldier was poorly armed.

Other advantages to the North were an established government, a strong navy, a regular army of 12,000 men, and few natural barriers to hinder its grand strategy of invasion. The Mississippi, Tennessee, and Cumberland rivers spread into the heart of the Confederacy like the spokes of a wheel, and the rivers of Virginia and its great valley invited invasion.

The naval blockade of the Confederacy which President Lincoln established April 19, 1861, guaranteed the isolation of the new nation. Matériel and population of the entire non-American world could be utilized to widen the discrepancy in resources between the warring sections. Foreign soldiers and munitions, if needed, could be added to the Federal supply; such reinforcement would be denied to the South.

Political isolation of the South was almost as complete. Its leaders had committed a crime against the dominant patriotism of the nineteenth century. At a time when progressive statesmen of the world were proclaiming the necessity of national integration, the Southern region of the United States was preaching national disintegration. Was not continental solidarity the ultimate goal of American politics? On this point the often-evasive Lincoln was clear. "You have," he told the secessionists in his inaugural address, "no oath registered in heaven to destroy the government, while I shall have the most solemn one to 'preserve, protect, and defend' it." He would not recognize the right of the Confederacy to exist, and largely because of his attitude no other nation was bold enough to give it diplomatic recognition.

The new nation also suffered from a moral blockade. It was stigmatized as the region of slavery—an institution which Harriet Beecher Stowe and other abolitionists had taught the world to regard as an unforgivable sin. Lincoln, after a period of politic hesitation, turned the war into a crusade for human freedom, thereby arraying the moral indignation of progressive men against his enemies. Isolated from the rest of the world by an iron ring of triple thickness, the Confederacy suffered almost uninterrupted defeat in everything except in the realm of actual fighting. There alone did the beleaguered nation win victories. It failed dismally, however, in its naval, industrial, financial, propagandist, and diplomatic endeavors.

Never before or since did local political leadership suffer such a decline in prestige in the eyes of Southerners as during the period between 1861 and 1865. The South was unable to develop a national consciousness sufficiently intelligent and disciplined to give stability to the nation they were attempting to create. Perhaps Lincoln was correct in assuming that their better natures were against their bid for nationhood. "Physically speaking," he said, "we cannot separate." No "impassable wall," he added, could be erected between the sections.

Despite its great inadequacies, the Confederacy survived for four long years of warfare. It enrolled a defense army of 800,000 men, equipping them with arms sufficiently effective to make them a formidable opponent. About 190,000 stands of small arms were seized from United States arsenals. Already in possession of Southerners were some 300,000 arms of varied antiquity. Munitions were captured on the battlefields and trickled in from the North or from Europe. Josiah Gorgas, the energetic chief of the Ordnance Bureau of the War Department, was so successful in providing the Confederacy with munitions that it could be said that "the supply never failed to be equal to the actual emergency, and no disaster was ever attributed to its scantiness." Gorgas scattered munitions works over the Confederacy where weapons of war were altered, repaired, and manufactured. The Tredegar Iron Works was a sort of scientific headquarters which produced torpedoes, submarines, plates for ironclads, propellar shafts, cannon, machinery for war production, and many other weapons of war.[3]

At the beginning of the war, at least, Southerners were better equipped for military life than their Northern rivals. Their outdoor activities had accustomed them to field exercises and they were trained in the use of firearms because they had followed the chase and guarded against slave insurrections.

Southern respect for rank and family led to prompt recognition of natural leaders, many of whom had graduated from West Point. In the Old South, as in Prussia, aristocrats favored the profession of arms. Since the Confederacy was fighting a war of defense, it required the services of fewer soldiers than its Northern attackers. To Southerners,

[3] E. Merton Coulter, *The Confederate States of America, 1861–1865*, pp. 203, 207.

states' rights and secession were sacred principles, and slavery was a domestic institution registered in heaven with the human family. Southerners, from their point of view, were fighting for elemental things—for freedom and independence, for hearth and home, for white supremacy. They were ready to resist to the end because they felt that defeat would involve the ruin of their way of life.

Many Southerners in 1861 believed that the interests of the Northerners were not great enough to warrant their participation in a war to suppress Southern independence. They felt that Northerners would not fight to destroy the fundamental rights of statehood, and that they would not endure the economic and social consequences of eliminating Southern trade in cotton and other commodities considered essential to Northern welfare.

Leroy P. Walker, while canvassing Alabama in support of secession, said that he would wipe up with his pocket handkerchief all the blood shed as the result of the South's withdrawal from the Union. Many of those who anticipated war thought of it as little more than a glorified muster. Southerners were convinced that what they lacked in military and naval equipment would be outweighed by their superior intelligence, bravery, and hardihood. Common opinion held that one Confederate was the match for at least three Yankees. Had not the American colonies, who were weaker than the South, defeated England, a nation stronger than the North? The Confederacy need only stand on the defensive, win a few victories, and the unheroic Yankee would quickly withdraw from the hornets' nest. Jefferson Davis and other thoughtful leaders, however, did not share such popular fallacies; they believed that there would be a long war against a merciless foe. Robert E. Lee wrote his wife that it might last for ten years; some thought that this revolution, like the American Revolution, would last for seven years.

It was true that in Abraham Lincoln the Confederacy had an implacable enemy. Behind that white face and black beard of a St. John the Baptist was the statesman willing to use the methods by which great leaders of modern times have built or maintained empires. This meant nothing less than imposing forcibly the will of the strong upon the weak. With Lincoln the word was "charity to all men," the reality "blood and iron."

The President's objective was clear: the complete destruction of the Confederate government, and the restoration of its constituent states to the Union. In his opinion the contest between the states was not a war, but rather an attempt to put down domestic insurrection which had become too formidable for ordinary officers of the law. The withdrawal of the Southern states and their subsequent organization into a new nation was declared illegal. To come to terms with the Confederacy necessitated a great war, but the canny theorist in the White House called it an endeavor to re-establish constitutional authority. Accordingly, the President mobilized armies and inaugurated a military struggle without asking Congress for a declaration of war. He launched an invasion against powerful armies without extending to them the formal belligerent rights customary among civilized warmakers. The Confederacy was blockaded to deprive it of basic necessities. The Federal armies moved forward not to come to terms with a legal enemy, but to possess militarily and politically the territory of outlawed rebels. When the policies of blockade and invasion were not immediately successful, novel methods of warfare were employed. Lincoln's Emancipation Proclamation, issued after Lee's advance into the North had been stopped at Antietam, at least by implication, was designed to demoralize Southern society and to give the war the character of a crusade in which righteousness was buttressed by vengeance. Provinces were devastated to break their will to resist.

When victory and the cessation of hostilities came, there was no armistice or peace treaty with an humbled foe, but surrender by an adversary who had been cut to pieces. The Confederacy was dissolved and its constituent parts reincorporated into the United States.

The Southern people entered the war with high hopes. Dissenting elements were swept in line with the majority by the enthusiasm created by secession, and by indignation over Lincoln's position after the fall of Fort Sumter. Disloyal elements within the Confederacy were probably much smaller than similar groups in the North.[4] An Alabamian felt that the Confederacy was "destined to become the proudest and most powerful country that ever flourished in the tide of time;" and James D. B. De Bow promised that the South would be "more than a match, when fighting upon her own soil and in sight of her own homes, for any twenty million which could be organized against" it.[5]

A permanent constitution for the Confederacy was adopted on March 11, 1861; laws of the United States not inconsistent with those of the new government were continued in force; the Stars and Bars became the flag of the new nation. Commissioners were appointed to carry on peaceful negotiations with the United States and foreign countries, and in June, 1861, the seat of government was transferred from Montgomery to Richmond. In a war message on April 29, President Davis answered President Lincoln in a tone of proud defense. "The crooked paths of diplomacy," he asserted, "can scarcely furnish an example so wanting in courtesy, in candor, and directness as was the

[4] Wood, ibid., p. 61.
[5] Coulter, op. cit., p. 69.

course of the United States Government toward our commissioners in Washington." It was extraordinary in his opinion, for the President of the United States to call "for an army of 75,000 men to act as a *posse comitatus* . . . in States where no courts exist whose mandates . . . are not cheerfully obeyed . . . by a willing people." The Confederacy, Davis pointed out, was a peaceful nation drawn into war by aggression from without, and desired peace at any cost save that of honor and independence. In the autumn of 1861 Davis was elected President without opposition for a regular term of six years, and on the following February 22 he was formally inaugurated.

Jefferson Davis was the logical choice for the difficult task of directing the Confederacy. He was a Southern gentleman by training if not by birth, possessing the necessary broad acres, high-born wife, refined countenance, and ornate rhetoric. His experience was broad. He had served successfully as a soldier and an expounder of the Constitution, as an administrator and a senator, as a secessionist and an advocate of Southern nationalism. He had the courage, integrity, and energy needed to achieve that which he considered wise and just. At the beginning of the war he had the respect of an overwhelming majority of the people of the South.

His cabinet members were chosen for their efficiency rather than the political influence they might inspire. Only two, Robert Toombs and Leroy P. Walker, belonged to the governing class, and they later resigned after disagreements with Davis. The only member who was both distinguished and brilliant was Judah P. Benjamin, but he was hated because he was a Jew and a foreigner, and because he possessed an irritating suavity. "A grander rascal than this Jew Benjamin does not exist in the Confederacy," declared Thomas R. R. Cobb of Georgia. The cabinet as a whole was composed of loyal servants of the Confederacy, but it was adjudged "a farce" and "a ridiculous cypher" by the critics of the Davis administration; and there were demands from the Confederate Congress for the dismissal of the entire body. The President made thirteen changes in its composition, but he seldom pleased his critics.

By the early months of 1861 President Davis and his cabinet were able to deploy an army large enough to give reasonable certainty of holding a defense line fully a thousand miles long. They developed an offensive-defensive strategy—a defense against the invader of home territory, which, when the opportunity came, could efficiently become an offense. The Confederacy was rich with leaders to carry out this plan. "No other nation has ever had commanders of such calibre at the very beginning of a great war."

There was the incomparable Robert E. Lee, personification of the

Virginia legend, and Stonewall Jackson, a modern Covenanter; curly-locked Jeb Stuart, a knight from the pages of Sir Walter Scott, and the bishop-soldier Leonidas Polk; Albert Sidney Johnston, Joseph E. Johnston, Ambrose P. Hill, and Daniel H. Hill. West Point furnished the Confederacy with 148 generals—attractive figures who monopolized the popular imagination to the exclusion of political leaders.

Yet, in a sense, their virtues were weaknesses. They were gentlemen who regarded war as a game of the governing classes, its cruelties regulated by the code of chivalry. The common people were considered mere auxiliaries or limited participants. Reluctantly the Confederate generals adopted the realistic view of their great antagonists, Sherman and Grant, that the Civil War was a people's war, involving the widest possible mobilization of men and resources, and directed toward crippling nonmilitary aspects of the enemy's life and economy. They did not understand, at first, that their Northern enemy had the will to fight as long as men and resources lasted. They did not realize why the enemy devastated Southern areas; they saw no reason why they should retaliate in kind. A Richmond editor caustically called Lee's Gettysburg campaign "a gigantic window shopping," and an Englishman who had seen the ravages of Northern troops in Southern towns spoke of the forebearance of the Confederate troops as "most commendable and surprising." [6] Limited warfare was consistent with the Southern idea that the contest was a defensive struggle, and that the enemy would quit as soon as he was driven off Confederate territory.

The execution of the Confederacy's offensive-defensive strategy was handicapped by a policy of dispersal to suit the whims of governors and others more interested in the defense of particular states than in that of the Confederacy as a whole. Localism was so deeply embedded in the Southern mind that little enthusiasm could have been engendered for the war had not strong forces been maintained in the states. Such an attitude made the Virginians feel that the loss of Richmond would have been the loss of the war and to have their way in the demand for the concentration of forces around that city. This made it possible for an adroit enemy to batter down the western doors of the Confederacy and bring about disintegration from the rear.

Emphasis on a strategy of defense was equally disastrous. President Davis wanted to show the world that the South did not want the war and would do nothing more than defend itself against the unjust aggression of the United States. This was derisively called the "digging and ditching policy." It did not take into account the likelihood that the time element was on the side of the contestant with most of the

[6] Lieutenant Colonel Arthur J. L. Fremantle, cited in Coulter, *op. cit.*, p. 347.

resources of the world at its disposal and that the weaker contestant's only chance to win was through lightning strokes.

The Southern people as a whole were too uninformed and too provincial to understand the difficulties of modern warfare confronting them. Enterprising to a certain point, they were hard to discipline and were intolerant of governmental interference in private affairs. Sacrificial in the obvious sense of that term, they were yet unwilling to submit to the hardships of tax measures that might have put the Confederacy on a sound financial basis, or to accept compulsory service which would have placed each man where he was most needed. The gentry, more accustomed to control than to be controlled, found it difficult to take orders from their military superiors. Robert Toombs, while serving as a brigadier, stormed at his superiors and disobeyed orders; he might have been shot in an army better disciplined.

The heavy hand of Federal aggression was most widely felt through use of the blockade, imposed in the spring of 1861. The complex shore line of some 3,500 miles was almost impossible to guard. Yet Lincoln, determined to cripple the Confederacy, placed an arc of naval vessels around each Southern port; other ships patrolled the long coasts and those areas where Confederate vessels were known to lurk. Yet many Confederate vessels, particularly during the early months of the war, successfully ran this so-called paper blockade.

When the Federal navy strengthened its squadrons so much that running the blockade became hazardous to ordinary vessels, a special type of steamer was constructed. These blockade-runners were long slim vessels capable of such high speed that they were not easily overtaken by warships. They moved from Wilmington, Charleston, Mobile, and Galveston to Nassau, Cuba, and other West Indian islands. Nassau attained a prosperity it was not again to know until the twentieth-century era of the rumrunners. Operators of successful blockade-runners flaunted their prosperity in public, consequently acquiring an unenviable notoriety in the eyes of Southerners. Confederate authorities, seeking to have the blockade declared illegal by European states, cited impressive figures to prove its ineffectiveness. The historian Frank L. Owlsey, after careful investigations, concludes that in 1862 not more than one in eight blockade runners was captured, and only one in four in 1863. One vessel, he says, "chalked up 44 trips through the blockade."

The success of these small craft, however, does not tell the whole story of the Confederacy's foreign commerce. Large vessels which normally bore the bulk of ocean commerce would not risk entering Confederate ports. As the Federal squadrons became stronger the blockade grew increasingly tighter; in time large segments of the Southern coastline, including the ports of Beaufort and New Bern in

North Carolina and Port Royal in South Carolina, were captured. By 1865 virtually one out of every two blockade runners was seized. Until almost the end of the war Wilmington in North Carolina remained the only important leak in the war on Southern commerce. Cotton export, the basis of the Confederacy's financial operations abroad, was seriously curtailed. This, in turn, limited the importation of many articles from foreign markets necessary for waging warfare. Although the blockade did not cause starvation, it deprived the Southern people not only of such luxuries as tea, coffee, and fine raiment, but also of such necessities as medicine and sugar. "The blockade," says one writer,[7] "was the real destroyer of the South."

The Confederacy expected to be aided by European recognition or even intervention in breaking the blockade. The situation in Great Britain and France in some respects justified this hope. The United States had long been criticized by the English ruling class because of its encouragement of popular government and the alleged uncouthness of its people. To divide the potential power of this growing nation might conceivably have seemed a prudent move. The Confederacy, on the other hand, in the opinion of certain British, was no longer a wasteland of slavery, but a land of culture controlled by gentlemen similar to those of the mother country. Its struggle for independence appeared to be no different from honored nationalist movements of Europe. The advantages to English industry and commerce of its low tariff policies were contrasted with the disadvantages of the protectionist policies adopted by the United States in 1861. Most important, the Confederacy was the home of cotton, the commodity which fed a significant portion of English industry.

To these reasons for sympathizing with the Confederacy, France could add another. Its ambitious emperor Napoleon III had taken advantage of the American predicament to establish French authority in Mexico under the puppet ruler Maximilian of Hapsburg. The United States, under the Monroe Doctrine, opposed this imperialistic adventure, and it was quite clear that the existence of Maximilian's empire was contingent upon an independent Confederacy to act as a buffer between the French and the Americans.

Envisaging the possibilities of the foreign situation, the Davis government sent two missions to Europe—one in 1861 headed by William L. Yancey, and another in 1862 composed of James M. Mason and John Slidell. A concerted literary campaign was launched to convince Europeans of the wisdom and justice of the Confederate position. London published a newspaper and employed writers to describe the vastness and unconquerable strength of the South, the strategic importance of

---

[7] Nathaniel W. Stephenson, *The Day of the Confederacy*, p. 105.

King Cotton, the perfidy of the Lincoln government, the sacredness of the war for independence, and the advantage to Europe of the division of North America into two equal powers.

With a single exception, Confederate diplomacy brought no results. Queen Victoria extended belligerent rights to the warring nation; other European rulers followed her example. This action was a logical sequel to Lincoln's tacit recognition of the belligerent status of the Confederacy by declaring a public blockade instead of simply closing rebel ports to foreign commerce, but it irritated the Washington government, which insisted upon adhering to the official fiction that the war was a domestic insurrection.

Vainly Confederate agents sought diplomatic recognition. The Yancey mission left England in 1862 with the distinct impression that it had been snubbed. Southern hopes were briefly raised by the Trent affair. When the commander of a United States vessel removed the Confederate envoys Mason and Slidell from the British mail steamer *Trent*, relations between the United States and England were tense. Britain demanded an apology and reparations. A diplomatic break was avoided by allowing Mason and Slidell to proceed.

In the summer of 1862 the failures of the Federal commanders McClellan and Pope before Richmond and the prospect of Lee's launching an offensive so brightened the cause of the South that there was a move in the English cabinet to mediate in favor of the Confederacy. Russell, the Foreign Minister, wrote that the time had come "for offering mediation . . . with a view to the recognition of the independence of the Confederates." Gladstone, the Chancellor of the Exchequer, publicly declared that he believed the Confederacy had developed into a nation capable of maintaining a separate existence. Lee's repulse at Antietam, however, brought about a strict renewal of the British policy of neutrality.

The Confederate authorities insistently demanded that Britain declare the blockade illegal because of its alleged ineffectiveness, but Britain, in the spring of 1862, openly announced itself satisfied with the situation. Secretary of State Benjamin bitterly complained that Britain had "some unconfessed interest" in its maintenance. In March, 1863, Mason lamented that he had "no intercourse, unofficial or otherwise, with any member of the [British] Government." A few months later Benjamin paid an unwilling compliment to an opponent by admitting "the success of his [United States Secretary of State Seward's] policy of intimidation." After an acrid controversy over the activities of four British consuls in Southern cities, President Davis expelled them in October, 1863. Thenceforth it was clear that the Confederacy could no longer reasonably hope for British aid. Scarcely a ripple appeared on the diplomatic sea when the Confederacy played its last card. Mason intimated to Palmerston a month before the war's end that his country would abolish slavery as a condition of recognition.

For two years Confederate agents warned Napoleon III that the success of his Mexican adventure depended upon the success of the Confederacy. The Emperor had often expressed sympathy for the South. Although he realized that France suffered more than England from the interruption of the cotton trade, his failure to secure the co-operation of Britain forced him to remain aloof from the war. Slippery in policies and uncertain in convictions, he gave the Confederates the impression that he was trying to dupe them. He apparently believed the South would win the war; nonetheless, he hoped to retain Mexico without incurring the hostility of the United States. In the spring of 1864, however, the Confederate envoy Slidell bluntly advised him that the safety of the Mexican protectorate depended upon the friendship and independence of the Confederacy. If, in other words, France would not intervene in the American war, it must expect the Confederacy—if Slidell's government were victorious—to join with the United States in driving the French from Mexico. Napoleon was unimpressed.

The failure of the Confederacy to gain recognition or aid from either England or France may be attributed partly to personalities. Queen Victoria and the Prince Consort Albert exerted their influence on the Northern side, and Charles Francis Adams and his two sons, the Federal diplomats, skilled in the intricacies of the interational game, were more than a match for the agents the South sent abroad. Mary B. Chesnut, diarist of the South, regarded Yancey as a most unfortunate representative of the Confederacy: "Send a man to England who had killed his father-in-law in a street brawl!" [8] Britain veered away more and more from the Confederate side as the chances of Southern success grew ever dimmer following Lee's repulse at Antietam. Relations with the United States became less strained after the decisive Federal victories at Gettysburg and Vicksburg.

The fundamental cause, however, for the failure of Confederate diplomacy was the inability of King Cotton to play his expected imperial role. Southerners felt that the need for their cotton would press so heavily upon the British and French that they would intervene in the war to maintain the trade. Southerners regarded the blockade as a blessing in disguise. They voluntarily accentuated its effectiveness by passing state laws restricting cotton exports; they urged planters to withhold their crops from the market, limit their acreage, and even burn quantities as a patriotic duty. As the result of these activities, the cotton crop of 1862 was less than half as large as that of 1861.

[8] *A Diary from Dixie,* p. 126. Actually Yancey had killed his uncle-in-law.

However, "the old delusion that American staples run the wheels of industry in Europe" was, indeed, a fallacy. In 1861 the British textile industry had a surplus of 700,000 bales of cotton and 300,000,000 pounds of manufactured cotton goods. Cotton goods were selling at a loss, and some people believed that England was on the brink of an industrial panic. When the blockade cut off the main source of cheap cotton, manufacturers were able to dispose of their surplus at huge profits. The "cotton famine" did not come until 1862 and 1863, throwing a half million operatives out of work and closing many of the smaller mills. The industry, however, picked up late in 1863, and the number of unemployed textile workers gradually fell to a small figure. Cotton importations from Egypt, India, and Brazil, and woolen and linen industries greatly expanded. One historian believes that this attempt to destroy the Southern cotton monopoly helps to explain England's aversion for slavery, as that calculating nation felt that the South could not raise cotton without slave labor.[9]

English industrialists reaped handsome profits from the sale of war materials, and the English merchant marine benefitted from the decline of American shipping. The nation of shopkeepers was generally earning more money from America at war than it had made from America at peace. Why disturb the war? Moreover, the economic hardships which England encountered because of the severing of communications with the Cotton Kingdom were less severe than those it might expect if it intervened in the war. Such interference would have cut off the profits accruing to the British from the sale of munitions to the North, and would have prevented the importation of American wheat —a product on which the English masses depended for their very bread.

In addition to practical considerations favoring nonintervention, British idealism was a deterrent. The liberal sentiments of England, and of Europe as a whole, were enlisted by Lincoln, who, with an eye on its international effectiveness, issued the Emancipation Proclamation in September, 1862. John Bright, William E. Forster, and Goldwin Smith, English pro-North agitators, were now believed when they asserted that the cause of the Union was the cause of freedom. Karl Marx led a meeting of British workingmen in the declaration that the success of free institutions in America was a matter of great importance to them. Henry Ward Beecher, in a triumphal tour of England in 1863, brought the message of the American common man to his English brother. Although the South had eminent preachers who believed in slavery as firmly as Beecher advocated freedom, none of them was capable of agitating for slavery in the foreign field.

[9] Coulter, op. cit., p. 188.

Confederate leaders could be proud of their large army in the field in February, 1862. Two months later President Davis achieved one of his greatest successes—the passage of the first Conscription Act of the Confederacy, calling white males between the ages of eighteen and thirty-five into the national army for three years. At the same time, however, Confederate authorities were far less successful in solving the grave financial, economic, and social problems with which their people were beset. "It would have required," says a writer on the Confederacy,[10] "a miracle of statesmanship to solve these difficulties."

Southerners could work near miracles only on the battlefield; they were unprepared to meet exigencies which they could not foresee. Primarily they were agriculturists, dependent for their livelihood on the export of their staples; when war cut off these shipments, they were economically helpless. An individualistic people accustomed to pay only those taxes needed to maintain the minimum functions of government, they could not accept the idea of a central administration exercising more than the limited powers assigned to it by the Constitution. No government, state or national, they believed had the right to interfere with an individual's social life or economic interests. From the viewpoint of those who have witnessed the wars of the twentieth century, it is clear that nothing would have provided a solution of the economic problems of the Confederacy except a total mobilization of resources of the beleaguered nation—conscription of physical assets as well as of men. Such a Herculean remedy was too much to expect of people of Southern background.

The Confederacy lacked adequate specie and banking resources, was unable to make free use abroad of its excess quantities of cotton, rice, tobacco, and naval stores, and was handicapped by the states' rights philosophy of its politicians as well as by the inability of its people to realize the necessity of submitting to heavy taxes. The Southern government was forced to support its operations by extravagant borrowing and by reckless printing of paper money. All this appears to have been the inevitable consequence of difficult circumstances, but the government's confidence in King Cotton led it to project financial plans with genuine hope of success.

Early in the war, Confederate agents abroad purchased arms, medicines, ships, and many other necessities of war. The Confederate treasury chiefly relied upon the seizure of specie in the Southern branch of the United States Mint and the coaxing from Southern banks of large portions of their specie in return for $15,000,000 in Confederate bonds. Although this loan was immediately successful, it placed the Confederacy in a dangerous financial position because the purchases made from

[10] Charles W. Ramsdell, *Behind the Lines in the Southern Confederacy*, p. 3.

its returns served to drain the country of gold. The tax measure of August 19, 1861, was intended as a direct property tax of one-half of one per cent. Since the Confederacy had no tax collectors of its own, however, the burden of collection was imposed upon the states, which solved the problem by borrowing from the people what was due the Confederate government. Thus a tax was converted into a loan.

In the summer of 1861 the Richmond government floated bonds which it exchanged for 400,000 bales of cotton and quantities of turpentine and tobacco. Against this cotton surplus Slidell in 1863 was able to negotiate through Émile Erlanger, a French financier, a loan of $15,000,000 in exchange for cotton bonds. Slidell was forced to make almost ruinous concessions. Erlanger realized handsome profits by taking over the bonds at 77, selling them in the financial markets at 90, and then collecting a commission of 5 per cent on the transaction. At that stage the Confederate government took the easiest road out of their difficulties and issued great quantities of bonds and paper money, to be redeemed two years after the winning of Southern independence. The final debt of the Confederacy climbed to $2,000,000,000 one half of which comprised paper money obligations.

A devastating period of inflation set in. The gold value of Confederate notes plunged from 90 in 1861 to 6.3 in 1863, to 1.7 early in 1865, and to zero with the fall of the Confederacy. The Confederate Congress tried to establish values more substantial than its own currency. As already indicated, it acquired cotton and other products of the land which it was able to dispose of advantageously by means of blockade-runners.

Part of the general tax measure of April 24, 1863 was a "tax in kind" of one tenth of the products of the land—a measure naturally unpopular with the farmers. It was the first general tax to be levied upon the low-income group of the South. In addition to enforcement of the produce levy was the commandeering or impressment of slaves, animals, tools, and food for the use of the army. This was virtually equivalent to having the soldiers "live off the country"; it was most burdensome in those sections of the country near railroads and army camps. Against such tyranny Robert Toombs railed, "I would rather see the whole country the cemetery of freedom than the habitation of slaves." Discovering that his labors in favor of ordered and responsible governmental finances were unavailing, Secretary of the Treasury Christopher G. Memminger resigned on June 15, 1864, utterly disheartened. His successor George A. Trenholm could do no better, but presided over ruin that soon dissolved into chaos.

Depreciating currency, says Charles W. Ramsdell,[11] aggravated

[11] *Ibid.*, p. 12.

"every difficulty that beset both people and government." It first expressed itself in the sensational rise of the price of salt, a commodity widely used in the curing of pork. This was followed by increases that sent other commodities out of reach of families with moderate incomes. Among these items were flour, corn, meat of all kinds, cloth, and domestic utensils, with some prices rising as much as 400 per cent. A pair of shoes cost $100; it was more than a sorry joke that persons were said to take their money to market in baskets and bring their provisions home in pocketbooks.

Those who lived on plantations untouched by the destructive violence of war enjoyed a rude plenty to the very end of the Confederacy. The poor of the cities suffered much; especially was this true in Richmond, where inhabitants endured hardships from overcrowding, traffic congestion, and the tendency of country folk to hold back commodities in anticipation of high prices. Charity alone kept many people from starving. The condition of the poorer families in the country, particularly those whose male members were in the army, was even worse. Although the wife of a soldier was able to raise a little corn and forage, she had no money with which to buy shoes and clothing for her family except what her husband was able to send her from his monthly pay of $11. "We are all Soldiers' Wives or Mothers . . ." was the vein in which many complained to the governor of their state.[12] "How far will eleven dollars go in a family now when meat is from 75 cents to $1.00 pr pound, flour, $50 pr bll, wood from 4 to 5$ per load, meal and b[ran] 4 to 5 dollars pr bushel, eggs 50 to 60 cts pr dz . . . Now Sir how we ask you in the name of God are we to live?" There were many bread riots. In Richmond April 2, 1863, a mob of a thousand women looted stores and was quieted only by speeches from Governor Letcher and President Davis.

There were outbursts of rage against the speculators. "Extortion, pitiless extortion is making havoc in the land," Bishop George F. Pierce told the Georgia legislature in 1863 "We are devouring each other. Avarice with full barns puts the bounties of Providence under bolts and bars, waiting with eager longings for higher prices." Heroic remedies were attempted. Governors Joseph E. Brown of Georgia and Andrew B. Moore of Alabama seized salt from the speculators. Several states prohibited monopoly of markets in the vain hope of restraining prices. More effective in meeting the needs of the people was the radical reduction in 1863 of acreage devoted to cotton so that there might be increases in the supply of grains, potatoes, beans, sorghum, and other foodstuffs. As additional protection to the food supply, authorities of

[12] Mary C. More to Governor Zebulon B. Vance, cited in Ramsdell, op. cit., p. 49.

six states enacted regulations prohibiting the manufacture of alcohol from grains.

These somewhat negative measures were followed in 1863 and 1864 by positive public acts designed to remedy deficiencies in the economy. All the states of the Confederacy appropriated large sums for the relief of indigent families of soldiers, establishing elaborate machinery for the administration of these funds. The proceeds of taxes in kind were freely distributed. Georgia appropriated $6,000,000 for relief in 1863, and the next year distributed 97,000 bushels of corn among mountain families who had suffered crop failures. The Virginia legislature authorized Governor William Smith to set up an agency to sell materials for manufacturing cloth. As a final expedient, Virginia and Mississippi resorted to impressments as relief measures.

States took active parts in the production of commodities. At first the production of salt was encouraged by subsidies to private producers, but later the states participated in its production and distribution. They entered into contracts with manufacturers to furnish clothing and shoes for the destitute; a few states set up factories of their own. Texas established a successful textile mill in its penitentiary and sold or donated its products to the people. Governor Henry W. Allen of Louisiana exchanged with Mexico cotton for medicines, cotton cards, and other necessities. The energetic Allen established a state medical dispensary, two textile mills, and a foundry for the manufacture of cooking utensils. Seeking to bring relief to their people, state governments entered the business of blockade-running. Governor Vance of North Carolina was so successful with his steamer, *The Advance*, that the governors of Virginia, Georgia, and South Carolina also purchased blockade-runners.

The evil effects of inflation and the blockade were increased by the inadequacy of the Confederate system of communications. Railroads were unsuited for the tremendous task of moving men and supplies in sufficient number to maintain a battle line stretching a thousand miles. Constructed for the local purpose of carrying crops to river towns or seaports, the rails were mostly narrow strips of wrought iron and at least eleven different gauges in the South made transfer of cars from one line to another impossible. Under the stress of war, rolling stock and rails wore out, and facilities for repair or replacement became ever scarcer. The Confederate government, pressed by immediate military necessities, sometimes routed cars and engines to dangerous areas where they frequently were lost, abandoned, or captured. The inevitable delays and stoppages resulting from these conditions defeated, to a large degree, the most successful economic measure of the Confederacy—

providing enough food for the sustenance of a blockaded people. It was a just complaint that abundant stores glutted railroad warehouses while the soldiers or the civilian population of cities were half starved and half clothed.

Almost as paralyzing to Southern economy as the breakdown of railroad transportation were the deficiencies in nonmechanical transportation. Wagons wore out under the long trips which the inadequacies of railroads necessitated, and often they could not be replaced or repaired. Although it was recognized that the production of food required work animals on the farms, they were often taken over by the army. Artillery and cavalry services seized horses and mules in a highhanded fashion and when Union forces raided Confederate territory they made off with all available animals.

Symptomatic of the weaknesses and confusion which characterized the internal affairs of the Confederacy was the reaction of the Southern people to nearly every proposal of the zealous man who directed their government. Although it has since been realized that almost all of Prsident Davis' measures were necessary for winning the war, the people and their leaders were displeased. Davis' personality was in part responsible. He lacked humor and frankness, displaying an irritating self confidence and little insight into human nature. He failed to recognize his own lack of military genius, and wasted his own time on military excursions which might better have been used for civil affairs. A sense of personal loyalty prompted him to retain officials whom the people despised. When the military offensives of 1862 were followed by disappointing retreats, Davis was severely, though unfairly, criticized. Although these difficulties were beyond the power of the Confederate government to correct, the President was too secretive to take the people into his confidence and tell them the facts—that their armies were not equipped for an offensive.

Davis was dogged by two apostles of states' rights who had no conception of the national unity necessary to repel the enemy. One of these critics was Governor Joseph E. Brown of Georgia, who believed that his state should raise its own armies, keep out Confederate tax gatherers, resist conscription, and promote the Southern cause independently. A Georgia editor declared that Brown had a hallucination which made him "imagine himself, alternately, the State of Georgia and the President of the Confederate States." The other critic was Governor Zebulon B. Vance of North Carolina, a masterly hero of the common people who cunningly played upon the belief that North Carolina was being exploited by the rest of the South. He believed that Davis, in making civil appointments and military promotions, prefered Democrats and secessionists over old Whigs and former unionists.

Vance opposed conscription policies and insisted that the products of his state be used exclusively by North Carolina troops.

Critics railed at Davis' program of conscription, denying that it was "absolutely necessary" for the success of the Confederate armies. "Conscription checks enthusiasm," was the cry; "we are invincible under a system of volunteering, we are lost with conscription." The laws permitting the hiring of substitutes for the draft and the exemption of one overseer for each plantation of twenty slaves gave credence to the charge that the President was conducting "a rich man's war and a poor man's fight." On the other hand, his proposal that the government's industrial demands be met by the purchase or confiscation of slaves created suspicion among the rich. Authority to suspend the writ of *habeas corpus* was requested by Davis and repeatedly granted by the Confederate Congress. Desertion from the army, organization of subversive societies, and sabatoge against military establishments created grave problems. Although in suspending the ordinary processes of justice the President exercised his authority with great moderation, he was arraigned by the "martinets of constitutionalism" who had long been important in Southern politics. They counted as nothing the wholly abnormal circumstances with which Davis was surrounded.

"Now I am beginning to doubt his good intentions," wrote Vice-President Stephens of the President in 1864, ". . . His whole policy on the organization and discipline of the army is perfectly consistent with the hypothesis that he is aiming at absolute power." When Davis tried to control prices to prevent speculators from exploiting the poor, he was told that he was violating the Constitution. "Every step we have taken during the past four years," grimly commented the *Montgomery Mail*, "has been in the direction of military despotism." There was even agitation to impeach this offender against the Constitution; friends of that much-disputed document seemingly preferred to lose the war according to rules rather than to win it by the exception.

The most disgraceful chapter in the history of the Southern War for Independence deals with desertion from the army. Unquestionably it "contributed definitely to the Confederate defeats after 1862 and . . . to the catastrophe of 1865." At critical times the absence of men from the ranks prevented Confederate generals from following up successes. President Davis was probably correct when he declared shortly after the Battle of Gettysburg that if every Southerner liable for military service would do his duty, the Confederacy would be invincible. According to official reports, there were 100,000 desertions from Confederate ranks. There were occasions when "whole companies, garrisons, and even regiments decamped at a time." Some of the deserters banded together in the Carolina mountains or the Florida wilds and organized raids to seize cattle and military stores; others hid in woods or caves, emerging when women signaled that army agents were not in the vicinity.

Desertions can be explained by the difficult conditions of the times. Conscription forced into the ranks men who, as unionists, had no sympathy with the Confederate cause. Others were poor whites, too ignorant to understand the meaning of the struggle, or vaguely convinced that it was a slaveholders' war. The great majority of the desertions, however, were caused by the hardships of military service—inferior food and clothing, a shocking lack of sanitation in the camps, the almost worthless wages the soldiers received. Many deserted because of deplorable conditions at home—wives and children without support, raids or rumors of raids by Confederates, unionists, Negroes, deserters, and even Indians. "Before God," one wife wrote her soldier-husband,[13] ". . . unless you come home, we must die."

The South had its share of cowards, too—men who employed every pretext to get out or stay out of the army, and selfish women who did their utmost to keep their men at home. Easygoing physicians issued certificates of ill health when it did not exist, and clever lawyers grew rich discovering loopholes for their unpatriotic clients. There was a rush to enter the professions and occupations exempted under the conscription law. Schools were opened by persons who had never taught before, hesitating patriots sought election to state offices, and men suddenly became apothecaries, collecting "a few empty jars, a cheap assortment of combs and brushes, a few bottles of 'hairdye' and 'wizard oil' and other Yankee nostrums." Strict constitutionalists sanctioned such practices. "If agents of the Confederate government," declared Congressman Henry S. Foote of Tennessee, "had the right to go in and take the men belonging to that state, how were states' rights and state sovereignty to be maintained?" The chief justice of North Carolina discharged two deserters who killed a man while resisting capture on the ground that a state had nothing to do with the enforcement of Confederate conscription.

President Davis informed the Confederate Congress in 1864: "In certain localities men of no mean position do not hesitate to avow their disloyalty and hostility to our cause, and their advocacy of peace on the terms of submission and the abolition of slavery." The Peace and Constitutional Union Society was strong in Alabama, Georgia, North Carolina, and Tennessee; the Heroes of America had members in southwest Virginia and in the neighboring counties of North Carolina and Tennessee. These two organizations gave information to the enemy, encouraged desertion from the Confederate army, and aimed at the

[13] Ella Lonn, *Desertion during the Civil War,* pp. 13, 23.

overthrow of the Confederacy and the restoration of the Union.

The peace movement came to a head in North Carolina where William W. Holden, editor of the *North Carolina Standard*, in 1863 and 1864 formulated plans which probably sought to detach North Carolina from the Confederacy and make peace with Lincoln. Holden's program was crushed, however, when Zebulon B. Vance defeated him for the governorship in August, 1864. Thereafter, the peace movement took on a less seditious and more unrealistic character, with certain prominent leaders of the Confederacy hoping that a settlement might be reached before Washington forced a military decision.

The leader of this fatuous group was Vice-President Stephens, who assumed early in 1865 that President Lincoln would consent to negotiating peace on terms short of a surrender. This led to a conference at Hampton Roads on February 3, 1865, between Lincoln and Secretary of State Seward on one hand, and Stephens and two other Confederates on the other. Lincoln, as might have been anticipated, rejected any peace other than total surrender. A wave of enthusiasm swept over Richmond, and President Davis enjoyed his final triumph.

On September 23, 1862, President Lincoln unleashed his principal moral weapon against those besieged by his armies and ships. It was the Preliminary Emancipation Proclamation, declaring that "persons held as slaves" within areas "in rebellion against the United States" on January 1, 1863, would be "then, henceforward, and forever free." On that day the Final Emancipation Proclamation invoked "the considerate judgment of mankind and the gracious favor of Almighty God." However, it was not applied to those portions of the slave states under Federal authority, an area which included the border states, Tennessee, and specifically designated sections of Virginia and Louisiana.

Like Lincoln's other state papers, the Emancipation Proclamations were the work of a subtle man who wished his well-wrought words to convey a different meaning to various groups. He gave comfort to the legalists who objected to his act as a direct violation of the protection given to slavery by the Constitution, pointing out that it was "warranted by the Constitution *upon military necessity*." In order not to offend proslavery Unionists of the border states, freedom was decreed only in those regions under Confederate control. When such a procedure had been suggested to him by a group of clergymen in the summer of 1862, Lincoln had declared that it would be "like the Pope's bull against the comet." Such, in truth, was its immediate effect. Slaves of the Confederacy continued their accustomed tasks, apparently unimpressed by the fact that a measure had been taken to change their manner of life. Not one slave rose in rebellion. The white South, sensing a bid for a slave revolt, felt inspired to fight more tenaciously, angrily hurling Lincoln's words back at him. "No public man in our country," said Governor John Letcher of Lincoln,[14] "has exhibited such depravity, . . . has displayed so atrocious a spirit as is manifested in this proposition." Anticipating this accusation, Lincoln, in the Final Emancipation Proclamation, cautiously counseled the persons declared free to abstain from all violence except in necessary self-defense.

In counseling no violence, Lincoln laid down a pattern of conduct for the Negro that the responsible benefactors of the race have since demanded of it. The demand is that the Negro must never be aggressive and always must depend on his white friends for social uplift. This meant that the Negro in 1863, unlike the French peasants in 1789, was not to have the radical benefits which result from successful revolts. Had the Southern slaves risen in revolt, Lincoln not improbably would have had to put them down with Northern soldiers.

While moderates were comforted, abolitionists, both at home and abroad, saw in Lincoln's words the fulfillment of their desires. Brushing aside literal interpretations, they lauded the President as the Great Emancipator, and Julia Ward Howe, in her hymn for marching men, perceived in the proclamation the "glory of the coming of the Lord." It cannot be proved that the abolitionists were wrong in giving so broad an interpretation to the meaning the President wished to convey. Horace Greeley and other leaders of a growing radicalism among Northerners had exerted immense pressure upon Lincoln. Moreover, through letters from England, he had been informed of the effect of his abolitionist policy upon European public opinion.

The Emancipation Proclamation was jubilantly hailed by the people of the North with the firing of guns. It was endowed with an origin as dramatic as that with which Moses received the Decalogue on Sinai, and the man who bore it down to earth was made a god in the pantheon of humanity. The war for the preservation of the Union was glorified into a crusade for freedom, and the federal armies, as they pushed further and further into the Confederacy, struck the shackles from the wrists and ankles of the bondsmen. At the sight of men in blue beating drums and singing songs of freedom, Negroes caught the spirit of the times. They rushed forward to meet their liberators in joyous abandon. Here, at last, was their Day of Jubilee. Lincoln furthered the process of freedom by abandoning previously expressed scruples against the arming of former slaves, and many of them joined the Union army. Some people, commented Lincoln, considered "the emancipation policy and the use of colored troops . . . the heaviest blow yet dealt to the rebellion."

While the slaves were being freed in the rebellious states, the border

[14] Cited in Edward Channing, *A History of the United States,* VI, 545.

ROBERT E. LEE. *The benign but firm countenance of this photograph indicates why the South believes that the leader of its greatest military effort was the most outstanding character in its history.*

SHERMAN'S MEN. *This contemporary sketch shows Union soldiers foraging in South Carolina in 1865.*

CIVIL WAR REFUGEES. *Driven from their homes, whole families took refuge in the Southern wilderness with such of their possessions as they could save and transport.*

states of West Virginia, Tennessee, Missouri, and Maryland of their own volition abolished the condemned institution, leaving only Delaware and Kentucky with slaves. The Thirteenth Amendment to the federal Constitution went into effect on December 18, 1865, granting the sanction of the supreme law of the land to what Lincoln and the armies had already done as a supposed necessity of war.

That the Confederacy was able to survive for four years was due in no small measure to the devotion of its slaves and the heroism of its women. The 3.5 million blacks could have arisen in a horrible insurrection that would have paralyzed the Confederacy. Instead, they remained so loyal to their masters that one writer sweepingly asserts: "The slaves supported the war unanimously (albeit somewhat involuntarily)." [15] Conspiracies and plots, in truth, were unearthed and the alleged participants were whipped or hanged in states as far apart as Virginia, Alabama, and Arkansas. In 1863 there were rumors of a slave plot of gigantic proportions, but its fruition was prevented by Confederates who discovered evidence of it months ahead. Most of the slaves uncomplainingly cultivated the fields of the Confederacy; they cared for women and children whose white husbands and fathers were on distant battlefields, and as body servants and trench diggers they performed many useful services of a type for which their descendants, in subsequent wars, were allowed to wear the uniform of their country. Indeed, the faithful wartime slave became one of the legends of the South.

Why were the Negroes so loyal? Partly, of course, it was due to the blind habit of obedience inherent in their humble state and to the dreadful punishment they would have received had they raised their hands in revolt; yet, like their white masters, they possessed more than passive emotions. They served the South because they were genuine Southerners as deeply devoted to their land as were white men, and they loved the old ways that the invaders were threatening, as many volumes of reminiscent literature testify.

The women of the Confederacy were burdened with more than their usual duties. They sent their men forth to battle with gaudy banners, and danced and sang with the soldiers on furlough. They nursed the sick and the wounded in the numerous ghastly hospitals of the Confederacy, even extending their kindly services to prisoners of war. They provided the men at the front with many necessities the government was unable to furnish—clothes they themselves had spun and woven, blankets and suits cut from carpets and curtains. Women of the upper classes watched the disappearance of accustomed luxuries without complaint, sharing their meager comforts with those in worse cir-

[15] Robert S. Cotterill, *The Old South*, p. 317.

cumstances. In many instances women and children of the lower classes stoically faced hunger and want and the necessity of following plows through their tiny fields. Women of all classes felt the awful anxiety for absent soldiers, suspense over the outcome of battles, and grief for the dead. Some wandered futilely from camp to camp and from hospital to hospital in the faint hope of finding those reported lost or dead.

Mistresses assumed the full responsibilities of plantations, managing the slaves and directing the planting and harvesting. They brought forth spinning wheels and looms from the attics to make homespun substitutes for cloth that could not be imported. They devised replacements for the shortages of the times—parched corn or wheat for coffee, sassafras for tea, sorghum molasses for sugar, and smokehouse drippings for salt. Advance of the enemy and fear of ruthless outlaws caused many women to flee to remote places where they endured privations in strange surroundings. Others wisely remained at home to face the invader with a serene and haughty courage. They were robbed, pillaged, and sometimes even burned out of their homes. Yet seldom were they subjected to personal violence by intruders drunk or sober. A legendary respect for the Southern lady evidently inspired prowling outlaws and Negroes as well as those who wore the uniform of the United States.

The Confederates had as great a faith in God as any people in modern times engaged in war. The voice of prayer mingled with the din of battle, and it was generally believed that the God of Battle would not let a just cause fail. Benjamin M. Palmer, James H. Thornwell, Stephen Elliott, Charles T. Quintard, and the other great preachers of the South went among the soldiers fighting sin and holding revival meetings. As many as 150,000 soldiers were converted and baptized; among them were Generals Joseph E. Johnston, John B. Hood, and William J. Hardee. Many Confederate leaders needed no conversion, for religion was already a dominant force in their lives. Among such persons were Jefferson Davis, Robert E. Lee, Stonewall Jackson, and John B. Gordon; they gave the Lord credit for their victories. The fact that the priestly office and command in battle could be blended was demonstrated by the words of the Reverend William N. Pendleton, Lee's chief of artillery, to his men concerning the enemy: "While we kill their bodies, may the Lord have mercy on their sinful souls—FIRE!" Other ministers who became active generals were Bishop Leonidas Polk of Louisiana and the Reverend Mark P. Lowrey, a Mississippi Baptist.

So tonic was the influence of religion on the morale of the Southern people that it might have accomplished the miracle of permanent victory. This did not happen, one student of the problem believes,[16] because religion had not as yet become a vital interest to the lower masses of the Southern people.

While the Confederacy was bleeding internally because of blockade, inflation, desertion, disloyalty, and other ills, the armies of the United States were pressing forward determined to destroy the Confederate government and reincorporate its territories into the Union. Between General Irwin McDowell's invasion of Virginia in July, 1861, and the surrender of the principal Confederate army at Appomattox early in April, 1865, stretched three years and nine months of costly warfare. Confederate resistance was so stubborn and heroic that the cost in human lives was the greatest in American history to that time: 110,000 Union soldiers and 94,000 Confederates died of battle wounds; 260,000 Federal troops and 164,000 Confederates succumbed to other causes.[17]

Each year of the war was marked by definite progress by the Union armies in their tremendous task of trampling out the lifeblood of the Confederacy. The year 1861 saw the Union forces secure their positions in the border states and occupy northern Virginia, Port Royal in South Carolina, and the northeastern coast of North Carolina. In 1862 Virginia was saved from conquest by Stonewall Jackson's Valley Campaign and by Lee's repulse of the Union armies before Richmond and Fredericksburg; but the same year witnessed vast federal advances in the West. The fall of Fort Donelson early in 1862 was followed by Federal occupation of all western and middle Tennessee and strong points on the Mississippi north of Vicksburg. In the meantime Federal naval forces captured New Orleans and occupied the whole length of the Mississippi south of Port Hudson. In 1863 Lee's smashing victory at Chancellorsville again saved Richmond, but the fall of Vicksburg and Port Hudson gave the Federals command of the entire Mississippi and cut off the Confederacy from Louisiana sugar, Texas beef, and Mexican firearms. These events were followed by the capture of Chattanooga, key to the Confederacy's center.

In 1864, for the third successive year, Lee kept the Federals out of Richmond, forcing them to halt there and at Petersburg for a nine-months' siege. William T. Sherman, Federal commander in the West, meanwhile captured Atlanta and by Christmas, 1864, had reached Savannah after his famous march of 300 miles through Georgia. In January, 1865, this bold general advanced through the Carolinas—a strategy designed to cut into Lee's defenses from the rear. That great Virginian

[16] Coulter, op. cit., p. 523.
[17] Estimate of James G. Randall, *The Civil War and Reconstruction*, p. 687.

soon realized that a gigantic encircling movement made his position untenable. This was the price he paid for concentrating all his energies in defense of his beloved state.

Thrice in its history the beleaguered Confederacy had opportunities to break the blockade which was tightening its coils around the stricken South. Efforts to take advantage of these situations somewhat brightened a scene otherwise dominated by the gloom of impending defeat. The first such opportunity was naval in character; the other two were military. On March 8, 1862, a strange craft steamed out of Norfolk to attack the Union fleet on blockade duty near Hampton Roads. It was the ram *Merrimac* equipped with ten guns and apparently made invincible by four inches of plate iron over its low hull. While its armor remained impenetrable to hostile fire, the wooden ships before it were destroyed—seemingly the first step in the destruction of the naval blockade. But when the *Merrimac* returned to finish the job next day, it was met by a craft as strange as itself. This formidable opponet was the *Monitor*, an ironclad vessel constructed for the specific purpose of fighting the Confederate ship.

The two vessels fought desperately without inflicting great damage on each other. The *Merrimac*, however, was forced to retire because of defective engines, and when the Confederates evacuated Norfolk it had to be destroyed by its own crew. The blockade could now be tightened as the Washington government turned its superior resources to building an ironclad navy.

Scarcely five months after the *Merrimac* had failed to break the naval blockade, Lee's victories in the Seven Days' Battle and at the Second Bull Run enabled him to penetrate into enemy country. At the head of an army singing "Maryland, My Maryland," the Southern leader crossed the Potomac in the late summer of 1862, hoping to arouse latent Southern sentiments among Marylanders, break the North in two by severing rail connections in Pennsylvania, and perhaps dictate a favorable peace from one of the great Northern cities. The Marylanders, fully aware of superiority of Northern power, did not respond, and after the bloodiest single day of the war at Antietam Creek, Lee was forced to retreat to Virginia.

The second and final chance for a grand Confederate offensive came in 1863 when Lee, after winning his last important victory at Chancellorsville, carried the war into the rich pastures of Pennsylvania at the head of an army of 73,000 men. Following his failure to dislodge the Union forces from Cemetery Ridge on the third day of the great Battle of Gettysburg, the Confederate chieftain again withdrew to Virginia. The offensive power of the Confederacy was spent. The work of tightening the iron coil around its neck progressed relentlessly during 1864. Early in 1865 Lee was in a hopeless position at Richmond as Sherman began closing in upon him from the South.

In order to crush all resistance of the Confederacy, Federal commanders waged war on the civil population as well as the armed forces. This was total war, which Lee had refused to permit when he marched into Pennsylvania. "We are not only fighting armies, but a hostile people," affirmed Sherman, advocate of total warfare, in December, 1864, "and we must make old and young, rich and poor, feel the hard hand of war, as well as their organized armies." He had already put this idea into practice in Mississippi in 1862–63, and General Philip Sheridan had applied it on his march through the Valley of Virginia, when he burned or carried off so much that he was able to boast that "a crow flying over the country would need to carry his rations."

In his march through Georgia, Sherman cut a swath sixty miles wide which reeked with the stench of butchered animals and the smoke of houses wantonly destroyed. As he entered South Carolina, this ruthless Union chieftain wrote to his superior: "The truth is the whole army is burning with an insatiable desire to wreak vengeance upon South Carolina. I almost tremble for her fate, but feel that she deserves all that is in store for her." The work of destruction was more thorough than in Georgia. Columbia was left in ruins and the people of a wide belt in middle South Carolina were largely deprived of the means of subsistence. To be sure, Sherman's and Sheridan's work might have been even more terrible had murder and rape accompanied pillage and destruction.

Confronted by an enemy dissatisfied with anything less than an annihilating surrender, the Richmond government attempted heroic remedies. "Let us then," said the still-confident President of the Confederacy, "unite our hands and our hearts, lock our shields together, and we may well believe that before another summer solstice falls upon us, it will be the enemy that will be asking us for conferences and occasions on which to make known our demands."

Constitutional scruples and jealousies were set aside to concentrate supreme authority in the one man in whom the whole South had unstinted confidence. On February 6, 1865, Robert E. Lee was made general in chief of the armies. Six weeks later, with his endorsement an outstanding Southern prejudice was sacrificed in the interest of national survival. The enrollment of Negro troops in the Confederate army was authorized at approximately the same time that James M. Mason proposed the abolishment of slavery as the price of British recognition.

These measures, however, came too late. The Confederacy never lived to experience the invigorating influence of Lee in supreme command with loyal blacks behind him. On April 2 Davis and Lee were forced to abandon Richmond. Davis made a futile flight southward, which ended in the dissolution of his government and his capture in Georgia on May 10. Lee retreated westward to Appomattox Courthouse, where his hungry and reduced army of 26,000 was trapped by the vastly superior forces of General Grant. In this great extremity Lee's officers pledged to continue the duel by means of relentless guerrilla warfare if he would give the word. But Lee counseled acquiescence, and his advice was accepted.

Never before in history was a defeated aristocrat treated by a plebeian rival with such modesty and generosity as was Lee when, on April 9, he entered the McLean House at Appomattox Courthouse to receive Grant's terms of surrender. The appearance of the handsome Virginia gentleman, attired in a new uniform with the jeweled sword of honor Virginia had given him at his side, strongly contrasted with that of the victor who wore a shabby private's uniform with nothing to show his rank except the three-starred shoulder straps. Grant permitted the Confederate officers to retain their side arms and personal belongings, and Lee was not deprived of his sword. The Union chieftain fed the famished army, paroled officers and men, and allowed them to go home with their horses on condition that they would not take up arms again. Amid tears the Confederate general told his men, "Feeling that valor and devotion could accomplish nothing that could compensate for the loss that would have attended the continuation of the contest, I determined to avoid the useless sacrifice of those whose past services have long endeared them to their countrymen." As he made his last ride down the lines, the men broke ranks to take his hand, to touch his sword, or to stroke his horse. Grant and his officers stood bareheaded until their foe had disappeared. On orders from the Union commander, victory salutes were silenced in respect for a fallen adversary. The War for Southern Independence was over, and the surrender of Joseph E. Johnston to Sherman on April 26 was merely an anticlimax.

Grant's terms to Lee were too simple to dissolve the many complex forces in the tragic struggle. His conditions were of a purely military character based on the intelligent recognition by both sides of the fact that the Confederate army was defeated and without the power or will to renew the struggle. The problems of peace were indeed complicated, concerned as they were with the reconciliation of political, economic, and social interests more baffling than the conflicts of war. These would be the problems of Reconstruction.

CHAPTER XVI

Problems of Peace

>>>

WHEN surrender stopped the invader, physical destruction was apparent in many places. Lands were devastated, plantations wrecked. Accumulated capital had disappeared in worthless stocks, bonds, and currency. The banks had failed; factories had been dismantled; and the structure of business intercourse had crumbled. Two billion dollars invested in slaves had been wiped out, without the compensation which Lincoln himself had regarded as equitable. This had been characterized by a modern historian as "the most stupendous act of sequestration in the history of Anglo-Saxon jurisprudence." [1] Cotton worth $30,000,000 had been confiscated by federal Treasury agents. Public buildings used for war purposes had been destroyed or taken over by soldiers. Such cities as Richmond, Charleston, Columbia, Atlanta, Jackson, and Mobile had been targets of fire or bombardment. Columbia, in the words of a Northern traveler,[2] "is now a wilderness of ruins. Its heart is but a mass of blackened chimneys and crumbling walls." Arlington—Robert E. Lee's proud estate on the Potomac—had been seized by the federal forces and converted into a soldiers' cemetery.

Wherever the armies had passed, the population had paid for their stubborn resistance. That portion of South Carolina through which Sherman had moved "looked for many miles like a broad black streak of ruin and desolation—the fences all gone, lonesome smokestacks surrounded by dark heaps of ashes and cinders, marking the spots where human habitations had stood; the fields along the road wildly overgrown with weeds . . ."

[1] Charles A. and Mary R. Beard, *The Rise of American Civilization*, II, 100.
[2] Sidney Andrews, *The South since the War*, p. 33.

In the Tennessee Valley, according to an English traveler, the trail of war was visible "in burnt up gin-houses, ruined bridges, mills, and factories, of which latter the gable walls only are left standing, and in large tracts of once cultivated land stripped of every vestige of fencing." [3]

The eighty miles from Harpers Ferry to New Market was described by a Virginia farmer as "almost a desert." "We had," he explained, "no cattle, hogs, sheep, or horses or anything else. The fences were all gone. . . . The barns were all burned; chimneys standing without houses, and houses standing without roofs, or doors, or windows."

The disruption of normal channels of production and exchange had resulted in a widespread prevalence of broken windowpanes, dishes, and furniture. "A set of forks with whole tines," an observer stated, "is a curiosity. Clocks and watches have nearly all stopped. Hair brushes and tooth brushes have all worn out; combs are broken. . . . Pins, needles and thread, and a thousand such articles, which seem indispensable to housekeeping, are very scarce." On once-luxurious tables could be found "neither tea, coffee, sugar, nor spices of any kind." Candles had been replaced by cups of grease with pieces of cloth for wicks.

The once wealthy were often reduced to humiliating poverty. Six years after the war James S. Pike, then in South Carolina, described the situation of the head of a well-known family, rich and distinguished for generations. "The slaves were gone. The family is gone. A single scion of the house remains, and he peddles tea by the pound and molasses by the quart, on a corner of the old homestead, to the former slaves of the family, and thereby earns his livelihood." [4]

Nearly every old Southern community had similar cases. The destitution was even more general among the lower white classes. There were eyewitness accounts of "almost thorough starvation from the failure of last year's crop"; of "ten beggars here to one in Washington"; of conscripted men returning "to their poor wives and children destitute and unable to get work"; of women and children "begging for bread from door to door." In December, 1865, an estimated 500,000 white people in three states of the lower South were without the necessities of life, and some of them even starved. [5]

Similar destitution among the blacks was followed by the flight of population. Many refugees fled before or after the Union armies, because they feared they would be punished for exercising the privileges of freedom; others, vainly believing that some development would make it no longer necessary for them to work, gravitated toward towns and

[3] Robert Somers, *The Southern States since the War*, p. 114.
[4] James S. Pike, *The Prostrate State*, p. 119.
[5] Walter L. Fleming, *The Sequel of Appomattox*, pp. 13–14.

army posts. In some states the general movement of these deluded people was toward the seacoast, where they hoped that lands would be distributed. Everywhere Negroes traveled in crowds like packs of gypsies, not knowing how they would exist when they came to their journey's end. A Northern visitor in the summer of 1865 was convinced that "the race is, on a large scale, ignorantly sacrificing its own good for the husks of vagabondage." Many died for want of proper food, shelter, or medical attention.

Poverty was prolonged and rendered more acute because of inadequate communications. Roads and bridges had fallen into disrepair; vehicles, horses, and mules were scarce; steamboats had almost disappeared from the rivers. Postal facilities were entirely lacking for several months after Lee's surrender, and two thirds of the railroads were destroyed or crippled and inactive. The Charleston and Savannah line, to cite an example, was "a mere wreck; every bridge and trestle were destroyed . . . ; the depot in Charleston was burned, as well as the depots and buildings at eleven of the way stations, and nearly the whole track torn up." The most effective method of crippling was the heating of the rails and the twisting of them around trees. The rolling stock of most lines, when not worn out, had been greatly reduced through capture, destruction, or wrecking.

The physical destruction and social disorder of the times made themselves felt in the decline of land values. Properties which had previously brought $50 or more an acre were now sold at $3 to $5. The poorer lands could not be disposed of at any price. To be sure, the soil remained, but there was a scarcity of agricultural tools, stock, seed, and labor. The Negroes were demoralized and in some sections half the white men of military age had been war casualties. Fifteen years after the war only the frontier states of Texas, Arkansas, Mississippi, and Florida had as many acres under cultivation as in 1860.

The most pressing problem was to rebuild that which had been destroyed and to relieve the prevailing destitution—a task requiring arduous labor but facilitated by the common realization that it must be done. This was not true of many social and political issues of the period, for the victory of the Union armies merely settled two controversies beyond dispute: the Negro was free, and the Union was restored. By their presence and actions, the invaders had made the bondsmen free. This was an experience so exciting for the Negroes that it permanently destroyed the emotional spell of slavery.

The doctrines of nullification and secession were smashed by the logic of brute force, and the Confederate government had been so completely annihilated that no one thought it could ever be revived. However, the settlement of these two fundamental controversies created a number of intricate problems: What would be the position of the Negro in the new society of freedom? His relations to agricultural and other occupational pursuits must be determined, his political and social status defined. A system of education to fit him for his new role must be devised. Possible solutions of these difficulties ranged from minimum accommodation to changes demanded by external forces, to a reordering of society making the freedmen the equal of white men. Then, too, what would be the position of the defeated states in the re-established Union? Should they be treated as subjugated provinces, or allowed to resume their status as equals of the victorious states? How could broken religious, cultural, and social relations of both a racial and sectional character be restored?

Here were baffling questions that involved many individual adjustments as well as consummate statesmanship of a nonpolitical nature. The general reordering of social and political relations had to be accompanied by emotional changes. Too much blood had been spilled; the tens of thousands killed in battle left behind a hatred that somehow must be obliterated before there could be more than an official restoration of the Union. The situation demanded an abler leadership than that which had launched and won the war. Grotesque and tragic mistakes were made, but the fact that the victors of Appomattox did not impose a peace that required a second war to undo it is a tribute to the wisdom of American statesmanship.

The victors held the power to take the initiative in the reconstruction of Southern society. Northerners were united in the determination that the triumph of unionism and freedom should be followed by measures that would lend these principles reality in the life of the defeated states. Nevertheless, opinion was divided on how these fruits of victory should be secured.

The spirit of vengeance was strong in the victorious North at first. There must be punishments for the crimes of secession and slavery. "Treason is a crime," declared President Andrew Johnson, "and must be punished as a crime. . . . It must not be excused as an unsuccessful rebellion to be . . . forgiven."

This spirit culminated in wrath over the assassination of President Lincoln. Public opinion approved of the military trial of the conspirators and the execution of four of them, including Mrs. Mary E. Surratt, whose complicity in the crime had not been active. Also executed was Henry Wirz, previously in charge of the prison pen at Andersonville, Georgia. Loud demands were made for the life of Jefferson Davis. He was dubbed the great criminal responsible, at least indirectly, for Lincoln's assassination. Women cried for his blood and children learned to lisp "Hang Jeff Davis on a Sour Apple Tree" to the tune of "John Brown's Body."

Because Southerners refused to be friendly, the federal army of occupation resorted to irritating retaliations. Women required to go to military headquarters for any favor were forced to take ironclad oaths of national loyalty. The wearing of Confederate uniforms was forbidden and when this order was enforced among men who had no other clothes scenes of unforgivable humiliation resulted. Negro garrisons were imposed seemingly as an affront to white prejudice. Elated over their uniforms and guns, the Negro soldiers took delight in humiliating white persons and in instilling insubordinate notions in the heads of the freedmen. Occasionally they committed atrocities. Their behavior was more than the Southern temper could bear, and race conflicts frequently ensued.

Church buildings were seized and turned over to agents of Northern denominations, and ministers were not allowed to preach unless they agreed to conduct "loyal services, pray for the President of the United States, and for Federal victories." Direct refusal of Protestant Episcopal clergymen to substitute in their liturgy the name of the President of the United States for that of the President of the Confederate States resulted in the closing of churches and the dispersal of congregations.

In addition, there was the burden of discriminatory war taxes and the confiscation laws of Congress. Federal Treasury agents threaded their way through the occupied areas seizing 3 million out of the 5 million bales of cotton which had not been destroyed. They corruptly enriched themselves. "I am sure," said the Secretary of the Treasury, "that I sent *some* honest agents South; but it sometimes seems very doubtful whether any of them remained honest very long." A special tax of from 2½ to 3 cents a pound on cotton yielded the federal treasury $68,000,000. Because of its effects on the economy of a prostrate region, this levy was called by the United States Commissioner of Agriculture "disastrous and disheartening in the extreme." As soon as the federal troops got a foothold in the South property was seized and sold for nonpayment under the Direct Tax Act. Under this law Arlington and much land in coastal South Carolina fell into alien hands. Pathetic sacrifices were made. One estate, for example, worth $15,000 sold for $300. It is estimated [6] that federal taxes collected in the South in 1865–68 exceeded the entire amount the federal government and private Northern agencies spent on Southern relief and reconstruction during that period.

Vengeful emotions gradually subsided, however, and traditions of

[6] *Ibid.*, p. 8.

law and humanity reasserted themselves. Jefferson Davis was not delivered to the mob; in fact, he was never brought to trial. Among the thousands of Confederates who surrendered, Wirz was the only one executed and if he had not been a friendless foreigner, his life might have been saved. Relations between the army of occupation and the Southern whites were, on the whole, not bad. The higher commanders bore themselves well, and much of the violence attributed at the time to organized troops was later discovered to have been the work of irresponsible individuals. Indeed, many communities welcomed the presence of troops as a protection against lawlessness. The relief afforded by Northern charitable agencies, although subsequently forgotten, was momentarily appreciated by many destitute Southerners.

A local journalist remarked that it was "a matter of gratitude as well as surprise for our people to see a Government which was lately fighting us with fire and sword and shell, now generously feeding our poor and distressed. . . . The Confederate soldier, with one leg or one arm, the crippled, maimed, and broken, and the worn and destitute men, who fought bravely their enemies then, their benefactors now, have their sacks filled and are fed." Relief organizations in the North, sponsored by such furious enemies of the Confederacy as Henry Ward Beecher and Horace Greeley, raised almost $3,000,000 for the distressed people of the South during the two years after the war.

Moderates in the North—Democrats of the border states and conservatives—wanted the defeated states restored to their traditional status under the Constitution with minimum interference in the Negro and other social problems. Although their position would prevail ultimately, because it was rooted in established custom concerning the proper sphere of the states and the Negro in the national life, it was too simple a remedy to give immediate satisfaction to a people stirred by great victory. It conceded freedom to the Negro and repudiated secession, yet it failed to provide adequate guarantees that those who had been guilty of slavery and rebellion would not, through indirection, negate those achievements.

The failure of the moderates to secure such guarantees enabled the radicals to capture Northern public opinion. This group justified the penalties which war had imposed upon the states of the former Confederacy as the retribution of a righteous God. Henry Ward Beecher, the nation's most noted preacher, declared at Fort Sumter shortly after the fall of Charleston: "We look upon this shattered fort and yonder dilapidated city with sad eyes, grieved that men should have committed such treason and glad that God hath set a mark upon treason, that all ages shall dread and abhor it." The radicals were willing to impose measures sufficiently harsh to secure their aims. As a rule, they were not interested in vengeance for its own sake. Reformers nurtured in the uplifting atmosphere of nineteenth-century liberalism, they sought to impose upon the benighted land of secession and slavery progressive concepts of social morality. They wanted Southern class distinctions eradicated and universal suffrage inaugurated.

The realistic observer could detect glaring weaknesses in the radical program which would in time cause its collapse. White opponents were not so helpless as their conquerors imagined, and the Negro was incapable of living up to expectations. Their plan was too simple for the complicated society of the defeated states. Perhaps it was not what these states needed; certainly it was not what they wanted. Moreover, with the North divided, there was danger that the Democrats would regain power and undo what may have been accomplished. Cherished constitutional principles preventing the interference of outsiders in the internal affairs of states were bound to reassert themselves. Lastly, the motives of the radical interventionists contained the seeds of failure for their program.

Those who acted from self-interest became corrupt and lost Northern support while others who had been originally disinterested joined the greedy or retired from the South when their enthusiasms subsided. Northern public opinion easily abandoned the idea of making over the South, once the crusading emotions of war had cooled and it became apparent how difficult were the problems of Reconstruction.

Under the plans of the radicals, no one was to be punished unless he stood in the way of their program of regeneration; amnesty and pardon were not denied to those who had supported the Confederacy. Nevertheless, application of radical rule was scarcely less trying on the vanquished than an outright program of vengeance would have been. The sweeping accusations against Southern standards of civilization, the tactless manner in which reforms were applied, the interference with race relations—all this struck Southerners as the cruelty and insolence of a hypocritical foe. They felt the peace imposed by a victor before the age of uplift and humanitarian reform might have been preferable. Such a peace would have required indemnities and executions, but it would not have involved meddling with established social institutions. Nor would it create the impression that the purpose of Northern policy was to uproot all unique aspects of Southern culture so that the humiliations of radical Reconstruction seemed even crueler than the bloodshed of the long war. Southerners learned from Aristophanes:

"There are things, then, hotter than fire, there are
    speeches more shameless still
Than the shameless speeches of those who rule the
    City at will."

The Negroes were central figures in the peace settlement. The war supposedly had been won for their benefit; they did not have cause to mourn the loss of relatives or property; and they could rejoice in their new gains. Still, they were woefully deficient in many of the qualities necessary for the competent exercise of the rights of freedom.

In the first place, the freedmen were very poor. They inherited no property from slavery, and attempts to give them lands only made for confusion and false hopes. One band of colored refugees was described: They were "partly covered with every conceivable thing that could be put on the back of a biped. Some of the women had on old, cast-off soldiers' coats and 'crocus bags,' fastened together with their own ravellings, for shirts, and bits of sailcloth for head handkerchiefs. Many of the men had strips of gay carpeting or old bags, or pieces of blanket, in which they cut armholes and wore as jackets. Their pants were tied below and above the knees and around the waist with pieces of rope to keep them on."

The Negroes were not inclined to remedy their poverty through thrift. They loved idleness and were "improvident to the last degree of childishness." Robert E. Lee testified that they composed an "amiable and social race" who looked "more to the present than to their future condition." Generally they were spendthrift and gullible, easily influenced by peddlers and storekeepers. They bought brass rings, earrings, breast pins, and gaudy handkerchiefs at ten times their worth.

A greater weakness than poverty was their inexperience in exercising with wisdom the opportunities brought by the great revolution. Under slavery there had been no social clubs, no hoarding of wealth, little training in individual initiative. Accordingly, it was inevitable that confusion would result from following false suggestions; much of the rejoicing with which freedom was celebrated was a surface effervescence that hid genuine bewilderment. That the race was able to survive the ordeal of freedom was due more to its large numbers and to the blind instinct of self-preservation than to purposeful social habits.

It should not be assumed, however, that the Negroes were altogether devoid of qualities helpful in the new situation. They were capable of hard manual labor and had knowledge of the language, social customs, religion, morals and industrial crafts of the new society to which they belonged. They knew how to live on little and, in a restricted sense, possessed the white man's powers of adaptability; they had been moved about as slaves and could minimize their hardship.

Then, too, the freedmen possessed qualities of temperament that were advantageous. Whatever may have been their boasts in moments of excitement, they were usually too wise or too timid to attempt actions beyond their powers. Seldom vindictive, they avoided bloodshed in situations that would have provoked the white man to violence, and they were not likely to go to extremes in contests that would endanger relations and make them intolerable to the dominant white race. Capable of an almost pathetic loyalty to old institutions, they were contented under conditions that would have made a more sensitive people miserable. They knew how to dance and sing in the midst of physical distress, and could almost turn a funeral into a joyful occasion; by some magic, they could even give rags the semblance of fancy dress.

Nor were the Negroes completely lacking the higher equipment of civilization. A quarter million of them had never been slaves and were accustomed to look out for themselves. One hundred thousand had gained valuable experience in the Federal army, and by the gradual extension of emancipation by the invading Northerners. The "grapevine telegraph" among Negroes and information imparted by whites had made the meaning of freedom widespread.

Most Negroes were better equipped for freedom in 1865 than they had been in 1861. More than 5 per cent of the freedmen knew how to read, and the race generally was adept at imitating the whites in dress, manners, and speech. A few exhorters had experience as religious leaders. Others had closely observed the habits of white politicians and, when the occasion arose, would prove to be political organizers and orators of ability.

The defeated Southerners were expected to make the sacrifices necessary for reforms favoring the Negro. They were willing to recognize the defeat of the Confederate armies, the freeing of the slaves, and the restoration of the Union. A considerable number with the fear of summary punishment before them were ready to repudiate the Confederacy with unseemly haste. A few—the first scalawags—were prepared to adopt the beliefs of the conquerors. One patriot at least, the aged Edmund Ruffin, killed himself in despair.

For the great majority, however, the tragic outcome of the war increased their hatred of Northerners, made Southern doctrines more precious, and invested the war leaders with an aura of heroism. Only the minimum demands of the victor were to be accepted. As soon as it became clear that the North would not be as vindictive as some imagined every reform suggested from the outside was contested bitterly.

Those among the conquerors who imagined that military defeat had reduced the white Southerners to impotence were to be unpleasantly surprised. Although defeated, these people were not without material resources. Despite threats of confiscation the land remained mostly in their hands, and agricultural possibilities partially compensated for decline in land values. All tools were not destroyed and many cities were unscathed or only partly wrecked. Fortunately, miles of railroads and great stretches of the back country had not been touched by war. The sale of cotton, the release of hoarded gold and silver, and the circulation of money by the army of occupation to some extent relieved the distress caused by the collapse of Confederate currency.

The whites faced their difficulties with superb courage. "While clouds were dark and threatening," wrote a Northern newspaper reporter, "I do not believe there was ever in the world's history a people who bear their afflictions with more philosophy and Christian fortitude than these unfortunate people." [7] Women cheerfully retreated to the kitchen and men turned to manual labor. A philosophy of hard work and close economy was preached, and every expedient which might lead out of the impasse of poverty and social stagnation was advanced.

The war had accustomed men to hardships, and women had learned to manage plantations, maintain slave discipline, and endure privations. Certainly there was no ground for the belief fostered by the romantics that Southerners were a lazy and improvident lot who were helpless unless ministered to by faithful blacks. Actually, they were ready to assume duties previously exercised by Negroes, at the same time resisting Northern assaults on their inherited privileges.

The whites generally had competent leadership. From the old regime they acquired experienced counselors who had lost many of their fire-eating qualities under the sobering influence of defeat. These men were usually able to check the passions of the mob and when violence did occur—often accomplishing purposes with which these leaders were sympathetic—they knew how to avert punishment from Washington.

They were backed in their policies by an assertive country folk who were accustomed to dwell on lands of their own, and who had a profound contempt for Northerners and for Negroes except as servants. These rural people had proved their stamina while serving in the Confederate army. They were ready to terrorize Yankees and Negroes alike if members of either group attempted to upset the traditional social order.

The wisdom of Southern leadership is best illustrated by the manner in which the prevailing pessimism was met. Some were convinced that the victor would enforce intolerable terms, and that an orderly and industrious society was impossible where free Negroes were numerous. Mass emigration was suggested, and arrangements were made for settlements in foreign countries. A considerable number of ex-Confederates went to Brazil, and even more to Mexico. Matthew Fontaine Maury, the Virginia scientist, attempted to establish colonies in that country under the protection of Emperor Maximilian.

[7] Cited in Francis B. Simkins and Robert H. Woody, *South Carolina during Reconstruction*, p. 22.

This solution, however, did not appeal to such generally loved and respected Southern leaders as Wade Hampton and Robert E. Lee, who advised the people not to move. All Southerners, declared Lee, should remain at home and "share the fate of their respective States. . . . The South requires the aid of her sons now more than at any period of her history." There were no wholesale migrations, and gradually the Southerners realized that life at home could be made tolerable even with the Negro free and the Northerner dominant.

A competent authority believes that had the South been assisted by skillful publicity in 1865, much misunderstanding between the sections might have been avoided. Although the North and South knew little of each other, the victors were eager to discover whether their defeated countrymen were willing to accept measures by which Union and freedom might be secured. The South, for its part, believed the words of its leaders.

Wade Hampton wrote President Johnson: "The South unequivocally 'accepts the situation.' . . . She intends to abide by the laws of the land honestly, to fulfill all her obligations faithfully, and to keep her word sacredly." General Lee wrote the governor of Virginia: "All should unite in honest efforts to obliterate the effects of war, and to restore the blessings of peace. They should remain, if possible, in the country; promote harmony and good-feeling, qualify themselves to vote; and elect to the State and general legislatures wise and patriotic men, who will devote their abilities to the interests of the country and the healing of all dissentions." Lee set an example of unselfish patriotism by becoming president of Washington College at Lexington.

The testimony of Hampton and Lee was not supplemented by sustained reports of the details of Southern life. Hence Northerners, their curiosity aroused, swarmed into the South. Some were able journalists who gave accurate reports. Others were speculators bent upon exploiting an unhappy land. A third group consisted of offensive bigots who gave advice, condemned customs, asked obtrusive questions, and published tactless statements. The South, regarding inquiry as humiliating, refused to be catechized. By failing to deny, it confirmed the impression that it was a strange land, not quite normal, not wholly American.

President Johnson sought to heal the breach. He dispatched observers to secure for the Northern public a true picture of Southern affairs. One of these was Benjamin C. Truman, a New England journalist who emphatically denied that Northerners were being persecuted in the South, and deplored the circulation of incendiary falsehoods about Southerners. Referring to conditions early in 1866, he declared that the South was "more loyal now than yesterday, and that it will be more loyal tomorrow than today." General Ulysses S. Grant reported "that the citizens of the Southern States are anxious to return to self-government within the Union as soon as possible."

The general's testimony, however, was contradicted by a third observer, Carl Schurz, sent by the President. This German-American wrote of the "incorrigibles" of the South, of the detestation of Yankees, of the fact that treason did not appear odious, of the Southerner's lack of "communion with the progressive ideas of the times," and of the want of "hearty attachment to the great republic." Obviously, the President had not been able to command a concerted opinion upon which a moderate policy of reconstruction could be based.

All available testimony expressed more or less accurately the prevailing conflict of ideas. Contentions over the terms of peace were almost as acrimonious as those which had brought on four years of war. There was potential trouble between radicals and moderates of the North, and between the whites of the South on one hand, and the Negroes and their Northern allies on the other.

Southerners accepted the destruction of slavery and the renunciation of state sovereignty, but they would not profess that they were ashamed of the achievements of the Confederate army, or that they loved the Union against which they had recently fought. They considered the Negro free but inferior, and they expected to settle his economic and social status in their own way.

Against these convictions was set the Northern determination that there should be repentance for the supposed sins of slavery and secession, and guarantees that the Negro not only was free, but would be given an ample measure of the democratic equality which the Declaration of Independence promised all Americans.

CHAPTER XVII

Process of Reconstruction

⋙-⋙

THE REHABILITATION of the society of the defunct Confederacy had religious, social, industrial, and agricultural aspects. But political readjustment had to come first. The Constitution had to be reapplied to the relations of states to the national government. Legally trained statesmen who dominated political life demanded the settlement of most governmental matters on a theoretical basis, and in 1865 each one formed his own concept of Reconstruction. They ranged from the radical views of Charles Sumner and Thaddeus Stevens to the ideas embodied in the Crittenden-Johnson resolution of July, 1861—that the war was being fought to maintain the Union under the Constitution, and should end with the attainment of this objective.

Charles Sumner contended that when a state forcibly denied the supremacy of the Constitution by secession or other revolutionary act it committed suicide and its territory fell under the exclusive jurisdiction of Congress. The "rebels" of the South should be punished by giving civil and political rights to the Negroes and educating them in the same schools with the whites. Thaddeus Stevens believed that the victors should treat seceded states as "conquered provinces" whose "proud nobility" should be subjected to punishments "longer remembered than death." Southern leaders, he felt, should be deprived of their estates and reduced to the social and economic level of the common people.

The policy first applied was that of President Lincoln. To him Reconstruction was an executive function to be performed by encouraging the establishment of provisional state governments as the military occupation of the South progressed. A highly intelligent opportunist who

((259))

had been sobered by the war, the President was anxious to secure a speedy restoration of national authority with as little friction as possible. He understood better than most Northerners the problem of the races, the weaknesses of the Southern unionists, and the advantages of securing the co-operation of the South's traditional leaders. Lincoln brushed aside as a "pernicious abstraction," "good for nothing at all," speculation on whether or not the states had left the Union. "We all agree," he said, "that the seceded States, so called, are out of proper practical relation with the Union, and that the sole object of the government . . . is to again get them in that proper practical relation."

By his proclamation of December 8, 1863, Lincoln offered pardon to all Confederates, except specified classes of leaders, who took oaths to support "the Constitution of the United States and the Union of States thereunder"; and he promised that if a tenth of the number who had voted in the presidential election of 1860 should qualify by taking such oaths and establishing state governments with slavery abolished, the Executive would recognize these governments as legal. He required that new governments be established because previously existing state organizations were deemed illegal since they had been disloyal to the United States. Having concluded that slavery must be eliminated, Lincoln raised no objection to the extension of suffrage to Negroes who were "the very intelligent, and especially those who have fought gallantly in our ranks."

The Lincoln plan was tried in four states that had partly fallen under the control of Union armies early in the war—Louisiana, Arkansas, Tennessee, and Virginia. Military governors were appointed, and in Louisiana, Arkansas, and Tennessee, unionist constitutions were ratified by the required 10 per cent of the voters. State governments were organized and subsequently received recognition from the President. Parson William G. Brownlow, a noisy unionist agitator, was elected governor of Tennessee, but the procedure differed in Virginia. A "restored government" was established at Alexandria under the leadership of Francis H. Pierpont before Lincoln proclaimed his plan. This government formulated a constitution under which slavery was abolished and the Union recognized. The President affirmed its legitimacy and at the same time recognized the establishment of West Virginia without later demanding the reorganization of Virginia under the 10 per cent plan.

Lincoln never succeeded in putting his plan into full effect in any state. The task of reorganization was rendered difficult by the negligible number of unionists and ex-Confederates willing to take the oath. Impatient with Presidential direction of reconstruction, Congress expressed its opposition in the Wade-Davis bill of 1864, which asserted the right of Congress to control restoration and provided for the proscription of the very ex-Confederates whom Lincoln invited to participate in his scheme. The President vetoed the bill, but Congress sustained its position by denying representation to any of the states of the Confederacy that had fallen under Lincoln's care. In a tone that contrasted strikingly with his assumption of authority in other fields, the President made concessions to the Congressional stand. In July, 1864, he signed a proclamation which excluded from the Presidential electoral count all Southern states, including those that had complied with his plan of Reconstruction. His assassination in April, 1865, put an end to his projects.

Had the great war President lived, he might have established a peace acceptable to the men of moderation of both North and South. He was tactful, possessed great personal influence, and—unlike the radicals and his successor in office—was not a doctrinaire. His purpose had been to anticipate the needs of the times with a specific plan for Reconstruction to be put progressively into operation as more and more territory came under Union control. Lincoln wished to guide and direct but not force the Southern people; persecution and vindictiveness were not parts of his plan. On the last day of his life he discussed with his cabinet a course of action similar to that later announced by President Johnson. It is problematical, however, whether such moderation would have been approved by an aroused public opinion. Lincoln himself was apprehensive lest his scheme meet Congressional opposition, and as a good politician might have yielded to his legislature in order to prevent a parliamentary deadlock. His plans were almost entirely political in nature, and not comprehensive enough to solve the revolutionary social and economic problems which the war had forced upon the South.

Lincoln's successor took office under difficulties for which the new President's honesty, devotion to duty, and powerful, if not well-disciplined, mind were not adequate compensations. Although Andrew Johnson loved the Union and the Constitution, he adhered to old-fashioned Southern dogmas of states' rights, apparently unaware that they had been rendered impracticable by the war. Of an origin as homespun as that of Lincoln, he possessed many of his predecessor's virtues, but lacked the latter's skill in handling men. An accident had thrown this Southern Democrat into the unenviable position of heading the government of the victorious North. Johnson played into the hands of his enemies by returning unjust abuse with imprudent and tactless language.

Johnson at first appeared willing to co-operate with the radicals. Bluff Ben Wade, one of their leaders, expressed their confidence: "Johnson, we have faith in you. By the gods, there will be no trouble now in running the government!" The new President replied: "Treason is a crime and crime must be punished. Treason must be made infamous and traitors must be impoverished." These vindictive words, however, represented only a passing phase of his attitude. After the excitement caused by the Confederate defeat and the assassination of Lincoln subsided, Johnson sobered under contemplation of the heavy tasks ahead. He quickly adopted the essentials of the Lincoln plan of Reconstruction, holding to the theory of the indestructibility of the states. The Southern states, he contended, had never been out of the Union, and their constitutional relations to the federal government were unaffected; but, until loyal governments were re-established, their functions were deemed suspended.

Although Johnson abhorred secession, he willingly recognized that the disbanding of the Confederate armies proved that the South had relinquished that doctrine. The states would be restored not through the army, but through loyalist elements actuated by the traditional processes of state-making. He assumed that the task of restoration was a Presidential function. Taking advantage of the long recess of Congress, which began when he took office in April, 1865, he hoped to present the national legislature with a *fait accompli* when it resumed its sessions the following December. At that time Congress learned that all former Confederate states except Texas had completed, under Presidential direction, the elaborate process of state-making.

Johnson accepted the policy which had been adopted by other governments—that, following civil strife, when former rebels renewed their allegiance, forgiveness should be granted to them. Accordingly he prefaced his plan of restoration with the Amnesty Proclamation of May 29, 1865. Without requiring impossible promises, it granted pardon to all who would swear to support the Constitution and laws of the United States, excluding fourteen specified classes of persons assumed to be inveterate rebels. These comprised high civil and military officers of the Confederacy, those who had resigned from federal service, and persons possessing more than $20,000. The President believed that wealthy Southerners had caused the war; to the excepted classes, however, he held out the possibility of special pardon through petitions endorsed by prominent officials or Southern unionists. Johnson granted about 13,500 pardons out of more than 15,000 applicants.[1]

On the day of the Amnesty Proclamation the President issued an order appointing William W. Holden provisional governor of North Carolina and outlining a plan of restoration. Holden was authorized to reorganize the government of his state, and to call a constitutional convention elected by those who had taken the amnesty oath. The President delegated to this convention the task of defining the qualifications

[1] E. Merton Coulter, *The South during Reconstruction, 1865–1877*, p. 33.

for future officeholders and voters. Determination of these qualifications was adjudged "a power which the people of the . . . States . . . have rightfully exercised from the origin of Government to the present time." Resumption of federal activities in the states was authorized, and the army ordered to assist civil authorities. Identical proclamations following the North Carolina model were issued for six other states of the former Confederacy by June 13. Virginia, Tennessee, Louisiana, and Arkansas were considered already reconstructed.

Unionist provisional governors executed their tasks with dispatch and efficiency. State governments which had existed under the Confederacy were outlawed, but all court decrees and statutes, except those sanctioning slavery, were recognized, and local officials willing to take the oath of loyalty were reappointed. Poverty of state governments was relieved by license taxes on trades and professions, and their prestige enhanced by unobtrusive aid from federal troops kept in the South for that purpose.

The President prescribed three duties for constitutional conventions which met in the fall of 1865: formal abolition of slavery, repudiation of the Ordinances of Secession, and rejection of Confederate war debts. These conditions were fulfilled except by South Carolina, where the Confederate debt was not repudiated. There was much quibbling over whether the Ordinances of Secession should be "repealed" or declared "now and always null and void," and over whether slavery should be abolished by state action, or had already been abolished by war. Old state constitutions were left intact except for the abolition of slavery and the apportionment of legislative representation on a basis of white population. This latter expedient was designed to lessen the influence of the Black Belt in favor of white democracy of the hill country. Legislatures and state officials were elected and the federal Secretary of State issued proclamations retiring the provisional governors in favor of those chosen under the new constitutions.

Thus was completed the presidential plan of Reconstruction, based fundamentally on the restoration of political rights without reference to past conduct, upon the reaffirmation of federal allegiance. It appeared that the way was clear for the recall to power of traditional leaders— men who had led the Southern states into the Confederacy. The constitutional conventions had left to the legislatures they created many pressing problems growing out of the freeing of the slaves. President Johnson had tentatively proposed that the vote be extended to blacks of education and property, but did not insist when this suggestion was not adopted. Although there was no discussion of the Negro suffrage issue in the conventions, certain white leaders loudly proclaimed: "This is a white man's government and intended for white men only."

Many historians have endorsed the Johnson plan of Reconstruction because of the dispatch with which it was put into operation and its respect for constitutional practices, and find fault only with the President's boldness in failing to await Congressional approval. Such a practice was frowned upon in an age dominated by legalists who exaggerated the letter of the Constitution. This, however, was not the most significant weakness of the presidential plan, since Johnson closely adhered to Constitutional tradition. Johnson considered it quite proper to surrender the recently conquered states to those who had led them into disastrous defeat. He appeared to disregard the fact that a great war had been fought and that hates must be satisfied and revolutionary reforms achieved. So obsessed was he with the supposedly changeless character of the Constitution that there existed no place in his constructive thinking for the enormous economic and social changes—largely centering around the Negro—which Northern victory made inevitable.

Johnson should have imposed upon his Reconstruction leaders specifications for the reform of Negro society as moderate and constructive as his plans for constitutional rehabilitation. Yet he evaded the Negro suffrage problem, leaving the solution of all race questions to ex-Confederates. It is customary for historians to ascribe the adverse reactions his policies provoked to hate and greed. While it is true that these sordid emotions played their part, there was a natural demand that the fruits of victory be guaranteed by more than a mere reordering of the old society. Johnson's radical opponents hoped that phases of democracy might be applied to that one tenth of the American people who had been slaves. The Southern unionist who was President failed to respond to this demand.

When the Congress met in December, 1865, it crippled the prestige of the newly constituted states by refusing to seat their members-elect. By exercising this undisputed constitutional prerogative the national legislature indicated its intention of disputing the presidential Reconstruction program. Moreover, it was already evident that Johnson's plans were being imperfectly realized. Reorganization of the federal administration in states of the fallen Confederacy was handicapped by lack of competent officials who could qualify under the ironclad oath of loyalty enacted by Congress in July, 1862. Under this oath a prospective officeholder swore that he had never willingly aided the Confederacy in any capacity. The Freedmen's Bureau—established at the same time as the Johnson governments—assumed authority over the Negroes. The army of occupation interfered with the free operation of civil authority. Everywhere in the South uncertainty and conflict between officials prevailed.

The Congress that refused seats to the Southern representatives began its grand strategy to defeat the President by the creation of a Joint Committee on Reconstruction to inquire into the conditions of the states lately in rebellion and to let Congress know when these states should be readmitted into the Union. This body was composed of fifteen members, headed by the dour Thaddeus Stevens. He openly favored "the punishment of traitors," and the confiscation of "rebel" property and its redistribution among the freedmen. The committee collected a mountain of testimony from 144 witnesses; all but 30 were "men whose private interests or prejudices strongly biased them against the Southerners, or made them eager to paint the picture as black as possible." Incriminating questions with self-evident answers were asked: Would a Southern jury convict Jefferson Davis of treason? Would Southerners prefer Confederates in elections over unionists? Would Southerners give the Negro the vote? The inevitable conclusion was that the treatment of the loyalist element in the South necessitated the retention of the army and the Freedmen's Bureau for most elementary protection; that if the whites were allowed to control the states, these governments would constitute a danger to the Union; and that free Negro labor was successful although the whites were hostile to it.

The findings of the Stevens body were accompanied by a campaign of misrepresentation and abuse designed to convince the North of the necessity of dealing drastically with the South. As feeling against the President grew stronger, the campaign became more and more unscrupulous. Newspapers regularly ran columns headed "Southern Outrages," exaggerating any mistreatment of Negroes by whites. These tales were supplemented by disturbing reports from radical leaders. Albion W. Tourgée, a distinguished carpetbagger, for example, had scarcely arrived in North Carolina before he began telling of a millpond out of which had been fished seven dead Negroes; federal Judge John C. Underwood suggested that the Republicans would gain votes if they could induce Barnum to exhibit a Negro girl whose back had been burned by Virginia fiends. It seems as though during 1866 every Southerner began to murder or beat Negroes. As time passed, agencies of the reconstructed governments secured firmer control over lawless elements so that abuse of Negroes decreased. Fortunately for the radicals, however, and unfortunately for the South, riots in Memphis and New Orleans led to large-scale killings of Negroes, confirming the accusation of lurid informists.

Congress took steps to protect the Negroes. It passed the Civil Rights Act of 1866, making the Negro into a citizen and giving him all the rights enjoyed by the whites. The substance of this law was submitted to the states in a proposed addition to the Constitution which became the Fourteenth Amendment. This document made the Negro a citizen of the nation and of the state in which he resided. It prohibited the states from abridging the privileges and immunities of a citizen, of depriving a person "of life, liberty, or property, without due process of law" and of denying him "the equal protection of the laws." Although it did not confer on the Negro the suffrage outright, it provided for the reduction of representation of any state which did not allow him to vote. It denied to many Confederates the right to hold office and provided that only Congress could remove their disabilities. It repudiated the Confederate debts and guaranteed the federal debts.

Radical aggressiveness caused the South to become recalcitrant. The tendency toward political division among the white population was checked, and only the most extreme unionists were willing to affiliate with the radicals. Public opinion frustrated an attempt on the part of some upper-class leaders to forestall the Stevens party through a compromise on radical measures. All Southern legislatures except Tennessee rejected the Fourteenth Amendment. The great majority of whites, while necessarily accepting federalism and abolitionism, were not willing to consent voluntarily to a proclamation of their own guilt. They took refuge behind the traditional barriers of race consciousness and states' rights, and became bitterly uncompromising.

Meanwhile, realists among Southern whites and Northern radicals were wrestling with the problem that pressed most heavily for solution—that of the newly freed Negro. Both groups agreed that emancipation of the blacks meant that family life, social conduct, and labor contracts must be regulated, legal status determined, interracial contacts stabilized. and various types of educational guidance adopted.

The white South's answer to all these perplexing questions was the Black Codes passed by the Johnson legislatures in 1865 and 1866; the radical North's answer was the Freedmen's Bureau created by Congress in 1865. These two groups differed in their viewpoint of the Negro problem. Southerners frankly felt the need to keep the blacks in a position of social and economic inferiority; Northerners insisted that constructive efforts be made to save them from the subordination and exploitation prescribed by Southern custom.

Their newly found freedom did not lead all Negroes to become disorderly and thriftless. Some remained on the plantations quietly continuing to work for their former master who found them cheerful and free of vindictiveness, but the majority of ex-slaves were ignorant, poor, and in many cases intoxicated by so much liberty. A predominantly agricultural race demonstrated a distressing tendency to move to cities and to become vagrants lacking responsibility. Agriculture, notably in the rice swamps of South Carolina, declined. Unaccustomed to their obligations, the freedmen wandered from place to place, subject to disease and death, neglecting family ties, and at times committing crimes.

Confronted with these conditions, the Johnson state governments imposed disciplinary measures upon the erring blacks. The slave codes were no longer operative and existing laws regulating the behavior of the small Negro class previously free were deemed unsatisfactory because of their severity. Accordingly, new social codes for Negroes were enacted, based on the vagrancy laws of both Northern and Southern states, on the customs of slavery, on the old free Negro statutes, on British West Indian legislation, and on the regulations of the Freedmen's Bureau and other federal agencies seeking to cope with the problem of the ex-slave.

Their sponsors were not conscious of any attempt toward oppression, believing that the most significant feature of their decrees was the extension of rights that Negroes had never before possessed. It seemed to them that the freedom they were giving exceeded the restrictions they were imposing; yet it cannot be doubted that the laws were primarily made for the protection of the ex-masters. The men who wrote them were simply pessimistic regarding Negro capabilities.

The new laws relegated to a distinct caste all individuals possessing a certain amount of Negro blood, usually one eighth. These were called "persons of color," and provisions were made for their marriage; existing slave unions were declared legal. Rights to make contracts, to acquire and hold property, to sue and be sued, and other ordinary civil liberties were given to colored persons. At the same time, various restrictions placed them on a social plane below the whites. Marriage between the races was prohibited. In some states Negroes could testify only in cases involving their own race and required permission to carry weapons. In Mississippi colored persons could own land only in towns; in other states their holdings were confined to the countryside. In South Carolina blacks were forbidden, except under special license, to engage in any business other than husbandry or domestic work. In most states they were subjected to very broad apprenticeship and vagrancy laws. The penalty for "enticing away" apprentices was severe, and in Mississippi Negro orphans were bound out, preferably to former employers; the definition of vagrancy was enlarged to include Negroes not at work and those "found unlawfully assembling themselves together."

Nearly all punishments for petty offenses consisted of hiring out, usually to ex-masters. South Carolina farm laborers had to "rise at dawn," perform their tasks properly, and "retire at reasonable hours," and servants were enjoined to be civil to the "master and his family, guests, and agents." Whipping and the pillory were permitted in Florida, and in South Carolina a master might "moderately correct" servants under eighteen years of age. Many of the rules concerning employer and servant strongly resembled those previously laid down for master and slave, but the sober historian records that "in general the legislation was faithful on the whole to the actual conditions with which it had to deal."

Congress created the Freedmen's Bureau on March 3, 1865, to unify the various federal organizations which sprang up during the war to meet the needs of the liberated Negroes. It had general headquarters in Washington and local offices in all former slave states, except Delaware. General Oliver O. Howard, a fair-minded and tactful soldier, was its chief; other army officers held subordinate positions. The agency assumed the ambitious function of effecting the material relief of the blacks and their economic and social adjustment. Food and other necessities were distributed, employment secured and wages fixed, the writing and execution of labor contracts supervised, and transportation of the dislocated to their former homes directed. Hospital and other medical services were provided, many schools were opened, and protection was invoked against the normal tendency of Southern communities to discriminate socially and legally against former slaves. Altogether, the Freedmen's Bureau proved a blessing to a childlike people struggling in the toils of poverty, disease, and other social and economic consequences of the sudden collapse of a paternalistic slave system. It distributed 22 million rations; it set up forty-five hospitals, and within a year treated 148,000 patients; it transported 32,000 displaced persons back home or to places of employment; it aided 9,503 teachers in the instruction of Negroes. Fisk University in Tennessee, Atlanta University in Georgia, St. Augustine College in North Carolina, and Hampton Institute in Virginia are today monuments to its efforts.[2]

Both the Black Codes and the Freedmen's Bureau were, from opposite viewpoints, wise attempts to meet the realities of Negro life. In theory and largely in detail they were intrinsically sound, but both were to be short-lived and unsuccessful because of the disapproval of outsiders. The greatest fault of the Black Codes was the failure of their creators to consider the prejudices of the Northern conquerors. A distrustful North interpreted such legislation as a systematic attempt to relegate the freedmen to a subjugation differing only slightly from that existing before the war.

The radicals sounded a shrill note of alarm. "We tell the white men of Mississippi," said the *Chicago Tribune*, "that the men of the North will convert the State of Mississippi into a frog pond before they will allow such laws to disgrace one foot of soil in which the bones of our soldiers sleep and over which the flag of freedom waves." The Black Codes were never given a fair trial. Reacting to Northern public opin-

[2] *Ibid.*, pp. 72, 82.

ion, the army and the Freedmen's Bureau suspended them before they went into effect.

Agents of the Freedmen's Bureau were neither numerous enough nor sufficiently trained to handle the multiform and intricate measures required to regulate effectively the industrial and social life of the Negroes. Many of these officials meddled in politics, and some were corrupt. The best among them sought enforcement of abstract principles of justice that ignored realities. Actually, the whites, who owned the land and were the inheritors of social privilege, were able to sit in judgment on economic problems. They angrily rejected the dogma of the equality of the races in judicial and agricultural matters which the Freedmen's Bureau tried to enforce, and succeeded only in giving it an evil reputation. The bureau's concepts were too paternalistic for the theories of government dominant at that time, and the sponsors permitted its abolishment in 1872.

Not until after President Johnson and the Freedmen's Bureau had tackled the Southern problem did Congressional leaders, two years after the surrender at Appomattox, launch their program of radical Reconstruction. This intentional delay gave the vengeful Stevens time to overcome formidable opposition in Congress and among moderate Northerners, and allowed Sumner to convince Congress that it must treat the Negro according to the teachings of the Declaration of Independence. During that two-year period, Southern legislatures affronted public opinion by enacting the Black Codes and electing former Confederates to office, and by rejecting the Fourteenth Amendment. The President weakened his position by tactless talk; in the election of 1866 he lost so many votes in Congress that opponents could override his vetoes.

By New Year's Day, 1867, the tide had moved so strongly in Stevens' and Sumner's direction that the average Republican citizen believed that unless the Negro were enfranchised Democrats and ex-rebels would gain control of the national government. Prospects of Southern influence in federal affairs were brighter than before 1865 because after the abolition of slavery Negroes were counted as whole men instead of three fifths in the apportionment of Congressional representation.

Congress declared its will in the Reconstruction Acts of March 2 and 23, 1867, which pointedly affirmed that "no legal State governments or adequate protection for life or property" existed in ten of the eleven states of the former Confederacy. Tennessee, already under a radical government, was the exception. Thus the Johnson governments were formally pronounced illegal and "subject to the paramount authority of the United States to abolish, modify, control, or supersede the same."

In order to accomplish this purpose effectively, the ten states were divided into five military districts. Virginia became the First Military District; the two Carolinas, the Second; Georgia, Florida, and Alabama, the Third; Mississippi and Arkansas, the Fourth; and Louisiana and Texas, the Fifth. Each district had its military commander with powers superior to those of existing state governments. He could make arrests, conduct trials by military commission and suspend the functions of civil government whenever necessary. His main objective was to direct the calling of a convention consisting of delegates "elected by the male citizens of whatever race, color, or previous condition." This convention must frame a constitution embodying the same rules of suffrage; the constitution must be ratified by the people and authorized by Congress; and a legislature elected under this instrument of government must approve the Fourteenth Amendment. The local boards for registering voters consisted of persons who took the ironclad oath which barred anyone who had voluntarily given aid to the Confederacy. Everyone who registered as a voter was required to subscribe to an oath which somewhat vaguely excluded those who had participated in the rebellion, or who had given aid to the Confederacy after holding state or federal office.

The Reconstruction Acts were passed over the vetoes of the President and were supplemented by legislation to prevent him from frustrating the will of Congress. That body excluded the Southern states from representation in the electoral college, declared certain military orders affecting these states void, and under the Tenure of Office Act usurped control of the cabinet. The Supplementary Reconstruction Act of July 17, 1867, placed the commanders of the five military districts under the authority of Ulysses S. Grant in his capacity as General of the Army instead of under the President as constitutional Commander in Chief.

Finally, through impeachment procedure, Congress unsuccessfully attempted to expel Johnson from office. The President, after accompanying his vetoes with vigorous denunciations of the Reconstruction measures, deemed it his duty to abandon official opposition, and promptly appointed distinguished major generals of the army to command the military districts. John M. Schofield was assigned to the First District, Daniel E. Sickles to the Second, John Pope to the Third, Edward O. C. Ord to the Fourth, and Philip Sheridan to the Fifth.

The reign of the major generals, established with little friction, lasted in all ten states from March, 1867, until June, 1868, and continued in Mississippi, Texas, Virginia, and Georgia until 1870. Northerners were surprised by the absence of violent opposition; less than 20,000 troops were required to keep order. The men who had surrendered at Appomattox were not disposed to resist the United States

Army. Many whites were bewildered by the turn of events, not fully comprehending the threat of Negro suffrage to their pattern of civilization.

Some Southern leaders like Generals Lee, Beauregard, and Longstreet, even though they did not approve radical Reconstruction, advised co-operation with the military authorities in order to salvage the most possible from a difficult situation. Rude honesty characterized the military administration, and tactless generals such as Sickles and Sheridan were replaced by men more acceptable to Southern ways. Successful attempts, too, were made to cope with economic and social disorders. In South Carolina, for example, the commanding general abolished imprisonment for debt, stayed foreclosures on property, made the wages of farm laborers a first lien on crops, and prohibited the manufacture of whisky.

In registration and elections Congress demonstrated a thoroughness which assured that control of most of the revised state governments would remain with the radicals and their allies. Admitted to the registration books were 703,000 Negro voters and 627,000 white voters. There were black majorities in Alabama, Louisiana, South Carolina, Florida, and Mississippi; in other states the Negroes and their white allies had majorities. The large number of white registrants in every state proved, however, that wholesale denial of political rights to the traditionally dominant race was not attempted. It has been estimated that only about 150,000 whites were disfranchised.

Nevertheless, it should not be assumed that the white South was unaware of the harsh aspects of military rule, such as flagrant disregard of civil rights. Confederate veterans' organizations, their parades, and other innocent symbols of the lost cause were repressed. Six governors were replaced, civil courts suppressed, and thousands of local officials supplanted by Negroes and carpetbaggers. Legislatures of three states were purged of their recalcitrant members, and much state legislation, including that of providing artificial legs and free education for crippled ex-Confederates, was set aside. All these measures reflected the will of Congress.

Enforcement by the district commanders of Congressional decrees was marked by one of the most noteworthy accomplishments in the history of American politics—creation among Negroes of an enthusiastic desire to register and vote. It is an easy task for high authority to give an unsophisticated and humble people the right to vote; it is quite another matter to instill in them the wish to exercise this privilege. Yet this well-nigh miraculous achievement occurred among the great masses of the most lowly and uneducated English-speaking Americans. The freedmen, despite their appalling ignorance, poverty, and lack of social and political training, were impressed with the necessity of engaging in political activities along with their former masters. Their inexperience was not interpreted as a reason to remain aloof from politics; in fact, friends of Negro suffrage hoped that their assumption of political power would broaden their social opportunities.

The way for this transformation had been prepared by the officers of the army and the Freedmen's Bureau who from the day of Emancipation inculcated political ambitions in the blacks. The process of systematic organization began when Congress officially decided in favor of Negro suffrage. First came the "visiting statesmen," men like Senator Henry Wilson of Massachusetts and Representative "Pig Iron" Kelley of Pennsylvania. Before large and interested audiences of freedmen, they delivered glowing homilies on the uplifting influences of universal suffrage. Registration officials laid the groundwork by promoting the exclusion of whites from their lists by day and organizing units of the Republican party by night.

Then came those who were derisively called carpetbaggers, because they were supposed to have brought all their possessions in carpetbags. They were a few thousand adventurers from the North who settled in the South for the primary purpose of organizing the blacks politically. Some of the carpetbaggers were honest missionaries who believed that the salvation of the Negro and the South could be secured through universal democracy. Others were knaves or fortune hunters bent upon aiding the Republican party as a means of attaining public office for themselves. Many were astute demagogues who through vague speeches and tricks of mass organization won the confidence of the naïve Negro. Horace Greeley described them as "stealing and plundering, many of them with both arms around negroes, and their hands in their rear pockets, seeing if they cannot pick a paltry dollar out of them."

These interlopers allied themselves with those who were called scalawags, a term previously used for filthy sheep, scaly pigs and other vile creatures. Scalawags were Southerners willing to espouse Republicanism for reasons of opportunism. When the pro-Negro policies of the carpetbaggers caused the scalawags to desert Republicanism, Northern leaders, conscious of the power of numbers, to an ever greater degree relied upon pure Negro support.

The principal agency of the carpetbaggers was the Union or Loyal League. Founded in Northern cities as a means of sustaining the war spirit after Federal reverses of 1862, this organization entered the South with the conquering armies. Initially it was composed almost entirely of white unionists with patriotic rather than political aims. As the plans of Congress unfolded in 1867, its main purpose became the organization of Negro voters. In some counties of the lower South whites were dis-

A RUINED CITY. *Richmond in 1865, shortly after its capture by Union forces, showing Jefferson's classic capitol rising intact over devastated factories, wharves, and warehouses.*

AFTERMATH OF WAR. *A picture that might be Berlin in 1945, this photograph gives some idea of the damage wrought in the heroic defense of Richmond against the Union armies that captured it on April 3, 1865.*

LEVEE AT NEW ORLEANS, 1881. *The postwar revival of this great Southern seaport is shown in this view made three years before the Exposition of 1884–5. Masts of ocean-sailing vessels are visible behind the river steamers loading in the foreground.*

couraged from joining; one Virginia official pointed out its *raison d'être* as "the humane objects and purpose of those in the North who believed that the ballot in the hands of the Negro would be preferable to bullets in the muskets of a standing army." In every Southern community trusting Negroes were organized into secret lodges of the order which indulged in mummery and high-sounding platitudes. In its heyday the Union League was said to have more than 200,000 members.

Ceremony, talk about freedom and equal rights, sententious references to the Declaration of Independence, accompanied by the clanging of chains, the burning of weird lights, and prayers and songs—all had their compelling effect upon the Negroes' emotions and thoughts. They were repeatedly reminded that their interests were eternally at war with those of Southern whites, and that their freedom demanded the continued supremacy of the Republican party. As a consequence of these teachings, the Union League "voted the Negroes like 'herds of senseless cattle.'" One member described it as the "place where we learn the law." When asked why he voted Republican, another member replied, "I can't read, and I can't write. . . . We go by instructions. We don't know nothing much." [3] During the presidential campaign of 1868, the Union League in North Carolina declared that if Grant were not elected, the Negroes would be remanded to slavery; if elected, they would have farms, mules, and hold public office.

One fact is of fundamental importance in understanding the course of radical Reconstruction: the Negroes were aroused to political consciousness not of their own accord but by outside forces. This revolution in Southern behavior, unlike the more lasting political revolutions of history, was not a reflection of accomplishments in other fields. Attainment of political equality by the Negroes, in other words, was not attended by social and economic gains, possibly not even signifying a general demand for these advantages. Such lack of support not only meant that the radical political experiment could be destroyed almost as easily as it was created, but that participation of the Negro in politics would be erratic and irresponsible. Even if it had not been that way, it would have been so regarded, because the Negroes did not preface their attempt to win political equality with the attainment of respect in other fields of social endeavor.

The Southern whites were slow to comprehend the full significance of this political mobilization of a group who had previously shown little interest in politics. Only a few leaders, such as Governors James L. Orr of South Carolina and Joseph E. Brown of Georgia, James L. Alcorn of Mississippi, and General James Longstreet of Louisiana, continued to

[3] Cited in Francis B. Simkins and Robert H. Woody, *South Carolina during Reconstruction*, p. 80.

counsel compromises that might lead to the control of the constitutional governments; the majority hoped that the federal courts would destroy the Reconstruction legislation as a violation of states' rights. When the United States Supreme Court in a decision appealed by Mississippi refused to do this,[4] the leaders decided to meet the impending revolution · with inaction. "A brave, sensitive, and suffering people" preferred a continuation of military rule to the reordering of the state governments along radical lines. By refusing to co-operate, they hoped to delay or even check the processes of Congressional Reconstruction.

Congress met this recalcitrance by obligating the military commanders to execute its will regardless of the Southern attitude. Leaders of the whites thereupon abstained from voting in elections that were to determine whether or not state constitutional conventions would be held, and to choose delegates to these proposed bodies. Thus the leaders hoped to prevent a majority vote in each state, for, under the Reconstruction Acts, no convention could be held unless a majority of the registered voters actually cast ballots for or against a convention. After this plan failed, it was tried again with more unity of purpose when the question of ratification of the proposed constitutions was submitted to the voters. This stratagem worked in Alabama where, in the referendum of February 4, 1868, only 70,000 of the 167,000 registered voters participated. Then Congress decreed that a majority of the votes actually cast sufficed to put a constitution into force.

The inaction of the whites and the aggressiveness of carpetbaggers and blacks resulted in overwhelming numbers in favor of the constitutional conventions and the election of huge radical majorities to these bodies. In Georgia, for example, the issue of the convention was carried by a vote of 102,283 to 4,127; in Florida, by a vote of 14,399 to 203. In Alabama out of a total of 100 delegates only 4 were conservatives; Louisiana had 2 from a total of 98; Florida, 2 out of 45. Approximately one third of the delegates were conservatives in Virginia; Louisiana had as many Negroes as whites; and there were 76 blacks to 48 whites in South Carolina. Negro delegates were definitely in the minority in other states, but in all except North Carolina, Texas, and Virginia the combined vote of Negroes and carpetbaggers exceeded that of native whites. Carpetbaggers in Alabama and Arkansas held majorities without Negro support. Although conservative delegates were fairly competent, they were too small in number to play an important part in the conventions. A few Negro delegates were also men of ability, but most were illiterate and ignorant, content to vote as the more experienced white men directed. Leadership rested with the carpetbaggers and scalawags, some of

[4] *Ex parte McCardle*, 7 Wall, 506.

whom were able and educated men; but the majority were conscience-less political soldiers of fortune.

Instruments of government created by the carpetbaggers and scala-wags and their Negro supporters contained many progressive innova-tions that have remained permanent parts of the constitutional fabric of the Southern states. That they were copied from the constitutions of Northern states did not detract from their usefulness. They included the principle of the equality of all men before the law, the apportionment of legislative representation solely on a basis of population, and state obligation to provide free education for all children. Such constructive measures were supplemented by some that were too eccentric or radical to be effective. Among these were the ban on the use of the words "Yankee" and "nigger," and the attempt to abolish the color line in schools and in social relations.

The only radical innovation of great significance was the establish-ment of universal manhood suffrage without restrictions of race or color. A South Carolina delegate expressed the revolutionary sentiments of new rulers of the South when he declared that the right to vote "belongs alike to the wise and the ignorant, to the virtuous and the vicious. . . . I hope the music of the nineteenth century will inspire every man upon this floor to view it in the light of progress and reason, and strike out every word that puts a limitation upon the manhood of the citizen, so far as regards the right to vote." [5] Although the voting requirements adopted by all the conventions except that of Texas ex-tended beyond the Fourteenth Amendment, there was no general dispo-sition to disfranchise permanently those whites who accepted radical Reconstruction. Only Louisiana, Alabama, and Arkansas actually ap-plied suffrage and officeholding restrictions against whites. Disabilities and disqualifications were taken out of the Mississippi and Virginia con-stitutions before ratification. North Carolina, South Carolina, Florida, and Texas in no way obstructed white men either in voting or in hold-ing office. Desire for reform rather than vengeance dominated the de-liberations. It was hoped that dissentions and discriminations of the past would disappear in a democratic future.

In hopes of making Negro suffrage permanent, Congress in 1869 enacted the Fifteenth Amendment and made its ratification one of the conditions precedent to the readmission into the Union of states in which the process of Reconstruction had not been completed. These were Virginia, Texas, Mississippi, and Georgia. Under this condition ratification went forward with a rush, and on March 30, 1870, the amendment was declared a part of the Constitution. It provided that the

[5] Alonso J. Ransier, cited in Simkins and Woody, *op. cit.*, p. 96.

right of citizens to vote "shall not be denied or abridged by the United States or by any State on account of race, color, or previous condition of servitude."

By July, 1868, seven of the eleven states of the former Confederacy complied with the remaining requirements of Reconstruction and were accordingly readmitted into the Union and granted seats in Congress—Arkansas, North Carolina, South Carolina, Louisiana, Georgia, Alabama, and Florida. They had ratified the new constitutions by popular votes, elected legislatures and state and local officials, and their legislatures had ratified the Fourteenth Amendment. Tennessee had already been recognized by Congress as reconstructed because under the exceptional leadership of Governor Brownlow it had ratified the Fourteenth Amendment when that proposal was first presented to it in 1866.

Virginia, Texas, and Mississippi were not readmitted into the Union until 1870. Virginia's new constitution was so severe in its provision for disfranchisement of ex-Confederates that the district commander refused to authorize expenditures or to put it to a vote. In Texas strife between the moderate and radical factions of the Republican party delayed the framing of a constitution, and Mississippi rejected the new constitution by a majority of 7,600 votes. When Grant became President in 1869, Congress placed in his hands the problem of reconstructing these three refractory states, with the proviso that they must ratify the Fifteenth Amendment. Virginia and Mississippi were permitted to submit separately the constitutions as a whole and their disfranchising clauses, and Texas deleted that objectionable clause from its constitution. Under these circumstances the radical constitutions were ratified in all three states; the disfranchising clauses were rejected in Virginia and Mississippi. In Texas and Mississippi the radicals gained control of the new governments, but in Virginia a conservative combination triumphed.

A peculiar situation developed in Georgia after its readmission into the Union in June, 1868. The legislature expelled its twenty-eight Negro members on the ground that a Negro had a right to vote, but not to hold office. Congress then remanded Georgia to military rule. After purging the legislature, reseating its Negro members, and ratifying the Fifteenth Admendment, Georgia was readmitted into the Union in 1870 along with Texas, Mississippi, and Virginia.

Thus, within five years after the Civil War, conditions supposedly promoting peace and harmony were imposed upon the rebellious states. President Johnson's moderate plan, based upon a continuation of white supremacy, had been replaced by Congress's bold experiment in the political equality of the two Southern races. Some thought that this dictated peace would be followed by genuine accord, but the struggle that persisted in certain respects was even more bitter than the physical conflict that had ended at Appomattox.

CHAPTER XVIII

Black Reconstruction

-»»-«««

THE PERIOD during which carpetbaggers and Negroes played a dominant role in the government of the Southern states is called Black Reconstruction. It is usually considered as lasting the eight or nine years
between the summer of 1868, when radical state constitutions were
effected, and the spring of 1877, when final contingents of federal
troops were withdrawn from state capitals. Actually, only South Carolina, Louisiana, and Florida experienced radicalism that long; Georgia,
Virginia, and North Carolina escaped after brief periods. The five other
states of the former Confederacy endured radical control for four or
five years.

Radical governments rested on the support of the 931,000 Negroes
whose names ultimately were entered in the voting books and who
apparently were given permanent protection in the exercise of political privileges by the adoption of the Fifteenth Amendment in 1870.
Blacks outnumbered whites in South Carolina, Alabama, Mississippi,
Florida, and Louisiana, and with the somewhat uncertain aid of the
scalawag element were able to control the majority in other states.
They were under the well-disciplined leadership of carpetbaggers and
scalawags who skillfully employed all the tricks of the demagogue to
keep these credulous creatures faithful to Republicanism.

After the retirement of President Johnson in 1869, the experiment
in Negro suffrage for eight years had the undivided support of the government and the political party which defeated the Confederacy and
imposed peace terms. Ulysses S. Grant, the new President, although at
first considerate of those who had fought him so bravely, showed willingness to co-operate with the radical majority in Congress. Basically

ignorant of Southern politics, this simple soldier fell under the control of radical advisers who played up the rebellious tendencies of the former Confederates, citing the need to protect Southern radicals from Democratic gains. Whenever the Southern state governments weakened, Congress granted them necessary support by legislation and gave the President required military force.

At first Southern whites could not effectively oppose this apparently invincible combination of Negro, carpetbagger, scalawag, and federal power. In 1868 approximately 150,000 Southern whites were disfranchised and about twice that number disqualified from officeholding. They were not so well led as in ante-bellum times. The abstention policy followed in 1867 and 1868 was supplemented by a cynical indifference toward civic responsibilities when they discovered that the Negro was deaf to their political appeals and that the dominant party in Washington regarded them as unpatriotic and unworthy of trust.

The radical combination that controlled the South was compounded of that mixture of the ignorant and idealistic, the calculating and the sordid which often creates and sustains a cause. There were Negro voters so morally obtuse that they refused to cry down officeholders repeatedly proved to be dishonest; and there were others so ignorant that they carried to the polls sacks in which to put their suffrage or halters with which to bring back the mules they believed would be given them. There were carpetbaggers and scalawags who were blatantly dishonest and profit seeking. Some politicians in Washington saw in corrupt Southern governments a means of sustaining a national party that in certain respects was as corrupt as its Southern branches. On the other hand, there were Negro voters who recognized political participation as a means of elevating themselves to that equality with other men guaranteed by the Declaration of Independence and the three war amendments to the federal constitution. Among carpetbaggers were those who combined a critical understanding of the defects of Southern society with a constructive desire to impose upon it some of the advantages of Northern progress.

Certain radical leaders in Congress and the Grant administration wished to give the South—white as well as black—the benefits of that brand of nationalism, democracy, and capitalism which had worked wonders in the North. These last-mentioned objectives explain why the radical experimenters, despite their excessive knavery, corruption, and ineptitude, never completely forgot their obligation to reform and uplift a less advanced section of the United States toward the standards of a more progressive group. Actual accomplishments were made in this direction.

Due to the scarcity of competent men for local office and the lawlessness of the opposition, the builders of radical strength in the South greatly increased the authority of the state governor, including his powers of appointment, disbursements, control of the militia and constabulary, and management of elections. Some of the men who exercised these augmented powers, such as William G. Brownlow of Tennessee and William W. Holden of North Carolina, were honest but vindictive and narrow. Others were forced by necessity to be unscrupulous in their public acts, and a third group of officials was flagrantly dishonest and corrupt. Franklin J. Moses, Jr., of South Carolina confessed to bribery; he admitted spending ten times his salary on extravagant living. Henry C. Warmoth and William P. Kellogg of Louisiana retired from office with large fortunes. The number of lesser officials greatly increased with the expansion of administrative functions and the lure of new spoils.

C. P. Leslie, a South Carolina carpetbagger, declared, "South Carolina has no right to be a State unless she can support her statesmen." He and others lived according to this principle. "By the exercise of the most rigid economy," was the explanation offered by the manager of a Georgia state railroad for his accumulation of a fortune on a small salary. Negro members of the Florida legislature formed "a smelling committee" to ferret out possibilities of graft.[1] Even the judiciary, pride of the Old South, became tainted. The chief justice of the Louisiana supreme court was convicted of fraud, and a South Carolinian associate justice offered his decisions for sale. Illiteracy was widespread among the lesser magistrates. Daniel H. Chamberlain, a carpetbag governor of South Carolina, asserted that 200 illiterate trial justices presided in his state. Federal officials participated in the corruption. Federal Judge Richard Busteed in Alabama enjoyed a rich harvest of bribes and federal Judge Edward H. Durell became so completely a part of the corruption in Louisiana that he resigned under pressure.

For several years following 1868 the radicals had overwhelming majorities in seven state legislatures and buffoonery and corruption ran riot. Votes were for sale everywhere at fixed prices; for example, $600 would buy a senator in Louisiana. In Florida sealed envelopes containing $100 or more were freely passed around on the occasion of any important vote. Conditions were at their worst in South Carolina, where Negro majorities prevailed from 1868 to 1874. State House "supplies" paid out of public funds included ladies' finery, liquors, table delicacies, furniture, and horses and carriages. In little over a year of radical rule more was spent for public printing than in seventy-eight years of the old regime.

The Republican journalist James S. Pike vividly pictured the colored

[1] Walter L. Fleming, *The Sequel of Appomattox*, pp. 223–6.

legislators as barbarians triumphing over civilization and described the South Carolina slave as "rioting in the halls of his master." They were of all colors, from the lightest quadroons to the blackest Africans, in clothing ranging from secondhand frock coats to the "coarse and dirty garments of the field." Their proceedings were marked by clamor, squabbling, interruptions, "bellowing and physical contortions." Although guffaws frequently greeted the speaker when he rapped for order, the dusky lawmakers took themselves seriously. "Seven years ago," notes Pike, "these men were raising corn and cotton under the whip of the overseer. Today they are raising points of order. . . . It is easier and better paid. . . . It is their day of jubilee." [2]

Attempts were made to meet the very real menace of counterrevolution by the organization of a sympathetic militia. Governor Brownlow of Tennessee and Governor Holden of North Carolina depended on white recruits, while Governor Powell Clayton of Arkansas depended on men of both races. South Carolina, Louisiana and Mississippi ran the risk of centering on armed Negroes. Governor Robert K. Scott enrolled 90,000 black South Carolinians and armed 20,000 of them.

This bold experiment carried with it the possibility of providing the radical governments with the physical protection necessary for them to survive under the constant menace of white violence. It might remove the embarrassing necessity of states having to call on the United States army for the enforcement of their laws. The Negroes seemed ideal soldiers. They were experienced in the use of firearms and they loved the uniforms and the mumbo jumbo of military exercises.

The whites, of course, were bitterly resentful. There was much talk of black soldiers "galloping about, cursing, threatening," but little proof of actual violence. Generally the militiamen quailed before white opposition. Governor Warmoth of Louisiana was relieved when lawfully deprived of the authority to arm his black followers against the whites. Eventually, radical governors were forced to depend on the protection of federal troops for the survival of their regimes.

Inevitably public expenditures were greatly enlarged. In Alabama and Florida current expenses of state governments increased 200 per cent, in Louisiana 500 per cent, in Arkansas 1,500 per cent. Consequently tax rates in Alabama rose 400 per cent, in Louisiana 800 per cent, in Mississippi 1,400 per cent. For these and other reasons, property values in some states declined as much as 75 per cent. Newspapers were full of reports of sheriff's sales of depreciated land which could not meet the burden of higher taxation.

State governments floated large bond sales to create additional revenues. By 1873 the public debt of South Carolina climbed from 7 to 29

[2] *The Prostrate State*, pp. 12–21.

million dollars; by 1871 that of Alabama from 7 to 32 millions; and that of Louisiana from 14 to 48 millions. Corrupt New York financial agents who sold Southern bonds below par values facilitated the creation of these mountainous debts.

The greatest cause of corruption was the endorsement of railroad bonds by the states. This practice, inherited from the Johnson administration, was continued with the connivance of both Democratic and Republican lobbyists. Railroad bonds in some instances were endorsed before the roads were built, and excessive issues were tolerated. Such grants under the Holden administration in North Carolina exceeded $27,000,000; Alabama issues have been estimated from $17- to 30,000,-000; a ring of twenty men in Arkansas got state loans of more than $5,000,000 for eighty-six railroad projects. When the companies defaulted, as most of them did, the states were left with the burden. Lobbyists and politicians alone profited. Little of the accumulated capital went for actual construction purposes.

Without an ignorant and irresponsible electorate such extremes of extravagance and corruption could not have taken place. The ex-slave allowed himself to be led to the ballot box by Republican politicians with the same submissiveness with which he had once been ordered to church or the cotton fields by his master. The Negro's great enthusiasm for politics never took the form of a demand for civic rectitude. In reply to the assertion that the race was not responsible for the Reconstruction iniquities, a famous Negrophobe said later: "The negroes put the little piece of paper in the box which gave the commission to these white scoundrels who were their leaders."[3] Yet the blacks were dupes rather than rascals. The more important bribes fell to the carpetbaggers and scalawags; to the Negroes went merely minor positions and smaller sums.

Carpetbaggers got a majority of the high offices in the states where the Negro population was large. Four of the governors and ten of the United States senators of the seven states admitted to the Union in 1868 were carpetbaggers. Nineteen of these outsiders ultimately went to the Senate. In Virginia, North Carolina, Tennessee, and Texas the scalawags ruled.

Only in South Carolina was the legislature dominated by blacks. Negroes became lieutenant governors in South Carolina, Mississippi, and Louisiana; all other state offices in some state at one time or another were filled by them. Only South Carolina had a justice of the state supreme court who was a Negro. Not one was elected to a governorship, although the mulatto Pinckney Benton Steward Pinchback served

[3] Benjamin R. Tillman, cited in Francis B. Simkins, *Pitchfork Ben Tillman, South Carolinian*, p. 302.

for a few weeks as acting governor of Louisiana and the Negro Alexander K. Davis frequently acted as governor of Mississippi during the absence of Governor Adelbert Ames. Hiram R. Revels and Blanche K. Bruce, both of Mississippi, served in the United States Senate; only fifteen of their fellows were elected to the national House of Representatives during the Reconstruction period. Those Negroes who held important offices were neither worse nor better than their carpetbag and scalawag compeers.

If race, then, does not explain the misdeeds of the reconstructionists, should they be attributed to the peculiarly evil nature of the Northerners who came South and to the weak characters of their Southern henchmen? Undoubtedly the Southern states had more such men in responsible positions during that period than in normal times, but in all probability most of those who committed fraud were prompted by circumstances rather than by inclination. Reconstruction was an era of unhealthy politics which called forth the evil in men that under happier conditions would have been suppressed.

It is an error, however, to treat those years as an example of isolated evil. If Reconstruction was a time of rampant corruption in Southern history, this was also true of the same period in the Northern states. The contemporary scandals of the Grant administration in Washington and the Tweed ring in New York City were fully as regrettable as events in Southern capitals. Conservative governments of the Southern states which preceded and followed the radical regimes were not spotless; for example, numerous Democratic land agents stole public lands in the time of President Van Buren, and the Brown-Gordon-Colquitt coalition after Reconstruction in Georgia behaved unscrupulously. All these examples of corruption and extravagance, including those of the radical legislatures, may be construed as part of a national era of expansion which prompted lavish and unwise use of public funds to promote business.

The enlarged scope of governmental activities necessary to remedy the destruction of war, to care for the confused freedmen, and to satisfy the demand that the states assume new social functions was responsible for much of the increase in expenditure. Buildings and roads had to be repaired, poverty relieved, and schools built. Even the attempt of South Carolina's legislature to endow Negroes with homesteads—sometimes cited as a prime example of radical folly—was not an act of madness, but an effort to supplement political with economic enfranchisement, an experiment not without precedent among progressive European nations.

The extravagance of the radical governments is conventionally compared with the economy of the planter and Bourbon regimes that preceded and followed these governments. Yet the activities of the two conservative white regimes may be interpreted as a false economy achieved only by sacrificing functions which progressive observers think the states should assume. On the other hand, increases in tax rates and debts characteristic of the radical governments are insignificant in comparison to similar increases in the same Southern states under the control of white Democrats in the twentieth century. As E. Merton Coulter points out,[4] Illinois in 1870 had a tax rate of 45 mills as compared with only 15 mills for the eleven states of the former Confederacy, and in the same year these states collected only $32,000,000 in state, county, and municipal taxes; whereas the state of New York collected $48,000,000. Conceding that the expenditures of the Southern radicals were high, they were still not great enough to stifle the significant agricultural and commercial progress of the Reconstruction period. That reputed utopia, the Old South, was responsible in a sense for the ignorance and incompetence of Negro voters and officeholders of the post-bellum period. For if the radicals in Congress were unwise in conferring political and social privileges upon ex-slaves, the rulers of the Old South were equally shortsighted in keeping down these unfortunate people.

Radical Reconstruction was not without positive benefits. State constitutions as drawn up by the carpetbaggers were so harmonious with progressive tendencies that they have substantially survived to the present day. These constitutions achieved reforms in the organization of the courts, in the codes of judicial procedure, in the systems of county government and school administration, in the manner of electing public officials, and in methods of taxation. Through them Southerners learned of the equality of all men before the law, the right of all children to attend state-supported schools, and—potentially at least—the privilege of all to enjoy political, civil, and social liberties. With the overthrow of the Reconstruction regimes, the South trampled upon many features of the democratic concept envisioned by the radical experimentalists. But this ideal had been embedded in the fundamental law of the land through the Fourteenth and Fifteenth amendments, and not forgotten by those in whose interest it had been created.

The new governments had scarcely been established before they showed signs of weakness which resulted in their overthrow within eight or nine years. This occurred in Tennessee in 1869; in Virginia, North Carolina, and Georgia in 1870; in Alabama, Arkansas, and Texas in 1874; in Mississippi in 1875; in Louisiana, Florida, and South Carolina in 1877. Counterrevolutions were effected by local whites; both federal and state authorities yielded before them after some struggle.

[4] *The South during Reconstruction, 1865–1877,* p. 156.

Extravagance, ignorance, and corruption of the radical voters and officeholders have been advanced to justify the overthrow of the regimes they supported and directed. However, malfeasance was not the fundamental cause. Radical Reconstruction was an assault upon the theory of white supremacy, the doctrine that gives the South distinctiveness as a region. From the time Negroes were first introduced in large numbers until the present day the South has clung to the belief that in no aspect of social relations may blacks equal whites. It is true that the reconstructionists made no persistent attempts to break this tradition in its social and economic aspects, but racial political equality was actually achieved. There, at least, the Negro was the equal and often the superior of the white man. Such scandals as white politicians fraternizing with Negroes, occasionally dancing and banqueting with them, became commonplace.

This explains why it seemed that the whites "had gone crazy with anger or were obsessed with some fearful mania" when confronted with "gibbering, louse-eaten, devil-worshipping barbarians from the jungles of Dahomey" in legislative halls. A Southern scholar says: "All the misfortunes of war itself are insignificant when compared with the suffering of the people during the era of Reconstruction." [5] Corruption and extravagance increased the intolerance with which the Negro regimes were regarded. Yet even if these regimes had shown exemplary statesmanship they would have been unacceptable to white Southerners as long as Negroes comprising any part of them were regarded as political equals. "A good Radical is no better than a corrupt Radical," asserted a leader of the common whites.[6] To destroy Negro equality the white man determined to employ all weapons at his command—even force when its use did not involve too great a risk of conflict with federal authority.

The superior economic and social strength of the whites meant that Negro and carpetbag rule could be maintained only with the support of federal power, such as it manifested in the purging of the Georgia and Alabama legislatures, the passing of the Fifteenth Amendment in 1870, and the Enforcement of Federal Election and Ku Klux acts in 1870 and 1871. These laws sought to sustain the Negro's civil and political rights by national authority since the radical governments obviously were unable to do this alone.

In the North, meanwhile, a countercurrent of opinion developed, questioning the wisdom of continued federal interference in internal affairs of the states. Important Northern states early in the Reconstruction period refused to grant suffrage to their Negro minorities and the

---

[5] Unsigned article in *Encyclopedia Britannica* (11th ed.), XXV, 504.
[6] Benjamin R. Tillman, cited in Simkins, *op. cit.*, p. 57.

national convention of the Republican party in 1868 refused to supplement its demand for Negro suffrage in the Southern states by demanding the same concession in the Northern states. The North would have to relent or else stand convicted of permanent hypocrisy. The North relented. The passions engendered by war gradually subsided as the American sense of fair play reasserted itself. Congress passed the Amnesty Act in 1872. This law re-enfranchised some 150,000 whites and omitted only 500 prominent leaders of the lost cause, among them Jubal A. Early and Jefferson Davis. Radical majorities in Congress were replaced by liberal Republicans and a resuscitated Democratic party. Americans generally were becoming disgusted with the corruption of the Grant administration and its Southern minions. Republicans lost control of the lower house of Congress in 1874. Northerners, plagued by sectional political problems and primarily interested in their own material development, cooled in their enthusiasm for universal brotherhood and the attendant controversies of Reconstruction.

The indecision of Southern whites that contributed to the triumph of the radicals in 1867 and 1868 gradually was replaced by activity. All members of the "superior caste," excepting only a diminishing number of scalawags, united in one political group which became known as the Conservative party to avoid the partisan associations identified with the name Democratic party. By 1870 this group, aided by a calculated use of Ku Klux threats and violence, won control in Virginia, North Carolina, Tennessee, and Georgia, where they held majorities. Factional quarrels among carpetbaggers, Negroes, and scalawags weakened the radicals' position. In those states where blacks possessed whole or near majorities the conservatives experienced greater difficulties, and between 1870 and 1874 made little progress against radicalism.

Alarmed Washington authorities met Ku Klux outrages by dispatching military reinforcements and federal deputy marshals to disturbed areas. Although arrests were numerous, the whites became entrenched in the states they had recovered during these years. Border states arrayed themselves more solidly with the conservatives, and radicals in Congress and in Southern legislatures declined in number. Earlier extravagances of the radical state governments gave way to poverty and bankruptcy. Property holders refused to pay taxes and Southern bonds could be sold only at great discounts. Carpetbaggers and scalawags departed, leaving the Negroes to flounder by themselves.

A constant threat to radical supremacy was the growing tendency of whites to meet with violence the political and social insubordination of the blacks. Every prominent radical feared assassination when he ventured into rural areas on political missions; the more timid prudently remained in cities and towns behind the protection of federal troops. In spite of their large numbers and experience in the use of firearms, the Negroes were powerless to resist the whites' demonstrations of force. The clever ruse through which they had been endowed with the arms and insignia of militiamen did not succeed, and they almost always quailed before members of the former master class. Race riots of 1866–67 were followed by those of 1873–74 with identical results: more Negroes than whites were killed. At the riot at Colfax, Louisiana, in 1873, for example, fifty-nine Negroes were massacred while the white casualties were only two; in the same state at Coushatta the next year six white Republican officeholders were killed after their surrender. The six were murdered, said the *New Orleans Republican*, "for the crime of Northern birth and Republican principles." Less than three weeks after the Coushatta disturbance a clash at New Orleans resulted in the loss of forty-four radicals and only twelve conservatives.

Without outside interference whites could easily have rid themselves of the radicals by direct action. Such action, however, almost always provoked federal intervention which resulted in a tightening of the radical yoke. More subtle tactics became necessary. These took the form of secret revolutionary societies generally known as the Ku Klux Klan. These groups sought to destroy radical political power through intimidation and terrorism. At first ante-bellum Negro patrols were reorganized and vigilance committees set up. Later more formal organizations became numerous, varying from local police bodies to great federations covering large sections of the South. They went by such names as Constitutional Union Guards, the Pale Faces, the White Brotherhood, the Order of the White Rose, and the Knights of the White Camelia.

The most famous of these organizations was the Ku Klux Klan proper. From a modest beginning at Pulaski, Tennessee, in 1865 as a secret lodge for innocent fun, it rapidly spread into many localities of the South, attaining its greatest scope between 1868 and 1871. Popular imagination was stirred by the night-riding, white-robed and hooded Klansmen, mounted on sheeted steeds. With a "grand wizard" and ten "genii" at its head, the order of the Ku Klux Klan was governed by such officials as grand dragons and hydras, titans, furies, and nighthawks, given to weird incantations. The cyclops was the master of the local lodge or den and members were known as ghouls. The so-called provinces and realms allegedly were federated into an invisible empire covering all former slave states except Delaware. Of the actual existence of the federation, however, there is but slight evidence. The activities of the order were usually confined to local efforts to destroy radical political organizations rather than a general conspiracy. The night-riding activities of the disguised were in part pranks, in part ghostly intimidations of superstitious blacks.

There is the story of one of these travelers who called at the home of a Louisiana Negro in order to frighten him into flight. The visitor appeared to drink three buckets of water, then asserted that he had traveled nearly 1,000 miles within twenty-four hours and it was the best water he had tasted since being killed at the Battle of Shiloh. Not infrequently, however, the hosts of these strange visitors, sensing actual weapons beneath the disguises, were more frightened by possible violence than by any ghostly affectations.

The Klansmen did much to revive historic social customs that had been shattered by war and Reconstruction. Union Leagues were destroyed; Negro militiamen whipped; political and religious agitators silenced. The worst of the Reconstruction officials were expelled and hostile gatherings of Negroes dispersed. In the opinion of a competent authority the Ku Klux Klan by 1870 had aided in re-establishing white supremacy in four states.

However, the Klan failed to achieve general restoration of white supremacy. Its founders did not develop effective central controls, and local units fell into the hands of irresponsible men. Frequently these men used the order as a cloak for murder and thievery and as a means for expelling Negroes from communities. After 1868 many prominent men resigned from the order, and in 1869 General Nathan Bedford Forrest, the grand wizard, proclaimed its formal disbandment. The units that continued to exist, notably those in South Carolina, were largely composed of men from the hills who sometimes shot, whipped, or even mutilated the victims of their raids.

Acting under the authority of the Ku Klux Act of 1871, President Grant in October of that year declared nine counties in South Carolina in rebellion and placed them under martial law. A Congressional committee made investigations in several Southern states, taking a vast amount of evidence on the so-called Ku Klux conspiracy against national security. In the ten years following 1870, thousands of Southerners were arrested and charged with Ku Klux violence. Convictions were obtained in about 1,250 cases. By 1871 violence disguised under the name of the Ku Klux Klan had been suppressed by federal authority. Still the ugly spirit that had been invoked persisted, continuing to come to life under a variety of names whenever the Negro appeared to be insubordinate.

Northern dissatisfaction with the radical solution of the Southern problem became increasingly pronounced in the years following the suppression of the Ku Klux Klan. The success of conservatives in Tennessee, Virginia, North Carolina, and Georgia seemed to point to the impossibility of maintaining radicalism in those states; at the same time Northern public opinion was being prepared for its destruction in other states. As Southern conditions became better understood, thousands of Northerners who had previously favored the radicals readily sympathized with fellow members of the white race suffering from the humiliations of Negro rule. The books of James S. Pike and Charles Nordhoff and evidence obtained by the Congressional committee investigating the Ku Klux Klan promoted a better understanding of Southern conditions. Reports were published which successfully contradicted further attempts to excite Northern opinion concerning "the horrible scenes of bloodshed and violence throughout the South." Albion W. Tourgée, after much experience as a carpetbagger, declared that "ignorance, poverty, and inexperience" were the chief characteristics of the Republican party in the South; and *The Nation*, an important New York weekly, declared that this group was "largely composed of trashy whites and ignorant blacks." Many who had once befriended the Negro became convinced of his political shortcomings; others wearied of the constantly recurring Southern problem.

This general trend was expressed in 1875 by President Grant's reply to a request for troops in Mississippi: "The whole public are tired out with these annual autumnal outbreaks in the South and the great majority are ready now to condemn any interference on the part of the Government." As an outgrowth of this feeling the Democrats won a sweeping victory in the Congressional elections of 1874 and Congress abolished self-government in the District of Columbia because of its large numbers of politically active and corrupt Negroes. This action at the national capital contrasted with the policy by which radical regimes were prolonged in the predominantly Negro states of the South.

Northern public opinion was especially influenced by striking scandals and disorders that kept occurring in South Carolina and Louisiana. In the former state a Negro majority of 30- to 40,000 was impervious to the arguments of coalitions of conservatives and reforming Republicans; blacks held a majority of the public offices and elected as governor the notorious scalawag Franklin J. Moses, Jr. When the facts concerning government in the Palmetto state became known through the writings of Pike and others, Northern public opinion concluded that the punishment imposed was too great for even the original state of secession.

The situation in Louisiana was more dramatic than that in South Carolina. In the Pelican state in 1873 Stephen B. Packard, United States marshal, and Henry C. Warmoth, carpetbag governor, engaged in a violent factional dispute over election returns. Warmoth recognized the election of a conservative legislature, while Packard secured the aid of United States troops and a federal court to prevent the meeting of this legislature and substitute a radical one in its place. Two governments were organized in New Orleans with both conservative John McEnery and radical William P. Kellogg claiming to be the legal governor. When Washington authorities failed to recognize either claimant Louisiana fell into anarchy, and serious clashes occurred between the races. Disorderly conditions were renewed in 1875 when federal troops, acting at the request of Governor Kellogg, expelled enough conservatives from the legislature to enable the radicals to take control. Two legislatures came into being when the conservatives organized separately.

Although General Philip H. Sheridan condemned the leaders of the whites as "banditti," the high-handed conduct of the troops under his command aroused feelings in the North and the Republican members of a Congressional committee stigmatized the conduct of the Louisiana radicals as unjust and illegal. This dispute was finally settled by a compromise under which the conservatives were given control of the lower house of the legislature. The presence of federal troops alone prevented the whites from sweeping the radicals from the state. The situation in Louisiana, declared William A. Dunning, "displayed to the people of the North the *reductio ad absurdum* of Reconstruction through Negro suffrage and a regime of carpetbaggers." [7]

To achieve the final overthrow of the Radical governments the South adopted two policies: one was to meet halfway Northern offers of conciliation; the other was to punish with calculated violence the obstinacy of carpetbaggers and unregenerate Negro voters. Without really sacrificing the doctrine of white supremacy, Southern leaders received Northern investigators with such tact that a leading statesman of Massachusetts admitted that former rebels "manifested in their home lives some of the human traits and even virtues that prevailed in New England." In 1875 a Georgian declared in Congress: "We are in the house of our fathers, our brothers are our companions, and we are at home to stay, thank God." There were even vague predictions that the South if freed of carpetbaggers and federal soldiers might accept Reconstruction to the extent of respecting the civil and political rights of the Negro. When the opportunity came for a Southerner to be magnanimous, Lucius Q. C. Lamar, the most eminent of Southern aristocrats in Congress, rose to the occasion. In April, 1874, he delivered in the House of Representatives an eloquent tribute to Charles Sumner, who had died the previous month. That a former rebel should find anything to approve in the collaborator of Thaddeus Stevens, save possibly Sumner's death, arrested attention in North and South alike. Here was an emotional basis for a spiritual reunion of the sections. The South, indeed, was soon forgetting itself sufficiently to grow as indignant as the North when foreign nations now and then insulted the Stars and Stripes, as in 1873 when Spain shot some of the crew of the *Virginius*.

[7] Dunning, *Reconstruction, Political and Economic*, p. 219.

Behind this façade of reconciliation, however, lurked the determination of the states still in the thralldom of radicalism to rid themselves of carpetbaggers and Negro voters at any cost except the renewal of dirict resistance to federal authority. At first conciliation would be tried, but if that failed force must be employed. The whites of the Negro-dominated states were tired of force bills, federal troops, Negro voters, and government by incompetents. They felt no gratitude for the supposed generosity of the North in not resorting to confiscations and executions, no repentance for war, no feeling that the Negro had been wronged by slavery. To them the magnanimity of Grant at Appomattox had been destroyed by the severity of his Southern policy as President. Accordingly, they tightened the color line and created a more homogeneous white society. The white masses were vengeful, the leaders shrewd, narrow, and calculating.

Without the suspected disguises, rituals, and formalities of the Ku Klux Klan the whites formed bands similar to the notorious organization that Grant's soldiers had suppressed. The new associations were known as the White League in Louisiana, the White Line in Mississippi, the White Man's Party in Alabama, and the Rifle Clubs or Red Shirts in South Carolina. Their plan of campaign was variously known as the Mississippi plan, or the Straightout, or the Shotgun policy. When persuasion failed to win the votes of the Negroes, threats and violence were used. If riots ensued, the superior discipline and stamina of the former master class was expected to prevail over black numbers. The small number of federal troops on hand for police duty was considered insufficient adequately to protect the Negro's political rights. The race riots which occurred were almost always at points beyond the reach of the soldiery. The troops, tired of the task of suppression imposed upon them, could be depended upon to show sympathy for the whites whenever interracial conflicts developed.

Through their organizations for violence the whites carried the elections in Alabama, Arkansas, and Texas in 1874. In Alabama a faction-torn radical party encountered the racial barrier. A conservative legislature and governor, George S. Houston, were elected. A great many election frauds and one serious race riot marked the proceedings. In Texas after the radical governor, Edmund J. Davis, refused to acknowledge his defeat by conservative Richard Coke, a near civil war developed between armed whites and the radical militia. Davis had to yield to superior force after vainly requesting federal intervention. A conflict developed in Arkansas between rival claimants for the governorship; known as the Brooks-Baxter War, it resulted in the loss of some 200 lives. A compromise ended in a constitutional convention and the election of Governor Augustus H. Garland, a conservative who had once served in the Confederate Senate. Attempts after 1874 to revive radicalism in Alabama, Arkansas, and Texas were unsuccessful. Conservatism had scored permanent triumphs in all three states.

In 1875 General James Z. George carefully laid plans for counter-revolution in Mississippi. The problem was to win a state with a large Negro majority and radical control of the election machinery without provoking federal intervention. The Mississippi plan was not based on the use of force, but on the ever-present threat that it could and would be employed if necessary to re-establish white supremacy. Democratic clubs were converted into armed bands which ostentatiously demonstrated at Republican meetings. Despite the restraining influence of General George, there were bloody clashes at Yazoo City and at Clinton, where more Negroes than whites were killed. Governor Adelbert Ames, a carpetbagger, asked for federal troops, but the Grant administration refused to send them for fear of ruining the chances of Republican success in an Ohio election. Ames resorted to the dangerous experiment of a Negro militia; he declared that none but colored people had respect for the state government. There would have been a war of races if federal emissaries had not effected compromise. Under it the Negroes, but not the Democratic clubs, were disarmed and the Democrats promised a fair and peaceful election. The election was generally peaceful; it was, says a historian,[8] "a peculiar quiet" induced by the fact that the Negro had been cowed into surrendering his political rights. Counties that had previously voted Republican majorities now returned few Republican votes. Indeed, the Democratic triumph was so overwhelming that advocates of federal intervention lost all courage to continue the struggle.

The intimate ties between federal authority and the Reconstruction governments of the Southern states were clearly illustrated in the election of 1876. This contest of ballots proceeded with only three states still under radical control—South Carolina, because of its great Negro majority; Louisiana and Florida, because of the power of their state boards to determine elections arbitrarily. In each of the three states two governments sprang up after the election, each claiming to be legitimate, each calling upon federal authority to settle the dispute in its favor. Still more extraordinary was the fact that because of the dual character of the governments of these three states there were disputed electoral returns. A final count of these votes would decide whether a Democrat or a Republican would be the next President of the United States. Samuel J. Tilden, the Democratic candidate, had 184 electoral votes—one less than a majority. But if all nineteen of the disputed votes of the three Southern states could be counted for Rutherford B. Hayes,

[8] Vernon L. Wharton, *The Negro in Mississippi, 1865–1890*, p. 195.

the republican candidate, he would have the necessary 185 votes.

This was the most momentous political struggle waged in South Carolina since 1860. Throwing aside despair, the whites girded themselves for action. Moderate leaders of the low country, believing in the invincibility of the Republican majority, favored coalition with Daniel H. Chamberlain, the radical governor who had struck mightily at the corrupt elements of his own party. To the men of the upcountry, a reforming Republican was not to their liking; the all-important consideration was white supremacy. Under the leadership of Generals Matthew C. Butler and Martin W. Gary they devised the Edgefield or Shotgun policy, modeled on the tactics so successfully followed in Mississippi in 1875. The bitter passions aroused by the race riot at Hamburg on July 8, 1876, enlisted white sentiment on the side of the uncompromising men of the upcountry and won for General Wade Hampton the Democratic nomination for governor.

This moderate aristocrat erected a façade of promises calculated to reap Negro votes and placate Northern public opinion. Meanwhile the white masses, organized into armed bands known as Red Shirts or Rifle Clubs, dealt directly with Negro voters. During the Ellenton Riot of September 15–20, they killed a considerable number of blacks, various reports ranging from 15 to 100. They also demoralized Republican gatherings by injecting Democratic speakers in their midst, and intimidated Negro voters and carpetbag leaders by brandishing weapons. On election day they barred Negroes from the polls and stuffed more votes in ballot boxes than there were names on voting lists. As a result of these tactics, returns revealed small majorities for Hampton and the Tilden electors. The state board of canvassers did not overrule the Hampton majority, but reported in favor of the Hayes electors. Neither conservatives nor radicals were satisfied. Two state governments were installed, one under Hampton, the other under Chamberlain, and two sets of presidential returns were sent to Washington.

Events in South Carolina were repeated in Florida on a smaller scale. Democratic majorities were achieved by intimidations modeled on the Mississippi plan, but the board of state canvassers, acting upon the behest of "visiting statesmen," decided in favor of the Hayes electors and Republican candidates for state offices. A careful scholar concludes that a "fair count" would have given the state to Tilden, but that a "free election" would have thrown it to Hayes. Finally, George F. Drew, a Democrat, won undisputed control of the governorship, but there were two sets of presidential returns.

The 1876 returns in Louisiana gave the Democrats clear majorities; however, the state board revised these results on orders from Northern Republican leaders. By rejecting whole polls, sometimes entire parishes,

Republican majorities were achieved. This behavior was justified by reams of evidence purporting to prove that the White League of Louisiana had resorted to the tactics of the South Carolina Rifle Clubs. The McEnery faction, sustained by white public opinion, claimed to be the rightful government, while the Kellogg or radical faction enjoyed recognition and support of the federal authorities. Dual governments resulted; a Democratic legislature declared Francis R. T. Nicholls governor, and a Republican legislature named Stephen B. Packard. As in South Carolina and Florida, two sets of presidential election returns were dispatched to Washington. An informal police force of White Leaguers now assumed the initiative, spreading Nicholls' authority so far and wide that Packard's rule scarcely extended beyond the walls of the state capitol.

The complication of dual governments in Southern capitals and an undetermined presidential election in Washington ended in compromise. To correct the failure of the United States Constitution to provide means for settling double election returns from the same state Congress created an electoral commission of fifteen, composed of seven Democrats, seven Republicans and one Independent. The fifteenth membership fell to a Republican when the Independent failed to serve, and the commission decided all contests by a strict party vote of eight to seven in favor of Hayes. Commanding 185 electoral votes, the Republican candidate received official recognition on March 2, 1877.

In order to allay Democratic opposition to this procedure the Hayes politicians assured influential Southerners that support of Southern radicals by federal troops would be discontinued when Hayes took office. Cries of treason came from the Northern wing of the Democratic party over this sacrifice of Tilden. But Southern Democrats in Congress by remaining steadfast had assured the success of the bargain. They had been promised Congressional support for Southern railroads and Southern public works by railroad lobbyists working for Hayes. This was the same kind of support that had been severely criticized by Democrats when given to Northern and Western interests by the Grant Administration.[9]

Troops were withdrawn from South Carolina and Louisiana in April, 1877, whereupon the Chamberlain and Packard governments promptly collapsed. Thus ended the experiment of radical Reconstruction. That the acknowledgment of this failure came from a Republican President who had been helped into office through an understanding between Southern statesmen and Northern business interests and politicians made for the future stability of the South under white rule.

[9] C. Vann Woodward, *Reunion and Reaction, passim.*

CHAPTER XIX

Reconstruction:
Social and Economic

⇛⇛⇛

A COMMON blunder of historians of Reconstruction is to treat the period as a melodrama involving wild-eyed conspirators committing bloody acts. This attitude springs from placing too great an emphasis on the behavior of scoundrels and idealists who participated in the politics of the most corrupt state governments in Southern history. However, political conduct is not always an accurate barometer of the social behavior of a people. This especially applied to the artificial and irresponsible Reconstruction governments imposed by the North and never in harmony with Southern life, socially or economically. Quite apart from the much-chronicled political events of the period were the educational, religious, economic and social developments of lasting constructiveness.

The detachment of Reconstruction politics from the realities of contemporary life is strikingly illustrated by the radicals' failure to accompany their political revolution with the establishment of general social equality for the Negro. Although universal manhood suffrage was adopted, Negroes were not allowed to manage political affairs, and whites continued to dominate even such extreme radical organizations as the Union League. Prominent politicians of both races generally observed the etiquette of Southern race distinctions. White politicians consorted with blacks only when absolutely necessary, and Negro politicians were usually deferential toward former masters and mistresses. The ex-slave who refused to vote for his employer did not necessarily make a poor servant or field hand. Legislatures did not try to extend theories of social equality further than halfhearted attempts to enforce

((295))

the most elementary civil rights. The Civil Rights Bill, passed by Congress in 1875, was more a memorial to Charles Sumner than an effort to change the currents of Southern society. In abolishing some aspects of the color line, carpetbaggers sought to estrange the blacks from scalawag leaders rather than to elevate them socially. Although intermarriages and mixed schools were lawful in some states, they seldom were to be found. Berea College in Kentucky was the only two-color school that survived. Indeed, the experiences of Reconstruction actually sharpened race distinctions and few attempts were made to check this development.

Even though the period was marked by many outbursts of race hatred and conflict, on the whole it was characterized by racial harmony. Except in the political field, Negroes were not generally insubordinate, usually according to their former masters the same respect as before. The tipping of hats and curtseying to passing whites still was to be seen and the words master and mistress were in general use. Social ties between the races, aside from those already ruptured by the shock of emancipation, were unbroken. In fact, as post-bellum life became more settled social relations destroyed by emancipation were renewed in numerous instances.

The Negroes were too genuine Southerners to be interested in the class struggle; they observed class distinctions within their own caste and respected class distinctions within the white caste. Although possessed of a great desire to own land they wished to break away from the communal practices of the slave plantation and own property individually and not collectively. They were not to any degree stirred by the contemporary Marxian ideas of revolution.

Dunning observes that the newly liberated Negroes were "fascinated with the white man's culture." They did not attempt—as is sometimes loosely asserted—to revert to the life of their jungle ancestors, turning South Carolina and Louisiana into African provinces. Reconstruction was a definite step forward in the Americanization, not Africanization, of the blacks. They recognized formal education as the most certain means of assimilating the white man's culture. Paradoxically, as Negroes grew more independent of white society they became more imitative of white customs. In their churches they adopted the rites and customs of the white churches from which they had withdrawn. Their political misbehavior had no African precedent; their poor manners were those of American rustics. Various dialects continued to be spoken in the years after the war, but even in the Gullah speech of the South Carolina sea islands African words were rare.

The primary cultural objective of the free Negro was to continue, with modifications, the slave's habit of imitating the manners of the whites. His uncritical view of their behavior often provoked the ridicule of contemporaries. There were stories of dusky females donning veils and gloves, carrying umbrellas, calling each other Mrs. and Miss, and retiring from the cotton field to become ladies of leisure. The spectacle of Negro politicians trying to emulate Daniel Webster or Charles Sumner caused many a jest, and there was amazement over attempts to fill the curricula of Negro schools with items of classical culture imported from New England. These aberrations had psychological compensations—evidences of a growing pride in the imitation of the substantial as well as the trivial aspects of the manners of those who had imposed their values upon the country.

Negroes assumed many habits of Anglo-Saxon family life. They readily responded to the suggestion of the Black Codes and the Freedmen's Bureau that they enter into formal marriages. They acquired surnames to supplement the lone Christian names which had designated them as slaves. Usually they adopted the names of former masters, especially those with an aristocratic flavor; many became Washington, Jefferson, and Lincoln. Black farmers, except in the Louisiana Sugar Bowl, abandoned communal living in slave quarters and demanded establishment of homes scattered over the land in the familiar American manner. This permitted the development of a more distinct family life and a subsequent decline in the sexual promiscuity that characterized the slave system. The women did not always desert the fields to become idlers, but often devoted themselves to rearing children and other domestic duties. The dingy and ugly appearance of the average Negro dwelling caused qualms among observers. For most blacks, however, it represented a living standard at least equal to that they had known under slavery. Christian morality was proclaimed, if not practised, as an ideal toward which colored society moved slowly.

The Negro race, however, had a long way to travel before approximating these ideals. Freedom brought much moral and social license. A fundamental disrespect for law and convention along with lying and stealing—heritages from slavery—were prevalent. Larceny was most frequently brought to the attention of the courts, and crimes of violence were numerous. Although fear often prevented open violence against white men, Negroes did not hesitate to fire upon them stealthily, to subject women and helpless persons to brutal treatment, or to apply the torch to barns and gin houses. For the first time in Southern history, rape was recognized as a real problem.[1] Among themselves the blacks

[1] Ulrich B. Phillips, *Life and Labor in the Old South*, p. 165, shows that 73 slaves were executed or deported under Virginia law for rape between 1780 and 1864. Yet according to Sir Harry H. Johnson, *The Negro in the New World*, p. 464: "Allusion to the rape or attempted rape of white women or girls, by negroes or mulattoes, are rare in the literature of the United States prior to 1870."

committed crimes of jealousy and passion—murder, mutilation, and wife beating. In the last year of radical rule in Alabama eight times as many blacks as whites were convicted of felonies, and 64 per cent more were convicted of misdemeanors. Laxity in the administration of justice only partially explains this disparity between the races. A more fundamental cause was the failure of Negro society to impose moral penalties upon criminals; persons convicted of serious crimes did not suffer social ostracism.

The cabins of the blacks were usually rude one- or two-room structures without windowpanes and ceilings. The food, generally coarse and poorly prepared, consisted of hominy, corn bread, fat bacon, and vegetables slimy with grease. The Negroes rarely respected the obligations of marriage, and chastity was believed to be an exception among their women. Tens of thousands freely lived together, and married persons were constantly abandoning their mates to form illicit unions. The disruptive influences of freedom encouraged male philandering, imposing responsibility for the family upon the woman. Often the breadwinner, she behaved with an independence equal to that of the most sanguine feminist of the twentieth century. Relations between parent and child were barbaric. Children were whipped until they bled, confined to the house all day while their mothers worked, and put into the field as soon as they could handle a hoe. The clothing of the blacks was often stiff with mingled grease and dirt, and filled with holes or variegated patches.

These people were seemingly happy with a low standard of living which encouraged thriftlessness. An acute observer noted that they were content "to burrow in a hole. They will buy an acre or two, build a cottage, move in, and live in sloth and filthiness on what they can raise on half their cultivated lot." An exasperated British traveler declared, "Nothing on earth can make them wash." [2] The worst crime the Negro committed against himself was the careless expenditure of his earnings. "You all think," Wade Hampton told a Congressional committee, "that the Negro is actuated by the same feelings as white men, but this is a mistake. They [the Negroes] have no provision; they have no forethought at all; they are content to live from hand to mouth; they do not pretend to lay up anything." Negro death rates increased greatly; in Charleston from 26.45 annually per thousand before the war to 43.33 afterward. Major diseases, except yellow fever and alcoholism, took a greater toll among blacks than among whites. The scientist Josiah C. Nott declared in 1866 that Negroes around Mobile were hud-

<hr />

[2] Belton O'Neall Townsend, cited in Simkins and Woody, *South Carolina during Reconstruction*, p. 330; and Charles W. Dilke, *Greater Britain: A Record of Travels in English-Speaking Countries during 1866 and 1867*, p. 28.

dled in shanties, "stealing, burning fences for fuel, dying of diseases and want."[3]

These social and economic maladies largely account for the Negroes' failure to make pronounced progress along the paths pointed out by their liberators. Despite their land hunger, as late as 1890 only 121,-000 Negroes owned the farms on which they worked. The race advanced little in business and in the professions, except in petty trades, the ministry, and teaching. The ex-slaves were taking a holiday from the hard labor and industrial skills that slavery had imposed upon them, and a marked decline in their efficiency became apparent. They were able to effect but the slightest alteration in the caste system; in fact, the contentions and bitterness of Reconstruction hardened the resolution of the master race to strengthen race distinctions. To secure the tolerance and good will necessary for his existence, the Negro was compelled to respect the superior social position the whites demanded for themselves. This necessitated a continued deference not unlike the servility of the slave. The black man lacked sufficient stamina to resist the social aggressions of the whites. In a fight the Negro always fared badly; the more politic among his race yielded to white demands without a struggle. The Negro also failed to develop a culture or social pride of his own; his path of progress remained the humble one of imitating the ways of the white man.

When the period of the Negro in politics closed, definite achievement was apparent in only one field of social activity, formal schooling. The illiteracy of the blacks was reduced from 90 per cent in 1860 to 70 per cent in 1880. In a typical town of the black belt, described by an English traveler in 1878, the colored "aristocracy" consisted only of public officials and a few lawyers in criminal practice. One or two tailor shops and a small harness-making establishment owned by colored men remained; in addition there were colored hack drivers, carpenters, and one storekeeper. There had been a colored physician, but he had been accused of extortion and left town. All other Negroes were engaged in unskilled labor, leaving the white minority the economic and social rulers of the community.

In a very real sense the Civil War freed the common white man to a greater degree than the Negro. While the blacks were on their industrial holiday, whites secured employment from which they had been excluded by slave competition. They learned to grow the great Southern staple whose cultivation under slavery had been dominated by Negro labor. By 1880 the less fertile soils of the Southern uplands were producing with white labor more cotton per acre than the richer lands of the black belt with black labor. It was discovered that the hot South-

[3] Cited in Coulter, *The South during Reconstruction*, p. 55.

ern sun did not harm the white man. The importation of Northern ideas of the dignity of labor reconciled him to many forms of work from which aristocratic prejudices had previously kept him. Moreover, the breaking of the industrial alliance between rich whites and slaves destroyed the wealthy man's incentive to maintain certain labor monopolies for the Negro. As a result, the common white man, using the prestige of race and a greater social discipline, could deprive the free Negro of many types of employment. Negro labor thus became of less significance in Southern industry.

Not all the social ills of the postwar period belonged to the blacks. The poor whites, who comprised a considerable part of the South's population, lived on a plane lower than that of the average Negro. Their conditions were not improved by the changes of war and reconstruction. Their cabins, declared an observer in 1867, "are dens of filth. The bed, if there be a bed, is a layer of something in the corner that defies scenting. If the bed is nasty, what of the floor? What of the whole enclosed space? What of the creatures themselves? Pough! Water in use as a purifier is unknown. Their faces are bedaubed with the muddy accumulation of weeks." Their children were described as "puny, unwholesome-looking creatures, with tangled whitish hair and a complexion of a dingy straw color." [4] A few of the women were led by poverty and ignorance to cohabit with Negro men.

In some cities whole sections which had been damaged by the war went unrepaired for years. In many towns sanitary conditions were bad, typhoid was common and some outbreaks of yellow fever occurred. Especially in the black belt, mansions that had been the chief glory of ante-bellum society were now neglected and dilapidated. Some old towns were as shabby as the plantation houses, and many new ones which had sprung up during Reconstruction were crude, almost barbaric. On week days loafers rescued the towns from the appearance of utter abandonment. They perched on merchants' counters and in front of the stores, complaining of the unwillingness of the Negro to work. Reluctant to put their hands to the plow, they expected to eke out a livelihood through Negro labor. One told a Northern traveler: "If you work with a nigger, he despises you for equalizin' yourself with him. Any man is a dog-goned fool to work, when he can make a nigger work for him." [5] Families of any social pretensions relied upon Negro servants. "To be waited upon is the normal arrangement of Southern life," complained a reformer.[6] Washerwomen who damaged clothes were tolerated, along with wasteful cooks adept at hiding dirt. Alcoholism

[4] *New York Herald*, May 7, 1867, and *The Nation* I, 625 (November 23, 1865).
[5] Stephen Powers, *Afoot and Alone*, pp. 38–40.
[6] D. Wyatt Aiken, cited in Simkins and Woody, *op. cit.*, p. 320.

increased as many sought escape from their misfortunes. The wider distribution of ready cash and the growth of the country store stimulated drinking among the lower classes. On Saturdays the ordinarily quiet streets became veritable bedlams of loud profanity, vagrancy, murders, and assaults upon argumentative Negroes. Unwilling to expose themselves to these dangers, women and children stayed off the streets on Saturdays.

The fundamental cause of such behavior was the failure of many Southerners to recognize that the old regime had died with the war. A few dreamed of the day when the landed aristocracy would be restored to social dominance; a larger number resigned themselves to supine admiration of a past that they knew could not be revived. They hated the Yankee and the Negro as the principal disturbers of the times; often they claimed aristocratic privileges although the possession of slaves, public office, and military rank had disappeared. They still assumed that their women were burdened with the frailties of Sir Walter Scott's ladies and therefore should not engage in the strenuous activities common to Northern women. The literature they admired was the poetry of "smooth sentiments and sonorous verses," "the rhythms of outworn music."

That all whites were not plunged in despair over the lost war and the scandals of Reconstruction was demonstrated by the wide prevalence of social activities. "I never knew," wrote Joseph LeConte of a Southern town, "so much real enjoyment in Columbia as in the years 1866 and 1867." A Tennessee observer reported at the same time that people everywhere were viewing life "with a commendable spirit of philosophy dispelling gloomy memories in successive merry-makings and literally strewing our forward path with flowers."[7] There was a disposition then, as in war times, to extract a maximum of pleasure from a minimum of resources. Calico balls grew up out of Southern poverty, making it financially easy for all to dance. Lodges, race courses, and agricultural fairs were promptly restored; and the young men of country communities had scarcely laid down the weapons of warfare before they took up the mimic lances of the ring tournament. Banqueting on a large scale soon grew common in many clubs, and there were numerous amateur musicals and theatricals, traveling shows, circuses, Negro minstrels, and magic lantern exhibitions. The Mobile Mardi Gras festival was revived in 1867 and the Parade of the Krewe of the Knights of Momus became a feature of the New Orleans festival in 1872. The building of the DeGive Opera House in Atlanta in 1871 and of the Grand Opera House in New Orleans the following year indicated an awakening interest in the professional stage. The urban aristocracies re-

[7] Joseph LeConte, *Autobiography*, p. 236; and Coulter, *op. cit.*, p. 296.

vived dancing clubs, such as the St. Cecilia Society of Charleston, while the people of the rural areas held informal community gatherings. Innovations of the period were amateur baseball and the annual Memorial Day in honor of the Confederate dead. The Fourth of July which had once been noisily observed was studiously ignored since the Negroes turned it into a second Emancipation Day. Christmas, on the other hand, was celebrated with a week's holiday.

The Negroes imitated activities of the whites; in addition they had others all their own. Festive evenings around cabin doors were so mirthful that one writer said it was impossible for the blacks "to repress their laughter, songs, dancing and merrymaking." Whisky was passed around, and after corn shuckings or logrollings, dancing began to the rhythm of the fiddle and the stamping of feet. The "lay-by season" in August was the time of camp meetings, picnics, militia drills, and munching watermelons with neighbors. The coming of the circus demoralized the blacks; they promptly abandoned work for the day, and with money saved, begged, or borrowed, entered the tent of wonders. The Ninth of April, the Fourth of July, and New Year's Day were occasions for large parades celebrating emancipation. Gorgeously dressed militiamen, fire fighters, Union Leaguers, and members of other fraternities marched; there were readings of the Declaration of Independence, and speeches proclaiming the benefits of Republicanism and freedom.

Of greater practical importance than the adjustment of political problems was the settlement of agricultural difficulties created by the war. Four million people torn from their moorings by emancipation must be anchored again in the interest of an ordered and industrious society. Agricultural conflicts were as great as those over politics. To the setbacks caused by depletion of land were added the disagreements between landlord and laborer, white man and black man. Who should own the soil, under what conditions should the ex-slave work, what should be his wages, and how must they be paid? Many Negroes dreamed of freedom from work, enjoyment of pleasures previously denied them, "forty acres and a mule," voluntary migration to other communities or states, perhaps even to the far-off African homeland of their ancestors. Hopes of the whites were often almost as visionary; many clung to the pessimistic and unjustified belief that farm life with the Negro as a freedman was an impossibility. Many planned migration to Mexico or Brazil; others hoped the Negroes would migrate and be replaced either with European immigrants or Northern purchasers of plantations.

These ideas of both blacks and whites proved impractical as a means of solving Southern agricultural problems. The attempts of state and federal agents acting through the Black Codes and the Freedman's Bureau also failed. It remained for the white landlords and black laborers to bargain with each other and reach agreements over the complex problems of land and labor. That they succeeded in devising an ordered agricultural economy lasting many decades is proof that they were more realistic than the official guides who tried to help them. Although this system had its defects, it resulted in arrangements tolerable to both.

The planters preferred to engage the laborers for stipulated wages and to work them in gangs with the whole plantation as a unit of production. In addition to a monthly wage of ten or twelve dollars, each laborer received food, shelter, and garden privileges. Although some of the Negroes accepted this arrangement, most of them objected to it as smacking too much of slavery. By allowing landlords to compete for their services in what had actually become a free labor market, they could generally secure more favorable terms. A small percentage, taking advantage of the low price of land, became landowners; others were able to rent places. The landlord was often suspicious of the managerial ability of his tenants; nevertheless, this arrangement frequently proved profitable to both parties.

Most laborers accepted the sharecrop system of tenancy under which the landlord furnished land, a house, fuel, and varying amounts of seed, fertilizer, farm implements, and farm animals. In return the landlord received one half, one third, or possibly one fourth of the crop, depending upon the extent of his concessions to the tenant. As a rule one third of the crop went to the tenant in return for his labor and one third to the landlord for rent, with the remaining one third divided between them in proportion to the supplies each contributed. The degree of independence allowed the tenant under sharecrop arrangement was not so great as when he rented outright, as the landlord reserved the right to decide what should be grown and to supervise its production.

New credit arrangements known as the crop-lien system developed along with the sharecrop method. A tenant at the beginning of the growing season could mortgage his anticipated crop in exchange for necessary household and farm supplies. The merchant-bankers who advanced the supplies designated the crops to be planted and charged high prices, because of the great risks taken on crops not yet grown. This system enabled the thrifty and ambitious laborer to become an independent farm operator, but it worked mischief with the average tenant, encouraging him to be improvident. Frequently he saw no money at the end of the harvest season because all his products were taken to satisfy his mortgage.

The creation of many new farm operators and the dispensing of considerable small cash in the form of wages and advances on crops stimulated retail markets to a degree unknown during the ante-bellum period. These business activities made possible a great increase in the number and size of commercial villages and towns with their new stores and banks. The new centers of trade were owned by an emergent economic group, the storekeepers. As Thomas S. Stribling has shown in his novel *The Store*, they were more important figures in the realities of Reconstruction than the better-known carpetbaggers and scalawags, and they dominated the Southern community as effectively, if not as glamorously, as the planters before them. The merchants were the town's leading citizens, often becoming bankers, church deacons, and state senators. Their power was based on the profits of the crop-lien system.

Various Southern religious denominations during Reconstruction were confronted with problems not unlike those that troubled the political life of the section. In the church as in the state conflicts arose between blacks and whites, between Northerners and Southerners; religious contentions inevitably paralleled those of politics. However, the leaven of Christian charity eliminated much of the bitterness present in political controversies. Moreover, no great doctrinal or material interests were at stake. The clash was purely racial and sectional with no struggle over rival systems of theology or over the possession of valuable church properties. Southern churches were relatively poor and, unlike the political state, had no extensive powers of taxation and police authority to be redistributed.

To Southerners the attitude of Northern churchmen toward the problems of Reconstruction seemed to promote the bitterest feelings. Northern churchmen reasoned that since slavery and Southern nationalism had brought about the organization of separate churches, the destruction of these causes by the war would effect immediate ecclesiastical reunion. Most Northern churchmen insisted that the expected reconciliation must take place under terms stipulated by the "loyal" or Northern churches; that the Negro must come under "loyal" church direction; that ex-Confederate "sinners" must confess the enormity of their crimes before they could again be received in Christian fellowship. In other words, they demanded that the same destruction, reordering, and rebuilding that Lee's surrender had necessitated in the field of government must take place in the sphere of religion. Was it not in keeping with American tradition for the church, though independent of government, to accommodate itself to political revolution? "Even the rebels and traitors," asserted a leading Northern religious weekly, "will soon refuse to receive the Gospel except from those who have shown their fear of God by loyalty to the Nation." Bishop Gilbert Haven of the Northern Methodist church dreamed of an approaching brotherhood

BOOKER T. WASHINGTON. Recognized by everyone as the greatest Negro in American history, and by some as "the greatest man, save Robert E. Lee, born in the South in a hundred years."

HENRY W. GRADY. Editor-orator, spokesman for the faith in industrial progress and in national reconciliation that has possessed the South since the 1880's.

CARONDELET STREET, NEW ORLEANS, 1901. *Center of the financial section of the city that Jefferson in 1803 saw as vital to Southern development. Jefferson's fear of city life would only have been augmented by the vigorous development that did take place in the following one hundred years.*

"when the white hued husband shall boast of the dusky beauty of his wife, and the Caucasian wife shall admire the sun-kissed countenance of her husband." Methodist, Baptist, and Congregational missionaries were sent to the South to effect the purposes of their churches.

The missionaries experienced some success with the blacks. Many Negroes flocked to their schools, listened eagerly to their political preachments, and accepted the discipline of the Northern churches. But the Southern whites, scornfully rejecting the terms of the Northern churches, were unwilling to confess sins which they were not conscious of committing. An Alabamian expressed the opinion of most white Southerners when he said: "Perhaps the greatest liars and the most malignant slanderers that the North has spewed out upon the South since the close of the war, are the reverend blackguards that have been sent among us as ministers of religion." A tendency toward reunion among the Presbyterians was checked by Northern insolence, and several Presbyterian bodies joined to form a strong separate southern church. "How," a committee of Southern Presbyterians asked their Northern coreligionists, "will you justify, on Presbyterian principles, your intrusion in their [the Southerners'] field of labor, your scattering their flock, your use of military power to keep possession of their church property? By what authority does your committee intrude into the diocese of another? Are you lords of God's heritage among us?" [8]

Southern Baptists expressed a desire to maintain their separate existence by reorganizing the Southern Baptist Convention. The Southern Methodist bishops effected a quick reorganization in August, 1865, rejecting suggestions of reunion by asserting that Northern Methodists had become "incurably radical" and were too much involved in politics. The bishops warned their flocks against the missionary efforts of Northern coreligionists.

The reorganized Southern denominations not only had the support of the majority of Southern white Christians, but also won the allegiance of many Baptist associations, Presbyterian synods, and Methodist conferences of the border states that previously had Northern affiliations. The Protestant Episcopal church was an exception to the rule of continued sectional disunity. Northern Episcopalian missionaries were not sent into the South, and the Southern Episcopalian bishops were welcomed back into the general convention of the national church without humiliating apologies. Episcopalian missionary and educational funds available for Southern use were dispensed through native agents.

Although the Southern churches retained their white members and even gained congregations in the border states, they were unable to

[8] Citations in Simkins and Woody, op. cit., pp. 375, 377; and in Coulter, op. cit., pp. 64, 334.

retain their Negro members. The whites were naturally reluctant to surrender the rigid control of the Negroes which they had exercised through the churches under the slave regime. Negroes, on the other hand, reasonably felt that their inherited habit of religious subordination to the master race was incompatible with their supposed status as free men. They demanded the elementary American constitutional right of religious freedom, including separate church organizations and congregations, and ministers and church officials of their own race and choosing.

The whites tried to forestall this separatist movement by granting concessions. Baptists authorized separate Negro congregations and associations, and the Methodist general conference of 1866 provided for separate congregations and conferences as well as bishops and presiding elders. These concessions were of little avail. During the first year of freedom the Southern Methodist church lost three fourths of its 400,000 colored members.

Realizing that separation was inevitable, the whites allowed the blacks to withdraw in peace, often helping them financially in the building of separate churches. Typical of what happened was the experience of the First Baptist church at Montgomery, which came out of the war with 300 white members and 600 colored members. When it was felt wise to separate, the two races co-operated in the erection of a new church for the colored members, who continued to use the old church while the new was being built. When all was ready, the colored congregation was launched with the blessing of the whites. The whites of Montgomery, as elsewhere in the South, were confident that structural independence would not be accompanied by doctrinal innovations abhorrent to Southern tradition. It is a tribute to the Christian tolerance of both races that this parting of the ways took place without the acrimony that characterized the political estrangements of the Reconstruction period. The South fortunately had no heritage of racial hatred along religious lines.

Thousands of Negroes joined the churches of the Northern missionaries; others flocked to the Colored Methodist Episcopal church, a body created for them by the Southern whites. A few became members of the separate congregations that the Protestant Episcopal bishops devised for them. The Roman Catholic church, which had been strong among the slaves of the Louisiana Sugar Bowl, retained most of its Negro members despite the fact that the only concession it made to the separatist tendencies of the times was to establish separate Negro congregations under white priests. Elsewhere in the South the great majority of Negroes adhered to churches of their own creation. A large number were drawn to the African Methodist Episcopal church and the African Methodist Episcopal church, Zion—Negro organizations imported from the North. A great many more became members of the thousands of independent Negro Baptist churches that sprang into existence under the Baptist tradition of congregationalism.

The creation of independent Negro churches was one of the most important consequences of emancipation and reconstruction. It meant religious freedom for the blacks for the first time in their history and opened up to Negro leadership at least one field of social endeavor. To this day not even the most reactionary Southern white challenges the right of the Negro to determine his own religious concepts. The separation and independence of the races along religious lines has become one of the immutable features of Southern life.

Partial recovery from the staggering blows of war brought on immediate demand for the rehabilitation of neglected or destroyed educational institutions. Colleges and academies reopened, and the Johnson state governments made appropriations for the maintenance of public schools. The question of Negro education, similar to that of religion and politics, aroused conflict of race against race, of Northerner against Southerner.

Teacher-missionaries came South imbued with the idea that education would dispel the "ignorance and barbarism" that allegedly enveloped the region, elevate the Negro to the white man's level, and perhaps apply the historic mission of the American common schools of ironing out class distinctions to the sharpest of all American class distinctions, that between white and black. President Thomas Hill of Harvard spoke of the "new work of spreading knowledge and intellectual culture over the regions that sat in darkness." The Negro received this evangel with an enthusiasm unique in the history of education, accepting it as a means toward social and political progress. Indeed, it promised sufficient culture to bring about the Negro's social equality with the white man. The radical constitutions of Louisiana, South Carolina, Mississippi, and Florida provided for mixed schools. That of Louisiana boldly declared: "There shall be no separate schools or institutions of learning established exclusively for any race by the State of Louisiana."

Southern whites, on the other hand, frowned upon such cultural innovations, inheriting from slavery the belief that literary instruction should be denied the blacks. In their opinion, the stringent post-bellum years were no time for the adoption of a general educational program for an inferior caste whom they considered innately incapable of learning. The few Southern clergymen and prominent citizens who thought differently saw their plans frustrated by the tactlessness of the educational missionaries. These Northerners were made to feel the effect of a merciless social proscription.

Despite conflicts and mistakes, the South emerged from Reconstruction with the foundations of its future educational progress securely laid. The theory of universal education for both races was established by the reconstructionists and, unlike the political theories of these innovators, not repudiated but amplified by those who came after them. The Northern concept of universal, state-supported education met the needs of both races and was too much in harmony with the spirit of nineteenth-century progress to be rejected by even the most reactionary Bourbons.

The education of the free Negro was begun by Northern missionaries and teachers who swarmed into the South in the wake of the armies. They were the agents of the Freedmen's Bureau, the Northern churches, and the various freedmen's aid societies. In three years the Freedmen's Bureau spent $16,000,000 on Negro schools. Southern whites were bitterly hostile to these new teachers in their midst, partly because they were basically opposed to anything outsiders might do to uplift the ex-slaves, and partly because these strangers were using the schools as an aid to remodel Southern society along radical lines. The educators were charged with ignorance of social conditions, fraternizing with the blacks, and teaching them that their former owners had been cruel taskmasters who wished to restore slavery. Many instructors stressed "book learning" too much, regarding it as a panacea for the numerous social ills of an inexperienced and impoverished race. The free Negro, to his great detriment, now neglected many of the industrial skills formerly fostered by slavery.

Some teachers treated their work in the South as an emotional jaunt to be abandoned once they discovered how difficult the inexperienced Negro child found the journey along the road to learning. There were exceptions, however. Some Yankee schoolma'ams gave many years of work to the Negro, and manifested keen intelligence in educational methods and objectives. Gifts excited the pupils' interest; their penchant for singing, shouting, and parading was cleverly utilized as an instructional device; domestic economy and manual training received almost as much attention as reading and writing. "We are convinced," said one teacher of her students,[9] "that plenty to eat would harmonize and Christianize them faster than hymns and sermons; and that needle and thread and soap and decent clothing were the best educators and would civilize them sooner than book learning." Hampton Normal and Industrial Institute, which was founded in Virginia in 1868 by General Samuel Chapman Armstrong, an officer of the Freedmen's Bureau, was based on such observations.

Enthusiasm for universal education among the Negroes, aroused by

[9] Elizabeth H. Botume, cited in Simkins and Woody, *op. cit.*, p. 431.

the missionaries, bore fruit in the provisions of the radical state constitutions for publicly supported systems of universal education. Southern states were given outlines of educational systems resembling those already established in New England and the Middle West. In every Southern state the legislature filled in the constitutional outline with laws providing for a state superintendent of public instruction, teacher training facilities, and direct taxation for educational purposes.

State superintendents made sincere efforts to put the laws into operation, but did not wholly succeed in their endeavors. Prejudice against the new schools ran high, especially against the constant, if never realized, threat of racially mixed classes. Negro children experienced difficulty in disciplining themselves to the habit of regular attendance, and much poverty existed among the pupils. School revenues were meager and the radical politicians, practicing their general policy of thievery, made no exceptions in favor of educational funds. In North Carolina, for example, $136,076 was collected for school purposes, yet the state superintendent of education received only $38,931. Nevertheless, in several states radical superintendents in charge of schools were able to submit encouraging reports on instruction of their pupils. The Negro superintendent in Florida, for example, in 1873 informed the National Education Association: "The census of 1860—ante-bellum—showed that Florida had in its schools 4,486 pupils at the expense of $75,412. Today Florida has 18,000 pupils in school, at the expense of $101,820, fully four times as many pupils." In states unable to report such great advancement during Reconstruction, conservative successors to the radicals adopted their plans, putting into effect universal education for both races. "It was a great thing," says a writer, commenting upon the work of the radicals in one state, "to commit the old commonwealth to the American ideal of universal education; to secure appropriations from the legislature even if they were not paid with regularity; to awaken into life a body of three thousand native teachers."

The constructive achievements of the ten or twelve years of active federal intervention in the internal affairs of the states of the former Confederacy were considerable. They included progress in education, rebuilding of houses destroyed by war, and adjustment of agricultural, religious, and social relations between the races. Foundations were laid for systems of legislative representation and public administration in harmony with the democratic spirit of the times. Nevertheless, Reconstruction could not be adjudged successful, primarily because of the failure of 4 million ex-slaves to win recognition as the equals of other Americans. Although the spectacular phases of the battle that ended so dismally occurred in the realm of politics, these results of the Reconstruction experiment had broad social and economic implications. Because the blacks did not emerge from the war in a position to compel the whites to grant them social and economic equality, there were no solid foundations on which they could base claims of political equality. Hence, radical measures of Congress and state legislatures were doomed to defeat. This great political failure gave occasion for re-enforcing upon the Negroes the social subordination to which they were accustomed. The race equality threat of Reconstruction evoked bitter memories that the whites were unwilling to forget. Yet, as Holland Thompson wisely observes, it is doubtful whether Reconstruction essentially changed the beliefs of the South. Left to itself, the region would not have accorded the Negro the vote or other manifestations of equality; after Reconstruction, when the South was free from Northern interference, it deprived the Negro of his rights.

CHAPTER XX

Bourbon Rule

❯❯❯-❮❮❮

WHEN Southern whites resumed full control of the area after 1876, their recollections of the period following Lee's surrender were bitter, and permanent reconstruction, they believed, was actually still to be accomplished. They were faced with the immediate problem of instituting some political adjustment between the races which would be both practicable for their needs and acceptable to federal authorities and Northern public opinion. Sectional hatreds engendered by war and intensified by Reconstruction had in some way to be ameliorated; Negroes and carpetbaggers had to be stripped of their power.

After the expulsion of the carpetbaggers would be the problem of dealing with a new group of Northern invaders. These were the business men who came as capitalistic agents of the victorious section of the nation. Debts accumulated by the radicals had to be paid or adjusted. The apathy observed by travelers—an aftermath of Reconstruction—had to be overcome if what remained of the South was to be preserved in the face of the great material advances of the reunited nation as a whole.

Naturally enough, white Southerners turned to the men who had led them in war to replace the vanquished carpetbaggers. Defeat, instead of discrediting the chieftains of the Confederacy, further endeared them to the Southern people. Every general became a popular hero, and Jefferson Davis—most unpopular of war leaders—achieved the stature of a beloved martyr after his imprisonment by federal authorities in 1865. A people who had not learned to look to the future rather than the past determined to give their former leaders an indefinite lease of political power. These leaders flocked to the capitals of all Southern states as the federal soldiers marched out, and their voices were raised in the halls of Congress to defend the Southern position. In the Congress of 1876, 9 senators and 49 representatives had seen service in the Confederate army. Typical delegations were Alabama's 8 Confederate veterans in its 8 Congressional seats in 1878, Georgia's 7 out of 8 that same year, and Arkansas's 5 out of 5 in 1883.

The Confederate Brigadiers, or Bourbons, as these leaders were derisively named by the few dissenters, sounded the keynote of every political contest; and a military record became almost a prerequisite for political success. At political rallies the deeds of Confederate soldiers and the horrors of carpetbag rule were reiterated before audiences that never seemed to tire of such talk. Indeed, a wooden leg or a battered eye acquired on a Virginia battlefield enhanced a candidate's chances more than the possession of actual qualifications for the office to which he aspired. Holland Thompson believes that without radical Reconstruction some of the ex-Confederate leaders might have been adjudged inadequate for the new age; the unpleasant post-bellum years in no way decreased their prestige. The necessity of white unity in opposition to the carpetbaggers permitted no experiments with new leadership; confidence could prudently be bestowed only upon the tried. War veterans were singularly fitted for the semimilitary task of driving the Negroes from the polls and preventing the carpetbaggers' return to power.

Confederate Brigadiers were not chosen merely to relive their glorious past; theirs was the duty of setting the future course of the South. The guiding principle of this course was to be the maintenance of white supremacy, an issue that the Southerner could not regard as absolutely settled by Reconstruction. They feared further federal intervention in the internal affairs of the states and a possible repeal, in the late seventies or early eighties, of the Hayes compromise of 1877 by a revived radical party just as the Johnson compromise of 1865 had been overthrown by the original radicals in the late sixties. Under the unchanged war amendments to the federal Constitution, Negroes still were legally entitled to the privileges of voting and holding office; as recent practitioners of these rights of American democracy, they were unwilling to yield them without a complaint.

It cannot be too often emphasized that white supremacy, as defined by Southerners, meant more than mere dominance of a white caste. It signified absolute elimination of the Negro from every social activity that involved one iota of equality with the white man. Reconstruction had been fervently opposed not because it established Negro equality, but because it gave him opportunities in the important field of political action. In the opinion of most whites, a system that tolerated such behavior, even if only a few Negroes voted, was scandalous, and protests

against it were continuous. This attitude of the white South resembled
that of certain countries of past centuries toward the few religious dissenters remaining after a campaign of suppression. All such heretics had
to be eliminated to insure peace and comfort in the community. Similarly, protracted use of the semimilitary methods of the Reconstruction
period were demanded in the South until all political privileges of the
blacks were destroyed or circumvented.

Obviously the most effective means of maintaining white supremacy
was through political unity under the banner of the conservative party,
as the Democratic party was for a generation called so as not to give
offense to former Whig members. This concept of the Solid South was
far more difficult to secure than later generations of Southerners, enjoying its fruits, have realized. Before the war Southerners were divided
into Whigs and Democrats. While Grant thundered at the gates of
Richmond, Confederate politicians disputed fine points of constitutional
interpretation and Southern unionists carried their differences with the
Confederates into the field of actual battle. However, in those regions
of the South where Negroes were an important part of the population,
Reconstruction experiences solidified white sentiment. As early as 1868
an Alabamian was able to declare: "There is but one party for true
Southern men, or true National men, and that is the Democratic
party." [1] Only certain sections of Tennessee where white leaders supervised the voting of the Negro masses provided exceptions to this rule.
In most areas it could be said, "There are only two kinds of people
—Democrats and Negroes." All public issues were subordinated to
white supremacy. Differences of opinion were suppressed, and platforms and editorial writers tried to avoid controversy by ignoring
questions on which white men might seriously disagree.

Established custom required that minorities within the Democratic
party accept loyally, if not always cheerfully, all decisions of the majority. "In other States it may be different," wrote the editor of Mississippi's leading newspaper in 1882. "In this State for some time to come
there is but one issue. All know what it is." Edward Mayes, the historian
who was chancellor of the University of Mississippi proudly announced
eight years later: "In all my life I have never voted any other ticket [but
the Democratic], I have never failed to vote, I have never scratched a
ticket, and I would not, no matter whom the party might nominate for
its candidate." [2] According to Wade Hampton, high priest of Southern
orthodoxy, a political bolter or independent was lower than a radical,
even as a traitor was considered worse than an enemy. To organize the
Negro politically amounted to treason to one's race, and called for

[1] E. Merton Coulter, *The South during Reconstruction, 1865–1877*, p. 377.
[2] C. Vann Woodward, *The Origins of the New South, 1877–1913*, pp. 51–52.

suppression, if necessary, by the same sort of fraud and violence that prevailed during the last phase of Reconstruction. The small group of active Republicans who maintained a skeleton organization of their party was believed to be composed of scheming rascals motivated by greed for federal office. The name of General James Longstreet was removed from the people's list of heroes when he led a force of Negro police through the streets of New Orleans during a Reconstruction riot. A similar fate overtook General William Mahone, hero of the Battle of the Crater, because he organized an independent political movement in Virginia. Weaknesses or ineptitude in duly nominated candidates for office were overlooked in the interest of white unity.

Decisive victories by the Democrats caused radicals to retire from the Southern capitals. A Northerner facetiously remarked in 1877 that all the Republicans in Texas could be hauled out in a few omnibuses; and the Republicans in Florida were able to show a few signs of life only because of the presence of native Negroes and Northern consumptives.[3] Yet a small Republican organization dominated by a few whites with courage to brave the disapproval of public opinion continued to exist in every Southern state. The primary interest of these leaders appeared to be the salaries attached to the offices given them by the Republican administration in Washington. Certainly, they were incapable of contesting equally with the leaders of the local whites, but their presence broke the unanimity of the white South; moreover, they were supported by thousands of Negroes who elected a few of them to Congress and the legislatures. For years North Carolina and South Carolina each sent at least one Negro to Congress, and in the Negro-dominated counties of several states were colored local officials. The Negroes remembering the experiences of Reconstruction still hoped for the reestablishment, through federal intervention, of their rights supposedly guaranteed by the Constitution.

White leaders acted against this alleged threat to white supremacy with a ruthless determination restrained only by fear of federal interference. Reconstruction promises to protect the blacks in the exercise of suffrage were repudiated or forgotten. Negroes were expelled from legislatures and carpetbaggers exiled by dread of punishment for their crimes. In many communities intimidation of Negroes took the form of threats of eviction or of loss of employment; continued Democratic victories at the polls were thus to be secured. Stronger methods were employed in those areas where the Negroes had large majorities. As during Reconstruction, armed men in distinctive dress patrolled the roads on election days and warningly shot off their guns in front of Negroes bold enough to approach the polls. "Men actually or apparently

[3] Coulter, *op. cit.*, p. 378.

the worse for liquor might stagger around, seeking an excuse for a fight." Negroes who discussed politics were cautioned to hold their tongues, and if these warnings were ignored physical violence ensued. The continual repetition of riots along the pattern established during Reconstruction continued to be a feature of Southern life. The Louisiana election of 1878 cost more than thirty lives, and after the election of 1884 sixteen bodies were found along the Bayou Teche.[4]

A Mississippi champion of white supremacy declared in 1890:

It is no secret that there has not been a full vote and a fair count in Mississippi since 1875—that we have been preserving the ascendency of the white people by revolutionary methods. In plain words, we have been stuffing ballot-boxes, committing perjury and here and there in the State carrying the elections by fraud and violence until the whole machinery for elections was about to rot down.[5]

Some years after the overthrow of the Reconstruction regimes methods which had a greater appearance of legality were utilized in suppressing the Negro vote. Gerrymandering became universal. "Our main object," explained a Tennessee senator, "was [so] to redistrict the State that for the next ten years not a Republican can be elected to the Legislature. . . . I believe in the law of revenge. The Radicals disfranchised us, and now we intend to disfranchise them." [6] Election laws required the registration of voters several months before elections and the possession of certificates at the time of voting. Bipartisan management of elections was not required, and each party had the obligation of providing ballots. It was therefore possible for the usually dominant Democratic officials to tamper with the registration books, to use boxes with false bottoms, and to stuff ballot boxes. The most interesting of these stratagems was "tissue ballots," half a dozen of which might be conveniently dropped into a ballot box by a single voter. The blindfolded officials commissioned to extract the surplus ballots before the count were guided by the difference of texture in withdrawing an undue number of Republican ballots. Illiterate Negroes were placed at a disadvantage by laws requiring separate boxes for various offices and declaring ballots placed in the wrong boxes illegal.

This practice reached a climax in the Eight Box law of South Carolina, which required a separate box for each office. Confusion overcame the poor illiterate who, after his ballots had been arranged by a friend in correct sequence, discovered that in the meantime the boxes had been so shifted that he had only one chance in eight to deposit a single ballot in its right place. White boys of eighteen sometimes voted, and young

[4] Woodward, *op. cit.*, p. 57.
[5] Judge J. J. Chrisman, cited *ibid.*, pp. 57-8.
[6] *Ibid.*, p. 55.

Negroes unable to produce evidence of their age were assumed not to have reached their majority. So well did these tactics work that in some counties the Democratic votes exceeded the entire adult male population. When Republican majorities could not be overcome in counties of overwhelming Negro populations, local self-government was relinquished and county officers were appointed by state authorities or indirectly by electors centrally designated. Thus, in terms as unmistakable as the Constitution and laws of the United States allowed, the whites gave notice that they were determined to free the politics of their states from Negro participation.

Whites resorted to subterfuge and trickery to eliminate Negro voters because no practical way of securing repeal of the Fourteenth and Fifteenth amendments offered itself. Provisions for the civil and political equality of the Negro could only be circumvented by indirection. Although the whites undoubtedly preferred orderly and legal methods to accomplish their purpose, they were willing to resort to any means —legal or illegal, orderly or disorderly—if necessary. They firmly believed that the maintenance of their very broad conception of white supremacy was the *sine qua non* of decent civilization. By book, pamphlet, memoir, and official investigation they sought to prove that the Negro by his very nature was incapable of intelligently participating in the higher features of citizenship.

The success of the whites in eliminating the Republican vote as an important factor in Southern politics contributed significantly to national Democratic victories, notably the election af a Democratic President in 1884. Republicans noted the increased Southern representation in Congress since 1865 when the Constitutional provision counting only three fifths of the Negro population in the apportionment of seats had been abolished. They also observed that the average number of votes cast in a Congressional contest in five Southern states was less than eight thousand, while in five Northern states this average was five times as great—a disparity explained by the elimination of Negro voters. The Negro was being punished for his loyalty to a Republican party unable or unwilling to protect him in the exercise of constitutional rights.

When a sufficient number of Republicans felt that something could be done to alter this condition, Henry Cabot Lodge of Massachusetts introduced in Congress in 1890 a measure which Southerners jeeringly referred to as the Force Bill since it called for the supervision of Congressional elections by federal officials. Although the bill passed the House it failed in the Senate; Southern leaders had once again made it clear that they would maintain white supremacy. The Atlanta *Constitution* had called for a revival of "that glorious era" when "the indomitable spirit of the freedmen of Georgia was equal to the emergency. . . .

What we did twenty years ago we can do again." The only lasting result of the agitation was the strengthening of the Solid South concept.

The North as a whole, if not the Republican high command, had come to realize before 1890 that the elimination of the Negro from politics must be recognized if spiritual reality were to be given to the political reunion forcibly re-established at Appomattox. This change of attitude became evident in actions of the United States Supreme Court. In 1883 it openly admitted that federal courts could not secure Negro rights supposedly guaranteed by the Fourteenth and Fifteenth amendments. It held that these provisions did not authorize the national government to protect citizens from each other, but merely from discriminatory state legislation, giving protection only when such laws made distinctions on grounds of race or color, and in civil, not social rights.[7]

Such a confounding by the highest judicial authority of a policy to which the national government had been committed for two decades was followed in 1884 by Northerners co-operating with Southerners in electing a Democratic President and Congress. This President, Grover Cleveland, chose Lucius Q. C. Lamar of Mississippi and Augustus H. Garland of Arkansas for membership in his cabinet, with John G. Carlisle of Kentucky as Speaker of the House and Roger Q. Mills of Texas as Chairman of the House Committee on Ways and Means. For the first time since 1860 Southerners were given a fair share of the patronage. The President signed a bill granting pensions to all—mostly Southerners —who had served in the Mexican War, while refusing to approve certain pension measures for veterans of the Union army. In addition, he ordered the return to their respective states of Confederate flags captured by Union troops. If such measures did not prove, as Northern critics asserted, that the Confederate Brigadiers were once more "in the saddle," they did make Southerners feel that they were part of the Union again.

Ex-Confederate political leaders of the South served their people most usefully by encouraging Northern public opinion to accept the fact of white supremacy. Without compromising their conviction that the white race was ordained to rule, Southern leaders took every opportunity for several decades to enlist the sympathies of Northerners.

General John B. Gordon of Georgia sounded the keynote at Boston in 1878 when he said: "The causes that divided us are gone, and gone forever. The interests which now unite us will unite us forever." Although they made no specific pledges to protect the blacks' constitutional rights, Southern orators did not openly attack the theories of democracy and equality which had been established by the war amendments to the Constitution. The regaining of white supremacy was not

[7] *U. S. vs. Harris,* 106 U. S. 629.

depicted as a campaign against the North for the benefit of the Democratic party, but as a bid for good government and civilization in general. This evasiveness did not please old-fashioned Northern idealists who saw discrepancy between the words of Southern spokesmen and their actual treatment of Negroes. Southern irreconcilables of the school of Jeffeson Davis and Robert Toombs viewed this apparent compromise with Northern principles as a repudiation of Southern ideals. For the most part, however, a responsive note had been struck, a new and convenient harmony created between North and South that would not be disturbed again in matters of importance.

After Reconstruction Southern leaders were often called Bourbons, men so wedded to the ideals and practices of the past that they forgot nothing and learned nothing. Unwilling to adjust themselves to current demands for political and social reform, they repeated the negative catchwords of that liberalism which functioned most effectively during the early days of the Republic. They were the belated proclaimers of the virtues of Jeffersonianism and Jacksonism. Doubtless, the Bourbons were no more attached to the ideals of the past than the Southern masses who loved to hear orations on the Old South.

To be sure, in one respect these so-called reactionaries looked to the present and future rather than to the past. They were quite willing to sacrifice inherited tenets of agrarianism and states' rights in return for the South's participation in the great wave of industrial development which was bringing plenty to other sections of the United States. With almost the same logic their fathers had used to justify slavery and the agrarian way of life, they acknowledged the evils of slavery, the one-crop system, and secession, and pleaded for factories, crop diversification, adequate schools and a tolerance of those actions that had made the North materially great. In their inspired moments the Bourbons asserted that the white man should banish inherited prejudices against work and take advantage of the revolutionary opportunities which the Civil War placed before him. It became a commonplace to say: "It is the white man of the South more than the Negro who had been freed by the Civil War." In this fashion Southern leaders aroused new hope among their people.

The fresh attitude toward Southern problems embodied in the phrase "the New South" was often discussed in the 1870's and the early 1880's. Henry W. Grady, editor of the Atlanta *Constitution*, made it the subject of a talk before the New England Society of New York on December 21, 1886. After pointing out that the war was over, that former foes had learned to love each other, and that the South, while glorying in its tragic past, no longer repined over lost battles but instead was learning lessons of thrift and industry, he described how the section had "found her jewel in the toad's head of defeat." Although this picture of alleged change was unoriginal and overly enthusiastic, the effect of the address was widespread. Grady became a popular hero because, without demanding an apology for past mistakes, he strengthened Southerners' hopes that they might share the material prosperity previously regarded as a monopoly of the victorious North.

Undoubtedly, Grady and those who applauded him were motivated by the thought that reconciliation with the North would bestow benefits upon all classes of Southerners. Their actions, however, were not entirely idealistic; behind their fine phrases was the desire for private gain. As their first move, Bourbon politicians allied themselves with native merchants and bankers who had won financial power through the new agricultural credit system. Politicians furnished the prestige of great names; merchants and bankers supplied the money. Next, the politicians and their journalist friends took action that had the earmarks of scalawagism. Northern businessmen, a sort of second generation of carpetbaggers, invaded every Southern state in search of profits, offering the gospel of material prosperity. They invited the traditional leaders of the South to what one historian has picturesquely called "the Great Barbecue." [8]

The Bourbons eagerly accepted a place at the table in order to participate in the profits of the new business era. They became businessmen or hired lawyers of local or Northern capital. This practice reached a grotesque extreme when Generals Pierre G. T. Beauregard and Jubal A. Early, veritable paladins of the Confederacy, accepted handsome salaries to supervise the drawings of the Louisiana state lottery, a notorious institution of carpetbag origins and Yankee ownership. In Georgia the unscrupulous machinations of the Bourbon triumvirate composed of Joseph E. Brown, General John B. Gordon, and Alfred H. Colquitt became a public scandal, whereupon Grady temporarily abandoned his attempt to lend respectability to self-made men, speculators, and other agents of sordid materialism. Georgia's historian Charles C. Jones told a gathering of Confederate veterans: "I call you to witness that behind this fan-fare of trumpets proclaiming the attractions and growth of the New South may be too often detected the deglutition of the harpy and the chuckle of the hireling." [9]

Such traditional leaders as William M. McCardle, John H. Reagan, Isham G. Harris, Jefferson Davis, and Robert Toombs stayed away from the Great Barbecue to munch cold victuals; they would remain unreconstructed rebels, true to the Old South. Lesser men—Ben Tillman of South Carolina, Reuben F. Kolb of Alabama, and Tom Watson

[8] C. Vann Woodward, *Tom Watson, Agrarian Rebel*, p. 52.
[9] Cited *ibid.*, p. 125.

of Georgia—were not invited to the feast. They represented the farmers who, because of falling agricultural prices, were not sharing the benefits of the new industrial order. Still the Great Barbecue went on, enjoying much popularity. The object was to make the New South's industrial development into a booming reality. In encouraging this progress and prosperity, the Bourbon statesmen were conferring lasting benefits upon their section of the country. But they paid the price of allowing important resources to fall into the hands of alien capitalists. The transactions by which this was done were less spectacular than those of Reconstruction; but they were just as unscrupulous and had more lasting results.

Unscrupulous procedures in Georgia had their counterpart in other states. Tennessee, the first ex-Confederate state restored to Democrats, fell under the control of Colonel Arthur S. Colyar and a succession of governors whose chief interest was the gaining of favors for railroads in which they had investments. The redeemers of Virginia from radical rule enacted two laws of importance. One of these provided for the sale, at a sacrifice, of the state's valuable holdings in railroads to private hands, usually into the hands of expanding Northern railroad systems. The second law was the Funding Act which fastened upon an impoverished commonwealth annual interest charges almost equal to the entire revenue of the commonwealth. Virginia had bowed to the pressure of bankers, bondholders, and railroads.

Kentucky was now as Southern in its sentiments as any state that had seceded and was under the leadership of Kentucky Colonels with the standard mustaches and goatees. But it willingly served the interests of invading capitalists. The Louisville and Nashville Railroad was the most aggressive of these invaders, winning favors through the hiring of legislators and public officials. Its chief lobbyist was the chivalrous ex-Confederate, Basil W. Duke.

Northern capitalists contributed heavily to the campaign chest of George S. Houston, the Democrat elected governor of Alabama in 1874. The new governor adjusted the debt of the state in a manner highly satisfactory to the railroad interests. The redeemer of Florida for the Democrats was Governor George F. Drew, a native of New Hampshire who had purchased large tracts of timber during Reconstruction. Harriet Beecher Stowe, now a resident of Florida, assured Northern capitalists that they were most welcome. William D. Bloxham, Drew's successor in office, improved handsomely upon this promise by granting to visiting capitalists much public land.

Louisiana lived up to its reputation of being the only Southern state perpetually corrupt. During this period the people of the state tolerated close ties between the Louisiana state lottery and its Democratic politicians. In the tense days of 1877 the owners of the lottery bribed Republican legislators into joining the Democrats and thereby aided in the redemption of the state from radical rule. In 1879 it won protection from the state constitutional convention. Then followed the ten most prosperous years in the history of the institution, in which it collected $28,000,000 annually through the sale of its tickets and "debauched legislators, muzzled the press, and made and unmade public officials." [10]

Sectional, business, and race relations were not the only problems confronting the Bourbons when they regained control of the state governments. There was the question of financial adjustments. Within a few years after 1869, debts of eleven Southern states reached $140,000,-000—a heavy burden for governmental units emerging from an impoverishing war. Nor did this include the military obligations repudiated under the requirements of the Fourteenth Amendment.

Although the larger portion of the debt was due to the carelessness and corruption of the carpetbaggers, this did not apply to the entire amount. Some of it was accumulated interest on obligations contracted before or during 1860, some for bonds issued by the carpetbaggers and still deemed legitimate by their Democratic critics. Nevertheless, all Southern states except Texas and Mississippi resorted to a general scaling down of their obligations. Arkansas and Alabama each repudiated $13,000,000; North Carolina $22,000,000; Louisiana $38,000,000; Florida $4,000,000; Georgia $9,000,000; and South Carolina an undetermined amount. Virginia, after much internal political struggle and a controversy with West Virginia extending over fifty years, reduced a debt of $43,000,000 to $19,000,000. The states justified partial repudiation on the ground that their debts were beyond their capacity to pay, and that they derived no benefits from what had been borrowed. True or not, the states were protected in their actions by constitutional immunity against suits by private individuals. Naturally, the defaulting states were loudly denounced by their creditors, and loss of financial prestige greatly retarded Northern investments in Southern securities. The prompt payment of interest on the accepted parts of the debts, however, gradually restored the integrity of Southern governments, and their bonds sold at par before long.

One of the reasons why faith in the credit of the Southern states was re-established so promptly was the thoroughness with which the Bourbons turned their backs on the extravagances of the carpetbaggers. The Bourbons met a temporary loss of financial standing and the prevailing poverty of their constituencies by a policy of rigid economy, necessitating little credit and only the lightest of taxes. Economy became

[10] Woodward, *Origins of the New South*, pp. 2–22.

almost an obsession of the Bourbons, with salaries of public officials fixed at absurdly low figures. There was an uncritical reaction against the expansion of governmental functions so characteristic of the radical period; social legislation was neglected; appropriations for higher education, if made at all, were not sufficient to restore state colleges to their ante-bellum level of usefulness; insane asylums and other charitable institutions were kept alive, but failed to obtain sufficient revenues.

This determined avoidance of previous extravagances led to the belief that low taxes were to the greatest governmental advantage. This attitude was at first justified by the prevailing poverty but when returning prosperity made heavier taxation feasible, parsimony had become so fixed that little heed was given to the social needs which governments customarily meet in progressive communities. A climax of asininity was reached in the 1880's when Southern leaders opposed the Blair bill, a proposal providing for the distribution of surplus federal revenues to state schools in proportion to the prevalence of illiteracy. The South —poorest and most illiterate section of the United States—would have received $11,000,000 of the $15,000,000 appropriated for the first year. This was more than the entire sum spent on public schools in the South in 1880. A majority of Southern senators and educators favored the plan, but complications developed. The patronizing remarks of some of the Northern sponsors of the measure and the fear of a return to federal benevolence similar to that provided by the Freedmen's Bureau proved too great for Southern sensibilities. Furthermore, Democrats saw a Republican plot to dispose of the surplus revenue without the necessity of lowering the tariff.

Appropriations of state legislatures were too small to allow much stealing by unscrupulous officials, and the high standards supposed to have dominated the public service under Bourbon control led a competent historian to declare: "No governments in American history have been conducted with more fidelity than the governments of the Southern States during the first years after the Reconstruction period." [11] But a more recent scholar [12] hoots at this idea and parades before his readers a gallery of Bourbon rogues.

Investigation of Governor Colquitt's administration in Georgia resulted in the impeachment and resignation or conviction of several state officials and the disclosure of scandals in the administration of the convict-lease system. In 1883 state treasurers in Tennessee, Alabama, and Arkansas were proved to have made away with state funds totaling the astonishing sum of $928,000. The Tennessee defaulter was a member of the illustrious Polk family. The most brazen thief in Bourbon annals was

[11] Holland Thompson, The New South, p. 25.
[12] Woodward, Origins of the New South, pp. 66–74.

Major E. A. Burke, an adventurer of obscure origin who won the favor of the conservative faction in Louisiana because of his services against the radicals in 1877. As state treasurer Burke profited to the extent of $1,777,000 through the sale of state bonds which were supposed to have been destroyed. This theft was not discovered until after Burke had safely embarked on another career in distant Tegucigalpa.

These and similar defalcations did not leave lasting memories. The South was more inclined to overlook sin among native white men than among carpetbaggers or Negroes. It was unwilling to conceive that men who had been brave on Confederate battlefields might be knaves in civilian life. Corrupt alliances between business and government were so much in accord with the moral patterns of the times that little criticism arose.

The unprogressive phase of Bourbon leadership was best illustrated by the conduct of those southerners sent to Congress. Generally athletic, handsome, and patriotic men, they were enveloped in a romantic aura because of their war records. They were often chided in debate in the hope that indiscreet answers would furnish campaign material for the "bloody-shirt" politicians of the North. As a rule, however, the Rebel Brigadiers kept their tempers, failing to fall into the traps set for them. Not equipped with the greatness of genuine statesmen, they accomplished little for section and nation. As representatives of a defeated minority, they were forced into a defensive position that left scant opportunity for positive achievements.

These Bourbons were simple men, survivals of the American agrarian age, with little understanding of the new forces that were reshaping the nation. In set speeches they clung to the inherited doctrines of the Democratic party—low tariffs, economy in expenditures, and opposition to paternalism—and never tired of repeating their ancestral aversion to the growth of federal power at the expense of the states. Although not adverse to picking up the crumbs left by ruling Republicans, they were usually too unimaginative to take advantage of the policies of protective tariffs and federal subsidies through which the party of Lincoln and Grant enriched Northern businessmen. On the other hand, they were deaf to pleas for reform, regarding, for example, President Cleveland's proposals for civil service reform as the arrogance of a stiff-necked Yankee.

It is inaccurate to state that the Bourbons were wholly blind to the progressive needs of their constituencies. They never repudiated the principles of universal suffrage or legislative representation according to population—for the white race. In deference to rising democratic sentiments, they gradually extended the practice of substituting party nominations by direct vote of the white people for convention nominations. This was the direct primary. That ex-Confederate officers still dominated public service was the will of the white masses.

The demand for public education was not overlooked by the Bourbons, and after their initial reaction to the overthrow of the carpetbaggers, schools were voted as much revenue as they had ever received. Although this support was not generous, it was a significant beginning. Conservative politicians praised universal education in much the same manner as the radical missionaries had.

The Bourbons also met the demands of many Southern farmers who had become class conscious under the burden of agricultural distress in the 1880's. Following the example of Western states, Southern legislatures created railroad commissions, regulated railroad rates, fostered agricultural societies, and provided for fertilizer inspection. Federal subsidies for agricultural and industrial education were supplemented by state appropriations which led to the establishment of technological colleges.

Certain features of Bourbon rule lent credence to the charge of oligarchy; to leaders of the one third of the Southern population that was Negro and Republican these were most apparent. Some Southerners regarded as beneficiaries of the wholesale disfranchisement of the blacks likewise felt the charge justified. There were whites who complained about the one-party system, the suppression of vital political issues, the frustration of popular will through the manipulation of nominating conventions by lawyers and courthouse rings, and the conduct of public services in the interest of commercial minorities to the neglect of rural majorities. The undignified zeal with which impecunious gentlemen of the governing cliques took all available offices for themselves aroused envy and hatred and called forth the ridicule of those who recalled an aristocratic past when politics was an avocation rather than a profession. In the seventies and eighties the Granger movement stirred class consciousness among the farmers, and dissatisfied politicians like Martin W. Gary in South Carolina and Thomas M. Norwood in Georgia claimed that the Bourbons had not carried the anti-Negro reaction far enough. The independent William M. Lowe was elected to Congress in Alabama in 1878, and in 1880 in the same state the People's Anti-Bourbon party polled 42,000 votes for its candidate for governor. Two years later Wash Jones, Greenback candidate for governor of Texas, polled 150,000 votes. William H. Felton, a caustic critic of the Democratic oligarchy, represented a Georgia district in Congress from 1875 to 1881. In Virginia the Readjuster party, dedicated to scaling down the state debt, captured control of the government between 1879 and 1881 and sent its leader, General William Mahone, to the United States Senate. In return for his co-operation with the national Republicans, Mahone received the support of the Republication state organization and that of the Negro voters. His machine appeared invincible.

Still these evidences of dissatisfaction were not portents of general revolt against Bourbonism. The Granger movement declined after a brief popularity, and few Southerners would risk the condemnation of their neighbors by voting for the Greenback independents. Felton lost to a regular Democrat in 1880, and a drawing of the color line brought about the defeat of the Virginia Readjusters in 1883. To the white masses of the South Mahoneism was a warning of the dangers to white supremacy of a division among white men. To vote for the Bourbon was to play safe. Thus, in the middle of the 1880's the South fell into political doldrums, as proud of its Confederate Brigadiers as ever. Apparently, the apathy would last, since these gentlemen could not envisage revolution.

CHAPTER XXI

Progress in Industry and Agriculture

>>>->>>

THE SLAVEHOLDER's boast of the supremacy of cotton and the agrarian way of life was silenced by the events of 1865. Southerners recognized that Northern industrial diversity, as contrasted with an economically homogeneous South, largely had contributed to the failure of the Confederacy, and they hoped that industrial enterprises would follow the victorious Northern armies. Indeed, before the war ended, their expectations led General Adam Badeau, a Northerner living in South Carolina, to coin the descriptive phrase "The New South." Obviously the South faced an economic as well as a political and social reformation. Defeat of the Southern trio of aristocracy, agriculture, and political decentralization, Southerners believed, cleared the way for the incorporation of the defeated section in the new nationalism of industry ruled by the money-makers.

Patriotic Southerners, bewailing the ways of the Old South, early preached industrialism. In 1868, for example, Francis W. Dawson, the gifted Charleston editor, declared that the disasters of war "have taught the Southern planter that he cannot live by cotton alone," and diversified industry was needed. A cry for the full use of Southern brains and brawn to accomplish this purpose was coupled with a demand for the investment of Northern capital and the encouragement of white immigration. Southerners reportedly were saying: "This country will do nothin' till we have some Northern men and capital."

For two decades after the surrender at Appomattox an industrial

((326))

revival vainly was awaited. Northern capitalism, although an expanding giant, found the building of the great Northern factories and Western railroads more remunerative than investments in the South with its apparently exhausted fields, Negro disturbances, and bankrupt state governments. The interest of Northern banking houses in the region was mostly limited to financing railroads and investments in state bonds. The attractiveness of such investments was considerably negated by corruption and repudiation. Efforts to stimulate immigration to the South proved abortive; European and Northern settlers found the West more alluring. Unwilling to compete with the low wage standards prevailing among Negroes and poor whites, they feared the hostility of the natives of both races. Actually, population movements pointed in the other direction, with ambitious Southerners moving to the North and West in large numbers in search of industrial opportunities. A returned traveler gloomily observed in 1879: "Fifteen years have gone over the South and she still sits crushed, wrecked, busy displaying and bemoaning her wounds." [1]

While vainly awaiting the influx of outside capital and labor, the South did not entirely neglect its own industrial rehabilitation. This especially applied to the cotton textile industry, whose 160 mills with 300,000 spindles had been partly destroyed by war. There were fewer mills in 1870 than in 1860; by 1880, however, there were as many mills as in 1860, and twice as many spindles. The high price of cotton had created capital for investment in cotton textiles.

An even better example of industrial progress was that of the railroads. The 10,000 miles of Southern track existing in 1860 were largely destroyed or worn out. By 1873 Northern capital repaired or rebuilt the original mileage and constructed an additional 8,000 miles; by 1880 the South possessed a modern railroad system twice as great as that of 1860. This progressive system of transportation was to remain much the same until the coming of the automobile and paved highway. Definite strides were also made during Reconstruction in the tobacco, iron, and fertilizer industries. By the late 1870's the South industrially recovered all that it had possessed in 1860; yet this development was modest when compared with Northern achievements during the same period. If all 542,048 spindles of the Southern cotton textile industry had been concentrated in one state in 1880, that commonwealth would have ranked only seventh among the cotton manufacturing states of the country.

A combination of circumstances made the two decades following 1880 the most sensational in the industrial history of the South. Decline of the planter class weakened the appeal of agriculture as the road to

[1] Whitelaw Reid, cited in C. Vann Woodward, *Origins of the New South*, p. 107.

wealth and social distinction and made propaganda for factory building more popular. The planters of the Old South had invested their profits in slaves and land; the successful merchants and farmers of the post-Reconstruction period were inclined to put their profits in manufacturing. The re-establishment of white supremacy increased confidence in local investments, and lessened preoccupation with political affairs. The great depression of 1873 came to an end in 1879 and released Northern and English capital for Southern investments. In 1877 stimulus was given to the exploitation of timber and mineral resources by the opening for private sale of the vast federal domains of Alabama, Arkansas, Florida, Louisiana, and Mississippi. The feeling prevailed that the South might win back, through peaceful efforts, some of the advantages it had lost on the battlefield. Defeat of the Democratic party in the election of 1880 was interpreted as a challenge to the South to accomplish in another field what it failed to do in politics, and beat the North at its own game of industrial prosperity.

To give direction to these efforts there arose a group of young leaders of vision, both willing and able to act. They included Richard H. Edmonds of the Baltimore *Manufacturer's Record*, Walter Hines Page, Daniel A. Tompkins, and others. This group preached the doctrines of the self-made man and of industrial wealth as a means of lifting the South out of the difficulties into which a mistaken agrarian and political leadership had lured it. They wanted what one of them called "the real 'reconstruction' which active trade will inaugurate"; they wanted hard work instead of mourning over the losses of war. These new leaders, unlike those of the industrial revolution in England a hundred years before, prophetically foresaw the great change, and on the eve of that event, the Charleston merchants toasted their state: "South Carolina—a new era of prosperity is about to dawn upon her; increasing commerce, manufactures, agriculture and population are echoes of its coming." This newborn enthusiasm culminated in a series of industrial expositions at Atlanta, Louisville, New Orleans, and Richmond between 1881 and 1888, all emphasizing the achievements and possibilities of Southern enterprise.

Between 1880 and 1900 a new empire of cotton manufacturing sprang into existence in the piedmont area of the Carolinas, Georgia, and Alabama, from Danville on the Virginia border to Sylacauga, with extension into the flat regions below the hills wherever water power was available. During this period Southern cotton mills increased in number from 161 to 401; spindles from 542,048 to 4,200,988; mill operatives from 16,741 to 97,559. It pleased the South to discover that it was challenging the near monopoly in cotton manufacturing heretofore enjoyed by New England; the older manufacturing section's proportion of spindles declined from 81 per cent of the national total in 1880 to 68 of the total in 1900. The federal census soberly stated in the latter year that the growth of the cotton industry in the South was "the one great fact in its history during the past ten years"; a prominent advocate of the new development declared that the section had "entered upon one of the most remarkable periods of economic development to be found in the history of the modern industrial world."

Even more remarkable were the methods by which this revival was effected. Turning away from hopes of attracting Northern capital, Southerners resolved to build the mills themselves. Since there were no great Southern capitalists to call upon, funds had to be subscribed locally in each community where a mill seemed feasible. With a spirit similar to that which characterized Southern political revolutions and religious revivals, it was persuasively argued that the establishment of mills would give employment; that raw materials and water power were available; that public authorities would grant tax exemptions; that mills already established were making money; and that Northern manufacturers of mill machinery were extending easy terms. At Salisbury, North Carolina, a mill owed its existence to the preaching of an evangelist. He asserted that it would give work to those whom idleness had made vicious. Savings from cotton growing, merchandizing, and banking were eagerly subscribed.

Popular participation in raising capital was facilitated by selling stock in small shares, with weekly payments in installments of only fifty cents or one dollar. It was not uncommon for a $100,000 mill to have a hundred or more stockholders. An ample labor supply was drawn from the underprivileged whites of the mountains and farms surrounding the mills. These folk eagerly sought industrial employment as a means of improving their low economic status. The hiring of women and children was hailed as a boon not only by the millowners, but by those to whom it gave a livelihood.

There were self-appointed prophets who held that the Southern people were incapable of manufacturing cotton, and should content themselves with the production of raw materials for the New England mills. To be sure, serious obstacles were encountered. Many new mills made the mistake of buying obsolete machinery discarded by the New England mills. Labor picked from the farms had to be trained in habits of skill and regularity. When Northern overseers imported for these purposes sometimes proved too exacting the operatives concluded that they had exchanged the economic and social handicaps of the tenant farm for the regimentation of the company-owned mill village where wages were paid in scrip redeemable only through purchases at the company store. Northern writers, motivated by what the South regarded as jealousy of its newly found prosperity, painted lurid pictures of the allegedly bad working conditions in the mills, thus giving the Southern factories an evil reputation.

Eventually, these and other obstacles were mainly overcome. Purchasing agents for the mills soon learned to buy the best machinery with the latest devices. Native managers drawn from stores, banks, and farms were readily adaptable to the larger activities of the mills. So successful were the laborers from Southern farms in applying themselves to the relatively simple operations of the mill machinery that Daniel A. Tompkins, after considerable experience as a millowner, believed that they were drawing upon ancestral experience held in abeyance during the period when cotton growing ruled supreme.[2] The assaults of Northern writers on Southern labor conditions had no effect upon mill operatives. They remained docile, ignorant, and proud, deaf to appeals that they forget their inherited prejudices and join labor unions advocating social legislation. Rather, they abandoned their traditional indifference toward religion and became the most religious group of industrial workers in the United States.

By 1900 the victory for cotton mill construction was won. In that year investments in the Southern section of the industry amounted to $124,596,874. Net profits averaged 15 per cent and frequently were as high as 40 to 60 per cent. These successes were so stupendous that the building of mills became almost a religious craze. By 1915 the number of mills in the cotton states exceeded those in the rest of the country. Two new classes had been added to Southern society, the mill operative and the millowner. The latter often outdid the town merchant and banker in wealth and prestige. His mansion overshadowed the small cottages of the mill village in much the same manner that the big house of the planter once had dominated the slave quarters. This new regime was almost as feudalistic as the earlier economy. If the millworkers, in the exercise of their prerogatives as white men, were not so docile as Negroes, they certainly did not question the economic and social preeminence of the mill master, or his right to control the moral, political, and industrial life of the usually unincorporated mill villages. It was a mild form of bondage in an age supposedly dominated by individual self-expression.

As in the English industrial revolution, the growth of the cotton industry stimulated other Southern production. There were demands for improvement in farming, and a renewed interest in the extension of cattle and sheep raising, also in the building of railroads and telegraph and telephone lines. The moral enthusiasm thus engendered stimulated

[2] In The South in the Building of the Nation, VI, 58–61.

the growth of temperance societies and campaigns against duelling and rural lawlessness.

Two new industries were by-products of cotton, one of which was the cottonseed-oil mill. It was discovered that cottonseed had other uses than as feed for cattle or as fertilizer. The oil proved to be a satisfactory substitute for lard and olive oil as well as an important ingredient of oleomargarine. The cake or meal from which the cottonseed oil had been pressed, if not palatable for man, was valuable as a fertilizer and as food for cattle. Unlike the cotton textile industry, the cottonseed-oil mills were scattered over the length and breadth of the cotton states. Texas, the largest producer of raw cotton, was also the chief manufacturer of cottonseed-oil products. In 1914 Southern states valued these goods as $212,000,000. The use of cottonseed cakes for soil improvement led to the establishment of fertilizer departments in more than a hundred cottonseed-oil mills. The expansion of cotton growing into the uplands brought about a need for other types of fertilizers. Peruvian guano was imported and phosphate rock mined extensively, first in South Carolina, later in Tennessee and Florida.

Scarcely less impressive than the expansion of the cotton mills was the development of the iron and coal industries. Like cotton textiles, the iron industry was concentrated in a well-defined area—the Birmingham-Chattanooga district of northern Alabama. In the 1880's a feebly organized, dispersed, and antiquated iron industry was modernized and expanded. Subsequently the production of southern pig iron increased from less than 400,000 tons in 1880 to four times that amount ten years later. Birmingham, founded in 1871, became the center of the steel industry, rivaling in spirit—if not in quality and quantity of its products—Pittsburgh's great steel development. Also in the 1880's for the first time modern methods of exploitation were applied to Southern beds of bituminous coal. Their output increased from 6 million tons in 1880 to 26 millions in 1890, and to twice that amount ten years later. The industry was centered in West Virginia and Alabama, with extensions into Tennessee, Virginia, and Kentucky. Analogous to cotton textiles, Southern coal and iron industries were mainly the products of local faith and capital, although Northern money played some part in their development.

Three railroad systems—the Chesapeake and Ohio, the Norfolk and Western, and the Virginian—gave the coal of the Virginias access to various markets. They represented Southern enterprise supported by Northern capital. Once the Birmingham area proved its ability to produce pig iron profitably, Northern bankers financed the consolidation of its industries. In the 1890's the Tennessee Coal, Iron and Railroad Company initiated a policy of expansion resulting in the absorption of Southern iron and steel by national corporations. The United States Steel Corporation, greatest of them all, became the chief Birmingham operator. For a time the output of this Alabama city was retarded because the phosphorous content of its ores was too high for the Bessemer process to be used. This handicap, however, was overcome around 1900 through the use of the open-hearth process for turning the basic pig iron into steel.

The quantity of timber taken from Southern forests more than doubled between 1880 and 1890, giving the South first rank as the source of the nation's lumber. Factories were founded to convert lumber into finished products. The wagon, buggy, coffin, agricultural machinery, and street car industries flourished, and small, scattered factories for manufacturing plowshares, spokes, shuttle-blocks, pails, and the like, were set up. The most important Southern wood industry, furniture-making, began at High Point, North Carolina, in 1888, spreading into other communities of that state, and into Virginia and Tennessee. The industry's great advantage was its proximity to hardwoods and its low labor costs.

Tobacco was not to be outdone by cotton, its great rival staple. In the 1880's large profits accrued from doubling the productive capacity of the factories devoted to its manufacture. The small ante-bellum establishments producing snuff, twist, and plug tobacco were supplanted by larger and more numerous factories. James B. Duke merged the industry into the American Tobacco Company in 1890; this consolidation sharply reduced the number of factories. Some were bought by the Duke interests, their brands transferred to larger plants, and the establishments closed; others, fearing the competition of the larger organization, shut down voluntarily. Nevertheless, the total tobacco output steadily increased with the plug and smoking tobacco industries primarily confined to North Carolina, Virginia, Kentucky, and Missouri. Florida and Louisiana led in the manufacture of fine cigars made from Cuban leaf, while the city of Richmond headed the production of cigars and cheroots from the domestic product.

The most sensational development of all was that of cigarettes. Their manufacture in unlimited quantities became possible in 1884 when the expanding Duke interests acquired from James A. Bonsack, a Virginia inventor, the privilege of using his cigarette machine. Durham, Richmond, Winston-Salem, and Louisville were the centers of this new industry. Despite the conviction of many devout Southerners that cigarettes were more harmful than tobacco in other forms, the industry grew rapidly, supplying world as well as national markets. The Duke family partially stifled religious opposition by diverting some of their huge cigarette profits to the endowment of Methodist educational and charitable institutions.

Industrial expansion in the 1880's and 1890's was accompanied by a growth of cities comparable to that of the commercial villages and towns during the fifteen years preceding 1880. Some cities were the offshoot of industrial developments. Birmingham, the site of a corn field in 1869, had 38,000 people in 1900, and during the same period Durham grew from a small village into a thriving tobacco center. Older towns like Richmond and Chattanooga became boom cities of the New South; Norfolk owed its expansion to railroad and shipping developments, while an adjacent tidewater plantation became the thriving shipbuilding city of Newport News. Big Lick, a Virginia village of 400 inhabitants, grew by 1892 into a manufacturing center of 20,000. It assumed the native name of Roanoke as though to disguise the fact that Philadelphia capitalists had called it into being.

The most spectacular of the new cities was Atlanta, whose population between 1880 and 1890 increased from 37,000 to 65,000. Through its network of railroads, Atlanta became the chief distributing center of the Southeast—"the wrist of a hand whose fingers reach the five principal ports of the Gulf and the Atlantic coast," as General William T. Sherman put it. The cotton factories, because they were scattered over the countryside, did not contribute to the growth of large cities. Such towns of the cotton mill area as Charlotte, Greenville, Greensboro, Spartanburg, and Columbus were the homes of merchants, bankers, and professional men who served the farms and the neighboring mill villages.

One of the main reasons for the industrial development of the New South was the low labor costs of that section, expressing itself in three ways: low absolute and relative wages, lax legal requirements as to hours of work and age of workers, and lack of interest in labor organizations. The rural South amply supplied cotton factories with white labor; both whites and blacks furnished the necessary labor for lumbering, for the cotton-oil mills and tobacco factories, and for the steel industry. This abundance of native labor accounted for the failure of ill-advised attempts to import European or Northern workers.

The people of the farms and mountain coves who trekked into the new cotton mills were moved by a variety of impulses. They were seeking in village life relief from the dreary isolation of sparsely settled rural areas with poor roads and scant social diversions; still more, they wanted fair wages to mitigate the grinding poverty of a depressed agriculture and a miserable tenant and credit system. To persons receiving less than $200 in cash yearly, stories of single families earning from $15 to $25 a week seemed fabulous. Both black and white workers were attracted to the tobacco, iron, and furniture industries by the same motives that led others into the cotton mills.

Because of the abundance of labor, the wages of Southern textile operators during the early period of expansion were much lower than those paid in New England at that time. Over a period of seventy-eight years, as Clarence Heer has demonstrated,[3] the wages earned by Southern operatives were, in fact, from 30 to 40 per cent lower than those paid in the rest of the country. Wages for male workers were as low as 40 cents a day, and there is a record of mills in North Carolina that paid 10 or 12 cents a day for child labor. Moreover, during the early history of Southern industry there were no restrictions upon hours of work, age or sex of operatives, or conditions of employment. Inevitably, as in all countries first turning to factories, abuses arose. Hours were long, often seventy-two and in some cases seventy-five a week. Wages were often paid in scrip good at company stores but redeemable in cash only at infrequent intervals.

Children were often victimized by the connivance of millowners, incompetent or parasitic parents, or those too blind to distinguish between working on the farms and in the mills. "So the children went into the cotton factories and stayed there," said Holland Thompson.[4] "If illiterate when they entered, they remained illiterate." There were several hundred so employed who were not over ten or twelve years old, and possibly there were a few who were still younger.

Local sentiment against these abuses was slow to be aroused. Organized labor, socialist agitators, and professional philanthropists—groups from which such crusades usually spring—were few in number south of the Potomac. Local sentimentalists steeped themselves in religion and in patriotic legends. Moreover the South continued to think of its problems in terms of the agricultural society Jefferson idealized. It was considered improper for the state to regulate either industrial or agricultural labor. If working children were not physically abused and preferred labor to learning, that solely concerned themselves and their parents. Attempts to apply reform pressure from the outside proved wholly ineffective, and the exaggerations of Northern muckrakers caused resentment that probably hindered rather than helped the cause of social legislation. Every true Southerner believed that the pitiful stories written by these agitators were mostly false. Their statements angered mill operatives as much as millowners and the general public, and were substantially refuted. Apologists pointed out that Southern living standards and costs were less than those in the textile areas of

[3] *Income and Wages in the South*, passim.
[4] *The New South*, pp. 114–15.

New England. Certainly, Southern rentals and fuel costs were lower and workers were unaccustomed to the many expenditures of the New England laborer. The fact that men, women, and children worked in the mill greatly increased the total family income. There was compensation in the friendly personal relations which often existed between the millowner and the millworker, in the overseer's tolerance of leisurely work habits, and in a paternalistic system under which the company provided houses at low rent, subsidized schools and churches, and allowed the worker the feudal privilege of gathering wood and of pasturing the family cow on the company's lands. The wretched living conditions in mill villages described by investigators were caused as much by the ignorance and indifference of poor whites turned mill operatives as by poverty. Furthermore, there was an abundance of land to which the Southern operative could return if dissatisfied with conditions of employment. Instead of doing so, farm people moved to the mills in ever-increasing numbers.

During the early history of the Southern textile industry, wages probably were higher per unit of product than those paid in New England. The Southerner, being a beginner, was less skilled than the New Englander and actually operated his newer and more expensive machinery at a slower pace. As for the prevalence of child labor, Northern critics greatly exaggerated this factor. For technical reasons, children were excluded from most processes of clothmaking except spinning, and there the possible percentage of workers under sixteen varied from 35 to 45 per cent. Doubtless, children in Southern cotton mills fared better than those in English mills a hundred years earlier or, for that matter, on the Southern farms from which the millworkers migrated. Of the 1,077,950 Southern children who were breadwinners in 1900, more than 843,000 worked on farms; of the remaining 234,000, only 28,000 were employed in the textile industry.

Working conditions among Southern textile operatives gradually improved. An increase in the number of mills and rising standards of rural life enabled prospective laborers to demand higher wages and better living conditions. Physical and moral conditions in the mill communities were vastly improved. Payment of wages in cash became the rule, and the hours of work were voluntarily reduced from a maximum of 72 to 69 or 66 hours. Some millowners assumed a patriarchal attitude toward their workers, contributing to the support of schools and providing libraries, parks, and recreational and social diversions. Even the most backward among them encouraged community churches. Attempts to better conditions through the initiative of the mill operatives themselves were less successful for they were inherently "the eternal poor whites"—improvident, slovenly, migratory. Nevertheless, some operatives learned to save, to buy property, and to make their surroundings attractive.

That the cotton mill people were white and not black promoted public sentiment in their favor; in fact, sentimentalists romanticized them into "our people of purest Anglo-Saxon descent," and praised the many inherent virtues not possessed by Negroes or by white people of other descents. This attitude effected, after much delay, a considerable body of social legislation in favor of the millworkers. Limitations upon age and hours of employment and upon night work for women and children were imposed; Negroes were excluded from the mills; compulsory education laws were rigidly applied to mill villages. The change to the white primary as the means of electing public officials lent millworkers in several states an importance out of proportion to their numbers. Living in piedmont counties where nonvoting Negro populations were small and voting whites large, they outvoted lowland counties sparsely inhabited by whites. It became impossible, especially in South Carolina, for politicians who had the ill will of the millworkers to win elections.

Despite the blandishments of chambers of commerce and other boosters of industry, the advances of the 1880's and 1890's did not give manufacturing a dominant position in the life of the Southerners. As in the past, in the New South agriculture continued as the most important occupation. True, in some areas the economic life of the people was completely altered by industrialism, but the majority of Southerners remained rural, apparently unaffected by the vigorous and supposedly contagious prosperity of the new cotton and steel mills. In 1910 only 15 per cent of Southerners gainfully employed were engaged in manufacturing, or half the proportion so employed in the United States as a whole. As late as 1930, 67 per cent of the people of the South Atlantic states and 72 per cent of those of the east South Central states were rural; the comparative figure for the United States as a whole was 44 per cent. In Arkansas less than 44,000 of 519,000 persons gainfully employed were in factories.

Southern cities at the beginning of the twentieth century were small in comparison with those of the North; their inhabitants retained the habits and ideals of country folk. Rich merchants and millowners invested part of their surplus wealth in farm lands so that they might pass their last years as country gentlemen. Some Southerners, answering those who sang the praises of the New South and its industries, asserted that the rural ways of their ancestors were nobler and more satisfying than those of the new era.

The decades that followed the overthrow of the carpetbaggers saw agriculture progress as substantially, if not so sensationally, as industry. Achievements in agriculture should not be underestimated by the student of Southern history because they were exceeded by contemporary achievements in Northern industry and Western agriculture. Southern agricultural advancement in no small measure was speeded by progress in the United States as a whole. This fact is strikingly illustrated by the South's readiness to make use of discoveries in scientific agriculture. In 1872 Virginia and Alabama established agricultural colleges, and by the end of the century all the Southern states had followed their example. Agricultural experimental stations were established and scores of agricultural journals tried to spread improved methods.

Seaman A. Knapp, a distinguished agricultural reformer in the employ of the United States Department of Agriculture, developed in 1903 a new technique of impressing upon the farmers the advantages of scientific agriculture. A farmer of Terrell, Texas, was induced to conduct his farm, under the watchful eyes of his neighbors, according to Knapp's specifications. The neighbors were impressed by the demonstration, and the Terrell farm became the inspiration of thousands of model farms established over the South in the next ten years.

Although cotton growing never recovered the national and international prestige it had enjoyed before the Civil War, it continued to be the South's major occupation. Indeed, it dominated the lives of even a larger section of the South than heretofore, and by 1879 the yield of the fleecy staple surpassed that of 1860. The 1879 crop of 5,475,000 bales rose to 8,458,000 bales in 1899, and to 13,587,000 bales in 1908. Between 1900 and 1913 the number of acres in cotton cultivation climbed from 25 to 37 millions. The chief significance of this increase in acreage was the continued westward expansion of the Cotton Kingdom. By 1900 Texas production came to twice that of any other state; its 3,438,386 bales represented 34 per cent of the national total.

The westward movement developed through improved transportation, the ravages of the boll weevil in the moist regions east of the Mississippi, and greater efficiency of white labor in the newer sections as compared with Negro labor in older regions. The decline of cotton in the eastern states was relative, not absolute. Only Alabama and Louisiana showed decreased production in 1879 compared with 1859, and Tennessee was the only state producing cotton in appreciable quantities that decreased its output between 1879 and 1899. Despite the westward movement, both North and South Carolina produced increased proportions of the total crop between 1859 and 1876. The ability of these older cotton states to hold their own could be attributed to greater use of commercial fertilizers which increased the yields per acre, and also to the extension of cotton culture into piedmont areas worked by the more efficient white labor. The less enterprising black labor of the lowlands adhered to cotton growing because it was familiar to them and bore their neglect. Everywhere cotton received preference under the prevailing system of credits. The ravages of the boll weevil, while real enough, were not sufficient to destroy the supremacy of the staple. In 1913, after the pest had spread for twenty years over the entire cotton belt, the United States Bureau of Agricultural Economics reported that the loss of cotton due to this insect was but 6.69 per cent "of the estimated crop in the absence of the boll weevil."

Critics of the alleged tyranny of King Cotton had many sound arguments on their side, but not all. Although cotton growers suffered from the maladies of the one-crop system and overproduction, they were not alone among American farmers in these respects, and their hardships were not so severe as some writers imagined. For two and one half decades after the Civil War, there was a growing demand by the cotton mills of the United States and Europe for that product which the South, because of the farming habits of its people as well as its unique climate, could supply so abundantly. During this period cotton always enjoyed a ready market at prices usually above production costs. The value per acre of cotton produced exceeded that of land devoted to grains, and a cotton crop was less likely to be a total failure than other forms of agriculture.

The ravages of war brought a radical decline in tobacco culture. In six Southern states the output dropped from 346 million pounds in 1860 to 190 million pounds in 1870; however, it increased in the decades after 1870. By 1900, the figure reached 658 million pounds, and there were increases in all tobacco-producing Southern states except Virginia and Maryland. This expansion of production could be accounted for by a considerable rise in the per capita consumption of tobacco both at home and abroad—in the United States from 1.6 pounds annually during the Civil War period to 5.5 pounds forty years later, with accompanying increases in western European countries dependent upon America for their supply. The shifting of the center of cultivation from Virginia and Maryland to newer and more fertile fields in Kentucky, Tennessee, and North Carolina also contributed to higher production. More intensive cultivation and closer attention to the problems of soil conservation could be given to the small farms which had been formed by breaking up the plantations.

These factors, together with the increased use of commercial fertilizers, stimulated a steady rise in the yield per acre—from 757 pounds in Kentucky in 1880 to 830 pounds in 1902, and from 472 to 608 pounds in North Carolina during the same period. The tobacco belt followed the example of the cotton states in adopting the sharecrop and crop-lien systems, without employing the undesirable one-crop practice. Diversification was the rule among tobacco growers. In 1900 approximately one third of this group derived more than 40 per cent of its income from tobacco exclusively. Less than 10 per cent of the acreage of tobacco farms was devoted to raising tobacco, with the remainder engaged in producing foodstuffs.

The Civil War wrought even greater havoc with the sugar industry of Louisiana than with the tobacco growing of the upper South. Production fell from 236,000 tons in 1861 to 9,000 tons in 1865; but by 1893 it equaled that of 1860 and in 1904 reached 356,000 tons. This expansion was made possible by the introduction of labor-saving machinery for both cultivation and harvesting, the importation of improved varieties of seed, use of scientific manuring and more effective flood control, and maintenance of a protective tariff or bounty.

Rice plantations of South Carolina—the source of so much antebellum wealth—never fully recovered from the devastating effects of war, which left labor demoralized, and canals, dams, and floodgates destroyed or choked with shrubbery. The yield of Carolina rice fell to 52 million pounds in 1880, to 27 million pounds in 1895, and vanished altogether in the first decades of the twentieth century. Labor problems, plant diseases, and unprogressive methods of cultivation speeded the extinction of this industry. However, the main cause was the competition of the rice fields of the Louisiana Gulf Coast, where farmer migrants from the Northwest, under the guidance of Seaman A. Knapp, in 1884 solved labor difficulties and increased yields tenfold by utilizing machinery with which they had become familiar in the wheat fields. The United States Department of Agriculture brought from Japan an improved variety of rice seed, known as the Kiushu, which produced greater yields. In 1895 Louisiana rose to first position among the rice-growing states with a yield of 127 million pounds; by 1905 its production exceeded that of all the states in 1860. Louisiana's enormous crop of 519 million pounds in 1908 represented more than half the rice crop of the entire nation. Texas and Arkansas also produced considerable quantities of rice.

The vast expansion of grain production in the Western states during the decades after the Civil War adversely affected Southern grain growing. In 1899, the South produced less than one third of the nation's Indian corn—a decrease of 20 per cent since 1859. Agricultural writers complained about Southern farmers who had corn cribs in Cincinnati and smokehouses in Chicago. However, the South showed definite progress in the production of foodstuffs. In the forty years preceding 1899 its output of cereals doubled. Indian corn occupied approximately three fourths of the acreage devoted to such foods. There was a marked increase, too, in the production of wheat in Kentucky and Tennessee, and in Southern states west of the Mississippi.

Considerable advances were made in the development of forage crops as substitutes for the general lack of natural meadows and pastures characteristic of a sunny climate. This need was partly met by recognition of the benefits of crimson and burr clover, alfalfa, Bermuda and Johnson grasses, and the all-prevailing cowpea. These forage crops helped to solve such fundamental problems of the section's farm economy as cattle feeding, soil restoration, and crop rotation.

The foremost innovation in Southern agriculture during the postbellum period was the expansion of truck farming. It came as a natural complement to the development of rapid and safe transportation of perishable edibles to the great markets of the North. The Southern vegetable and fruit industry may be said to have had its beginning when Clayton A. Cogwill raised Florida produce for the market as early as 1865. A Georgia planter in 1870 set out 5,000 hills of watermelons and sold many melons weighing thirty-five pounds. Robert Somers, an English traveler, was impressed as early as 1870 by the number of peach orchards he found in Georgia.[5] In 1866 peaches and tomatoes were first shipped from Crystal Springs, Mississippi, to New York City, and in 1872 the first refrigerator car of strawberries reached Chicago from the lower Mississippi Valley. By 1900 more than 60,000 of these cars were in operation. Annually they hauled $24,000,000 worth of vegetables and $28,000,000 worth of fruits from Southern to Northern markets. The major crops consisted of Irish and sweet potatoes, green vegetables, strawberries, watermelons, oranges, apples, and peaches. Advantage was taken of the longer growing seasons of the South, where all these products matured earlier than in the North. Southern truckers enjoyed an ample supply of cheap labor, concentrated manures stimulating early maturity, and sprays as protection against insects and fungous diseases. The perils of frosts to early plants were minimized by placing orchards and gardens near the moderating influence of the Gulf of Mexico and the Atlantic Ocean.

Sidney Lanier asserted in 1899 that "the notable circumstance" of the South for the period since the Civil War was the "quiet rise of the small farmer." In this conclusion the Georgia poet was buttressed by the census of 1880 which showed that in the nine principal cotton-planting states the size of the average farm declined from 347 acres in 1860 to 156 acres in 1880, and that during this period the number of farms increased from 450,000 to 1,110,000. But what had really happened was a revolution in the labor system and not in land tenure. The plantations had been parceled out to sharecroppers who worked their allotments

[5] E. Merton Coulter, *The South during Reconstruction*, p. 222.

separately in place of the gang system of slavery times. By 1880 share-croppers cultivated 302,000 of the farms of the nine cotton states. The ante-bellum plantations had not been broken into small proprietorships. What was true of one state may be true of the entire South. A study of representative areas of Louisiana proves that the plantation as a unit of ownership in that state "not only survived but also expanded after the Civil War" and that small farms actually decreased to such a degree as partly to destroy small proprietorships.[6]

"The main feature of Southern agriculture since the war, as slavery was previous thereto," wrote an authority in 1897,[7] "was the crop-lien system." Few white tenants and practically no Negroes could acquire the capital to operate the farms in which the plantations had been divided. Consequently they were forced into the practice of asking the country merchants for advances. This applied to many landowners also. In the months before crops were gathered both tenants and landlords depended upon the merchants for items necessary for their very existence—meal, bacon, flour, molasses, cloth, tobacco, and other articles of personal consumption, and occasionally tools, farming implements, fertilizers, and work animals. When harvest time came merchants took their portion of crops in settlement of accounts. Although they did not charge interest, the difference between cash and credit prices often amounted to practical interest charges of from 40 to 100 per cent.

Merchants were protected by laws governing the crop lien and chattel mortgage. Under contract arrangements, farmers pledged their planted or unplanted crops, their farming implements, cattle, horses, and land. It was a serious statutory offense for debtors to hold back any crops until accounts were settled, and nine tenths of the farmers in some sections of the South fell into debt. Frequently merchants exacted additional interest charges by crediting the encumbered crops at prices lower than in free markets. Crops were often worth less than the advances, and an unfavorable balance was carried over to the following year. Since no merchant would extend credit to a farmer whose accounts with a former creditor were not cleared up, farmers in these circumstances were reduced to a state of peonage or debt servitude. Since the bookkeeping was handled by the merchants and could not be understood by many illiterates among the tenant farmers, there were chances for cheating by unscrupulous individuals.

Naturally the merchants assumed close supervision over the purchases and farm operations of their debtors. At the beginning of the year amounts varying from $50 to $200 were lent to each tenant, but

[6] Roger W. Shugg, *Origins of the Class Struggle in Louisiana*, pp. 235–40. Cf. Woodward, *op. cit.*, pp. 175, 178–9.
[7] Matthew B. Hammond, *The Cotton Industry*, p. 122.

he could only draw on his credit gradually over the season of growing and harvesting. Otherwise, most of the debtors might have exhausted their credits months before the crops were gathered, and merchants would be forced to make additional advances or see debtors move to avoid starvation. Because merchants extended credit even before crops were planted they could demand those commodities which assured an adequate return on their investments.

Invariably the choices were cotton and tobacco, as both these staples possessed comparatively large value in comparison with their small bulk and could be stored conveniently. Moreover, neither was difficult to sell or liable to total failure, and neither tempted the thief before they were grown. A crop of wheat might be abandoned before harvesting in favor of a cotton contract on a neighboring plantation; a crop of corn might be stolen or consumed while still green. Besides, encouraging the growth of foodstuffs would merely serve to cut down profits on the sale of imported flour, meal, and bacon. Thus was perpetuated a one-crop system even more burdensome upon the health and economy of its victims than in the days of slavery.

It is not true, as some critics of Southern rural economy maintain, that a general conspiracy existed to keep the Negro and other lowly tenants in debt servitude. Certainly landlords would have preferred thrifty and prosperous tenants capable of assuming the full responsibilities of renting without haggling for portions of the landlords' none-too-fluid capital. The merchants preferred business on a cash basis. Despite their exorbitant interest charges and many opportunities for cheating, experience taught them that the crop-lien system was a risky business. Droughts or floods or abandonments of fields by shiftless, ill, or dishonest debtors all too frequently reduced harvests below the level of outstanding mortgages. Consequently, merchants accumulated many bad debts, and the wealthy among them had been either extremely shrewd or lucky. The denial of the right to acquire lands was not included in all the restrictions and conditions of Southern life imposed upon the blacks. Almost everywhere Negroes could buy land on the installment plan with modest initial payments. A significant albeit small minority availed themselves of this opportunity.

The crop-lien system despite its many faults possessed one important advantage: it enabled the agricultural laborer to carry on operations independently and permitted him, if he wished, to become debt-free by applying the profits of one year's crop to that of next season. In most cases, however, Negro and white tenants refused to do this because Southern agricultural laborers were among the most improvident of Americans and failed to seek independence from their merchant-creditors. A careful student of plantation economy cites: [8] "The money from a crop already gathered is theirs, to be spent as fancy suggests, while the crop to be made must take care of itself, or be taken care of by the 'white folks.' "

The complaints of critics in slavery times against living conditions among the poor whites could be reiterated with almost equal justice several decades later. These neglected folk improved their lot somewhat through migrations to new industries, and their ability to supplant the blacks as growers of cotton and tobacco. More than one fifth of the South's arable land in 1910 was cultivated by 886,000 white tenant farmers. Their farms were larger than those of the blacks, averaging 83.8 acres as contrasted with the Negroes' 39.65, and on the whole they were more prosperous. Many of them, however, were as improvident and as impoverished as the Negroes. They were the victims of the credit system, large families, lack of moral stamina, and physical disabilities often arising from improper diet and poor sanitation. They especially suffered from malaria, hookworm, and pellagra. Neither books nor physical conveniences lightened the discomforts of their overcrowded homes. Unlike Negroes in the same economic status, they had no social life other than a journey to church in a springless wagon; their overworked womenfolk usually led hermitlike existences, cut off from contact with anyone except their numerous broods.

The expansion of the textile, coal, iron, tobacco, and furniture industries in the last decades of the nineteenth century made for a degree of prosperity which the South had not experienced since the advent of cotton and slavery. No such unqualified statement can be made concerning Southern agriculture of the same period. To some extent it was characterized by what Henry George called the great enigma of the age—the prevalence of progress along with poverty. The 1870's and 1880's saw a steady increase in production of the great staples, and a pronounced prosperity based on the growth of fruits and vegetables. At the same time, however, there was the appalling poverty of the poor whites and Negro tenants. In the late 1880's forces were developing throughout the United States as a whole which made the contrast more striking between the progress and poverty of the different classes. During the same period in the South these forces tended to place all agriculturalists—both the possessors and nonpossessors of land—in the poverty class. The cause was the "poverty" of low prices induced by the "progress" of overproduction.

[8] Alfred H. Stone, *Studies in the American Race Problem*, p. 189.

CHAPTER XXII

Agrarian Revolt

⤞⤞⤞

"THE WHEELS have dropped out of balance," declared a leading agricultural journalist in 1887. "The railroads have never been as prosperous, and yet agriculture languishes. The banks have never done better or more profitable business, and yet agriculture languishes. Cities and towns flourish and 'boom' and grow and 'boom,' and yet agriculture languishes. Salaries and fees were never as temptingly high and desirable, and yet agriculture languishes." The truth of these assertions was brought home to the farmers through radical declines in the prices of their commodities. According to the United States Department of Agriculture, cotton prices per pound fell from 15.1 cents for the 1870–73 period to 9.1 cents for 1882–84; to 7.8 cents for 1890–93; and to 5.8 cents for the years 1894–97. The returns received by the farmers were actually less than these figures because of transportation charges, merchants' commissions, and deductions made for cotton below standard quality. Falling prices were accompanied by mounting costs of production including charges computed on advances under the crop-lien system, and the use of ever-increasing quantities of commercial fertilizer on depleted soils.

Daniel A. Tompkins, a thoughtful student of Southern economy, believed that, as a whole, cotton was produced at a loss after the Civil War. A report of the United States Senate Committee on Agriculture in 1893 specifically declared: "It is the general consensus of opinion that cotton cannot, except under the most favorable circumstances, be raised profitably at less than eight cents a pound, nor without a loss under seven cents." According to Holland Thompson the larger crops produced after 1870 because of improved methods of cultivation hardly brought the monetary returns of smaller crops of earlier years.

Conditions against which Thomas P. Kettell and other economists of the Old South had complained were accentuated by circumstances prevalent after the Civil War. The Northern victory resulted in the triumph of commerce and industry over agriculture. This meant that under the existing capitalist system more than a fair share of the profits of rural endeavor went into the pockets of merchants, bankers, and manufacturers. Farmers, landlords, and tenants alike, became ever poorer while city people grew increasingly richer.

The federal government fostered this state of affairs through policies of high tariffs and currency contraction, and failure to impose effective controls upon business. The middlemen regulated prices the farmer paid as a consumer and received as a producer. Through trade combinations business could direct production and distribution as a means of preventing losses caused by overproduction. The farmers—growers of Western wheat and corn as well as Southern cotton and tobacco—were told that overproduction accounted for the low prices. It was pointed out that the westward expansion of farm lands, improved methods of farming, and the enormous extension of ocean and railroad transportation had thrown upon the markets of the United States and the world more corn, wheat, cotton, and tobacco than the public could consume. The radical remedy for this condition should have been an organization of combines for the reduction of agricultural production similar to those of merchants and manufacturers. However, the farmers were not masters of the intricate tricks utilized by the capitalist economy; but they did attempt remedies of another nature.

The first organization of farmers to relieve the situation appeared soon after the Civil War. In 1866 Oliver H. Kelley, a clerk of the United States Bureau of Agriculture, distressed by the conditions of Southern farms, organized an association to promote agricultural welfare. The Patrons of Husbandry, better known as the Grange, by 1873 had 7,000 local organizations with ramifications in all but four states.

Despite the turmoil of Reconstruction, the Grange was firmly established in the South by 1871; two years later its membership totaled 210,000 in the states that had seceded. Since Negroes were not admitted to membership, the proportion of Southern whites in the organization was probably as high as that of whites in other sections of the country. The Southern farmer, notwithstanding his prejudices growing out of war and Reconstruction, had discovered that he had common interests with the farmers of other sections. The Grange claimed that it had fundamental remedies for rural ills. Through its frequent meetings and ceremonials in which women were allowed to participate it partly relieved the loneliness of the Southern farmer and his wife, whose isolation was almost as depressing as that experienced on Western ranches. The Grange's grandiose plans of co-operative buying and selling promised relief from capitalist demands. Nevertheless, after 1875 the organization disintegrated, its promises unfulfilled, its business enterprises mismanaged. Southern farmers were not ready to follow Western Grangers into independent political action; they prudently continued to accept the Democratic leaders who were freeing them from Negro rule. Nor were they willing to emulate Westerners in placing radical restraints upon the profits of railroad companies, because their services were too highly appreciated. Still the Granger movement was not without lasting influence on Southern life. Bourbon legislatures were persuaded to pass moderate railroad rate legislation. The Grange helped to develop class consciousness among farmers; it established a community of interest with the West; it implanted in people's minds the notion that legislation of an economic character, even as a remedy for poverty, was desirable. Other organizations were built upon foundations laid by the Grange.

In the New South, as in the Old, the thesis was proposed that the real remedy for agricultural distress was a partial adoption of more profitable nonagricultural undertakings. Thus towns, cities, and factories were built to alleviate in some measure the outstanding weakness of Southern economy—a one-sided devotion to agriculture. Some struggling landowners became clerks, prosperous merchants, or mill-owners, and many tenant farmers improved their incomes by becoming laborers in the new industries. Such moves, however, provided no remedy for the thousands who remained in agriculture. The fact that centers of industrial prosperity were shifted from distant cities to local towns only served to heighten the contrast between urban prosperity and rural poverty. The farmer now had additional reasons to bemoan his troubles.

Henry W. Grady suggested relief from the crop-lien system by encouraging loan companies such as those lending money on Western lands at relatively low interest rates. The insistence of loan companies on long-term credit failed to meet the short-term credit needs of the Southern landowner, and the loan companies had nothing to offer numerous tenant farmers with no land to mortgage. The lien merchant continued his exactions, quite willing to adjust his business to the necessities of those who sought short-term advances on growing crops.

A simpler, yet more fundamental, proposal from Grady was agricultural diversification as a direct remedy for overproduction of the great staples. The folly of unswerving devotion to cotton, and the consequent liberal purchase of food and feed in the face of ever-declining cotton prices was too obvious not to be fully recognized. Actually a considerable amount of diversification existed, but it was overlooked by Grady and others who exaggerated sectional ills. If the majority of farmers gave too much attention to cotton for their own good, it was because the lien merchants demanded this. The concentration on cotton had its advantages, and the ignorance of many farmers made the propaganda for diversification unintelligible to them. Many poor and uninformed farmers met the problem of falling prices caused by overproduction by still more production. When prices dropped, with balances against them mounting at the stores, they saw no escape except to rent more land and grow more cotton.

Whatever may be the opinion of the critic on the consequences of overproduction, southern farmers did not blame themselves for their plight. Conscious of their own virtues, they were accustomed to regard themselves as the "bone and sinew of the nation," the producers of "the largest share of its wealth." They resented the charges of provincialism and unscientific methods that city critics leveled against them. They complained "that it has become fashionable for every quill driver in the land to inform us, 'that we are not abreast of the age, that we don't know how to farm.'" They could not understand why those who had moved to towns and cities prospered while they did not; nor could they grasp why the harder they worked the less became the returns from their commodities. Evidently someone was "walking off with the surplus" and there were "certain influences at work, like thieves in the night."

Southerners joined Westerners in complaining against discriminatory freight rates and the merchant's right to fix prices on what the farmers bought and sold; and against tariff-protected trusts and financial policies that necessitated the payment of debts in dollars worth more in farm commodities than when these debts originally were contracted, so that a deflated dollar could buy twelve pounds of cotton when formerly it had bought six. There were protests over fertilizer, jute, and cottonseed-oil trusts which cheated farmers. To these grievances were added other complaints by Southerners. The grinding burden of the crop-lien system was supplemented by extensive chattel and land mortages. In Georgia, for example, evidences of foreclosures on chattels could be seen in the "pitiful heaps of . . . rubbish" that "commonly disfigured the court-house squares." Taxation added to the heavy load of the Southern farmer. His land was the principle source of public revenue, while other forms of wealth were often able to dodge or win exemption from taxation.

In the 1880's farmers formed the bulk of Southern population and, consequently, their grievances were paramount in explaining the political disturbances of the decade that followed. There were, however, sources of dissatisfaction not directly agrarian. The Bourbon statesmen, through the one-party system, continued to dominate the political life of the section. Although they generally furnished honest rule and satisfied the anti-Negro and anti-Northern prejudices of their constituencies, they were unconscious of any antiagricultural inclinations on their part. They gave the farmers moderate railroad rate legislation along with a certain amount of agricultural education and fertilizer inspection. In many cases, however, their selfish interests came first; they manipulated the political machines so that the rewards of office mostly fell to themselves and their friends. Indeed, their very impecunity and honesty made them especially avid for the spoils of office.

The Bourbons associated with important people of the towns—merchants, bankers, railroad executives, manufacturers, and lawyers—and they came to share the social and economic views of these business men. They enacted lien laws favorable to the merchants and maintained a *laissez faire* attitude toward the activities of railroads and other corporations. As advocates of the salvation of the South through industrialization, they did much to promote local business and to encourage the investment of Northern capital. While assiduously guarding business, however, they were in many respects blind to the farmers' needs.

A constant cause of resentment on the part of the humbler whites was the continued political dominance of the inhabitants of the lowland regions of those states having many more Negroes than whites. In many instances the Black Belt planters became heirs to the carpetbaggers in their ability to outvote the men of the hill country by marching submissive Negroes to the polls. In South Carolina, Wade Hampton proudly boasted that he was the first man in the South to advocate giving the Negro the right to vote. In Georgia, Benjamin H. Hill marched "arm in arm" to the polls with a Negro, "glad to be voted by a colored Democrat." Despite the upland dogma that Negroes were absolutely unfit for public office, members of that race were often given minor positions which otherwise would have been filled by petty white politicians.

True enough, the Negroes gradually became almost completely disfranchised through the violence and tricky election laws we have described.[1] Representation in legislatures and party conventions, however, continued to be apportioned according to population instead of the actual number of voters. This gave white politicians and landlords of the black sections an influence in state politics out of proportion to their numbers. Even in those states where the population of the Negro areas was less than that of the hill counties, the ability of lowland

[1] See above, p. 315.

politicians to manipulate conventions more than balanced preponderance in numbers. Thus white minorities located in the black belts and frequently in alliance with city politicians were able to direct the destinies of states. As early as 1876 the lowland bosses were warned, "The people are tired and heartily sick of the caucus rule. They long for an opportunity to throw off the galling yoke." [2]

Oppressive grievances were not enough to cause the white agricultural masses to revolt against urban and lowland rule. "The silent poor who never complain," in the South, as elsewhere, had neither the stamina nor the intelligence to seek their own salvation. The Negroes, the most abject victims of these agricultural maladies, showed no tendency to arise, and such reforms as others projected were designed almost exclusively for the white race. In fact, one complaint was that the Bourbons had not been sufficiently extreme in the suppression of Negro rights, so that white farm tenants were nearly as victimized by the agricultural system as the Negroes. These whites were enfranchised and played useful parts in the fight for farmers' rights; they were "the wool hats," "the plowboys," "the horny-handed sons of toil," and "the one-gallus boys" who put the ballots in the boxes. Yet within their own class they lacked leaders and political knowledge with which to acquire constructive benefits. The same applied to the small landowners, if in a lesser degree.

The large farmers and planters alone had the necessary intelligence and leadership to carry on an effective campaign against the Bourbons, the city politicians, and their business allies. These farmers suffered along with their tenants and less prosperous neighbors from the low price of cotton, from mortgages, and from the requirements of lien merchants. They resented the authority the lien laws gave merchants over small farmers and the pronounced tendency of the merchants to become landlords themselves. They were a proud group, more closely identified with the agrarian tradition of the Old South than were the merchants and the industrialists and their Bourbon friends. Although willing to seek novel remedies, they were too imbued with Southern traditions to go to extremes that might alienate public opinion. Perhaps their greatest contribution to Southern life was the promotion of the spirit of democracy through their appeals to the common white man. But with this forward step they satisfied inherited prejudices of their constituencies by furthering the Negro's political debasement.

The discontent of the 1880's found expression in a combination similar to the Grange of the 1870's—the Farmers' Alliance. This organization had its inception in Lampasas County, Texas, around 1875 when a group of frontier farmers combined to protect themselves

[2] C. Vann Woodward, *Origins of the New South, 1877-1913*, p. 81.

against cattle kings and foreign-owned land syndicates, and to purchase farm supplies co-operatively. In 1879 a Grand State Alliance was formed in Texas, and by 1887 this organization had spread to many counties of the state; by 1889 it attained widespread importance in the South. For a time the alliance served primarily as a social organization. But conditions were ripe for more extreme demands, and consequently the Texas group gained prestige by requesting adequate taxing of railroads, new issues of paper money, and laws for the regulation of interstate commerce. Meanwhile the agricultural Wheel and Brothers of Freedom of Arkansas and the Farmers Union of Louisiana were formed.

Under the leadership of Dr. C. W. Macune, a gifted agitator who had lived successively in Wisconsin, California, Kansas, California, and Texas, all these orders were consolidated into the National Farmers' Alliance and Co-operative Union of America, known as the Farmers' Alliance. Missionaries were sent forth to bring the entire cotton belt under its influence. Convinced that it would aid them financially, Southern farmers flocked into the organization by the tens of thousands. At a convention held at St. Louis in 1889 an attempt was made to merge the Southern group with similar ones that sprang up in the Middle West. Although this failed because of sectional prejudices and the insistence of the Southerners on secrecy, the two groups co-operated sufficiently to propose joint declarations favoring financial reforms of an inflationary nature, government ownership of railroads, the abolition of national banks, and legislation against the trusts and the sale of public lands to anyone except bona fide settlers. The following year the Southern Alliance adopted the famous Ocala platform; its chief feature was the Sub-Treasury plan, which called for the federal government's construction of warehouses for agricultural products. In these buildings the farmers planned to deposit their nonperishable products; in return they would receive 80 per cent of the market value in greenbacks. The Southern farmers had gone radical.

Ostensibly the main purposes of the Farmers' Alliance were of a social, educational, and commercial character. There were frequent lodge meetings and picnics; lecturers and farm journals spread enlightenment; co-operative buying and selling were attempted with temporary success. The real mission of the alliance, however, was political, for it was necessary to influence government in the interest of the reform program. Nevertheless, the Southern farmers did not organize a separate political party; only a minority joined members of the Western Alliance in 1891, and the Populist party in 1892. As an easier route to their objective, the majority chose to enter the Democratic primaries. The unfortunate experiences of Texas and Arkansas with independent farmers' parties taught the wisdom of not affronting Southern leanings toward the one-party system as the means of maintaining racial unity.

In state after state trained demagogues aroused among farmers the feeling that they were oppressed. The hatred of the "money power," "the trust," and the "hirelings of Wall Street," was locally reflected in sharp dislike for merchants, lawyers, and other residents. The dominant conviction prevailed that only farmers were wealth producers and other persons were parasites who fattened on the fruits of agricultural labor. This resentment extended to old political leaders whom the farmers once had venerated. Because the agricultural part of the voting population was in the majority, in many states the old leaders were replaced by farmers and their friends.

The most spectacular and far-reaching changes took place in South Carolina. There the contrast between the disabilities of the white masses of the rural districts and the privileges of the politicians of Columbia and Charleston was greater than in other states, and there the farmers found a man of unusual sagacity and daring to give direction to their discontent. He was Benjamin R. Tillman, a one-eyed rustic whose partial failure as a farmer stirred him to rebel against the privileges of the politicians and townsmen. Organizing the farmers of his state into an association, he later joined forces with the Farmers' Alliance, and in 1890, 1892, and 1894 won smashing victories that made him governor, United States senator, and complete political master of South Carolina.

Tillman raged up and down the state, frankly preaching class war. He made a clean sweep of the public offices, retiring United States Senators Wade Hampton and Matthew C. Butler, among others. Constructive reforms were introduced. The liquor business became a public monopoly known as the State Dispensary, under which no liquor could be consumed on the premises and the amount allowed each purchaser was limited. Tillman hoped that the evil of excessive drinking would be eliminated and that the profits of the monopoly would result in tax reductions. These aspirations, however, were not realized, and scandals concerning liquor purchases kept the state in a turmoil for two decades. Other Tillman legislation met more success. An agricultural and mechanical college for men, Clemson, and a normal and industrial college for girls, Winthrop, were established. Tax reforms were instituted and railroads were more effectively regulated. With one hand Tillman reduced the Negro to abject political impotence; with the other he increased the political power of the common white man. He accomplished the latter by arousing the political consciousness of the white masses and by extending the operations of the direct primary.

In other Southern states the farmers won victories in 1890 almost as signal as that of Tillman in South Carolina. In Georgia the Farmers' Alliance possessed sufficient prestige to nominate and elect a governor, most of the legislature, and six of the ten congressmen. Thomas E. Watson, a fiery and erratic young lawyer, was one of these congressmen. Leonidas L. Polk, president of the national Farmers' Alliance and editor of the *Progressive Farmer*, gave North Carolina's farmers effective leadership. They gained control of the machinery of the Democratic party, forced its state convention to express sympathy with "the efforts of the farmers to throw off the yoke of Bourbonism," and elected legislators and congressmen who endorsed agrarian reforms. Alliancemen captured 52 of the 100 seats of the Florida legislature. In Tennessee they named the governor and gave the legislature an agrarian slant by electing 14 of the 33 state senators and 40 of the 90 members of the lower house. In Alabama Reuben F. Kolb, the state leader of the alliance, was defeated for governor by a combination of Black Belt politicians, but the farmers claimed 75 of the 133 assemblymen. James S. Hogg was swept into the Texas governorship by an agrarian combination consisting of the alliance and his personal political machine.

The Farmers' Alliance was defeated in most Southern states in 1892 because it refused to heed Hogg's and Tillman's advice to remain within the Democratic party. The leaders of the farmers bolted to the Populist party because they were stirred to wrath by the continued control of the Democratic party by Grover Cleveland and his conservative Eastern friends. Among the bolters were men of substantial property and cultural interests like Leonidas L. Polk of North Carolina and Thomas L. Nugent of Texas, as well as Virginians with the names of Ruffin, Beverley, Cocke, Page, and Harrison, who were conscious of continuing the agrarian ideas of their ancestors. But most Southerners were shocked by the revolutionary language in which Populist orators such as Thomas E. Watson of Georgia and "Cyclone" Davis and "Stump" Ashby of Texas indulged. Southerners were worse shocked by the instances in which Populists cooperated with Republican and Negro minorities. Populist platforms denounced lynching and called for a defense of Negro rights. Some Negroes were given representation in the party councils. To an outside observer "the colour line seemed to have broken down." [3]

The Southern whites depended on unity within the Democratic party to prevent Negro participation in politics and were unwilling to tolerate any movement that might destroy this unity. Political pressures in the familiar Reconstruction pattern were exerted against the Populists. There were boycotts, ostracisms, discharges from jobs, and

[3] Charles B. Spahr, cited *ibid.*, p. 257.

appeals for campaign funds from Northern business and political interests. Populist orators were mobbed, fifteen Negroes were killed in Georgia, and James B. Weaver, the Populist candidate for President, was frightened out that state. In no Southern state did Weaver receive more than 37 per cent of the vote. Kolb in Alabama and Watson in Georgia suffered calamitous defeats.

In North Carolina alone, the insurgency of 1892 presaged future victory. There, in 1894 a combination of Republicans and Populists won control of the legislature, the two senatorships, and a majority of the congressional seats. Two years later this same coalition, aided by a law permitting each party to participate in the control of the election machinery, won the governorship and reaffirmed its control of the legislature and the congressional delegation. North Carolina temporarily experienced the distinction of being the only Southern state which allowed non-Democratic elements to participate freely in elections. This created the *bête noire* of Southern politics—the election of Negroes in considerable numbers. In 1898 North Carolina whites, with the sympathy of the entire South behind them, successfully rebelled against such infamy. Populist principles were thus proved less fundamental to Southern farmers than their inherited aversion to Negro rule.

Southern agrarianism did not die out with the widespread defeat of the Populists in 1892. Their rejection merely meant that the majority of Southern farmers refused to risk white unity for the untried benefits of a third party. Although they failed to dislodge Cleveland and his followers that year, they were, nevertheless, able to force Alliance and Populist doctrines upon Democrats in many states. In the elections of 1894 they retained what they had won, and in 1896 joined the radicals of the West to remove the Democratic presidential nomination from Cleveland's friends.

The victory of the reform element within the Democratic party was facilitated by President Cleveland's unpopularity, and by widespread endorsement of the free silver principle which the Chief Executive steadfastly opposed. Free coinage of silver was offered as a convenient means of inflation, enabling farmers to secure higher prices for their commodities and to discharge their debts for less than the prevailing standard of exchange. This was the essence of Populism.

The most ardent Southern champion of this doctrine was Tillman of South Carolina. A Democrat to the core because of his extreme aversion for Negro participation in politics, he nevertheless did not hesitate to denounce Cleveland. "Send me to Washington," he said to the cheering mobs who elected him to the Senate in 1894, "and I'll stick my pitchfork into his old ribs." The Silverites won control of all

Southern delegations to the national Democratic convention, including Virginia, a state that previously had lagged in reform movements. Southern Democrats had the pleasure of seeing Populism as a distinct political movement killed by their own party's adoption of Populist principles. Tillman destroyed his bid for the Presidential nomination by tactlessly admitting on the floor of the convention that the agrarian movement was sectional in character. To the more cautious William Jennings Bryan, a Westerner, went that honor. The white South accepted Bryan without general dissent, and the tradition of unquestioned loyalty to the Democratic party was re-established.

After Bryan's defeat in 1896 class consciousness among the farmers declined. The prosperity and higher prices that followed the Republican victory of that year softened demands for a more elastic currency. Sectional animosities gave way to the great wave of patriotism with which the South welcome the war with Spain in 1898. The Farmers' Alliance promptly disappeared from the American scene.

There is substance in the argument of twentieth-century radicals that the radicalism of the 1890's was superficial. That the farm leaders were not serious in their revolutionary profession is indicated by the fact that they elected General John B. Gordon to the United States Senate in 1890, that the alliance governor of Tennessee in the same year proved as conservative as his predecessors, and that several governors with farm support opposed the Sub-Treasury plan as a dangerous venture into state socialism. The supposed capture in 1896 of the Democratic party by men with Populistic beliefs had its sequel: the stifling of many of these beliefs by the conservatives in the old party. The most prominent Southern Populist who stood out against the merger understood what had happened when he wrote: "Our party, as a party, does not exist any more. Fusion has well nigh killed it." [4]

The agrarian revolt in the South merely served as an awkward interlude in the forward march of business, so auspiciously begun under the name of the New South. After 1898 more enterprising Southerners in increasingly large numbers flocked to the towns and cities; urbanism, industrialism, and commercialism achieved a firmer grip, and none remained in the rural areas with sufficient courage to organize other farmers' movements. Once again the conventional type of postbellum Southern politician took possession of popular fancy. He combined the pretentious chivalry of the Bourbon with an exceedingly practical, if unostentatious, championship of business interest; more often than not he was the hired attorney of one or several huge corporations. Those agrarian politicians who survived were Ben Till-

[4] Thomas E. Watson, cited *ibid.*, p. 289.

man, Tom Watson, and Jim Hogg. The South Carolinian became a conservative senator who repeated the phrases of his Bourbon predecessors. The Georgian retained a precarious hold upon the popular imagination by coupling an appeal to the sentiments of the Old South with attempts to incite anti-Catholic, anti-Jewish, anti-Negro, anticlerical and antiwar prejudices of the rural masses. The Texan sought Eastern capital for Texas investments and amassed a fortune as an old company promoter.

It should not be assumed that the agrarian revolt was without permanent effect. The farmers made another forward step toward the abandonment of their traditional individualism. Future requests for government intervention in the economic problems of the farm would be more far-reaching than under the Sub-Treasury plan. The demands of the Farmers' Alliance for the regulation of railroads, a graduated income tax, popular election of United States senators, and free delivery of rural mails were enacted into laws. The legislatures of the Southern states achieved advances in the regulation of corporations, in public education, and in the creation of more equitable tax systems.

Rural mass opinion hastened the legal ban upon the sale of alcoholic liquors. When Georgia and Oklahoma adopted statewide prohibition in 1907, 825 of the 994 counties in the former Confederacy had already secured this effect by local option. Even in Kentucky, the home of both a powerful liquor industry and of a still more powerful Baptist church, the cause of good bourbon had been lost in three fourths of the counties. By 1914 ten Southern states were wholly dry, and when national prohibition was submitted to the states some years later, all those below Washington were prompt in ratification. The antiliquor crusade in the South was essentially imposed by the whites of the rural and hill regions upon cities and lowland areas with large Negro populations. The evils of drink among all classes of both races became so evident that the majority among voters set aside their traditional prejudice against sumptuary laws in an heroic attempt to banish alcohol. The efforts of these reformers were disappointing, as liquor regulations were the most frequently violated laws among a people not distinguished for their law-abiding habits. Temporarily, however, prohibition made the purchase of alcohol more difficult and consequently reduced its consumption.

By overthrowing the Bourbon oligarchies the agrarian movement advanced the cause of political democracy. White masses were taught to exercise more effectively their inherited rights of suffrage and through the white primary were given an adequate means of using this power. Men like Ben Tillman and Tom Watson consistently demanded that the Declaration of Independence be used as a justification for the common white man's advance toward equality with the more privileged groups. After the agrarian revolt stirred the people, politicians of most Southern states encountered difficulties in gaining office when not in close touch with the common man. Although some of the leaders chosen for high office recalled the best traditions of Southern statesmanship, many were mediocre statesmen or even blatant demagogues who appealed to vulgar prejudices.

The most permanent result of the rise of the common white man was of a reactionary character. Despite many progressive manifestations, the triumph of agrarianism primarily meant the return of the most conservative region of the United States to its traditions. The awakening of the farmers constituted a revolt against the Bourbon cultivation of a new generation of carpetbaggers who settled in the South as business men. This feeling was brought to the surface by a realization that dissension between Bourbons and agrarians threatened white unity—a unity providing protection against carpetbaggery and Negroism. In South Carolina the Bourbons tried to defeat Tillman through an independent movement. Farmers in Alabama and Populists in other states also organized independent movements. Most shocking to Southern consciousness was the fact that for four years North Carolina had a non-Democratic government in which Negroes were conspicuous if not dominant. These developments were accompanied by Northern attempts to help Negroes obtain the votes their numbers justified.

The Lodge Force bill of 1890, providing for federal supervision of Congressional elections to the South's great alarm, had been defeated by an extremely narrow margin. Once more the South stood solid against the threat of Negro participation in politics. It was ready, as in Reconstruction days, to use fraud and violence to prevent any such "calamity." More reputable devices were sought to circumvent the Fifteenth Amendment legally without, at the same time, disfranchising the majority of Southern whites. Upon recalling that this section of the Constitution merely prohibited suffrage restrictions on grounds of race, shrewd men recognized the possibility of acting against the Negro's political rights on other grounds.

In 1890 Mississippi led the way with a new state constitution requiring long residence in the state and precinct and payment, on a more or less voluntary basis, of a two-dollar poll tax eight months preceding regular elections. Although these requirements theoretically applied to both races alike, they were designed to discriminate against the blacks. This they actually accomplished, because the Negro was notoriously migratory and generally too poor or improvident to pay for the privileges of voting far in advance of elections.

To insure double protection, the Mississippi constitution further provided that in addition to the poll tax and residence requirements the prospective voter must be able to read a section of the constitution, or "be able to understand the same when read to him, or give a reasonable interpretation thereof." Since no provision was made for bipartisan representation on the registration boards, there were obviously many opportunities for discrimination on political or racial grounds. "A reasonable interpretation," in the presence of white Democratic officials, could mean requiring a difficult or impossible explanation from a Negro, and the exact opposite from a white man. By 1896 the Republican vote in Mississippi had become negligible.

For a number of reasons most Southern states in the two decades after 1890 adopted their particular versions of the Second Mississippi plan. The subsidence of agrarian agitations made it possible for all factions of the Democratic party to unite against the old enemy of white supremacy: the Negro vote. A growing number of Republicans joined the Lily-White faction of their party which aimed at respectability through the elimination of the Negro from politics. The Second Mississippi plan became the American way when the United States Supreme Court in 1898 accepted as constitutional the suffrage provisions of the Mississippi constitution,[5] and when in the same year a Republican administration in Washington applied race discriminations in the newly acquired dominions of the United States. The implications of what was being done in Hawaii and the Philippines was not lost among Southern Democrats.

In 1895 residential and poll tax requirements similar to those of Mississippi were supplemented in South Carolina by a somewhat different "understanding clause." Until January 1, 1898, any male South Carolinian who fulfilled the residence and poll tax requirements and could read any section of the Constitution, or could understand and explain it when read by a member of a registration board consisting of "three discreet persons," earned the right to have his name entered on a permanent list of voters. The "understand and explain" alternative applied to the great mass of illiterate and non-property owning whites. After January 1, 1898, the prospective registrant was required to read and write any section of the Constitution, or to show proof that he paid taxes on property worth at least $300. Moreover, South Carolina's list of disqualifying crimes emphasized those of which Negroes were most commonly guilty.

Louisiana, in 1898, added the "grandfather clause" in order to protect those whites threatened with the loss of suffrage through application of the Mississippi and South Carolina literacy-or-property stand-

---

[5] *Williams v. Mississippi,* 170 U. S. 213.

ard. The latter requirement was waived in the case of those who had voted in any state before 1867, or were descendants of such persons, provided the prospective voters complied with residence and poll tax specifications as in Mississippi and South Carolina. Accordingly, suffrage in Louisiana was opened to white illiterates but closed to the unlettered Negro since none of his race had voted in Louisiana before the passage of the Reconstruction Acts in 1867. Governed by the constructive principle that it devolved upon white men of the future to equip themselves educationally for suffrage, the Louisiana consti- tution-makers allowed a grace period—a few months only—in which a person could avail himself of the chance to achieve a place on the vot- ing lists.

The new constitution which North Carolina adopted in 1900 made more liberal provisions for white illiterates. Any one whose voting was based on the suffrage of his post-bellum ancestors was permitted to continue this privilege until December 1, 1908. Alabama combined the South Carolina and Louisiana plans in 1901 by creating a per- manent voting list composed of veterans of wars and "men of good character who understand the duties and obligations of citizenship under a republican form of government." Oklahoma, although pos- sessing only a small Negro population, resorted to extreme suffrage dis- criminations in 1910. Unlike any other state, Oklahoma attempted to disfranchise permanently illiterate Negroes, while allowing their white counterparts to vote forever, and placed no time limit on registration under its "grandfather clause." In the meantime Georgia, Tennessee, Florida, Arkansas, and Texas accomplished disfranchisement by means of the poll tax and other devices.

Oklahoma's foolish desire to make the "grandfather clause" per- manent did not escape the vigilant eye of the United States Supreme Court. In June, 1915, that tribunal declared it unconstitutional on the grounds that a state could not re-establish conditions existing before the ratification of the Fifteenth Amendment.[6] The objectionable pro- vision, meanwhile, had allowed a whole generation of illiterate whites to enroll as voters, and the development of the Southern public school systems since 1900 made a loophole for illiterates scarcely necessary after 1915. Although other suffrage provisions of Southern constitutions were almost as obvious as the "grandfather clause" in their violation of the spirit of the Fifteenth Amendment, the Supreme Court failed to at- tack their validity. Possibly the tribunal felt the practical necessity of deferring to the white man's determination, within or without the law, to keep Negro voting at a minimum. Force, when needed to maintain white supremacy, was used unhesitatingly, as vividly illustrated by

[6] *Gwinn v. U. S.*, 238 U. S. 347.

occurrences in 1898 at Wilmington, North Carolina, and Phoenix, South Carolina. White mobs imposed bloody vengeance upon blacks for political activities in both these places.

A recent student of Southern politics [7] suggests that the formal methods of disfranchisement just described merely recorded an accomplished fact "brought about, or destined to be brought about, by more fundamental processes." Among these "more fundamental processes" was a means more effective in keeping the Negroes out of politics than either force or constitutional restrictions. It was the Democratic primary, a nongovernmental agency through which political contests were settled and in which only white men were allowed to participate. All candidates in primaries were pledged to support party nominees so as to present a united white Democratic front in the general elections. Since Republican opposition was usually negligible, general elections degenerated into formal ratifications of the primary results. So great was the prestige of the primaries that dissent from their results was synonymous with political and social suicide. The exclusion of Negroes from Democratic organizations was based on the claim that these were private associations which, like social clubs, were not subject to constitutional dictation concerning membership. When state legislatures converted primary rules into statutes in order to secure state government aid in preventing election frauds and other irregularities, the United States Supreme Court called a halt. In 1927 it declared a Texas statute excluding Negroes from Democratic primaries a violation of the Fifteenth Amendment.

The white South, however, refused to be checkmated in its determination to ban Negro suffrage. Some states removed the anti-Negro provisions of the primary laws from their statutes, leaving these discriminations to the party; others permitted a nominal number of blacks to vote, and depended upon custom and white administration of the primary machinery to exclude the bulk from politics. A more moderate group of states—Kentucky, Tennessee, and Maryland—allowed a considerable number to vote, with the proviso that they were "good" Negroes, who made no effort to champion men or measures deemed inimical to white interests. For a Negro to seek an elective office in a Southern state was abnormal; for one to achieve the nearly impossible feat of being elected would have caused a public scandal.

During the first decades of freedom saloons and soda fountains served the two races at the same bars; many eating places served the two races in the same rooms at separate tables; parks and public buildings were often interracial; and segregation was not strict in churches and public conveyances. The law only prohibited interracial marriages

[7] V. O. Key, Jr., *Southern Politics in State and Nation,* pp. 533-5.

and interracial schools. But in the New South, as in the Old South,[8] race distinctions increased with the growth of white democracy. This fact found expression in the Jim Crow laws. These acts of Southern legislatures prohibited, as far as practicable, all contacts between the two races implying or establishing social equality. Beginning with Florida in 1887, by 1907 all Southern states had separated the two races on railroad cars and other public conveyances. "A person of color" was broadly defined as one possessing a small fraction of Negro blood, usually one eighth. The prohibition of interracial schools was supplemented by bans on interracial associations in penal and charitable institutions, factories, restaurants, theaters, hotels, and most public places except the streets and the stores. Enforcement of these laws was facilitated by the United States Supreme Court decision of 1883 declaring the federal Civil Rights Act of 1875 unconstitutional and by its decision of 1897 declaring constitutional "separate, but equal" accommodations.[9]

Extension of the Jim Crow principle to additional aspects of race relations was officially checked in 1917, when the Supreme Court declared unconstitutional the ordinances of various cities requiring residential segregation on racial lines.[10] This decision, however, did not prevent the continuation and even extension, through legal subterfuge and social pressure, of the long-established custom of residential segregation. Almost the same fate has overtaken a series of Supreme Court decisions in the 1940's outlawing racial segregation on public conveyances engaged in interstate commerce.[11] Some Negroes eat in dining cars along with whites and continue to sit in unsegregated cars on trains moving into the South, but up to date, in 1952, Negroes in most Southern conveyances gravitate to the sections of trains and buses custom assigned to them.

By 1910 the third period of Southern politics since the Civil War had run its course. The first of these was Reconstruction, which failed in its principal objective to give the Negro political rights; it survived only as a promise of the equality supposedly guaranteed all Americans. The second period was Bourbon rule, which re-established the cult of the Southern gentleman, and taught the wisdom of seeking political power through co-operation of the statesman and businessman. It came to an end because it did not heed the demands of progressive democracy. During the third period—the subject of this chapter—the common man sought to win rights for the agricultural majority, and for the great masses of whites in general. Notable re-

[8] See above, p. 108.
[9] *Plessy v. Ferguson*, 163 U. S. 537.
[10] *Buchanan v. Warley*, 245 U. S. 16.
[11] *Morgan v. Virginia*, 328 U. S. 373.

sults were accomplished; the common whites were taught to exercise effectively their political power through the Democratic primaries; discriminatory legislation against the political and social rights of the Negro created the sort of equilibrium the South had long desired.

Doubtlessly the era of the common man was more lasting in its results than either of the two periods that preceded it. Still it fell short of the needs of the second and third decades of the twentieth century. Revived traditions and the spread of popular culture called for leaders less crude than those inherited from the agrarian revolt. There was a renewed demand for the Southern gentleman, and for leaders in close touch with business interests. The new age sought leaders whose conception of government was broad enough to satisfy a multitude of social needs.

CHAPTER XXIII

Educational Revival

>>>->>>

THE TWIN enthusiasms of statesmen of the New South were industrial and educational development. For numerous reasons the industrial revival of the 1880's was not accompanied by comparable educational activities. Poverty and debts inherited from war and Reconstruction led to sharp cuts of all tax levies, including school revenues. Some men of means opposed school taxes for selfish reasons, but most of the antagonism came from the poor and illiterate. "It has sometimes seemed," remarked Holland Thompson,[1] "that the poorer a man and the larger the number of his children, the greater his dread of taxation for education." Informed persons, clinging to the conservative tradition, held that education should not be a function of the state any more than provision for food and shelter. Governor F. W. M. Holliday of Virginia considered public schools "a luxury . . . to be paid for like any other luxury, by the people who wish their benefits."[2] Thousands of rustics with individualistic traits resented the curbs that schools necessarily imposed upon the freedom of family life, and were slow to recognize the somewhat intangible advantages of education. Sparsity of population and rural isolation, in the New South as in the Old, were barriers to an institution that always thrives best in well-populated centers. There were those who opposed public education because it interfered with already existing schools supported and directed by religious denominations.

A few conservatives like the theologian Robert L. Dabney objected to the leveling effect of public education—the creation of a condition

[1] *The New South*, p. 170.
[2] Cited in C. Vann Woodward, *Origins of the New South*, p. 61.

((362))

in which "the children of the decent must become companions of the children of the vile." [3] Opposition grew appreciably when it was suggested that this leveling might include both races. Mixed schools were not to be tolerated; hence, if universal education were to be effective, two school systems would have to be established—one for whites, the other for blacks. Many of the whites resented taxes to support Negro schools. The experiences of Reconstruction convinced them that educating the blacks would only make them unfit for the subordinate role assigned them in Southern society. It was generally asserted, "An educated Negro is a good plowhand spoiled." Indeed, the smattering of education the average Negro received improved neither his efficiency nor his morals; his initial enthusiasm for "book learning" was succeeded by a dull indifference and a general reluctance to attend school at all.

A list of the deficiencies of the schools at the end of the nineteenth century seems unbelievable in the light of subsequent improvements. In 1900 the amount provided for each child of school age ranged from $.50 in Alabama and North Carolina to $1.46 in Florida and Texas. At that time the average for the United States as a whole was $2.84. The school term for the South averaged less than 100 days out of the year against 145 days for the United States as a whole. Teachers were poorly trained and earned an average annual salary of only $159 as compared with a national average of $310. Kentucky alone among Southern states required school attendance of children; consequently in the South as a whole less than 40 per cent of the potential school population attended regularly. Only one pupil out of ten who enrolled remained in school long enough to reach the fifth grade. Administration and supervision were often left to unsuccessful lawyers, broken-down ministers, or other incompetents, and courses of study were determined by the whims or capacities of individual teachers. School-houses, especially those in the rural districts, were frequently dilapidated structures lacking windowpanes and classroom equipment. The average value of school buildings was $276. Outside the cities little attempt was made in the public schools to bridge the gap between the grammar grades and college.

What a German emigrant found in a South Carolina school in 1890 scarcely exaggerated general conditions. His teacher, writes Ludwig Lewisohn,[4] "sat by the window, smoking a pipe and chewing tobacco at the same time. There, in a weary mechanical way, he heard the lessons which we were supposed to have prepared in the other bare

[3] Cited in Thomas C. Johnson, *The Life and Letters of Robert Lewis Dabney*, p. 397.
[4] *Up Stream*, pp. 46–8.

room or on the porch of the windy and abandoned cottage. The ten or twelve pupils played and studied behind the sunken-eyed old man in a half-hearted kind of way; the manner and the mood of the place float to me across the years in images of chill discouragement and mouldering desolation."

The educational deficiencies found expression in the survival in 1900 of 1,198,744 native white illiterates and 2,637,774 colored illiterates ten years of age and over. This was approximately 12 per cent of the South's whites and 50 per cent of its Negroes. Ironically this condition could be explained—even justified—by the circumstances of Southern life. The number of children to educate in proportion to adult population was twice as large in the South as in the North. The amount of taxable wealth per child of school age was so small that the Southern school tax rates would have been five times as great as those of the North to provide equal school funds. Furthermore, the South bore the extra expense of two school systems for the two races.

The period around the turn of the century held some measure of educational promise. There was no deliberate or general repudiation of the obligation assumed by the states under Reconstruction to give free education to all children of both races. Negro schools were maintained and were less discriminated against in the distribution of funds than were those of later generations. Under white supervision colored schools were purged of many of the social and intellectual heresies that had made them so repulsive to whites during Reconstruction. Reduced school appropriations were gradually restored to former levels as public opinion leaned toward general education.

This sentiment was most pronounced among members of the new middle class created by industrial and commercial advancement. Increased wealth inevitably resulted in higher school revenues; cities and towns, despite the prevalence of restrictive legislation, learned to levy supplementary taxes for educational purposes. The establishment of teachers' institutes, reading circles, and normal schools improved the quality of instructors of both races. The school term was gradually lengthened and, in many instances, fairly adequate school buildings replaced commonplace cabins.

The public schools of the South greatly profited by the generosity of George Peabody, a Massachusetts banker. Between 1867 and 1869 he set aside an endowment of three and a half millions for this purpose. The first active administrator of this fund was the Reverend Barnas Sears, president of Brown University. He was not the conventional Yankee missionary with an uncompromising social and educational philosophy. Sears, co-operating with Southern educational officials, established model schools, provided subsidies through which

existing institutions could be improved, and fostered teacher training. The Peabody Normal College was founded at Nashville in 1875.
Legislatures, school trustees, and interested citizens were tactfully
given advice whenever they requested it.

After Sears died in 1880 Jabez L. M. Curry became administrator.
This Southerner supplemented a military and political career by service
as a Baptist minister and professor in a Baptist college. A thoroughgoing native with a gift for oratory, he could speak more freely of
the value of education for both races than his predecessor. Addressing
legislatures from the Potomac to the Rio Grande, Curry proved the
most persuasive champion of schools that the South had possessed up
to that time.

During the Bourbon period efforts of the common schools were
supplemented by the academies and colleges which were revived or
created in the post-bellum years of recovery. The academies were
few in number compared with the high schools that later supplanted
them; they had scant scientific apparatus and few books and were
not well graded; their courses of study were limited and unconcerned
with the actualities of contemporary life; their teachers were unacquainted with the concepts of progressive pedagogy. But many instructors developed a genuine passion for Latin, mathematics, and
rhetoric, and sent to the colleges students who were thoroughly, if
narrowly, prepared. Of the Charleston school of this type, Ludwig
Lewisohn observes that he was "taught to study with thoroughness
and accuracy under pain of tangible and very wholesome penalties" by
a principal who followed the precepts of Arnold of Rugby. The same
could be said of the Bingham School in North Carolina, the Webb
School in Tennessee, the Episcopal High School in Virginia, and a
dozen or more academies scattered throughout the South.

The colleges suffered the losses of ante-bellum endowments. The
total available annual income of sixty-six colleges and universities in
seven Southern states in 1901 was less than that of Harvard alone.
Southern institutions enjoyed the income from only $14,000,000 of the
$157,000,000 endowments of all American colleges and universities. The
problem of higher education in the South was accentuated by an over-
abundance of colleges competing among themselves for tuition fees.
Many of them, moreover, were bound by standards of religious orthodoxy and sectional prejudice that hampered the free play of the mind.
Professors were poorly paid. Their average annual salary in forty-four
of the better white colleges was about $840. Most of the professors
lacked extensive formal training, and few could claim distinction in
letters or scholarship. As a whole they were little influenced by the
newer concepts of education that were entering the United States from

Germany by way of Harvard and Johns Hopkins. The New South produced no Jefferson to broaden its ideas of higher education.

Nevertheless Southern colleges were making some progress. Under the stimulus of the federal aid afforded by the Morrill Act of 1862, auspicious beginnings were made in agricultural and mechanical education. A few professors trained in German seminars found their way into the more progressive universities, and beginnings were made in literary and scholarly expression. Moreover, the Southern colleges had certain strong points not taken into account by the quantitative analyses of the educational experts. What the clergymen and gentlemen on teaching staffs lacked in technical training and scholarship was compensated for by their striking personalities, genteel worldliness, and high ethics. Such characteristics probably were more impressive to many students than a greater amount of scholarship.

Professors of the Bourbon period were not spiritual or social outcasts; rather, they were forces for social and intellectual uplift in their communities. Their students were serious, conducting themselves in the classrooms as men, not as boys. Many of them were twenty-five to thirty years of age, men whose education had been postponed by war and Reconstruction. They were interested solely in study and fostered no organized athletics, no dramatic or musical clubs or other extracurricular activities, except the literary societies that provided training in public speaking.

Forces in operation at the beginning of the twentieth century opened the way for educational progress. Among these were the increase of industrial and commercial wealth, the appearance of an ambitious middle class, the awakening of the farmers to the need of reform, and the subsidence of political phases of the race issue. In addition, there was need for organized agencies to spread information and lead people into accepting a broad definition of the educational function. Toward that end, Robert C. Ogden, a New York philanthropist, inspired and financed a series of annual conferences on education. The first meeting of the Ogden movement was held at Capon Springs, West Virginia, in the summer of 1898. Influential people from North and South were brought together to consider the educational problems of the South and related topics. Agencies were organized to collect funds and to inaugurate campaigns for better schools. The field work was directed by eminent Southern educator-orators such as Jabez L. M. Curry, Edwin A. Alderman, and Charles D. McIver.

An unparalleled enthusiasm for public schools seized most sections of the South, culminating in the great fourth meeting of the Ogden Conference at Winston-Salem in April, 1901. Delegates came from all sections of the region, and Ogden brought on a special train a number of prominent Northerners including John D. Rockefeller, Jr. Intensive state canvasses were carried on in North Carolina in 1902, in Tennessee in 1903, in Georgia in 1904, in South Carolina, Alabama, Virginia, and Mississippi in 1905, Louisiana in 1906, Kentucky and Arkansas in 1908, and Florida in 1909. Popular opinion held that it was the duty of public authorities to prepare for the time when "grandfather clauses" in state constitutions would no longer confer on illiterates the right to vote. Taking advantage of this trend, educators enlisted the aid of political leaders, including Governors Charles B. Aycock of North Carolina, Andrew Jackson Montague of Virginia, Braxton B. Comer of Alabama, Napoleon B. Broward of Florida, and Hoke Smith of Georgia. The chief contributions of the governors was to dispel opposition to the inclusion of the Negro in the new dispensation.

Results were immediate. The educational provisions of state laws and constitutions were revised; between 1900 and 1910 school revenues were generally increased 100 per cent, in some states twice that much. In the short span of ten years, illiteracy decreased from 27 to 18 per cent and the school term grew from an average of 96 to 121.7 days. A rise in teachers' salaries was accompanied by the establishment of additional normal schools and departments of pedagogy in colleges and universities, and the enforcement of standards of teacher certification.

The movement for the consolidation of small rural schools into larger graded units was inaugurated, followed by the setting up of rural libraries, school improvement leagues, and parent-teacher associations. Tennessee, North Carolina, Virginia, Arkansas, and Louisiana wrote compulsory education into their statutes. Although there was still much to be done, the carpetbaggers' promise of universal education in the South approached fulfillment in 1910; native leaders, of course, had succeeded the men who originally imported the idea from New England.

Forward strides taken in the second and third decades of the twentieth century practically realized the ambitions of the educational agitators of 1900. With interest in public education so widespread, a phenomenal increase in school appropriations became inevitable. In one state where the zeal of the people for education was by no means unique the value of school properties increased one hundred times between 1900 and 1930. During these three decades annual appropriations of all Southern states for public schools rose from $28,000,000 to $415,000,000, or fifteen times the original sum. In Oklahoma appropriations were 48 times as great, and in North Carolina 38.

Although the 1930 expenditures for the education of the average Southern child was far below the national average, "five Southern states ranked higher than the average for the nation in the percentage of total income appropriated for school purposes." [5] Southern states maintained a larger ratio of their total population in schools than other states. In Mississippi the ratio was 34 per cent compared to less than half this percentage in Rhode Island, New Hampshire, and Delaware. Many Southern towns and cities developed schools that were in a class with those of similar communities in the North and West. The municipal high school supplanted the privately directed academy by 1930, and only in the more sophisticated centers did rich men feel the need of supporting select private schools to prepare their children for college. Multiplication and improvement of high schools were largely due to the expert advice of professors of secondary education in the state universities. A continued backwardness of the rural schools was partially remedied by additional mergers of small, ineffective schools into larger, better-graded units. The consolidation movement became possible through a growing willingness of communities to provide the improved roads and motor buses necessary to transport children beyond walking distances. More than one third of the nation's school buses operated in the South.

Another aid to rural school was fiscal reform, which tended to shift the burden of support from local administrative units to the states. Thus, the richer centers of population were compelled to help support the schools of poorer and less populated communities. Federal support of vocational education made this principle nationwide by forcing the country as a whole to share its bounties with the poorer Southern section. This type of support was inaugurated in 1914 and 1917. Legal barriers protecting the low attendance records of the Southern schools were cleared in 1918, when Mississippi became the last state of the section to adopt a compulsory attendance law. Following the example set by North Carolina in 1919, all Southern states to a greater or lesser degree shouldered the obligation of caring for dependent, delinquent, and defective children. Instead of rejecting these pupils, schools assumed the difficult task of correcting their deficiencies. Reformatories were provided for incorrigibles and criminals.

Schools broadened their functions further. "Illiteracy commissions" and "moonlight schools" were founded to eliminate what was regarded as the shameful prevalence of adult illiteracy. The traditional three R's were supplemented by health education and inspection, courses in citizenship, attention to vocational education—especially home economics and agriculture, and by general acceptance of the belief that the main task of the school was to prepare the modern child for his complex and ever-changing environment.

[5] Howard W. Odum, *Southern Regions of the United States,* p. 103.

The educational triumphs of the South during the twenty-odd years since 1930 have been almost as spectacular as those during the thirty years before that date. The section was stirred into action by those who emphasized the deficiencies of its schools and by the conviction that education was the key to social and material progress. It was willing to spend for this purpose a larger proportion of its total public revenues than the rest of the nation. Total annual expenditures for operating the public schools rose from $415,000,000 in 1930 to $1,214,000,000 in 1951. In every town there arose an edifice of learning comparable in size and equipment to the cathedrals of medieval Europe. The number of teachers employed in Texas rose to 50,000; Virginia, with 20,000, had a larger corps of teachers than Lincoln had soldiers when the Civil War began. Teachers' salaries rose from an average salary of $159 in 1900 to averages ranging between $1,462 in Mississippi and $3,100 in Texas.

Education, analogous to other planned projects of Southern life, was primarily for the benefit of the white two thirds of the population. The interests of the Negro minority, however, were not entirely neglected by white officials who controlled the schools. If the greatest progress of the Negro during the Reconstruction period was in the field of education, this was also true in the years following the overthrow of the carpetbaggers. While experiencing stagnation and even retrogression in many aspects of political, social, and economic life, the race enjoyed unchecked advances in formal schooling. The illiteracy rate of the Southern Negro fell from about 70 per cent in 1880 to about 10 per cent in 1940. In 1920 one half of the Southern Negro children were enrolled in school, but the attendance record of the race was gradually catching up with that of the whites. In South Carolina, for example, 59.1 per cent of the Negro children were enrolled as compared with 60.7 per cent of the whites, while in Oklahoma the difference in length of school term in favor of the whites was only twelve days, and in North Carolina only thirteen days. By 1950 these differences had been generally destroyed because of the zeal of truant officers and administrators interested in the lengthening of school terms.

The movement for the establishment of Negro high schools assumed South-wide proportions by 1920, and 1,860 such institutions existed by 1928. The number of Negro high-school graduates increased from 9,640 in 1930 to 31,180 in 1944. The $3 spent in 1910 for the education of the average Negro child rose to four times that amount by 1930, and the average annual salary of Negro teachers climbed from $106 in 1900 to $423 thirty years later. By that time some states were spending as much on Negro schooling as all education had cost in 1900.

These evidences of advancement in Negro instruction were accompanied by a gradual awakening of the more enlightened segment of white opinion to their educational needs. Governor Aycock of North Carolina, although favoring the political repression of the Negro, willingly conferred upon him the benefits of universal education. His views were shared by such progressive leaders as Henry W. Grady, Walter Hines Page, and a large company of newspaper editors and churchmen. Booker T. Washington, perhaps the most distinguished Southern Negro of all time, dispelled prejudice by postponing political and social ambitions for the race, and by stressing the needs of industrial education. He put his theories into practice at Tuskegee, an institution founded in Alabama in 1881 on the model of Hampton Institute in Virginia.

State appropriations for Negro education, although substantial, were meager in comparison with the sums provided for white education. This disparity was partly remedied from other sources. Federal subsidies for vocational education were divided equally between the races, and Northern and Negro missionary agencies continued to maintain numerous private schools as during Reconstruction. In 1916 the annual income of 653 schools of this type was more than $3,000,000.

Efforts of the Peabody Fund and the General Education Board (a John D. Rockefeller philanthropy) in behalf of the education of both races were supplemented by Northern funds devoted to Negro schooling exclusively. The John F. Slater Fund, established by a gift of a million dollars in 1882, encouraged teacher training. The Anna T. Jeanes Fund of the same amount was used to employ rural school supervisors, and the Caroline Phelps Stokes Fund, amounting to almost a million dollars, was applied to research in education and kindred problems. Julius Rosenwald, president of Sears, Roebuck and Company of Chicago, donated many millions to help build 5,357 Negro schools in fifteen states under a plan by which the Rosenwald gifts were supplemented by subscriptions of private individuals and local government agencies. The Negroes themselves were thereby encouraged to give what they could to the Rosenwald schools.

The development of Southern public schools in the twentieth century was accompanied by a growth almost as striking in the field of higher education. By 1900 Southern colleges were emerging from the doldrums of the post-bellum period. Their first need was to obtain adequate revenues and enrollments to support the numerous institutions fostered by separatist trends in race, religion, or sex. In 1930 there were 120 four-year colleges on the accredited list of the Southern Association of Colleges and Secondary Schools, some of them representing "faith and hope or denominational zeal rather than accomplishments." Since good preparatory schools were few and colleges were largely dependent upon tuition fees for their survival, standards of admission were low. One college president frankly admitted, "We are liberal about letting young men into the freshman class but particular about letting them out." [6] Vanderbilt University, founded in Nashville in 1872 through the generosity of Cornelius Vanderbilt, set an example to other institutions by insisting upon adequate preparation for entrance. The Southern Association of Colleges and Secondary Schools, founded in 1895, partially succeeded in fixing higher standards.

Among other endowed institutions were Tulane University, established in New Orleans in 1884, and Emory, which moved to Atlanta in 1919 to become a university. The General Education Board gave $3,-000,000 to various Southern institutions of higher learning. Educational endowments reached their peak in 1924 when James B. Duke gave Trinity College at Durham $40,000,000 to enlarge it into Duke University. The legislative appropriations for the average Southern university rose from $117,000 in 1906 to a figure many times that sum twenty-five years later. Technological, medical, and teachers colleges enjoyed similar increases. As a result by 1930 the Southeastern states were spending on higher education a greater percentage of their total income than the rest of the United States, 0.30 per cent compared with 0.19 per cent for the Middle states.[7]

Through extension courses and other less deliberately planned activities, institutions such as the University of North Carolina and the Virginia Polytechnic Institute affected the lives of thousands not within academic precincts. In 1930 more than half of the 7,545 agricultural extension workers of the nation operated in the South.

Admittedly many Southern institutions of higher learning were more distinguished for the size of their buildings and the number of their students than for the quality of their instruction. All too frequently their reputations rested upon the excellence of their football teams and the seating capacity of their stadiums, rather than upon the number of books in their libraries or their capacity to disseminate knowledge. The desire for increased enrollments often prevented more than a fictitious raising of standards, and led to the admission of thousands of poorly prepared students from many new high schools. Some college and university presidents unabashedly sacrificed tolerance and culture for endowments from capitalists and politicians. Toward the benefactors of their institutions they were sycophantic, and toward dissenting faculty members and students, tyrannical. An atmosphere of indifference and often hostility toward artistic and literary values frequently

[6] Cited in Holland Thompson, *op. cit.*, p. 187.
[7] Odum, *op. cit.*, p. 103.

prevailed, even in institutions provided with adequate libraries and expert teaching staffs. Campus book stores where students could purchase tools of learning other than those in immediate demand in classrooms were practically nonexistent; too often, students could merely appreciate the vocational and tangible.

By 1930 scarcely a single Southern college for men had attained the standards reached by fifteen or twenty colleges of the Eastern states. By relinquishing quality, however, Southern universities and colleges performed a worthy function of democracy: the duty of bringing to rural youths benefits which in more conservative communities were the exclusive possession of aristocrats and townspeople. Moreover, Southern universities were not devoid of scholarly achievement. The University of North Carolina, under the leadership of Professors Eugene C. Branson, J. G. de Roulhac Hamilton, and Howard W. Odum, introduced scientific, historical, economic, and social research to provide a rational explanation of the section's past and present. The English departments of Vanderbilt University and Louisiana State University vied with each other as centers of literary criticism and creative writing. Louisiana State University won fame for its researches in sugar culture, as did North Carolina State College in the textile industry. A University of Oklahoma group thoroughly studied the culture of the Indians, and others at the same institution made important contributions to the findings of the oil industry. *The Virginia Quarterly Review* (University of Virginia) became one of the "quality" magazines of the nation. Other faculty-sponsored magazines of the same standard but more limited in their appeal were *The South Atlantic Quarterly* (Duke University), *The Sewanee Review* (University of the South), *Social Forces* (University of North Carolina), *Southwest Review* (Southern Methodist University), *Books Abroad* (University of Oklahoma), *The Journal of Southern History* (Louisiana State University and University of Kentucky). The University of North Carolina Press, under the direction of William T. Couch, ranked as one of the foremost university publishing agencies of the nation. It produced many significant books on Southern subjects. The presses of the University of Oklahoma, Duke University, and Louisiana State University rivaled in productiveness that of the North Carolina institution.

Students of Southern progress stress the fact that according to almost all accepted norms educationally the South lagged behind the rest of the United States in 1930. This was true despite the enormous strides that the schools of the section had taken since 1900. In 1930 the annual school term in the South was shorter than the national average by a month and a half; the typical Southern child attended school less than three fourths as many days as children elsewhere in the country; the average salary of the Southern teacher was only 60 per cent of the national level. In the same year the expenditure per pupil for the nation was $99 as compared with $44.31 for the Southern white child. Despite the vast material progress which has been made since 1930 the comparative deficiencies of Southern education have not been destroyed. In 1951 the lowest average teachers' salaries were paid in Mississippi, Arkansas, South Carolina, and Kentucky.

The situation appears worse when the Negro is brought into the comparative rating. The average annual expenditure for the Southern Negro child amounted to only $12.57—one eighth the national average, or one fourth of that for the Southern white pupil. Mississippi spent only $5.45 on each Negro, or less than one ninth the white average for the state. In the thirty years preceding 1930 the proportion of school revenues provided for the average Negro child declined from one half to one fourth of the white average. During the same period the average salary of Negro teachers decreased from 65 per cent to 47 per cent of the usual salary of white teachers. Evidently twentieth-century educational progressives were unwilling to grant to Negroes as large a share of the school revenues as their conservative predecessors of the late nineteenth century. In the rush to advance the white child the Negro often was forgotten.

In higher education this comparative neglect was almost as great. In 1938 South Carolina spent $82,500 on the higher education of Negroes and $1,445,900 on that of whites; for Alabama these figures were respectively $76,600 and $1,906,000. The same proportions in the South as a whole prevailed in 1944 as in 1930. Negro colleges got only 5.8 per cent of the total college and university revenue.

Since 1940, as we shall see,[8] much progress had been made toward equalizing the educational facilities of the two races. But still there is much to do. In 1952 the best available statistics indicated that a capital outlay of $1,596,000,000 would be necessary to bring the Negro schools of the South up to the level of the white schools, and that at least $81,-000,000 would have to be spent annually to maintain this parity.

The disparity in the educational opportunities of the two races becomes more acute when it is realized that unintelligent use of the meager funds provided for Negro education occurred frequently. It seems that neither Booker T. Washington nor his white sponsors were aware that the type of industrial education provided by Negro schools was concerned with handicrafts which were being supplanted by machine production. The students of these schools, as true Americans with ambition, "follow other than the industrial pursuits when they are graduated." [9]

[8] See below, p. 574.
[9] W. D. Weatherford, *Negro Life in the South*, p. 50.

The numerous Negro "universities" and "colleges" failed to fulfill their objectives; only three of them could properly be called colleges in 1916 —Howard University in Washington, and Fisk University and Meherry Medical College in Nashville.[10] In 1932 six Negro colleges were placed in Class A of the Southern Association of Colleges and Secondary Schools; but in 1949 only three Negro colleges were recognized by the American Association of Universities and Colleges.[11]

The Negro colleges suffered from an exaggeration of the evils of the white colleges. The cultural background of the average student was poor and did not improve with increased enrollments. Students and faculty lived in the isolation of upper-class Negro society where "a real scholar is still an oddity." [12] The Negro college president was frequently a unique type of autocrat responsible only for his many sins against scholarship—and sometimes against morals—to distant Northern trustees or to indifferent white politicians.

The most fundamental inadequacy of Negro education was its failure to promote social equality, a service American education is expected to perform. The white South justified its failure to provide this service because of its standards of race purity and white supremacy. The fact that the schools were forced to separate the races in the classrooms meant to the Negro child denial of opportunities for cultural contacts with members of the supposedly superior white race. The intellectual and mechanical practices of the racially segregated school, however excellent they may have been in themselves, were not adequate substitutes for free and democratic association with those who controlled cultural, industrial, and social opportunity. Therefore, the actual cultural inferiority of the Southern Negro was far greater than one might infer from an uncritical examination of statistics of educational progress.

The relative backwardness of Southern schools could not be attributed to some malevolent conspiracy against public welfare which might be remedied by constructive propaganda, but to seemingly immutable circumstances of Southern life. In 1930 the South spent on education a greater portion of its zeal and total resources than the North; the difficulty was that its total resources were too meager to provide schools as good as those of other sections of the United States. The estimated value of all Southern property divided by the number of the section's children of school age gave a figure only one third as high as that of the North. For each 1,000 males in the South there were 1,300 children; the corresponding figures for the North and West were, respectively, 800 and 600. Moreover, the school population of the South

[10] United States Bureau of Education, *Negro Education*, II, 16.
[11] E. Franklin Frazier, *The Negro in the United States*, p. 485.
[12] *Ibid.*, p. 480.

was not only more scattered than that of most sections of the North, but expensive duplication of separate school systems for the two races was imposed by the Southern social order. The difference in the income of these two systems was accepted by the public. It was claimed that the Negroes received in educational services more than they paid in taxes. The Virginia state auditor, for example, pointed out that the Negroes of his state paid in taxes about $60,000 annually and received $420,000 for school purposes.[13] The districts which voted for high school taxes had comparatively few Negroes; besides, colored teachers in the free labor market were paid less than their white colleagues because other fields of employment did not compete for the services of educated blacks. Among Negroes, too, there was little demand for the more expensive types of schooling.

For seventy years following Reconstruction Southern schools consistently made progress. The meager funds provided for them during the Bourbon period found compensation in a steady adherence to the doctrine of education for all children, including those whose parents had been slaves. The colleges in existence then were poor in material goods and restricted in the range of studies and freedom of expression; yet they afforded a training at once thorough and morally inspiring. The first decade of the twentieth century witnessed an educational resurgence comparable in emotional intensity to the great religious revival which captured the imagination of Southerners some hundred years earlier. Indeed, education became a second religion. Faith in organized Christianity, as a means of achieving moral rectitude and heavenly salvation, was supplemented by a firm belief in public education as a shortcut to worldly success. Southern schools became more pretentious and expensive and attracted greater attendance than churches. Unlike the churches the schools were allowed to invoke the power of the state to compel financial support and attendance. Certainly Southern schools made vast quantitative progress between 1900 and 1930. That period marked the erection of numerous buildings of expanding colleges and universities and the consolidation of elementary and high schools, attracting thousands of students daily. Yet there were reasons to believe that the quality of Southern schools in 1930 showed no improvement over that of 1900. The white schools continued to fall behind those of the North, the Negro schools behind those of the white South. Emphasis was placed on elaborate building programs and physical demands rather than on the quality of teachers and instruction. Fine institutions of learning were often confused with good buildings. A more subtle deficiency was the unwillingness of Southern people to accept the intellectual discipline necessary to give their high schools and colleges

[13] Colonel Ruffin, cited in Thomas N. Page, *The Old South*, p. 336.

high scholastic standards. Superficiality, even sham, characterized the schools of the South to a marked degree. Friends of education, however, did not despair; they asserted that these deficiencies were the inevitable results of a relatively young school system assigned the difficult task of promoting rural democracy.

CHAPTER XXIV

Society in the New South

⇛⇛⇛⇛⇛⇛⇛⇛⇛⇛⇛⇛⇛⇛⇛⇛⇛⇛⇛⇛⇛⇛⇛⇛⇛⇛⇛⇛⇛⇛⇛⇛⇛⇛

THE MOST important development in Southern society after the Civil War was the shift of control from the agricultural aristocracy to men of industry and commerce. Earlier chapters described how the Civil War smashed the power of the great landowners and how that struggle was followed by the economic rise of merchants, bankers, and industrialists. The storekeeper assumed the position held by the planter, and Bourbon political leaders, despite their fine manners and old-fashioned oratory, were modern enough to heed the demands of business men, the actual masters of the counties and states they represented. Just as the enterprising citizen of the Old South aspired to become a planter with slaves and broad acres, his counterpart in the New South was eager to become a wealthy business man with holdings in town property and mortgages on farm lands. He knew that the continued pursuit of farming involved low prices and probable economic ruin, while a mercantile career might lead to material success.

This contrast explains the growth of commercial and industrial towns, and also the immense popularity of the New South movement with financial ambitions similar to those of the contemporary North. The Old South, according to Henry W. Grady, clung to the agrarian way when the progressive world decided in favor of industrialism, but the New South did not perpetuate this fallacy. Its leaders employed the "boundless" resources of the section to create nonagricultural forms of wealth, calculated to earn the fealty of the multitude. Thus the South acquired a new governing class.

Most of the agrarian aristocracy that survived this change was shabby. As one writer observes, in the post-bellum decades "carriages still rolled along the sand tracks and red gullies"; and "the more earnest exponents of gentility" still wore long-tailed coats; the ladies still appeared in silks and satins. "But these were tired old carriages, drawn by sad-eyed, introspective nags"; the long coats hid patches; the silks and satins were faded and hid petticoats of homespun cotton.[1] Under such conditions it was difficult to maintain a semblance of old-world elegance and extravagance. "Men rarely fight duels," wrote an observer in 1877 [2] "when death may mean starvation to their families. . . . Pistols are not drawn as quickly as of old, and the tendency is to brandish rather than shoot, so little can our hot bloods now afford the expense of a legal trial." Gentlemen were careful how they spent their money. "Southerners still make largesses to servants, stand treat, game and run into debt," added Townsend, "but they can ill afford to be lavish with their money. Fees and bets are small in amounts, and the aristocrat, who would not wait to receive change, or would pocket it without looking at it, will now count it when handed him. Treats are as often invited as proffered, and cheaper refreshments are selected than formerly."

The fortunate few who were able to adjust themselves to the postbellum system of labor and land tenure still retained the old style. However, the majority of the former planter class took one of three possible courses: an escape into storekeeping, law, politics, or other nonagricultural occupations; like the characters in Ellen Glasgow's novels, the maintenance of old ideals, outward appearance, and the traditional way of life through rigid economy and heroic pretense, continuing to enjoy the fine old silver and furniture amid austere surroundings devoid of modern conveniences and luxuries; or adjustment to the ruins in the manner of William Faulkner's characters. Scattered over the South were hundreds of crumbling mansions, victims of the decay that had set in during Reconstruction, and inhabited by the discouraged descendants of once-lordly planters. Roofs leaked, plastering sagged, porches rotted. Such a house was described as early as 1875. Within, "the stuccoed ceiling lay all around, the frieze mouldings were hanging in decay, the carved balustrade was a wreck, the staircase had found its way to the cellar. What had been a wine vault held a one-horse wagon; a pile of manure was heaped up close to the window of the parlor; a calf was penned under the carved porch." [3]

The plantations, as has been explained,[4] failed to break into small proprietorships in the decades after the Civil War. But this does not mean that the ante-bellum planters were preserved also. In the Louisiana

[1] Wilbur J. Cash, The Mind of the South, p. 108.
[2] Belton O'Neall Townsend in The Atlantic Monthly, XXXIX, 467-8 (June, 1877).
[3] Charleston News and Courier, May 17, 1875.
[4] See above, p. 341.

Sugar Bowl there was a "revolution in land titles" resulting in a new sugar aristocracy composed partly of Northerners. What was happening elsewhere is revealed by the estimate in 1881 of the president of a cotton planters' association that not one third of the cotton plantations of the Mississippi Valley were "owned by men who held them at the end of the war." A study of the background of 254 industrialists of the New South reveals that "about eighty per cent came of non-slaveholding families." A Third Estate had arisen in the South, wrote a New Englander in 1890, "to challenge the authority of the old ruling class." [5]

Despite these harsh realities, the attitude of the agrarian aristocracy of the Old South continued to be a living part of Southern tradition, not only for the thirty-five years after 1865 but for the twentieth century as well. A war that destroyed most of the old regime at the same time attached so much tragic grandeur to it that this era could not be forgotten. Although the Old South would never reappear after the Civil War, it could still be dreamed about and imitated. The Southern youth "had continually before his eyes the vision, and heard always in his ears the clamorous hoofbeats, of a glorious swashbuckler, compounded of Jeb Stuart, the golden-locked Pickett, and the sudden and terrible Forrest." The march toward America's ideal of democracy was stayed in order that the splendid legend of the Old South might be preserved. "Perpetually suspended in the great haze of memory, it hung, as it were, poised somewhere between earth and sky, colossal, shining, and incomparably lovely." [6] Everyone paid fealty to this ideal, including men of such different ambitions as Thomas E. Watson and Daniel A. Tompkins; the Georgian Populist to write a poignant novel on plantation life, the North Carolina industrialist to pen romantic pictures of life in the Old South. Everyone who claimed to have been a planter was metamorphosed into a Marse Chan or a Squire Effingham. The slave period was represented as the summit of human achievement and social justice. When the indignant Yankee reminded the Southerner of lashes and other symbols of slavery, he was answered by the sentimental Southerner, who explained the bonds of slavery in terms of understanding and trust.

The frustration of living on poverty-blighted lands was offset by proud boasts of relationship with departed leaders of the old days. Ancestor hunting became a vital part of the Southern social strategy. "Even today from Virginia to Texas," wrote William A. Percy in 1941,[7] "ten thousand crepuscular old maids and widows in ghostly

[5] Roger W. Shugg, *Origins of Class Struggle in Louisiana*, pp. 248–9; C. Vann Woodward, *Origins of the New South, 1877–1913*, pp. 152, 179.

[6] Cash, *op. cit.*, pp. 121–4.

[7] *Lanterns on the Levee*, p. 38.

coveys and clusters are solving such insoluble problems." The socially ambitious tied themselves to baronial planters, and some persons—if we accept the word of Stark Young and James Branch Cabell—even traced descent from the ten lost tribes of Israel. Southern womanhood and virtue were glorified as in the days of the Old South. Thousands of ex-slaves remained obsequious to old masters even when they could not feed them. Love of rural life, like that among the English gentry, survived. And the feeling persisted that poverty notwithstanding, the Southern gentleman possessed a glorious tradition which elevated him above all mankind, Yankees included.

The survival of social ideals of the Old South prevented the new ruling classes from attaining a prestige equal to that enjoyed by the plantation aristocracy. Merchant, banker, and industrial groups of the New South won economic power without achieving that social dominance which America in all areas outside the South accorded to business leaders. The spirit of community consciousness forced Southern business men to turn to the Bourbons for political leadership. To win social prestige the successful merchant had to assume the trappings of aristocracy. This meant the purchase of land and the discovery of real or imaginary ancestors among once-prominent slaveholders. The businessmen lacked distinction of their own; they were overshadowed by the more successful industrialists of the North, whom they imitated in dress and economic concepts. Their progressive ways smacked too much of Northern values to win the wholehearted approval of the Southern masses. Moreover, the business leaders of the New South were without stability and frequently failed in business before they could establish families. Among them were few dynasties comparable to the great planter class of the Old South, or to the millionaire families of the industrial East.

One reason for this was the insecurity of investments arising from the basically weak agriculture; also, many of the better commercial opportunities were pre-empted by the more powerful businessmen of the North. Still another reason was lack of business skill and social sophistication among Southerners. Usually of agricultural background, they were caught in pitfalls carefully avoided by men of mercantile training. These self-made men did not know how to educate their sons to the responsibilities of wealth and did not always appreciate the importance of placing their daughters in exclusive educational and social circles. Family fortunes were frequently scattered through impractical marriages. It is not surprising, then, to discover that the history of the New South, socially and economically speaking, records the rise and fall of dominant groups in rapid succession.

Commercial developments of the Reconstruction period allowed the small town or country merchants to assume a position of power and prestige in many respects like that of the ante-bellum planter. They gained wealth from the trade of the greatly increased number of farm operators and added to their fortunes by acquiring mortgages on farm lands and crops. The storekeepers built showy homes typical of the Gilded Age, and if not members of the plantation aristocracy by birth, they frequently married into it. The more successful merchants eventually became bankers and plantation owners and were subsequently honored with church offices and state senatorships.

These men are often represented as the horse-trading, money-making type, who turned their backs on "the vague largeness of outlook" associated with the planter aristocracy. Although they charged high interest rates, their risks were equally high. Liens on crops and depressed farms were most uncertain. The many who failed outweighed the few shrewd enough to succeed. The whole system of merchant-farm credit was smashed by the depression of 1929. The chain store, with its cheap cash arrangements, replaced the local merchant, who was relegated to the status of the neighborhood grocer. Bankers were the only surviving local magnates comparable in importance to the older credit merchants. Those not wiped out in 1929 continued to enjoy a certain standing in the life of most Southern communities until the present.

Emerging later than the merchants were those who won fortune and prestige through the lumber industry. They cut down the huge forests of the South and shunted the logs behind dinky engines to sawmills, where they were made into building materials. This class did not secure a permanent place in specific communities, because its members wasted the forests or allowed them to be decimated by fires. Even more transitory were the turpentine barons of the Southeast who bled resin from the pines. After attaining brief power in the community, they moved on to other harvests. Most mushroomlike of all were the peach and pecan kings who in several sections of the South periodically planted enormous orchards. They prospered for a time, only to have their fortunes ruined by the failure of crops, the collapse of prices, or by the competition of Western producers.

The wealth created by the vast industrial development of the 1880's inevitably produced a privileged class. This was composed of industrial capitalists, men who established and maintained the South's cotton and steel mills, its coal mines and furniture factories. Here was a new group to impose itself upon Southern communities along lines already familiar to those who knew the history of English and Northern industry. The Southern factory owners built fine houses for themselves, demanded and received favors from public authorities, and advocated social and political reform. Their power was peculiarly Southern. Unconsciously copying the planters, they established their workers in villages which resembled the slave quarters of old. In return for this "benevolence," they received a feudal obedience from their workers.

The quickening business enterprise of the twentieth-century South produced a crop of millionaires. Prominent among them was the Reynolds family, whose mighty fortune came from tobacco. Extensive tobacco warehouses and factories, above which arose the impressive office building called Reynolds Tower, proclaimed these lords of Winston-Salem. Billboards and magazine advertisements apprized American smokers of the merits of such Reynolds products as Prince Albert smoking tobacco and Camel cigarettes. One hundred miles east of Winston-Salem was Durham, where tobacco warehouses and factories, a towering hotel, and a university testified to the industrial success of the Duke family. Costly advertisements called nationwide attention to the Duke's products, Bull Durham smoking tobacco and Lucky Strike cigarettes, and the family fortune was further increased by investments in electric power. A third fortune of a magnitude comparable to those of North Carolina's tobacco manufacturers was made by the Candler family of Atlanta. In the 1880's Asa Griggs Candler, a druggist, bought controlling shares in the Coca-Cola formula, originally perfected by Dr. J. S. Pemberton, a patent-medicine producer. Under Candler's direction the popularity of this nonalcoholic drink soon rivaled that of coffee and tea. Atlanta's great office buildings, its real estate developments, and its Candler-subsidized university and hospital bespoke the power and prestige of the Candler name. The Cheeks of Nashville made their millions from Maxwell House coffee; the Pattens of Chattanooga from Wine of Cardui, a tonic; the Cannons of Kannapolis from towels; the Rosses and Hoggs of Texas from petroleum; the Prices of Greensboro and the Craigs of Nashville from life insurance; the Cones of Greensboro in textiles; the Belks of Charlotte in chain stores.

The plantation aristocracy had given outward evidence of its power in porticoed churches, courthouses, and manors. The more pretentious new aristocracy owned magnificent suburban estates and won public popularity by endowing hospitals, universities, and other philanthropies. Cardui, Coca-Cola, Grove's chill tonic, and Cannon towels vied with Camels and Lucky Strikes in giving national fame to Southern magnates. The Candler, Reynolds, and Duke names appeared in gossip columns along with those of the Astors and Vanderbilts. The millionaire's way of life set the social standards for the South. Around the mansions of Greensboro, Durham, Winston-Salem, Nashville, Atlanta, Memphis, Birmingham, or Dallas were built homes of less grandeur and these, in turn, were imitated by many others. The rich man of the twentieth century captured the Southern imagination nearly as completely as the planter of the Old South did before him.

More recent in origin that other segments of the Southern governing class were representatives of Northern owners of Southern life insurance, electric power, coal and steel, automobiles, railroads, hotels, airplanes, telephones, moving pictures, and mail-order and chain-store products. The great Northern corporations maintained regional branch offices in Atlanta, New Orleans, Dallas and Memphis, with subregional headquarters in Richmond, Raleigh, Greensboro, Charlotte, Columbia, Jacksonville, Montgomery, Nashville, Jackson, Houston, Fort Worth, and Little Rock, and with sales agencies in thousands of smaller cities, towns, and villages. In 1941 it was estimated that Atlanta alone possessed 1,300 branches of national businesses.[8]

Other communities were dominated by specialized activities, frequently owned by absentees—shipbuilding at Newport News; sports and tourist trade at Miami, Natchez, Charleston, and Asheville; petroleum manufacturing at Houston; cigar manufacturing at Tampa; naval stores at Brunswick; steel and iron at Birmingham. Managers of the alien-owned businesses were called distributors or regional overseers. Many of them were merely hired clerks in charge of the distribution of popular products, and their modest salaries precluded the possibility of their becoming important citizens except in small communities. Some of these overseers, however, had charge of the distribution of commodities requiring high business skill in order to extend markets and outdo their competitors. To command this service, national organizations paid large salaries or generous commissions to their Southern agents, and sometimes allowed them to own local or regional distributing agencies. For instance, the state manager for a big life insurance company, the city distributor of a certain brand of gasoline, beer, or soft drink, the Ford, Chevrolet, or Plymouth agent in even a small town, enjoyed more wealth and position than that accorded most independent businessmen. Although their power was delegated and could be withdrawn, the overseer class developed considerable influence in Southern communities. Most of them were natives and those of Northern origin were not carpetbaggers in the traditional sense; they accepted Southern race and class prejudices.

The overseers directed the lobbies of state legislatures, hired politicians as company lawyers, and colored the news, editorial, and advertising policies of the newspapers. They felt no compulsion for the stability of residence and intimate community pride traditionally associated with a governing class because they filled the highly standardized needs of whole states and regions rather than those of specific com-

[8] Arthur F. Raper and Ira De A. Reid, *Sharecroppers All, passim.*

munities. Just as the lesser men of the Old South depended upon planters for their sustenance, so did the masses of "the new urban plantations" look to overseers of commerce for their livelihood. The garish advertisements and dazzling colors of the chain stores, the standardized comforts of new mechanical and electrical contrivances replaced the mellow charm of the ante-bellum plantation. If the commercial overseers could be accused of draining the resources of the Southern people by dispatching them to offices in distant cities, perhaps they were no worse offenders than the planters whose prosperity sprang from slavery and soil depletion.

In a very real sense, the lawyers and politicians who ruled the Old South continued to hold their traditional position after Reconstruction. In 1900, 1933, or 1945, almost as much as in 1800 or 1850, they were the only group able to achieve national fame along with local importance. The main reason for their continued prestige was their ability to retain exclusive possession of public office and direction of public expenditures and court procedures. With the passing of the planters, the Confederate brigadiers, and the farmer-politicians, their monopoly tightened. New business leaders failed to strip them of their direct control of politics. Of all Southerners they were the most adaptable to changing conditions. When occasion demanded, they could assume the courtly manners of the plantation aristocracy—the long coat, the broad-brimmed hat, the flowing oratory, the Latin phrases; they also knew how to affect the rough dress and colloquial speech of common folk, or the smooth ways of the successful businessman. They were indestructible, rich in the gifts all Southerners admired. The day seemed distant indeed when law and politics would fail to attract the more ambitious and talented Southerner.

It is evident that the cream of Southern society was composed of a variety of groups. There was the planter class whose contemporary importance had declined but whose heritage of manners and ideals gave tone to all segments of the upper classes. Added to this section were remnants of the storekeeper group, the lumber barons, the turpentine distillers. Then came the prominent millionaire families, their imitators, and the commercial overseers and their aides. And, of course, there were the perennial lawyers and politicians. Supplementing these were doctors, dentists, higher public officials and also army officers whose importance grew as the social functions of government expanded. There were ministers of the Gospel, college professors, and newspaper editors who lent a moral and cultural note to discriminating social groups. A few Negro doctors, ministers, teachers, and businessmen might be considered in the "ruling" class because of their influence over the Negro masses.

Although the upper classes comprised no more than one tenth of the Southern people, they formed an aristocracy all their own, and were an integral part of society as a whole. Like the governing classes of England, they adjusted themselves to changes, even receiving talented recruits from the lower orders. Unlike their predecessors of the Old South, these new rulers had no fixed institution to defend. They were either too wise or too practical to make themselves an object of attack by emulating their ancestors who had argued for slavery so strenuously. When they felt obligated to defend their position, they spoke in terms as acceptable to the twentieth century as the proslavery argument had been unacceptable to the nineteenth century. If their rule was tyrannical, it resembled the social domination of the contemporary North to such an extent that outside critics could make no devastating accusations.

Southerners knew how to make social distinctions—for example, who not to receive in the intimate circle of their homes or clubs. Ellen Glasgow in her novels distinguishes between "good family" and "good people," and sociologists discovered among the white inhabitants of a small city of the Deep South a social pyramid consisting of no less than six classes, each with its social ritual—the upper uppers, the lower uppers, the upper middle class, the lower middle class, the upper lower class, and the lower lower class.[9] As genuine Americans, however, Southerners did not know how to draw class lines in the European manner. In a society in which so many wore ready-made clothes and owned automobiles, those with exclusive tastes could not dress or ride very differently from others. There were few private schools where children of the upper classes could escape from the social promiscuity of public institutions. The South could not avoid the social confusion so typically American. A friendly critic notes "a feeling of neighborliness, and almost pioneer closeness among the people of all walks of life." The young man or the young woman of anonymous origin could enter the inner circles of society if he or she possessed a requisite amount of charm, good looks, and dancing ability.

"It may easily happen," wrote Holland Thompson in 1919,[10] "that in the afternoon you may purchase a collar or a pair of shoes from a young man whom you will meet in the evening at the house of the local magnate." "Any Sunday in the social columns of the state newspapers," wrote a North Carolinian twenty years later, "a picture of some mill town bride may appear alongside that of the mill owner's daughter." This same observer[11] noted that the millowner called his workers by

[9] Allison Davis, Burleigh B. Gardner, and Mary R. Gardner, *Deep South, passim*.
[10] Thompson, *The New South*, p. 207.
[11] Cash, *op. cit.*, pp. 212–13.

their first names, moving among them "full of the small teasing jests and allusions to kinfolk so dear to the Southern heart," and that "he might pick up the whole crew, man, woman, and chit, and carry them off to a barbecue or picnic, where as likely or not, his women might appear, a little cool and remote it might be, but sweetly gracious after the tradition of the South." It was not socially demeaning for girls of good families to be stenographers or trained nurses, or for the boys of the best families of small towns to wait on tables or be filling-station attendants. The pride of ancestry was so widely exercised that, paradoxically, it made for social democracy. Almost any Southerner could become an aristocrat of a sort by tracing his descent from genuine or spurious forebears of distinction.

Perhaps the most striking characteristic of upper-class Southern society was its almost complete absence of intellectual interests. Leaders of the post-Reconstruction era were Confederate heroes, primitive men whose strength lay in geniality and physical prowess rather than in mental attainments. The next generation of leaders grew up during the cultural famine of war and Reconstruction; some were city-bred with an aristocratic heritage, but the majority sprang from the uncultured yeomanry. Although members of the third generation of leaders were often college-bred, they usually specialized in "campus courses," football, and fraternities. They were induced by editors and professors to support museums and orchestras, but displayed little understanding or enjoyment of these institutions. Theirs was the company of the perpetual Philistines to whom it meant social suicide to discuss intellectual or esthetic subjects. The ladies of the upper classes often attended better colleges than the men and demonstrated little opposition to higher learning. Yet, after graduation, they found more satisfying activities than the pursuit of themes outlined for them in college lecture halls. Domesticity remained the chief obligation of the Southern wife and daughter. Less attractive members of high society—or those who were too old for dances or babies—went into women's clubs with their study groups and musicales. Not so the ladies of high personal charm and social standing, who were too busy with their many diversions to tolerate the tedium of lectures and recitals.

Inevitably, such cultural immaturity was reflected in much outright boorishness. Strangers found it difficult to converse with ladies who prattled about their neighbors and were too provincial to discuss topics of general interest. They were disappointed by the soft hands, pink faces, and general corpulence of business men as contrasted to the tanned countenances and lithe figures of the old-time planter. Nor were they prepared to find "hooch" in place of mint julep, the fox trot instead of the Virginia reel, and most of all, perhaps "the grafting of Yankee backslapping upon the normal Southern gentility."

Strangers also discovered that the chivalric code of Southerners meant one set of morals for women, another for men, with much talk about "feminine honor" and "Southern virtue" by those who tolerated a low legal age of consent for illicit relationships. Such shortcomings further indicated the immaturity of the newly rich and the backwardness of the lower classes. The discriminating minority sedulously preserved the aristocratic traditions of good manners and good morals. If money in this society, as elsewhere, was the final arbiter, pride in its possession expressed itself in terms of superior standards inherited from the Old South. Accordingly, impoverished old families could still dictate to the *nouveau riche*, and when a marriage took place between an old and new family the standards adopted were always those of the old.

The governing families, then, possessed modesty and good breeding in ample measure; much informal geniality without familiarity; a marked social distinction that was neither deliberate nor self-conscious. Indeed, the best families of the South were the most delightful segment of the American elite. Southern charm reached its culmination in the Southern lady, a creature who, like her plantation grandmother, could be feminine and decorative without sacrificing any privilege except the masculine prerogative of holding public office. Count Hermann Keyserling in 1929 was impressed by "that lovely type of woman called 'The Southern Girl,' " who, in his opinion, possessed the subtle virtues of the French lady.[12] What at times appeared to be ignorance, vanity, or hypocrisy, frequently turned out to be the innate politeness of the Southerner who sought to put others at ease.

To a greater degree than other Americans, Southerners practiced what may be regarded as the essence of good manners: the idea that the outward forms of inherited or imposed ideals should be maintained regardless of what went on behind the scenes. Southern ideals were more extensive and inflexible than those prevailing elsewhere in America. To the rigid code of plantation days was added, in the late nineteenth and early twentieth centuries, the repressions of puritanism imposed by the Protestant clergy, who demanded that the fiddle be silenced and strong drink eschewed "on pain of ruin in this world and damnation in the next." As the land outwardly became more moral, the Southerner expressed his primary love of play and conviviality by "sneaking into the woods with his cards, foregathering with his cronies over a jug behind the barn, slipping away over the river in the nighttime

[12] "The South—America's Hope," *The Atlantic Monthly*, CXLIV, 607 (November, 1929).

to a cockfight or a breakdown." [13] Although Southerners were among the hardest drinkers in America, one reason they refused to vote for presidential candidate Al Smith in 1928 was because he openly defended drinking. Many critics called this attitude hypocrisy, even deceit; the Southerners, however, insisted upon making a distinction between hedonistic tendencies and long-established ideals. If such evasiveness did not create a perfect code of morals, at least it helped to repress the indecent.

The New South supplemented a heritage of grace with a heritage of violence. Dueling by 1890 had passed into history as an extravagance of a more glorious age; it was supplanted by the custom of "toting a gun" and "shooting on sight." South Carolina, with less than one fourth as many people as New England, had three times the number of homicides in 1890. In that year the states of the middle South, with one third the population of Italy, had as many persons charged with murder as a country with a bad reputation for homicides. A Mississippi editor declared in 1879 that there was an average of a murder a day in that state; and six years later a Kentucky editor demonstrated that there had been an annual average of 223 murders in his state since 1880. The state auditor of Alabama in 1881 valued the tools and farming implements in his state at $305,613; the guns, pistols and dirks at $354,247. [14]

Race violence and lower-class lawlessness explain only in part this appalling record. The newspapers before and after 1900 were crowded with accounts of homicidal frays among lawyers, planters, doctors, even preachers, and particularly editors. Francis W. Dawson and Narciso G. Gonzales, South Carolina's two most distinguished editors since the Civil War, were victims of assassin's bullets. Homicide was an important means of preserving the Southern code of decorum and puritanical chivalry. Sometimes lives were exacted for offenses as trivial as an argument over a dog; others were exacted for offenses as vital to Southern honor as the cursing of a gentleman, the slander of a lady, or the seduction of a daughter.

In the decades after the Civil War the family was the core of Southern society; within its bounds everything worth while took place. No one recognized to be a Southerner's social equal dined anywhere other than in his own house or in that of a friend. Good Southern dishes—hot biscuits, fried chicken, custards—could be had only in the home, and the sole type of architecture that appealed was domestic in nature. This absorption in household affairs explains why strangers unacquainted with Southern home life found the social scene so dismal. They saw ugly main streets deserted after business hours and noted an almost com-

[13] Cash, op. cit., p. 133.
[14] Woodward, op. cit., pp. 159–60.

plete lack of public entertainment. The hotels were poorly equipped, the restaurants so drab and filthy that they repelled persons of good taste. Southerners who preserved the traditions of comfort and good manners seemed altogether oblivious to these conditions.

After 1910 there were changes in Southern domestic life. Urbanization and industrialization meant an increase in apartment houses and the abandonment of the family roof by youths seeking the opportunities of a changing economy. The Southerner was frequently lured away from home by the temptation of the automobile and good roads, and became itinerant like other Americans. Hotels became numerous and often achieved the standards of other American public places; restaurants multiplied, and the suburban and rural areas blossomed with community centers given to dancing, dining, and drinking. Public places continued to be almost as backward as in the nineteenth century, however. In the vast distance between Washington and New Orleans, only with difficulty could the traveler find a restaurant of distinction. The numerous roadhouses were places of bad food, raucous and indiscriminate conviviality, even ruffianism and immorality. They were merely centers of escape for young people tired of the gentility of the home. When these young people married, they joined their elders in losing interest in what happened along the roadside after dark.

There was no significant uprooting of family life. The home in the twentieth century remained the core of a social conservatism fundamentally Southern, still harboring "the tenacious clan loyalty that was so mighty a cohesive force in colonial society." This explains the interminable visits among brothers and sisters, the sheltering of elderly aunts and distant cousins, the care of old family servants, the seeking of favors from relatives in high places, and the tribal conferences whenever a daughter married or a son changed employment. There were two living symbols of the prevailing domestic stability. One was the rush of millions to the suburbs after World War II to build cottages away from crowded apartment houses; the other was the porch where, in the leisure of the rocking chair, the Southerner endlessly contemplated the past. Here nothing important had happened since the Civil War, except that the screen of trees and banisters had grown more protective.[15]

The most obvious indication of the tenacity of home life was the survival of the Southern style of cooking. Assaults upon it came from the outside, with scientists claiming that monotony and lack of balance in the eating habits of millions resulted in such diseases as pellagra. National advertising imposed Northern food products upon those Southerners who would heed. Federal subsidies after 1914 enabled home economics teachers to carry the new science of nutrition into Southern

---

[15] American Guide Series, *Georgia*, pp. 3–7.

communities and schools. As a result, the so-called protective foods—milk, fresh fruits, and leafy vegetables—became widely consumed. Yet no revolution in diet took place. Possibly the home economics teachers overstepped the mark when they sought to introduce the culinary customs of Battle Creek and Boston. Their attempted revolution failed for the same reason as that of the Yankee schoolma'ams during Reconstruction. The South in 1915 was as unwilling to become a dietary province of New England as it had been unprepared in 1865 to become an educational adjunct of that section. If champions of scientific nutrition had not compromised with the local diet the entire home economics movement would have had little effect upon the South. Actually, changes which they effected in provincial peculiarities of diet were not so intensive as those during the Civil War and Reconstruction period. The poverty of those times forced the upper and middle classes to turn to chitterlings, cowpeas, cracklings, and other foods of the Negro and poor white.

Southerners of the twentieth century remained such unabashed champions of the traditional diet that they spread its virtues and defects wherever they went. Ben Tillman and Madame C. J. Walker were different from each other in most respects, but both were Southerners crying out in Northern exile for the same type of food. The statesman from South Carolina insisted upon supplementing the diet of his Washington hotel with collards, fried chicken, and pork; the colored manufacturer of hair straightener from Louisiana topped off a New York wedding supper of caviar and champagne with chitterlings and mustard greens. Huey P. Long touched the Southern heart when he proclaimed to the nation the virtues of corn pone and "pot likker." It was not uncommon for Southerners living in the North to send home for such specialties of the native larder as corn meal ground by old-fashioned water mills, and hams cured in family smokehouses.

"In the small homes . . . and in the 'big houses' where 'Aunt Nancy' still measures by hand and taste," declared a North Carolinian in 1939,[16] "the art of cooking famous old dishes still lives on." Hot biscuits enjoyed the greatest renown of all; in fact hot biscuits bound the Southern province together with an authority as general and as intimate as the doctrine of white supremacy. They were a mixture of flour, lard, soda and buttermilk, lightly kneaded, rolled, cut out, baked in an oven until brown, and served while still hot. As typically Southern as biscuits, but declining in popularity, were the several varieties of corn bread, including the simple corn pone shaped with the hand and dropped into a greased pan. At the other extreme were elaborate preparations consisting of meal mixed with milk, soda, and eggs.

[16] American Guide Series, *North Carolina*, p. 103.

The cook fried many foods: meats, vegetables, even pies and breads. The ever-popular fried chicken called for an unjointed fowl seasoned with salt and pepper, rolled in flour, then sizzled in hot lard. Chicken in other forms also delighted the Southern palate—served, for example, with red giblet gravy—also chicken salad or pie, chicken dumplings, chicken hash, and smothered chicken. Equally enjoyable were the almost endless varieties of pork. At the lower extremes of taste this meant the chitterlings, pig's feet, cracklings, and jowls. Choicer parts of the hog were the spareribs, backbones, fresh hams, and sausages. Most delicious of all was the boiled, baked, or fried country-cured ham, swimming in gravy. The most useful part was the bacon, variously called fat back, salt pork, middlin', sowbelly, or simply "meat." When not eaten alone, bacon was used to season string beans, black-eyed peas, cabbage, mustard, poke, turnip tops, collards, and other vegetables dear to the Southerner of all classes and both races. The juice left in the container after the vegetables were removed was called "pot likker," and reputedly contained almost magical nutritive values, especially for Negro babies. The cooking of two or three vegetables or other foods together was widely practiced; string or butter beans were combined with corn, okra with tomatoes, black-eyed peas with rice. The sweet potato was cooked in a variety of forms: baked in the peelings, fried, or made into pies.

The invention of artificial ice around 1850 enabled Southerners of later generations to become the world's greatest consumers of Coca-Cola and other soft drinks. Ultimately coffee as a table beverage partly gave way to iced tea. Southerners joined other Americans in taking to all types of alcoholic beverages, the exigencies of prohibition and high prices notwithstanding. When choice was possible, the Southern male usually selected the drink traditional to his section—corn whisky—in preference to the lighter and smoother varieties of alcohol imported from Europe or the North. Under the more elegant name of bourbon, this drink came from the great distilleries of Kentucky and Maryland, but when prohibition cut off that source, corn whisky was obtained deep in the mountains, woods, or swamps. This illicit liquor was a barbarous concoction known as "corn likker," "moonshine," "white lightnin'," or "rot gut," yet it satisfied many Americans who lived outside the section of its origin.

The revolution in sanitary and health practices which enveloped the progressive world in the late nineteenth century effected greater changes in Southern life than the much-heralded changes in political and social life. The region below the Potomac possessed a practical monopoly within the nation of hookworm, pellagra, and malaria; its problem of tuberculosis and venereal disease was aggravated by the careless habits of poor whites and Negroes; and cities of the Deep South were annually terrorized by the fear of yellow fever. In the great epidemics of 1878 and 1879, this horrid pestilence killed more than 9,000 persons in four cities. So demoralizing was its effect on Memphis that a historian writes of two cities—"one which existed prior to the pestilence, and a second metropolis which sprang up like some fungus growth on the ruins of the first." [17] Sanitary conditions in a typical town were described as late as 1906 by an unsuccessful candidate for mayor:

The condition of the town is simply something to contemplate. The streets are unkempt. Back lots reek with filth. Hog pens are allowed in the populous portions of the town without any sanitary regulations of the same. The smell from them rises up under the windows.[18]

Inevitably typhoid fever was rampant every summer, and the cemeteries of every Southern town were dotted with the graves of upper-class youth who were victims of this disease.

Southerners joined others in making contributions to the solution of their region's health problem. Walter Reed, a Virginian, identified in 1899 the mosquito that carries yellow fever, supplementing the discoveries being made by non-Southerners concerning the causes of malaria, typhoid fever, and venereal disease. William C. Gorgas, an Alabamian, demonstrated in 1902 the uses of these discoveries during the building of the Panama Canal. In 1902 Charles W. Stiles, a native of New York, established the widespread existence of hookworm infection in the Southern states. Joseph Goldberger, a non-Southerner, in 1927 carried on an experiment in Mississippi proving dietary deficiencies as the causes of pellagra.

The awakening soon came. In 1905 occurred the last yellow fever epidemic. All the Southern states after 1906 created state boards of health, with ever-increasing authority to enforce sanitary regulations and to dispense inoculations The use of central water supplies and pasteurized milk became widespread, and pigs and cows were banished from backyards. The Rockefeller Sanitary Commission for the Eradication of Hookworm was organized in 1909 and, through the treatment of 440,000 infected persons, in a large measure banished a debilitating disease to the pages of history. At a later date the same fate overtook pellagra, malaria, and venereal disease. By 1933 the death rate among Southern whites and Southern Negroes had fallen respectively to 8.9 and 15.2 per thousand.

Reforms in health practices were followed by a revolutionary atti-

[17] Gerald M. Capers, Jr., The Biography of a River Town: Memphis, p. 204.
[18] William P. Calhoun, in the Edgefield [South Carolina] Chronicle, August 14, 1906.

tude toward the sun. Beginning at the time of World War I the South learned to regard its very hot and very bright sun as a beneficent friend instead of as a cruel tyrant. Sunbonnets and the habiliments of Victorian parents were cast aside in favor of the loose and lighter garments. The modesty of the Southern maiden was replaced by a nakedness almost as complete as that of a pagan goddess. The sun's rays were proclaimed as protection against inadequate diets and lack of sanitary devices. Sun baths were indulged in for two reasons: because of health and because of an aesthetic revolution that holds that a brown skin is more beautiful than a fair one. The acme of Southern comeliness became blue eyes, blond hair, and brown skin.

CHAPTER XXV

Social Diversions

➤➤➤-➤➤

WHETHER within or without the approved standards of chivalry and puritanism, Southerners have managed to extract the maximum pleasure from the seventy years that have elapsed since Reconstruction. This applied equally to the difficult decades that followed 1865 and the more affluent times of the twentieth century. During the earlier period materials were ingeniously utilized; old jewels, laces, fans, and shawls were refurbished; mothers became expert dressmakers and devised refreshments of a simple type. Special stress was placed on the charm and beauty of the Southern girl and an aristocratic self-esteem which blinded the observer to the sound of a creaking floor or the sight of a faded garment. Twentieth-century wealth added material comfort to the social scene, a circumstance that did not necessarily blot out gentility. Some of the social diversions that grew out of these factors survived or developed during the post-bellum period, while others emerged from twentieth-century conditions.

The desire of many Southerners to cast aside, occasionally, their strict domestic code in favor of untrammeled indulgence is best illustrated by what went on in New Orleans in the years preceding World War I. In that city of the lower South big-scale gambling received official sanction when the Louisiana lottery was legalized in 1868. This institution, before its abolition in 1895, twice yearly awarded a capital grand prize of $600,000. Legalization of prize fights by Louisiana in 1890 made it possible for these bouts to be staged openly with few restrictions other than the requirement of the use of gloves, and New Orleans became the boxing center of America. In 1892 the 21-round knockout victory of James J. Corbett over John L. Sullivan was fought

((394))

there for a $21,000 purse and a $10,000 side bet. The following year saw the longest bout in boxing history—the 110-round draw between Jack Burke and the Negro Andy Bowen that lasted over seven hours.

Under the stimulus of legalized gambling, New Orleans became a haven of prostitution, with old mansions converted into brothels. During the Cotton Exposition of 1884, newly installed electric lights exposed "many saloons and gambling houses which throb with raucous sounds of pleasure-bent men and women," while elsewhere in the city men stood on the streets to catch "a glimpse of female limbs draped in gauze of pink and blue." In 1897 prostitution was confined to certain sections of the city on the theory that it could then be better controlled. This restricted area was derisively dubbed Storyville in honor of the alderman who created it. It was at once the show place and the scandal of the city, "one of the most amazing spectacles of legalized vice that had ever been seen." It was a world of tinseled gaiety, of "honky-tonks," "dives," "palaces," and "cribs." Some of the "palaces" were lavishly furnished in plush, gaudy drapes, and gilt statuary; the "cribs" were bare one-room structures closely placed together, their occupants plainly visible to the passerby. *The Blue Book*, official directory of Storyville, contained the names and addresses of all prostitutes, with special articles and photographs extolling their qualifications.

Because of its size and Latin background, New Orleans displayed its moral delinquencies more flagrantly and on a grander scale than any other Southern city. However, by the end of the nineteenth century every sizable Southern city had its dens of iniquity and red-light district. Men of all classes, including college boys and men from the pious homes of small towns, congregated there nightly. During World War I, Josephus Daniels exerted his dictatorial powers as Secretary of the Navy to close every red-light district near a military or naval establishment. This decree meant the end of legalized vice in all Southern cities. Some of the prostitutes took refuge in suburban tourist camps, others settled in the larger commercial hotels, where bellboys brought them together with pleasure-seeking guests. For the generation between the two World Wars, almost all the hotels of Southern cities harbored women of loose morals. With the passing of the Daniels era, police-protected houses of prostitution were revived in many cities. They were never so blatant, however, as before 1917, and were subject to harsh treatment from police, who were prompted by outraged reformers.

Although most forms of approved entertainment were in the home, large numbers of people from Southern cities and towns attended dramatic performances. The theater of that day, however, was not sufficiently creative to justify its discussion under literature and the fine arts. A perambulating affair imported from New York City, it acquired in the Southern environment little that was significant. The general public showed a preference for the extravagant and sentimental, without, however, excluding the classical and restrained. There was no opportunity for such originality as marked the Little Theater movement after World War I.

Despite its handicaps, the Southern theater of the post-Reconstruction period was an extensive, lusty, and varied institution. Every town or city built an "Opera House." Davis Hall, with a seating capacity of 4,000, arose out of the ashes of Atlanta in 1865; six months after the railroad reached Dallas in 1872 that town had a playhouse; by 1873 Little Rock had its Grand Opera House "elaborately decorated with crimson velvet hangings, prism-glass chandeliers, and new scenery." A similar building in Louisville was described as "constructed and finished in the highest style of modern art . . . and one of the most substantial and elegant theaters in the world."

Such buildings were often equipped with decorated façades, balustraded verandas, and several tiers of seats for persons of different social classes. Not the least interesting of these was the highest gallery, reserved for the demimonde and the Negroes. On the stage below appeared stars of the American theater, including New Orleans-born Minnie Maddern Fiske, Adah Isaacs Menken, Cora Urquhart Potter, and Edward Hugh Sothern. The St. Charles Theater in New Orleans claimed that it featured more famous actors than any other stage in the South. Actress Irene Franklin stated that she spent fifty weeks in Texas frontier towns doing one-night stands. Italian companies were heard in performances of *Faust, Rigoletto, Il Trovatore, Mignon,* and other favorites of the French and Italian opera. Their Shakespearean heritage made audiences receptive to the plays of the Bard, as well as other classics of the English and Continental stage. Interest in the higher type of drama was not only demonstrated by cities like Charleston, Richmond, Louisville, and New Orleans, but by the newer communities of Texas and Arkansas. As early as 1869, for example, Little Rock saw successful performances of *Camille, The Robbers,* and *The Bride of Lammermoor.* Less exalted forms of drama, naturally enough, were nearer to the hearts of the Southern people, and popular taste ran in the direction of such melodramas as *Ten Nights in a Bar Room, The Drunkard, East Lynne,* the Gilbert and Sullivan operettas, and American comedies like *Toodles* and *Under the Gas Lights.* Spectacle shows with ingenious mechanical thrills were the delight of simple folk—for instance, a locomotive rolling across the stage in *Under the Gas Lights;* a chariot race in *Ben Hur,* and a gristmill with splashing water, creaking machinery, and flying dust in *Hearts of Oak.* People of such unsophisticated tastes were certain to enjoy vaudeville and burlesque shows, which appeared in many Southern cities after 1900. When censorship was exercised the crowds turned to motion pictures. Conditions created by World War I gave the final blow to the traveling theater in the South.

The traveling theater was supplemented by various tent shows. Some of these were chautauquas with lectures and recitations presented for genteel tastes exclusively. Others were frankly vulgar, featuring sights and sounds attractive to children, Negroes, and country folk. Southern audiences never tired of the black-faced minstrels with their stereotyped Negro characters. This form of entertainment culminated in the performances of Blind Tom, a Georgia Negro who was mentally deficient as well as blind. For forty years before his death in 1908, he displayed a remarkable musical instinct which won him popularity as a pianist and a composer. Tremendous crowds were drawn to the one-day stands of circuses and the week-long visits of tent carnivals. Although the latter had its innocent features, chief popularity sprang from what disapproving moralists called the displays "of fat women, giants and disgusting monstrosities, and the nameless hosts of gamblers and swindlers."

More unique were the showboats, which anchored along the bays and rivers of the Atlantic seaboard and Mississippi valley. Announced by the blaring of calliopes and the flutter of multicolored flags, these floating theaters were joyously greeted by the entire populations of river towns and plantations. Sometimes they were merely flatboats with rude superstructures, but occasionally they were "floating palaces" with full theater equipment as well as sleeping quarters for the actors. Their melodramas and musical entertainments conformed to standards less critical than those prevailing in theaters ashore. The showboat reached the height of its popularity between 1870 and 1890, gradually giving way after 1900 to the novelty of the flickering film.

Every state capital and many county seats possessed a fenced-in space called the fair grounds, where exhibitions were held each fall. There were stalls for livestock and booths for agricultural and industrial exhibits, and a race track for trotting matches, sometimes with an athletic field in the center. Apart from agricultural displays, there were the street carnivals where the rustics could momentarily forget their furrowed fields. The fair was the occasion of much "neighboring," much friendly rivalry over exhibition prizes, and considerable feasting at hot dog stands and barbecue pits. Each fair had its special feature. At the State Fair in Columbia it was the Clemson-University of South Carolina football game; at the State Fair in Dallas the encampment of farm youth; at Bandera in Texas, the revival of old frontier activities including spinning and weaving contests; in Neshoba County, Mississippi, a political jamboree at which candidacies for office were announced.

The fair reached its peak in the regional expositions, which attracted national attention. The first of these was the Cotton Exposition of 1881 in Atlanta, where 1,113 exhibits were viewed by 350,000 people. Most recent were the Dallas and Fort Worth Expositions of 1936 celebrating the centennial of Texas independence. Between these events were the Cotton Centennial Exposition at New Orleans in 1884–85, the Southern States Exposition in Atlanta in 1895, the Charleston Exposition of 1902, and the Jamestown Exposition of 1907. Although these events were not comparable in magnitude and originality with the great world's fairs at Philadelphia, Chicago, New York, and San Francisco, they were effective methods of making Southerners acquainted with each other and with the industrial progress of the section.

Of twentieth-century origin were the annual festivals in honor of the chief agricultural products, flowers, or animals of various Southern communities. Virginia had its Apple Blossom Festival at Winchester, its Tobacco Festival at South Boston, and a Dogwood Festival at Bristol. North Carolina held the Tulip Festival at Washington, Dahlia Show at Durham, Cotton Festival at Gastonia, and a Rhododendron Festival at Asheville. Charleston gave an Azalea Festival. Kentucky had its Strawberry Producers Revel at Paducah, Strawberry Carnival at Beaver Dam and a Tobacco Festival at Lexington; Tennessee promoted the Dogwood Festival at Knoxville, Strawberry Festival at Humboldt, Rhododendron Festival at Gatlinburg, and a Cotton Carnival at Memphis. Not to be outdone, Alabama featured an Azalea Trail at Mobile, a Flower Show at Tuscaloosa, a Dogwood Trail at Birmingham, and a Strawberry Festival at Cullman. In Louisiana and Texas, a background of French-Catholic and Mexican-Catholic culture gave the flower and crop festivals a variety not possible in states of purely Anglo-Saxon and Protestant background. Louisiana presented a Spring Fiesta at New Orleans, an Azalea Tour at Lafayette, a Strawberry Festival at Hammond, a Cotton Carnival at Tallulah, a Rice Carnival at Crowley, and a Sugar Festival and Carnival of Flowers at New Iberia. Texas gave a Citrus Fiesta at Mission, an Oleander Fete at Galveston, a Rose Festival at Tyler, and a Forest Festival at Lufkin.

The utilitarian triumphed over the esthetic in the Potato Tour at Robertsdale, Alabama; in the Blessing of the Berries at Parksville, Kentucky; in the Onion Festival at Raymondville in the Rio Grande Valley. There was even a Turkey Trot at Cuero, Texas, and an appropriately named "Yamboree" in honor of the sweet potato of Gilmer in the same state; also there was Mule Day at Columbia, Tennessee, an all-day affair for the "orneriest and workingest work-critter living." [1]

Seasonal celebrations had parades of floats displaying the specific fruit, flower, or animal of the occasion, and a court of "royalty" with

[1] American Guide Series, *Tennessee*, p. 133.

a queen, maids of honor, and "nobility" drawn from first families of the community. To a great extent these festivals manifested the wholesome pride of a garden-loving and field-loving people in the products of the soil which conferred fame, wealth, or beauty upon their respective localities. However, as time passed, these celebrations became so numerous and repetitious that they aroused a suspicion of commercialism. Many were products of the age of advertising, more the creations of trade boosters than spontaneous expressions of joy over the triumphs of the harvest.

The talents of the South's largest, most distinctive city were expressed in the most elaborate festival of them all—the pre-Lenten carnival season at New Orleans. It was the most unique display of its kind in America. The gaiety began late in December and terminated with the Mardi-Gras (Fat-Tuesday) parades on the day before the beginning of Lent which prohibited all but the leanest pleasures. First came a series of upper-class balls in honor of the season's debutantes. Between these affairs were many breakfast, dinner, and supper dances, cocktail parties, receptions, musicales, and operas. After several weeks of these activities, the spirit of gaiety gradually spread to the public at large, and burst into unrestrained hilarity when, a week before Ash Wednesday, the Krewe of Momus inaugurated the parades. These were organized by numerous secret clubs from whose "dens" floats emerged at the appointed time. Parade followed parade with much dancing and merrymaking.

Interested visitors—in some seasons as many as 100,000—crowded hotels, restaurants, and night clubs. On Mardi Gras the entire city and its guests turned out for one of the liveliest street scenes in the United States. Attired in every conceivable disguise, maskers converged on Canal Street to cavort in dancing, buffoonery, and joviality, while they awaited the coming of Rex, the Lord of Misrule, and his splendid retinue. Increasingly animated became the scene as night fell, and then Comus paraded with brilliantly colored floats, illuminated by oil flares carried by hundreds of Negroes. With the coming of Lent at midnight, the crowds scattered, and New Orleans resumed its normal appearance.

Despite the prevalence of the automobile after 1910, the Southerner showed no more tendency to cast aside his traditions of horsemanship than other aspects of his heritage. Perhaps the adoption of the automobile as the common mode of transportation placed greater emphasis on the horse as a means of pleasure and sport. Horse shows became annual events in all important cities. Tennessee developed the Plantation Walking Show where the three easy gaits, once enjoyed by planters and their overseers, were displayed. In Marshall and Bedford counties of that state, an extensive network of bridle paths was used by the walking horse. Although in most communities fox hunters traveled in automobiles. the English custom of riding to the hounds was practiced in northern Virginia and in eastern Texas and there were mounted hunt clubs in Tennessee. "More polo ponies," said a local authority in 1940,[2] "are trained in Texas and more polo is played in Texas than in any other place." This sport was not widely practiced elsewhere in the South, being largely confined to Camden and Aiken in South Carolina, and to Miami in Florida, where wealthy Northerners congregated.

Ring tournaments continued to be popular after Reconstruction. These demonstrations of pageantry, fine horsemanship, and flowery speeches enjoyed their greatest popularity in the last decades of the nineteenth century, but they survived until after World War II in many localities. "Knights" in colorful costumes mounted on caparisoned steeds and tilted with wooden lances at metal rings suspended at intervals along straightways. The champions chose queens and crowned them at the balls that followed the field meets.

The roundups of cattle of the plains were often followed by riding and roping contests, in which cowboys were both spectators and participants. When the fencing-in of the plains made these roundups obsolete, their feats of horsemanship became public spectacles known as rodeos. One of the earliest of these was held at Pecos, Texas, on July 4, 1884, when local ranchmen engaged in a roping, racing, and riding contest. The Pecos exhibition became an annual affair. One of the most popular rodeos was held each Saturday night at Saint Jo, another Texas town. Perhaps the best-known show of this type was presented annually at Fort Worth as part of the Southwestern Exhibition and Fat Stock Show. Although the rodeo enjoyed especial favor in the cattle country of Texas and Oklahoma, its independence from the roundup transformed it into a traveling entertainment on a commercial basis. Among well-known rodeos of this type was the 101 Ranch Wild West Circus which the three Miller brothers first sent out in 1908 from their huge ranch near Ponca City, Oklahoma.

The grand sport of the ante-bellum gentlemen had a checkered career after the Civil War. Horse racing at first suffered from the prevailing poverty and from the seizure by Yankee raiders of the best horses. Racing tastes had to be satisfied by old nags. When horses grew better, jocky clubs were organized, and cities like Memphis, Nashville, Montgomery, and Little Rock held races blessed by crowds of smiling ladies fashionably attired. Then arose a worse enemy than poverty and Yankee raiders. It was a rising moral consciousness which found gambling offensive. Race courses were outlawed by the antigambling enactments of Southern legislatures. Consequently at the beginning of the twentieth century racing took the form of tame trotting contests at

[2] American Guide Series, *Texas*, p. 119.

state and county fairs. In the years that followed it existed on a grand scale only in New Orleans, Hot Springs, Arkansas, Miami, and in the Blue grass region of Kentucky. In New Orleans and in the two resort cities there was little opposition to the sport. The Kentuckians learned to reconcile piety with pleasure, seeing no incongruity in poring over race forms on Saturday and crowding the churches on Sunday.[3] When a puritanical legislature outlawed horse racing in 1908 its Kentucky partisans proved resourceful. They unearthed an old law permitting parimutuel betting. In 1907 an act of the Arkansas legislature closed the Hot Springs course; however, in 1935 the legislature permitted parimutuel betting.

The race course at the Fair Grounds in New Orleans was decorated with shrubbery, flowers, fountains, and artificial lakes. Each year, beginning at Thanksgiving, it offered one hundred days of racing. Operating in midwinter was the Hialeah Track at Miami, surrounded by royal palms, landscaped grounds, and picturesque pink flamingoes and black swans. After the New Orleans and Miami races came those at Hot Springs where the track's white rails were set against the green foothills of the Ouachitas. The most congenial home of the race horse was Kentucky. The Bluegrass region with its firm turf, its layer of limestone, and its long easy roll of hills developed the required strength and fleetness in that highly bred animal. The most famous racing event in the United States—the Kentucky Derby at Churchill Downs, Louisville —has been held each May since 1875. Matt Winn assumed its management in 1902, and turned it into a national festival. "It is," said a Kentuckian in 1939, "a dramatic climax to the Kentucky legend . . . of 'My Old Kentucky Home' acted before your eyes." It caused 70,000 visitors to spend a million dollars annually. Noisy revelers were treated indulgently, and all the juleps served made "a long, long drink." Important politicians and movie stars mingled with stenographers and collegians. A million radios throughout the United States tuned in to listen, and a blanket of roses was bestowed upon the champion horse.

After General Lee's visit to White Sulphur Springs in 1867, the springs of Virginia became once more the center of Southern society. There each summer the Confederacy was born again. The courtesy which Lee showed his enemies of a few years previous encouraged Northern visitors to such a degree that they gradually monopolized White Sulphur and Hot Springs. But Southerners for five or six decades after Lee died continued to visit the numerous hotels which sprang up in the pleasant groves which surrounded mineral springs in all sections of the South. There were Indian Springs and Warm Springs in Georgia; Blount Springs and Bladen Spring in Alabama; Glenn Springs in South

[3] Thomas D. Clark in American Guide Series, *Kentucky*, p. 6.

Carolina; Hot Springs in Arkansas, and Allison Wells in Mississippi. By 1920 most of the springs lost their popularity because of loss of faith in their health-giving properties.

The South of the post-Reconstruction period had few formal holidays. Except for picnic dinners on church grounds, Sunday meant abstinence from pleasure and work. Apart from the Lutheran, Episcopalian, and Catholic minorities, churches were still too Protestant in their traditions to make religious festivals of Christmas and Easter. Thanksgiving had too much of a New England flavor to excite any real enthusiasm. The Fourth of July continued, as during Reconstruction, to be a Negro holiday; while blacks paraded and listened to oratory, whites remained at home. National Memorial Day was seldom celebrated by the whites, but it had a solemn substitute in Confederate Monument Day or Confederate Memorial Day to honor their heroes. For the former occasion, crowds gathered to dedicate Confederate monuments in every courthouse village or town. For the latter event, cited an observer in 1877, "the whole population of a town turns out in procession, headed by the Ladies Memorial Association, and decorates the graves. Poems, too, are commonly recited, either specially written for the occasion, or such old, old stories as Collins' ode, 'How Sleep the Brave.' " These occasions were as extended as the most elaborate festivals in Catholic countries; indeed they so elaborate that sometimes nineteen pages of a newspaper were required to describe all the details of one of them.[4] The legislature of every state of the former Confederacy set aside a day for this purpose, and in 1894 the various memorial associations were consolidated into the United Daughters of the Confederacy, an organization which had a membership of some 40,000 in 1936. Interest in Confederate Memorial Day naturally declined in the twentieth century, with flower and crop festivals serving as adequate substitutes. A revival of interest in the great American holidays came with the growth of national reconciliation. Southerners of the World War I era celebrated the Fourth of July and Thanksgiving almost as enthusiastically as Northerners, and took part in such national holidays of twentieth-century origin as Mother's Day and Armistice Day.

In the years following the Civil War both blacks and whites remained devoted to Christmas. It was the Southern festival *par excellence*, the only holiday of the year that completely captured the anticipations and desires of the whole people. It was an occasion for simple, domestic joys rather than public rites of a religious or festive character. On Christmas Day the typical Southerner stayed at home, leaving the religious services to the older people and the community Christmas tree to the children of the poor. Preceded by two weeks of

[4] Katherine D. Lumpkin, *The Making of a Southerner*, pp. 114-20.

brisk buying at the stores, the great day was hailed at dawn by fire-crackers and the examination of gifts left by Santa Claus. There was much drinking of eggnogs and other cheering potions at the homes of friends. The main event, of course, was the Christmas dinner at which Southern cooking reached a climax of profusion and quality.

The Southerner's failure to emphasize the religious aspects of Christmas does not mean that he did not find in religion a means of social satisfaction. The inherited ban on Catholic feasts enabled a Protestant people to devise church pleasures both original and consistent with natural inclinations. One of these was the camp meeting. By 1900, it had long since passed the zenith of its popularity; however, it survived at such places as Epworth, South Carolina, Crestwood, Kentucky, and McHenry in Stone County, Mississippi, although it had a twentieth-century flavor. Bush arbors, tents, and pine torches were replaced by substantial wooden buildings and electric lights. The advent of the automobile perpetuated the religious and social features of the camp meeting without the necessity of maintaining dormitories. The congregation drove from their homes to church daily during the ten-day period of the meeting. Noon lunch under the trees was the only meal provided at the gathering.

Since these affairs no longer necessitated camping, their names were changed; they were called protracted meetings, revivals, or simply "big meetings," at which the sermon remained the featured event. It was a reiteration of the traditional Christian theme of the wreckage wrought by sin, followed by a shout of triumph as possible damnation was replaced by the hope of heaven. The social aspect of protracted meetings was important. They were, in fact, social clubs, news exchanges, and marriage marts, centers of rest and recreation, and of a certain amount of merrymaking which did not have the approval of the church.

An interesting feature of the summer religious gatherings was the alternation of the sermon with singing. This was the old *fa, sol, la* music of the Southern uplands written in four parts, with each one carrying a degree of melodic pattern all its own. Traveling music masters trained the singers. Pupils adjudged proficient were organized into singing conventions or sacred harp associations. For days on end, they harmonized the deep rhythm of the white spirituals. There were county and state conventions, the largest of them the Sacred Harp Association of Alabama with several thousand members. The summer's activities came to a climax with a singing convention in Jefferson County Courthouse, Birmingham, followed by a basket picnic in Woodrow Wilson Park.

As much a part of the entertainment of the people as the church gatherings were the political meetings. During the campaigns before primaries almost every county seat and rural community from South

Carolina to Texas held its political rally. The all-day speaking bout was interrupted by a barbecue lunch. When there was a debate between an aspiring demagogue and a Bourbon statesman, the crowd around the speakers' stand grew large and attentive; interest waned, however, before a politician's denunciation of Republicanism or Negroism.

Sometimes the summer pageant of speaking resembled vaudeville or minstrels, with the serious issues of state subordinated to unalloyed entertainment. Such was the War of the Roses of 1886 in Tennessee, when the brothers Bob and Alf Taylor were rivals in a good-humored race for the governorship. Their weapons were droll anecdotes, repartee, and a matching of skills with the fiddle. In 1903 James K. Vardaman, dressed in white with his long raven hair hanging loosely about his shoulders, campaigned for the governorship of Mississippi behind white oxen. There were the campaigns of 1938 and 1940 in Texas when the flour salesman W. Lee O'Daniel, nicknamed "Pass the Biscuits Pappy," successively won the governorship and United States senatorship by haranguing crowds between renditions of hillbilly music featuring his three children, Mickey Wickey, Patty Boy, and Molly. That such antics are still effective in middle of the twentieth century is evidenced by the part the singing over the radio of "You Are My Sunshine" had in the election of Jimmy Davis as governor of Louisiana in 1944, and the part a coonskin cap played in the election of Estes Kefauver as senator from Tennessee in 1948.

Since Reconstruction, Southerners have taken a growing interest in all American sports with particular stress on baseball. The game originated in the North in the 1840's and 1850's, and captured the Southern imagination between 1865 and 1875. At first the baseball nines were composed of amateurs; later they were supported by professional pitchers and catchers. The earlier matches were not arranged according to schedules but simply through an exchange of challenges between neighboring communities. Professional baseball became a Southern institution when cities in Georgia, Alabama, and Tennessee were organized into the Southern League in 1885. After the failure of this combination the Southern Association was formed in 1891. Other successful combinations were the South Atlantic League and the Texas League. The Dixie Series, an annual runoff contest between the Southern Association and the Texas League, never attracted the attention given the World Series. Sports enthusiasts took pride in the fact that Ty Cobb, a Georgian, for twelve years led the American League in batting averages. The material prosperity and easy transportation of the twentieth century permitted even the smaller towns to maintain baseball diamonds where teams representing social, civic, and business organizations view with each other in amateur contests. Although the depression of 1929 limited many other activities, baseball was not included; it received fresh stimulus from the introduction of softball and night games under floodlights.

Almost twenty years after the first game of intercollegiate football was played at New Brunswick, New Jersey, in 1869, this American modification of English rugby was accepted by Southern collegians. It was first played at the University of Virginia in 1888,[5] then at Tulane University in 1890, at Georgia Tech in 1892, and at almost all the male colleges of the South by 1900. For twenty-five years Southern elevens enjoyed only local fame, apparently unable to compete successfully with celebrated teams of the North. The defeat of Virginia by Princeton in 1890 by a score of 115 to 0 was long remembered. Southern football was thought to be handicapped by an enervating climate, sectional isolation, and the distribution of players among small colleges. There were exceptions; for example, Coach Dan McGugin's team at Vanderbilt University scored a 4 to 0 victory over the famed Carlisle Indians of Pennsylvania in 1906, and the Praying Colonels of little Centre College in Kentucky enjoyed brief fame in 1921 by conquering the Harvard Crimson. Between 1926 and World War II, Southern elevens won many victories of national importance. On New Year's Day, 1926, the Crimson Tide of the University of Alabama, under Coach Wallace Wade, won the Eastern-Western Championship by defeating Washington State in the Rose Bowl at Pasadena, California. The University of Georgia defeated Yale thrice within four years. In 1930 Vanderbilt triumphed over Minnesota, Florida over Chicago, and Duke over the Naval Academy. In 1938 Texas Christian University, Tennessee, and Duke were rated among the foremost elevens of the country, because they went through the season without being scored on. Tennessee and Maryland enjoyed the same distinction in 1951. Georgia won the Rose Bowl contest in 1943, Alabama in 1946.

These and other triumphs encouraged enormous enthusiasm for football among Southerners. Scruples against professionalism and favoritism toward players, and against long training seasons were less pronounced than in sections of the country where academic standards were higher. Ardent alumni joined spectacle-hungry mobs in forcing timid college authorities to make the football team the principal purpose of academic existence. It was discovered that Southern climate was an asset rather than a liability, allowing what a writer in 1930 called "a medieval pageantry long forgotten in the East." Men in bare legs and wearing the lightest equipment played against a background of shirt sleeves, girls in summer dresses, and gallons of ice cream, Coca-Cola, and corn whisky. The "rah-rah spirit" was as prevalent among the collegians of the South in 1930 as it had been among their fellow Northerners in 1890. The

[5] Philip A. Bruce, *History of the University of Virginia*, IV, 142–3.

Southerners heartily endorsed feminine sponsors, pep meetings, brass-band rallies, and victory bonfires. To accommodate the crowds football stadiums were constructed in every city and on many campuses. The best known of these were the Sugar Bowl at New Orleans, the Orange Bowl at Miami, the Cotton Bowl at Dallas, and the Sun Bowl at El Paso. In imitation of Pasadena, the final games of the season were held on New Year's Day after wintry weather had closed the stadiums in colder climes. Southern attendance records rivaled—if they did not equal—those of the great Eastern and Western population centers. In 1938, some 52,000 people gathered at Durham to watch Duke play the University of Pittsburgh, and in 1941 the greatest Southern attendance record up to that time was attained when 73,181 assembled in the Sugar Bowl to see Boston College defeat the University of Tennessee. This record was broken in 1950 when 82,470 persons assembled in the same place to see Oklahoma defeat Louisiana State.

The development of mass participation in organized sports during the second and third decades of the twentieth century marked a radical change in Southern habits. Heretofore, most outdoor exercises were regarded as something for common laborers, sport-loving youngsters, and men enjoying a bit of roughhouse. Gentlemen made an exception only in favor of military drill and riding to the chase. "The Southerner of the small towns and cities," Holland Thompson wrote as late as 1919,[6] "puts away play with his adolescence. . . . Golf has gained no foothold except in the larger towns, and even there the existence of the country club is often precarious. Few males except college youth will be seen on the tennis court, if indeed there be one in a town of five thousand people." The direct rays of the sun were regarded as perilous to beauty and health. The fair sex confined its outdoor exercises to horseback riding and surf bathing under the protection of several layers of clothing.

Important changes became evident at the time of World War I. Colleges and schools popularized gymnastics. Northern tourists demonstrated the advantages of golf and other outdoor sports. Southerners appreciated the claims of certain Northern magazines concerning the benefits of physical culture. Women learned to play basketball, hockey, and other strenuous games. In an effort to rid themselves of the stiff formality acquired when they abandoned the plantation for the office, men of the upper classes returned to the short trousers of their boyhood days, and began swinging clubs and rackets. Swimming pools appeared everywhere; baseball, football, and basketball became as popular in the high schools as in the colleges. The introduction of softball marked a turning point in the history of mass sports. This game, substituting a

[3] *The New South*, p. 208.

softer ball for the hard and lively device of traditional baseball, was said to have originated in Florida. Its less adventurous character made possible the widest participation—by the very young and those approaching middle age, by girls and boys alike, by amateurs as well as experienced players. By 1930 many a vacant lot had been turned into a softball diamond, with thousands devoting their late afternoons to the sport.

Florida went to extremes in mass sports, even organizing older persons into clubs for lawn bowling, shuffleboard, roque, horseshoe pitching, checkers, dominoes, and bridge. One shuffleboard club in St. Petersburg claimed 4,000 members, and an annual card party in the same city attracted 3,000 players. More typical of the South as a whole was the development in Atlanta. For its vast system of supervised recreation that city in 1939 provided thirty-seven playgrounds that were used by 700 basketball players, 1,200 softball lovers, and 1,000 baseball participants. In addition, there were eighty-three municipal tennis courts, fifteen golf courses, and many swimming pools and gymnasiums.

The most esteemed sport of mature men and women of the middle and upper classes was golf. Although introduced into Georgia as early as 1756, not until the end of the nineteenth century did Southerners evince much interest in the game. However, by 1930 every city had its country club where the chief attraction was the golf course. Although it was a rather expensive form of exercise, clerks and others of the lower middle classes were tempted to imitate their social betters. Toward that end private links were supplemented by municipally owned courses.

Golf became almost as popular among men as baseball among boys. Every Southern state took pride in the number and quality of its golf courses; Florida boasted of 200, Georgia 150, Arkansas 51. Texas claimed to possess more public courses than any other American state, and North Carolina's 87 in 64 different places offered a wide variety of terrain from 8 to 4,000 feet above sea level. At Pinehurst, North Carolina, more golf was said to be played annually than anywhere else in the world. Many state, sectional, and national tournaments were played on the South's best-known courses. The section contributed its share of national and international golf champions. As famous as Ty Cobb in baseball and Wallace Wade in football was Bobby Jones, the Atlantan who captured the highest golf honors in 1930—the American Amateur, the American Open, the British Amateur, and the British Open.

The oldest, most democratic, and genuinely native sport of the South was the hunting of wild animals. It was practiced with as much zeal in the twentieth century as in the Old South. It was no more uniquely Southern than churchgoing; however, it was pursued with rare enthusiasm by both gentlemen and common folks. A considerable amount of surplus wealth went into hunting clubs. In the swampy regions of the Atlantic and Gulf coasts there were millionaires' estates from whose hunting privileges the common folk were as rigidly excluded as from similar lands in England. In Northern Virginia fox hunting was conducted with all the expensive artificialities of its English counterpart. Game laws of a growing complexity were enacted, generally for the purpose of protecting wild life.

The fields and forests of the South were so open and plentiful that hunting almost seemed a gift of nature, and hunters roamed over lands with impunity, failing to respect the laws of exclusion. The poorest and most primitive inhabitants of the land, whether mountaineer, poor white, or black cabin dweller, always possessed the minimum necessities of the chase—a shotgun and one or more hounds. Country youths were ever ready to put off their tasks in order to pursue any form of wild life. An ordinarily rough Southerner could be extremely sentimental over hunting dogs; they were supported in large numbers, fondled in old age, their memories cherished after death. Perhaps hunting dogs caused as many feuds and homicides in the South as overindulgence in alcohol.

The extent and variety of hunting would fill a long catalogue. Almost everywhere bird hunting attracted the largest number of sportsmen, with quail the favored game. In the marshes and lakes of the coastal areas and of the great Mississippi Flyway, thousands of hunters each year awaited the passage of ducks and other varieties of swimming and wading migrants. In the forested regions experienced hunters were able to lure the wild turkey within range of their guns. Tracking down rabbit, squirrel, 'possum, and raccoon was commonplace. Fox hunting was not the exclusive prerogative of the wealthy but also a sport for the plebeian without horses; the hunters moved on foot or in automobiles, or merely sat around fires and listened to the blended echoing of the dogs. Twentieth-century conditions enhanced rather than diminished the opportunities for hunting in the South. More intelligent game laws restrained the ruthless, and vast public and private game preserves were created for the protection and propagation of wild creatures.

The invention of the automobile considerably enlarged the area in which a quarry could be hunted. Reports from various states in the years preceding World War II afforded glimpses of expanding resources of the section. Texas placed the value of its wild life at $94,350,394, and in addition to ordinary animals boasted of its bears, wildcats, mountain lions, and wolves. The Southeastern Field Trials at Albany, Georgia, was a competition attended by "some of the best dog handlers with the finest bird dogs in the country." [7] Duck hunting became so popular in Arkansas that Stuttgart and other towns in the rice belt experienced

[7] American Guide Series, *Georgia*, p. 105.

mild business booms during the hunting season. Tennessee had its mounted hunt clubs and One-Gallus Fox Hunters' Association, shooting contests stemming from the rifle contests of pioneer days, and sensational wild bear chase made possible by the importation of that fighting animal from Russia. An indication that Florida did not intend to surrender hunting as one of its major attractions was its deliberate preservation of black bears, panthers, and wildcats in the swamps. In one preserve alone 5,000 deer were kept behind fences for restocking purposes.

The history of fishing in the modern South resembles that of hunting. There exists the same wide variety from tiny catfish to fighting sharks, tarpons, and other salt-water giants—everything from deep-sea catches to the fresh-water products of quiet lagoons and mountain rapids. Apart from fishing as a recreation, there is the industry which has no small share in feeding the nation.

In the use of the rod and reel Florida led the South. Its coastal cities had tarpon and sailfish tournaments; its lakes, rivers, and runs were stocked with black bass, and other fresh-water giants; even its radio stations broadcast fishing lore. Other states were less organized in their fishing activities but aroused almost as much natural enthusiasm for the sport as the state that developed a mere diversion into a major industry.

A survey of the South's social and recreational activities during the seventy-five years after Reconstruction leads to the conclusion reached in other aspects of the section's life. Although changes occurred, there was no fundamental alteration in its distinctive folkways. New classes rose to power at the expense of the old; new recreational activities were introduced with a revolution in the popular attitude toward outdoor exercises. These innovations destroyed the sectional peculiarities to no greater degree than corresponding developments in the realms of politics, industry, and race relations. The new ruling classes inherited the old ideals. The shifting of population and domestic rearrangements did not destroy the home as the anchor of Southern society. There were new foods, but no fundamental difference in eating habits. Modern diversions were made to conform to Southern customs and predilections. Significant in this connection was the fact that the ancient sport of hunting was retained as the most enduring recreation of all.

CHAPTER XXVI

Survival of Religion

⤜⤜⤜

ORTHODOX Protestantism in the Old South had been in a large measure responsible for the failure of the Negroes and non-slaveholding whites to regard abolition of slavery as a means of advancing their earthly welfare. The unrelenting hold of "the old-time religion" upon Southerners of the post-Civil War generations had a similar retarding effect. It partly explains why the section, in the face of revolutions in transportation, industry, and education, maintained its cultural identity in the twentieth century. The Word of God as revealed in the Book continued to provide the great masses with an unchanging and certain truth before which the demonstrations of scientists and social reformers seemed negligible. The modern Southerner accepted scientific technology, but he refused to be separated from the view "that man holds a position in the universe under divine guidance"; he refused to convert science into a religion or a philosophy of life. Such elementary orthodoxy explains not only the difficulty of arousing Southern churches to the need of social reform, but also the indifference of Southerners toward nonreligious themes except those of a political or purely practical nature. Public forums, even in larger cities, were rare and street-corner orators discoursing on other than religious themes were unknown.

Communistic and other radical doctrines were seldom understood below the Potomac. Northern Negro radicals were ignored by the majority of Southern Negro Christians, just as were Boston and New York journalists who since the days of William Lloyd Garrison had admonished Southerners to change their evil ways. Southern liberals with the Jeffersonian tradition of religious indifference had little direct influence beyond academic halls and editorial sanctums. One of this group after moving to the secular atmosphere of Harvard University in 1939 wrote despairingly that the pervading influence of religion had recreated an Old South unable to grow into a New South.[1]

Organized Christianity in the twentieth century tightened its hold upon the people of the South. Church membership in the section increased from 10,562,000 in 1906 to 15,678,000 in 1926. In the latter year 61.4 per cent of the adult population of the states of the Southeast were enrolled in church, the largest proportional membership in any section of the United States; this group was also spending a greater portion of their total incomes for church purposes than any other group in the country. This could not be said of Texas and Oklahoma, where a certain amount of frontier indifference to organized religion still prevailed. However, these two areas were traveling in the direction of other Southern states; in the twenty years after 1906 their proportional increase in church membership was even greater than that of the section lying east of them. Orthodox Protestantism dominated Texas and Oklahoma. Baptists, doctrinally the most conservative sect, were predominant, followed by the Methodists, the most aggressive morally and politically. In 1926 Baptists and Methodists comprised at least three fourths of the church membership of the two Carolinas, Georgia, Alabama, Mississippi, and Arkansas, as well as half the membership of all other Southern states except Louisiana.

During the twenty years prior to 1926 the more important Protestant denominations experienced greater growth in the South than in any section of the country except the new West. The 34.6 per cent increase in the Southern white Baptist church represented the largest expansion of any of the major churches of that period. One fact about the history of the Southern church not applicable to other sections of the civilized world, was that the advance of industry, urbanization, and education helped rather than hindered the advance of religious organizations. That church membership in Southern cities grew more rapidly than their whole populations proved as much. The comparative percentages of these increases between 1916 and 1926 was 19.3 in membership and 16.5 in whole population for Richmond; for Dallas, 81.7 and 66.8 respectively; for San Antonio, 55.7 and 48.3; for Birmingham, 58.0 and 29.4; for New Orleans, 35.1 and 13.4; for Memphis, 62.0 and 23.0.[2] In a typical Southern community one could seldom find a native adult of the middle or upper classes who had not been baptized into some Christian communion. The 38.6 per cent of adults of the Southeastern states who were not church members in 1926 were illiterates, isolated mountaineers, poor whites, and Negroes. These were the persons who might be

---

[1] Carroll Kilpatrick in *The Nation*, CLI, 311–12 (October 5, 1940).
[2] *Census of Religious Bodies, 1926*, I, 68–9.

expected to join the church when they became sufficiently educated to understand the Southern heritage.

The continued dominance of a fundamental orthodoxy among the common people did not prevent noteworthy changes in the theology and ritual of churches of the upper classes. Some of these changes met the approval of outside critics because they were in the direction of liberalism and enlightenment. This was possible because such centers of science and liberalism as the University of North Carolina, and Emory, Vanderbilt, Sewanee, Tulane and Duke universities imposed modern ideas upon the top layer of Southern society as well as the clergy who ministered to this group. Older churches of the cities and towns discarded the revivalistic emotionalism which originated with untutored Baptists and Methodists, and favored a more rational behavior and a ritualism approximating that of the Episcopal church. Episcopalian formalism gained in the newer cities the prestige it always enjoyed along the Atlantic seaboard; the increase from 129,000 members in 1906 to 256,000 in 1936 is only a partial record of its expanding influence.

The aristocratic tradition of the Episcopal church drew many persons of social ambition, wealth, and education who previously were members of more democratic faiths. Sophisticated congregations among Presbyterians, Methodists, and Baptists sacrificed simplicity for rituals similar to those of the Episcopalians. This tendency was expressed in the construction of elaborate churches, including Duke University Chapel, First Baptist Church at Richmond, Centenary Methodist Church at Winston-Salem, Scarritt College Chapel at Nashville, Idlewilde Presbyterian Church at Memphis, and First Methodist Church at Fort Worth. All were imposing and beautiful, but unoriginal in the sense that they copied the Gothic or classical. A church at once original and imposing was the Boston Avenue Methodist Church at Tulsa, conceived by Adah Robinson, a local artist. This striking example of modern ecclesiastical architecture had an illuminated tower of 290 feet and decorations of cubistic images, pointed arches, terra-cotta, and bas-relief of pioneer characters.

The Roman Catholic church in the twentieth century made moderate gains in the South. In fourteen Southern states it grew from 1,721,000 members in 1906 to 2,215,000 members in 1936. Its main strength was among the least Southern of Southerners: among the Louisiana French, among the Texans of Mexican origin, and among immigrants to the cities from the North or from Europe. The region between the Potomac and the Mississippi, with one fifth of the American people, possessed only one fortieth of the American Catholics. There was only one Catholic for every 60 persons in South Carolina;

only one for every 100 persons in Tennessee and Georgia; and only one for every 200 persons in North Carolina.

The Old World flavor of the Church of Rome continued, as in the Old South, to run counter to the English traditions and the deeply ingrained nativism of the Southern people. This church showed a preference for non-Southern priests; it refused to compromise with Southern puritanism, the Southern practice of dividing congregations on class lines, and the Southern practice of congregational rather than clerical control of church affairs. It was unwilling or unable to recover the aristocratic prestige which it possessed before the Irish took control away from the Maryland and Louisiana gentry.

In recent decades the Catholics have been active among the Negroes, abandoning the cynical belief that the Negro was emotionally and morally too unrestrained to tolerate the Catholic discipline. A seminary for the training of Negro priests was founded at Bay St. Louis, Mississippi, in 1923. Missions were established in various places of the South to make a systematic approach to the educational and recreational problems of the race. Outstanding was St. Jude's Mission in Montgomery, whose imposing buildings arose amid Negro slums.

Traditionally the Catholic church accepted the mores of the South to the extent of providing separate seats or separate church buildings for the two races. But of late church authorities have demanded a greater degree of race equality. The Archbishop of St. Louis instructed parochial schools to admit Negroes and the Archbishop of New Orleans refused to hold an outdoor meeting in a public stadium because a city ordinance required segregation. But it is not likely that this social radicalism will draw the Negroes to the Catholic church to any greater degree than a similar policy, eighty years ago, drew Negroes into the Northern Protestant churches. The Negro wants a greater measure of religious freedom than an institution as rigid in its discipline as the Catholic church is willing to give him.

The conservative forces that controlled most of the Protestant churches of the New South had one great weakness: lack of an intellectual defense of orthodoxy comparable to that with which Presbyterian divines of the Old South supported the doctrinal and social conservatism of their times. There was no eminent twentieth-century theologian to protect inherited traditions against the pressure of liberal theological and scientific thought which assaulted it. When the most sensational of these liberal attacks occurred in 1925 at Dayton, Tennessee, millions of orthodox Southerners were forced to adopt the defense advanced by William Jennings Bryan, a distinguished politician with little theological learning. Southern universities were on the side of the invading liberals, accepting in the twentieth century the materialistic science and psychology which Europe gave the North in the nineteenth. Even Southern theological seminaries of highest academic rating took a similar stand. Methodist Bishop Warren A. Candler was unable to preserve the orthodox character of the theological school at Emory University which his millionaire brother had named in the bishop's honor. Uncompromising conservatism sought refuge in the so-called Bible institutes, founded primarily to train religious workers insufficiently prepared to enter regular theological seminaries. When religious disputes arose, conservatives inevitably were forced to give ground.

In the South, as in other sections of the civilized world, the twentieth century brought a decline in clerical influence. This took several forms. The leadership in Southern thought, which in proslavery days had been shared by Presbyterians and politicians, now passed into the hands of nonclerical editors, educators, and businessmen. In the church itself businessmen usurped authority once held by clergymen; this especially applied to the trusteeships of denominational colleges. Nonreligious activities were encouraged and hotel-like buildings for social and recreational activities far removed from the spiritual were added to church auditoriums.

The minister's place in the charitable affairs of the community, although still important, tended to be overshadowed by that of the social worker or public-spirited businessman. Many progressive ministers permitted an interest in sumptuary legislation or in the improvement of race or labor relations to obscure the historic Protestant preoccupation with heavenly salvation. In this connection it is significant that the prohibition of alcoholic liquors was the most conspicuous accomplishment of Southern Protestants in the twentieth century. The marked division of the church along sectarian lines could be attributed less to doctrinal differences than to something as worldly as class distinctions. Episcopalians were considered the sophisticates and aristocrats, Presbyterians the cultured and refined, Methodists and Baptists were found in all classes; the premillennial faiths attracted the uneducated and poor.

The first of the doctrinal disputes in the post-bellum church centered around a question of fundamental importance: whether man was miraculously made by God in His own image, or whether he evolved from natural causes out of lower species, as described by the great nineteenth-century scientist Charles Darwin. To Southern conservatives Darwinism seemed to usurp a sacred prerogative of religion by attempting to explain origins and destinies, and by lowering man to the level of animals without the personal moral responsibility of Christianity. To Southern liberals, on the other hand, Darwinism seemed to offer the church an opportunity to discharge its historic mission of reconciling dogma with accepted scientific doctrine.

The issue came to the foreground in 1884, thirteen years after the publication of Darwin's *Descent of Man*. At that time, James Woodrow, who held the Professorship of Natural Science in connection with Revelation at the Presbyterian Theological Seminary at Columbia, South Carolina, published his address *Evolution*. This able graduate of the German university at Heidelberg maintained that "the Bible does not teach science" and that a sympathetic understanding of the theory of evolution did not lead to doubt, but to a more profound reverence for God's plan of creation. The writer of these affirmations was accused of teachings calculated to destroy the authority of Holy Scripture and, after four years of controversy, was removed from his professorship. But the courageous and enlightened manner in which Woodrow urged the claims of science on religion was an important step in the progress of free thought in the South. Thereafter the advocates of unyielding orthodoxy were in retreat. Their most formidable champion was Robert Lewis Dabney, once major on the staff of Stonewall Jackson. For three decades after the fall of the Confederacy in lectures and in books he energetically expounded the dogma that virtue had its origin in divine fiat, that the Civil War was a Christian struggle of a justified South against a wicked North, and that it was "a deadly mistake" for Southerners to become like their conquerors in praising "mines and banks, and stock boards, and horse-powers of steam, and patent machines." [3]

The freeing of higher education from clerical control is illustrated by Vanderbilt University's break with the authority of the Methodist church. When Chancellor James H. Kirkland attempted to carry out the liberal policies of the Methodist ministers in whose hands Commodore Cornelius Vanderbilt had placed the institution, he was attacked by conservative Methodist leaders. They desired the suppression of certain types of liberal thinking and sought the services of professors who were "zealous and active Methodists." The General Conference of the Southern Methodist church brought suit in 1910 to establish the contentions that the conference should elect the trustees of the university and that the bishops should have the right of visitation.

Although Southern popular sentiment supported church authorities, the Tennessee supreme court decided against them in 1914, emphasizing that the subscriptions the church provided through public appeal were insufficient to finance a large university. The church authorities subsequently withdrew from all affiliations with the school, and Kirkland,

[3] Dabney, cited in C. Vann Woodward, *Origins of the New South, 1877–1913,* p. 174.

with substantial assistance from the Vanderbilt family and wealthy alumni, lived to see Vanderbilt University free of the "narrow sectarianism and belligerent fundamentalism" which he despised. A plutocracy, liberal in theological but not in economic matters, had triumphed over mass orthodoxy. The beneficiaries of economic privilege, a professor had already complained,[4] had "found places on college boards of control, and now threaten both legislator and teacher who speak the truth about their doings."

Another example of the inability of the common people to control the thinking of a college community is afforded by Trinity College, the North Carolina Methodist institution which later became Duke University. In 1903 John S. Bassett, a professor of history who took a peculiar delight in describing the decline of the planter class, published in the *South Atlantic Quarterly* an article that offended orthodox racial views. He declared that Booker T. Washington, the Negro who induced Northern capitalists to spend money on the education of his race, was "the greatest man, save Robert E. Lee, born in the South in a hundred years."[5] This brought upon the head of the outspoken professor the wrath of Josephus Daniels, editor of the Raleigh *News and Observer*. Bassett offered to resign in the face of dire threats, but the trustees of Trinity College upheld the right of a college professor to express unorthodox opinions on social matters.

After failure to control Southern educational institutions by exerting pressure on their governing bodies, the adherents of social and religious orthodoxy attempted other tactics. In 1910 they formulated their views in twelve booklets entitled *The Fundamentals: A Testimony to the Truth*. This gave them the name of Fundamentalists, and as such they circulated their ideas freely among sympathetic multitudes of the South. Their opportunity for action came during the period following World War I when their narrow traditionalism was challenged by the unlicensed freedom of Southern universities. From academic halls came such revolutionary, perhaps even sinister, ideas as a mechanistic psychology that eliminated the soul, a sociology that minimized individual moral responsibility, a Freudianism in which sex motivation replaced spiritual values. This new freedom in teaching was reflected in student conduct, in jazz music and dancing, in excessive drinking, in a free association of the sexes that approached the scandalous. Yet Southern public opinion as a whole remained old-fashioned.

Edwin Mims, a Southern liberal, recognized in 1927 that there was room for the belief that the section's "solidarity in matters of religion is

---

[4] William E. Dodd, "Freedom of Speech in the South," in *The Nation*, LXXXIV, 383–4.

[5] Bassett, cited in Edwin Mims, *The Advancing South*, p. 148.

quite as well established as its solidarity in politics." [6] Was it not time for action on the part of those who saw their sons and daughters imperiled by the postwar freedom of the colleges? An Englishman had written, "The South is by a long way the most simply and sincerely religious country that I was ever in. In other countries men are apt to make a private matter of their religion . . . ; but the Southerner wears it on his sleeve." [7] Appreciating the political advantage of superior numbers, the Fundamentalists asked legislatures dependent upon the votes of the orthodox multitudes to outlaw the teaching of evolution in state-supported schools. Bills to that effect failed by narrow margins in the South Carolina and Kentucky legislatures in 1921. The Fundamentalists, however, had better luck in 1923. In that year the Florida legislature by joint resolution condemned the teaching of Darwinism in tax-supported schools. The disputed theory was interdicted at the same time by a clause of the free textbook law of Oklahoma. Two years later the Tennessee legislature, by majorities of 71 to 5 and 24 to 6, forbade any educational institution supported by public funds "to teach the theory that denies the story of divine creation as taught in the Bible."

Although law-enforcing agencies made no actual effort to execute the Tennessee antievolution law in the classrooms, the liberal consciousness of the nation and the world was shocked. Advocates of untrammeled teaching of science became aggressive. John T. Scopes, a high school teacher of biology at Dayton, Tennessee, deliberately violated the law in order to create a test case. The Dayton courthouse became the scene of a memorable battle between the orthodox people of Tennessee and outside forces demanding academic freedom unhampered by religion-motivated laws. The antievolutionists were led by William Jennings Bryan, proevolutionists by the renowned freethinker Clarence Darrow. Scopes was convicted in the Dayton trial, and the constitutionality of the law was upheld by the courts. The Southern Baptist Convention in the same year of the Dayton trial rejected "every theory, evolutionary or otherwise, which teaches that man originated or came by way of lower animal ancestry." Mississippi in 1926, and Arkansas in 1928, entered antievolutionary laws in their statute books.

The Fundamentalists had overshot the mark. The ridicule which Darrow and the Northern press visited upon Bryan for his inept prosecution of the Scopes case made most Southern legislative and prosecuting authorities reluctant to run the risk of similar trials. Accordingly, no other states followed the example of Tennessee, Mississippi, and Arkansas in passing antievolution laws. In North Carolina President Harry Woodburn Chase of the state university and President William

[6] *Ibid.*, p. 281.
[7] Sir William Archer, cited in Woodward, *op. cit.*, p. 169.

Louis Poteat of Wake Forest College turned the tide in the other direction by courageous arguments before legislative authorities. In 1927 the educational association of the Southern Methodist church expressed its conviction that "legislation which would interfere with the proper teaching of science in American schools and colleges is futile and can serve no good purpose."

Oklahoma promptly repealed its antievolution proviso; although Tennessee, Mississippi, and Arkansas did not do so, they took no steps to enforce their laws. The Bryan Memorial University, established at Dayton in honor of William Jennings Bryan, who had succumbed to overexertion induced by the Scopes trial, failed to achieve importance. Fundamentalism lost respectability because of the erratic and often disreputable conduct of its leaders. John Roach Straton, a Georgian who had established an outpost of Fundamentalism in New York City, was caught in financial irregularities by a hostile press, and J. Frank Norris, a Texan preacher whose special mission was the exposure of unorthodox professors before his congregation, was brought into court on charges of perjury, arson, and murder. By 1930 Fundamentalism as an organized movement had collapsed; nevertheless, it served as a salutary warning to Southern centers of learning. Most colleges and universities retreated from the immature license that marked their period of growth after World War I. They learned to exercise their freedom discreetly and to respect the opinions of the orthodox families who sent them their sons for education.

A significant example of the progressive tendencies of Southern religion was the healing of the ninety-five-year schism in American Methodism. On May 10, 1939, at a grand general conference at Kansas City, representatives of more than two million members of the Methodist Episcopal church, South, joined representatives of the Methodist Episcopal church and the Methodist Protestant church to form a nationwide body of nearly eight millions, called simply the Methodist church. As the sectional animosities created by slavery, Civil War, and Reconstruction faded into history, the need for this action had become increasingly apparent. Friends of unification cited that there had never been important differences of policy, dogma, or ritual between Northern and Southern Methodism. The Wesleyan emphasis on right living, rather than on right belief, and on Christ-likeness rather than on various concepts of Christ, prevented Southern Methodism from harboring conservative theology to the degree with which it was cherished by the more dogmatic branches of Southern Protestantism. With the advance of clerical education, Southern Methodist ministers learned to appreciate the advantages of closer fellowship with their coreligionists from more progressive sections of the country.

Because of the centralized character of Methodist church government, bishops were able to swing the councils of the church toward unification despite much opposition from laymen and lesser clergy. Participation of the Southern church in political and social agitations had proved to its leaders that their condemnation of the Northern church for conducting similar projects was wholly unjustified. This spirit of accord was even more strengthened when the Northern church laid aside its anti-Southern and pro-Negro propaganda to join Southerners in the prohibitionist issue. Both Southerners and Northerners recognized the practical necessity of checking the duplication of pastoral efforts in at least twenty-six states. In one year the two denominations spent $750,000 for the support of competing churches.

A joint commission on federation had suggested unification in 1911, but this group's proposal was not readily accepted. In 1925 the General Conference of the Southern church finally approved it by an overwhelming majority of 298 to 74; nevertheless, the annual conferences of the states failed to give the necessary three fourths majorities. Antiunificationists under the persuasive leadership of Bishops Collins Denny of Richmond and Warren A. Candler of Atlanta aroused much opposition. They charged that the integrity of social and religious institutions of the Southern minority would be endangered by organic union with a Methodist majority notorious for two types of radicalism: new tendencies toward theological liberalism, and century-old leanings toward race equality. The first objection was minimized by the growth of liberalism in the Southern church; the second was overcome by incorporating in the plan of union a compromise that reconciled conflicting views concerning the church relations of the Negroes. This was dispatched with an adroitness matching that of Southern statesmen a generation earlier in reconciling Negro disfranchisement with the Fifteenth Amendment. Under the plan of union the United States was divided into five jurisdictional conferences for white Methodists, with a separate jurisdictional meeting for most of the Negro members of the Northern church. The jurisdictional conferences were accorded much the same authority previously exercised by the two general groups which were uniting.

Segregation of the Negroes was necessary to satisfy immutable Southern custom, and was justified as the only means by which Negroes could be sure of controlling their own bishops and church life. Nearly two million Negroes who were members of the African Methodist Episcopal church, the African Methodist Episcopal church, Zion, and the Colored Methodist church were not affected by the plan of union. This document was first accepted by the Northern church; by 1937 all the local conferences of the Southern church except that of

Northern Mississippi had sanctioned it. In 1938 it was adopted by the General Conference of the Southern church by vote of 434 to 26. The act of unification was affected at Kansas City the following year. A minority led by Bishop Denny refused to accept the verdict and continued a small denomination under the old name of Methodist Episcopal church, South.

The collapse of Fundamentalism as an organized movement and the triumph of progressive nationalism among the Methodists should not lead to the assumption that the second decade after World War I witnessed a general decline of provincialism and obscurantism in the religious life of the South. Actually, many traditional attitudes remained unchanged. For the forward strides that caused liberals to rejoice there were perhaps as many backward steps toward illiberal standards of historic Protestantism, or even the accommodation of superstitions of the Southern backwoods. For Methodist unification the liberal nationalists had to pay a heavy price to Southern tradition—the Northerners' acceptance of the principle of race segregation. Moreover, Methodist unification was not emulated by other denominations important in Southern life.

The same year in which the Methodists acted, the Southern Baptist Convention forthrightly announced its refusal "to join hands with creed-makers and church-breakers in their merger movements." The 4,582 delegates to this assembly were too close to the 4,389,417 white Southerners they represented to compromise Baptist principles with those of other denominations. This was another example of Southern democracy expressing itself in reactionary channels. The Southern Baptists, like the Roman Catholics, tended to believe that theirs was the only road to salvation. For the absolutism of the One was substituted the absolutism of the Many. Certainly the Baptist multitudes of the South were unwilling to come to terms with the Northern Baptists, who were believed to be contaminated by a dangerous liberalism in social and theological matters.

The discrediting of Fundamentalist organizations was not an indication of the decline of orthodoxy. Religious orthodoxy, like racial or political doctrines, was so firmly established that prudent Southerners saw no need for excessively militant groups acting beyond the restraints of the traditional churches. To demand responsibility and decorum was as much a part of the conservative instinct in the South as elsewhere. In other words, the Fundamentalist organizations were discouraged for the same reason as the Ku Klux Klan movement. Besides, in the decades after World War I the South was influenced by many currents that ran counter to progressive forces. Orthodoxy and reaction took on startling forms not previously known to religion.

While upper-class churches in the cities and larger towns were assuming the formalities of liturgical churches, the middle classes were reinterpreting their faith in terms of their environment. Without altering historic Protestantism, they introduced modern imagery in their rituals. In thousands of Southern Baptist and Methodist churches sermons were delivered in the informal language of the streets by preachers in business suits. For subject matter the conventional biblical themes were often adapted to topics as contemporary as those that engaged the attention of politicians and editors of secular journals.

Yet these preachers were orthodox, often fighting alien ideas and theological modernism and advocating principles of race, nationality, and morality as Southern as the Ku Klux Klan. Hymns to tunes heard in the contemporary dance halls were rendered by modishly dressed girls to the accompaniment of modern musical instruments—the saxophone and slide trombone. Social life on church premises was modernized. To the churches were added banqueting halls, kitchens, parlors, and other facilities for social enjoyment. There, under clerical direction, arose new types of social intercourse in which the spiritual and the worldly were deftly blended. Dining alternated with games and diverse cultural activities. The puritan tradition, however, prohibited dancing, drinking, and card playing on church premises. The tradition of Christian charity prevented the ministers of conservative churches from condoning mob violence and race injustice.

Through the meetings of the twentieth-century traveling evangelists millions of Southerners entered into God's company of the redeemed. Sam Jones, the first and most interesting, as well as the wittiest and most genuinely Southern of these preachers, died in 1906; there were many imitators of his methods after 1910. Foremost among them were Mordecai F. Ham of Kentucky, "Cyclone Mack" (Baxter McLendon) of South Carolina, Billy Graham of North Carolina, "Fighting Bob" Shuler of Virginia, and the Texan J. Frank Norris. Imported from England and the Middle West respectively were Gypsy Smith, Jr., and Billy Sunday. "Multiplying in Dixie with a rapidity unexampled since the early nineteenth-century revivals," exhorters set up their tents in all Southern towns and cities. They were frequently self-confessed sinners called to preach by ecstatic experiences of conversion that overtook them in mature life.

Although they cast doubt upon the validity of church organizations and often incurred the dislike of the regular clergy because of their lack of schooling and vulgar manners and speech, they were ultraconservative in their theology. These evangelists viewed worldly society pessimistically and ignored the problems of social reform. A few, like Billy Sunday, especially catered to the rich, but most of them appealed to the masses in the tenement areas of the new towns. Disappointed or sick souls sought refuge from the confusion and discouragement of urban life in an old-fashioned gospel that blotted out transgressions, guaranteed salvation from a hard world, and offered a crown of life in eternity. Some revivalists blatantly measured success in terms of the money they were able to collect; however, many others derived the greatest satisfaction from providing a haven for many humble Christians lost through denominational neglect or through the cold formalism of rituals and sermons designed for those more fortunately situated.

The old Protestant tendency to be as primitive as the Apostles and to practice certain biblical injunctions literally was steadfastly observed by many Southerners. They were as numerous as those who fostered the sectional and doctrinal tolerance in the upper-class churches of the cities. Although the humble dissenters from progressive tendencies were ridiculed as "Holy Rollers" by the educated, the peculiarities of their faith had sound basis in Christian tradition. They revolted against the progressive churches' tacit acceptance of rational or scientific causations, and favored a divine Providence presumably interested enough in His children to minister to their needs. Accordingly, these sectarians were often divine healers, believers in heavenly intervention in favor of the sick. They reported varied experiences with the unknown tongue and pillars of fire, means through which God conversed with the faithful. Frequently they were Premillennialists, believers that Christ would not postpone indefinitely His Second Coming to save His troubled people. This emphasis on man's hopes for the future was more satisfying to practical Christians than the earlier explanations of man's origin. What is supposed to have happened had been discredited by the scientific data of the Darwinians; what was going to happen seemed beyond human criticism.

Many of these Holy Rollers were forceful demonstrators before God of the joys He bestowed. Given to prophecy, they believed that hidden in the obscurities of the Prophets and the Apocalypse were divinely inspired keys to future events. Each of the Primitivist sects was intensely separatist and intolerant of those who did not see God's truth from their viewpoint; still they introduced no unorthodox ideas to conflict with their Protestant heritage. These Primitivists differed most significantly from the great religions of the middle and upper classes in their unrestrained approval of accepted Christian doctrines. They were people who were often found shouting, screaming, and jumping; for to them the events narrated in the New Testament were still the most exciting news the human race has ever had. The South was not a favorable soil for such heresies as Christian Science or the Oriental mystery cults. Father Divine, although himself a Southern Negro, found few

Southerners of either race who would believe his audacious claim to divinity. Amidst sectarian diversity general doctrinal harmony prevailed, with no fundamental differences between the beliefs of the High Church Episcopalians and the Holy Rollers.

Some believers in Primitive Christianity were members of sects of pre-Civil War origin. For example, there were the 110,000 Southerners of both races who, in 1936, belonged to the Primitive Baptist church —a denomination founded a hundred years earlier in protest to the alleged unscriptural character of Sunday schools, missions, and other coordinating agencies of the majority Baptists. These dissenters believed in foot-washing and the full verbal inspiration of the Bible, but they opposed formal Biblical instruction as a barrier to individual interpretation of the Scriptures. Another of the older groups of foot-washing conservatives was the Duck River Baptists, a sect which in 1936 held the allegiance of some 7,000 Tennessee and Alabama highlanders. The Associate Reform Presbyterian church, a body with eighteenth-century roots and adherents among the upper classes, grew from 13,201 members in 1906 to 21,981 in 1936. The primitivism of this highly respected denomination was indicated by the exclusive use of the Psalms in praise and by emphasis on the strictest Sabbath observance. The Seventh Day Adventists in 1936 were a nationwide denomination whose Southern membership increased from 8,383 to 22,538 within thirty years. This group stressed the imminence of the Second Coming; in the interest of Scriptural literalism, it proclaimed Saturday as the Sabbath and enjoined the eating of pork and other foods condemned in the Old Testament.

Many Southerners, dissatisfied with existing opportunities to express their apostolic ardor, founded new Primitivist churches of their own late in the nineteenth century or early in the twentieth. Perhaps the most interesting of these new groups was the Church of God and the Saints of Christ, which owed its origin in 1896 to a heavenly vision of William S. Crowdy, an Oklahoma Negro cook on the Santa Fe Railroad. Crowdy claimed prophetic endowments and a call to lead Negroes to the true religion. His labors bore fruit in a religious body that had 213 churches and 37,084 members by 1936; this organization was directed from headquarters near Portsmouth, Virginia. Their belief that the Negro race was descended from the ten lost tribes of Israel prompted members of the Church of God and the Saints of Christ to use the Hebrew language in their rituals and to observe the Jewish calendar and feast days, especially the Jewish Sabbath. Similar to this group was the Church of God in Christ, organized at Memphis in 1895 by the Negro Baptist minister C. H. Mason. Its first church was "set up in an old gin [house] on the banks of a little creek," [8] near Lexington,

---

[8] *Census of Religious Bodies, 1926,* p. 381.

Mississippi. Inspired by the pentacostal revival which started at Los Angeles, California, in 1906 this sect developed into a body of 772 churches and 31,564 members. It encouraged "the possibility of entire sanctification, in evidence of which they [the members] are given the power of speaking with new tongues and gifts of healing." A small but growing Negro group was the Churches of God, Holiness, founded in Atlanta in 1914 when the Reverend K. H. Burress "began preaching the doctrine of entire sanctification." With most of its recruits from Georgia and South Carolina, this church grew to 2,278 members in 1926 and to more than twice that number in 1936.[9]

Among the whites were various Holiness bodies, one of which was the Pentacostal Fire-Baptized Holiness church. Organized at Nicholson, Georgia, in 1918, its membership reached 1,348 by 1936. Another group was the Congregational Holiness church, totaling 2,167 members, mostly Georgians, in 1936. The Church of Christ (Holiness), U. S. A., organized at Selma, Alabama, in 1894, by C. P. Jones, a Baptist minister, had 7,379 members, half of them Mississippians, by 1936. Still larger was the Pentacostal Holiness church founded at Anderson, South Carolina, in 1898 by representatives from ten states who felt the need of a separate church "as the result of a revival which had swept over the Southern and Western states." In 1936 this denomination numbered 12,-955 members, most of whom lived in North Carolina, Oklahoma, South Carolina, and Virginia. This church was described as "intensely alive to all questions of public morals"; it was premillennial and believed that "provision was made for the healing of the body" by Divine dispensation, without regarding "the practice of medicine as something essentially evil." The largest of the Holiness bodies was the Church of God, organized in 1907 in Bradley County, Tennessee, with only 150 members. By 1936, however, it had grown to 44,818 members from twenty-nine states; its main membership was in Tennessee, Florida, Georgia, and Alabama. The Church of God advocated "sanctification as a second definite experience subsequent to regeneration" which is in evidence "by speaking with other tongues as the Spirit gives utterance." The Tomlinson Church of God originated in 1922 as a secession from the Church of God. In 1936 it had 18,351 members. Its founder was A. J. Tomlinson who, on a mountaintop at the North Carolina–Tennessee border, received, after a night of prayer, the first vision of the Church of God of the Last Days. Its professed purpose was to aid "the spread of the glorious gospel of Jesus Christ . . . to every creature in the whole wide world;" its most impressive activity was an annual assembly and feast at Cleveland, Tennessee.

Hidden away in the depths of the Great Smoky Mountains were

[9] *Ibid., 1926,* II, 746.

Holiness bodies which eluded the vigilant census takers. "I have been told," wrote a searcher after obscure faiths in 1950,[10] "of the Runaway Church of God, so called because it fled from a pending church merger, pastored by an old man who rides a blind mule and cannot read, but knows the Bible and the Declaration of Independence." Another vague denomination was called the Church of Brother Jesus God Almighty. Perfectly clear because of the distaste it excited was the Church of God With Signs Following After. Its chief rite was a test of power to heal persons who had allowed rattlesnakes to bite them. Did not the last chapter of the Gospel of Mark say: "They shall take up serpents?"

The churches of the South were inevitably influenced by the forces of change and progress that moved the civilized world in the late nineteenth and early twentieth centuries. They lost to the universities and the new sciences that intellectual leadership of the people which pre-Civil War ministers of the Gospel wrested from the Jeffersonian liberals. The "old-time religion" was weakened considerably when the educated accepted so un-Biblical a doctrine concerning man's destiny as Darwinian evolution. The trend of the times among the upper classes was to substitute an imitative ritualism for the emotionalism and exhortation formerly regarded as the natural core of Southern religious devotions. Apostolic zeal apparently gave way to an easy and practical reconciliation with worldly ways.

The same could be said of Southerners as they entered World War II as when they embarked upon the Civil War: they were "one of the few religious peoples left in the Western World." The great masses of both races remained virtually untouched by the winds of modernism that swept in from the outside world. For the thousands among the educated who adjusted their ritual and religious outlook to these new influences, there were other thousands whose lower-class credulity impelled them to embrace forms of Christianity as primitive as those that attracted European peasants in the seventeenth century. Superficially, the dissimilarity between Holy Rollers and upper-class churchmen was the difference between intense emotionalism and mannered restraint. Nevertheless, both groups were fundamentally Southern, both dominated by orthodoxy, natural piety, and hostility to rationalism and the spirit of free enquiry in Biblical matters. Conservatism in religion did not rank far behind traditional racial attitudes as significant causes for the South's retention of its regional distinctiveness.

[10] Archie Robertson, *That Old-Time Religion*, p. 156.

CHAPTER XXVII

Literature Since the
Civil War

⇒⟩⟩-⟩⟩

CRITICS uninformed yet clever have often repeated what Donald Davidson calls the "delightful foolishness" that the South was a literary
"Sahara of the Bozart" until they discovered some twentieth-century
writer to conform to their ideas of genius. Had not William L. Yancey
once asserted: "Our poetry is our lives; our fiction will come when
truth has ceased to satisfy." Did not the *Encyclopedia Britannica* in
1886 declare that Southern letters had been "saved from sinking to the
level of Mexico or the Antilles . . . mainly by their connection with
the North?" Did not the Kentucky-born geologist Nathaniel S. Shaler
declare as late as 1909 that four years of civil war had ended "the higher
life" in the South and set its people "on a moral and intellectual plane
lower than they occupied when they were warring with the wilderness
and the savages?" [1]

The circulation of twentieth-century Southern books published in
New York City did not suffer when their authors began to awaken a
backward land that was reputed to be at once barbaric and romantic.
Yet informed persons were aware that the area below the Potomac possessed a persistent literary tradition that had its inception many decades
before the twentieth century. The Old South, with novelists like Simms
and Kennedy, a humorist such as Longstreet, and poets like Poe and
Timrod, certainly was no literary desert.

[1] Citations in C. Vann Woodward, *Origins of the New South, 1877–1913*, pp.
162, 165.

After Appomattox the South developed a literature that expressed in words the spirit of the new era as vigorously and accurately as conveyed in deeds by merchants and industrialists. The problem of writers, like that of businessmen, was to reconcile their section with the victorious North without a humiliating sacrifice of revered traditions. They accomplished this with brilliant success. If their work was too adaptive to possess the originality of genius, the same applies to other aspects of post-bellum endeavor. The New South was more imitative than creative; its deliberate achievements were predominantly local reflections of a great nation's inventiveness.

Writers of the post-bellum period first attempted to interest the people of the defunct Confederacy in a literature distinctively Southern. This effort inspired by the old spirit of Southern independence had an overtone of hatred for the North. Chief media for its expression were *The XIXth Century*, founded at Charleston in 1869 by William Gilmore Simms and a group of associates, and *The Southern Review*, established by Albert Taylor Bledsoe at Baltimore in 1867 and dedicated to "the despised, disfranchised, and downtrodden people of the South." Bledsoe interpreted the Civil War as a conflict between principle and brute force, and justified slavery and secession on the familiar constitutional and moral grounds. John Esten Cooke, veteran novelist of the Old South, wrote *Surry of Eagle's Nest* (1866) and its sequel *Mohun* (1869), which glorified the lost cause without making any adjustments to the new age. Simms's magazine failed in 1872, and Cooke doubtless earned more by writing occasional articles for a New York newspaper than from the sale of his novels. Despite an admirable indifference to financial rewards, Bledsoe's magazine after ten-years' trial was allowed to perish by apathetic Southerners. South Carolina's poet Paul Hamilton Hayne and Lousiana's historian Charles E. A. Gayarré dedicated themselves to the outworn dogmas of the Old South. Their attitude, however, ran counter to existing literary trends, and they could do little but complain to each other of the public's gross neglect.

The South was not adequately interested in an independent sectional literature to support it. In order to be recognized in the South, Southern books were forced to become sufficiently national in tone to secure New York publishers and appeal to Northern readers. A way had to be found to link what was deemed excellent and charming in the Southern tradition with the triumphant national spirit. The literary as well as the political and economic life of the people of the destroyed Confederacy had to undergo reconstruction. The Civil War had stimulated an interest in American themes and aroused buoyant pride in the native life; literature became almost a matter of human geography. Novelists became full-fledged members of the local-color school, obliged to do little more than describe the diversities of the national scene.

The South provided perhaps the richest of all American areas for this literature. Local color could be found in every corner of the South —in its geography, as well as in its social and racial contrasts inherited from the past. There were the romantic Creoles of Louisiana, crackers of Georgia, mountaineers of Tennessee, Kentucky, Virginia, and North Carolina, and innumerable varieties of Negroes and planters. These groups were set in backgrounds of swamps, mountains, cotton fields, cabins, verandas, yellow rivers, sea islands, and towns. Love of liberty existed beside slavery, refinement and hospitality close to ignorance and barbarism; a wistful longing for the Old South mingled with hope for the New. Most important of all was the spirit of elation in participation, albeit on the losing side, in America's most tragic war experience.[2]

A group of hopeful young Southerners deftly performed the task of presenting Southern life in a manner acceptable to the American reading public. They turned their backs on the deeply ingrained Southern prejudices which would have led to obscurity in order to attune their faith to the newer creed of national reconciliation. Although they sought to give the South a significant role in American letters, they were charged with worshipping mammon, with bowing too readily to Northern flattery, and with indifference for the refinements of the age of chivalry. Yet from the homespun virtues of the New South these writers built the foundations for a body of literature more significant than anything their section had known before. Lacking formal training for literary careers, they acquitted themselves remarkably well because they were equipped by experience to write spontaneously and simply about Southern customs, scenes, and traditions. Under their own names they produced writings of merit, but their chief accomplishment was their setting the scene for the local color quintet of the 1880's: George W. Cable, Joel Chandler Harris, Thomas Nelson Page, Mary Noailles Murfree, and James Lane Allen.

Pre-eminent among the writers of the transition period was the poet and critic Sidney Lanier. Born at Macon, Georgia, in 1842, his education in such authors as Froissart and Sir Walter Scott was supplemented by a lively interest in music, in the Victorian writers, and in the value of science in modern thought. Believing that secession marked the beginning of a nation which embodied all that was fine in government and society, the youthful Lanier enlisted early in the Confederate Army. His military career ended in capture in 1864 and imprisonment at Point Lookout, Maryland. Lanier aptly described his ordeal during the "dark raven days" of Reconstruction as: "Pretty much the whole of life has

[2] Paul H. Buck, *The Road to Reunion*, pp. 196-7.

been merely not dying." Consumption, inadequate employment, the responsibilities of a family, and the suffering of the Southern people were his burdens. Despite these practical difficulties, in 1873 he heroically resolved to devote the remaining years of his life to music and literature. His career as a musician was interesting if not creative. He learned the technique of the symphony, played the flute in the Peabody Orchestra of Baltimore, and in his posthumously published *Music and Poetry* (1898) wrote hopefully of the place of music in modern society. Other endeavors of minor importance were his renditions for boys of the medieval classics, and his researches in English literature entitled *Shakespere and His Forerunners* (2 vols., 1902), *The Science of English Verse* (1880), and *The English Novel* (1883).

This gifted Southerner also expressed himself in poetry, the one medium in which he showed possibilities of great achievement. His poems "Corn" and "The Symphony" were published in 1875; more successful was the series of poems on the marshes of his native Georgia, from "The Marshes of Glynn" (1878) to "Sunrise" written in his dying months (1887). By 1878 he had overcome every obstacle except his illness. Although endowed with spirituality and a sense of melody, Lanier did not achieve, except in a few poems, "that union of sound and sense" of truly great verse. Lack of tranquillity and a certain discursiveness prevented his development into a great poet. Nevertheless "An Evening Song," "My Springs," "The Song of the Chattahoochee," "The Revenge of Hamish," "The Poem of the West," and, above all, "The Marshes of Glynn" earned Sidney Lanier an eminent place in Southern literature.

Of lesser importance than Lanier was another Georgian, encouraged by the poet to write fiction around their native state. After spending the first forty-two years of his life as an educator, Richard Malcolm Johnston published *Georgia Sketches* in 1864 and more significant *Dukesboro Tales* in 1871. He continued the portraiture of the Georgia cracker that Judge Augustus B. Longstreet had begun in the prewar years, proving that middle Georgia possessed that dialect and local color which postwar realists deemed essential for good fiction. His stories are suffused with the kindness and humor of an agricultural people of sound character. Especial stress is placed on character and setting; as a result, Johnston's stories are weak in action, some almost without plot. Yet he accomplished for Georgia what the contemporary Hoosier Edward Eggleston did for Indiana.

The postwar popularizer of Negro character was Irwin Russell, a Mississippian. After an irresponsible and dissolute life, he died in 1879 at the age of twenty-six. Russell acquired an unusual understanding of human behavior through experiences on river steamers and in sailors' boardinghouses. Impulsively he turned from his profession of law to write Negro dialect poetry. He won national recognition when *Scribner's Monthly* published his "Uncle Cap Interviewed" in 1876. His masterpiece, "Christmas Night in the Quarters," appeared in that magazine two years later. Although not the first of the postwar poets to exploit the Negro theme, Russell exhibited a spark of genius and a spontaneous insight into the emotions of the Negro. He caught the thought processes of a race seemingly inscrutable to his predecessors, and discovered the new literary field of Negro dialect and Negro life.

Russell created a type that for generations would remain a conventional figure of American literature: the Negro as a superstitious, mercurial fellow, irresponsible and good-natured, shrewdly philosophical and possessing an astonishing exegesis of the Scriptures along with a fondness for the banjo and the 'possum. Recognition came to Russell with the publication of his *Collected Poems* (1888) nine years after his death. Mississippi honored him by placing his portrait in its Hall of Fame and by erecting a shrine to his memory in his native city of Port Gibson.

Illustrating perfectly the dependence of Southern writers on Northern recognition was Sherwood Bonner, a Mississippi girl. After the death of her mother and an unhappy marriage, she migrated to Boston in 1872 at the age of twenty-three to seek a literary career among those who had published some of her stories. Nahun Capen, editor of the *Boston Ploughman*, befriended her; Longfellow, for whom she worked as a secretary, became her literary adviser. The young writer turned for material to the section of the country she knew best. In her series of "Gran'-mammy Stories" she anticipated Irwin Russell's more brilliant achievements in Negro dialect. In 1878 she produced *Like unto Like*, a novel of Reconstruction in which the theme of sectional reconciliation is expounded. She wrote humorous tales of the Civil War, pointing up the virtues of both sides; in her stories of the Tennessee mountains she paved the way for the work of Mary Noailles Murfree. Shortly before her death in 1884, Miss Bonner published *Dialect Tales*, considered "peculiarly American" because they portrayed realistically "the secluded life of everyday folk."

These four writers, talented though they were, failed to develop local literature of creative significance. Lanier's and Russell's poems were fragmentary, and Johnston's and Miss Bonner's stories lacked that elusive quality which transforms regional realism into living romance. Nevertheless, they discovered the materials which would be effectively utilized by the five masters of literature of the New South who followed them. These five combined substance with the penetrating understanding and sustained effort required to meet prevalent standards of literary excellence. Their use of dialect was effective, the technical skill of their story form unexcelled. They found in their surroundings the universal interest that elevated their work above its provincial origin. Moreover, they exemplified the spirit of the New South. Practical enough not to offend the North, they disarmed their critics by cheerfully accepting the verdict of 1865. Yet they were responsible Southerners who were devoted to "dey good old days, dose times befoah de war." They drew a glorious picture of the "uncles," "mammies," "colonels," gracious ladies, and fair maidens of the Old South. The North responded by honoring in death a culture which had proved anathema in life. This repentance reached absurd extreme when Maud Howe, the daughter of the author of "The Battle Hymn of the Republic," declared in her novel *Atalanta in the South* (1886) that the Negro was happier in slavery than in freedom.

As in the literature of the slave controversy, in that of the New South the Negro remained the focal character. The loyalty of the slave was exploited; but unlike Uncle Tom, the Negro of the new school was not at the mercy of his master; instead, an impoverished and usually helpless master was represented as dependent upon the forgiving pity of the ex-slave. Actually the Negro became a handy device for a statesmanlike bit of propaganda. It was asserted that his problems under freedom could best be solved by preserving, as far as possible, the bonds of friendship between the races which had existed under slavery.

First among the five who lifted the Southern scene into national importance was George Washington Cable, born in New Orleans in 1844 of a Virginia father and a New England mother. His literary career began soon after the Civil War with a weekly miscellany, "Drop Shot," in the *New Orleans Picayune*. It was continued after 1869 in the strange romances he discovered through research in the archives of his native city. These stories were first published in *Scribner's Monthly*, then expanded in 1879 into the volume *Old Creole Days*, which was instantly recognized as the classic exposition of life among the French-speaking people of Louisiana. From Cable's pen came other Creole stories: *The Grandissimes* (1884), an elaborate historical romance; *The Creoles of Louisiana* (1884); *Dr. Sevier* (1885); *Bonaventure* (1888); and *Strange True Stories of Louisiana* (1889). His outspoken essays on the Negro and other Southern topics, collected in *The Silent South* (1885), aroused the resentment of his native region. The fact, coupled with the desire to be near his literary market, led him to the New England of his mother.

Cable's life thereafter was filled with reading tours, religious and philanthropic activities, and books on social questions. Later, he returned to romantic writing, producing eight volumes of this type between 1899 and 1918. He felt that he had the right to speak as "a native of Louisiana, an ex-Confederate soldier, and a lover of my home, my city, and my State." [3] But the old charm and cunning were lacking, and it was soon evident that his ultimate fame had to rest on what he had written before 1890.

In these tales of the vanishing French civilization of Louisiana, Cable opened up a new world that was highly picturesque and bizarre, yet a part of the American scene. In helping to discover that the native landscape and society were richer and more varied than previously was realized he achieved for the South what Bret Harte did for the West. The Louisianan's style is epigrammatic and Gallic in its swift shiftings and witty insinuations; he excelled as the creator of dainty femininity and exotic atmosphere. His picture of the Creole was sharply challenged by Grace King, Gayarré, and other informed Louisianians who charged that he drew his characters only from the lower levels of Creole society. Whether or not his backgrounds and characters are actual types is of little importance; they are alive and satisfying.

Joel Chandler Harris, the great delineator of Negro character, like Judge Longstreet, Richard Malcolm Johnston, and other representative humorists, was identified with the society of middle Georgia. He was born near Eatonton in 1848, the son of an Irish laborer who deserted his wife and unborn child. For the first fourteen years of the boy's life, his mother supported him by dressmaking. In 1862 he entered the service of Joseph Addison Turner as a printer's devil on *The Countryman*. Young Harris not only learned the trade of the journalist, but became thoroughly acquainted with the inhabitants—both human and animal—of his employer's plantation, especially absorbing Negro speech and folklore. Turner introduced him to his library and schooled him in the art of writing. After the destruction of the Confederacy he emerged as a humorist on the staff of the Savannah *Morning News*. In 1876 he joined the Atlanta *Constitution*, where he served as a miscellaneous contributor for all but the last eight years of his life.

Harris wrote his first animal tales with painstaking care, withholding them from publication until he was sure that he had faithfully reproduced the middle Georgia speech of Uncle Remus. The resulting tales were immediately popular, as welcome in the North as in the South. In 1880 appeared *Uncle Remus: His Songs and Sayings* and three years later a continuation of this book entitled *Nights with Uncle Remus*. The replies of this veritable Ethiopian Aesop, philosopher, and gentleman to the inquiries of the little boy with inexhaustible curiosity called forth two unforgettable books of American literature. This eighty-year-old sage of the Georgia countryside possessed an unconscious hu-

[3] Cable, *The Silent South*, p. 25.

mor springing from "the universal desire to correlate the unknown with the known, or to explain the most difficult things by reference to the most obvious." He was concerned with the mysteries of animal life, especially as embodied in the characters of the rabbit and the fox. Since the narrator had lived observantly through three periods of Southern history, he commented on many subjects other than animals within his own experiences—on Negroes, his favorite dishes, courtships, churches, religious revivals, Christmas, and witches. Uncle Remus was picturesque in phraseology, unexpected in comparisons, varied in figures of speech, most effective in the use of his limited vocabulary.[4] Eight volumes besides the initial two were added to the Uncle Remus cycle, but in these and in seven other books on various subjects Harris, like Cable, never advanced beyond his earlier successes. In the first two books he excelled all other American writers in three respects: ability to combine accurate research in Negro life and language with the style of the great artist, to harmonize a typical character with an individual type, and to excite the interest of both child and adult. Uncle Remus was the last of the old-time Negroes and as unique a character as one may find in Southern fiction.

If Harris expressed the genius of democratic Georgia through the conversations of a humble Negro, Thomas Nelson Page, in accents not entirely different, recorded the spirit of aristocratic Virginia. Born of a long line of aristocrats in 1853, his home was at "Oakland," a family plantation in Hanover County. As a Virginia gentleman he received a classical education and began his career as a lawyer. Success in his profession at first left opportunity for only desultory pursuit of his predilection for writing. Then *Century Magazine* published "Marse Chan," a dialect story of the Confederacy which was well received. Gradually, he turned from law to become a busy short-story writer, novelist, and essayist. The bulk of his writings dealt with the same periods of Virginia history that Harris treated in his Georgia stories.

Page's most popular books were *In Ole Virginia* (1887), tales largely in Negro dialect; *The Burial of the Guns* (1894), a collection of sketches and stories; *The Old Gentleman of the Black Stock* (1897); and two volumes for children, *Two Little Confederates* (1888) and *Among the Camps* (1891). Among works of nonfiction were *The Old South* (1892), *Social Life in Old Virginia* (1897), *The Negro, the Southerner's Problem* (1904), *The Old Dominion* (1908), and *Robert E. Lee, Man and Soldier* (1911). These were closely akin to his fiction in theme and spirit. Because the Virginian overemphasized the attractive side of plantation life, neglected its faults, and failed to penetrate beneath sur-

[4] C. Alphonso Smith in *The Cambridge History of American Literature*, II, 354–8.

face appearances, he was criticized severely. In the unrealistic manner of Sir Walter Scott, this romantic writer exploited the feudalistic splendor of the Old South. Page dedicated himself to the task of preserving from oblivion the virtues of a civilization of merit. Although he never represented on a large scale the tremendous tragedy of the Civil War, he, nevertheless, pictured a chivalric ideal possibly more important than the sordid details of Southern life portrayed by his successors. That Page's romantic concepts are recurrent in the tastes of American readers is proved by the immense popularity of such Civil War chroniclers as Stark Young and Margaret Mitchell.

Mary Noailles Murfree, novelist and story writer, came of a family sufficiently prominent to give its name to towns in both North Carolina and Tennessee. She was born in 1850 at "Grantlands," her mother's estate near Murfreesboro, Tennessee. Left partly paralyzed by a fever, she devoted more time to study than the normal child, learning French, playing the piano, and reading extensively in law, history, and literature. For fifteen years her summers were spent in the Cumberland Mountains, which provided the background for her fictional characters. Her literary career began in 1874 and 1875 with the publication of some stories in *Lippincott's Magazine* under the pen name of E. Emmett Dembry. In 1878 "Dancin' Party at Harrison's Cove" appeared in *The Atlantic Monthly* under the pen name of Charles Egbert Craddock. A collection of short stories entitled *In the Tennessee Mountains* created a literary sensation in 1884. Her masculine pseudonyms suited her robust and forthright style, and her editors were astonished to discover later that "Mr. Craddock" actually was a little crippled lady.

In the twelve years following 1884 eleven volumes of mountain stories came from her pen. They were followed by historical novels on the Civil War and the colonial history of the old Southwest. Her mountain romances reveal in rhythmical prose the pathos of a lonely and frustrated people and the solemn beauty of their surroundings. The dialect is faithfully reproduced with its dry wit and drawling intonations. Her style is marred by too many landscape pictures and a fondness for stately epithet and pedantic words. Descriptions of scenery, usually exaggerated (the moderate Tennessee ridges assume the proportions of the Alps or the Rockies), dominated Miss Murfree's books, leaving the characters as victims of nature and the plots scattered and conventional. Her work is that of the summer vacationist who gave external descriptions of mountain folk without intimate concern over their common humanity. Yet the Tennessee lady's talent for graphic detail and her charm as a storyteller attracted the readers of her day.

It was James Lane Allen who first described the peculiar colorings of Kentucky scenes and life. He was born in 1849 near Lexington of a sturdy line of farmers. As with many Southern writers of his generation, a happy childhood was disturbed by the misfortunes of war and Reconstruction. Allen struggled for an education against the handicap of poverty and learned from older people to love Kentucky birds, flowers, and woodlands, and to idealize the past of the South. He practiced the art of writing during thirteen years spent as a teacher, then turned to a literary career. A store of Kentucky lore and a deft and euphonious style were his twin assets. The Kentuckian's first story, "Too Much Momentum," appeared in *Harper's Magazine* in April, 1885; the year 1891 saw the publication of his first book, *Flute and Violin, and Other Kentucky Tales and Romances*. This was followed by *The Blue Grass Region of Kentucky and Other Kentucky Articles* (1892).

His reputation established, Allen left Kentucky to become a novelist in New York City. *John Gray*, a slight novel which appeared in 1893, was followed by such masterpieces as *Kentucky Cardinal* (1894) and *Aftermath* (1895), idyllic accounts of two lovers; *The Choir Invisible* (1897), a strong story of conflicting love based on historical facts; *The Reign of Law* (1900), an epic of the Kentucky hemp fields, reflected the author's interest in science and religion. Another book of scientific appeal was *The Mettle of the Pasture* (1903), dealing with the problem of the double standard. Nine additional books of lesser importance appeared between 1909 and Allen's death in 1925. Contemporaries were shocked by the bold frankness with which he handled social problems; a later generation of critics accused him of being uncritical of the chivalric past, of oversweetness, and of limiting his beauty and tragic meaning by sentimentality.[5] With all his faults, this Kentuckian expressed in sonorous English the quieter and more spiritual experiences of man, and made the Bluegrass region of Kentucky one of the best-known areas of the South.

In 1888 Albion W. Tourgée wrote: "A foreigner studying our current literature, without knowledge of our history, and judging our civilization by our fiction, would undoubtedly conclude that the South was the seat of intellectual empire in America and the African the chief romantic element in our population." [6] This reputation was gained by the quintet of local colorists and enhanced by a host of lesser writers. Carrying on the literary tradition of Georgia were William Nathaniel Harben and Harry Stillwell Edwards. Harben in numerous novels described with a sound if not powerful realism, and with a human if not large philosophy, the land and the people of north Georgia. Edwards produced human nature sketches in black and white, notably his brief *Aeneas Africanus* (1919), a genuine folk book of his state, Sarah Barn-

---

[5] Carl Van Doren, *The American Novel*, p. 222.
[6] "The South as a Field for Fiction," *The Forum*, VI, 464 (December, 1888).

well Elliott in *The Durket Sperret* (1898) supplemented Miss Murfree's treatment of Cumberland Mountain folk. Although lacking the poetic dignity of the older writer, Miss Elliott surpassed her in sympathetic characterizations. Armistead Churchill Gordon and George William Bagby were portrayers of Old Virginia. Their lively localisms touched Virginians, but failed to attain the national appeal of Thomas Nelson Page's writings. Francis Hopkinson Smith, engineer and painter turned story writer, in *Colonel Carter of Cartersville* (1891) created an unforgettable symbol of the patrician South, making his leading character generous, lovable, and genuine.

Margaret Junkin Preston, sister-in-law of Stonewall Jackson, wrote Civil War verse, and Constance Cary Harrison, wife of the man who had been Jefferson Davis' secretary, turned out numerous popular novels on superficial social themes, many of them about Virginia. Cable's exploitation of the Louisiana theme was supplemented by the writings of Ruth McEnery Stuart, Charles Étienne Arthur Gayarré, Grace E. King, and Kate Chopin. Mrs. Stuart created a full gallery of Southern characters—Louisiana Creoles, New Orleans people, Arkansas poor whites, and, above all, plantation Negroes. Gayarré, a competent historian who wrote artless novels, inspired Miss King to correct what both writers believed was Cable's false conception of the French people of Louisiana. Miss King's many stories of Creole life are French in idiom and incisive brevity, but English in language and Louisianian in background. In Mrs. Chopin's *Bayou Folk* (1894) and other books about the rural Creoles, she demonstrated a mastery of the short story and a sense of realism ahead of her time. John Fox, Jr.'s romances of the Kentucky and Virginia mountains, notably *The Little Shepherd of Kingdom Come* (1903) and *The Trail of the Lonesome Pine* (1908), made little contribution to the knowledge of their region, but they were immensely popular.

Knowledge of the Southern scene was expanded by two writers whose achievements extend beyond the scope of this book. One was Lafcadio Hearn—a veritable literary waif in origin and abode—who spent ten interesting years in New Orleans. One result of his residence there was "Chita," a tale of the terrible tidal wave that swept a Louisiana island. Many of his newspaper articles described the semitropical wonders of the Southern metropolis in prose distinguished for its beauty and exotic lyricism. The other writer was Mark Twain, a literary giant whose genius transcends sectional limitations. Important portions of his writings, however, possess an indelible Southern character, stemming from his Missouri childhood and his services as a pilot on the Mississippi River. Early associations with slaves were responsible for the significant part the black man played in *Tom Sawyer* (1876), *Huckleberry Finn*

(1884), and *Pudd'nhead Wilson* (1894). Nigger Jim of the first two stories excellently illustrated the device of creating humor through the superstitious and credulous comments of a black man on serious topics. Without subordinating his art to the argument of the Negro question in the manner of Cable and others, Mark Twain revealed in *Pudd'nhead Wilson* the tragedy of miscegenation, employing a frank realism usually associated with more recent literature. The book was not a study in heredity, but a portrayal of life as it was in the slave era. It depicted brilliantly the eccentricities and tragedies of race mixture, as well as the personal and social villainies of both master and slave.

Southern writers did not have to deviate radically from accepted practices to participate in the revival of the historical novel which engaged the enthusiastic attention of the most popular American writers at the turn of the century. Love of Sir Walter Scott, the great master of this genre, had long been the besetting passion of Southerners; it required no great changes to abandon the native realities in which local colorists set their stories for the unrealities of the past or of distant places. The South, whose sectional consciousness primarily sprang from a past replete with pathos and grandeur, eagerly shared the nation's desire to escape from the tedium of peaceful decades into the adventures of the Spanish-American War, which came in 1898. The historical romance reached its peak around the time of this war.

There arose a group of Southern writers who, relishing the colorful conventions of the romancers, dressed their historical characters in the habiliments of medieval knights, employed an ornate literary style, proclaimed fashionable class prejudices, and created cavaliers and ladies who lived in spacious houses amid mahogany, silver, and brocade. The Southern romancers were, in one respect, less extravagant than their Northern contemporaries; they confined themselves to the American past, leaving Europe to the more cosmopolitan Northerners. Of the 72 most popular historical novels published between 1895 and 1912 on American themes, 34 were written by 12 Southern authors, and 38 by 15 Northerners. Four of the 7 historical novels which sold more than 500,000 copies each were by Southerners.

Some of the Southern local colorists turned from their forte to write historical romance. James Lane Allen, in *The Choir Invisible* (1897), portrayed Kentucky in the eighteenth century. Thomas Nelson Page, in *Red Rock* (1898), wrote of Reconstruction. Ellen Glasgow, whose genius would subsequently express itself in other fields, was so influenced by the historical vogue that she produced *The Battle-Ground* (1902), a tale of the Civil War. There was Maurice Thompson, the Indiana poet and novelist whose Georgia childhood gave him material for *A Tallahassee Girl* (1881), and other pioneer sentimental novels on

Southern themes. Thomas Cooper De Leon wrote reminiscences and romances of the Civil War, and George Cary Eggleston, although born in Indiana, became a Virginian and a Confederate soldier; in later life he demonstrated his love for his adopted state by writing *Dorothy South* (1902), *The Master of Warlock* (1903), and *Evelyn Byrd* (1904), all idealizations of Old Virginia.

Probably the most powerful of the entire American school of historical romancers was Mary Johnston, a Virginia woman who early turned to the portrayal of the past of her native state. Born in 1870 of a family prominent in the military and legal life of Virginia, she spent a childhood amid the serene beauty of the Virginian mountains, absorbing her father's treasures of English literature and colonial history. Her delicate health prevented extensive formal schooling. While living in New York in 1898, she made her literary debut with *Prisoners of Hope*. This narrative of conspiracy and insurrection around the time of Sir William Berkeley's governorship of Virginia was told with marked respect for historical detail and atmosphere. Miss Johnston's next novel, *To Have and to Hold* (1900), became a best seller of record-breaking proportions. It proved that its writer had an eye for the picturesque along with the ability to say "just enough, not too much."

Some ten other novels in the same general pattern followed the Virginia writer's initial successes, chiefly *The Long Roll* (1911), and *Cease Firing* (1912), both concerned with the Civil War. With the decline of popular interest in the historical romance after 1910, Miss Johnston wrote *Silver Cross* (1922) in a wave of mysticism and threatened to dam the rapid flow of her art. However, in *1492* (1922), *The Slave Ship* (1924), and *The Great Valley* (1926) this mysticism was subordinated to the main stream of narrative so that the gusto of her earlier work was restored. Indeed, *The Great Valley* was described as "one of the finest narratives of Indian warfare and Indian captivity yet written."

Popularity in the case of the Southern historical romance should not be confused with lasting worth. Had Tourgée written again after 1900, he would not have been able to give the South as important a position in American literature as he had done in 1888. Critics were pointing out that Southern authors were becoming tiresome because they had created no schools or themes themselves, had overworked the Negro, the mountaineer, and other local color characters, and had serenely ignored the realities of contemporary Southern life. Significant in this connection is the fact that all twelve of the aforementioned popular historical novelists except Ellen Glasgow left their native states to live elsewhere. Although they continued to write about the South, they apparently felt that they had nothing more to learn about it.

The South did not participate in that chapter in the history of

American literature known as the generation of the muckrakers, covering roughly 1901–14. The writers of this period refused to escape into a charming past; instead, they exaggerated the evils of contemporary society in the hope of building a new society on the ruins. The only world worth striving for in the eyes of a people as religious as the Southerners was heaven itself. Indeed, they saw themselves, as fifty years earlier in the case of *Uncle Tom's Cabin,* the victims of outsiders. The muckrakers' exposure of such sectional evils as race prejudice and child labor was resented as the work of meddlesome Yankees.

Nor were Southerners able to evaluate their own literature through constructive criticism. So kindly a patriot as James Lane Allen was accused by Mildred Lewis Rutherford, a popular literary historian, of tampering "with subjects only fit for discussion in the privacy of one's room or at the dissecting table." [7] The school of literary commentators who collaborated with William Malone Baskervill in producing *Southern Writers* (2 vols., 1896–97) and with Edwin A. Alderman in publishing *The Library of Southern Literature* (16 vols., 1907) were too profuse in their praises. William Peterfield Trent, a perceptive young professor at Sewanee, left the South after the appearance of his *William Gilmore Simms* (1892) made life disagreeable there. With ruthless veracity this book analyzed the maladies of Southern literature. Apparently the South, without either muckrakers or discriminating critics, seemed unable to join the outside world in new literary fields. Long after Northern critics believed a chapter in literary history had been closed by the publication in 1907 of George Ade's satire on chivalry, *The Slim Princess,* Southerners continued to bask in the self-flattery of the historical romance. The result was that Henry L. Mencken in 1920 dubbed the South "the Sahara of the Bozart," an intellectual and literary desert.[8]

Mencken had scarcely spoken before the ruling critics of New York began to recognize that the South was in the throes of a new movement, which around 1920 was to grow into a major phenomenon of American literary history. Naturalism, after reaching maturity in France several decades before and taking root for some fifteen years in the more progressive sections of the United States, at last crossed the Potomac to dwell in a land allegedly brimming over with barbarism, romantic charm, and aristocratic pretensions. A significant group of Southern writers, courageously embracing the new movement, set out to produce "pleasure by the delineation of such objects as in reality excite displeasure and even disgust." They were "inspired by resistance against delusion and vain sentimentality, against mere decorum and mere propriety."

[7] Rutherford, *The South in History and Literature,* p. 588.
[8] *Prejudices* (2nd series, New York, 1920), p. 137.

Achievement in this type of realism proved difficult among a religious and polite people. Naturalism called for a note of gravity in delineating the behavior of the country Negro and the poor white, in understanding the Southern strain of violence, and in appraising the tradition of gallantry and femininity. These Southern writers were forced by outside criticism to examine the total Southern inheritance in a realistic manner, but theirs was "not a literature of protest but a literature of acceptance." In a modern manner, they portrayed a South of tragic virtues and vices. They had no easy solutions for the evils they discovered. As moralists in a Christian or classical sense, they found nothing to change and much to praise in Southern folkways.

By 1920 Ellen Glasgow and James Branch Cabell, chief practitioners of the new realism, had already published more than a score of volumes. Not until that date did these notables of the new movement receive the plaudits of New York's literati; simultaneously, they were acclaimed in the South. Beginning at Charleston and Nashville, poetry societies met in nearly every state of the former Confederacy. Little theaters were formed in leading cities, and a half dozen "little reviews" began fugitive existences. By 1925 these tentative manifestations of the new literature gathered momentum; some fifteen or twenty Southern volumes enjoyed national prominence. By 1932 Henry L. Mencken saw so much merit in the Southern literary output that, in the words of Donald Davidson, the Baltimore critic began "to look almost like a disguised Confederate raider who had chosen his own methods of devastating a too-Yankeefied civilization." [9]

The inaugurator and most eminent practitioner of Southern realism was a Virginia woman who, from the time she was 22 in 1897 until her death in 1945, labored with uninterrupted consistency in the construction of a world of her own. Ellen Glasgow wrote twenty-one volumes. William Gilmore Simms alone among Southerners rivaled her in the constant pursuit of a chosen theme over a full lifetime; but unlike the South Carolinian she was encouraged by friendly critics and readers. Her rearing and surroundings, at least in externals, adhered strictly to the Virginian pattern. Of aristocratic lineage, she was privately educated, fed upon inherited traditions by nurse and aunt. She passed most of her life behind the walls of her old Richmond home amidst furniture and shrubbery in the best Victorian taste. Yet her first novel, *The Descendant* (1897), struck a note of realism which proved that she had looked beyond her garden wall but at the same time had been protected by it from too much sentimentality. The young novelist had read Maupassant and Dostoevski, and other French and Russian realists. She had also absorbed the works of Darwin, Malthus, John Stuart Mill, and

[9] Davidson in William T. Couch, ed., *Culture in the South*, p. 196.

English radicals whom she might not have encountered had she gone to a Virginia school.

Miss Glasgow's first successful book was *The Voice of the People* (1900), the story of the rise of a member of "the poor white trash" to the governorship against the opposition of all classes. It was a pioneer discussion of the period of Southern agrarian unrest, and marked the beginning of a series of novels that constitute a complete social history of Virginia from the Civil War to the present. *The Battle-Ground* (1902) was Miss Glasgow's sole treatment of the Civil War. *The Deliverance* (1904) was significant for its objective appraisal of the merits and demerits of Virginia aristocrats and plebeians, and its depiction of a Southern lady who had only lies spoken in her presence. *The Wheel of Life* (1906) dealt with Virginians living in New York. *The Ancient Law* (1908) described the experiences of a released gentleman convict in a tobacco town. *The Romance of a Plain Man* (1909), concerning the trials of an aristocratic lady married to a simple man, was another departure from the standards of Southern fiction that is "by no means a departure from life." In *The Miller of Old Church* (1911) Miss Glasgow accepted the abolitionist doctrine that the humbler class of Southern whites possessed ambitions and capabilities suppressed by the social system inherited from slavery. In *Virginia* (1913), the complications of miscegenation were as frankly presented as in *Pudd'nhead Wilson;* it was the biography of a representative Virginia woman sacrificed on the altar of outworn notions of chivalry. *Life and Gabriella* (1916) presented a Richmond girl of good family who became a dressmaker to escape an unhappy marriage. *The Builders* (1919) was the story of a parasitic woman who got what she wanted by sacrificing others. In the opinion of many critics, Miss Glasgow reached new heights in *Barren Ground* (1925), the grim tale of a woman pathetically in love with soil gutted by a generation of shiftless tenants and landlords. By way of relief the Virginia novelist followed this novel with *The Romantic Comedians* (1926) and *They Stooped to Folly* (1929), in which, employing irony and high comedy, the author was charmingly malicious at the expense of respectable Richmond. In her last three novels, Miss Glasgow returned to the serious attitude of her earlier work. *The Sheltered Life* (1932) told of a Virginian bound by the women whom he cherished. *Vein of Iron* (1935) was a return to the country to portray the tragedy of folk uprooted from rural certainties by the lure of industrialism. In *This Our Life* (1941) older men representing an earlier Richmond were contrasted with a female of the young generation motivated by sinister irresponsibility.

Miss Glasgow constructed her elaborate history of Virginia with wit, keen observation, and consummate craftsmanship. She broke the sentimental tradition in Southern letters and brought to the foreground middle-class Southerners previously neglected by story writers. Going beyond a mere excitement of the interest of those concerned with Virginia's dark problems, she used her state as a medium for expounding matters of universal human interest. She was concerned with the endeavor of woman to conquer the injustices of man. In developing this theme she employed a humor sometimes grim, sometimes witty, but always more subtle and restrained than that of the usual feminist. Dominated by a note of profound pessimism, her recurrent theme was the power of the weak to wreck the strong. The New South, which she praised at least by implication in her earlier work, in her last novel was portrayed as no happier or more enlightened than the Old South she so effectively damned. She accepted too readily the harsh judgments of outsiders on Southern conditions and proved by her own studies that her assumptions concerning the willingness and ability of the lower classes to elevate themselves were illusory. Her realism was not entirely merciless; indeed, there was admiration for those quixotic, aristocratic, middle-class and poor-white Southerners. "An honorable end," said Miss Glasgow, "is the one thing that cannot be taken away from man."

The Virginia novelist James Branch Cabell, like Ellen Glasgow, was a lonely aristocrat who, unlike his feminine contemporary, refused to look beyond his cloister to record the trials of the common world. He was born in Richmond in 1879, received a classical education, traveled in Europe, worked on newspapers, and did extensive genealogical researches. He scorned realism as a mark of mediocrity. His first novel, *The Eagle's Shadow*, was published in 1905. He produced a Virginia romance, *The Rivet in Grandfather's Neck* (1915). However, he did not pursue the theme further, for Mary Johnston had already popularized material of this type. Cabell sought to write differently of a society that had escaped the wear and tear of life. Toward that end, he brought out a series of books which few understood or read until his novel *Jurgen* was brought into court in 1920 for alleged obscenity. Despite his escape into unreality, he was more of a naturalist than the woman author of the great dour chronicle of Virginia. Cynical instead of pitying, Cabell returned to the age of chivalry only to prove that the noble ideal of civilized man is sham and illusion.

Miss Glasgow was willing to dignify the commonplace by proving its existence; Cervantes and Mark Twain made kindly fun of chivalry; Cabell befouled it. His vast array of books is unified by a carefully wrought style and an artistic design rare in modern fiction. Many of his works were concerned with the biography of Manuel. It was the history of an imaginary medieval country, minutely constructed with all the trappings of royalty. This kingdom of Poictesme was peopled by an Arthurian circle of Cabell's creation whose main contact with reality was provided by their descendants living in Virginia. The plots and characters were complicated, and the reader is confounded by a myriad of names and genealogical references. If one has time to wade through this wilderness of words he may find a great parable, another medieval legend to inspire future poets and scholars.

Far more direct in approach to the ordinary circumstances of Southern life than Miss Glasgow was Thomas S. Stribling. He was born in 1881 at Clifton, Tennessee, of a father who ran a country store and newspaper. Preferring fame as a writer to the profits of trade, the boy early revolted against the standards of his community. He was amused by writing and bored by work. Forced by his family to become a lawyer, he again revolted in favor of writing, using Dickens and Tolstoy as models and earning his first money with moral adventure stories for Sunday-school magazines. Later, he wrote for popular magazines and in 1922 with the publication of *Birthright* was recognized as a novelist of importance. It was the tragedy of the new Negro turned loose in the South—a Harvard-educated mulatto vainly trying to uplift his people. A Negro *Main Street* was created, at once realistic, humorous, pathetic.

After writing novels of South American adventure, Stribling returned to his Tennessee hills in *Teeftallow* (1926) and in *Bright Metal* (1928). The first, a bitter tale of poor whites bound by an environment of bigoted ignorance, was a sharp thrust at the old-fashioned belief concerning the charm of the hill folk. His mountaineers were neither kind nor gentle. The second novel portrayed the trials of a cultured outlander married into the difficult Tennessee environment. Next came *Backwater* (1930) describing the love of a bootlegger's son for an aristocratic lady of an Arkansas town. Despite its melodramatic violence, it was not significant.

With *The Forge* (1931) Stribling produced the first of three novels which he planned as a long cycle of Southern history. It was concerned with the Viadens, a middle-class Alabama family just before, during, and after the Civil War. The second of the series was *The Store* (1932), which depicted the end of the Old South and the beginning of the New. The storekeeper triumphed over the planter largely by dishonesty and violence. The series closed with *Unfinished Cathedral* (1934), which introduced the storekeeper to a twentieth century of wealth, real-estate booms, and skyscrapers. Stribling's prose was graceless, his history composed of mere documents; his action was poorly organized and susceptible to coincidence. The characters were types invented for immediate purposes, not living individuals. The author's propagandist aims were crudely evident; he lectured his characters, satirizing their intentions and refusing to meet them on their own terms. He saw nothing good in the Southern heritage; all his Southerners except certain Negroes were villains. History was explained in terms of brutality; the religion of the people evoked fulmination. Perhaps Stribling was motivated by the desire to see the South achieve that material progress which Stribling's mentor, Sinclair Lewis, considered so despicable for other American areas. Despite his faults the Tennessee novelist had a humorous appreciation for vulgar souls and presented a convincing number of documents on the darker phases of Southern life. Southern liberals see virtue in many of the reforms he advocated.

Viewing the accepted standards of Southern life with Stribling's harshness was Thomas Wolfe. Born at Asheville, North Carolina, in 1900, he passed an unhappy and misunderstood childhood in his native town. In the stimulating atmosphere of the University of North Carolina he became a member of the Carolina Playmakers. His literary debut was modest—"The Return of Buck Gavin, The Tragedy of a Mountain Outlaw," in *Carolina Folk-Plays, Second Series* (1924). After receiving a Master of Arts degree at Harvard and traveling abroad, he became an instructor at the Washington Square College of New York University. Meanwhile, this overgrown, bushy-haired youth was indulging those prodigious powers of analysis and narration that eventually led to his exhaustion and death before he was forty. His first book, *Look Homeward Angel, the Story of a Buried Life*, appeared in 1929. A novel of epic proportions both physically and spiritually, it dealt with his own family at Asheville in the manner of the writer's master, Dostoevski. The book, universal in its tragic appeal, in no deep sense was a Southern problem novel. Wolfe did not look back wistfully to the Old South, or advance a program for sectional resurgence. Rather, he presented the conflict of his own spirit with those about him. A sequel, *Of Time and the River: a Legend of Man's Hunger in His Youth* (1935), contained a hundred stories richly experienced and deeply felt.

Wolfe's main fault was a fabulous prolixity. His first book ran to 626 pages or some 240,000 words; his second was reduced to 912 pages containing 450,000 words. The latter book has been described as "an awful curiosity of the literature of our times." Much that Wolfe wrote was trivial, rhetorical, and adolescent; the artistic principle of selection was violated; the narrative was often repetitious, overwritten, and confused. Gigantic virtues, however, offset these gigantic defects. Criticism of the author's unrestrained flow of observation is silenced by the dynamic force of the man and his work. Wolfe possessed humor, vitality, originality, and gusto, along with a sense of epic grandeur expressed in full-throated Biblical prose. He rose to universals, and turbulently portrayed the struggle of man in quest of himself. Had this "colt of American letters" lived longer, he might have developed the discipline necessary to produce the Great American Novel.

In the works of William Faulkner and Erskine Caldwell there is little that is artistically extraneous as in Miss Glasgow's pitying disapproval of things Southern or Stribling's anti-Southern preachments. Faulkner and Caldwell accepted the conditions of Southern life with a spontaneity as satisfying as that of Thomas Nelson Page and Joel Chandler Harris. In their most distinctive works, however, they were not admirers of roseate traditions. With a realism so startling that one suspects an escape into a romanticized hell they portrayed life among the filthiest dregs of rural society. Theirs is the Deep South, not of gentility and elegance, but of degeneracy and sordidness.

Faulkner was born in Mississippi in 1897 of a prominent family of politicians, and spent some years at Oxford, the seat of the state university. After serving in World War I as an aviator, he began his literary career with *The Marble Faun* (1924), a book of poems, and *Soldier's Pay* (1926), a tragedy of the returned soldier. His characteristic work did not begin until 1929 with the publication of *The Sound and the Fury*, the story of a Southern family of genteel birth turned drunkards, perverts, suicides, and idiots. This book was followed by *As I Lay Dying* (1930), the glaringly graphic tale of the journey of a poor white and his six sons with the decaying corpse of his wife across a rain-swept country to the place she wished to be buried. *Sanctuary*, written before *As I Lay Dying* but not published until 1931, established Faulkner's popularity. In it "a brooding atmosphere of obscene and bestial decadence" hangs over Mississippi hills inhabited by poor white moonshiners, half-wits, and prostitutes. The principal events of the novel, confessedly written as a money-maker, were brutal rape, two wanton murders, a lynching, and an execution. *Light in August* (1932) was made up of two stories: the journey of a pregnant woman in search of her lover, and the efforts of a bastard, who believes himself a mulatto, to get himself lynched. *Absalom! Absalom!* (1936) presented Faulkner's solemn recipe for avoiding incest. *The Wild Palms* (1939), like *Light in August,* presented two stories: one of a prison-farm convict who goes on a rampage while rescuing the victims of a Mississippi flood; the other of a wandering hospital interne who has escaped into the wilderness with another man's wife. *The Hamlet* (1940) was a riotous tale of the rise of a sharecropper and his verminous brood to supremacy in a small town in the canebrakes.

The world of William Faulkner echoes with the hideous clangor of lust and disease, brutality and death. His men and women are twisted shapes in the wreckage of a degenerate society; the Southern reader, however, is forced to recognize its existence in his midst. Whether or not such horrors should be recorded evidently did not trouble Faulkner, for he presented them with stark resolution. In the year that he produced *The Sound and the Fury* came *Sartoris*, the story of a witless suicide in whom the author implanted all the glory and the chivalry of an earlier Sartoris who served under Jeb Stuart. In *The Unvanquished* (1938), Faulkner surrendered to sectionalism to produce a romance of Civil War and Reconstruction in which the Colonel and his Lady pursue the Southern ideals without effectively halting the violence and degeneracy typical of the author's characters. In this book Faulkner was as conventional in his prejudices as any old-fashioned romancer. He condemned carpetbaggers and the upstart descendants of the slaveless, and glorified the moral code of the plantation aristocracy. In his opinion, the most frightful trick of fate was the inability of the descendants of this aristocracy to recover from the Civil War. This situation led Faulkner to create "a lightless and gutted and empty land" for which there was no future hope, but only a legendary past to lend dignity to the present.[10]

In *Intruder in the Dust* (1948) this legendary past comes to life in a Negro of immense dignity and in two boys and an aristocratic spinster who save the Negro from a mob. This chivalrous exploit is a parable of the South for hostile critics. In *Requiem for a Nun* (1951), a sequel to *Sanctuary*, Faulkner treats one of his foulest females with thoughtful sympathy.

Faulkner's interesting but intricate manner of recording the doings of his Mississippians through the mind-flow of his wretched creatures did not hamper Erskine Caldwell's efforts to expose the lives of similar folk in rural Georgia. He spoke with direct and brutal clarity, and his outrageous tales delight a large and growing public. The son of a Presbyterian minister, he was born in Coweta County, Georgia, in 1903. After a desultory education, he learned to know the poor whites while engaged in cotton picking, hack driving, and cooking. The drama from his novel *Tobacco Road* (1932) enjoyed one of the longest runs in the history of the New York stage. This story of the progressive degeneration of a family of Georgia poor whites living on exhauted lands that had once been the prosperous farm of their grandfather evokes instantaneous laughter because of its ribald humor, and the almost idiotic gravity with which its degraded creatures conduct themselves. *God's Little Acre* (1933) when hauled into court as obscene was declared by a broad-minded judge to be a legitimate attempt to tell the truth. It revolved around a lecherous Georgia farmer who spent fifteen fruitless years digging for gold. Shootings and suicides turn this rural comedy

[10] Malcolm Cowley in Allen Tate, ed., *The Southern Vanguard*, pp. 13–27.

into deadly serious drama. *Journeyman* (1935) was the story of a wild and vicious preacher against a background of gullible poor whites. *Kneel to the Rising Sun* (1935) was a collection of short stories concerned with "nigger-hunting," rape, murder, and other crimes committed by the whites of the countryside. *Trouble in July* (1940) described, from the viewpoint of white men, the lynching of a guileless colored boy caught in the embrace of a white nymphomaniac.

Caldwell's characters are a sex-ridden crew, and their tolerance of each other's philandering is in the vein of high comedy. Another poor-white trait emphasized by Caldwell is the deadening of normal emotions by poverty; he presents people without family feeling, insensitive to physical deformity. Yet in *Tobacco Road* and *God's Little Acre*, the Georgia writer creates what one historian says are the first full-length portraits in literature of Southern poor whites in all their tragic misery. The lives of the main characters are pictured without apology, sentiment, or ridicule; without gratuitous sympathy, or desire for betterment. Their callousness is balanced by a paradoxical sensibility, which gives their fall the element of high tragedy.

Bridging the gap between those interested in backwoods whites and those concerned with backwoods Negroes were Paul Green and Dorothy Scarborough. Green, a North Carolinian farm boy who became professor of philosophy at the state university, drew upon a wealth of experiences with common folk to write tragic drama. His plays were first produced by the Carolina Playmakers and subsequently had a limited run on the professional stage of New York. *In Abraham's Bosom* (1926) and *The Field God* (1927) were about Negro life, but *The House of Connelly* (1931) dealt with whites. In his work Green expressed a profound sympathy for the unhappy race that has "borne the brunt of our dirty work," and for whites caught in the meshes of religious fanaticism and tenant poverty. However, he was too gloomy, too much of a reformer to be successful on the New York stage. He shifted to more conventional endeavors.[11]

Miss Scarborough's *In the Land of Cotton* (1923) and *Can't Get a Red Bird* (1929) represented fine contributions toward understanding those who toil in Texas cotton fields. With the thoroughness and impartiality of the trained scholar, she depicted the cotton market, the one-crop system, tenancy, and other evils that beset her characters. More important, she offered solutions strangely prophetic of the measures later enacted by the federal government. Although her criticisms were wise and complete, she made no distinction between literature and sociology.

A group of Southern white writers in the 1920's made revelations

[11] See below, p. 464.

concerning the life of the humble Negro almost as startling as the Faulkner and Caldwell portraits of the poor whites. Buttressed by the sociologists' substantial research into the darker phases of Southern life, these writers interpreted the common Negro more intimately than a whole generation of Northern muckrakers and Negro publicists had been able to do. They abandoned the comic and obsequious character of traditional literature, and treated their Negroes seriously, endowing them with enough lustiness and pathos to prove that these lowly subjects were as human as the rest of mankind.

At the same time, with a courage worthy of Faulkner or Caldwell, they subordinated reform programs to the portrayal of Negro life on its own level. In other words, they wrote of harlots, beggars, gamblers, and rowdies, and did not create malcontents who talked like university professors. Their popularity in no small measure sprang from the great fondness for the Negro that possessed the American public in the years following World War I. It was the age of Negro spirituals and blues, of Negro art and letters, of colored actors and singers, and of anthropologists interested in the primitive and the near-primitive. Southern writers on Negro themes were enthusiastically received. The Negro threatened to become not only human, but superhuman. His portrayers, however, proved incapable of sustaining this note. "Negro life of the folk sort," one critic remarks, was perhaps "a shallow literary vein soon worked out." The reading public lost interest and returned to its traditional concepts of the Negro.

The first example of the new portrayal of the Negro was *Porgy*, written in 1925 by DuBose Heyward, a South Carolinian of an old family. He turned from the writing of poetry to stories dealing with the indolent and casual life of the Negroes he had learned to know while pursuing a business career on the Charleston waterfront. *Porgy*, in dramatic form and with an all-Negro cast, was a noteworthy success on the New York stage. The opera *Porgy and Bess*, with music by George Gershwin, also became a hit. In *Half-Pint Flask* (1929), Heyward dealt effectively, if briefly, with the occult influence of primitive blacks over a white man who had wronged them. *Mamba's Daughters* (1929) was the story of a colored cook of the Charleston underworld who served in the kitchen of an aristocratic family. Through the interrelations of the families of both races, the past and present of the New South was revealed. After *Mamba's Daughters*, the Charleston novelist delved into inconsequential themes. Yet in his two books of Negro life, this white Southerner wrote tenderly of the tragic difficulties of a despised folk whose minds had not been explored by previous writers.

Another white South Carolinian, Julia Peterkin, rivaled Heyward in intimate and sympathetic character analyses of the humble blacks. As her subject she chose the near-primitive Negroes of her husband's river plantation in middle South Carolina. Encouraged by her music teacher Henry Bellamann to record what she had learned, she published *Green Thursday* in 1924; it dealt with plantation life, emphasizing without prejudices the patient struggles of the Negroes against poverty and disaster. Her second book was *Black April* (1927), a chronicle of the daily lives of isolated black folk as seen through the experiences of a Negro foreman and his children. Gaiety and tragedy were blended to create a truly heroic character, and to reveal dramatically the folkways usually buried in less imaginative writing. Next came the Pulitzer Prize-winning *Scarlet Sister Mary* (1928), which described a reality common in Negro society—the black woman grows masterful after the desertion of her husband. Her triumphs and griefs were depicted with tragicomic effectiveness. Those who felt that after such a success Mrs. Peterkin had more to give were disappointed. Her single subsequent novel, *Bright Skin* (1932), did not equal it. In Scarlet Sister Mary she created one of the major characters of American literature. Her writings of the country Negro reveal an almost native comprehension.

Among those who wrote in the vein of Heyward and Mrs. Peterkin were two other South Carolinians. Edward C. L. Adams in *Congaree Sketches* (1926) and *Nigger to Nigger* (1928) described beliefs of blacks on a river plantation near Columbia. Ambrose Gonzales in *Black Border* (1922) and other books rendered the dialect and superstitions of the Gullah Negroes of the South Carolina coast so faithfully as to leave little opportunity for imaginative interpretation. Howard W. Odum's *Rainbow Round My Shoulder* (1928) was an impressive tale of a black Ulysses who wandered from one construction camp to another, from wife to wife, and from chain gang to chain gang. Emmett Kennedy, in *Black Cameos* (1924) and *Gritny People* (1928), portrayed primitive passions in the lowlands of Louisiana. Roark Bradford in *Ol' Man Adam and His Chillun* (1928) showed how the Negro reduced historic Protestantism to the consistencies of the Southern environment. Changed by Marc Connolly into the play *Green Pastures*, it was immensely successful on the New York stage.

The tainted atmosphere of realism which for the fifteen years after 1920 hovered over the region south of the Potomac was sensationally dispelled in 1936. That year saw the publication of Margaret Mitchell's *Gone with the Wind*, a reaffirmation of the legend of the Old South, which took the reading public—Northerners and Southerners alike—by storm. Within eighteen months after publication, 1,399,000 copies were sold; within ten years sales reached 3,625,000, the largest in the history of American fiction. The careful observer of Southern sentiment was not surprised; he knew that, in the heyday of the new realism of Glasgow, Stribling, and Wolfe, the average Southerner still clung to the romantic tradition. Steadfastly he ignored the New York critics who urged him to heed the voices in his midst telling him that Southern customs and conduct were far from perfect. Proof of this was the continued popularity of Thomas Dixon, whose romances of Reconstruction were extravagant protests against Yankee interference in the race question. *The Clansman* (1905) was read by millions of Southerners ordinarily unimpressed by fiction. Its moving picture version called *Birth of a Nation* (1915) so stirred the public that sometimes it had to be suppressed to forestall possible race riots.

As early as 1933 Donald Davidson, the South's first important literary critic, noted that the very citadel of the new realism was more receptive to the conventional view of Southern life than to the one extolled by the critics. Davidson contrasted the failure on the New York stage of Paul Green's *In Abraham's Bosom* with the success of *Green Pastures*, a play about Negro religious superstitions much closer to the inherited view of the subordinate caste.

During the decade and a half in which critics ignored the survivals of the period of historical romance, a group of Southern historians were justifying conservatism. They employed research techniques learned in Northern universities to refute the traditional Northern conception of American history, and to disprove those historians and sociologists who had furnished the realistic novelists with factual material. E. Merton Coulter, in many books, has delved deepest in the section's past. William Cabell Bruce in *John Randolph of Roanoke* (1922) effectively disposed of the strictures of Henry Adams against a great Southerner. Ulrich B. Phillips in *American Negro Slavery* (1918) and William E. Dodd in *The Cotton Kingdom* (1919) demonstrated the virtues of the Old South. John Donald Wade in *Augustus Baldwin Longstreet* (1924) exploited the much-criticized religion of Southerners; Douglas S. Freeman in the most complete of American biographies, *R. E. Lee* (1934–35), substantiated a glorious legend; Walter L. Fleming in *The Sequel of Appomattox* (1919) and George Fort Milton in *The Age of Hate* (1930) justified the South's solution of the Reconstruction problem; C. Vann Woodward in *Tom Watson, Agrarian Rebel* (1938) and *Origins of the New South, 1877–1913* (1951) exposed the betrayal of the agrarian tradition by the New South leaders.

Writers arose to protect sectional values against the deadening effects of national standardization. The Southwest regionalists, notably Mary Austin, J. Frank Dobie, and Stanley Vestal, based their writings on Indian and Spanish folklore. Southern Agrarians, whose symposium *I'll Take My Stand, the South and the Agrarian Tradition* (1930) has already been noted, questioned the benefits which industrialism imposed upon the South, and saw wisdom in a possible return to those agrarian practices which once gave the section wealth and distinction. Ammunition from the arsenal of European and New England humanism is used to refute the humanitarian and naturalistic novelists and sociologists. The agrarian reaction against attacks on the South culminated in the assertion of William A. Percy, the Mississippi poet-planter, in his *Lanterns on the Levee* (1941) that the Southern share-crop system is America's most equitable type of profit sharing. Justification for this viewpoint may be found in Ellen Glasgow's tacit admission in her later work that a reformed South to which she hopefully pointed in her earlier writings is no happier than the Old South from which she revolted originally.

The Southern Agrarians supplemented *I'll Take My Stand* with poetry and literary criticism in part stridently defensive of Southern traditions. John Gould Fletcher, after a long exile in England where he won fame as an imagist poet, returned in 1933 to his native Arkansas to write homely themes in prose and poetry. Donald Davidson of Tennessee was the spokesman for his state and region in *Tall Men* (1927), a narrative poem contrasting early and modern Tennessee; in *Lee in the Mountains* (1938), poems on Southern heroes; and in *Attack on Leviathan* (1938), essays defending regionalism. Allen Tate wrote controversial essays of a high critical order and poetry which is described as having "something of the flavor of the persimmon." John Crowe Ransom, Aristotelian critic, produced three or four volumes of poetry in which he meditates over the predicament of a divided sensibility. Robert Penn Warren, poet, essayist and novelist, was catapulted into popularity by the novel *All the King's Men* (1946), the tragedy of the Southern demagogue who fell into sin.

At the time the New York critics were bestowing so much praise on the Southern naturalists, a group of Southern women were quietly recording the brighter phases of life among normal Southerners. First in this group was Elizabeth Madox Roberts, a Kentucky poet who turned to a more popular medium to write deeply imaginative novels of the people of her state. *The Time of Man* (1926) told of trials and triumphs of a poor girl living in the Arcadian folk-world of Kentucky; the miseries of mountain existence were not ignored, but made subordinate to the appeal of beauty. *The Great Meadow* (1930) described the migration of Virginians to Kentucky; conventional complications were given a compelling significance by an exquisite presentation of the environment and mental reactions of the travelers. Miss Roberts's version of Kentucky superseded that of James Lane Allen; she was intelligent and poetic where he was sentimental and rhetorical.

Maristan Chapman in *The Happy Mountain* (1928) recounted a

simple idyll of the Tennessee mountains, rich in idiom and wit. Three others struck compromises between realism and romanticism: Anne Armstrong in *This Day and Time* (1930) covered old ground in por- traying a Tennessee mountain woman's triumph over adversity, but the poetical strain that ran through the book kept it from becoming trite. Olive Tilford Dargan in *Call Home the Heart* (1932) took a North Carolinian mountain woman through the ominous shadows of marital infidelity and new industrial developments to a happy home. Marjorie Kinnan Rawlings shrewdly chose a heretofore unexplored region for the setting of her novels. *The Yearling* (1938) was the story of a youth broken to the plow of life by the cruelties of the Florida wilderness. Anne G. Winslow with *The Dwelling Place* (1943) began a series of tenderly humorous novels in which traditional attitudes survive un- touched by vulgarity.

Chief among the rehabilitators of Civil War romance was Stark Young, a Mississippian who had won recognition as a literary journalist in New York City. *So Red the Rose* (1934) was a loving picture of all that was best and gracious and worth dying for in the civilization of the Old South. Young's Mississippi aristocrats pleaded their cause and re- called the culture of a bygone era. Despite its recording of deep mis- fortunes, the story failed to convey the menacing reality of a great war; however, it penetrated beneath the surface to catch the spirit of a vanished age.

Two years after *So Red the Rose* came *Gone with the Wind*, the first and only book of Margaret Mitchell, an Atlanta newspaperwoman. This 1,027-page story was set in Atlanta and North Georgia during the twelve eventful years of the Civil War and Reconstruction that fol- lowed 1860. The great figures of the times are offstage, but history is there in a less obvious sense. The first section of the novel reflected the graciousness of the plantation culture; the second strikingly portrayed the Civil War and its effects upon civilian life as seen through the eyes of women; in the third part, the narrative rose to imposing heights in depicting the rebuilding of raw, booming Atlanta from its own ashes and agrarian culture. Although it is history strictly from the Southern viewpoint, objectivity does not surrender to sentimentality, and there is a deft fusion of romanticism and realism.

The appeal of the book was its subordination of dull historical data to a long list of characters who glide gracefully or storm lustily through a veritable whirl of events. It will long command a wide circle of read- ers because it is more than a good tale; it is high comedy in the classical sense. Specifically, it is an American "success story" in the best meaning of that term. It blows like a cleansing wind over the areas of Southern fiction reeking of the stench of a whole generation of naturalistic writers. The book exudes optimism in portraying the triumph of an individual over adversity with the clarity of an old Christian drama. Although Miss Mitchell emphasizes worldly rather than spiritual values, her achievement is nonetheless effective.

Evidence that Southern literature was adhering closely to sectional traditions is the fact that Mississippi, long adjudged by the sociologists the most unprogressive of American states, in 1950 possessed a larger number of creative writers than any other Southern state. William Faulkner continued to dwell among his own people, refusing to be lured away to distant places. Eudora Welty developed her particular version of Mississippi with an unusual skill. In *The Robber Bridegroom* (1942) she creates a weird fantasy of the state's frontier, and in *Delta Wedding* (1946) a deft study of an old Southern family in decline. Frances Gaither in *Follow the Drinking Gourd* (1940) and *Double Muscadine* (1949) demonstrated the skill of a born storyteller. Cid R. Sumner in *Quality* (1946) portrayed the problems of a colored girl returning to Mississippi after acquiring Northern ways. James R. Peery in *Stark Summer* (1939) and *God Rides a Gale* (1940), and Elizabeth Spencer in *Fire in the Morning* (1948), created pictures of life in small towns and rural communities. Other Mississippians of literary distinction were William A. Percy, poet and plantation memorialist, and Hodding Carter, the liberal journalists who fought local injustice and explained to the nation the ways of the South. And there were natives of Mississippi such as Richard Wright, James Street, Tennessee Williams, Blanche C. Williams, David Cohn, and Henry H. Brickell, whose literary expression, whether in criticism, drama, memoirs, or the novel, carry into strange climates the flavor of the state which has not destroyed its folkways by an overdose of literacy.

The list of Southern writers since 1865 who made a deep impression upon their time is long. It includes Lanier, Cable, Harris, Murfree, Page, Allen, Johnston, Glasgow, Cabell, Stribling, Wolfe, Faulkner, Caldwell, Roberts, Young, Rawlings, and Mitchell. The accomplishments of these men and women become all the more evident when compared with the poor performances of Southerners in the nonliterary arts. A longer list of eminent personalities is aviable only in the field of politics.

These writers deserve the prominence bestowed upon them because they exploited almost every phase of regional life. The sectional history, the folklore, the behavior of all classes of society of both races were bases for imaginative explorations. The sordid results of poverty and ignorance are not ignored; neither are the no less real regrets of a people endowed with romantic ideals. No one can deny that a wide reading of Southern literature yields a complete and profound understanding of the region. At its best, this literature rises to universal values above the local or provincial materials in which it is rooted. One need not be especially interested in things Southern to derive instruction and entertainment from the best books of Harris, Johnston, Glasgow, and Mitchell. Uncle Remus, Scarlet Sister Mary, and Scarlett O'Hara are imaginative creations of far greater appeal than actual characters of Southern history in the post-bellum period.

CHAPTER XXVIII

The Fine Arts

>>>->>>

EVEN patriotic extollers of sectional achievements admit that the South experienced an artistic doldrums during the forty years of prostration and recovery which followed the Civil War. The principal activity in sculpture was the erection on every courthouse lawn or public square of a nondescript figure of a Confederate soldier which conveyed little of the high emotions of 1861. The impulse to memorialize in bronze or stone the great heroes of the Confederacy was largely held in abeyance until after 1900. Notable exceptions, however, were the recumbent marble figure of Robert E. Lee which Edward M. Valentine placed over Lee's tomb at Lexington after the great general's death in 1870, and Jean Antoine Mercié's equestrian statue of Lee with bared head, placed on Monument Avenue in Richmond in 1890. The Civil War stimulated a certain amount of painting. John A. Elder and Conrad W. Chapman created battle scenes, and copies of Elder's portraits of Lee and Stonewall Jackson adorned countless homes. William D. Washington's *Burial of Latané* was reproduced for display in hundreds of Virginia parlors. Architecturally the period was aptly described as having been "sliced off from its past by the sword of a destructive war."

Southerners of sensibility were forced to be content with such remnants of a glorious past as plantation mansions, patio houses of New Orleans, and the stately residences of Charleston. Louisiana-born Henry R. Richardson was the leading American architect of the 1870's and 1880's; his buildings sprinkled every section of the country except the South. The few men of wealth—the merchants, bankers, and factory owners —were too unimaginative to give judicious attention to the decorative. The dwellings and occasional public buildings they erected conformed to the inferior taste then prevalent everywhere. An example of this was the castellated Gothic structure which was the state capitol of Louisiana after 1880, and which Mark Twain described as "a whitewashed castle, with turrets and things—materials all ungenuine within and without, pretending to be what they are not." [1] Another example was the Female Institute of Columbia, Tennessee, which boasted of "its resemblance to the old castles of song and story, with its towers, turreted walls, and ivy-mantled porches." And there was the Jefferson Hotel built in Richmond in the 1890's—"a vision of old Seville conjured up by Carrère and Hastings, just back from setting up Spanish scenery for the Florida winter-resort stage." [2] It was truly a gaudy affair with its terraces, arches, fountain court, towers, and show of cream-colored brick and terra cotta. Fortunately, the Southern artistic doldrums of the postbellum period did not extend far beyond 1900. Indeed, it is possible, as Southern patriots have done, to make a formidable list of the section's achievements in the fine arts for the fifty-odd years of the twentieth century.

During these years there arose in every Southern city and town an impressive array of residential suburbs. Houses were so obviously rural in their expansive settings of lawns and native forests that it seemed impossible that they were only a few minutes' ride from commercial streets. Still, homes in these beautiful and comfortable settings were not so tasteful or distinctive as those of the Old South. The earlier ones were a medley of styles following the trend in other sections of the United States.

As the twentieth century advanced, however, there was a growing movement toward harmonious distinctions. Florida and the Gulf states in keeping with their climate turned to Spanish and Mediterranean houses. The Atlantic seaboard states veered toward sound traditions by recreating the classical revival and Georgian forms of the Old South. The restoration of the rotunda of the University of Virginia by Stanford White, after it had been wrecked by fire in 1895, prompted the revival of the Jeffersonian or early republican architecture of red brick and porticoed houses. This preference was most emphatically expressed at Atlanta where Neel Reid, an architect who became active in 1907, persuaded suburbanites to abandon their varied extravagances in favor of the simple reds and whites of the Georgian style set against the forests and hills. Thus Atlanta—and Southern cities that followed its example—came to possess some of the most beautiful suburbs in all America. A modern touch was given the larger Southern cities by their tall office buildings and hotels, the most notable examples of which

[1] Mark Twain, *Life on the Mississippi*, chap. xl.
[2] American Guide Series, *Virginia*, p. 184.

were in Atlanta, Birmingham, and Texas cities. No attempt was made, as in the North, to transform commercial areas into masses of skyscrapers. In older cities like Richmond and San Antonio modern buildings arose amid edifices of earlier generations, but in most Southern metropolises skyscrapers mingled with the stark ugliness of lesser commercial structures. Since the 1920's there has been a tendency to move businesses to suburbs where spaces are ample enough to dispense with tallness and to allow spacious lawns.

None of the many Southern colleges constructed or expanded in the twentieth century had an architectural distinction comparable to Thomas Jefferson's University of Virginia. Some, to be sure, exhibited a certain massive charm. There was Rice Institute at Houston, a group of buildings of the Venetian Renaissance effectively displayed by ample gardens. Southwestern College at Memphis erected seven buildings of variegated stone in collegiate Gothic arranged in an impressive quadrangle. The Mediterranean buildings of Louisiana State University at Baton Rouge made a bright mass against semitropical foliage. The most expensive architectural enterprise in the South was Duke University, whose Gothic towers culminating in a great chapel raised their tops above North Carolina's pines. European-like in its massiveness and intricacy of design, Duke University in the twenties attracted thousands of art-starved Southerners. Miami University, erected after World War II, was a bold experiment in the modernistic to meet the functions of an educational institution in a warm climate. Scarcely less arresting was colonial Williamsburg on the banks of the James, some 200 miles to the northeast of Duke University.

In the decade following 1926, this town was restored to its eighteenth-century elegance through the generosity of John D. Rockefeller, Jr. After infinite research in America and abroad, the Governor's Palace, the Capitol, the Raleigh Tavern, and some 130 other buildings were rebuilt or restored with unparalleled verisimilitude. Williamsburg houses, interiors, and colors were widely copied in the domestic architecture of many Southern states. Inspired by an antiquarian interest similar to the Williamsburg restoration was the Parthenon reproduced at Nashville, "the Athens of the South." It was a replica of the Greek temple in all its details, including pediment, sculptures, and metopes. Ultramodern and extremely ornate was the Louisiana state capitol, which Huey P. Long erected in 1932 at Baton Rouge to replace the building ridiculed by Mark Twain. In the main body of this edifice the classical style was modified in the interest of massive simplicity; for the Roman dome, traditional in state capitols, was substituted a great tower of offices at once useful and ornamental. A broad flight of stairs, magnificent bronze doors, a wealth of sculpture, and spacious gardens added to the impressiveness of this greatest of Southern statehouses. A monument to the union of sculpture and architecture was the Carillon Tower at Mountain Lake Sanctuary in Florida, built by Edward Bok, the Philadelphia capitalist, in 1929. In true Gothic tradition, the Bok tower—inspired by the Bell Tower at Malines, Belgium—was a mass of soaring loveliness enriched by elaborate sculpture.

In their domestic arrangements Southerners of the twentieth century unreservedly accepted all the modern conveniences Northern ingenuity could devise—plumbing, central heating, screens against insects, and electric lights, refrigeration, and other appliances. The dingy, overheated, and often unsanitary kitchens of the late nineteenth century gave way to kitchens so clean, cheerful, and practical that they often were displayed with pride. The modern trend included a passion for antique furniture. The golden oak, the plush, the enlarged crayon portraits, the bric-a-brac, and other relics of the late Victorian interiors were discarded in favor of Sheratons, Hepplewhites, and the simple beauty of old American survivals. Because there was not enough old furniture to satisfy the demand, so-called antiques were pulled out of attics, barns, and the shanties of Negroes and poor whites and carefully repaired.

The antique shop became an institution of the Southern roadside. Still the demand could not be met, so furniture in antique styles was manufactured; Biggs of Richmond became noted for such reproductions. Of course, there was much misrepresentation in the antique business, with dealers often deceiving customers concerning the antiquity of wares; in turn, these buyers frequently represented their purchases as having once belonged to famous ancestors. The first deceit in a sense was negated by the second, and the interiors of Southern homes were made more beautiful, whether adorned with furniture that was genuinely or spuriously old. The fact that not all antiques were authentic had a distinct advantage. It made possible improvements and adaptations in styles and forms to suit the more contracted and utilitarian living spaces of the twentieth century. It is probable that the modern Southerner, with his mechanical conveniences hidden behind real or simulated antiques, lives as tastefully, if not as spaciously, as his real or imaginary ancestors of the pre- or post-Revolutionary period.

The paucity of sculpture in the period immediately following the Civil War was somewhat redeemed by the scattering of a considerable number of sculptured monuments over the South in the twentieth century. Richmond became a "monumental" city, with its statues of Stonewall Jackson, Jeb Stuart, Jefferson Davis, Matthew F. Maury, and Hunter H. McGuire supplementing Jean Antoine Houdon's marble figure of Washington, and its Washington and Lee monuments of earlier dates. Charlottesville, like Richmond, had impressive monuments —Jefferson, Washington, Lee, Jackson, and the elaborate Lewis and Clark and George Rogers Clark memorials. Most original of all Southern statuary was the McConnell Statue by Gutzon Borglum on the campus of the University of Virginia. This is the bronze figure of a World War I aviator who, "with pinions on his outstretched arms, is poised on a globe as if for flight." In a low-country setting of live oaks, Spanish moss, and dark waters, Archer M. and Anna Hyatt Huntington adorned South Carolina's Brookgreen Gardens with 300 or more pieces of statuary, rivaling in quality and quantity the garden displays of the sculpture-loving people of Europe.

Although little of its sculpture was of artistic value, New Orleans had the appearance of a richly ornamented city because its monuments were in such attractive settings. Among its best were the Wounded Stag in front of the Isaac Delgado Museum of Art, the equestrian figure of Andrew Jackson in Jackson Square, the symbolic fountain at the entrance of Audubon Park, and the rich ornamentation on the Criminal Court Building. Sculpture was introduced into Texas by Elisabet Ney, a celebrated and bold artistic missionary from Germany. Austin displayed her monuments to Sam Houston and Stephen F. Austin, and her memorial figure of Albert Sidney Johnston. Dallas received Clyde Chandler's Sidney Smith Memorial Fountain featuring the Gulf Cloud, a symbolic figure. William M. McVey created the decorative sculpture on the San Jacinto Monument, as well as the one to James Bowie at Texarkana, and the bronze doors and exterior of the Museum of History of the University of Texas. At Nashville, Thomas P. Mims produced character studies of Tennessee Negroes, farmers, and backwoods types. At Stone Mountain near Atlanta Gutzon Borglum in 1923 began "the most stupendous sculptural undertaking . . . that has ever been conceived anywhere in the world." [3] His plan was to carve on the face of this gigantic cliff a vast panorama of the Confederacy centering around the figures of Lee, Davis, and Stonewall Jackson. What might have become an achievement of outstanding splendor was interrupted by a controversy while work on the three central figures was still in progress. Other additions to the South's sculptured monuments were made by Sir Moses Ezekiel, Augustus Lukeman, Karl Bitter, and F. Wellington Ruckstuhl.

In the South more attention was given to the creation and preservation of pictures than to sculpture. Painting was not only less expensive than carvings and not so dependent upon the co-operation of public authorities, but encouraged by an admiration for ancestral portraits inherited from the Old South. In 1932 the South had seventy art

[3] Ula M. Gregory in William T. Couch, ed., *Culture in the South*, p. 276.

schools. Although not comparable in importance to the great art centers of New York City, Chicago, and Cleveland, some of them turned out notable work. At the School of Arts at Sophie Newcomb College in New Orleans, under the inspiration of William and Ellsworth Woodward, materials at hand were utilized for the development of local color. The James Lee Memorial Academy of Arts, where some 500 students received free instruction, was founded at Memphis in 1925. In Richmond the creative urge was fostered by the art department of the Richmond branch of the College of William and Mary; local types of the Virginia scene were produced in profusion. The artistic impulses of Virginian Negroes found expression in ambitious scenes of Negro life and history executed at Hampton Institute under the direction of Viktor Lowenfeld, the Viennese exile. In 1938 an all-Virginian exhibition of painting appeared in New York City. In Atlanta, Charleston, Houston, and Sarasota, Florida, art schools were connected with museums. The most notable of these was in the Florida town at the John and Mabel Ringling Art Museum, which was founded in 1931.

The principal Southern collections of paintings were the Isaac Delgado Museum of Art at New Orleans, Houston Museum of Fine Arts, High Museum of Art at Atlanta, Gibbes Art Gallery at Charleston, and Virginia Museum of Fine Arts at Richmond. No Southern museum possessed the truly comprehensive collection of paintings seen in European or New York City galleries; rather, selectiveness was encouraged. During the three decades after World War I, museums flourished; both the wealthy and the lesser taxpayers increased their endowments and support. Their deficiencies were partly remedied by traveling exhibitions loaned by New York and other art centers. Groups of artists in every city south of the Potomac united in 1922 to form the Southern States Art League. Frequent art exhibits indicated a decline of public apathy in such matters.

The Southern painter and etcher demonstrated ability and willingness to depict the local scene with some of the completeness characteristic of the novelists and short-story writers. They pictured the varied landscapes of mountain, hill, and swamp, the sleepy streets, the flower markets, the old houses, the Negro in all poses, even the slums and other unhappy realities. No artist of the first order appeared, but Carle John Blenner, Hugh Henry Breckenridge, John E. Bundy, Murray P. Bewley, and Alice R. Huger Smith—to name a few—were pioneer painters of solid merit. William Woodward was inspired by the beauties of the Louisiana and Mississippi coasts; he was followed by a veritable galaxy of artists who have given color and animation to every aspect of the life and background of New Orleans. Robert J. and Julian Onderdonk, Frank Reaugh, Edward G. Eisenlohr, and Alexander Hogue painted the Texas landscape with its Spanish missions, Mexicans, and cattle; Gari Melchers and W. Sergeant Kendall portrayed the color and local types of the Virginia scene. The Southwest came to life in Samuel P. Zeigler's lithographs of oil wells, and in Ben Carlton Mead's illustrations for J. Frank Dobie's book, *Coronado's Children* (1931). Under the leadership of Elizabeth O'Neill Verner, the doorways and gateways of Charleston have become the subject of beautiful prints. Emma Langdon Roche of Mobile selected southern Alabama landscapes and Cajun types; Anne Goldthwaite, another Alabamian, achieved fame with her "golden canvases" of scenes in Montgomery, New Orleans, and Charleston.

In the 1930's the Works Progress Administration fostered numerous art projects which resulted in many impressive, sometimes startling murals of local history, scenery, and industry; they were placed in post offices and other public buildings throughout the South. Among the most noteworthy were the symbolic scenes from Negro history which Aaron K. Douglass, a Negro artist, painted in the 1930's in the library of Fisk University, Nashville.

The decades between World War I and II witnessed increased opportunities for Southerners to experience the joys of music. The radio became an institution in every upper-class and middle-class home, and through it for the first time Southerners could hear every type of music. Music received much emphasis in the public schools and many orchestras and choral clubs were organized. The existence of sixty-eight schools of music in 1930 indicated the South's substantial support of a type of instruction which long had been a part of its genteel tradition. The great heritage of German and English sacred music was sedulously preserved; perhaps its best expression was in the sunrise service held each Easter by the Moravians of Winston-Salem. Grand opera was produced at Louisana State University, at Bob Jones University in South Carolina, at the University of Florida, at the University of North Carolina, and at Memphis State College.

Every Southern city of importance received Paderewski, Caruso, Iturbi, Gigli, McCormick, and other musicians of international renown on their tours of the country. Sixteen Southern cities held annual musical festivals in which distinguished professional musicians co-operated with local amateurs in the production of classical music. Richmond, Atlanta, and New Orleans heard the great symphony orchestras of the North; the Chicago Civic Opera Company visited several Texas cities; and New York City's Metropolitan Opera Company made repeated visits to Richmond and Atlanta. Huge municipal auditoriums where large musical events were held became almost as common in Southern cities as football stadiums. In 1930, eight of the sixty-two symphony orchestras of the United States classified as of second rank were located in the South; Dallas' orchestra was best known. Because of inability to provide sufficient endowments, no Southern city could claim any of the eleven symphony orchestras deemed of first rank.

The section's most original contribution to music was its Negro folk songs. The most appealing of these were the Negro spirituals, outpourings of the religious feelings of the slaves which evolved from 200 years of intimate contact with biblical lore. Nevertheless, they were not adequately recorded or appreciated until Northerners William Francis Allen, Charles Prichard Ware, and Lucy McKim Garrison published in 1867 *Slave Songs of the United States*. Shortly thereafter, they received popular acclaim when sung by touring companies of students from the newly founded Fisk University and Hampton Institute. Some of these songs were joyous or humorous; others were plaintive, pathetic, even dignified. Best loved were *Swing Low, Sweet Chariot; Go Down Moses; Roll Jordon, Roll;* and *Steal Away to Jesus.* To the generation after World War I, Negro spirituals became a veritable passion, appealing to all Americans from conservative white Southerner to radical Northern Negro. They were proclaimed by some as the only distinctive folk music ever produced in America. The popularity of the religious songs led to recognition of other types sung by the Negro. Although more numerous than the spirituals, they neither deserved nor received so much regard.

Songs known as the blues were catapulted into fame in 1910 by the publication of *The Memphis Blues*, the work of William C. Handy, a Tennessee Negro. These songs expressed homesickness, jealousy, disappointment, lonesomeness, and a groping for material things quite apart from the heavenly hopes of the Negro spirituals. Out of the so-called hot music of ragtime bands grew jazz, an expression in raucous song and dance of "the syncopated bafflement of humans at the tempo of modern life." Jazz was introduced to Chicago and the outside world by musicians from New Orleans around the time of World War I. The ancient folk music of the mountain whites gained formal recognition through the White Top Festival, first held in 1931 on a mountain in Southwest Virginia, and through the publication in 1934 by John Powell of *Twelve Folk Hymns*. White folk music never gained the prestige of the Negro spirituals in cultivated circles, but it became immensely popular in the form of so-called mountain or hillbilly music featured in juke boxes, gramaphone records, dance halls and radio broadcasts.

Every Saturday night for four and one half hours millions listened to fiddlers and guitar singers of Grand Ole Opry at a Nashville radio station twanging hillbilly tunes. So great was the popularity of Grand Ole Opry among the plain folk that such star performers as Roy Acuff, Red Foley, and Hank Williams earned as much as $100,000 annually from gramaphone records and from personal appearances before the great crowds they were able to pack in city auditoriums.

A few composers, in the manner of the great musicians of Europe, used the Southern folk idiom as the basis of elaborate expression. The best known works of this type were created outside the South by Antonin Dvořák, the Bohemian who composed *New World Symphony* in 1893, and George Gershwin of New York whose *Rhapsody in Blue* (1923), and *Porgy and Bess* (1935) achieved enormous popularity. The most distinguished Southern work was *Negro Rhapsody* by John Powell of Virginia, *Negro Folk Symphony No. 1* by William Levi Dawson of Alabama, and *From the Southern Mountains* by Lamar Stringfield of North Carolina. Among numerous folk compositions of Louisianian origin are *Street Cries* and *Bayou Songs* by Ferdinand Dunkley, *Danse Louisianaise* by Christian Jordan, *Mississippi Suite* by Ferde Grofé, *Place Congo* by Henry Gilbert, and *Swamp River Suite* by Jacques Wolfe.

Texas cowboy ballads came into the limelight through songs of Oscar J. Fox of San Antonio and David W. Guion of Dallas. James A. Bland, a Negro of Southern ancestry whose birthplace was Long Island, glorified the land that held his ancestors in slavery. His *Carry Me Back to Old Virginny* (1875) was perhaps the most exalted song to win popular approval throughout the country. In 1940 it was made the official song of the state whose spirit it so faithfully captured. Another song adopted by the general public was *Deep River* by Henry Thacker Burleigh, another Northern Negro. Southern musicians who composed other than folk themes of the region were Frank van der Stucken and Harold Morris of Texas, Clifton Chalmers of Mississippi, William J. Reddick of Kentucky, and Paul de Launey of Alabama.

The visiting companies of players who delighted Southerners during the five decades after the Civil War were imported institutions which the South had no part in creating. This was not true, however, of the theater of the 1920's and 1930's. Thrown on its own devices, the South produced its own plays. All colleges and high schools developed drama clubs for which adequate auditoriums were conveniently provided by school authorities. Never before had the schools of the South evinced so much interest in dramatics. Acting, designing, and managing were added to the more familiar reading, writing, and arithmetic. A small group of Southern colleges—the universities of Virginia, South Carolina, North Carolina, and Louisville—undertook the serious and complete study of playmaking. Productions by members of college dramatic clubs were often based upon native folklore; Louisiana's North-western State College at Natchitoches perhaps gave most encourage ment to this type of drama. The best-known productions were those of the Carolina Playmakers of the University of North Carolina under the direction of Professor Frederick H. Koch. Amateurs of mature years made up the stage societies organized in almost every Southern city as part of the Little Theater movement which swept the United States after World War I. These groups of artistic crusaders experi-mented with all types of drama from miracle, Elizabethan, and Restora-tion plays of English to non-English productions of all countries and ages, from contemporary Broadway successes to original dramas by members of the little theaters themselves. If these productions failed to make the serious drama a popular Southern institution, at least they were enjoyed by the elite of many cities, especially by aspiring young actors and playwrights. Outstanding among the little theaters were Le Petit Théâtre du Vieux Carré, founded at New Orleans in 1916; the Richmond Theater Guild established in 1918; the Dallas Little Theater formed in 1921. The latter group won the Belasco Cup in the 1924 Little Theater competition held in New York City with John William Rogers' powerful one-act play, *Judge Lynch*. The Dallas Little Theater repeated this feat with other plays in 1925 and 1926.

In the years after World War II the drama showed a courageous vigor in scattered sections of the South. The little theaters repeated what they had done in previous years. Robert Porterfield's Barter Theater, organized in 1933 to give unemployed actors pay in country produce, entertained tourists at its home base in Abingdon, Virginia, during the summer, and gave town audiences in Virginia and elsewhere a taste of professional drama during the winter. Paul Green wrote two historical dramas for outdoor presentation with music and dance and verbal continuity spoken by narrators. For Nags Head in North Caro-lina the spectacle is "The Lost Colony" (1937), the story of the Roa-noke Island tragedy; at Williamsburg in Virginia the spectacle is "The Common Glory" (1947), a story of the American Revolution with Jefferson as the leading character. "Horn of the West," a drama by Kermit Hunter on Revolutionary patriots of the Appalachian high-lands, was inaugurated in 1952 at Boone, North Carolina.

Dallas in 1952 was the dramatic capital of the South, with six pro-ducing organizations of its own. Notable was the Civic Playhouse, basically an amateur organization which put on Broadway plays. More interesting was Margo Jones' Theater '52 which was in its sixth season successfully producing professional drama, some of which was original.

This incomplete catalogue of the South's twentieth-century achieve-ments in the creation and enjoyment of the beautiful should not be accorded too great significance. In the arts, as in agriculture, a record of substantial production by a wide area, over a long period, is not proof of genuine fertility. Indeed, the division of artistic creations over the extensive region between the Potomac and the Rio Grande meant a comparatively meager share for a given area of the South at any given time. Actually, in all the major arts except literature, the region between the two rivers represented one of the most barren territories of twentieth-century civilization. The prevailing notion of progress was too practical to permit liberal patronage and recognition of talent not essentially utilitarian. Southerners retained too many rural traits to allow sufficient development of those features of urban culture required for an artistic flowering above the level of folk expression. The twentieth century was primarily an age of mechanical marvels; ideas and articles, once created, could be easily reproduced and disseminated. The South contented itself with adopting Northern ideas in the realms of the beautiful and the decorative, and that of the purely useful. The inherent weakness of such imitativeness was that local creativeness became stifled; imported works of art often lost their inherent value because they were not in harmony with the specific locality and temperament of the South.

If, by some good luck, the South had produced an outstanding artist, there was only the remotest chance that his genius would have been recognized. The Southerner was accustomed to acknowledge greatness only in war and politics and, to a lesser degree, in literature and industry. The names of those artists which the section produced meant little to its people. Accordingly these artists were compelled to seek more favorable environments, or to express themselves in mediums enjoyed by strangers as well as neighbors. Such a medium was the novel, where the achievements of Southerners bear comparison with those of other areas. Another medium was painting, an art which Southerners practiced extensively, if not with the creative distinction of their novelists. A critical examination of Southern activities in several other major arts—those requiring the patronage of the community—reveals their essential shallowness.

The necessities of civilized existence in a progressive age led to considerable building. Many private homes demonstrated an artful adaptation of Southern experience to modern needs. There were exceptions, however. Every Southern city or town had its hideous bungalows. The newer suburbs were frequently attired in borrowed finery to hide genuinely creative interiors. An absurd passion for every variety of exterior presented a gaudy pageant resembling a parade of circus cages. All types of houses—Spanish, Venetian, and Dutch—were built, to the neglect of the typical American or Southern style of dwelling. Because of the tyranny of books and magazines imported from strange climates, Southerners constructed artificial lakes, treeless lawns, and low-roofed houses without porches or blinds. The lakes were often mosquito infested and slimy or muddy; the lawns were often bare; and the houses were often uncomfortably hot for six months of the year.

Commercial sections were mostly products of the post-Civil War period and, except for occasional warehouses, little remained from the Old South. Overdecorated façades of the Victorian period were supplemented by cheap imitations of Broadway with its garish lighting. The tall impressive office buildings were not numerous enough to obliterate their inharmonious surroundings. Despite its remarkable growth, the Southern business center retained "narrow and outmoded streets, grimy old buildings, and the settled placidity of middle age." Public buildings, with certain exceptions, were generally conceived in the poorest taste. School buildings were as plentiful and almost as large as medieval cathedrals, but they were uniformly dull in appearance—great masses of red brick and concrete set off in treeless squares, complete triumphs of utility over beauty. More ambitious church builders, on the other hand, strove for beauty at the expense of utility, erecting Gothic or Byzantine buildings unsuitable for Protestant ceremonies.

The charm of the ante-bellum college was not often copied by those who built the colleges and universities of the New South. Institutions such as the universities of Virginia and North Carolina refused to harmonize their new buildings with the universally acknowledged distinction of their original foundations. At North Carolina Thomas Wolfe observed: "post-Revolutionary buildings of weathered brick" were flanked by "other newer buildings, in the modern bad manner (the Pedagogic Neo-Greeky)." The most glaring example of rejecting beauty immediately at hand was South Carolina's World War I Memorial Building adjacent to the state university's old library. The library was a gracious, spacious, and well-lighted structure, an inspiration of Robert Mills; the memorial building was an odd sort of Persian tomb with sepulchral chambers.

A confession of architectural bankruptcy was manifested by a return to the remote past for models of some of the South's most deliberately wrought structures. In producing a Parthenon in concrete the Athens of the South admitted its inability to develop an art form of its own. The builders of Colonial Williamsburg, neglecting what should have been 200 years of progress in adapting inherited forms to Southern needs, created eighteenth-century models for the twentieth century. Duke University, planting an Oxford in the piney woods, attempted to adjust Tudor Gothic to the demands of modern education under the Southern sun.

Perhaps to a greater degree than other sections of the civilized world the South held sculpture as something apart, not as a natural means of expression. Consequently, anyone impelled to view a statue was forced to go out of his way. The average town's sole monument was that of a Confederate soldier in an unimaginative pose. Any impressive or elaborate sculpture usually was the work of alien hands, unfamiliar with community standards. When the sculptors resorted to the nude, there were distressing reactions. There were the outraged Charleston nursemaids who hurriedly rolled their charges past the naked male adorning the Battery as a memorial to World War I; the amused surprise of country people before the ample form of Virginia Dare in the North Carolina Historical Museum; the lack of understanding with which motorists from the Deep South received Georg J. Lober's bronze crucifix hanging on the roadside between Fredericksburg and Washington. The attempt at Stone Mountain to memorialize on a grand scale the immortals of the Confederacy failed to gain adequate support from the Southern people. They were too practical to recognize the wisdom of such an expensive monument, although the subject evoked feelings of patriotism. In this connection, it is significant that few of the section's memorials to World War I were in sculpture; the majority comprised utilitarian structures such as bridges, roads, and auditoriums; this is true to even a greater degree of the memorials to World War II.

The musical shortcomings of the Southern people were many. Local choirs and orchestras were almost always mediocre and amateur. Soloists who brought elements of the classical and professional into the larger churches were not appreciated by their unsophisticated congregations. Symphony orchestras of the cities were alien institutions, and the support they received was insufficient and uncertain. Resident professional musicians made their livings through teaching, not through concerts. Music of a sort enjoyed popularity, but it was of the simple or vulgar variety—sentimental survivals, ragtime, jazz, and hillbilly tunes. The juke box with its raucous rhythms attained undisputed dominion over the dance halls, and the radio became supreme in the homes. Radio programs originating in Southern stations were invariably of an inferior order.

Although the schools emphasized popular participation in music, there was a marked decline in such activities. The main reason was the triumph of mechanical music. Young girls who traditionally stayed indoors to practice piano lessons became fewer and fewer, nor did local prejudice against boys taking music lessons abate in the twentieth century. Indeed, the South considered it effeminate or suspiciously abnormal, something for boys to put aside at an early age. Therefore, with the exception of an occasional music teacher, the man who could perform well on the piano became a rarity in Southern communities. More often than not, such composers as lived in the section were strangers whose talents had matured before their arrival. Southern composers, unlike the native novelists, did not adequately exploit the rich field of folk music which surrounded them. Perhaps it was not accidental that outsiders created the best work of this type.

The theater's noteworthy revival after World War I never got beyond the academic and the amateurish. That the Little Theater managed to survive over two decades was due not so much to its intrinsic merit as to the audiences' interest in the productions and acting of friends and relatives. Since actors were not paid, budgetary problems were reduced to a minimum. The Carolina Playmakers, the most distinguished of the Little Theater groups, largely restricted themselves to one-act plays that were mere transcriptions of local life without the imaginative complications of great drama. The Barter Theater to be successful was forced to produce plays which had been tried on Broadway. Few Southern cities had a large and interested public to support theaters on a sound professional basis. Such repertory companies as were foolhardy enough to establish themselves in the South were starved out of existence. The moving pictures satisfied ordinary folk, while the upper classes partook of dinners and parties.

The Federal Theater Project was an attempt on the part of the Franklin D. Roosevelt administration to salvage, through governmental support, a profession bankrupted by the depression of 1929. Companies of competent actors were sent on Southern tours, but the plays did not have a chance to succeed in the face of profound indifference. The only professional drama that Southerners of the generation between World War I and II were willing to support were traveling plays featuring stars to whom New York City had already paid sustained homage. There was no room for an indigenous theater or for imported drama with mere competence to recommend it.

After the artistic doldrums of the period following the Civil War there were in the years that came after 1900 certain stirrings to indicate that the South would not remain artistically barren forever. As a result, a new artistic appreciation and some creative achievements became discernible. Examples could be found in the adoption of modern domestic conveniences, the passion for style and decoration in buildings, the fostering of museums, art schools, municipal auditoriums, and symphony orchestras, and the recognition of Negro and other folk music. In addition, there was the construction of dignified buildings in spacious settings, including such structures as Duke University, Colonial Williamsburg, and the Louisiana State Capitol; also the organization of choral clubs, amateur orchestras, and antique interiors adapted to mod-

ern purposes. Recognition of local color became apparent in a multitude
of paintings, and there was a scattering of sculpture over the land, culminating in the unique McConnell statue at the University of Virginia
and in the grandeur of the Stone Mountain conception. The flowering
of folk music, of formal compositions based on Southern themes, and
the development of the Little Theater were other evidences of art appreciation.

Such a list of achievements should not lead to excessive claims, or to
the assertion that Southern attainments in the fine arts were outstanding
among those of the country at large. The South's accomplishments in
this field were in no way comparable in importance to its successes in
imaginative literature. The region below the Potomac was too thoroughly devoted to the problem of material recovery to find time and
energy for artistic expression. Its god was Progress, not Beauty; its culture was too rustic and new to develop the urban civilization in which
the arts customarily flourish. The products of the Northern atelier and
factory proved so convenient to the South that it neglected to cultivate
its own artistic potentialities. Perhaps in the not remote future Southern
cities will mature culturally; possibly the upper classes will patronize
the arts more liberally and common folk will be educated in the direction of more refined tastes. In such an atmosphere, artists can produce
masterpieces as in other sections of the world. There is no reason why
the South should not produce fine musicians, painters, sculptors, and
architects when it has shown itself capable of giving the world great
statesmen, soldiers, industrialists, and writers.

CHAPTER XXIX

The Industrial Paradox

⇛⇛-⇛⇛

A DISTINGUISHED contemporary student of Southern society declares that the section's rich endowment of natural resources created the "optimum conditions for the development of vitality in culture and abundance in economy." [1] Southern industrial leaders of the twentieth century accepted this challenge by applying modern techniques to the resources at their command. Thus the industrial development so auspiciously begun in the 1880's and the 1890's was continued with unabated enthusiasm in subsequent decades. Older industries, such as cotton textiles, tobacco, fertilizer, iron, and lumber, expanded; among newer industries, petroleum, electric power, rayon, chemicals, and paper became important sources of wealth. Between 1909 and 1929 the South's share of the industrial output of the United States rose from 12 to 14 per cent; this represented an increase in the value of the section's manufactures from $2,637,100,000 in 1909 to $9,993,600,000 in 1929. In the latter year, the South had almost 64 per cent of the nation's spindles and produced 84 per cent of the cigarettes. For its newer industries it possessed the most modern and efficient machinery of any section in the country. The industries of the Southeast had 4.82 horsepower per wage earner, as compared with 4.56 horsepower per wage earner for the Northeast. This meant that the industry of the New South was more highly mechanized than that of the wealthiest section of the United States. By 1939 the South had regained in manufacturing what it had lost during the depression. This was not true of the nation as a whole. A measure of this relative gain was the fact that the wages paid the South's industrial workers had risen from 10 to 14 per cent of the national total. This in-

[1] Howard W. Odum, *Southern Regions of the United States*, p. 25.

dustrial progress, however, had not created a "vitality in culture and abundance in economy." For a variety of reasons, not the least of which was its methods of industrialization, the South entered the era of World War II as the poorest section of the nation. It was the wasted land of Gerald W. Johnson's book, the unhappy hunting ground of the very sociologists who proclaimed the virtues of the new techniques accepted by the South. It continued to be in the twentieth century what it had been in the late nineteenth: the most glaring illustration of Henry George's paradox of poverty existing amid progress.

Southern chambers of commerce and other business groups never ceased to urge outside capital to invest in the section's industries. The advantages they pointed up were tangible ones. Adequate transportation and power facilities gave access to stores of raw materials that were described as existing "in such quantity and variety for the increase and development of America's wealth as are found nowhere else." Attention was directed to the section's great deposits of coal, iron, and petroleum, and to its countless other mineral and agricultural products used by the industrial chemist; to a plentiful supply of cheap labor, as eager as in the 1880's to abandon impoverished farms for employment in industrial centers. New industries were amply rewarded for their willingness to utilize this labor exclusively, as soon as it could be trained by outsiders temporarily imported for this purpose. Native labor proved to be intelligent, industrious, loyal, and conservative. Southern factory workers adhered to the same principles as their employers, and were equally interested in the industrial prosperity of their communities; both groups sought to exclude radical proposals of outside labor organizers. There prevailed what was described as "the most wonderful spirit of understanding and sympathy between employers and employees."

Old-fashioned Jeffersonian ideals of liberalism and individualism lingered on in the twentieth century among the Southern ruling classes and hampered legislation calculated to control the free exploitation of labor and natural resources by industrial capital. So appreciative were Southern commercial and political leaders of new industries that such enterprises were lured into the section by gifts of land, buildings, and capital. Over a ten-year period the Tennessee legislature authorized the issue of almost $3,000,000 of bonds for these purposes, although the state constitution prohibited the practice. All Southern states except North Carolina and Texas indulged in tax exemptions for specified periods.

Southern statesmen joined those of other sections of the progressive world in believing that the key to a higher civilization was the application of the revolutionary advances of science and invention to the abundant natural resources at hand. A newer and happier agrarian life was envisioned through the utilization of cheap power, household conveniences and farm machinery, the automobile for marketing perishable foods and for transporting the once-isolated farmer and his family to recreation spots. From the sweet potato, peanut, cotton, wood pulp, corn stalks, clays, and resins, a hundred and one articles of consumption were made possible through the new chemistry. Southern merchants and industrialists anticipated great prosperity in their growing cities, rivaling those in the North.

Building upon a hundred years of moderate but solid progress, the South did much in the twentieth century to improve and extend its means of communication. Efforts were made to halt the decline in the use of inland waterways that became manifest after the coming of the railroads. The White House conference of 1908 sponsored by President Theodore Roosevelt focused popular attention upon these efforts and emphasized the need of federal subsidies. The necessary assistance, however, did not come until the demands of World War I resulted in transportation congestion. In 1916 Congress created the Inland Waterways Corporation to operate a fleet of river carriers known as the Federal Barge Line on the lower Mississippi and on the Warrior River in Alabama. After this undertaking was subsidized by Congress, a few large oil and steel companies began to run their own boats on the two rivers. The competition of motor vehicles and railroads militated against the success of the Federal Barge Line, but this did not prevent the national government from embarking upon a more ambitious project.

As part of the great Tennessee Valley development of the Franklin D. Roosevelt administration, it was proposed in 1934 that $75,000,-000 be spent for the improvement of navigation on the Tennessee River. The idea seemed impractical to some, because the Tennessee Valley had no heavy industries like those which had made the navigation of the Ohio successful; moreover, the meandering Tennessee was considered no fit substitute for the excellent railroads and highways that lead out of its valley. Some explained the project as one of the extreme measures of the Roosevelt administration to promote a prosperity through extravagant spending. A more acceptable explanation is that it was a blind to cover constitutional objections to the practical flood-control and hydroelectric projects of the Tennessee Valley Authority.[2]

Far more successful than the development of inland waterways was federal promotion of navigation along the Gulf and Atlantic coasts of the Southern states. Vast sums were spent in deepening the harbors of Baltimore, the Hampton Roads cities, and New Orleans and Houston, each of which was connected by railroad and highway with an extensive hinterland. The most unusual harbor improvement was the con-

[2] But see below, pp. 479, 499–500.

struction of a fifty-mile canal to join Houston to the Gulf of Mexico. An old and very interesting project was the Intracoastal Waterway, which linked the numerous bays, sounds, estuaries, lagoons, and rivers of the Atlantic and Gulf coasts. The Atlantic section from Massachusetts Bay to the tip of Florida was completed in 1937; by that date the Southern Louisiana and Texas Coastal Waterway furnished a protected route between Louisiana and the Texas cities. Sections of the Intracoastal Waterway near Baltimore and New Orleans carried much local freight, but as a means of moving long-distance cargoes the waterway could not compete with ocean and land transportation. Federal expenditures brought negligible returns in commerce. Of possible importance to Southern trade is the proposed 200-mile canal across northern Florida begun by the federal government in 1936 as a means of shortening the movements of ships between Atlantic and Gulf ports. Army engineers pronounced the project feasible, but whether the canal would be profitable to shippers was not clearly established. The coming of World War II caused its construction to be abandoned, at least temporarily.

Southern railroads of the twentieth century were free of many of the mistakes and controversies that marked water transportation during the same period. The reason was that by the end of the nineteenth century railroad communications were already established in all parts of the South except the extreme west. Expenditures were primarily confined to the improvement of existing lines; there was no demand by the railroads for the extravagant and often erratic subsidies the federal government bestowed on other types of transportation.

The railroad mileage of the Texas-Oklahoma region grew from 18,-222 miles in 1900 to 32,970 in 1920; this expansion was justified by the opening up of new regions which these lines served. In the thirties the South with one third of the population and area of the United States possessed one third of the railroad mileage, or 82,000 miles of track. Except in some mountain areas and in southern Florida, nearly every Southern farm was within ten or twenty miles of a railroad.

From the operators' viewpoint the section possessed a superabundance of railroads. In 1931 the Southern installations yielded only $2,150 in passenger revenue per mile of railroad, as compared with $3,228 for the nation as a whole; the corresponding freight revenue, excluding the highly profitable coal carriers of Virginia, totaled $10,394 per mile for the South, as compared with $13,414 per mile for the nation. More than half of the American railroad mileage in receivership was in the South, and most of the major companies of the section were not able to pay interest on their bonded indebtedness. This meant that the absentee owners of these enormous properties were giving the Southern people a generous service without receiving any profits. Financial losses were accompanied by a lowering of passenger rates and by improvements in service.[3]

Highways gave the railroads keen competition. "The building of the road system of the Southeast," says Odum,[4] "is one of the most brilliant chapters in the remarkable record of construction in the South since the Civil War." Emulating Northern achievements, Southerners espoused highway construction with as much enthusiasm as they accorded industrial and educational projects. Good roads became the third god in the trinity of Southern progress.

In 1894 Virginia held a Good Roads Convention, and the following year a National Roads Parliament met in Atlanta. Before the end of the century several Southern states organized highway departments, and in 1910 the Southern Railway Company sent from Alexandria a Good Roads Train which aroused as much excitement as the tour of a Presidential candidate. Not until after 1910, when the automobile became a Southern institution, did construction assume a truly modern meaning. Hard-surfaced highways stretching across states became imperative for adequate use of this new means of rapid transportation. Road construction was centralized in the hands of state highway commissions with sufficient revenue attained through the imposition of high gasoline taxes and automobile license fees and by securing federal subsidies.

Under the direction of Frank Page as chairman of the state highway department, North Carolina pioneered in the construction and maintenance of a system of hard-surfaced highways to connect all county seats. Between 1921 and 1925, a primary system of 7,500 miles had been built, with all main routes constructed of concrete or asphalt. Louisiana outdid North Carolina; between 1929 and 1936, under the dynamic direction of Governor Huey P. Long, it constructed 9,800 miles of paved and graveled roads costing $140,000,000. In addition, 400 bridges spanned the state's many waterways. The crowning achievement was the great Huey P. Long Bridge across the Mississippi on the outskirts of New Orleans. Soon other Southern states followed the example of North Carolina and Louisiana. The result was that by 1947 the South was spending $430,000,000 annually on the construction and maintenance of nearly one million miles of state and local highways. It enjoyed the distinction of having a larger percentage of its roads under the central control of state highway departments than any other section of the United States. These administrative agencies were highly efficient, taking advantage of the best engineering skill and emphasizing hard surface. By 1940 a motorist could travel from Washington to the Florida

[3] Odum, *op. cit.*, pp. 399–400.
[4] *Ibid.*, p. 361.

Keys or to El Paso without leaving the pavement. The cost of the trip in gasoline taxes was higher than in the North, but there were compensations. The traveler encountered fewer motor vehicles in proportion to the population than in the rest of the United States; nevertheless, in 1947 there were almost 9 million cars on Southern roads.

Twentieth-century expansion in transportation was accompanied by the growth of cities. Between 1900 and 1930 the number of urban people in the Southeastern states increased from 2.25 millions, or 15 per cent of the total population, to nearly 8 millions, or 30 per cent. Although most Southern states continued to be predominantly rural, 52 per cent of Florida's population was urban, 40 per cent of Louisiana's, and 32 per cent of Tennessee's. The number of Southern cities with a population of 100,000 or more increased from three in 1900 to twenty-two in 1930. In the latter year, there were twenty-four cities with populations of 50 to 100,000; thirty-six had 25 to 50,000. These figures indicate that cities grew faster than those of the nation as a whole; the only ones that lagged behind were the South Atlantic ports of Wilmington, Charleston, and Savannah and such interior places as Lynchburg, Petersburg, Danville, Fayetteville, Augusta, Natchez, and Lexington. The primary cause for this arrested development was the diversion of trade to other centers by the railroads.

New Orleans remained the section's largest city, with 459,000 inhabitants in 1930; Louisville's population reached 308,000; Richmond, 183,000; Nashville, 154,000; Houston grew to 292,000 inhabitants; Atlanta to 270,000; Dallas to 260,000; Memphis to 253,000; Jacksonville and Norfolk to 130,000. Other great cities were products of the twentieth century. For example, from a modest beginning of 4,000 in 1890, Oklahoma City's population climbed to 185,000 by 1930; Tulsa from a mere 1,400 inhabitants to a city 100 times as large thirty years later. El Paso, with 102,000, rivaled in growth the two Oklahoma cities, as did the Florida cities of Miami and Tampa, which grew from small beginnings in 1900 into cities of 111,000 and 101,000 respectively.[5]

The mushroom-like character of many Southern cities prevented them from manifesting the cultural traits usually associated with great centers of population. This very newness, however, had certain advantages. Modern transportation enabled their people to enjoy rural life within a few minutes' drive of towering office buildings. The oil magnates of Tulsa transformed their city into one of the most architecturally beautiful places in America. At Miami "mosquito-infested swamps, infertile sand dunes, and lagoons" became "cultural landscapes as attractive as the imaginary cities of the Arabian Nights." By 1930 Southerners turned their backs on rural tradition to become urban

[5] For other figures on city growth, see above, p. 333, and below, p. 589.

minded with the more talented among them moving to the cities. People were as proud of Atlanta, Birmingham, and Dallas as they once had been of the Old South with its plantations and mansions.

In the twentieth century the Southern branch of the American cotton textile industry became even larger than that of New England. The number of active spindles in the South increased from 4,369,000 in 1900 to 18,881,000 in 1937, while the number in New England during the same period fell from 13,171,000 to 7,131,000. In 1923 Southern spindles first exceeded those of New England. A goodly portion of this expansion was due to native enterprise and capital, but many New England manufacturers dismantled and rebuilt their mills in the South. There were reasons for this preference. Chief among them was the proximity of the Southern mills to the cotton fields. In 1929 the four leading cotton manufacturing states of the section produced 4,260,000 bales of cotton and consumed 4,219,000 in their industries. Constructing mills in rural areas meant cheaper lands, a greater degree of company control of governmental agencies, and lower taxes than in New England, where the mills were maintained in urban areas. The abundance and comparative cheapness of coal and hydroelectric power, and the very effective co-ordination of these two sources of energy, were conditions favoring the South. Moreover, the mills of the section had improved machinery, 71 per cent being automatic as compared with 38 per cent in New England.

By 1940 the South's lower wages and longer hours were finally adjusted through federal and state intervention, and through the growing social consciousness of Southern communities. By then child and female labor were no more prevalent in Southern cotton mills than in those of New England; nor was there any more evidence of squalor and mean living in Southern mill villages than in Northern communities. Extensive programs of social betterment raised millworkers to a more favorable position among the section's population. The disadvantages of rising labor costs were compensated by the increased skill of the laborers, and this, along with a traditional loyalty to their employers, led some observers to believe that Southern mill hands were more satisfactory workers than the class-conscious and only partly Americanized workers of New England. The superior quality of cotton goods produced in New England mills was gradually equaled by 1930 as Southern workers perfected their skills.

Southern industries established before 1900 showed pronounced progress in the first decades of the twentieth century. Between 1900 and 1930 the production of pig iron increased from 1,965,000 to 4,480,000 tons, and that of the related industry of coal mining from 54,510,000 to 202,092,000 tons. These figures represented an increase in the

South's share of coal production, but a loss in its iron output because of the exploitation of the rich Lake Superior deposits. In 1907 the United States Steel Corporation purchased the Tennessee Coal, Iron and Railroad Company, the chief operator in the Birmingham area. This saved the local company from financial ruin. Effective use was made of substances essential in steel manufacturing—iron ore, fuel, and flux—which were found conveniently near each other in the Birmingham area.

The fact that the Southeastern states produced 85 per cent of the nation's tobacco enabled them to retain their earlier-won supremacy in the realm of tobacco manufacturing. In 1929 they manufactured 60 per cent of the nation's tobacco products and 84 per cent of its cigarettes. The expansion of the tobacco industry was mainly the work of the American Tobacco Company under the able direction of James B. Duke. Concentration of the industry into fewer cities in larger factories, and the popularization of its products through advertising were part of the Duke strategy. The dissolution of the tobacco trust into several companies in 1911 was more nominal than real. "Gentlemen's agreements" concerning production and price were maintained, and such "competition" as appeared took the form of rivalry between four well-known brands of cigarettes to see which one, through clever salesmanship, could sell most to the American public.

Between 1899 and 1929 the South increased its share of the nation's lumber production from 32 to 47 per cent. The yellow-pine industry of the South became the leading endeavor of its kind in the country. In the twentieth century the section maintained the leadership which it had held for three centuries in the output of naval stores. Improved methods of extracting and distilling turpentine, increased uses which the chemist made of this substance, and the industry's ability to migrate into more southernly regions after the pines of its northern states were exhausted all contributed to this leadership. Southern furniture manufacturers kept pace with the accomplishments of earlier decades. In 1928 North Carolina surpassed other states in the quantity of lumber used to manufacture furniture; in that year, the South as a whole was producing one third of America's household furnishings. Improved quality and style of cabinets were made as well as those of cheaper grades. The American industry came to utilize more Southern hardwoods.

The most important industrial innovation of the South was the development of hydroelectric power and its auxiliary steam-electric power. First successfully applied in the North in 1882, electric power was introduced in the South five years later as a means of propelling the street railroads of Richmond. By 1888 the transformer and related devices were so perfected that distant transmission of electric energy could be accomplished. The first electric-powered cotton mill began operation at Columbia, South Carolina, in 1894; since then most Southern mills have been of that type. By 1929 the Southern Power Province had been created, capable of 5,460,000,000 kilowatts of electric generating capacity, or 17 per cent of the total electric energy of the United States. These figures were, respectively, 10,428,000 and 20 per cent in 1946, with engineers' schedules calling for the installation of 5,383,000 kilowatts of new generating capacity in the near future.[6] This phenomenal growth was made possible by the precipitous rivers of the Southern Appalachian region and the contiguous Piedmont, which was abundantly and regularly supplied with rainfall and topographically adapted to the construction of dams.

The Southern Power Province was conveniently divided into seven sections, extending from the Virginia-Maryland region to the relatively unimportant Ozark-Ouachita area. The most important power area was the Carolina-Georgia Piedmont, which generated 70 per cent of the electric energy of the Piedmont industrial area. The largest power developments of this section were the huge Murray Dam on the Saluda River in South Carolina, the six dams belonging to the Georgia Power Company on the Tallulah-Tugaloo River in North Georgia, and the Catawba-Wateree River developments in the Carolinas belonging to the Duke Power Company. So thoroughly do a series of dams utilize the 220 miles of the Catawba-Wateree's course that they capture for electric energy all but 304 of the 1,056 feet of the river's fall. The Southern Power Province was developed through private capital operating through some forty principal and subsidiary companies, which have largely absorbed the many small municipally owned power stations.

With the exception of the Duke Power Company, all Southern power companies fell under the financial control of large holding companies—Commonwealth and Southern Corporation, Electric Bond and Share Company, and the Mellon interests—with local management remaining in the hands of the already existing companies. By means of this consolidation nearly all electric plants of the Southeast, including the steam-powered units, were interconnected by high-voltage transmission lines, thus forming a more complete integration of power-producing and transmission capacity than existed anywhere else in the world. Consumers over a wide area were given an unvarying supply of power unaffected by low water or washouts in local areas. The linking of the steam plants into the system permitted advantageous use of these more expensively operated units during the summer seasons when water flows were normally low.

[6] Calvin B. Hoover and B. U. Ratchford, *Economic Resources and Policies of the South*, p. 135.

Popular resentment over high rates charged for electric energy and the unscrupulous methods employed by absentee financiers in organizing and operating the electric holding companies in 1933 led to the creation of the Tennessee Valley Authority by Congress. The federal government acquired vast water power in the heart of the Southern Power Province for the purpose of producing electricity in competition with private companies. However, it was not likely that this idea would be applied so extensively as to threaten capitalistic control of the greater part of the electric properties of the South. Monopolistic greed was resented by the people of the section, but not to the extent of tolerating government-supported enterprise which threatened to annihilate profit-seeking private interests.

From its beginning at Titusville, Pennsylvania, in 1859, development of petroleum had spread into West Virginia, Kentucky, and Tennessee by 1883. The discovery at Spindletop, near Beaumont, Texas, in 1901 of a gusher of unprecedented capacity marked the beginning of the great Southwest oil boom. New pools were soon opened in various sections of Texas, Oklahoma, and Louisiana. The growth of the oil industry in these three states was facilitated by the use of improved techniques devised in the older petroleum regions and encouraged by the increased demands of automobile drivers. By 1910 Oklahoma was producing 52,000,000 barrels; Texas, 8,899,000; Louisiana, 6,841,000. For some years Oklahoma and California were rivals as the nation's chief producer of petroleum, but Texas has surpassed both of them in recent years. By 1944 the South was producing over a billion barrels, or well over 60 per cent of the national total. In 1931 more than 150 oil refineries were located in the South and were handling about 40 per cent of the nation's crude petroleum. Since that date there has been a large absolute growth in the industry without much change in the South's share. Pipelines connected the producing fields with Northern and Gulf Coast refineries.

The discovery and opening of oil wells had a magic effect upon the sparsely inhabited regions of the Southwest. When, for example, a new oil field was opened in the panhandle of Texas in 1926, a ranch area in a few weeks was turned into an oil-producing city of 25,000 inhabitants; a nearby community, between a certain Sunday and the following Wednesday in October, 1929, was converted from a hamlet of 20 persons into a town of 1,500, with land values rising from $300 to $2,000 an acre. In 1929 Texas and Oklahoma had 326 citizens with annual incomes of $100,000 or more. According to expert estimates, the South has 70 per cent of the nation's oil reserves of 14 billion barrels; this augured well for the industry's future prosperity.

A Southwestern product of comparable importance was natural gas;

well over half of the nation's total came from that area by 1929. South-west cities were early supplied with this fuel, and by 1950 gas lines connected the Southwest with the principal cities of the East.

In 1930 the Southern states produced 25 per cent of the mineral output of the United States, or $1,809,000,000; in 1945 this figure was 32 per cent, or $2,616,000,000. Although a formidable proportion of the South's share was represented by coal, iron, and petroleum, the section contained innumerable mineral substances that proved economically workable. It continued to lead the nation in the old but important industry of digging phosphate rock, and produced some 5,527,000 tons annually, most of it from Florida and Tennessee. Salt production on a commercial scale was a Southern industry extending back to the eighteenth century; Louisiana produced 606,000 tons annually. Sulphur became an outstanding Southern commodity, because of Herman Frasch's invention of an effective method of extracting this valuable substance from wells along the Gulf of Mexico. Gulf Coast production got under way in 1903, and before long 356,000 tons were extracted annually; this figure rose to 3.8 million tons by 1945. The monopoly which Sicily had enjoyed previously was broken, and the South exported large quantities of sulphur in addition to supplying domestic needs. Because of the extensive road-building programs, cement mixing and the quarrying of stone and gravel became widespread in many sections of the South. The beautiful marble quarried at Knoxville, Tennessee, and Tate, Georgia, found markets throughout the United States. Bauxite, a mineral from which aluminum is manufactured, chiefly came from Arkansas; in 1945, $5,000,000 worth of this substance was mined in the South.

In the 1930's twenty major chemical industries of the South produced slightly more than one fourth of the entire chemical output of the United States. Among these were petroleum refining, natural gas production, and the distilling of naval stores; the rayon, wood pulp, and paper industries were also important. Many large chemical establishments are located in the South: Davidson Chemical Company of Baltimore (fertilizers); rayon plants at Covington and Roanoke in Virginia; Ampthill plant of the Du Ponts near Richmond; various industries of Hopewell which include the great nitrogen-fixation plant of the Solway Process Company; Chesapeake-Albemarle paper mills at West Point, Virginia; Masonite Corporation of Laurel, Mississippi, which explodes waste wood fiber with steam to yield a new type of insulating material; Celotex Company of Louisiana, which utilizes so much spent sugar cane in manufacturing insulation board that sugar is sometimes referred to as a mere by-product. The Tennessee Eastman Corporation at Kingsport converts wood into many essential chemical products.

Chemical industries were attracted to the South by the ample labor supply, the presence of hydroelectric energy, and the nearness of such basic raw materials as coal tar, petroleum, rare earths, cotton, pulp wood, sulphur, and phosphate rock.

Most of the research was done by outsiders. As late as 1946 only 6.5 per cent of the industrial research laboratories of the nation were in the South, employing 5,900 people, or 4.4 per cent of the country's total.[7] Among the section's few outstanding experimenters were George W. Carver, Negro researcher of Tuskegee Institute, who made many products from the sweet potato and the peanut; Thomas L. Willson of Spray, North Carolina, who discovered a commercial method of making calcium carbide in 1892; Charles H. Herty, a Savannah chemist, who demonstrated in 1934 that the pulp from Southern pine could be utilized for newsprint and even rayon, lacquer, and cellulose products.

The discoveries of Herty and others prompted manufacturers in the 1930's to turn to the South as a source of that most widely used and carelessly consumed of all American articles—paper. The 977.8 million cords of Southern yellow pine comprised the nation's largest forest reserve. It was nearer the great markets than the vast tracts of Canada, Alaska, and the West; moreover, if properly regulated, it could better withstand the perils of exhaustion. The growth of trees for pulp wood in Canada required from sixty to eighty years; the South needed from nine to twenty years. These unquestionable advantages for a time were offset by the fact that Northern paper mills were equipped to use their own forests. Nevertheless, Southern paper manufacturing progressed. It began with the making of kraft, a tough brown wrapping paper, which in 1919 utilized 234,000 cords of Southern wood. The Southern industry spread so rapidly that in 1937 fifteen or more paper mills, representing an investment of more than $100,000,000, were either in operation or under construction.

The process of duplicating the work of the silk worm by changing cellulose plant fiber into a liquid, then forcing this liquid through small openings to form threads, was first accomplished in France in 1884. The resulting product is known as artificial silk or rayon. Its manufacture in the United States began in Pennsylvania in 1911, but not until 1925 was the new substance accepted in this country as a basic textile. The first unit of the industry in the South was established at Roanoke in 1917 by British capital; in 1940 more than two thirds of the rayon of the United States was made south of the Potomac. The principal mills were at Roanoke, Covington, Waynesboro, Hopewell, and Ampthill in Virginia; at Rome, Georgia; at Nashville and Elizabethton, Tennessee; at Burlington in North Carolina and at Enka near Asheville. Rayon manufacturing came South for the same reasons that prompted other industries: cheap

[7] *Ibid.*, p. 387.

labor, cheap land, and abundant water power. In addition, the area possessed distinctive attractions for this industry: the soft water which was an essential, the proximity of other textile industries, and the presence of cotton and various fibers to mix with the artificial silk.

Emphasis on the growth of Southern manufacturing in the twentieth century should not relegate Southern agriculture to a secondary role. Then, as during the inauguration period of industry in the late nineteenth century, farming retained the greatest importance for the Southern producer. No other section of the United States exceeded the South in the variety and value of its agricultural products. Possessing less than one third of the land area, in 1933 it produced $1,409,000,000 worth of farm crops from a national total of $2,876,000,000, or nearly half.[8] The South owned most of the country's acreage of cotton, tobacco, peanuts, and rice. Even though it trailed in the production of wheat, oats, and hay. it had a fair share of the nation's corn production. Florida lagged behind California in oranges, Georgia's peach crop failed to equal that of the Western state, and the cane fields of Louisiana produced less sugar than the beet fields of the American midlands. Yet both Florida and Texas led California in grapefruit production, and a commercial truck crop valued at $65,000,000 gave the South a large proportion of the returns from providing the American table with fresh foods.

The hope that the South's emphasis on cotton would decrease was no more fulfilled in the twentieth century than in the decades after the Civil War. True enough, King Cotton was sick, as numerous analysists asserted, but not to the point of death. The weight of traditional agricultural practices, as well as the incomparable advantages of the Southern climate and soil, lent as much support in the twentieth century as in earlier years. If cotton suffered from falling prices, overproduction, foreign competition, and pests, so did other products of the Southern soil. Moreover, unlike other Southern farm commodities, cotton enjoyed an almost complete monopoly of the American market. Special maladies affecting cotton—the invention of paper and rayon substitutes, excessive soil depletion, the dwindling of exports—were considerably compensated for by the uses that chemistry discovered for both cottonseed and lint, as well as by the application of soil-building devices and diminishing competition from foreign textiles such as Japanese silk.

The realm of King Cotton in the 1930's continued to expand over some 1,200 miles from the Virginia southside to the heart of Texas. In this area some 40 million acres were devoted to the fleecy staple as compared with 25 million acres in 1900. The annual crops rose from 11 to 17 million bales between 1919 and 1931. This represented almost the entire crop of the United States and some 60 per cent of the world's

[8] Almon E. Parkins. *The South, Its Economic-Geographic Development*, p. 239.

supply. The high tide of cotton profits came in 1920 when the crop brought $2,034,650,000. After that date a marked drop in prices occurred. The average annual value of the crop between 1921 and 1931 was $1,400,000,000; it fell to $465,000,000 in 1932 with a consequent radical decrease in production in the years immediately following. However, as in the past, cotton staged a recovery from depression; scarcities created by world disturbances proved a stimulus.

Despite the decline of foreign markets and of the fertility of the soil, tobacco continued to play as significant a role in Southern economy in the twentieth century as in the preceding three centuries. Production in the United States rose from 808 million pounds in 1910 to twice that amount two decades later; 85 per cent of this crop came from the South. The increased intensity of cultivation enabled the tobacco farmer to obtain a yield of $75 to $150 in value for each acre employed. Because of its extensive areas of soils suitable for cigarette tobacco growing, North Carolina in 1927 assumed the leadership previously held by Virginia and Kentucky, and in 1929 produced five times as much of the popular weed as the Northern states combined. After World War I, the older tobacco fields of Virginia, Maryland, North Carolina, and Kentucky were supplemented by the development of important fields in eastern South Carolina, south Georgia, and northern Florida.

In the twentieth century the rice-sugar area of Louisiana and Texas continued to hold its established position in the economy of the South. By 1930 the area was producing 34 million bushels of rice, enough to supply the American market and some 12 million bushels for export. The use of machinery and superior organization permitted a single worker to produce 60 times as much rice as an Oriental farmer. The well-being of Louisiana's sugar industry was threatened by the competition of foreign sugar and by the fear of tariff changes in 1916. Before the "free sugar" clause of the tariff became operative, World War I nullified its effect, and Louisiana planters turned actual or expected losses into profits. In 1921 another protective tariff was imposed, and the industry survived.

The most widely distributed Southern crop continued to be corn; in 1930 every Southern state except Arkansas devoted more than one fourth of its cultivated acreage to this staple. Rivaling corn in distribution were cowpeas, soybeans, velvet beans, and peanuts. Twenty-six per cent of Florida's cultivated acreage was devoted to these and similar foodstuffs; Georgia and Alabama utilized only slightly less land in their production. Wheat was grown in the Southeast, but its importance declined as a result of the greater accessibility of Western granaries. The coming of railroads in 1887 permitted the semiarid regions of Oklahoma and the Texas panhandle to shift to wheat as a primary commodity. The future of these regions, however, was limited by the possible recurrence of dust storms like those of 1937.

Apples became one of the most profitable crops of the South, where a more or less constant annual production of 12 million bushels increased 60 per cent in price between 1929 and 1948. The orchards were centered in the Shenandoah-Cumberland valleys, on the eastern slopes of the Blue Ridge, in the southern Appalachians, and in the highlands of Arkansas. Winchester in Virginia, with its Apple Blossom Festival, was called the Apple Capital of the South.

Peaches grew in the apple regions and in warmer parts of the South. The largest area was middle Georgia, which sent the first refrigerator car to New York City in 1889; at about that time the Elberta variety was perfected. The number of peach trees in Georgia rose from 3.8 million in 1890 to 15 million in 1925. Since then, however, the number of Georgia's trees has declined, and the peach industry has shifted to the piedmont slopes. Southern peaches enjoyed the advantage of reaching the Northern markets in successive relays. Those of Georgia came first, followed by those of the Carolinas, Tennessee, Virginia, and Maryland. Its perishable character made the peach less satisfactory for marketing than the apple, and the Southern varieties in canned form were never able to compete in quality with those of California; too, producers of the South lacked the advertising skill of West Coast growers.

The most signal progress in twentieth-century citrus fruit production in the South occurred in the region of the lower Rio Grande, where advances in irrigation and grafting encouraged the development of large orange and grapefruit orchards. In this area 4.2 million grapefruit trees and 1.8 million orange trees were planted between 1920 and 1930. The Texas grapefruit was "conceded to be by the Federal agricultural experts, the best in the world," superior even to the boasted product of Florida.[9] Despite the vigorous competition of Texas and California, Florida brought about a revolution in the eating habits of Americans within the past century by changing oranges and related fruits from luxuries to necessities. Mass planting resulted in cheap prices which, in turn, led to wholesale consumption. Satisfaction of this demand was partially insured by the growers' utilization of precautions to reduce the perils of frost. When Florida fruit growers learn from their California rivals the many skills of cultivation, grading, and advertising, as well as the art of dickering with governmental bodies over protective laws and freight rates, they will capture a fuller share of the markets. Already the Florida Citrus Exchange has made a beginning in this direction.

[9] *Ibid.*, pp. 295-8.

The twentieth-century South developed inland market gradening to meet the growing needs of nearby cities. More uniquely Southern, however, was the continued growth of early vegetable markets in connected zones along the Gulf of Mexico from the Rio Grande to Florida, and along the Atlantic from Florida to the eastern shore of Virginia. Railroads and new highways provided rapid transportation; the ever-growing predilection of Americans for fresh foods at all seasons furnished the demand; the Southern climate supplied the sunshine and showers while the plants were fed fertilizer with a precision based on scientific knowledge. Each vegetable locality could count on two or three weeks' priority in crop maturity over the next zone to the north as the trucking season swung up the Atlantic Coast. Florida and the Rio Grande Valley began the profitable procession with lettuce at Thanksgiving, green beans in November, tomatoes and cucumbers in December, celery and cabbage in January, white potatoes in March, and green corn in May. The season closed in early summer with the products of the Chesapeake Bay area well in advance of those from the fertile fields of Pennsylvania and New Jersey.

The enormous industrial and agricultural strides described in this chapter created a prosperity unparalleled in the annals of the South. The region ended the first quarter of the twentieth century with a gross wealth four times as high as at the start of the century—an increase from $17,000,000,000 in 1900 to $70,000,000,000 in 1922. Deposits in Southern banks rose from $1,728,000,000 in 1909 to $5,959,000,000 in 1923. Seemingly, the South had passed out of the vale of poverty caused by the Civil War. If Frederick Law Olmsted, who had complained so vigorously of the meager comforts and primitive culture of the Old South, could in 1930 repeat his journey through what he had called the Back Country, he would have found much to admire. "Had he come again then," remarks Howard W. Odum,[10] "he would have passed thousands of homes and suburban places surpassing all that he had seen in the ante-bellum country. Instead of his crowded rooms, inadequate linen, and sordid conditions, he would have found comfort and surcease. If he had been invited to a private home, he would have been provided with his desired private room and bath, soft curtains and gentle lights, a warm house or cool according to season, music and books and pictures, recreation and conveniences, gardens and flowers and fruits. . . . He would have found Southern wealth and resources far beyond the limit of any ante-bellum dream."

Indeed, Southerners were so elated over their material progress that they pictured their region as a place "in which to live better and make more money" than in other areas of the world. "Good schools, good

[10] *An American Epoch*, pp. 315–16.

roads, and churches, added to the healthful climate," they told prospective colonists, "make the Southland a most attractive place to rear your
children and to have something left over after the end of your year's
work." Of course there were contrasts with the still greater prosperity
of the North and with the "mile after mile, area upon area" of the "limited and sordid conditions" under which poorer Southerners lived.[11]
That existing conditions made it impossible for all Southerners to enjoy
the comforts of the section's new industrial civilization was brushed
aside as irrelevant by staunch defenders. Had not the more fortunate
Southerners of modern times established standards of living toward
which their underprivileged brethren could aspire?

There was, however, another side of the picture of Southern material development, which could not escape the attention of socially
minded critics. The South in contrast with the North was a land of
waste, inefficiency, exploitation, and poverty. In the 1938 report of the
National Emergency Council to President Roosevelt on *Economic Conditions of the South*, the region was designated as "the Nation's economic problem No. 1." Stark figures and facts were presented to sustain
this conclusion; coming from such a high source, it jolted Southerners
out of their complaceny.

The National Emergency Council and censorious sociologists were
quick to cite the material shortcomings of Southern life. In 1929 the
South with approximately the same population as the states of the
Northeast had less than half the gross wealth of that group of commonwealths. In per capita wealth certain Southern states averaged $1–2,000
as compared with $4–6,000 in favored Northern states. Seven Southern
states with average bank resources of $150 per capita stood lowest in
this respect among all the states. The per capita bank resources of eight
Northern states were three times the amount of Southern states with the
highest average. The per capita savings deposits of six Northern states
were ten times as great as in seven Southern states. The $44.93 average
of income tax payments for Delaware's whole population contrasted
with the $0.39 average of Mississippi.

Average cash farm incomes of many Southern states were under
$1,000 as opposed to California's average of $4,000. The Southeastern
states, with 13.2 per cent of the wage earners in the nation's factories,
received only 8.4 per cent of the wages, or $844 per person as against
$1,364 for the Northeast, and $1,447 for the Middle states. Even wealthy
Southerners did not receive a proportional share of the national income.
Among those individuals who enjoyed incomes in excess of $100,000,
the Southeast had only 441 from a national total of 14,677.[12]

[11] *Ibid.*, pp. 317–20.
[12] Odum, *Southern Regions of the United States*, pp. 49–77.

These material deficiencies were inevitably reflected in living conditions. The South was no exception to the universal rule that poverty breeds ignorance and slovenliness indicated by an unintelligent use of meager resources. The depressing slums of all Southern cities seemed practically unlimited as one perused the gloomy documents which sociologists and novelists compiled. There were the cheap, tumbledown shanties, unimproved by whitewash, paint, flower gardens, or adequate water supply. Their inhabitants refused to produce for themselves such commodities as eggs and milk to meet minimum dietary requirements.

The Federal Bureau of Home Economics recommended that 83 per cent of an adequate farm diet should be raised at home; however, poorer Southern farmers purchased as much as 58 per cent of what they consumed. Nevertheless, Southern purchases were comparatively meager. In retail purchases per capita, ten Southern states averaged less than $250 annually, as compared with a dozen other states averaging twice that amount. Therefore, either from necessity or choice, millions of Southerners continued to subsist on the three M's—meal, meat, and molasses. Human happiness and life itself were needlessly sacrificed to pellagra, tuberculosis, rickets, anemia, and other diseases resulting from dietary deficiencies. The death rate, especially from malaria, typhoid fever, childbirth, and pellagra, was much higher among Southern whites than among Northerners, and still more appalling among the Negroes. Higher death rates were in part responsible for the fact that the average Southerner was younger than other Americans. In 1930 South Carolina was the only state with more than half of its population under twenty years of age.

The most obvious explanation for the comparative poverty of the South was its adherence to many of the more harmful phases of a traditional agricultural economy—primarily, continued emphasis on commercial agriculture such as the raising of cotton. The preference of both landlord and tenant for the staple that could be most easily converted into money led to the neglect of products necessary for home consumption. The section in 1930 had "the lowest ratio of income from livestock production, the lowest per capita purebred livestock, the lowest production of milk and dairy products, a low ration of pasture land, a low carrying capacity for pasture lands." [13] Purchases of the necessities of life in markets controlled by merchants inevitably resulted in accumulating more debts. The exhaustion of capital meant increased tenancy, or even banishment from the land, since no capitalist would assume the risks of credit. Between 1880 and 1935 the number of tenants increased from one third to one half the total count of farmers.

Careful studies proved that communities with the largest ratio of

[13] *Ibid.*, p. 41.

tenants not only produced fewer crops for sale, but less for domestic consumption. The continuation of tenancy and the one-crop system, and the elementary neglect characteristic of poverty caused the vast soil exhaustion that cursed the South far into the twentieth century. In 1933 it was discovered that nearly two thirds of the eroded land in the United States was in the South. In many areas of the section "vast gullies and gulches, wagon wide and tree deep, spotty hillsides and great stretches of field marred like some battlefield—each year destroyed more and more, each decade added ugliness and havoc to the landscape." [14] If all the vast tons of potash, nitrogen, and phosphoric acid that had been washed away through the process of erosion could have been added up, one authority believes, "the staggering cost would run into billions." The irony of the situation was that the great science of chemistry enabled Southern farmers to remain on their depleted lands without any radical remedy for the erosion. This was because the leached and eroded lands could be kept in operation by feeding them the fertilizer which chemistry provided in ever-increasing quantities. The Southeast's annual purchase of 5,514,000 tons of fertilizer cost $161,000,000, or twice the amount spent by the rest of the United States.

In the Southeast, farms under 100 acres increased from 68.9 per cent of the national total in 1900 to 79.9 per cent in 1930; in the latter year farms of more than 500 acres were less than 1 per cent. This continued breakup of the land into small rentals presented another irony of Southern agriculture. It did not bring about any greater degree of rural prosperity than had existed in the days of "the chimera of land concentration," which liberal critics had often blamed for the ills of Southern farming. Possession of these small holdings, either as tenantships or as peasant proprietorships, did not indicate initiative and thrift so often associated with independent farming. Actually, the freedom of poor and ignorant tenants to manage their farms brought about as much abuse of the land as would have occurred if landlords had operated the farms themselves. The Tobacco Road farm of the independent Jeeter Lester was a scene of desolation more appalling than if "the proud Jeeter had been under direct control of the most stupid and autocratic landlord."

Emphasis on the forward strides of the section's industries should not blind the observer to the fact that its proportion of the national industrial output was small. In 1929 barely 9 per cent of this output was produced in the states of the Southeast, as compared with 42 per cent for the Northeast and 36 per cent for the Middle states. Southern industry produced only $5,355 worth of products per wage earner, as against $7,577 for the Northeast and $8,744 for the Middle states. The value of

[14] *Ibid.*, p. 341.

products per horsepower for the Southeast was $1,111, as compared with $1,661 for the Northeast and $1,810 for the Middle states. To some people, this justified the relatively lower industrial wages paid in the South; it was chiefly due to a lack of balance in Southern industrial economy comparable to the same deficiency in Southern agriculture.

Although the South excelled in some types of mechanical equipment and in the production of certain products, its range of technology was so incomplete that it has been described as "essentially colonial in its economy." Its industries were operated primarily for the profit of outsiders rather than for the natives themselves. Manufacturing mainly was confined to elementary processes; it fabricated its own cast-iron pipes, steel rails, bridges, and oils, but not its hardware, locomotives, and automobiles. The South did not produce radios, clocks, surgical instruments, dynamos, clothing, drugs, radiators, and many other finished articles requiring the highest skill to produce and bringing in the largest profits. It did not demonstrate leadership in a single one of the nation's ten major industries. For example, it had only 5 of the 161 concentrations of the 29 iron and steel industries, and 28 of the 195 concentrations of the nation's 16 foremost food products industries. More important, its machines were not what Walter P. Webb calls "mother machines that have within themselves the reproductive capacity." This absence of machine manufacturing permitted outside dictation of the types of industry the South should choose. It sometimes meant, as in the case of the Texan milk bottle company cited by Webb, the destruction of a Southern industry to protect Northern patent monopolies.[15]

Another cause of the South's comparative poverty was absentee ownership of many of its businesses and industries. By the end of the first quarter of the twentieth century, the great financial houses and corporations of the North controlled most of the section's strategic industries. The second generation of carpetbaggers, who participated with Southerners in the first industrial development in the 1880's, was followed by a third and far more successful invasion in later decades. Huge impersonal Northern corporations with Southern labor and managerial ability founded factories or purchased those already established by local enterprise. Since they lacked wealth for large-scale investments and were charged relatively high interest rates when they attempted to borrow, Southern leaders welcomed the ingress of outside capital; to them it represented potential industrial prosperity. Although the textile industry of the 1880's was created by local capital, in the twentieth century a substantial share passed directly into Northern hands—approximately 15 per cent of the cotton spindles and 13 per cent of the looms. The newer textile mills of the Deep South were to a greater degree

[15] Webb, *Divided We Stand*, pp. 73, 83–99.

Northern-owned—36 per cent for the cotton mills of Alabama, with higher percentages for the rayon and silk mills and the newer hosiery mills. The South's vast coal and iron reserves were held by the nation's financial titans—the Morgans, Fords, Mellons, and Rockefellers. The United States Steel Corporation dominated the Birmingham branch of the iron industry. All sixteen corporations controlling the section's oil fields were nonlocal in ownership, with the Mellons, Rockefellers, and Morgans again in top place.

The National Emergency Council, in its *Report on Economic Conditions of the South*, continued the story: "All the major railroad systems are owned or controlled elsewhere. . . . Most of the great electric holding companies, whose operating companies furnish the light, heat and power for Southern homes and industries, are directed, managed and owned by outsiders. Likewise, the transmission and distribution of natural gas, one of the South's greatest assets, is almost completely in the hands of remote financial institutions." Only nine of two hundred prominent corporations in the country had their headquarters in the South. Contrary to popular belief concerning the supposedly wide distribution of the stocks of these corporations, incomplete evidence indicates that not more than 6 per cent of these investments were Southern-owned. Direct ownership of Southern property was by no means a full measure of Northern control. Even that part of the textile industry owned directly by Southern capital was dependent, in many instances, for its financing on banks which were Northern dependencies. Southern agricultural lands, because of their depressed status, did not attract direct investments of Northern capital, except where large acreages were taken over by banks and insurance companies through foreclosures of mortgages. There was no real independence for farms if one counts the actual, albeit devious, dependence that came through the linking of Southern and Northern banking and marketing institutions.

As in the colonial, ante-bellum, and post-bellum eras, the South in the twenties and thirties remained an agrarian society in debt to wealthier industrial and commercial areas. The Southern farmer bought in markets dominated by quantity-reducing combinations of businessmen, and he sold in markets beset by an almost ruinous competition of farmers among themselves. He was too individualistic and hidebound to be successful in the organization of marketing and crop-reducing co-operatives; through such methods he might have obtained a fair share of what consumers paid for farm products. As a result his profits were small, and his more ambitious sons departed for commercial and industrial areas. An authoritative estimate established that between 1920 and 1930 the rural areas of the United States surrendered to the urban areas some

$3,500,000,000 in the form of inheritances, rents, and interest. A goodly portion of the Southern half of this sum enriched bankers, brokers, and merchants in the fast-growing cities and towns of the South, but much of it also passed into Northern hands. The Northern drain on Southern resources through ownership of industries was further augmented by the purchase of Northern luxuries and other manufactured articles usually more expensive than the unadorned and unfinished products of Southern farms and factories.

In a few businesses, notably in life insurance, a considerable share of the profits ultimately remained in the South. Through the control of certain "specialty" articles—Cannon Towels of Kannapolis, North Carolina, and Coca-Cola of Atlanta—Southerners by effective advertising realized inordinate profits from consumers. The city of Dallas made the experiment of trying to be a style center and thereby capture some of the glamor and billions New York enjoys from its dictatorship over what men and women wear. Of the thirty-nine specialty advertisers in the *Saturday Evening Post* for June 27, 1935, only two were Southern businesses. Among 4,664 firms listed in 1944 as manufacturers and distributors of druggists' supplies, only 466 were Southern.[16] Retail profits once enjoyed by Southern merchants were siphoned out of the section in ever-growing proportion to the rise of Northern-owned chain stores. The Southern businessman increasingly became a mere factor or agent of Northern principals, who controlled both production and distribution. His function was to sell the gasoline, automobiles, mechanical refrigerators, alcoholic beverages, clothing, insurance policies, foodstuffs, and a hundred and one other articles endeared to the Southern public through advertising.

The burden of these purchases on a poor people was devastating. In 1937 David C. Coyle [17] estimated that the South was paying out one billion dollars in excess of its income. It balanced its credit by selling property to investors from other sections of the country, by borrowing, by going bankrupt, and by destroying lands and forests to secure immediate incomes. The federal government, through its policies of protective tariffs, constitutional immunities to corporations, railroad rate discriminations, and patent monopolies, favored the older manufacturing sections of the country. The possibility of revolt against its debtor status, in the manner of the Revolutionary planters against their British creditors, was ruled out by the Civil War. Legislative remedies were also eliminated through decisions of the Supreme Court against confiscatory legislation by states. Southern leaders reconciled the sons and

[16] Webb, *ibid.*, p. 19.
[17] In *Virginia Quarterly Review*, XIII, 192 (Spring, 1937).

grandsons of those who had followed Robert E. Lee and William Jennings Bryan to the domination of their section by Northern centers of industry and trade.

"We are confronted," said a Southern historian in 1942,[18] "with a paradox more amazing and ironical than any ever conjured by the imagination of Gilbert and Sullivan. The people of the South, who all their lives have suffered deprivation, want, and humiliation from an outside financial imperialism, followed with hardly a murmur of protest leaders who, if indirectly, were nonetheless agents and attorneys of the imperialists." "On the other hand," answer two economists,[19] "the South has realized substantial advantages from absentee ownership. When a large concern establishes a plant in the South, that plant brings with it the accumulated technology or 'know-how' which the concern has built up over years and the right to draw on the research facilities of the company. It may also bring with it a higher scale of wages than prevails in the region and other employee benefits which are more advantageous to workers—such as health insurance, vacation and retirement privileges, and better systems of personnel administration."

Both a symptom and a cause of the plight of the South was the emigration of its people. Between 1900 and 1930, nearly 3.5 million more inhabitants left the South than came there to live. The primary reason for this exodus was overpopulation caused by a high rural birth rate. This abundance of Southerners had its advantages, however, since it attracted industry to the section. It also provided a means of imposing Southern ideals and prejudices upon those regions where emigrants settled. Nevertheless, the disadvantages outweighed the advantages. In the opinion of some students the overpopulation problem "lies at the heart of most Southern economic dilemmas." As a major cause of low wages, it meant that the Southern people received less than a fair share of the returns of production. Southern states spent more than $2,000 to nurture each of its young people only to have millions of them, upon reaching maturity, move elsewhere to expend their productive energies and take along their inheritances. Financially minded sociologists estimated the loss through the outflow of the aforementioned 3.5 million people at $5–10,000,000,000, since many of these emigrants were among the most talented of native-born Southerners. This partly accounted for the scarcity of Southern residents in many fields of national leadership.

The Wilson administration which came to power in 1913 attempted to correct sectional inequalities by lowering the tariff, imposing a graduated federal income tax, and decentralizing banking through the Fed-

[18] Benjamin B. Kendrick in *The Journal of Southern History*, VIII, 19 (February, 1942).
[19] Hoover and Ratchford, *op. cit.*, pp. 74–5.

eral Reserve System. The effects of these corrective measures were blunted by World War I. The United States was so enveloped in prosperity that Northern business willingly shared its gains with the less wealthy sections of the country. Southern industries boomed; cities expanded; Southern businessmen became rich; wages rose; land increased in value. In 1919 Southern cotton reached 38 cents a pound, the highest price since 1866. All this naturally converted the South more thoroughly than ever to the wisdom of Northern leadership in business. Its people gladly participated in the magic prosperity that continued for ten years after the war. They joined in a veritable orgy of industrial activity, buying, selling, and speculating in stocks, lands, and luxuries. "In every town," remarked an observer,[20] "businessmen quit their occupations to sit in hard chairs before a blackboard and figure the profits as they were chalked up by the boy with the crayon and rag eraser."

The South's special contribution to postwar prosperity was the Florida land boom, a contagion which spread over the country and involved land as far north as Asheville, North Carolina. This vast real estate enterprise was prompted by the desire of the newly rich to enjoy the mild winter climate of the far South. Semitropical Florida increased in population from 752,619 in 1910 to 1,265,549 in 1925; Miami rose from 5,471 to 69,754. Unattractive swamps and barren beaches were transformed into villas and gardens where hundreds of thousands gathered to mix pleasure with profits.

The region below the Potomac was so imbued with the current craze for prosperity that in 1928 seven of its states set aside inherited political prejudices to help Northern majorities elect a Republican President who promised a continuation of this prosperity. A year later, on October 24, 1929, New York's stock market crash ushered in the depression of the thirties. The South suffered in much the same manner as the rest of the country. Fortunes were lost; bankruptcies, a collapse of values, decreased wages, and increased unemployment prevailed throughout the South. Such yardsticks of prosperity as construction contracts, car loadings, and bank debits were affected as much in Southern centers of trade as elsewhere. Although tobacco and textile interests were less severely hit than branches of the iron, steel, and lumber companies, the organization of Southern economy was such that reverses in these industries brought dire consequences. The fact that the section devoted such a large share of its agricultural energies to money crops caused havoc when the prices of cotton and tobacco tobogganed to points below the cost of production.

The sectional income from cotton fell from $1,245,000,000 in 1929 to one third that amount in 1932. Because of this and other price

[20] Webb, op. cit., p. 128.

declines, Southern farmers were often without funds for necessary articles of consumption. Forced sales of farms rose from 26 to 45 per thousand between 1927 and 1932. There followed an exodus from the land where many poor whites and Negroes had not lived much above the level of subsistence even in normal times. The rural unemployed or dispossessed went North, or crowded into various Southern cities. Only a few states continued to show increases in population; South Carolina and Georgia actually lost 10 per cent of their Negro inhabitants. This disgorging of farm peoples depressed industrial wages out of proportion to the decline of industrial output and prices. In 1925, four years before the collapse of the New York stock market, much of the spirit had been already taken out of Southern business by the collapse of the Florida boom, when the bidding up of real-estate values to fantastic levels was followed by an inevitable break in the market. Then came the bankruptcy of the many sanguine speculators and those units of local government which lent support to the whole enterprise. The condition of Southern real estate explains why the section suffered more than its proportional share of bank failures—a total of 3,011 between 1920 and 1930, or 39 per cent of all bank failures in the United States.

Because of its misfortunes in the depression the South was receptive to President Roosevelt's New Deal, involving federal intervention in business and agricultural enterprises in order to promote economic recovery. Those measures which especially affected life and economy included agricultural and unemployment relief, the protection of labor, and the development of hydroelectric power.

The Agricultural Adjustment Act of May 12, 1933, attempted through law enforcement to do what the Southern farmer had for generations been told to do for himself, but had been unable or unwilling to accomplish. Production of such staples as cotton, tobacco, and rice was to be curtailed so that growers of these commodities might secure fairer prices. The great trusts and unions had succeeded in obtaining higher prices and wages through limitations of production; accordingly, the impoverished farmer, when confronted with reduced American consumption and the collapse of foreign markets, called upon his government for relief from the curse of overproduction.

To remedy this condition each cotton, tobacco, or rice grower agreed by contract with the government to reduce the acreage of his commercial crop, and to use the resultant surplus lands for soil-improving crops and commodities for home consumption. Since this contract was not entered into until after the cotton planting of 1933 had started, provision was made for the plowing under of 10,500,000 acres of surplus cotton for that year. The farmer, in return for his acreage destruction or reduction, was to receive "benefit payments" in addition to the higher prices anticipated from the artificially created scarcity. Benefit payments were to come from excise taxes on the first conversion of cotton, tobacco, or rice into some other goods; for example, cotton into cloth. This "processing tax" was disliked by some because it tended to raise consumer prices, but others claimed that it provided aid for the farmer analogous to the protective tariff given to the manufacturer. The Secretary of Agriculture was authorized to supply the difference between current market prices of the regulated commodities and the "parity price" deemed just for the farmer's share. The parity price represented an adjustment between what the farmer had to pay and what he realized; the aim of this arrangement was to restore his purchasing power to the point it had attained during the four years immediately preceding World War I. Southern farmers entered into the reduction contracts enthusiastically and received much material benefit from their operation; in a series of referendums, they approved their continuation.

In 1936 the processing tax feature of the AAA, which supplied the funds for the entire program, was declared unconstitutional by the United States Supreme Court. The Roosevelt administration, however, was not to be dissuaded from its production and price-control activities, and secured from Congress the more elaborate AAA of 1938. Under this act the national legislature was obligated to make direct appropriations to take the place of the invalidated tax. The new law endeavored to maintain parity prices by withdrawing commodities from the market when they were abundant and releasing them when crops were scarce. Thereby the government was authorized to allot average acreage quotas for normal domestic and foreign demands, and for the creation of surpluses for lean years. To avoid constitutional objections, farmers were not compelled to sign quota agreements, but those who did not do so were deprived of subsidies. If overproduction resulted despite restrictions, the government was prepared to make loans to farmers against crops stored on farms or in public warehouses; if two thirds of the producers of a basic commodity agreed, the government was authorized to restrict sales to marketing quotas, and to impose fines on farmers selling more than their quotas.

This ambitious plan was widely criticized. It was pointed out that the prices of the great American staples, especially cotton and tobacco, were determined by world conditions beyond American control; that to raise prices through curtailments stimulated the production of cotton in Egypt, Brazil, and elsewhere; that these foreign increases would again lower prices, and foreign markets once held by America's low prices would be lost beyond recovery. Conservatives asserted that the measure deprived farmers of economic freedom by subjecting them, in a matter of private concern, to the decrees of distant and impractical bureaucrats; that the expense to the federal government for benefit payments and unredeemed loans on surplus crops was prodigious; that the spirit of the Constitution was as much violated by the AAA of 1938 as by the AAA of 1933. Radicals argued that the price advances contemplated were a sharp blow in the face of the consumer; that it was unjust to remedy low prices by creating a scarcity which would aggravate the hardships of millions of Americans who were underfed and poorly clothed. A Communist magazine carried a cartoon of a shirtless tenant farmer plowing under cotton. Moreover, it was asserted that the chief beneficiaries of the law were the more prosperous farmers and landlords. This particularly applied to the South, where the disfranchised masses of black and white tenants had little control over administrators chosen by political oligarchies. Too large a share of the benefit payments, intended for tenants and landlords alike, went to the landlords; indeed, the degree to which this was practiced became scandalous in some areas. Crop restrictions threw many thousands of laborers and sharecroppers out of work. They joined thousands of others whom the depression and overpopulation had torn from the land. Opponents of AAA were unable to suggest constructive alternatives.

Southern farming was plagued with too many cultivators of cotton and tobacco; restriction of production, by one method or another, was the inevitable remedy. Since voluntary agreement apparently was beyond the capacity of the Southern farmer, Federal intervention seemed imperative. Because cotton had been plowed under in 1933, its price rose from six cents to ten cents a pound; from this source and from benefit payments, the farmers reaped twice as much for the cotton crop that year as they had received in 1932. The gross income from cotton increased $276,000,000 by 1935. The farmers gave the two thirds majorities necessary for implementing the second AAA, and by 1939 four and one half million crop contracts had been executed in the South, at a cost to the government of some $900,000,000. When the inequities practiced toward tenants and farm laborers became known partially successful efforts were made to correct them. The President's Committee on Farm Tenancy collected the doleful facts and provision was made for tenants to receive larger shares of the crop allotments; also limitations were placed upon the amounts which wealthier planters could receive.

The Resettlement Administration was created in 1935 with authority to remove destitute farmers from submarginal lands and to establish them in co-operative communities. A few such settlements were begun in the South. Far more in keeping with prevailing traditions was the Farm Security Administration, known as FSA. Between 1935 and 1941, this agency loaned $570,000,000 to more than 900,000 needy farm families, half of them Southerners. These loans were used by tenant farmers, croppers, and farm laborers for the purchase of farms and necessary stock and tools, the creation of more diversified agriculture, the replenishing of the soil, and the establishment of health centers. The land-purchasing activities of the FSA were disappointing, because available funds were inadequate for a comprehensive attack upon the enormous problem of Southern tenancy. Much good, however, was accomplished in improving income and living conditions among economically depressed families. Traditionally considered "bad credit risks," these families met their obligations with such surprising promptness that government losses were small. The Civilian Conservation Corps—CCC—spent $570,000,000 between 1933 and 1940 for the employment of 586,000 boy members of poor Southern families, the majority of whom were rural. From each boy's $30 monthly wages $25 was given to his family while he was engaged in reforestation, soil conservation, and other projects useful to agriculture.

The soil conservation and diversification programs of the various federal farm agencies added uncounted millions to the value of an agriculture whose chief weaknesses were land wastage and the one-crop system. Proof that "the shackles of the one-crop system were being rent asunder" was the fact that the cash income of Southern cotton farmers in 1939 reached only $598,000,000, as compared with the $666,000,000 of Southern raisers of live stock. Thriving beef and dairy industries developed in the Black Belt of Alabama and Mississippi, once the exclusive domain of King Cotton. Similar changes took place in the tobacco region.

Federal laws designed to better the wages and working conditions of labor held especial significance for the South, whose workers had long been underpaid. The National Industrial Recovery Act of 1933 —NIRA—established minimum wages, shortened hours, banned child labor, and fostered the organization of labor unions as a logical counterpart of the law's encouragement of industrial agreements among capitalists. NIRA's codes and contracts were criticized by some for allowing lower wage scales for Southerners in general, and Negroes in particular. Its efforts to create more jobs through distribution of work, and to increase profits by the curtailment of production proved impractical; the NIRA was invalidated by the Supreme Court in 1935.

It had not been banished, however, before Southern labor learned the advantages of increased wages, shorter hours, and the establishment of labor unions. When it became evident after the demise of the NIRA that industry was expanding and taking advantage of the expected breakdown of Southern labor standards, workers joined forces with Northern interests to demand a substitute for the defunct government agency. Relief came in the form of the National Labor Relations Act of 1935 and the Fair Labor Standards Act of 1938, which gave federal guarantee to the right to organize labor unions and in a wide variety of commercial and industrial employments placed the minimum wage at 25 cents an hour and the maximum work-week at forty-four hours, with plans for subsequently raising wages, lowering hours and ironing out differentials between North and South.

By 1941 Southern labor was receiving $100,000,000 annually in increased wages, and "honest business" was allegedly satisfied with the elimination of "labor chiselers," and the increased purchasing power of Southern workers. The attempt to effect a sweeping elimination of wage differentials between the sections met only partial success. Socially minded Southerners felt that their section might then be placed at a competitive disadvantage that would result in industrial stagnation or even ruin. The National Labor Relations Board—NLRB—directly encouraged unionization in a region customarily backward in this practice, and a reformed Supreme Court proclaimed the "fundamental right" of the workers to organize. Employers were forbidden to discriminate against union members or to support company unions. Elections were held to determine which of the two labor groups, the AF of L or the CIO, should have the allegiance of a specific group of workers. Southern employers and public opinion at first reacted militantly to the demands of union organizers, who were abetted by the extremists originally making up the NLRB. The foes of unionism acted in keeping with the traditional Southern pattern of violence. Opposition to unions decreased when the Roosevelt administration remained firm in its championship of labor and when the NLRB acquired a less radical leadership. Unionization proceeded apace in certain major mass-production industries of the South, notably in steel, coal, textiles, and tobacco. Both the AF of L and the CIO were able to report increased Southern membership.

The problem of unemployment relief became acute in the South because it was a low-wage area where workers had little resources to fall back upon when the depression threw them out of work. The Federal Emergency Relief Administration—FERA—was created to assist local authorities in bearing the burden of the unemployed. Small monthly allowances were made; in 1935 this sum averaged $15.14 for Southern families. In that year the Works Progress Administration—WPA—was created to furnish the unemployed with work not requiring large expenditures on materials. Although Southerners were paid lower wages than workers in the rest of the country under this plan, thousands of them were saved from destitution while taking part in many useful projects. The scorn which more fortunate Southerners visited upon WPA workers was undeserved.

The Social Security Act of 1935 was an attempt by the New Deal to provide insurance for the unemployed and the aged, and assistance to the afflicted, to dependent children, and to old persons. Both employers and employees were required to contribute to a trust fund in the Federal Treasury which is used to pension employees over sixty-five years of age. All the Southern states adopted unemployment insurance plans to administer funds provided by a federal payroll tax.

These measures proved a boon to a section where voluntary savings were at a minimum. Although at first farmers, domestic servants, and other low-paid persons were excluded from the benefits, many persons in these classes have subsequently been included. The Social Security Act has caused the public welfare expenditures of the Southern states to grow from $21,000,000 in 1929 to $309,000,000 in 1948. Although the average monthly payment to needy Southerners was much less than the national average, the percentage of Southerners getting such assistance was much higher. In 1948, 228 persons per 1,000 population aged sixty-five and over in the nation as a whole were receiving payments; the median number for the South was 439.[21]

The New Deal experiment which most aroused the hopes of those concerned with the economic backwardness of the South was the Tennessee Valley Authority. TVA was created in 1933 as a means of applying the intelligence and resources of a great government to a portion of the South which presented "some of the worst examples of eroded soil and handicapped humanity in the United States." Those sections of Virginia, Kentucky, North Carolina, Tennessee, Georgia, Alabama, and Mississippi through which the Tennessee River and its tributaries flowed became the scene of what was grandiloquently described as a "monumental work of agricultural planning," "a laboratory in which solutions of the problems of the Tennessee Valley's, and America's rural population are being studied scientifically and hammered out" on the anvil of experience.

Specifically the objectives of TVA were threefold: (1) to improve farming through the manufacture and distribution of cheap fertilizers, through prevention of soil erosion, and through the teaching of crop diversification; (2) to provide electric energy at a fair rate to some communities and to force down, through TVA competition and the measuring power of the TVA yardstick, the excessive rates charged by the privately owned electric power companies; (3) to foster the development of flood control, navigation, and electric power facilities in order to attract industries to the Tennessee Valley and raise the standard of living among its inhabitants. The nucleus of this ambitions experiment was the dam and nitrate plant which the federal government

[21] Hoover and Ratchford, *op. cit.*, pp. 212–13.

had constructed at Muscle Shoals on the Tennessee River during World War I. It was tangibly expressed in the construction or renovation, at the cost of $700,000,000, of twenty other dams, the most noted of which was the Norris Dam, completed in 1936.

The benefits of these hydroelectric developments were impressive. The regulation of the river flows checked floods on the Ohio and Mississippi, as well as on the Tennessee and its tributaries. By 1944 an installed electric capacity of 2 million kilowatts was furnishing power for municipalities at low rates, with especial stress upon the electrification of rural areas and the development of new uses for electric energy. The program of fertilizer distribution, soil conservation, crop diversification, and reforestation was effectively advanced, as was the development of native industries and of recreational areas along the shores of the lakes behind the dams. Even in the dubious field of water transportation, the TVA fulfilled its promises. Between Knoxville and the Ohio, 589 million ton-miles of water traffic moved in 1951 through an intricate system of locks and lakes where only 33 million ton-miles had moved in 1933. It is impossible to prove, however, that TVA has been a dominant force in the economic advances of its region. The growth of the region's population and of its industrial, agricultural, and financial resources has been about the same rate as that of the rest of the South.[22]

The whole scheme was energetically attacked by Wendell Willkie and others as an unjust expenditure of public funds, and as an unwarranted invasion of the field of private enterprise. The much-heralded electric-power yardstick was termed an unfair measure of comparative costs between the products of privately owned enterprise and those enjoying the support of the public purse. After the Supreme Court refused to invalidate the TVA in 1938 the privately owned electric companies bowed to the inevitable. They sold their Tennessee Valley plants to the government agency, and thoughtful critics saw in the TVA program many aids to private business.

Some economists regarded the heavy expenditures of the Roosevelt administration as a means of lessening, or even abolishing, the annual billion-dollar excess of expenditures over receipts which an uncontrolled system of capitalistic enterprise had imposed upon the South. It was believed that the levying of huge federal income and corporate taxes according to ability to pay, and the expenditure of these revenues according to the degree of human needs, meant a vast shifting of resources from the wealthier North to the poorer South. During the first six years of the New Deal, the nonrepayable expenditures of the federal government in the South amounted to $5,400,000,000, and the repayable

[22] *Ibid.*, 241-3.

loans to $2,900,000,000. Much of this outlay was of immediate benefit to millions of impoverished Southerners; to Southern commonwealths overtaxed to support schools and highways; to farming and business enterprises burdened by very high interest rates. It has been roughly estimated that the federal government spent in the South from 20 to 25 per cent of its total average annual budget of $40,000,000,000, which was from 5 to 8 per cent above federal tax collections in the region. This indicated that the South gained $2–3,000,000,000 from the financial operations of the federal government.[23]

To state that such outlays resulted in a lasting redistribution of wealth reveals a misunderstanding of the purposes of the New Deal. Many of its measures had the effect of guaranteeing the economic *status quo* by protecting private business through loans, regulations, and generous contracts. If rich men were taxed in order that poor men might spend, the federal government was careful that these expenditures be made within the framework of privately owned economic institutions, not through publicly owned agencies scattered throughout the United States. Hence the money of the government's beneficiaries went into the pockets of those in the habit of furnishing consumer goods—in other words, to the great corporations of the North—in about the same proportion as before the coming of the New Deal. Expenditures of the Roosevelt agencies far exceeded tax collections; the difference was covered by vast bond issues. Therefore, instead of paying heavier taxes in ratio to incomes, the several sections of the United States bought federal bonds in proportion to their wealth. The New Deal, then, imposed upon the American people a sizable mortgage to guarantee the principal and interest of its huge loans. The South, whose comparative poverty prevented the purchase of a large share of these bonds, had an added tribute inflicted upon it in favor of the bondholders of other sections.

The twentieth-century South continued the economic progress begun so auspiciously in the 1880's. Old industries like cotton textiles, iron, fertilizer, tobacco, and furniture flourished, while other industries practically unknown before 1900 made their appearance. Among these newcomers were electric power, petroleum, natural gas, paper, rayon, and other chemical industries. There was a revolution in transportation: the supplementing of the railroad by the automobile moving on paved highways. Yet agriculture remained the chief occupation of the Southern people. The section still ruled in the realms of cotton and tobacco, and still played a significant role in furnishing rice, sugar, fruits, and vegetables to the country and the world at large. New highways provided the means by which Southern farm products could be transported in

[23] *Ibid.*, pp. 223–6.

larger quantities to the tables of the growing numbers employed by the new industries. Industrial and agricultural advancement created an unprecedented prosperity and a renewed optimism.

The South was proud of itself. Yet these achievements seemed illusory to those who looked beyond the circles of the more fortunate into the lives of the common people. The plain truth was that Southern incomes and living conditions were the lowest in the United States. The one-crop, credit, and soil-exhausting practices of the post-Civil War period persisted in the twentieth century. The industrial and commercial systems were lopsided, emphasizing the production and marketing of less profitable commodities. Many of the newer manufacturing and marketing agencies were owned by Northerners who drained off a considerable share of the section's wealth. Debts mounted, and ambitious Southerners sought careers in the North and West. No remedy for these difficulties offered itself, but a temporary solution came with World War I and the attendant prosperity that lasted for several years. Then the depression of 1929 accentuated the plight of "the Nation's economic problem No. 1"—the South. Federal intervention appeared in the form of the New Deal. Before the results of this conscious attempt to lessen the sectional inequalities became fully effective, war again drowned the South's miseries in a wave of prosperity. World War II gave Southerners the greatest abundance they had ever known.

CHAPTER XXX

The Negro Contrast

>>

THE NUMBER of Negroes in the United States grew from 4,442,000 in 1869 to 8,864,000 in 1900, and to 14,894,000 in 1950. During six of these eight decades, the white population increased more rapidly. This signified a gradual decline in the Negro proportion of the national total, from 14.1 per cent in 1860 to 11.9 per cent in 1890, and to 9.7 per cent in 1930. By 1950 this proportion rose slightly, to 9.9 per cent. The Negro population of the South rose from 4,097,000 in 1860 to 7,923,000 in 1900, and to approximately 10 million in 1950. The relative decline of the South's proportion of the nation's total Negro population was from 92 per cent in 1860 to 90 per cent in 1900, to 73 per cent in 1940, and to 63 per cent in 1950. In the North the number climbed from 340,000 in 1860 to 881,000 in 1900, and to almost 5 million in 1950. In the latter year, New York City had 774,000 and Chicago and Philadelphia together had 885,000. In 1860, 37 per cent of the people of the South were Negroes, with colored majorities in Mississippi and South Carolina. By 1900 this proportion declined to 32 per cent, with colored majorities still prevailing in Mississippi and South Carolina. In 1950 the ratio stood at 21 per cent, with no Negro majority in any state.

Nevertheless the continued presence in the South of two thirds of nearly 15 million people whom the American majority insisted on keeping in a separate caste made the Negro problem in the twentieth century as much a Southern responsibility as the slave problem had been in 1860. In 1940, 180 counties, stretching from Virginia to Texas, had Negro majorities. Only 20 of the South's 1,415 counties had no Negroes.

The failure of the Reconstruction experiment permitted the South to reassert its Southernism. This meant the reaffirmation of the doctrine of white supremacy, with the blacks in the position of an inferior caste as the main condition under which the dominant whites tolerated them in their midst. Although Negroes protested against this obvious denial of the heritage of equality and liberty which Americans define as democracy, most blacks realized that the whites had both the will and the means to compel submission. Therefore, they accepted their lot, thankful that Civil War and Reconstruction had effected some improvements. The more realistic Northern friends of Negro uplift recognized the impracticability of trying to revive the Reconstruction vision of race equality.

It was not accidental that the most important sequels of Reconstruction were affirmations of the white South's solution of the race issue. First came decisions of the Supreme Court cutting the heart from federal laws designed to give political and social equalities to the Negro. In 1875 that tribunal held that a state might require a reasonable prerequisite, such as the payment of a poll tax, before a citizen could vote in Congressional elections.

In 1883 the anti-Ku Klux Klan laws and the Civil Rights Act of 1875 were declared unconstitutional because the Supreme Court believed that it was not the function of the federal government to guarantee Negroes and other persons admission to theaters, accommodations in hotels, equal transportation facilities, and protection against conspiracies of disguised persons who would deprive them of their rights. It ruled that remedies for such personal affronts must be sought from state authorities. This was equivalent to saying that there was no redress whatsoever, because authority in Southern states rested with those least inclined to fulfill the promises of the Reconstruction laws. The Supreme Court diverted the Fourteenth Amendment from its alleged primary purpose of protecting Negroes against the tyranny of the states to the protection of corporations against such tyranny. Between 1890 and 1910 only 19 of the 528 cases before the Court involving the Fourteenth Amendment applied to Negro rights; 228 of these cases referred to corporations. Taking advantage of the Supreme Court's obvious indifference toward Negroes, in 1894 a national Democratic administration cleared vestiges of the Reconstruction legislation from federal statutes.

Into the vacant space created by the destruction of the Reconstruction laws the Southern states placed other important measures affecting Negroes—the Jim Crow laws and the constitutional restrictions on voting described elsewhere in this book. These enactments legalized existing race discriminations. They were followed by a reinterpretation, in the light of changed conditions, of the ante-bellum concept that the Negro was innately inferior to the white man, and therefore incapable of exercising freedom and democracy wisely.

There arose in the South a group of popular leaders who, while ascribing all the Jeffersonian virtues to the common white man, denied them to the Negro. Notable among the proclaimers of white superiority and black degradation were Ben Tillman of South Carolina and James K. Vardaman of Mississippi. They supplemented the ante-bellum arguments of race inferiority derived from the Bible and Aristotle with the fresher viewpoints of the evolutionists and anthropologists. The son of Ham became "the missing link" between the lowly ape and the exalted Caucasian. Although a human being, the Negro was adjudged so far down the evolutionary scale as to be unworthy of equality with those who had climbed higher on the Darwinian ladder. Advocates of Negro inferiority maintained that it was fallacious to assume that the race progressed through education; they cited the large number of Negroes in prison, and declared that literacy and criminality went hand in hand.

The South's reactionary views on slavery and Christian Fundamentalism provoked the relentless opposition of the outside world. This was not true, however, of its attitude toward the Negro, at least for several decades following Reconstruction. Eminent historians, philosophers, scientists, and psychologists—both European and American—sustained the Southern position. Among affirmers of the doctrine of Negro inferiority were such distinguished Europeans as Charles Darwin, Francis Galton, Thomas Carlyle, Joseph Arthur de Gobineau, and Cesare Lombroso, as well as outstanding American students of the race problem like Nathaniel S. Shaler, Albert Bushnell Hart, Madison Grant, and William McDougall. To the evidence advanced against the Negro by the anthropologists and biologists of the nineteenth century were added the findings of psychologists of the twentieth century. Intelligence tests applied to the American soldiers during World War I professed to show that the American Negro ranked 10.37 in mental age, as compared with 13.08 for the American white.[1]

This verdict, however, never won universal approval among reputable thinkers and was sharply challenged in the decades following World War I. A group of scholars, notably Franz Boas, Alexander Goldenweiser, and Robert H. Lowie, preferred to blame the backwardness of colored people on lack of opportunity rather than on a deficient mentality. They claimed that all races on the average possess the same mental capabilities. Indeed, the issue of the comparative ability of the Negro was so confused by political and social controversy and by the inability of researchers to isolate inborn characteristics from environ-

[1] Jerome Dowd, *The Negro in American Life*, p. 391.

mental influences that there could be no accepted verdict among careful and unbiased scientists. The white South, when necessary, could ignore the controversial science of race, justifying its racial attitude on the irrefutable fact that the Negro, as he actually functioned during the period after Reconstruction, was on a lower level than the white man in most cultural achievements. Whether this fact should be explained in terms of biology or of environment seemed academic. If the progressive manner in which Negroes of the twentieth century seemed to react to social improvements strengthened the environmental explanation of their inferiority, advocates of white supremacy could take refuge in a much-emphasized principle of modern psychology: that the blacks inherited from their caste experiences an inferiority complex which prevented their behaving as white men even when in the same environment and with equal opportunities. Thus psychological conditioning entered into the perennial argument.

The Southerner of the post-Reconstruction period saw around him a black caste which failed to measure up to the American standards of civilization. In the first place, the Negroes were dreadfully poor, among the ten per cent of America's most impoverished people. Unlike the immigrant groups, they had not been able to acquire those material advantages which the American environment supposedly offered to humble folk. The explanation was that many opportunities were denied them either because of color or because they failed to cultivate the habits of thrift and social discipline necessary to rise in the world. In 1890 only 121,000 of the 1,689,000 Negroes engaged in agriculture owned the land they tilled.

The masses continued to live, as during Reconstruction, in shanties whose main protection against inclement weather was heavy blinds and walls plastered with old newspapers. A tumbledown appearance, indicating the utmost indifference, was nearer the rule than the exception among these dwellings. The absence of screens, privies, and protected water supplies demonstrated neglect of rudimentary domestic sanitation. The average Negro's work clothes were so tattered and grimy with several weeks' accumulation of filth that the white South clung to its contention that the Negro preferred such clothes to those that were clean. When bright and whole outer garments were worn for church or other social gatherings, the absence of clean underwear and washed bodies betrayed a stench so disagreeable that the sensitive whites believed the odor to be congenital.

Despite a significant revolution in educational policies, 57 per cent of the race was illiterate in 1890. This official finding represented an underestimate of the vast amount of ignorance, superstition, and pure illusion to which the Negroes were condemned because they were denied free cultural intercourse with the race by whose standards they were judged. The school of local color writers of the 1880's and 1890's transformed the Negro into a picturesque and praiseworthy character since he could derive so much contentment and joy from his lowly state. But the practical effect of such artistry was to justify what was indeed misery, if conditions were measured by cold realities. Squalor and superstition—no matter how picturesque in print—should not have blinded readers to the fact that these conditions resulted in an annual death rate of 33 per thousand in 1890, a rate closer to that of India or China than of the United States as a whole.

The inferior position of the Negroes was concretely illustrated by their occupational status. They continued to experience the ill effects of the freeing of labor markets by Emancipation, and the consequent shattering of the dictatorial powers of slave masters to give them employment. Accordingly, they were worsted by white labor in competition for better types of employment. They fell from a position of dominance of the skilled crafts in 1865 to a minor role twenty-five years later. In 1890 the percentages of Negroes engaged in the following crafts were: carpenters, 16.1; masons, 28.2; painters, 10.9; plasterers, 33.2; machinists, 2.5.[2] The blacks were completely excluded from the new textile industry except for a few thousand entrusted with the heaviest or most disagreeable tasks. They were freely employed in such unskilled and poorly paid occupations as railroad building, brickmaking, quarrying, street cleaning, sewer digging, and scavenging. The lumber, iron, and tobacco industries also made good use of them.

The almost universal practice of employing blacks for menial work at low wages was justified by the firm conviction that they were lazy, shiftless, and unreliable in the higher industrial callings. Employment restrictions caused them to fall back upon their traditional occupation—agricultural labor. All Negro farmers, except a small percentage, took refuge in cotton, the South's most depressed crop; more than two thirds of these black cotton cultivators were in the bottom rank among Southerners gainfully employed. One third of all employed Negroes in 1890 were domestic servants, mostly women forced by economic necessity to neglect their own domestic obligations for those of white families. They were the lowest-paid American workers, able to keep body and soul together only through judicious begging and petty thievery. Obviously the free Negro, like the slave, was the mudsill of Southern economic life. Certainly one principle of Southern economy was definitely established: no position that a white person wanted and could fill as well as a black man or woman was denied to him. This generally meant the

[2] Abram L. Harris and Sterling D. Spero in *Encyclopedia of the Social Sciences,* XI, 339.

confinement of Negroes to work which was poorly paid, backbreaking, or menial. In practical respects, then, the Negro was worse off in 1890 than he had been in 1860.

Innate social weaknesses and the workings of the caste system combined to give the blacks the highest criminal record of any civilized people. In 1890 the race comprised 11.9 per cent of the population and 30.4 per cent of the criminals—a crime rate triple that of the whites. As a part of his very genuine Americanism, the Negro carried to extremes the national trait of lawlessness. More impulsive and less self-controlled than the white man, he seemed naturally prone to violence—a tendency encouraged by his environment. His jealousy was aroused by the conduct of his womenfolk; his rights as an individual were disregarded by associates of both races. Without property and economically insecure, he had ten times as many opportunities to steal from the white man as to be the victim of theft. The savage severity with which "the white folks' law" prosecuted Negroes accused of crimes against white men logically evoked acts of brutal retaliation. On the other hand, this law allowed blacks to carry knives, pistols, and razors, and to use them on members of their own race with comparative impunity.

The most appalling fact about the Negro crime record was that the forces of progress to which the race was heir did not reduce it. The Negro prison population of the United States as a whole increased from 24,879 in 1890 to 38,701 in 1910. Between 1890 and 1923 the Negro section of the entire population decreased from 11.9 per cent to 9.3 per cent; however, the proportion of Negro prisoners rose from 30.4 per cent to 31.3 per cent. In 1939 three times as many Negroes were in prisons as there were whites in proportion to their respective numbers. Not even education had turned the trick; indeed, the cynics asserted that it merely widened the criminal opportunities of the blacks. If such a claim seems like arrant anti-Negroism, there is sound statistical evidence that migration had an evil effect. Negro migrants from rural areas gave Southern cities such as Memphis, Birmingham, and Charleston the highest criminal records in the country. Negro migrants to the North got in the clutches of the law more often than those who remained in the South. In 1939 in the North 149 out of every 100,000 Negroes were in prison; the corresponding figure for the South was only 86. An example of the high crime rate of those who moved North is the fact that in 1945, 74 per cent of the adults arrested in the District of Columbia were Negroes, although Negroes constituted only one third of the population. More than eight times as many Negroes as whites were charged with aggravated assault and three times as many Negroes as whites were charged with murder and housebreaking.[3]

[3] E. Franklin Frazier, The Negro in the United States, pp. 646-7.

The most sensational evidence of the sad plight of the blacks was the mob murders of those who had committed real or imaginary crimes against the code of interracial relations. Among 4,672 persons done to death by mobs in the United States between 1882 and 1936, 3,383, or nearly three fourths, were Negroes, and only 1,289 were whites. Since 1900 the trend in the number of lynchings has been downward, as indicated by an annual average of 154 for the years 1890–99 to 31 for the period 1920–29. With the disappearance of frontier lawlessness, which was the original reason why communities took the law into their own hands, Southern Negroes became the main victims of lynchings. For the 1890–99 decade, 13 per cent of these offenses were outside the South and 28 per cent of the victims were non-Negroes; for the period 1920–29, only 5 per cent were not in the South and 10 per cent were non-Negroes.

Mob execution became a weapon of white supremacy, an instrument of race justice more summary and biased than the established courts with their traditions of deliberation and comparative impartiality. Lynchings were considered necessary remedies for deeds of unrestraint, the most notorious of which was rape or attempted rape of white women. Although by actual count such crimes accounted for only one fourth of all lynchings, the fact that the Negro at times could be guilty of such a crime against the whites created enormous prejudice against him. Almost any offense was likely to be considered sufficiently sinister to lead to lynching.

More frequent than rape as a cause for mob violence was the murder of a white man. Other causes extended from crimes as serious as arson to those that seemed trivial to outsiders, but important to Southerners interested in "keeping the nigger in his place." Among the minor offenses were slapping children, using offensive or boastful language, and seeking political or other employment not deemed proper for members of an inferior caste. Lynchings, in the majority of cases, were the acts of young men of the uneducated classes dwelling in rural communities of the middle South, where the races were divided more or less evenly. Race contacts of the competitive type which might lead to irritation and violence were at the maximum there. In the cities and border states there was less interracial competition, greater popular respect for law, and more tolerance of Negro rights. In regions of black majorities the Negroes were protected from white lawlessness by the weight of numbers, by their own social conservatism, and by their comparative isolation from contacts with lower-class whites.

A lynching often took place in the presence of hundreds, sometimes thousands, of white persons motivated by curiosity, excitement, or the desire to gratify a feeling of race superiority. In the minority were relatives or friends of the person wronged, eager to be avenged. When the accused was captured or taken from the officers of the law, he was generally slain by a volley from the guns of his assailants, if not first hanged and then riddled with bullets. Sometimes, however, death was inflicted by the tortures of slow burning, mutilation, or dragging the culprit behind automobiles. Occasionally, this medieval savagery was accompanied by the distribution of such gruesome souvenirs as the teeth and toenails of the victim.

The decline of lynching in the twentieth century was mainly due to the growing disapproval of upper-class Southerners, who made their influence felt among the masses. Through press, school, and pulpit, responsible leaders spoke of the South's reputation, and of the senselessness of mob vengeance in the face of locally controlled courts. Improved methods of capture and transportation at the command of the twentieth-century police made it easier for sheriffs and their deputies to put accused persons beyond the reach of mobs. Antilynching legislation by Congress was impeded by the filibusters of Southern senators, but the South took warning from this threat of intervention by federal authorities in its internal affairs and assumed the initiative in suppressing lynching. Cynically minded persons interpreted the decrease in lynching as a transfer of the mob spirit to the courts. It was pointed out that no need of extralegal executions of Negroes existed in communities where white judges and juries had the power and will to impose the extreme penalty in summary fashion. In some cases only thirty-six hours elapsed between a crime and the imposition of the death penalty by regular courts.[4]

Outsiders were astonished, on the other hand, at the leniency with which whites dealt with certain types of Negro crime. In thousands of instances servants guilty of the theft of such articles as a watch or a pistol were not arrested, and frequently not even discharged by employers. White men of prominence used their influence and wealth to free Negroes in whom they had a personal interest. Southern justice, however, generally illustrated the penalties of the caste system. Household stealing was regarded as an inevitable and unenviable weakness of the blacks, and considered some sort of bonus to compensate servants for their miserable wages. Juries were prone to be charitable toward Negroes guilty of crimes against their own race, because of a reluctance to grapple with problems of law and order which did not directly concern the whites. The stabbings and shootings of Darktown were tolerated with a half-amused, half-cynical indifference, in striking contrast to the attitude toward most crimes of Negroes against whites. If a Negro other than a domestic servant robbed a white man, more severe

[4] Francis W. Coker in *Encyclopedia of the Social Sciences*, IX, 639–43.

penalties were imposed than those tolerated by progressive countries since the eighteenth century. When a Negro committed homicide, rape, attempted assault, or burglary against a white person, juries were not inclined to listen to extenuating circumstances. It was almost a foregone conclusion that the penalty would be death.

Such was the disciplinary rule of the caste system. This selfsame system demanded leniency for white men accused of crimes against blacks. If such offenders were even so much as brought into court, they were either promptly acquitted or given the lightest of sentences. White men were not punished for the rape of black girls, and "the unknown parties" who committed lynchings were seldom identified officially. There have been several convictions of lynchers in North Carolina, but when in May, 1947, twenty-eight self-confessed lynchers were brought to trial at Greenville, South Carolina, a jury acquitted the entire group.

Selfish interest as often as human sympathy prompted influential white men to help Negroes escape the law. They paid fines and lawyers' fees in order that black offenders might be bailed out to them for periods sufficient to work off the debts incurred in the transactions. This form of peonage or temporary slavery was sanctioned by the law on the theory that impecunious Negroes should have opportunities to escape jail sentences equal to those of persons able to pay their fines and lawyers' fees. Although the period of servitude in most cases terminated at the end of the specified time without injustice, the granting of such powers over Negroes often led to abuses by unscrupulous whites. Between 1900 and 1920 they even took the form of extreme cruelty or murder. The worst of these cases was that of John S. Williams, a planter of Jasper County, Georgia, who murdered eleven Negroes he had bailed out of Atlanta and Macon stockades and retained unlawfully after they had served their legal periods of peonage.

An abuse still more widespread was the convict-lease system. This practice became common during the post-Reconstruction period as a means of relieving the overcrowding and costly idleness prevailing in state penitentiaries. The convicts were hired out to individuals or corporations for a stipulated sum per capita. They were put to work on railroads, in mines, factories, sawmills, brickyards, phosphate beds, and turpentine stills. Thrifty Governor Ben Tillman of South Carolina hired convicts to contractors engaged in the construction of Clemson and Winthrop colleges, and Jones S. Hamilton, Mississippi politician and speculator, made a fortune leasing a small army of convicts. The convict-lease system was very profitable both to the states and the contractors, but it was received with opposition by organized labor. Moreover, it was so loathsome from the humanitarian viewpoint that it was abolished in all Southern states by 1928. Julia S. Tutwiler of Alabama described the practice in 1893 as a system "that combines all the evils of slavery with none of its ameliorating features."

The demand for good roads in the 1890's prompted county sheriffs in Georgia, Florida, South Carolina, North Carolina, and other Southern states to hold many of the convicted Negro criminals for labor on local highways. This was the origin of the convict-camp system, generally known as the chain gang. The convicts were identified by striped garments and shaven heads. To prevent escape they were shackled with chains while working and at night were often confined to wheeled dormitories not unlike circus cages for wild animals. The chain gang, like the convict-lease system, was profitable to public authorities but had little to commend itself from the convicts' viewpoint. Conditions in some of the camps were horrible. The guards were often poorly paid, ignorant white men given to cursing and using guns and whips rather than understanding the needs of the prisoners at their mercy. Many convicts were cruelly punished; a large number lived under deplorable sanitary conditions. Bedding often was tattered and vermin-infested, and bathing and sewerage facilities either absent entirely or very inadequate. Frequently the food was bad or insufficient; ill men did not receive prompt medical attention, and those infected with tuberculosis or syphilis were herded with the healthy.

After protests on humanitarian grounds led to inspections by state welfare agencies, county chain gangs were abolished or reformed in many instances. The trend in this direction was accelerated by the introduction of road machinery which antiquated the gang system of labor. A partial substitute was the state convict farm, but expert supervision eliminated the worst features of the convict-labor system.

In the 1930's the South adhered to the belief that most convicts should be employed productively. In 1929 of the total number, 78 per cent were employed, as compared with the national average of only 58 per cent. The South's high percentage, the *Encyclopaedia of the Social Sciences* affirmed in 1933,[5] "with its consequent low maintenance costs, is secured at a terrible price to society and to the individual prisoner."

Negroes did not have an entirely black sky above them. There were many stars of hope to guide them on the path of opportunity which a rich and progressive America offered its people. There were disappointments as well. Some failed to attain their ambitions because they were too unrealistic or because they were stopped by immutable caste barriers. Other hopes were partially realized. Yet there was enough progress

[5] Louis N. Robinson, *op. cit.*, XII, 418.

for the historian to recognize a steady improvement in the Negroes' position in the seven decades that elapsed since Reconstruction.

Some students saw a solution of the Negro problem in a frank recognition of the fact that the African in the United States was as much a minority race as those who suffered at the hands of nationalist majorities in Europe. Certainly, the discriminations that the white two thirds of the South imposed upon the black one third were comparable to those visited upon Jews and Poles in Germany and Russia, and upon Russians and Germans in Poland. It was proposed that territorial segregation of the blacks be tried as a means of relieving the tensions and injustices caused by the two races living together in the same communities. To remedy the dislocations of Negro populations during the Civil War and Reconstruction, it was suggested that states such as Mississippi or South Carolina be turned over to their Negro majorities. The idea, had it been taken seriously, would have been rendered impractical by the bitter and effective opposition of white minorities.

The return of the Negroes to their original dwelling place had once been advocated by Thomas Jefferson and Abraham Lincoln as a solution to the slave problem; after the Civil War it was advanced by Henry M. Stanley as a solution of the Negro problem. In the 1870's a few Negroes joined those who had already left for Liberia, and the decade of World War I witnessed the organization of the Universal Negro Improvement Association by the Jamaican Marcus Garvey. Its purpose was to build a great Negro empire in Africa under American Negro direction. Garvey denounced the traditional mulatto leadership of his race and the idea of improving its status in an America dominated by the white man. As Provisional President of Africa he employed some 900 orators to plead for his project. His theatrical methods appealed to the imagination of the Negro masses more than other agitations in the past. Thousands of Negroes in the United States were enlisted in his cause, and $1,000,000 was collected. In 1921 a band of skilled Negro workers embarked for Liberia to begin the rehabilitation of the Dark Continent.

This grandiose scheme collapsed under the searching scrutiny of less credulous Negroes, who discovered that Garvey had spent the money entrusted to him in extravagant living and foolhardy ventures. After serving a term in a federal prison he was deported to his native island. Although completely failing in his immediate objective, he succeeded in one important respect: among a basically humble and imitative people, he had aroused an unaccustomed pride in their race and heritage.

Many educated Negroes who opposed the back-to-Africa movement advantageously exploited the racial patriotism created by Garvey. They believed in cultural autonomy and, emulating European methods, discovered past events on which to build. They found Negro heroes in American annals and dug up various African legends; they extolled Negro music and other unique aspects of American Negro life, and professed to see in black skins and profiles a comeliness as inherently attractive as that attributed by whites to fair coloring and fine features. Although no attempt was made, in the manner of European minorities, to create a separate Afro-American nation, there was an endeavor to encourage a sense of independence, and even a certain contempt bordering on hatred for the majority caste. The separate social existence which the dominance of caste forced upon the blacks made some of these developments inevitable and necessary. Nevertheless, there were limitations to Negro cultural autonomy. There could be no radical revolt because the black man had inherited no distinctive culture of his own. His African heritage had been practically destroyed by the peculiar manner in which slaves migrated to America. Almost all that the Negro knew—his language, religion, dress, skills, and so on—was derived from the whites. The realities of American life forced most members of the Negro race to concede that the ways of the white man represented the only road to freedom and progress.

The Negro in revolt against the tyranny of the white man was caught in the same trap as the feminist in rebellion against the despotism of man. Both made no innovations; their passions for reform led them to imitate that from which they were attempting to revolt. Just as the feminist leader became more masculine, so the black reformer embraced white culture. This tendency reached the extreme in efforts of Negro progressives to eliminate the one African characteristic not already destroyed by a long history of imitation—physical appearance. Many Negroes indulged in hair-straightening and skin-bleaching preparations. Selective breeding proved a more effective means of disseminating the precious heritage of white blood with which miscegenations of slavery endowed the colored caste. Mulattoes, octoroons, and quadroons were the privileged members of Negro society, and in all but the least discriminating social circles fairer women were preferred as wives. Such upbreeding resulted in one of the outstanding accomplishments in practical eugenics ever to be recorded. Within the last seventy-five years this has meant the substitution of a brown race for the black one brought from Africa. Some students of the race problem believe that the desire of colored people for lighter-skinned mates is so great that, were the American color line abolished, Africans would gradually merge with whites and lose their identity entirely.

The inability of the black man to escape into Africa or to develop an independent society of his own indicated that he was as genuine an American as the most pronounced blond of Anglo-Saxon descent. Possibly he was too American, carrying to extremes many typical traits. He was the most emotional of all Americans in religious demonstrations, the most extravagant in expenditure of his means, the most unsettled and migratory, the most subject to disease and crime, and too willing to accept the superstitions of the backwoods. He excelled in the national passion for bombast, parade, oratory, and song, rather than in the more cosmopolitan forms of self-expression. Although the least able of all Americans to improve his position, he characteristically cherished illusions of doing so; the most underprivileged of Americans, he yet believed in the equality of opportunity. Often failing to perform his work as well as the white man, he was deluded by the hope of advancing himself by wandering from one job to another, and from one place to another. Like many other American workingmen he did not appreciate the advantages of labor organizations, and preferred a business or professional career to co-operation with fellow workers.

His desire for social betterment also accounted for the failure of the elaborate industrial training provided by the schools to function as effectively for the blacks as it did for whites. The Negro ambitious enough to remain in school usually wanted to become a preacher or a teacher. He was such a pronounced victim of inferiority complexes that sometimes he lived uncomfortably under the authority of deliberate rules of etiquette. A Negro writer [6] claimed that among the upper circles of colored society were those who felt constrained to eat chicken, pork chops, and watermelon secretly, because of the frequent gibes over the black man's weakness for these characteristic Southern dishes. When the Negro failed to realize the promises of American life he was likely to react to crime, like the youth in Richard Wright's *Native Son*.

The Negro's hopefulness and wanderlust led him to seek occupational opportunities in sections of the United States outside the South. First, in 1878 and 1879, came the attempted migration of some 200,000 blacks, mostly from Mississippi and Louisiana, to Kansas and other Western states. They were impelled by agricultural depression and various unfavorable features of Southern life. The movement was discouraged by whites in both the South and the West. The Southern planters wished to keep their labor. The Westerners did not want the competition of Negro farmers. Most of the migrants, lacking the resources and ability necessary to adjust themselves to a non-Southern agriculture and climate, returned to their Southern homes. About 30,000, however, permanently settled in Kansas and sourrounding states. During the thirty-five years following 1879 the gradual flow of Negroes to Southern and Western cities was proportionately less than the corresponding

[6] Eugene Gordon, "The Negro's Inhibitions," *The American Mercury*, XIII, 165 (February, 1928).

movement of Southern whites. Then came the great migration during and after World War I, when approximately half a million Negroes crowded into the industrial states of New York, Pennsylvania, and the Middle West. They settled in large numbers in New York City, Philadelphia, Chicago, Pittsburgh, Cleveland, Detroit, St. Louis, and East St. Louis.

In an attempt to stop this exodus, the South ceased complaining about the Negro, and began to appreciate his role in the sectional economy. But the call of higher wages and the hope of freedom from persecution and discrimination swept the great tide northward. The Negro fell into the breach created by the discontinuance of European immigration, enlistments in the army, and the enormous expansion of war industries. Some Negroes returned to the South when their war jobs expired. The northward movement, however, continued in the post-bellum years of industrial upsurge and agricultural depression; half a million more Negroes left the South in the early twenties. Later movements were more orderly and devoid of many of the hardships during World War I. Between 1910 and 1930 the Negro population of the Northern states increased from 1,027,674 to 2,409,219, or from 10.5 per cent to 20.2 per cent of the country's total.

The sustained character of the northward movement of the Negro indicated that there were solid benefits from it. The lure of higher wages persisted, despite increased living costs. Many Negro migrants had better lodgings than previously; some acquired property. Life in the North gave the Negro a sense of emotional well-being—he could ride on any seat in a public conveyance, he enjoyed freedom of the ballot and could even exact political gains from bosses of large cities.

It should not be assumed, however, that the northward movement of the Negro in any comprehensive sense solved America's perplexing race problem. It was startlingly clear that the North had no room for a Black Utopia. As one of the bitterest ironies of American history, those who gave the black man freedom had after the Civil War denied him a share in the heritage of public lands, freely bestowed upon all comers except the Negro. It was reasonable to expect that such discrimination would form a pattern for the future. This proved to be true in many social and economic matters.

So bitter was the hostility of the Northern working classes to the employment of Negroes that between 1880 and 1890 as many as fifty protest strikes were held. Antagonism deepened when Negroes were imported as strikebreakers. Trade unions, controlled by the skilled crafts, regarded the Negro as an interloper and made no serious efforts to allay the tension. The comparative freedom with which the earlier labor organizations admitted Negroes was followed by a general policy of exclusion when the American Federation of Labor rose to power in the 1880's. In 1900 there were not more than 33,000 Negroes in this organization.

The sudden movement of the proscribed race into the congested Northern industrial centers during World War I precipitated feelings of hatred; barriers of caste imposed upon the new arrivals in some respects were more severe than those from which they had fled. If Northern whites showed more respect than Southern whites for the legal and political rights of the blacks, they were less inclined to tolerate intimate personal relations. Although the Northerner might love the Negro in a general or abstract way, he was hostile toward him concretely and individually. The residential segregation imposed upon him in Northern metropolises was more rigid than that of old Southern cities like New Orleans and Charleston. Northerners were angered because colored competition depressed wages and decreased the value of certain residential areas. Leagues were formed to prevent the rental of houses to Negroes, and serious race riots ensued. In 1917 at East St. Louis thirty-nine Negroes and eight whites were killed; twenty-six race riots occurred in 1919, the worst in Chicago and Washington.

Police intervention alone prevented a general expulsion of Negroes from certain cities. They remained there under trying conditions and were despised by the white majorities. This was especially true in Washington, where the average white objected to Negroes occupying any seat in a public conveyance, using the same cafeterias and washrooms in public buildings, and securing federal employment in other than menial capacities. Segregation was intensified. This meant crowding and charging rentals out of proportion to those demanded of whites. Bad living conditions coupled with boisterous and undisciplined habits turned the colored sections of Northern cities into veritable bedlams. In 1938 tuberculosis, a disease of crowded tenements and sleepless nights, killed five times as many blacks as whites in forty-six cities.

The Communist party sought to convert the Negro to its plan of world salvation. It flaunted American race distinctions to the extent of encouraging its white girl members to make social engagements with Negro men. In 1940 the Communists nominated James Ford, a Negro, as their candidate for Vice-President. In 1931 they dramatized race discriminations by assuming the leading role in the litigation growing out of the Scottsboro case, in which eight Negro boys were sentenced to death in Alabama on a flimsy charge of rape. A reversal was obtained from the United States Supreme Court through an exposure of the Alabama practice of not allowing Negroes to serve on juries. The spirit of protest among the black masses of Northern cities was aroused to fever pitch.

Few Negroes, however, were converted to Communist principles. The party's plan for a Negro "republic" in the Black Belt was so obviously absurd that it failed to capture the blacks' imagination. The bid to join whites in united working-class opposition to capitalist oppressors appealed neither to the aspirations of the Negroes nor to their observation of reality. Like other Americans, they wished to improve their class status and enjoy the privileges of American democracy and equality. They saw around them a world prejudiced against race rather than class, where fraternization was possible only with fellow Negroes. They suspected the social evangelism of their white Communist friends. "Even after a revolution the country will be full of crackers" was a reflection heard in Negro communities.[7] There were never proportionally as many Negro as white Communists. The Committee on Un-American Activities declared in July, 1949, that there were only 1,400 Negroes in the party, or less than one tenth of one per cent of the total Negro population.[8]

Far more in harmony with the realizable promises of American life was the plan of salvation which Booker T. Washington offered the Negroes long before the Communists presented themselves. From the vantage of his rise from a humble position to that of the most distinguished American Negro of all times, Washington proposed a program that was genuinely American. In his opinion, the Negro should take advantage of the popular belief that the way to get along in the world was to begin at the bottom and through skill, enterprise, and thrift work one's way up the ladder of material success. To give direction to such a procedure he advocated the widest acceptance of the Hampton and Tuskegee idea through which he had achieved such phenomenal success. Hampton and Tuskegee were schools designed to train the blacks in the skilled trades and agricultural and domestic arts in which they had obtained experience as slaves but from which, as freedmen, they were excluded largely because of apprenticeship and trade-union practices.

Aware that, at least for the present, the dream of social equality was unattainable, Washington urged the blacks to accept their status and to ask no privileges that were not granted freely. This patient attitude secured for him the good will of Northern and Southern whites. Washington emphasized the material and moral advantages that would benefit both races through a dedication to mutual interests, and he won favor with the upper classes by advising blacks not to join labor unions. In his Atlanta address of September 18, 1895, the Negro leader told his white listeners: "In all things that are purely social we shall be as separate as

[7] Gunnar Myrdal, *An American Dilemma*, I, 509.
[8] William A. Nolan, *Communism versus the Negro*, p. 206.

the fingers, yet one as the hand in all things essential to mutual progress."

He was severely criticized for these remarks by the advocates of political and social equality. However, it is not true that he accepted political and social bondage for his race in favor of industrial progress and opportunities. He favored advancement through the only policy which he and other leaders considered practical at the time. When he told the blacks: "Cast down your bucket where you are," he meant that they should take advantage of the very real opportunities for economic, education, and social progress which even the post-Reconstruction reaction had not denied them. "No race," he said, "that has anything to contribute to the markets of the world is long to any degree ostracized." Thus Washington believed that the political and social barriers of caste would melt when the blacks through thrift and industry proved themselves worthy of the full respect of other Americans. With this end in view he organized the National Negro Business League.

Washington's views enjoyed wider acceptance than those of any other Negro in American history. To the masses of Southern Negroes he was Moses who offered deliverance from the wilderness in which they had been wandering since the failure of Reconstruction. To the Northern friends of the Negro his program seemed to offer a statesmanlike alternative to the necessity of leaving the Negroes at the mercy of Southern reactionaries, now that the radical plans of social equality were beyond redemption. His disposal of the specter of social equality enabled all Southern whites of liberal and progressive tendencies to applaud his pronouncements; he made them feel that the general material and cultural uplift of their specific section was identified with improved conditions among the repressed portion of the population.

Naturally there was some dissent from the Washington program. Gathering up the scattered fragments of the Reconstruction doctrine, a group of Negro leaders, mostly Northern mulattoes, would tolerate no compromise with white supremacy; they insisted that the abolition of social and political inequalities was a necessary prelude to any plan to elevate the race. These forthright advocates of complete equality stigmatized Negro leaders who co-operated with Southern whites as "Uncle Toms" and "white folks' niggers." Their leader was W. E. Burghardt Du Bois, a Massachusetts octoroon who turned from a career of historical scholarship in 1910 to direct the activities of the militant National Association for the Advancement of Colored People, and to edit its fiery monthly, *The Crisis*.

Du Bois attacked Washington's championship of industrial education on the theory that higher education provided a means of fostering the "talented tenth" deemed necessary for leadership. He fought for social and political rights equal to those of the whites: the right of the Negro to enter all public places, use public conveyances, receive educational equality, live anywhere, seek any employment, and vote freely. "A disfranchised working class in modern industrial civilization," Du Bois declared, "is worse than helpless. It is a menace, not simply to itself, but to every other group in the community; it will be diseased; it will be criminal; it will be ignorant; it will be the plaything of mobs, and will be insulted by caste restrictions."

Washington and Du Bois agreed that it was possible to establish a fundamental harmony between the two races and called on well-disposed and influential white men to aid them. Both men believed in education as a primary means of race improvement, merely differing in the kind they thought best. Actually the objectives of the two leaders were not at variance; each sought to eliminate lynchings, the injustices of the white courts, and the unequal accommodations provided in schools and on public conveyances. The ultimate aim of both was to abolish caste prejudices so that the Negro might attain the quality of other Americans. If Washington could be accused of subordinating this objective to piecemeal gains, his rival could be charged with seeking the immediately impossible. Du Bois urged the somewhat narrow social and political reforms of the abolitionists and the reconstructionists; he failed to take into account the economic and psychological changes which twentieth-century analysts asserted were necessary for the important shifts in race relations that he demanded so loudly. The essential difference between him and Washington was in tactics: Washington was diplomatic and conciliatory; Du Bois put principle above discretion. Accordingly, Washington was far more successful in enlisting Southern co-operation for his program.

Among organizations which approved Washington's teachings were the University Commission on Southern Race Problems, founded in 1912; the Commission on Interracial Cooperation, founded in 1919; and the interracial groups sponsored by the Southern churches and the Young Men's Christian Association. Unlike the National Association for the Advancement of Colored People, these organizations avoided direct challenges to Southern opinion. They wished to appeal to the better conscience of Southern whites in an effort to remedy obvious injustices. They won the active support of such eminent representatives of Southern enlightenment as James H. Dillard of New Orleans, President William L. Poteat of Wake Forest College, President Robert E. Blackwell of Randolph-Macon College, Bishop Theodore D. Bratton of Mississippi, and the Reverend M. Ashby Jones of Atlanta. Through widespread publicity and many interracial conferences these groups succeeded in influencing thousands of Southern whites. In 1925 the

Commission on Interracial Cooperation was reputedly active in hundreds of Southern communities. This commission frequently prevented friction and violence, induced the proper public authorities to correct abuses in administering justice and allocating public funds, and dispelled much of the ignorance concerning the accomplishments of upper-class Negroes which prevailed in Southern white society.

Although denied many of the economic, social, and political rights so freely bestowed upon other Americans, Negroes received a fair share of what men of wealth like George Foster Peabody, John D. Rockefeller, Julius Rosenwald, and Edward S. Harkness were willing to spend on human welfare. Their endeavors to improve the lot of Southern blacks proved more successful than similar efforts of the Reconstruction period. The resources of great capital were attuned to the actual needs of a people in physical and educational distress. The co-operation of the Southern upper classes was secured by carefully avoiding any assault upon the color line. The establishment of this happy understanding between Northern charity and Southern white sentiment in the interest of Negro welfare was among the greatest achievements of Booker T. Washington. The Du Bois school of Negro leadership accepted the benefits of this policy, thereby tacitly admitting that in the first decades of the twentieth century no program of social uplift could be successfully applied in the South without the co-operation of whites.

An outstanding feature of Southern history in the twentieth century was the progress of the Negro. Despite caste discriminations, advancement of the race could be chiefly attributed to such aid and tolerance as whites were willing to bestow upon them. The educational achievements described elsewhere were the clearest example of this, but they were by no means the only one. Loss of opportunity for employment in certain vocations was partly offset by new industrial, commercial, and professional opportunities. Forward strides were made in the battle to overcome poverty, ill-health, and bad living conditions typical of Negro life. A strong sense of race solidarity was demonstrated by an expressive Negro literature. Partial compensation for failure to break into Southern politics was found in successful participation in Northern politics. These evidences of progress were accompanied by a more generally enlightened and humane attitude on the part of the dominant whites that to a considerable extent lessened the burden of color.

In 1930 in the United States 5,503,538 Negroes were gainfully employed. This meant that the race that comprised 9.7 per cent of the country's population furnished 11.3 per cent of its workers. This high proportion was due to the large number of Negro women who worked as domestic servants. The Negro domestic retained her status in the South and often replaced foreign workers in Northern homes. The number of Negro domestics increased from 1,122,251 in 1910 to 1,516,-205 in 1930. In this same year the number of Negroes in agriculture totaled 1,967,839. This represented a sharp decline over the 2,834,969 farming in 1910, but agriculture was still the principal occupation of the race. Some 219,000 Negroes owned farms in 1920, as compared with 121,000 in 1890. A large proportion of these landowners made a good living and were among the most contented members of their race in America.

In the twentieth century Negroes began to regain their position in the skilled crafts. The number in industry grew from 655,906 in 1910 to 1,024,656 in 1930. In many Southern communities they were still employed in the building trades, and in numerous ports of embarkation in the North and South they were preferred as longshoremen. They enjoyed a virtual monopoly as Pullman porters and dining-car waiters, and were accepted by the thousands in the meatpacking and automobile industries of the Middle West. Their many skilled jobs in the South's tobacco industry and around blast furnaces were based on the assumption that the race possessed greater manual dexterity than the whites, and could endure heat better.[9] For once race prejudice demonstrated itself in favor of Negro superiority. Between 1910 and 1930, the number of Negroes in clerical occupations rose from 19,052 to 40,549. Limited clerical opportunities were open to them in Negro colleges and business enterprises. During the same period Negroes in public service increased from 22,229 to 50,203. Most of them were postmen and postal clerks, who retained their positions with truly exceptional tenacity.

Headway was made in the 1930's toward a more equitable treatment of Negroes by labor unions. They were freely admitted into the unions of longshoremen, hod carriers, common building laborers, and tunnel workers. The Brotherhood of Sleeping Car Porters presented an outstanding example of a union composed of Negroes exclusively. The Franklin D. Roosevelt administration exerted the powerful influence of the New Deal in favor of black unionization. The CIO, which began to rival the conservative AF of L for the allegiance of American labor in 1935, outlawed exclusion from membership on racial grounds and made a concerted effort to recruit the unskilled trades in which Negroes were so largely concentrated. By 1944 there were over 400,000 Negro union members. In such cities as Chicago, Pittsburgh, Detroit, and Gary, the proportion of Negro factory workers in unions exceeded that of whites.

Extensive educational facilities coupled with their ambition for social improvement brought marked progress to Negroes in the professional fields. The number climbed from 68,350 in 1910 to 136,925 in 1930. The most popular profession was teaching. Although many colored teachers

[9] Edwin R. Embree, *Brown America*, p. 151.

continued to be underpaid employees of rural schools, steps were taken toward equalizing salaries with those of white teachers. The various Negro colleges had 1,500 competent professors, a few of whom were productive scientists or scholars. In the later class were the biologists E. E. Just and Charles E. Turner, the historians Carter G. Woodson, W. E. B. Du Bois, and John Hope Franklin, and the sociologists Charles S. Johnson and E. Franklin Frazier.

The clergy was the second most popular profession among Negroes. Many of these ministers were poorly educated, but a growing minority moved steadily toward white standards of excellence. The colored clergy continued to exert a greater influence among their people than the corresponding group of whites. By 1930 the number of colored physicians reached 4,000, and Negro dentists totaled 1,500. The laws of the states required that their professional standards be as high as those of whites. Negroes were rapidly learning to turn to colored practitioners in cases of illness. Barriers of race held down the figure of Negro lawyers to 1,000 in 1930.

Lack of prestige by the colored attorney found compensation in the rise of the Negro journalist, entertainer, and artist. Every sizable city had a Negro newspaper. Large numbers of Negroes, especially in New York City, made their living as actors, musicians, and showmen, and a small but important segment of the race turned to art and literature. The enthusiasm that the Negroes themselves bestowed upon their entertainers and artists was supplemented by white admiration for this group. Here, again, the color ban worked in the black man's favor. Perhaps for sentimental reasons or because of admiration for what was supposedly primitive, many whites accorded a black artist more attention than a white artist of equal talents.

Booker T. Washington's hope for Negro participation in business had a limited fulfillment. In 1930 some 70,000 Negroes were engaged in profit-seeking enterprises. Significant gains were made in the fields of insurance, banking, restaurants, retail groceries, and real estate. In 1939 Negro insurance companies numbering twenty-seven had assets of $15,000,000. The most successful of these was the North Carolina Mutual Life Insurance Company of Durham, which was founded in 1898 by John Merrick, and by 1941 had some 300,000 policyholders. In 1927 there were thirty-three Negro savings and commercial banks with assets of $15,292,820, and between thirty and forty Negro loan and investment associations. The concentration of Negro populations in cities led to the employment of 1,500 Negroes as rental agents and as buyers and sellers of property. Every Southern town of any size had at least one Negro undertaker.

A few Negroes achieved business success of the type to excite the admiration of the average American; among prominent financiers were Charles C. Spaulding and William G. Pearson of Durham. Anthony Overton, son of a former slave, successively became a manufacturer, banker, insurance executive, and newspaper publisher of Chicago. A. F. Herndon of Atlanta supplemented a very successful barber business by the organization of a life insurance company. Madame C. J. Walker, whose career started modestly enough over a Louisiana washtub, made a fortune from an "anti-kink" hair preparation. Her spacious residence at Irvington-on-the-Hudson was substantial proof of her rise in the world. Mrs. A. E. Malone of St. Louis and Chicago made a fortune through the manufacture of Poro hair and skin products, which supplied the numerous Negro beauty shops.

Ignorance and poor health—the two besetting sins of the free colored man—were somewhat alleviated by 1930. Between 1890 and that date the illiteracy rate of the race fell from 57 to 16 per cent. What the school accomplished in dispelling ignorance was supplemented by knowledge gained from military service and migrations to urban centers. The annual death rate of the race fell from 33 per 1,000 in 1890 to 12 in 1949. Compared to the death rate of 10.6 for the United States as a whole, this figure was not very discouraging. The great scourges of the black race continued to be tuberculosis, venereal disease, and the maladies of childbirth and infancy. All were primarily the result of inferior living conditions; however, they were gradually being ameliorated through the advancing economic status of the blacks and their attainment of more leisure, better housing, and improved medical and hospital facilities.

World War I gave the blacks their second significant opportunity to bear arms in the service of their country. Between June 5, 1917, and September 12, 1918, more than 2.25 million Negroes registered for military service, and 367,710 were inducted into the armed forces. Some 200,000 went to France, totaling one tenth of American forces sent overseas, or precisely the race's quota of its proportionate population. Despite predictions to the contrary made by those unable to appreciate the genuine Americanism of the race, the Negro remained completely devoted to his country's cause; he had none of the problems of divided loyalty which beset other American minority groups. He responded as fully as other sections of the population to the rousing words of President Woodrow Wilson.

Negro soldiers received the same military pay as white soldiers and were accepted into every branch of the service except aviation. A Negro officers' training camp was established at Fort Des Moines, Iowa, and some 1,400 Negroes were given commissions. The Ninety-Second Division of the United States Army was composed entirely of blacks, with the exception of the highest officers, and engaged in active combat with the enemy. The first soldier of the American Expeditionary Force to receive the Croix de Guerre with star and palm was a colored sergeant; a Negro organization, the Fifteenth Regiment, New York National Guard, was cited for exceptional valor during the Meuse-Argonne offensive.[10]

Those who thought that the Negro's service in the great American crusade to make the world safe for democracy would raise his status were disillusioned. Public opinion forced the army to segregate Negro troops almost as rigidly as in civilian life, and when colored officers or enlisted men tried to overstep the color line they were subjected to indignities, even occasional violence. More than half of the colored soldiers shipped overseas were put to work on road building and unloading boats; the remainder was usually denied opportunities for spectacular service or high military rank. Colonel Charles Young, the Negro of highest military rank, was sent on a futile mission to Liberia. Army authorities generally lacked confidence in the Negro as combat material. Colored officers were necessarily inexperienced and because of the racial handicap were unable to inspire sufficient respect for their leadership.

Politics, not military sense, prompted the risk of massing Negroes in large combat units rather than following the French practice of scattering them among other commands. A certain amount of wrangling occurred between officers of the two races. The unaccustomed social freedom that the French bestowed upon the blacks so alarmed American General Headquarters that a confidential circular was issued to French authorities on August 7, 1918, warning that the Negro must not be treated as an equal; that he was a natural ravisher of women, and therefore should not be received in French homes. So fearful was General Robert Lee Bullard that soldiers of the Ninety-Second Division might rape French women that he ordered his men home as soon as the Armistice was signed.[11]

Back in America, Negro veterans were subjected to the same discriminations which plagued them before and during the war. Helping to win the crusade for democracy did not carry with it social and political advances comparable to those won by Negro participants in the Civil War. World War I resulted in greater freedom for Poles, Yugoslavs, and Czechoslovaks, but not for the American Negro. The whites saw that he returned to the selfsame position he occupied previously. He was even excluded from active participation in the councils of the American Legion, organized for veterans. By 1940 there were only two Negro combat officers in the regular United States Army, and none in

[10] *Ibid.*, p. 193.
[11] Jerome Dowd, *op. cit.*, p. 224–32: Myrdal, *op. cit.*, I, 420.

the United States Navy; of the 100,000 officers in the reserves only 500 were Negroes.

The failure of the Negro to realize social gains from his war experiences stimulated a militant race consciousness. This found expression in the writings of a gifted group of young Negroes who in the artistically free atmosphere of New York City cried out bitterly against the restrictions on their race and asked for manifestations of culture independent of the disdainful whites. The poets Claude McKay, Countee Cullen, Langston Hughes, and James Weldon Johnson proved beyond doubt that blacks were richly endowed with the emotions of tragedy and exaltation along with humility and humor. Novelists like Richard Wright protested against the frustrations of colored youth, and historians like Du Bois and Woodson depicted a people struggling to free themselves from the manifold oppressions heaped upon them by Anglo-Saxons. A few Negroes, like Frank Yerby and Willard Motley, wrote best sellers not specially concerned with the problem of race.

The expression of the New Negro was not altogether doctrinal or negative. It was demonstrated that the black man could stand on his own feet artistically. James Weldon Johnson, for example, found high inspiration in the sermons and prayers of the conservative Negro preacher. The Negro spirituals were interpreted as a glorious version of Christian triumph in the peculiar idiom of the Negro. "A wail of trouble too poignant to know, swings upward in three brief verses to a shout of hallelujah." The blues expressed a groping for material blessings in contrast to the heavenly hopes of the Negro spirituals. Plays were especially written for Negro actors so that they might convey the serious, as well as humorous, side of their people. In 1921 a delighted public applauded the joyous singing and dancing of *Shuffle Along,* in which Florence Mills set the pattern for the Negro revue. Then came Charles S. Gilpin in Eugene O'Neill's tragedy, *The Emperor Jones.* New heights were reached by the Negro stage with Richard B. Harrison in *Green Pastures,* a play portraying the struggle of a country folk endowed with naïveté and spiritual power. The artistic expression of the New Negro lacked the elaborateness and thoroughgoing independence of a great national art and attracted the public's especial attention to its unique songs and dances. One of the most original of American expressions, it created among the blacks themselves a pride of race. The Negro could turn to his own experiences for literary and artistic endeavors.

During the era of World War I the Negro press became important. Beginning with Samuel Cornish and John B. Russworm's *The Freedom's Journal* in 1827, it had grown a century later into some 150 newspapers with a combined circulation of about 1.5 million. In addition there were thirty-odd magazines. These publications attested to the modern Negro's inventiveness, comparable only to the free Negro church which arose in the last half of the nineteenth century. The Negro press, like the Negro church, was patterned after the white example, but it had a flavor all its own. Directed and owned by Negroes, it appealed to black readers exclusively. Although more radical in its outlook than the church, it enjoyed that institution's right to speak as it pleased.

Outstanding among Negro magazines was Du Bois's *The Crisis*. Its militant racial radicalism enabled it at one time to reach a circulation of :oo,ooo. Second in importance was *Opportunity*, the organ of the National Urban League, which presented Negro attainments and aspirations in a variety of fields. The radical tempo of Negro newspapers was set by the Chicago *Defender*, founded by Robert S. Abbott in 1905. Among other prominent Negro newspapers of the North were the Pittsburgh *Courier* and the Baltimore *Afro-American*. The best known cf the South were the Norfolk *Journal and Guide*, New Orleans *Louisiana Weekly*, Houston *Defender*, and Atlanta *World*.

Almost without exception Negro newspapers were weeklies, being unable to secure the advertising necessary for financially sound ventures in daily journalism. They allowed their readers to depend on white dailies for general news, while they concentrated on items about Negroes. The Southern Negro newspapers were more moderate in tone than their Northern counterparts, stressing news of local interest—religious, school, and athletic functions, and the social activities of the colored elite. The Northern press bent its main energies toward crusading for the abolition of all race distinctions. In pursuit of their objective, these newspapers were often bitter, blatant, inaccurate, and frenzied in their hatred of the white South. There was talk about "the crafty Caucasian" and "the white devils of the South." The fundamental weakness of Negro journalism was its overpraise of Negroes slighted by white newspapers, and an apologetic treatment of Negro crime in answer to its overemphasis by the white press. Such license was not resented by white people because they never read Negro newspapers. Still, it created an unwholesome spirit of animosity among those forced to live in a white world.

Neither World War I nor other agitations of the period effected much change in the political status of the Southern Negro. True, in some communities—notably in San Antonio and Memphis—local political machines made use of black votes; in some states—Virginia and North Carolina—Negroes learned to vote in limited numbers in the Democratic primaries. Nevertheless, the policy of exclusion established by the disfranchising state constitutions of the 1890's and 1900's and by the white primaries was generally maintained. It has been estimated that of a total Negro adult population of 3,651,256 in Alabama, Georgia, Mississippi, Louisiana, Florida, Texas, South Carolina, and Arkansas in 1940, only 80–90,000 voted.[12]

No Negro was taken seriously as a candidate for an elective office in the lower South; no Negro was ever appointed to public office, except school principals, public welfare agents, and a few policemen patrolling Negro communities exclusively. Any attempts by the few who voted to exercise this reputed liberty, except as dictated by interested whites, met with instant repression. Thus, in any but a technical sense, the Southern Negro was as completely disfranchised in 1920 or 1940 as he had been in 1840 or 1860. In recognition of the Negro's political failure, the national Republican party after 1920 sanctioned the "lily-white" policy of excluding Southern Negroes from the party's councils; in 1940 it deprived them of a full voice in its national convention by denying representation to congressional districts with less than 1,000 Republican voters.

However, the northward migration of the blacks gave them their long-awaited voice in politics. Abandoning their traditional loyalty to the Republican party, they bargained with the machines of Northern cities, and in return for their votes they received a limited share of the political plums—minor elective offices, municipal, state, and federal appointments, and all civil rights. Chicago since 1929, and New York City since 1945, have each had a Negro congressman. Negroes have become judges and sat in the legislatures of numerous Northern states. Northern Negroes exerted even greater influence in national politics. They constituted from 4 to 5 per cent of the voting population of such states as New York, Ohio, and Illinois, and apparently held the balance of power between the two great parties and accordingly were able to influence the councils of these two rivals for national leadership. This new power was strikingly illustrated during President Herbert Hoover's administration, when Negroes played a significant role in the Senate's rejection of John J. Parker as a Supreme Court Justice.

The Negro vote in the second, third, and fourth elections of President Franklin D. Roosevelt was rewarded by appointments of Negroes to high office. President Roosevelt allowed the blacks more than their proportional share of relief expenditures, and strove to eliminate discriminations against Negroes working in industries which operated under federal contracts. Northerners, with the tacit backing of the Roosevelt administration, secured the approval of the lower house of Congress for a bill outlawing the payment of poll taxes as a prerequisite to voting. Successful filibustering by Southern senators in 1946 and the following years prevented its passage. If this obstacle is not overcome,

[12] Myrdal, *op. cit.*, I, 475.

the desired purpose is being accomplished by the action of the Southern states themselves.

By 1952 the poll-tax provision had been repealed in North Carolina, Louisiana, Florida, Georgia, South Carolina, and Tennessee, and similar movements were being considered in the five remaining poll-tax states. The South, although seeking to forestall Northern criticism and Congressional interference, was reasonably certain that the change would not give added political power to the Negro. Louisiana furnished a likely example; the poll tax was repealed there in 1934, yet only some 2,000 Negroes registered in 1936.[13] The inflation of the forties reduced the poll-tax fee to less than the price of a pint of whisky. Events of the forties and fifties as we shall see,[14] increased the Negro vote in the Democratic primaries, but the control of these primaries still rests firmly in white hands. The whites were almost as determined in 1950 as they were in the 1900's to keep the blacks politically inactive.

Negrophiles feared, with reason, that the aggressiveness of Negro newspapers, the National Association for the Advancement of Colored People, and similar organizations would do more harm to the race than any good these militant groups might accomplish. In substantiation of this fear were the lynchings, suffrage discriminations, more rigid caste barriers, new Ku Klux Klan, race riots, and a new crop of Jim Crow politicians, like "Cotton Ed" Smith of South Carolina and Eugene Talmadge of Georgia, who were as rabid in their Negro-baiting as the Tillmans and Vardamans of their day. Nevertheless these reactionary influences were more than counterbalanced by significant improvements in the treatment which whites accorded to the subordinate race.

A group of Southern white social scientists, blazing the trail for reform, refuted the pessimistic and sinister predictions made twenty-five years previously by such eminent scholars as Frederick L. Hoffman and Alfred H. Stone. Without wincing at the rude facts of Negro life, the social scientists, led by Jerome Dowd of the University of Oklahoma, Willis D. Weatherford of the Southern College of the Young Men's Christian Association, and Howard W. Odum of the University of North Carolina, endeavored to explain the status of the race in its historical and social aspects, rather than in terms of immutable biology. Their enlightening analyses, accompanied by programs of reform, were concrete without violating Southern sensibilities. Their presentation of fairly convincing evidence that the best way to improve the status of Southern whites was to raise that of Southern blacks received effective support. The doctrines of these scientists were freely propagated in the classrooms of a hundred Southern colleges, and in the editorial columns

[13] *Ibid.*, I, 482.
[14] See below, p. 609.

of newspapers as widely scattered as Richmond, Norfolk, Raleigh, Louisville, Chattanooga, Birmingham, Montgomery, and Macon. Among political leaders who demonstrated racial liberalism were Mayor Maury Maverick of San Antonio, and Senators Claude D. Pepper of Florida and Hugo L. Black and Lister Hill of Alabama.

As a result of these activities, a liberal consciousness respecting the Negro made itself felt among the upper classes and among the bureaucrats of a score of Southern state capitals. The conversion of the latter to this attitude was very important, because it came at a time when the states were expanding the social welfare agencies directed by state officials. Concrete reforms were effected; obvious abuses such as the convict-lease system, county chain gangs, and crowded jails were corrected. Lynchings declined almost to the vanishing point, and the revitalized Ku Klux Klan was frowned out of existence. The governors and courts of a number of states, at least in *causes célèbres*, now carefully investigated before they sanctioned executions of Negroes convicted of capital crimes. The South showed a pronounced tendency to fall in with the democratic theory of public expenditures which provided that money raised by taxation be spent where it was most needed, regardless of the amounts that needy groups contributed as their share. This meant increases in expenditures for Negro education, with a veering toward actual equality in states like North Carolina, Virginia, and Oklahoma. It also meant establishing excellent reform schools for colored juvenile delinquents in many states and expansion of the ordinarily adequate service accorded to colored insane along with better, if still inadequate, clinical and hospital facilities. The public health authorities of North Carolina, South Carolina, and Alabama pioneered in providing Negro women with birth-control information.

Despite the militancy of certain Negro groups and the ameliorative reforms instituted by white liberals, Negroes still belonged to an inferior stratum of Southern society in 1920 and 1940 as in 1880 and 1900. Indeed, there was evidence that in recent decades the color line was more sharply drawn than formerly. Although the Jim Crow laws remained a controversial issue, the principle which they symbolize was still accepted as an unchangeable condition of Southern life. These laws treated all Negroes in the same manner, thereby weakening the tendency of whites to make distinctions. "All coons look alike to me," was a common saying.

Without available statistical proof, there were reasons to believe that miscegenation had declined; concubinage almost ceased to exist. Due to the invention of labor-saving devices and the development of manual skills of their own, the whites gave a broader application to their resolution to reduce to a minimum intimate contacts with the blacks. Northern philanthropy recognized the growing rigidity of caste by carefully respecting its conventions; so did most federal relief and military agencies previous to and during World War II. Southern liberals adopted the same attitude—the blacks meeting in Durham, the whites in Atlanta —when they assembled in 1943 to suggest improvements in race relations. Edwin R. Embree, a distinguished representative of the movement for interracial accord, in 1933 admitted the impossibility of "spontaneous and informal associations" between the most well-disposed and enlightened members of the two races.[15] Ironically enough, those members of Southern society most vocal in the advocacy of Negro rights belonged to the three professions which least permitted social contacts with Negroes under Southern caste conventions. They were the ministers, college professors, and editors, whose arguments might have a less liberal tinge if their professional duties threw them in daily contact with the downtrodden race.

As progressive Southerners were ever ready to demonstrate, much good could be accomplished within the limits of caste. On the other hand, no observant student of Southern life could deny that these barriers represented a dreadful handicap. They denied to nine or ten million Americans the self-reliance and self-expression which are the very essence of American democracy. The benefits bestowed upon the black man were aristocratic in origin, the largess of strong men to their weak inferiors. It was but human for these donors to contemplate their kindnesses, forgetting the many exclusions and denials which kept the Negro poor and humble.

Democracy as it actually existed in the South was the imposition of the selfish will of the white majority upon the black minority. Students of Southern problems knew that the restraint the common white man imposed upon the Negro was generally less kind than that of upper-class whites. In the issue of race against race, the student of Southern problems knew who would come out behind. It was the Negro who was lynched, who had the scales tilted against him in legal disputes, and who was forced to yield to his so-called superiors in employment and business opportunities. Outsiders ascribed such injustices to individual wickedness, but more often it was the logical outgrowth of the idea of "keeping the nigger in his place." Caste distinctions were supported by a system of justice that respected differences between individuals and consigned to the vengeance of the mob those members of the lower caste who attempted any familiarity with women of the higher caste. Nevertheless not a single lynching took place in the South in 1952.

The common Southern white, like the Negro and other ordinary Americans, felt it to be his inherent right to improve himself economi-

[15] Embree, *op. cit.*, p. 226.

cally and socially. In so doing, Southern whites could be as aggressively selfish as anyone else, often at the expense of the Negro. The latter was overcharged and underpaid, restricted in his movements, and deprived of opportunities. Cruel though this attitude seemed to outsiders, Southern whites had a string of grievances against the Negro to excuse almost any extreme of conduct. Paradoxically, the white man was more dissatisfied with the Negro than the Negro was with the white man. He reproached him for his social ambitions, for his alleged inefficiency and dishonesty, and for enjoying more than a fair share of allotted public funds. Such a state of mind represented a threat to the many gains won by the Negro since Emancipation. To a marked degree, it resembled the aggressiveness which had overthrown the Reconstruction regimes and created disfranchising state constitutions. How it manifested itself in a field of greatest importance during the twentieth century will be explained presently.

A striking illustration of the inadequacy of aristocratic prescriptions for Negro uplift was the black man's failure in business. Although there were some 70,000 Negro business enterprises in 1930, up to that time little headway had been made toward attaining an independent Negro economy within the confines of white society. Negro business endeavors were generally unimposing; they included many small huckstering and grocery establishments and enterprises in the field of personal service to Negroes in which whites did not care to function. In the latter class were beauty and barber shops, restaurants, and funeral parlors. Large mercantile establishments enjoying colored patronage were owned and managed by whites. Negro retailers obtained only two per cent of the $4,000,000,000 annual Negro trade.

On the other hand, the day of the Negro-owned barber shop, beauty parlor, restaurant, and grocery catering to the white trade virtually disappeared by 1930. The same applied to the Negro business contractor, who in the decades after the Civil War had played his small part in Southern economy. The most important Negro businesses—insurance companies and banks—were "defense enterprises," which owed their existence to the policy of the white banks and larger insurance companies who either refused to deal with Negroes or charged them higher rates. What were not good investments for white banks and insurance companies were no better for corresponding Negro firms, which explains why Negro businesses did not expand and prosper generally. Among the 134 Negro banks organized between 1888 and 1934, only twelve survived in 1936. Negro banks have been on firmer ground since that date because of war prosperity and because United States government obligations absorbed a large share of the increase in their resources. Several of the larger Negro insurance companies experienced difficulties; and their achievements do not seem impressive in the light of a 1948 estimate [16] that "one large white insurance company has insurance in force on Negro lives amounting to more than twice the insurance in force in all Negro insurance companies."

Negroes were necessarily inexperienced in business, and their properties were poor securities for loans. The restriction of trade to a single race with limited purchasing power hampered individual projects and prohibited large-scale enterprises. No Jim Crow laws or other conspiracies among influential white men kept the Negro out of business. The cause was more subtle and fundamental: the continued existence of the color line. Behind that barrier the black man could not provide the security of character and assets required to obtain credit for business ventures. Experience proved that Booker T. Washington was a mistaken prophet when he proclaimed it possible for his handicapped race to forge ahead in the business world. The colored leader's belief that business success would destroy race prejudice could not be tested. With few exceptions, the Negro race in the fifty years that elapsed since Washington spoke never produced the millionaires and captains of finance and industry who might have aroused the admiration of success-conscious Americans.

Jobs seemed to be growing scarcer due to increases in population, the closing of the frontier, and the invention of labor-saving and skill-saving machines. Inevitably, the competition for employment produced evidences of Negrophobia. As already cited, the Negro scored the first triumph in this contest by taking advantage of the industrial opportunities created by World War I. The Northern white workingman retaliated with race riots and by excluding colored men from labor unions and desirable jobs. Then came the depression of 1929, which struck a devastating blow at labor, Negroes included. Had these employment difficulties of Negroes been the result of temporary business reverses, there would be no need of special discussion here; the fact that unemployment among blacks far exceeded that of whites indicates the need for a broader explanation. The National Urban League estimated that 1.5 million of the 5.5 million Negroes capable of work, or 27 per cent, were jobless in 1932–33. Thus, the depression years brought to a head the racial handicap constantly operating against job security among Negroes.

In 1930, as in 1890, it was possible for whites to take jobs away from blacks when members of the dominant caste were willing and able to perform the same tasks. This power was exercised in the years before, during, and after the depression to oust colored persons from jobs as

[16] Quotation from Joseph A. Pierce, *Negro Business and Education,* in Frazier, *op. cit.,* p. 401.

newsboys, messengers, waiters, bellboys, elevator operators, janitors, barbers, hairdressers, and even such menial or heavy labor as garbage removing, street cleaning, road building, and locomotive firing. Although Negroes formerly controlled teaming, trucking, and horse-drawn vehicles, they did not shift to taxi, truck, and bus driving in large numbers. If a new garment or shoe factory came to a Southern town, only whites were employed. "Give jobs to white men and women!" and "Blood is thicker than water!" were the cries. This decline in urban opportunities for Negroes was accompanied by their replacement as farm operators. Between 1860 and 1930 the number of Negroes on the land in seven Southern states of the Southeast fell from 71.3 per cent to 39.7 per cent of the total population so employed. During the same period for the South as a whole, Negro farm operators decreased 107,000 while whites increased 323,000.

Sometimes the replacement of black labor was accomplished by rude or dramatic processes out of the reactionary past. In 1932 the Black Shirts of Atlanta, the Blue Shirts of Jacksonville, and other proletarian clans frightened both black labor and white employers with the cry, "Niggers, back to the cotton field—city jobs are for white folks!" Inherited standards of civil liberty were threatened by the advocacy of laws depriving Negroes of the right to cut white persons' hair. In 1923 seven Negroes were murdered, seven wounded, and one flogged because they held jobs as firemen on the Mississippi division of the Illinois Central Railroad. In some instances, as described by Erskine Caldwell, Negroes were lynched as a warning to black laborers to leave farm communities.

The Negro unemployment problem was less a survival of the reactionary past than an adaptation of that bygone age to the progressive tendencies of the twentieth century. Negroes were dismissed not because they were hated but because they stood in the way of white men deprived of employment by the industrial competition of modern life and improvements in machinery. Although many whites discarded the class spirit of the Old South in favor of new liberal concepts, they preferred the services of a white barber or waitress to a black one. Socially minded employers felt obligated to give work to members of their own race, even when such discrimination involved inconveniences or sacrifices. Family clothing was often washed at home by machinery or at the commercial laundry so as to "avoid the contagion in shanty-washed clothes"; thus the Negro washerwoman was deprived of work. In the name of moral reform Negro bellboys were replaced by whites; the former were accused of bootlegging and establishing contacts between hotel guests and prostitutes. The most notable case of this type occurred in Atlanta in 1930 when there was a wholesale arrest of Negro bellboys in the downtown hotels. They were charged with selling liquor and "attempted rape." Although only given light fines, they were generally replaced by whites. Frequently white men wanted jobs held by Negroes because labor-saving machinery had been adopted or social legislation instituted. For this reason some Negrophiles favored the maintenance of wage differentials between the races, fearing that the elimination of inequalities would result in the whites appropriating jobs from the blacks. These people saw in low wages the only alternative to destitution and need of public relief.

With modern enlightenment a new occupational democracy began to invade Southern consciousness and replace the hereditary scorn for certain types of "nigger work." The Southern white discovered that almost any type of honest labor, however humble, could be dignified. It became acceptable for a white person to be a waiter, field laborer, barber, nurse, or even a janitor, garbage carrier, or street cleaner; only bootblacks, domestic servants, and heavy laborers were the exceptions.[17]

Any discussion of Negro history for the decades following Reconstruction carries with it the pertinent question whether or not the race has progressed or retrograded. Bereft of hope of political and social equality by the Reconstruction debacle, the Negroes' situation was indeed unfortunate toward the end of the nineteenth century. In that period, decisions of the Supreme Court prepared the way for repressive legislation by the Southern states. The doctrine of white supremacy appeared completely triumphant over the American creed of equality. Fresh arguments concerning the alleged incapacity of the race for improvement seemed to be confirmed by its own internal weaknesses: poverty, industrial inefficiency, crime, and ill-health. Nevertheless, before the nineteenth century terminated, a new hopefulness was born out of the teachings of Booker T. Washington and the response of Northern philanthropists and Southern white progressives to the great Negro leader's pleas for co-operation. There was progress in education and in new opportunities for employments, as well as advancement in the professions, a limited success in business enterprise, and a more realistic understanding of the blacks by Southern whites who sought to halt the Negro migrations to sections of the United States which promised them political and social betterment. Inspired by leaders who recognized the shortcomings of Booker T. Washington's program, some Negroes developed a militant race consciousness which sometimes proved effective in situations where persuasion failed.

A survey of Negro history, however, prompts the conclusion that there is danger of overemphasizing the forces of progress. Both those Negroes who remained in the South and the ones who migrated north-

[17] Arthur F. Raper and Ira de R. Reid, *Sharecroppers All, passim.*

ward continued to live under restrictions of caste as rigid in 1940 as they were in 1890. This fact necessarily crippled all phases of Negro advancement. There was educational progress without free social and economic opportunities and a continuation of political and civil inequalities. Poverty persisted along with new limitations on business and occupational openings. There was the necessity of becoming more and more Americanized, without removing the social and psychological barriers which prevented adequate enjoyment of the privileges of a great country. For these reasons it appears doubtful that in the years since Reconstruction Negro progress has outweighed Negro retrogression. As long as the black man is the victim of caste, the politician, capitalist, and labor leader will refuse to share any real power with him. Accordingly, he will be forced to remain a mere beggar for favors from a country not consciously unkind in its attitude. Perhaps the Negro will continue to improve materially, but he will need far more self-assertion and self-reliance before he attains the status of a respected American citizen.

CHAPTER XXXI

Politics in the Twentieth Century

᭤᭤᭤᭤᭤᭤᭤᭤᭤᭤᭤᭤᭤᭤᭤᭤᭤᭤᭤᭤᭤᭤᭤᭤᭤᭤᭤᭤᭤᭤᭤᭤᭤᭤᭤᭤᭤᭤

SOUTHERN political leadership in the early decades of the nineteenth and twentieth centuries has often been contrasted. Nine of the 12 Presidents of the United States prior to 1850 were native Southerners. For sixty years before the Civil War the Chief Justices of the Supreme Court were Southerners. Among 41 Americans adjudged by the editors of the *Encyclopedia of the Social Sciences* as "important in domestic affairs before the Civil War," all but 14 were Southerners; of the "figures important for the development of political theory" in the same period this authority selects 27 from the South and only 25 from the remainder of the country. Since the Civil War no resident Southerner except the accidental Andrew Johnson has been President, and the *Encyclopedia's* editors list only one Southerner as important in political theory.[1] This contrast is heightened if one compares the magnificent leadership Old Virginia gave the nation with the minor roles Virginians have played in national life recently.

The reasons for the New South's deficiencies in political leadership are not hard to find. Inevitably the decline in the section's proportion of the nation's wealth was accompanied by dwindling political influence. Likewise the shift of the nation from agricultural to industrial dominance took power and prestige from the agrarian section and gave them to those places where industrial wealth was concentrated. Southern leaders were unable to express their talents adequately because their

[1] Howard W. Odum, *Southern Regions of the United States*, pp. 131-3.

((537))

political party was generally in the minority. As inheritors of a defeated tradition they tended to stand for lost causes and outmoded ideas, leaving to Northerners the championship of realities and attainable aims. The quality of Southern leadership suffered through the reassertion of power by an uncritical democracy. The common white man who dominated in the balloting after 1900 often demanded representatives as undistinguished as himself. Gone were the days of the hereditary families—of the Lees, Randolphs, Masons, Tuckers, Prestons, Rutledges, Pinckneys, Pickenses, Butlers, Breckinridges, and other planter families—who could gain and hold high office without paying more attention to the prejudices of humble men than to the problems of statecraft.

Nevertheless the political leaders of the New South were more outstanding than those in any other field of regional endeavor, with the possible exception of literature. The public in the New as in the Old South was slow to recognize distinction in any field except politics, and almost as reluctant to choose a state or sectional hero from industry or engineering as from the ranks of artists or scholars. The Southern statesman possessed a distinctive sphere of activity in the political life of his state. The Southern industrialist or editor was inclined to accept the dictation of New York City, for his ideas, perhaps even the ownership of his enterprise, often came from there. This was not true of the Southern governor or senator, whose authority came from the state which neither in constitutional theory nor in practice accepted dictation from the outside. Therefore he could afford to be a definite personality, as provincial or as original as the state he represented.

The South of the twentieth century produced few statesmen of great national importance, but it produced many vivid personalities. John Sharp Williams of Mississippi, Augustus O. Bacon of Georgia, and Andrew Jackson Montague of Virginia were cultured gentlemen in the old tradition, while Carter Glass of Virginia, Joseph T. Robinson of Arkansas, Charles B. Aycock and Claude Kitchin of North Carolina, Oscar W. Underwood of Alabama, and James F. Byrnes of South Carolina were constructive statesmen. Thomas S. Martin and Harry F. Byrd of Virginia, and Furnifold M. Simmons of North Carolina were efficient state bosses as well as important United States senators. Jeff Davis of Arkansas, James K. Vardaman and Theodore G. Bilbo of Mississippi, Cole L. Blease of South Carolina, Huey P. Long of Louisiana, and Eugene Talmadge of Georgia were panderers to the pride and prejudices of their white constituents; as such, they objected to the injustices which the agrarian revolt of the 1890's had failed to remove. And almost forgotten are Hoke Smith of Georgia, Napoleon B. Broward of Florida, William Goebel of Kentucky, and Braxton B. Comer of Alabama, whose deeds refute the legend that the South did not participate in the Progressive movement of the 1900's made famous by Robert M. La Follette of Wisconsin.

Southern progressivism was largely indigenous. As was true of the reform movements of the Old South, it was for whites only. Its main argument for the extension of the system of primary elections was that the Negro had been eliminated from politics. Its leaders were professional men and businessmen of the cities, but they were as sectional in their appeal for mass support as were the rural leaders of the 1890's. They envisaged the enemy as the "foreign" interests of the Northeast which, through railroads, insurance companies, oil companies, public utilities, and banks, were in conspiracy against small enterprises.

Within the framework of sectional standards the Southern Progressives adopted many reforms. The state-wide Democratic primary was by 1915 extended to every Southern state. Railroad and public utility commissions were strengthened, corporation malefactors were hauled into court, freight and passenger rates were lowered, inspection laws for mines and factories were passed, and such progressive nostrums as preferential primaries, and initiative, referendum, and recall were toyed with. Prohibition, as we have seen,[2] was in this period triumphant. The commission form of city government originated in Galveston in 1900 to cope with the problems created by a flood which swept away a large part of that city. By 1913 it was used by most of the larger cities of the South and by many of the smaller ones. The city-manager plan was first tried by Staunton, Virginia, in 1908, and next by Sumter, South Carolina, in 1911. The wave of reform culminated in the Oklahoma constitution of 1907, which required 5,000 words to list the restrictions imposed upon corporate wealth.

The Southern reform governors were men of striking personalities and bold deeds. Hoke Smith of Georgia was a former member of Cleveland's cabinet and an Atlanta publisher who induced his legislature to abolish the convict-lease system, to establish prohibition, and to institute more reforms than the Georgia Populists had accomplished. Broward of Florida was an ex-seaman who won the governorship in 1904 as a champion of the Florida crackers against predatory railroads and those who were monopolizing the public lands. He suggested that the state go into the insurance business to stop the exactions of Northern companies. Goebel of Kentucky was the remorseless foe of the railroad interests who, four days after he was made governor, died from a wound he received while contending for that office. Without his leadership, his legislative friends were unable to accomplish much against the railroads. Comer of Alabama was a wealthy manufacturer who, as governor in 1907, got his legislature greatly to expand the authority of the

[2] See above, p. 355.

railroad commission, to reduce railroad rates, and to prohibit lobbying and free passes. He believed that high freight rates were thwarting the development of Alabama industries.[3]

There were other Southerners whose political urges were not fulfilled by the constructive programs of progressive businessmen. They were the great masses of the poorer whites who had nothing to ship by classified rates and no insurance policies to bother about; but they possessed the ballot under the Democratic primaries and in a blind sort of way wished to express their grievances against the rich man above them and the Negro below them. They turned to leaders who were willing to pander to their pride and their prejudices. These leaders were called Dixie Demagogues. They knew that they were more representative of the white majority than were the educated element that sought to uplift the South through constructive reforms. "I am an ignorant man," declared Huey P. Long, the most famous of the group.[4] "But the thing that takes me far in politics is that I do not have to color what comes into my mind and into my heart. I say it unvarnished. . . . I know the hearts of the people because I have not colored my own. . . . I have one language. Ignorant as it is, it is the universal language within the sphere in which I operate. Its simplicity gains pardon for my lack of letters and education."

Possessed of great oratorical ability, warm and magnetic personalities, and striking appearances often accentuated by picturesque dress and mannerisms, the Dixie Demagogues won the admiration of thousands by reaffirming those concepts to which the uneducated and frustrated were heirs. They attacked the rich, the city folk, the Jews, the Catholics, and the minions of Wall Street. The invocation of orthodox religious convictions was often curiously accompanied by drollery at the expense of the Protestant clergy. Of course, the main butt of these rabble-rousers was the disfranchised Negroes, whose faults—real or imaginary—were exploited to the limit. "The way to control the nigger," said Vardaman, "is to whip him when he does not obey without it, and another is never to pay more wages unless it is absolutely necessary to buy food and clothing." The fact that the demagogues were often devoted to the welfare of their constituencies, and more often than not honest in financial matters, did not prevent them from being occasionally indiscreet or even immoral in their personal relations. Perhaps the greatest tragedy of twentieth-century Southern politics was not that

[3] A full appraisal of the southern progressives is C. Vann Woodward, *Origins of the New South, 1877–1913*, pp. 370–92. See also Arthur S. Link, "The Progressive Movement in the South," *The North Carolina Historical Review*, XXIII, 173–90 (April, 1946).

[4] Odum, *op. cit.*, pp. 531–2.

such men were so popular, but that the admiration they aroused was not altogether undeserved.

They gave just expression to the aspirations of rural folk whose interests had been obscured by the rise of urban and industrial populations. Primitive emotions were appealed to by the curses, vituperation, and ridicule which these leaders directed against the privileged, while constructive programs for relief were sometimes nonexistent. These friends of the common man were not always negative; some were intelligent enough to supplement vulgar antics by programs aimed at political and social improvements.

The procession of twentieth-century Southern demagogues was led by Jeff Davis of Arkansas. Davis's public career began in 1899 when he was elected attorney general of his state; it continued with his tenure of the governorship from 1901 to 1907, and closed with one term in the United States Senate. Attired in a Prince Albert coat of Confederate gray, Davis stormed through Arkansas pitting class against class, and catering to the prejudices of the uninformed. He capitalized on the opposition of the newspapers by telling the hillbillies that, according to the editors, no one voted for him "except the fellow who wears patched breeches and one gallus and lives up the forks of the creek, and don't pay anything except his poll tax." When Davis was turned out of the Baptist church for drinking, he good humoredly called his accusers "quart Baptists," while asserting that he himself was only a "pint Baptist." He tried to apply a law against the price-fixing policies of nonresident corporations doing business in Arkansas, and when overruled by the state supreme court he secured legislation which led to the temporary retirement of leading insurance companies from the state. Although he never hesitated to repeat false stories, Davis resolutely championed the common people against grasping corporations. Under his direction, laws were passed prohibiting excessive charges of the trusts, dishonest banking practices, and mistreatment of labor, and favoring better schools and the direct election of public officials by the people.

James K. Vardaman owed his election as governor of Mississippi in 1903 to the white masses who had been given political power by the direct primary for nominations which had been adopted by the Democratic party the previous year. This editor-lawyer knew all the tricks necessary to swing the voters. He was spectacular, accentuating a naturally striking appearance by dressing in immaculate white, wearing his raven hair down to his shoulders, and riding in an eight-wheeled lumber wagon drawn by several yokes of white oxen. He established a brotherhood with the common folk by declaring that his first audiences were "barnyard inhabitants and jackasses," and by playing upon Mississippi's deep fear of a resurgence of its black majority. White supremacy, he declared, was endangered by the educational progress of the Negroes; they should have for their schools only such funds as they themselves contributed in taxes. He contended that there should be two types of justice in the South, one for white men, another for "niggers." "God Almighty," he said, "created the negro for a menial."

The attempt to take from the blacks the meager gains of Reconstruction brought upon the Mississippi leader's head the wrath of Southern liberals, but an anti-Negro policy was necessary to free this clever demagogue of the stigma of earlier Populist affiliations. His administration as governor was featured by laws attempting to curb the privileges which previous administrations had granted to railroads, lumber barons, and various corporations. "He fought, tooth and nail," says Ray Stannard Baker,[5] "the trusts and combines that were striving to gobble up the state's resources." He improved the services of the state charitable institutions, and put an end to the convict-lease system. Personally honest, he eliminated graft and inefficiency from public service.

After a bitter fight with conservative Democrats, he won a seat in the United States Senate in 1911. In Washington he incurred disfavor by opposing President Wilson's war policies. He belonged to that "little group of willful men" who in February, 1917, successfully filibustered against Wilson's Armed Neutrality bill, and was one of six senators who voted against war with Germany. His belief that war sacrificed the interests of the common man, not demagogic ambition, prompted Vardaman to take this stand. It led to his defeat for re-election in 1918 on orders from the White House, thus ending his political career.

Cole L. Blease took up the cause of the common man where Ben Tillman had left it. This South Carolina leader appealed not only to country people but to ordinary white men of the growing towns and cotton-mill villages. Blease, unlike Tillman, was not reared on the farm but in the friendly atmosphere of a small-town hotel and livery stable. He carried himself haughtily, dressed ostentatiously, and spoke vividly. After gaining much political experience through numerous unsuccessful candidacies for office, he was elected goveror of South Carolina in 1910, and re-elected in 1912. His bizarre manners and morals, his frequent indulgence in abusive speech, and his crude assaults upon Negro education earned for him the contempt of the educated classes. Their criticisms, however, prodded him to a greater degree of oratorical effectiveness, and made him the idol of the mobs.

As governor he kept South Carolina in a tumult by frequent quarrels and drunken extravagances. His most notorious deed was to pardon

[5] Cited in *The Journal of Southern History*, III, 301 (August, 1937).

some 1,800 convicts. He was accused of corruption, but the charges against him were not proved. His administration was almost entirely devoid of constructive legislation for the benefit of the poorer people who voted for him. He was defeated in his many campaigns after 1912 except in 1924, when he was elected to the Senate. His career in Washington was exhibitionist rather than distinguished. Nevertheless Blease succeeded in awakening the political consciousness of the poorer whites of South Carolina in an unforgettable fashion, and he was especially popular with cotton-mill operatives. Both he and his followers were too individualistic and proud of their South Carolinian heritage to desire social legislation; what seemed to satisfy them most were negative and unreasoning criticisms of the privileged classes.

Vardaman's successor in the esteem of the underprivileged whites of Mississippi was Theodore G. Bilbo, a former theological student. He served as governor of his state from 1916 to 1920, and from 1928 to 1932, and he became a United States Senator in 1935. Among his many irregularities as governor was the freeing of 634 convicts in one year, the demoralization of state finances and the discrediting of state colleges by discharging staff members to make places for his own henchmen. At the same time, Bilbo increased the physical equipment of state colleges, promoted public education, and sponsored more hospitals for the abnormal and underprivileged. Bilbo's senatorial career was featured by manifestations of race prejudice that aroused the ire of the Negro press and Northern public opinion. He renewed the old demand that the Negroes be sent back to Africa.

Eugene Talmadge, an heir to the sentiments which Tom Watson had stirred up in the 1890's, was three times governor of Georgia between 1933 and 1943, and was preparing to begin another term when he died in 1947. "The wild man from Sugar Creek," as the city people called him, made capital out of the county-unit system under which rural counties with 43 per cent of the population cast 59 per cent of the unit votes. In 1942 Talmadge caused the state institutions of higher learning to be taken off the accredited lists of educational associations by dismissing from the service of these institutions officials falsely accused of seeking to abolish race distinctions. Apparently Talmadge sought to make capital out of Southern resentment against the Roosevelt administration's attempt to eliminate certain evidences of race discrimination in war activities.

J. Thomas Heflin, member of the second Ku Klux Klan, and senator from Alabama from 1920 to 1931, won notoriety as "an anti-Catholic maniac who spent hours on end raving against the Vatican." Believing that there was a Jesuit plot to poison him, he took to peering under his bed and examining his food.

Gaiety was added to the pageant of Southern politics by James E. Ferguson and his wife Miriam. When "Jim" was removed from the governorship of Texas in 1917 after the state legislature found him guilty of malfeasance, "Ma" Ferguson became a candidate for that office in order to vindicate her husband. She was elected in 1924 and again in 1932. The support of the "one-gallus" farmers and of elements opposed to the revived Ku Klux Klan was responsible for her success. During her administration scandals occurred in the state highway department, and pardons were issued by the thousands.

Most picturesque among the lesser demagogues was "Alfalfa Bill" Murray, governor of Oklahoma from 1931 to 1935. His boorish manners and wordy assaults upon the rich and educated won him the approval of the common man.

All these leaders, with one or two exceptions, were defeated for high office after initial successes; all appealed to the prejudices and passions of the lower classes. Some drank heavily, lied blatantly, and consorted with lewd women. Their vices were so obvious that they were easily exposed. Perhaps the primary weakness of these men was a pathetic faith in outmoded ideals. Their faith in the power and wisdom of rural majorities was so great that they failed to come to terms with political machines made powerful by business and industrial interests. Their corruption was usually of a crude personal nature; as generally sincere champions of rural democracy, they opposed the common graft of big business and politicians. Consequently, the well-nigh invincible power of money was often arrayed against them. In a sense they were martyrs to the democracy which found expression in the power of the Southern common man. This democracy was rude and ignorant and in a state of decline in the twentieth century. Nonetheless, it was more real and honest than the type of popular government that money-controlled machines substituted in its place.

Southern leaders carried into the 1930's the pattern set by the Blease-Vardaman type. The most powerful one of all was Huey P. Long of Louisiana. He possessed "the swaggering, hell-for-leather bluster that the South demanded in its heroes and champions; in addition he had a kind of quizzical, broad, clowning humor, and a capacity for taking on the common touch." He extended demagoguery into new fields and modified it to suit new conditions. Although a genuine rustic by birth, this Louisianian ignored the old prejudices against Negroes, Catholics, Jews, foreigners, and Yankees, and addressed himself realistically to the immediate social and economic problems of the common man. Thus he attained stature with the American people as a whole as well as those of his own state and section.

Long did not let Jeffersonian traditions against expanding governmental functions and expenditures stand in the way of the opportunities which enormous accumulations of capital gave the politician for distribution. Possessed of a genuine sympathy for the underprivileged and an almost maniacal faith in his ability to better their conditions, he was no mere emotionalist conjuring up dying agrarianism. Long could "stand really apart from his people and coolly and accurately measure the political potentialities by the condition of the underdog." Unlike most of his predecessors adept in the art of popular appeal, he offered the masses material benefits in return for their loyalty and votes.

Huey P. Long was born in a four-room house in an upstate Louisiana parish. Before becoming a lawyer, he peddled books, soap, furniture, and patent medicines, and organized a cooking contest for the manufacturer of a lard substitute. Elected governor of Louisiana in 1928, he was elected to the United States Senate two years later. When he became their chief magistrate the people of Louisiana anticipated an unconventional regime, but the reality which evolved was beyond all expectations. The Kingfish—as Long was dubbed—administered shock after shock, adding discomfort to confusion, and flouting the traditions of an ordinarily dignified office. He conducted the affairs of state from his hotel bedroom, and once received the commander of a German warship in green pajamas. He indulged in fisticuffs and turned the state militia into a bunch of storm troopers. He tore down the beautiful executive mansion at Baton Rouge and substituted a building that looks like a cross between a museum and a post office. He craftily circumvented impeachment proceedings against himself and dealt summarily with the lieutenant governor who tried to take his office. Perhaps none of his indiscretions received more publicity than the encounter in which he received a punch in the eye from a man with whom he disputed the use of a Long Island toilet. Such conduct, however, failed to break his power. As senator he dictated Louisiana affairs through a subservient legislature. Hundreds of thousands inside and outside his state admired his daredevilry, or regarded his bad manners as irrelevant in the face of many constructive achievements.

Long made good his assaults upon corporate monopolies, newspapers controlled by the wealthy, and various machine politicians of New Orleans. He gave his constituency magnificent roads, free school buses and textbooks, the right to vote without paying poll taxes, and lower telephone, gas, and electric rates. He pumped new life into the football team of the Louisiana State University, and into its academic and scholarly activities as well. With Napoleonic audacity, this egotist hoped to supplant Franklin D. Roosevelt as the presidential candidate of the Democratic party in 1936, or at least to cause Roosevelt's defeat at the hands of a Republican rival. Long devised a scheme for federal spending far more lavish than that of Roosevelt and his New Deal—the Share-Our-Wealth plan. Under this plan the great fortunes of the United States were to be confiscated, so that each family might enjoy a home, an automobile, a radio, and a minimum income of $2,500 annually, and every promising child might receive an education. The popular response to this scheme took the form of mountains of mail and huge audiences for its originator.

The Kingfish's activities were abruptly terminated by his assassination on September 8, 1935. Despite his popularity, Long could not have won a national election in which he would have met the opposition of organized politicians, the billions of the Roosevelt administration, and the conscience of a nation whose conservative majority was offended by this Louisiana boss's morals and threats of violence. America was not ready for a Hitler or a Mussolini.

Less spectacular, but more symbolic of the destiny of the New South than the Broward-Goebel-Comer or the Davis-Vardaman-Blease-Long type, was another group of leaders. They were so diverse in their personalities and methods that the best way to define them is to say that they were not demagogues. As genuinely Southern as the most arrant demagogues, they promoted sectional faith in racial and religious matters; yet their main strength did not come from proclamations of sectional prejudices. They respected the doctrine of white supremacy to the extent of giving the white race the major share of the benefits of progressive reforms, but—except when cornered by the demagogues—they did this without heaping insults upon the helpless Negro. Some mixed benevolent intentions toward the blacks with a discreet respect for outside opinion on the race question. They did not resort to the extravagant showmanship, the violence of expression, and the sense of personal grievance typical of the demagogues; instead they appealed to the sober intelligence of the voters. Some did so because they were humdrum individuals unable to inspire mass devotion on which the demagogues thrived; others were men of exceptional ability who understood the instability of statesmanship based on mob hysteria. They mapped out programs considered beneficial to their constituencies and employed diplomatic means to achieve their objectives. That political progress in the South kept pace with achievements in other fields of endeavor was primarily to their credit.

A few radical intellectuals bitterly complained that these men were agents of the same business interests that tightened their hold on Southern economic life in the years between World War I and II. Here, it was claimed, was a group of "scalawags," who acted for Northern interests more effectively than those pilloried in the pages of history. "The native Southern elite" was pictured as guaranteeing "the protection of Northern imperialist interests in the region." [6] Co-operation with invading capitalists might possibly explain the excellent reputations such politicians gained for themselves.

These leaders were not compelled to stoop to the shabby tricks and downright thefts of the demagogues. The wherewithal for controlling votes and satisfying personal needs came from business interests in ways so conventional that few scandals occurred. The gifts they received took the form of attorneys' fees, business opportunities, and campaign contributions, which affronted neither the law nor the conscience of the community. The collaboration of business and politics stimulated the commercial and industrial progress that most Southerners welcomed. Frequently politicians defeated the passage of labor laws that in turn might have hindered business expansion; they cheerfully granted the favor of tax exemptions to industrial enterprises owned by outside interests. If these actions branded them as reactionaries or conservatives, then the people themselves were equally guilty for giving the politicians their votes.

Southerners as a whole evinced little enthusiasm for social legislation and labor unions; they were convinced that the public welfare was well served in offering political inducements to industry and commerce. The subservience of the Southern political leader to business interests sprang from the fact that his section represented a subordinate part of a great capitalistic country; individually, the Southern politician was as patriotic and honest as his predecessors of earlier decades when capitalism was less imperialistic. As heir to the Southern tradition of state sovereignty and agrarianism, he was more critical of big business than were the local leaders in nonpolitical fields. At times he was sufficiently provincial to defend the rights of farmers and small business against great national syndicates.

The wealthy lawyer of Uvalde, Texas, who in 1933 became the first Vice-President from the South since 1865, and who aspired to be President, clearly illustrated the more undesirable aspects of Southern politics and business working hand in hand. Although John Nance Garner had the reputation of being parsimonious and usurious, he was not too occupied with money-making to win the friends necessary for a political career. The Texas leader spent convivial nights drinking whisky and playing poker; finally Uvalde politicians made him a judge. A stroke of fortune was his marriage to Ettie Rheiner, a fiery moralist who broke him of gambling and became his secretary and most judicious adviser.

In 1903 Judge Garner won a seat in Congress; in 1923 he became

---

[6] Benjamin B. Kendrick, "The Colonial Status of the South," *The Journal of Southern History*, VIII, 19 (February, 1942).

ranking Democratic member of the Ways and Means Committee and in 1928 House minority leader. He was exceptional among outstanding Southern politicians because his career was not marked by rough-and-tumble campaigns and close elections. Through his joviality and the support of powerful business interests Garner developed an invincible strength in his Congressional district. Among his friends were the oil magnates, the chief lobbyists of the state's sulphur monopoly, and the Texas representatives of the electric power trust. If Garner was not consciously a representative of big business, it was because he did not possess a sufficiently broad understanding of social and economic trends. A political hack, his existence revolved around his small Texas town and Washington politics. In the interest of party regularity, he fulminated against Secretary of the Treasury Andrew Mellon, high tariffs, a contracted currency, and other symbols of Republicanism. Although a legislator, he had no constructive plans; he drew strength from his knowledge of parliamentary procedure, his ability to debate at close quarters and to bargain behind the scenes. His lack of drama and oratorical prowess found compensation in the Garner legend. Newspapers represented him as a rugged soul whose customary silence indicated "uncanny political shrewdness," and whose love of baseball, poker, fishing, and whisky bespoke a sound Americanism opposed to radical innovations. In 1931 Garner became Speaker of the House, and in 1932 he received the Vice-Presidential nomination of the Democratic party in return for shifting to Franklin D. Roosevelt the 90 votes he polled for the Presidential nomination.

Garner began his career as Vice-President by applying his skill as a parliamentary manager toward furthering Roosevelt's aims. He considered the New Deal nothing more than an emergency measure soon to be abandoned for more conventional objectives. When, however, the President persisted in favoring organized labor and urging the reorganization of the Supreme Court, the Texan's innate conservatism proved stronger than his party loyalty. He secretly became the leader of a Democratic revolt against Roosevelt. The fact that this break was not openly acknowledged enabled the Vice-President to be re-elected in 1936 under the Roosevelt banner. In 1940 he was groomed as a conservative candidate for President, but his personal handicaps were too apparent. He was seventy years old, and remembered as an orthodox Southerner at a time when the Negro and labor votes were increasingly important in crucial states. John L. Lewis, the CIO chieftain, unjustly stigmatized him as "a labor-baiting, poker-playing, whisky-drinking, evil old man." Roosevelt won the nomination, and Garner's political career came to a close.

A less elusive and more attractive figure among Southern conservatives was Carter Glass of Virginia. This son of a Confederate officer began his career as a printer's devil in Lynchburg at the age of fifteen. Some twenty years later he came into prominence as the owner and editor of the town's newspapers. His vehement championship of Virginia and of Democratic principles brought the reward of a state senatorship in 1898 and membership in the convention called to rewrite the Virginia state constitution in 1901. In this assembly Glass won for himself a permanent position in the Democratic oligarchy, then gaining ascendancy in Virginia; he strenuously sponsored the poll tax and other provisions which deprived Negroes and the underprivileged of suffrage. His labors in the constitutional convention were promptly recognized by awarding him a seat in Congress.

After many quiet years in Washington, Glass became nationally prominent in 1912 when he threw the Virginia delegation to Woodrow Wilson in the national Democratic convention. He helped the Wilson leaders fashion the Federal Reserve Act and piloted that measure through the House of Representatives. In recognition of this service, Wilson appointed him Secretary of the Treasury. In 1920 he resigned from that office to accept the Virginia senatorship made vacant by the death of Thomas S. Martin. Virginia's political machine protected his seat in the Senate so thoroughly that Glass could dispense with speaking tours to insure his re-election.

This did not, however, mean that this Virginian had not the will and ability to be energetically vocal. A choleric little man with the habit of snarling out of the side of his mouth, for many years he arrested the nation's attention by his biting utterances. This won him the title of the Unreconstructed Rebel. He gave the otherwise colorless political machine of his state, of which the undramatic Harry F. Byrd was boss, a vivid and noisy leadership. It was best demonstrated by the manner in which Glass, a Methodist and prohibitionist, waged the fight in 1928 for the Presidential candidacy of Al Smith. He spoke in favor of Virginia's orthodoxies of party regularity and religious tolerance, and made unfair charges against Herbert Hoover, Smith's Republican opponent.

When Franklin D. Roosevelt started the New Deal experiment the Virginia senator was openly hostile; however, he did not endanger his position as a member of the Democratic organization by quarreling with the President personally, or by leaving the Democratic party. Glass criticized the "spendthrift policies" of the "dishonest and dishonorable" New Deal.[7] In committee meetings he graciously protected J. Pierpont Morgan against embarrassing questions. The Unreconstructed Rebel was a favorite of conservative finance.

More independent of machine control than either Garner or Glass

[7] Cited in Allan A. Mitchie and Frank Ryhlick, *Dixie Demagogues*, p. 179.

was Oscar W. Underwood of Alabama, the leading Southern statesman of Woodrow Wilson's administration. Entering Congress in 1895 from the Birmingham district, he demonstrated his independence of the iron and steel interests of his city by opposing the protective tariff. When the Democrats captured control of the House of Representatives in 1911, Underwood became House floor leader and chairman of the Ways and Means Committee. He won these distinctions because of his high character, winning personality, and unflagging industry. Under his direction a bill lowering the tariff was evolved. When President Taft vetoed this measure, tariff reform became the issue of the hour and its proponent a leading aspirant for the 1912 Presidential nomination of the Democratic party.

Underwood's candidacy for this high office was the most formidable of that of any Southerner since the Civil War. Although defeated by Woodrow Wilson, he remained consistently loyal to the administration, and he assumed a leading role in framing the tariff act which bears his name. Elevated to the Senate in 1915, Alabama's legislator played a constructive part in formulating the financial measures of World War I and in Wilson's unsuccessful fight for senatorial acceptance of the League of Nations. At the Democratic national convention of 1924 Underwood resolutely fought against the power of the Ku Klux Klan, failing by a margin of one vote to include an anti-Klan plank in the party's platform. His name came up for the Presidency, but his opposition to the Ku Klux Klan and prohibition alienated the South. Discouraged by the trends of the times, he retired from the Senate in 1927 and sought the sanctuary of his Virginia estate. From there, he proclaimed such Jeffersonian principles as the minimum of government and the maximum of personal liberty, and rejected such manifestations of modernism as federal regulation of child labor, woman suffrage, and federal development of Muscle Shoals. To the very end, Oscar W. Underwood embraced the principles of an austere ultraconservatism.

Another conservative who put independence above political expediency was John Sharp Williams of Mississippi, the son of a Confederate colonel who had been killed at Shiloh. An active cotton planter, educated at the University of Virginia and at Heidelberg, the younger Williams won prominence as a conservative Democrat during the sixteen years he was a member of the lower house of Congress. As the floor leader of his party, he co-ordinated its efforts, posed leading questions in his verbal battles with Republicans, and despite the opposition of William Jennings Bryan injected into party councils an old-fashioned Jeffersonianism. The moderate tone of the platform on which Wilson was elected in 1912 was chiefly the doing of this Mississippi conservative. After a bitter struggle in which the issue of aristocrat versus commoner was drawn, Williams was elected to the United States Senate over Vardaman in 1907. Since there was less Republicanism to fight in the Senate, he failed to attain the prominence there which he had enjoyed in the House. Disappointed over the defeat of Wilson's postwar policies and over Congressional concessions to the demands of ex-soldiers, Senator Williams retired from public life in 1923 with this parting shot: "I'd rather be a hound dog and bay at the moon from my Mississippi plantation than remain in the United States Senate." John Sharp Williams was the last of the Bourbons, the aristocratic planter who brilliantly represented what was left of the old-fashioned interests in the South's least progressive state.

The eclipse of such gentlemen as Underwood and Williams and of antiquated demagogues like Blease and Vardaman was due to significant changes in Southern political philosophy. The fundamental cause was the section's shift in interest from agriculture to industry. Although this change occurred toward the end of the nineteenth century, it did not become politically apparent until the beginning of the twentieth century. Its most obvious manifestation was a revised view of the tariff. While continuing to express a sentimental attachment to the sectional tradition of low tariffs or free trade, responsible Southern statesmen learned to seek the benefits of protection for Southern products. The tariffs, for example, which the Republican successors of Wilson imposed upon metals, cotton, peanut and sugar products were accepted cheerfully by Southern leaders. Few Southern congressmen insisted that the Roosevelt administration repudiate the protectionism inherited from the Republicans.

Another indication of changed philosophy was the willingness of the South to exchange Jeffersonian individualism and states' rights "for any three letters of the endowed alphabets"; that is, for such Roosevelt experiments as AAA, PWA, and NIRA. Previous to the New Deal the section had turned to the federal government for the enforcement of prohibition, aid to highways, more vocational education, and regulation of agricultural and business activities. Enthusiastically it accepted vast extensions of the functions of state and local governments, especially those affecting schools and highways. From a region once advocating low-tax policies, the Southern states became that section of the country which spent the largest share of its total income for public purposes. This meant an increase of 300 per cent in state and local taxes between 1913 and 1930, and the most widespread application by any group of states of both sales and personal income taxes. A pronounced tendency for expensive public services was best illustrated by the South's spending twice as large a share of its total wealth and income as the rest of the country on the maintenance of its unexcelled highway systems.

The demands of forward-looking businessmen, the stimulus of rival factions within the Democratic party, and the creation of co-ordinated political machines led to improvements in Southern governments as much in harmony with the demands of the Southern Progressives as was possible without antagonizing dominant business interests. One state after another expanded its educational functions, assumed the supervision of public health and sanitation, and constructed improved institutions to care for the insane, the blind, juvenile delinquents, and other unfortunates. County chain gangs and convict-lease systems were abolished, and the machinery of state governments underwent a general modernization. Several states, notably Virginia, North Carolina, and Tennessee, centralized executive responsibility in the hands of the governors, enforced standards of efficiency and workable budgetary systems, and streamlined theories of taxation. The former dependence of states upon the general property tax gave way to more discriminating classifications of property and to the inauguration of income and sales taxes.

Reforms in state and municipal administrations were not generally accompanied by changes in the affairs of the numerous counties and parishes into which the thirteen Southern states were divided. Most of these units of local administration continued to be controlled by oligarchies of officeholders, lawyers, and non-officeholding businessmen. The officeholders usually came from the white middle class, the policy-making positions went to members of the upper group, and the "dirty work" of law enforcement fell to the deputy sheriffs and policemen from the lower stratum. Men from the lower group, despite the democratic character of the suffrage, failed to be elected to office; however, they were generally pleased by the public benefits of improved roads and schools, and by the easy and friendly manner in which they were received by the not overworked county officials.

Courthouse cliques could not always feel assured of permanent tenure; once they allowed themselves to lose touch with changing popular tastes they might find themselves overwhelmed by rivals taking advantage of the waves of anti-Catholic, anti-Negro, and anti-business sentiments that periodically influenced the common man. The frequent inefficiency and occasional dishonesty of sheriffs and county treasurers led to defeats in the primaries, as did the demand for "rotation in office." Moreover, unenlightened politicians were at times forced to retire before the criticisms of reformers and experts who often dominated state administrations. Governors, for example, removed incompetent sheriffs or gave the powers of these officials to state police; state auditors smoked out inefficient local officials; welfare commissioners disturbed the peace of county commissioners who retained jails constructed before the Civil War.

The increased functions of state governments helped to develop political machines of a power undreamed of in earlier times, when public controls and services were less ubiquitous. Inevitably there were political potentialities in the deposit of huge public funds in favored banks, in the supervision of insurance companies and banks by public agents, in the allocation of enormous school funds, and in the armies of publicans who collected income, corporation, and excise taxes.

The power of governing politicians was most convincingly demonstrated through the road-building programs. State highway departments proved to be ideal instruments of machine politics. Customary legislative checks on executive absolutism were removed by allocating to highway commissioners control of the vast sums derived from automobile license and fuel taxes. A state commission's expenditure of $15-30,000,000 in a single year attached to the political fortunes of this body a powerful group of deposit holders, note brokers, contractors, cement manufacturers, engineers, supervisors, and laborers. Thousands of jobs were given away; every Southern capital possessed its mansions owned by highway contractors.

In some states it proved impossible to win elections without the co-operation of highway interests. By the use of this and other types of patronage, sinister machines developed in certain states. For example, the Ed Crump organization of Memphis, collaborating with Kenneth D. McKellar, in 1932 extended its tentacles to seize control of the whole state of Tennessee. Crump's strength lay in his ability to control almost unanimously the 50–60,000 votes of Memphis and surrounding Shelby county, including those of business, labor, and school organizations, as well as of a large number of Negroes. He held the balance of power between the factions in which the 300,000 Democratic voters of the state were divided. McKellar, who was a United States senator between 1917 and 1953, made full use of the federal patronage.

Similar to the Crump machine was the Robert S. Maestri organization of New Orleans, which obtained control of Louisiana. Most dynamic and menacing of all Southern machines was the state organization which Huey P. Long substituted for the New Orleans clique.

Several Southern states, including South Carolina, Texas, Mississippi, Florida, and Alabama, remained relatively free of boss rule, so that the Democratic voters in those states could select their own rulers. There the primaries were often spirited and closely contested, and issues arose involving personal, territorial and class differences. Virginia and North Carolina, on the other hand, fostered machines so autocratic and permanent that there were adjournments of the processes of popular government. However, the political juntos of these two states compensated for their cunning by furnishing the best governments south of the Potomac.

Controlled politics in North Carolina owed its origin to Furnifold M. Simmons. Like Carter Glass and other prominent Southern statesmen, he started as a crusader for white supremacy. Simmons broke the backbone of the coalition of Negroes, Populists, and Republicans who, as has been shown,[8] won temporary control of North Carolina in 1894. Elected to the United States Senate in 1900, he proved who was boss of North Carolina by his triumphant re-election in 1912 over liberal opposition. His strength was built on moral fervor for prohibition and white supremacy, staunch championship of Southern tariff interests, and use of county cliques and federal patronage for political purposes. Although President Wilson suspected his liberalism, the North Carolinian as chairman of the Senate Finance Committee loyally executed the dictates of his party chief in respect to the Underwood tariff and other Wilson policies.

The nomination of Al Smith by the Democratic party in 1928 proved too much for the prohibitionist boss of North Carolina. Simmons bolted the party and brought about his political ruin. In 1930 he was defeated for his Senate seat by Josiah W. Bailey, who shrewdly stressed disloyalty to the Democratic party as the worst of crimes. Subsequently the boss of North Carolina was replaced by a clique from the little city of Shelby, headed by O. Max Gardner, Clyde R. Hoey, and Otis M. Mull. The Shelby dynasty, operating through the state highway department and school system, has been guilty of absentee ballot frauds and threats against voters who failed to pay their poll taxes. Nevertheless, both the Simmons and Shelby machines gave North Carolina progressive rule. The state pioneered in paved highways and social welfare work. Its university was liberally supported and could criticize public policies in nonacademic fields. Although taxes were high in North Carolina, the state had a surplus revenue of $73,000,000 in 1945.

Virginia's organization was perfected by Thomas S. Martin, a successful but colorless lawyer of plain origin. He first demonstrated his power in 1894 by defeating for the United States Senate Fitzhugh Lee, nephew of the renowned Confederate general. The day of the Bourbon statesman was over, and that of the machine politician at hand. For lack of a picturesque personality and oratorical ability, Martin substituted a tireless attention to local political organizations, absolute personal honesty and loyalty, and a discriminating distribution of the patronage. His supremacy in Virginian politics was definitely recognized by 1900. In

[8] See above, p. 353.

the ensuing years he obtained financial assistance from the multimillion-aire Thomas Fortune Ryan and moral support from the Anti-Saloon League and its Methodist leader, Bishop James Cannon, Jr. The Martin-Ryan opposition to the Woodrow Wilson candidacy in 1912 threatened to create the anomaly of a state machine without the support of a national administration of its own party. When Martin came to terms with the victorious Wilson, federal patronage was exchanged for industrious legislative backing.

After Martin's death in 1919 his position was gradually assumed by Harry F. Byrd, a young veteran from Virginia's public service who was fast accumulating wealth through the publication of newspapers, apple growing, and other business enterprises. Byrd became governor of Virginia in 1926 after gaining prestige as the very prudent director of the state highway department. His regime was characterized by administrative reforms most pleasing to progressive businessmen, of whom he was the chief representative. Through the "short ballot" many previously elective officers became appointees of the governor. Rigid economy, the elimination of duplicating bureaus, and the establishment of a modern tax system bore fruit in a carefully balanced budget. Without sacrificing the spoils system, Byrd introduced high standards in public service. Gaining wide popular support because of his reforms, he maintained a hold upon his state more tenacious than that of any state boss since the time of Sir William Berkeley. Byrd won a United States senatorship in 1933, and for a number of years dictated his successors in the governorship almost without interference. The existence of the poll tax and other restrictions on suffrage, the absence of effective opposition in both the Democratic primaries and general elections, and the tact with which Byrd and his lieutenants avoided controversies, created so much harmony in Virginia's public life that it was indeed difficult to prove the reality of a political machine. When serious local opposition developed, however, the Byrd organization went into action, paying the poll taxes of voters and rallying beneficiaries and kinsmen to the support of imperiled cohorts.

The effectiveness with which the Virginia oligarchy held in abeyance the processes of democratic government was the despair of liberals. The absence of widespread popular support for these critics indicated that most Virginians were satisfied with the conservative methods of Byrd and his lieutenants. Indeed, the manner in which the machine handled the Al Smith crisis proved the utter wisdom of its strategy. It loyally supported the unpopular nominee of the national party while discreetly acquiescing in the determined majority of Virginians to vote for Smith's Republican opponent. Two years later the machine reaped the reward of this strategy when Virginians elected the machine's candidates for state offices. Unlike Simmons of North Carolina, Byrd did not bolt the Democratic party. For this reason he won the gratitude of those who had voted against Smith. They were prejudiced Southerners who, once they recovered from the shock of having an Irish Catholic as the candidate of their party, clung to the belief that a bolter was the worst political sinner of all. They punished Bishop Cannon for leading them in the 1928 bolt, and thereby freed the Byrd politicians of the unpleasant necessity of submitting to clerical dictation.

The conservative instincts of many Southern politicians were offended by the candidacy of Woodrow Wilson for the Presidency. This opposition centered in the combinations of Martin-Ryan of Virginia, Joseph M. Brown–Clark Howell of Georgia, and Oscar B. Colquitt–Joe Bailey of Texas. The Princeton educator was suspected as a newcomer who championed strange radicalisms; moreover, he had bolted the Democratic party in 1896, had expressed Federalist sentiments in his historical writings, and had been a "base ingrate" toward the politicians who made him governor of New Jersey. Nevertheless the candidacy of a Virginia-born son of a Presbyterian minister enlisted formidable Southern support. The ringing phrases of Wilson's New Freedom aroused the hopes of Southern liberals without being too specific to affront their fundamental conservatism.

Wilson's determination to carry high moral principles into practical politics stirred the enthusiasm of nonpolitical leaders. Pulpits and academic halls rang with his praises. The businessmen of the South's new cities saw in him an opportunity to eliminate many sordid features of the political practices inherited from the Agrarian Revolt. A group of publisher-editors, including Josephus Daniels of Raleigh, William E. Gonzales of Columbia, Frank L. Mayes of Pensacola, and Alfred A. Belo of Galveston, used the daily press to acclaim Wilson's candidacy warmly. Important politicians rallied to his banner, anticipating favors and local reforms. The most influential of these were the Texans Thomas B. Love, Thomas W. Gregory, Albert S. Burleson, Cone Johnson, Cato Sells, and Colonel Edward M. House. Thanks to the able support of these people, Wilson's candidacy created more enthusiasm in the South than that of any other Presidential aspirant since the Civil War.

In the initial balloting at the Democratic convention of 1912, most of the delegates from Virginia, Georgia, Florida, Kentucky, Alabama, and Tennessee voted for candidates other than Wilson. When it became evident that the Princeton educator would win the nomination, however, these states joined the other Southern delegates to insure this outcome. It was this shift of Southern support from Oscar W. Underwood to Woodrow Wilson that was the decisive factor in the proceedings. The efforts of Theodore Roosevelt—candidate of a third party—

to capture Southern votes by repudiating Negro affiliations proved entirely unsuccessful. The South voted solidly for Wilson.

Albert S. Burleson, the experienced Southern politician who became Wilson's Postmaster General, persuaded his chief to set aside scruples concerning appointments to favor a liberal distribution of the spoils of office to Southern congressmen and other influential politicians from their section. Southerners besides Burleson who obtained cabinet appointments were Josephus Daniels, Secretary of the Navy; James C. McReynolds of Tennessee and Thomas W. Gregory of Texas, successively Attorney General; William G. McAdoo, native Georgian, and Carter Glass of Virginia, successively Secretary of the Treasury; David F. Houston of Texas, Secretary of Agriculture.

The achievement of the President's legislative aims necessitated such favoritism since, under seniority rule, the chairmanships of the most important congressional committees were in the hands of Southerners. These congressmen rallied magnificently to Wilson's program. The liberal tariff of the administration was primarily the work of Underwood. The Federal Reserve Act was fathered by three natives of Lynchburg: Carter Glass, Senator Robert L. Owen of Oklahoma, and Samuel Untermyer, a New York attorney. Louis D. Brandeis, also of Southern birth, devised the antitrust law which was steered through Congress by Henry D. Clayton of Alabama. The charter of privileges of railroad workers bore the name William C. Adamson, congressman from Georgia. Legislation providing federal support for agricultural and home economics education was sponsored by two South Carolinians, A. Frank Lever and Ellison D. Smith. The only Wilsonian reforms Southerners would not champion were woman suffrage and liberal immigration laws.

When Wilson opposed intervention in World War I, Southerners acquiesced; when he decided that war with Germany was inevitable, the only Southern congressmen to vote negatively were Senator Vardaman of Mississippi, Representative Claude Kitchin of North Carolina, and two others. The national leadership in the war effort mainly rested with Northern industrialists, but Southern congressmen as a whole gave the support required of them by the chieftain of reform turned warmaker. Senators Benjamin R. Tillman and Claude A. Swanson of Virginia aided Josephus Daniels in developing the world's greatest navy; Senator Thomas S. Martin of Virginia sponsored huge appropriations; William G. McAdoo directed the co-ordination of railroads; Walter Hines Page, the liberal North Carolinian, while serving as ambassador to Great Britain helped to bring the United States into war on the English side; and Colonel House was the President's closest adviser and his roving ambassador in a Europe at war.

The most characteristic feature of the section's politics in the twentieth century was the survival of the Solid South—that is, the determination of all Southern states and practically every Southern county to vote for the Democratic party regardless of the issues and personalities involved. Cogent arguments were advanced by both political scientists and practical politicians against such a one-sided procedure. The very purpose of democracy was seemingly defeated by denying a voter the freedom of choice between two functioning parties. The failure of choice kept from the polls vast numbers who would have gone under more stimulating circumstances. In 1920, which may be taken as a typical year, only 21 per cent of the population of voting age cast their ballots in eleven states of the Solid South; in eleven non-Southern states of equal population in which the two-party system prevailed, three times this percentage of eligible voters cast their ballots.

Popular government in the South was largely destroyed in favor of increased power to self-perpetuating oligarchies. Steadfast adherence to one party seriously affected the influence of the section in the councils of both parties, since little was to be gained by courting the favor of states whose votes were predetermined. Defenders of the one-party system, however, offered arguments convincing to the majority of articulate Southerners. They felt that political division would threaten white supremacy as long as the Constitution of the United States continued to guarantee, even theoretically, the political privileges of the Negro. Accordingly it was deemed necessary to maintain Democratic dominance by retaining many of the post-Reconstruction restrictions on voting. When Republicans adopted the "lily-white" policy of repudiating Negro suffrage, Southern moralists pointed to the disreputable character of local Republican organizations, which seemed to exist for the corrupt purpose of distributing federal patronage. Against the assertion that the one-party system worked disadvantageously to the South in national elections was the fact that this system insured long tenure to Southern congressmen who secured influential committee assignments.

The result of these factors was that the Republican party, despite its great success in national elections in the years following World War I, enjoyed no lasting increases in its Southern vote. The Republican electorate approached the vanishing point in many Southern states; in 1932, for example, only 100 of the 1,743 members of the Southeastern state legislatures belonged to the party of Lincoln and Hoover; by 1949 this number had sunk to 53.[9] The one-party system in state politics appeared to be an immutable feature of Southern life.

[9] Howard W. Odum, *Southern Regions of the United States*, p. 129; and V. O. Key, Jr., *Southern Politics in State and Nation*, p. 408.

That the traditions which tied the South to the Democratic party could be reinterpreted in the light of modern conditions was proved by the revival of the Ku Klux Klan immediately after World War I. This second Ku Klux Klan was not, as some have maintained, an un-American aberration created by the semi-insane. Rather, "in its essence the thing was an authentic folk movement," "a meaningful witness of the continuity of the Southern sentiment," [10] lending vigorous expression to inherited prejudices against Negroes, Catholics, foreigners, and religious liberals. It enhanced its prestige by drawing from the South's past a historic regalia and ritual, and an equally historic pattern of violence. At the same time it was progressive in the perverse sense of that term; it recognized the new nationalism by failing to emphasize anti-Yankee sentiments, and by applying its concepts to twentieth-century problems. To a people troubled by Darwinism it affirmed Protestant Fundamentalism. To a country harassed by the diversities of culture and economic philosophy introduced by European immigrants it avowed the Anglo-Saxon way of life. To a Nordic majority allegedly threatened by the ambitions of Negroes, Jews, and south Europeans it held out the discipline of violence.

The second Ku Klux Klan was organized in October, 1915, "under a blazing, fiery torch" on top of Stone Mountain, Georgia, by Colonel William J. Simmons and thirty-four associates. It remained a Georgia group exclusively with only 5,000 members until 1920, when two professional publicity agents, Edward Y. Clarke and Mrs. Elizabeth Tyler, began a nationwide campaign for membership. The nationalistic, red-baiting, alien-hating America of the postwar years was ripe for their propaganda. By 1925 between four and five million Americans had enrolled. Fiery crosses burned in many parts of the United States; hooded Klansmen denounced Negroes, bootleggers, adulterers, Jews, pacifists, Bolsheviks, Catholics, and evolutionists; politicians in many states effectively used the Klan to win high office. Although it became more than a Southern organization, its greatest influence remained in the section of its origin. It dominated the politics of Texas, Oklahoma, and Louisiana. Membership was principally confined to the lower middle classes; however, men prominent in business and politics maintained relations with it, and the rural clergy of several states welcomed it as an agency of moral censorship.

The organization became more conservative when Hiram Wesley Evans succeeded Simmons as its chief in 1922. This change, however, did not prevent its decline after 1926. Northern newspapers exposed its secrecy, exaggerated its acts of violence, and ridiculed its ceremonials as mummery. The Southern press, along with such political leaders as

[10] Wilbur J. Cash, *The Mind of the South*, p. 335.

Oscar W. Underwood and Governor Thomas W. Hardwick of Georgia, joined in the chorus of condemnation. The Southern upper classes did not feel the need of an extralegal organization of their "inferiors" to maintain standards of race, patriotism, and religion already amply protected by law and custom. By 1928 the Ku Klux Klan had lost most of its Southern members; yet it was more than a passing phenomenon. Its standards of social and civic morality were those of the South, and should they again be threatened, it is likely that the hooded order or a similar group would arise.

At the time of the decline of the Ku Klux Klan the South graphically illustrated the lasting vitality of one of the cardinal principles of this much-criticized organization. In 1928 the national Democratic party stretched the loyalty of the section to the breaking point by nominating a Catholic for President. Most of the Democratic state organizations supported Al Smith, but the people of Virginia, North Carolina, Florida, Tennessee, and Texas cast majorities for his victorious Republican opponent, Herbert Hoover. The South opposed Smith because he was a Roman Catholic, an antiprohibitionist, and a product of the notorious Tammany Hall machine of New York City.

There would have been no objections had the party candidate been a high church Episcopalian professing Catholic doctrines, but nationalistic prejudices were offended by his allegiance to a church so largely alien in its composition and having as its head an Italian potentate. The Southern sense of propriety was offended by Smith's brown derby, his vaudeville manners, East Side dialect, plebeian wife, and his drinking habits. The vote against Smith did not mean that the South had turned Republican; actually, the more prejudiced Democrats of the anti-Yankee, anti-Negro, and anti-Catholic variety were responsible. Once their votes had removed the Catholic menace, these recusants returned to the old party.

The South remained solidly Democratic because to do so did not preclude vital intraparty contests in many states. Dissent was permissible in state and county elections within the not too narrow limits of race and party. Suffrage requirements in primary elections were broad enough to include the majority of whites of both sexes who wished to qualify, and the contests were often sufficiently spirited to attract most of the eligible voters. Contrasts in personalities and principles of rival candidates were frequently striking and sometimes fundamental as, for example, between progressive businessmen and agrarian demagogues. Over and above the fulsome proclamations of loyalty to race and party which the South always demanded of its office-seekers were interests of class and economics as vital as those that divided politicians in other sections of the country.

HARRY FLOOD BYRD. *The conservative South finds its most satisfying expression in this businessman and farmer who has been the unchallenged ruler of Virginia in the twentieth century for a longer period than that enjoyed by Sir William Berkeley in the seventeenth century.*

ELLEN GLASGOW. *First among the South's women novelists, this Virginian combined realistic observation and subtle imagination to produce the most complete and intimate history of a Southern state.*

WILLIAM FAULKNER. First among the South's men novelists, he tells, with tragic insight, of a grand civilization fallen into decay because of its sins and the sins of Yankee aggressors.

HUEY LONG. By methods as ruthless and as violent as are possible on this side of the Caribbean Sea, he tried to capture for the common man a fairer share of the wealth created by a triumphant industrialism.

The South rallied to the support of the second Democratic president of the twentieth century as it did in the case of Woodrow Wilson. The aristocratic manners and speech of Franklin D. Roosevelt appealed to the genteel tradition, and his professed love for the common man stirred the Southern masses, especially the disfranchised Negro. While Roosevelt, unlike Wilson, could not claim Southern birth, his repeated visits to a Georgia health resort enabled him to regard the South as his second home. A product of the New York political machine, he depended upon a group of young intellectuals known as the Brains Trust, to which the South furnished not a single member. Nevertheless, Roosevelt pleased the South by allowing James A. Farley, his patronage boss, to distribute offices more lavishly than Wilson would have tolerated. The poorest section of the nation soon recognized obvious advantages in the outstanding feature of the regime—liberal spending to relieve distress. Alarm over the fact that Negroes were to be included in this policy was allayed by placing these expenditures in Southern white hands. In this way racial discriminations were possible. Southern public opinion accepted the New Deal, and the majority of Southern congressmen voted for such earlier measures as AAA, NIRA, and the relief laws.

In 1937, however, a group of distinguished Southern leaders began to quarrel with Roosevelt radicalism. Senators Harry F. Byrd, Carter Glass, Walter F. George of Georgia, Ellison D. Smith of South Carolina, Josiah W. Bailey of North Carolina, and Millard E. Tydings of Maryland attempted to obstruct the New Deal at every turn, while Representatives Howard W. Smith of Virginia and Eugene Cox of Georgia specialized in attacking its labor laws. Representative Clifton A. Woodrum of Virginia opposed its relief expenditures, and Representative Martin Dies of Texas sought to expose the alleged communism of certain officials. The dissenting Southerners manifested profound alarm over the President's reputed desire to change the Constitution by enlarging the Supreme Court. They were promptly accused by Roosevelt's more radical friends of being agents of big business who were protected from the people's wrath by the restricted franchises of their states. Taking advantage of his immense personal popularity, Roosevelt tried to prevent the re-election of the two Smiths, Tydings, and George in 1938; however, this attempted purge failed. When the genial Chief Executive appeared to be kindly disposed toward these candidates, Southern voters, putting personalities above principles, refused to take literally Roosevelt's advice to vote against his friends. They re-elected the reactionary congressmen, at the same time indicating their intention of voting for Roosevelt again if given the chance.

Despite this group of dissenters, there were Southern congressmen

who served Franklin D. Roosevelt almost as effectively as their prede-
cessors had supported Wilson. The administration's floor leaders in the
Senate were, successively, Pat Harrison of Mississippi and Alben W.
Barkley of Kentucky; the party whip was James F. Byrnes of South
Carolina. Vice-President Garner for a time aided the administration
as a manipulator of the parliamentary machinery. Robert L. Doughton
of North Carolina proved tireless in his services as chairman of the
House Ways and Means Committee.

Cordell Hull of Tennessee, Secretary of State, enjoyed considerable
respect as the Roosevelt mouthpiece in foreign affairs, and as the nego-
tiator of the Hull Tariff Reciprocity treaties. Hugo L. Black of Alabama served the President ably, first as senator, later as a member of
the United States Supreme Court. This one-time member of the Ku
Klux Klan became a distinguished liberal; as a legislator, he sponsored
the Wagner Labor Relations Act; as a jurist, he defended the civil rights
of Negroes, and destroyed the conception of the federal common law
as a protector of corporations against civil suits. Among Southerners,
James F. Byrnes served Roosevelt with greatest distinction. He graduated from the Senate to the Supreme Court and subsequently became
Director of Economic Stabilization, Director of War Mobilization, and
Secretary of State. Byrnes was virtually an Assistant President of the
United States, a liaison officer between Congress and the administration, an arbitrator in economic and social matters related to the conduct
of World War II, and spokesman of the nation's policies in the difficult
postwar period.

No Roosevelt innovation caused more suspicion below the Potomac
than the radicalism of the administration toward the Negro. Without
violating the Southern caste system by the appointment of Negroes to
office in the South, Roosevelt won colored support by giving the race
a fair share of relief funds along with that economic and social democracy identified with the New Deal. Negroes in limited numbers were
appointed to federal office in the North. To these measures were added
the activities of the First Lady of the land, who associated with blacks
and spoke freely against denials of their constitutional rights. The South
grew alarmed but did not break with the administration. Some observers read in Eleanor Roosevelt's conduct not true interracial frater-
nity, but merely an aristocrat's benevolence toward the underprivileged.
Opportunists secretly applauded a policy which strengthened the
Democratic party with Negro votes in the border and northern states
without interfering with the political status of the race in the South.

The wisdom of this attitude was questioned in 1942 when a filibuster
by Southern senators alone prevented a combination of Northern Democrats and Republicans from pushing through Congress a measure

abolishing the poll tax as a requirement for voting in congressional and Presidential elections. In that year Virginia, South Carolina, Georgia, Alabama, Mississippi, Tennessee, Texas, and Arkansas still enforced this requirement. Apprehensions over the effect of its possible repeal were not altogether justified. Realists doubted the constitutionality of over-throwing the time-honored practice of leaving the regulation of elections to the states. They knew that apart from the poll tax there were other barriers to the free exercise of suffrage under the South's complex primary and election rulings. Some even doubted the sincerity of the sponsors of the anti-poll tax bill, and pointed out that genuine advocates of Negro suffrage would have sought to enforce the provisions of the Fourteenth Amendment allowing reductions in the congressional representations of states which deprived citizens of the suffrage.

Between 1900 and 1940 the South did not assume as important a role in American politics as it had a hundred years earlier. The new South produced no presidents of the United States and no great philosopher-statesmen who in the manner of Jefferson and Calhoun could offer elaborate justifications of the sectional interests and ambitions. Loss of a sense of destiny made for mediocrity among Southern political leaders. Nevertheless eminent politicians continued to enjoy, if they did not always deserve, public esteem. Some were eloquent demagogues who gave poignant albeit confused expression to the grievances of the poorer classes; others were enlightened conservatives who carried old common-wealths along the road of economic and social progress. In administrative reform and welfare work several Southern states stood abreast of certain Northern and Western states with greater reputations for progressiveness. If local government in the South was less advanced than in other sections, at least it was conducted with comparative honesty. When national administrations of the Democratic party gained power, Southern statesmen demonstrated capacities for leadership at once constructive and conspicuous. A sober conservatism, pleasing to men of common sense, was the salient characteristic of those Southerners who carried weight in national councils. Certain phases of Southern politics prompted sharp criticisms, among them the one-party system, the suppression of voting privileges of Negroes and other humble persons, the electorate's tolerance of rabble-rousers, and the growth of machine politics. These alleged evils are explained by the historian in the light of the social and economic circumstances of Southern life; perhaps they were no more pronounced than similar practices in other sections of the United States.

CHAPTER XXXII

World War II

--»»-«««

WORLD WAR II exerted a powerful influence upon the South. The greatest war in history enveloped the quiet land below the Potomac in a whirl of activities that in many places altered its actual appearance. Southerners by thousands went to work in the great war industries of the North and to fight in distant regions of the world. Others flocked to the war-expanded cities of their own section. A traditionally impoverished people enjoyed the greatest prosperity it had ever known. Strenuous efforts were made to convert Southern habits to the ideals of a nation fighting to break the barriers of race and caste erected by dictatorships overseas. A sifting of the evidence, however, reveals that the patterns of social behavior that lent distinction to the prewar South underwent remarkably few changes as result of the war. The region was prepared to make all sacrifices necessary to win the war for the Four Freedoms, but it felt that external enemies, not Southerners, had committed the sins that made the war imperative. Germany and Japan were the targets of this bloody crusade, which Southerners believed could be won without injecting the Southern issue.

That the South did not regard the national aims as inimical to its interests is evident by the zeal with which all sections of Southern opinion accepted the challenge of war. This applied to conservatives and New Dealers, whites and Negroes alike. Its feeling in the national controversy between interventionists and isolationists was revealed by the vote of its representatives in Congress on the first Lend-Lease measure in the spring of 1941. Only one Southern senator and five representatives were among the 202 congressmen who opposed this desire of the American people to give material support to the enemies of the

Axis powers. Robert R. Reynolds of North Carolina, the one senator who voted in the negative, lost public favor to such an extent that he did not stand for re-election in 1944. So great was the enthusiasm of Southern congressmen for the war effort that they set aside beliefs concerning the sacredness of private property in order to vote solidly for a provision of the Selective Service Act broadening the power of the President to seize defense plants when production was interrupted.[1] When the Gallup poll of public opinion in the autumn of 1941 asked whether it were preferable to keep the United States out of war or to defeat Germany, 88 per cent of the Southern people, in comparison with 70 per cent in the nation as a whole, thought Germany's defeat more important.

The proportion of Southerners who enlisted in the army before the draft was organized was so unusually large that an Alabama congressman asserted that the federal government "had to start selective service to keep our Southern boys from filling up the army." [2] As early as 1940 Canadians began to call their air corps the Royal Texas Air Force. "To Southerners, then," said the novelist James Boyd in 1944,[3] "Pearl Harbor was no shock; it was a relief. Better still, it was, in their notion, an overdue reminder to the Yankees to cast off their stupor and gird themselves for what had long been obvious to their more astute fellow citizens below the Potomac."

There are many explanations of the warlike inclinations of the Southern people. They inherited to the greatest degree the pro-British, antiforeign, and military inclinations of Americans. Their preachers, editors, and professors had given ample lip service to the pacifist dogmas popular in the twenties and thirties. However, such doctrinal novelties had no profound influence upon a people whose model Christians were Robert E. Lee and Stonewall Jackson. The relatively poor population of the section saw in the anticipated lavish expenditures of war unparalleled opportunities for employment and for the winning of personal distinction and gain. The most specific explanation of the South's views was that war leadership would be in the hands of their party chieftain, to whom they were accustomed to giving blind allegiance.

In 1917 Southerners had hesitated to go to war when their leader, Woodrow Wilson, essentially dedicated to peace and neutrality, struggled against entering the contest. There were no such inhibitions in the 1938–41 crisis, because Franklin D. Roosevelt was neither neutral nor pacifist. Indeed, he was the type of Christian warrior whose preachings

[1] V. O. Key, Jr., *Southern Politics in State and Nation*, p. 372.

[2] Luther Patrick cited by John Temple Graves, "The Fighting South," *The Virginia Quarterly Review*, XVIII, 61 (Winter, 1942).

[3] "The South and the Fight," *The Atlantic Monthly*, CLXXIII, 53 (February, 1944).

appealed to the South, and it accepted with alacrity his division of mankind into the peaceful and the aggressor nations. Southerners believed with him that the way to regain the soul of a nation was to lose it in a great crusade. Leaders such as Harry F. Byrd who disapproved of the New Deal's vast expenditures hoped to drown that experiment in the still vaster expenditures of war. Southern liberals, on the other hand, recognized in a war for American ideals a chance to lift the South out of its past. For the region to forget for a time its hates in favor of the primary problems of the world, wrote a liberal journalist in 1942,[4] "may do something to save the South from the mess of Communism and Ku Kluxery after the war."

Never before did the South experience such an upsurge of its population. Three million people left its farms and small towns to enter the armed forces or war industries. A few were bitter over the country's demands for unaccustomed hardships and sacrifices, and many knew the meaning of tragic news from battlefields. Nevertheless the Southern people as a whole derived keen exaltation from their war experiences. The lack of understanding of war aims characteristic of the more ignorant segments of the population in 1917 was not apparent in 1941. Public schools and the radio were largely responsible for this. The Southerner, more than the average American, could make use of both the exalted and the debased in the national ideals.

A people who cherished the memory of Woodrow Wilson, who had produced an international moralist of the caliber of Cordell Hull, and possessed a small army of ministers, editors, and professors proclaiming democracy and Christian brotherhood, were not slow to see in Hitler and Hirohito the very embodiment of racism, militarism, antidemocracy, denial of personal rights, and subjection of religious and cultural liberty. On the other hand, Southerners easily succumbed to the belief that the sins of such an enemy were analogous to those of certain minority groups in the United States. The cause was race. The Japanese were regarded as hideous persons of color, endowed by nature with a unique and cunning cruelty. The Germans were considered blond beasts whose diabolical notions of superiority necessitated a ruthless reckoning.

The war brought certain personal gains. The wealthy and commercial classes obtained large profits from rentals, retail sales, and war contracts. Main streets near the army camps took on the brisk tempo of busy metropolises. The equalitarian procedures of the army and other federal agencies warmed the hearts of simple folk. There was the satisfaction of knowing that a wealthy neighbor had no more sugar or gasoline than oneself; that his son was drafted into the army under exactly

[4] Graves, *loc. cit.*, p. 71.

the same conditions as one's own boy, and might come home on furlough with no higher military rank or more ribbons and medals. Many Southerners, for the first time in their lives, gained a feeling of social security and economic well-being, because they had sufficient clothing, food, wages, family allotments, and other benefits that a generous government bestowed upon its soldiers and war workers. The arrival in Southern camps of young men from all sections of the United States afforded local girls welcome opportunities for romance on a scale unknown since the days of the Confederacy.

The Negro, despite the continued handicaps of caste, derived an exaltation from the war in some respects more intense than that of the Southern white man. He was confronted with a Japanese enemy so unattractive that, in comparison, he was an angel of light and a god of beauty. The German was represented as a racial enemy who would destroy all the realities and promises of democracy and place the black man in the lowest category in the hierarchy of races. Quota restrictions had to be placed upon Negro enlistments to prevent the army from becoming overloaded with blacks. There were visions of a new world, some sort of second Emancipation by which the American dream of politico-economic equality would be realized by its underprivileged tenth. President and Mrs. Roosevelt became a second Massa and Missus Lincoln. From the free atmosphere of Northern cities came strident cries from Negro intellectuals who demanded that Southern conduct be squared with the democratic professions of the nation.

Southern liberals used the social and economic readjustments of war to improve race relations, and Southern church groups demonstrated an unprecedented awareness of the disparity between Christian professions and practices. The white clergy, on formal occasions at least, fraternized with the black clergy to the extent of breaking bread with them. Negro girls and women found work in war plants and joined the army. As proof that the promised equalities of war were no mere dream, colored soldiers by the hundred thousands experienced the benefits of liberal pay, ample clothing and food, and contacts with unprejudiced whites. Photographs came back of colored soldiers warmly welcomed in Australia, England, and France, and parading before the emaciated populace of India, or joining their white countrymen in lording it over the conquered master race of Germany.

It should not be assumed that the hell of war abroad resulted in a heaven at home. World War II produced its irritants and its trials. A serious difficulty was the depletion of labor springing from the largest emigration in Southern history. Nearly 3 million Southerners moved to the industries of the North and the West; Southern farm population fell by 3,203,000 as compared with a corresponding decrease of only

1,867,000 for the rest of the United States; Southern farm acreage fell 7 per cent, while that of the rest of the nation increased 15 per cent.[5] Unable to meet the wage competition of the war industries, many farmers were forced to suspend or curtail operations. They accused the federal government of imposing impossible price ceilings upon farm products, thus encouraging flight of farm labor into the army, of fixing artificially high wage scales, and of encouraging indolence through payments to soldiers' families.

These complaints were met by the liberalization of draft exemptions of farm laborers, and by the attempt of the War Manpower Commission to compel agricultural workers to stay on their jobs. These efforts, however, were largely negated by relentless demands of draft boards and by the organization among Negroes of some sort of second underground railroad through which they escaped to the high wages of the cities.

The privileged classes of the South resented the rationing, high income taxes, and rent controls necessitated by total war. In Texas and in the states of the upper South they expressed their disapproval by voting against the Roosevelt administration. Most irritating to the middle classes was the Negroes' desertion of domestic service, with colored women quitting in favor of higher-paying war jobs. As the result of allowances from soldier husbands and sons, many abandoned the care of white households and children in order to look after their own families. "The inconvenience of being without the familiar Negro domestics," said a colored writer in 1944,[6] "has proved to be one of the most intimate effects of the war in many households." Although this movement was the natural result of new opportunities provided by war industries, the white South interpreted it in personal terms. It was adjudged a disagreeable form of social insubordination, inspired by the words and deeds of Mrs. Roosevelt. Servants allegedly were organizing Eleanor Clubs and Disappointment Clubs to celebrate their new-found freedom from household drudgery.

What employers lost through the upheaval of war became their employees' gain. The poorer classes of the South once more resorted to their main weapons of defense—migration from economically depressed areas to regions offering better opportunities. The whites moved first, entering the more skilled and higher-paying positions; the Negroes were not far behind, taking advantage of ever-increasing manpower shortages to advance their economic status. The Hampton Roads-Newport News area gained 200,000 in population between 1940 and 1943; the Mobile section, 150,000; the southern Florida, Charleston, Jacksonville, and

[5] Calvin B. Hoover and B. U. Ratchford, *Economic Resources and Policies of the South*, p. 92.

[6] Charles S. Johnson in *Social Forces*, XXIII, 29 (October, 1944).

Knoxville regions, between 40 and 80,000. "In Waco," came a report from Texas in 1944,[7] "the population has increased from 55,000 to 110,000 within the past two years. . . . Waco's growth is small compared with that of Houston, Dallas, and Fort Worth." The number of persons employed in manufacturing increased from 1,650,000 to 2,835,000. Those employed in shipbuilding and aircraft construction rose from 20,000 to twenty-five times that number. In the Southeast alone, unemployment dropped from 626,000 to 80,000; many of the unemployed were persons moving from one job to another.

The bottom of the Southern manpower barrel had been scraped. "A number of elderly men have turned up and surprisingly many middle-aged women," wrote one who visited the employment office of a great Gulf city in 1943.[8] "There are children still of high school age who have taken courses in metal working, women whose husbands and sons have gone to war . . . , gray-haired men who wrenched themselves loose from habits of a lifetime and gone to school again in the machine shops. . . . By themselves at one end in dusty overalls stand a group of very black back-country Negroes." The income of the Southern people became higher than ever before; total wage payments rose from $308,923,-727 for the second quarter of 1940 to $738,500,977 for the same period in 1943, with the average weekly wage increased from $18.60 to $30.75. Those who were dissatisfied with the South's wage scale journeyed northward and secured employment in the industries of Detroit, Pittsburgh, and Chicago at almost fabulous wages.

"Due to conditions arising out of the war," wrote Dillard B. Lasseter in 1944,[9] "the South has undergone more economic changes in two years than in any previous fifty." For a variety of reasons a majority of military installations were developed south of the Potomac and the Ohio —Langley Field and camps Lee and Pickett in Virginia, Fort Bragg in North Carolina, Fort Jackson in South Carolina, Fort Knox in Kentucky, Fort Benning in Georgia, Maxwell Field in Alabama, Fort Sam Houston and Corpus Christi Naval Station in Texas. The business of supplying the South's chain of military establishments gave employment and prosperity to thousands, and turned large areas into bustling centers of production and trade.

Economically more stimulating were the war industries. The federal government and private industry spent $4,500,000,000 for the construction and expansion of chemical, ammunition, shipbuilding, and other industries in the South. By 1944 six Southern states had been awarded $7,000,000,000 in war contracts. "A bird's-eye view of large-scale South-

[7] *Christian Century*, LXI, 149 (February 2, 1944).
[8] John Dos Passos, "The People at War," *Harper's Magazine*, CLXXXVII, 260 (August, 1943).
[9] *Social Forces*, XXIII, 20 (October, 1944).

ern industry," wrote the chairman of the War Production Board in 1944,[10] "makes you feel that the South has rubbed Aladdin's lamp." The largest combination powder and explosive plant in the country operated near Birmingham; the biggest bomber and modification plant was at Marietta, Georgia. Huntsville, Alabama, possessed the largest chemical warfare plant, and from Maryland to Texas other great chemical plants turned out high explosives and synthetic rubber. Dallas had one of the world's largest aviation factories; other great airplane-producing centers in the South were located at Birmingham, Nashville, New Orleans, and Houston. Shipbuilding areas dotted the Southern shore from the Chesapeake to Corpus Christi; ships were going to sea from places as far inland as Memphis, Nashville, and Decatur in Alabama. In every section of the vast Southern woodlands men hewed materials for the pulp wood industry, whose fifty mills turned out 2.5 million tons of kraft paper and board. Southern cellulose and lignin were increasingly employed to make rayon, cellophane, lacquer and plastic products, and from Southern turpentine came isophene, important in the manufacture of synthetic rubber. The most sensational industrial development of the entire war occurred at Oak Ridge, Tennessee, where atomic bombs were produced.

One of the most remarkable features of the war period was the Southern people's adaptability and inventiveness, almost Yankee-like in its ingenuity. The war industries made skilled and semiskilled workers of many farm boys, while executives handled difficult problems with an ability comparable to that of their ancestors who directed the destinies of the South during the Civil War. Conversions of peacetime industries to war uses excited the admiration of the chairman of the War Production Board, who described a citrus-canning machinery industry manufacturing parts for merchant ships; a mechanical-pencil manufacturer making bomb parts and precision instruments; a chenille-bedspread mill manufacturing mosquito netting; and concerns which once made cotton-gin machinery producing ordnance.

The heightened activities of war, despite their rushed appearance, were accompanied by a thoughtful regard for the South's industrial future. Plans were formulated for the time when it would be feasible to beat the sword into the plowshare. There developed what one writer calls "an entirely new attitude towards raw materials." [11] This took the form of plans for the conservation of forest, petroleum, gas, and other natural resources. Agencies were established for the discovery of better methods of exploiting the regional wealth. These researches were car-

[10] Donald M. Nelson, "The South's Economic Opportunity," *The American Mercury*, LIX, 423 (October, 1944).
[11] William Haynes, *Southern Horizons*, p. 15.

ried on in the laboratories of state universities and engineering colleges, by the Cotton Research Committee of Texas, by the Southern Regional Laboratory at New Orleans, by the North Carolina Textile Foundation, and by the Callaway Institute at La Grange, Georgia.

The co-operative efforts of powerful business interests were applied to industrial advancement through the Southern Research Institute, founded at Birmingham on October 4, 1944. Within six months of its inception, this organization had on its laboratory work benches projects concerned with cotton textiles, cottonseed products, tobacco, peanuts, citrus by-products, essential oils, metallurgy, and mechanical problems. Among many discoveries stimulated by wartime needs were the improvement of cotton-picking machines, the perfection of a mechanical saw for cutting timber, the development of tung-oil plantations in northern Florida and southern Mississippi, the culture of ramie fiber in the Everglades; and new uses were found for the sweet potato, cotton, and other products of Southern fields and forests.

A long fight against railroad freight-rate discriminations, of which Southern shippers were the victims, was brought to a head by Ellis G. Arnall, the dynamic young governor of Georgia. He spoke of "the freight-rate cartel" which hindered the industrial development of the South, and appealed to the Supreme Court for relief. While this litigation was pending, the Interstate Commerce Commission put into effect on August 1, 1945, an order which Arnall exultantly declared "will make it possible for Southern industry to compete on the domestic market." The ruling of the Interstate Commerce Commission advanced "class-freight rates" 10 per cent in the North and East, and reduced them 10 per cent in the South and West. Although, as will be shown,[12] it is doubtful that this decree will fulfill Arnall's hopes, it represented a definite beginning in the direction of destroying one of the outstanding obstacles to Southern industrial progress.

The South's willingness to help defeat those nations conspiring to destroy democracy and equality was not enough; to satisfy outside opinion it must abolish, or at least modify, its own racial attitude. A government and a people waging a desperate war against a European country whose chief crime was the proscription of a supposedly inferior race felt logically bound to discourage similar practices among its own citizens. Only filibusters and other dilatory tactics by Southern senators prevented Congress from making lynching a federal offense and outlawing poll taxes as a voting requirement in national elections. The United States Supreme Court in a Texas case of 1944 declared the exclusion of Negroes from white primaries a violation of the Fifteenth Amendment; in a Virginia case of 1946 the court ruled that a state

[12] See below, p. 593.

could not require the segregation of races on buses crossing state lines. The United States Army, consistent with anti-Nazi standards, issued orders against segregation, and in 1943 published a pamphlet citing the biological equality of races.[13]

While President Roosevelt at Warm Springs, Georgia, in 1938 inveighed against the anti-Jewish Nuremberg laws of Hitler, the First Lady, at nearby Birmingham, denounced the Jim Crow laws of Alabama. Wendell Willkie called upon Hollywood to change its Negro stereotypes, and film audiences were introduced to new Negro talents. Plays on the New York stage like *Strange Fruit* and *Deep Are the Roots* showed the effects of segregation, race prejudices, and conscious discriminations in the South. The mass-circulation magazines to some degree departed from conventional treatments of Negroes in favor of articles proclaiming their achievements and disputing the findings of theorists. When the D.A.R. refused the use of its Washington hall to Marian Anderson in 1939 there was a great outpouring of high officials, as well as common folk, to hear the banned artist sing from the Lincoln Memorial.

Negro leaders were bitter over denials to their race. As the novelist, Pearl Buck, stated, they felt that "what they have been taught and have believed is not true—namely, that if the colored people can be patient and good and show themselves obedient and humble they will inevitably prove themselves worthy citizens and will therefore receive the rewards of full citizenship." They belligerently demanded that the federal government order a nationwide abandonment of segregation. They protested the government policy that established shipyards and army aviation units exclusively for Negroes, and asked for mixed army units of whites and blacks, with Negro officers commanding some of them. The War Department pointed out the difficulty of effecting such a revolution, whereupon it was charged that the American cause would suffer severely among the colored people of Asia and Africa. One Negro writer declared, "The military leaders would rather lose the war than see us have equality." When Southern Negrophiles warned that a radical policy would inevitably lead to devastating riots, the colored press would not concede sincerity of motive. White moderates were called "spiritual kinsmen of Hitler," colored moderates, "weasel-minded gentry who put property rights above human rights."

Most intransigent of the Negro leaders was A. Philip Randolph, president of the Brotherhood of Sleeping Car Porters, who organized the March-on-Washington movement. Colored persons were to converge on the national capital for the purpose of forcing concessions. "If

[13] Ruth Benedict and Gene Wellfish, *The Races of Mankind*, Public Affairs Pamphlet, No. 85, 1943.

the President," asserted Randolph, "does not issue a war proclamation to abolish Jim Crow in Washington, the District of Columbia, and all government departments and the armed forces, colored people are going to *march;* and we don't give a damn what happens. . . . Rather that we die standing upon our feet fighting for our rights than to exist upon our knees begging for life."

The South made certain wartime concessions to the Negroes. This partly was a response to the logic of wartime liberalism, partly an extension of that benevolence which Southern upper classes and public officials had learned to bestow upon the Negroes. Southerners, as in the past, professed what Gunnar Myrdal called the American Creed. It assumes the fundamental equality of all men and their inalienable right to freedom, justice, and opportunity.

Perhaps more in the 1940's than previously Southerners recognized the underprivileged position of the Negro as a century-long lag in public morals which demanded immediate action. As Christians or Jeffersonians they felt the need to put into practice their brotherly assertions; as statesmen and realists they believed they must act before outside revolutionary forces enveloped them in some such debacle as had befallen their grandfathers in 1865. "The real doubt," wrote a student of Southern life in 1944, "is that the region believes its own racial postulates as deeply as it believes in the fundamental implications of the American Creed." This faith made it impossible for the South "to exclude the Negro altogether from opportunities for education and self-advancement" and stirred hope of important changes.[14]

What actually can be chalked up in justification of such hope? The churches led the way. They devoted increased study to the race problem and acted to modify the harsher phases of racial incompatibility, in some instances abolishing the eighty-year-old custom of racial separation in clerical gatherings. Southern universities and colleges broke away from provincial patterns of thought to enter into the intellectual currents of the nation and the world at large. Southern newspapers bent backward to be fair to Negroes in their news columns and frequently used their editorial space to preach humane racial views. In 1943 at Atlanta the Southern Regional Council, composed of members of both races, was formed as the successor of the dissolved Commission on Interracial Cooperation.

Taking advantage of the increased revenues of wartime, state and municipal welfare agencies spent unprecedented amounts on Negro betterment. By 1944 most Southern states gracefully accepted federal court orders requiring the elimination of race differentials in the payment of

[14] Charles S. Johnson, "Race Relations in the South Today," *Social Forces*, XXIII, 29–30 (October, 1944).

public school teachers. "North Carolina," said the governor of that state,[15] "recognizes the justice of equal pay for all teachers." By 1944 Negroes were on police forces in twenty-one Southern cities. In 1943 an adverse vote of the state supreme court prevented Tennessee from abolishing the poll tax as a requirement for voting. In 1945 this provision was eliminated in Georgia, and some 80,000 Negroes voted in that state's Democratic primary in the summer of 1946.

Most radical of all war measures affecting the status of the Negro was that issued by President Roosevelt on June 25, 1941. The Chief Executive's order struck so near the roots of race discriminations that a Negro journalist termed it "probably the most revolutionary bit of legislation yet passed in America." [16] The Fair Employment Practice directive stipulated that "there shall be no discrimination in the employment of workers in defense industries or government because of race, creed, color, or national origin." To make this principle effective, contracting agencies of the United States government were required to include provisions in all war contracts by which they agreed to omit racial discrimination from their employment policies.

The Committee on Fair Employment Practice was created with authority to investigate complaints and to "take appropriate steps" to eliminate the discriminations forbidden by the order. Thus the President seized the opportunity to set aside the handicaps to free employment which always represented one of the principal burdens of the Negro. His decision was tantamount to telling the great producing agencies of the country that they were threatened with the loss of government contracts unless they were willing to treat the Negro fairly. Under the able direction of Bishop Francis J. Haas of the Roman Catholic church, the Committee on Fair Employment Practice exposed many cases of discrimination and promptly eliminated numerous abuses. Perhaps its most outstanding achievements were in the field of the federal civil service. The percentage of Negroes working for the government rose from 9.8 in 1938 to 12 in 1943.[17]

The nearest approach to revolution in Southern life was the immense gains which wartime employment gave to Negroes. Nonwhite workers in firms reporting to the War Manpower Commission climbed from less than 3 per cent early in 1942 to 8.3 per cent in November, 1944. A million and a half colored persons had been admitted into war industries. The 1945 ruling of the National War Labor Board providing equal pay for equal work was written by Frank P. Graham, a white North Carolinian. Perhaps even more significant than these employment gains was

[15] Joseph M. Broughton, cited in *Christian Century*, LXI, 89 (January 19, 1944).
[16] Arthur P. Davis in *The Journal of Negro Education*, XX, 12 (Winter, 1943).
[17] John A. Davis in *The Annals of the American Academy of Political and Social Science*, CCXLIV, 72 (March, 1946).

the fact that blacks in constantly growing numbers were allowed to join labor unions. By October, 1944, half a million Southern Negroes were members of these organizations. In the great new mass-production industries the objectives of labor could best be secured by organizing into one big union all workers regardless of skills or race.

For the first time since Reconstruction, Southern Negroes could participate in groups which exercised power over the destinies of the American nation. One fourth of those who attended the 1943 Southern War Labor Conference of the American Federation of Labor were Negroes. To a limited degree, notably in the Southern Tenant Farmers' Union of the Memphis area and among the mine and smelter workers of the Birmingham area, unions were formed with whites and blacks on an equal footing. Although the abandonment of peacetime restrictions on Negro labor was partially due to the proddings of the Committee on Fair Employment Practice and of liberal labor leaders and journalists, the main reason sprang from the necessity of meeting unprecedented labor demands. Engaged in total war, America could not permit racial prejudice to stand in the way of its objective. Southern whites demonstrated their eagerness to do their share by employing Negroes in new positions.

Governmental policy toward the Negro in the armed services during World War II was similar to that of World War I. The principle that the number of Negroes called to the colors should be in proportion to its percentage of the total population by the end of 1944 led to the enlistment of 701,678 in the Army; 148,769 in the Navy; 5,072 in the Marines; and 3,556 in the Coast Guard. The pay, insurance, and family benefits allowed Negro soldiers were exactly the same as those of whites. Because of certain cultural deficiencies the Negro benefitted more than others from the generous educational program in the armed services. More than half the colored soldiers were sent overseas. The Ninety-Second Division saw combat service in Italy, the Ninety-Third Division auxiliary service in the Pacific. The fact that a majority of Negroes were assigned to labor battalions did not keep them out of danger or prevent individuals from winning military citations. Negro labor was utilized most effectively in the construction of the 1,621-mile military highway connecting the United States with Alaska.

Through pressure exerted by Negro organizations, blacks received more advantages in war services than they had enjoyed during World War I. Dean William H. Hastie of the Howard University Law School was appointed civilian aide to the Secretary of War for Negro Affairs, and Benjamin O. Davis became the first Negro in American history to wear the star of a Brigadier General. For the first time there were colored army aviators, and the all-Negro Ninety-Ninth Pursuit Squadron saw combat service over Italy. Negro officers numbered 5,804 and were trained together with white men. Negroes served in the Navy in other than menial capacities; there were 28 Negro naval officers. Colored women were admitted to the Woman's Army Corps. Orders were issued prohibiting the segregation of races in hospitals and post exchanges. In the autumn of 1944, when all available manpower was needed for the final push into Germany, Negro volunteers from the less active branches of the service were organized into platoons. They performed effective combat service scattered among white units. "From many points of view," wrote an observer,[18] "the United States Army is at present doing more for the advancement of the Negro than has any other agency, governmental or private, since the Civil War granted the race its freedom."

Despite all these changes, World War II caused no fundamental alteration in the inherited patterns of Southern life. Southerners resisted with violence, or threats of violence, any interference with their customary racial standards. They opposed successfully all attempts of the Negro to assume political power and prevented the destruction of race distinctions both in the armed forces and war industries. The contacts of war did not stifle sectional prejudices, nor did the prodigious expansion of war industries alter the relative position of the South in the national economy.

The South's habit of resorting to violence when Negroes became "insubordinate" was applied with the proved effectiveness of bygone days. In 1942 several disturbances between white policemen and colored soldiers occurred. At Alexandria, Louisiana, on January 10 of that year, a dispute over the arrest of a Negro soldier led to a melee between colored soldiers and white policemen in which twenty-nine Negroes were injured. At Fort Dix, New Jersey, on the following April 3, three persons were killed in a fifteen-minute battle between Negro soldiers and white military police of Southern origin. The director of the Federal Bureau of Investigation in 1943 warned against "civil violence, race riots, and insidious campaigns against minority groups" which, he averred, were "rapidly approaching flood-tide proportions." [19]

True to this prediction, the race disturbances of 1943 were the worst since World War I. The most serious one occurred on June 20 at Detroit, where racial tensions of long standing were aggravated by the arrival of Southerners of both races to work in various war industries. A fight between a white man and a Negro precipitated a fifteen-hour battle in which 30 persons were killed, 700 injured, and considerable

---

[18] *The Americana Annual*, 1945, p. 526.
[19] Cited in *The Annals of the American Academy of Political and Social Science*, CCXLIV, 82 (March, 1946).

property looted or destroyed. The Detroit disturbance was followed by a riot less than two months later in the Harlem section of New York City. Negroes, aroused by false reports that a colored soldier had been killed by a policeman, engaged in indiscriminate looting. Order was restored by white and Negro policemen after five Negroes had been killed and $225,000 worth of property destroyed. The Zoot-Suit riots were noisy disturbances in several cities, notably in Los Angeles, between white sailors and Mexican and Negro youths dressed in the bizarre fashion affected by youths of the lower classes.

Although the South had no racial outbreaks of a magnitude comparable to those of Detroit and Harlem during 1943, more than a hundred incidents of sufficient importance to warrant the attention of the press occurred within its borders that year. On May 25 a riot broke out in a Mobile shipyard over the promotion of 12 Negroes to welding positions. After 50 persons had been injured, peace was restored by the intervention of military force. On June 16 a mob of whites, having heard rumors of the rape of two white women, descended upon the colored section of Beaumont, Texas, with such wild fury that the whole area was "literally stamped into the ground," and two persons were killed and 60 injured. During 1944 and 1945 there were no large-scale race disturbances.

The race riots of this period were not comparable either in magnitude or number to similar disturbances during World War I. The police in many cities organized special squads to suppress mob violence, and when incipient riots appeared imminent they utilized all the techniques and weapons at the command of modern law-enforcing agencies. Outside the South, especially in California, successful efforts were made to give policemen a better understanding of the difficulties of the Negro minority. By 1944 interracial councils had been organized in eighty-one cities, and these groups, together with numerous churches, spread the doctrine of interracial amity. The South was proud of the fact that the Detroit tragedy was not repeated within its borders; it commended the courage of the Beaumont sheriff who held off the mob at the point of a machine gun and the wisdom of the press campaign staged in Houston and Richmond against irresponsible rumors that Negroes planned to create disturbances during holiday gatherings.

The main reason, however, why race riots were not more numerous was that the Negro leaders did not try to implement their demands for social and political equality. The March-on-Washington movement was abandoned after Mrs. Roosevelt warned that such an action would be a "very grave mistake" which would "set back the progress that is being made in the Army, at least, towards better opportunities and less segregation." The Southern liberal Virginius Dabney, in an article "Nearer and Nearer the Precipice" warned that if radical Negro leaders did not desist from their campaign to destroy the color line, bloody riots like those of World War I would recur.[20] A Southern policeman continued to be "a promoted poor-white" [21] whose growing effectiveness even the most resentful Negro was not inclined to challenge. Young white men of the South in soldiers' and sailors' uniforms could be mobilized at a moment's notice to administer discipline with a zeal remindful of their training in subduing the Japanese. The older whites, without considering anything as outmoded as mob violence or as progressive as inviting Negro participation, organized extensive Home Guard units to put down local disorders. They did not wish to incur the wrath of liberals by creating a third Ku Klux Klan.

Although the wartime gains of Negroes in employment were real enough, they failed to threaten established racial standards. The radical Fair Employment Practice order had been enforced only to give Negroes wartime positions for which it was not possible or convenient to employ whites. "Even at the height of the war boom," writes a careful student of the problem,[22] "they were far from achieving their goal of economic parity, nor did they have nearly as good a chance of obtaining jobs as did whites." The same high percentage of Negroes in unskilled jobs prevailed in 1944 as in 1940; 98 per cent of the clerical and sales forces of the country remained white, as did 95 per cent of the professional, proprietary, and managerial groups.

Even President Roosevelt did not fully apply his Fair Employment Practice order. Unlike his Republican predecessor of the same name, he did not appoint a single Negro to federal office in the South or give any position of importance to a Negro in Washington. It was beyond the imagination of most Southerners that a Democratic President wished to prevent discrimination against blacks in industry. When federal agents attempted to enforce that policy, there were sharp reactions. Governor Frank M. Dixon of Alabama in the summer of 1942 refused to sign a contract with the government for the manufacture of cloth in his state's prison system. He charged that the clause in the contract against race discrimination sought to eliminate the color line. In December, 1943, Southern railroads defied an order of the Committee on Fair Employment Practice to cease depriving Negroes of jobs, or denying them deserved promotions. These companies explained that they could not afford to offend Southern sensibilities by rewarding Negro workers with better jobs, or keeping them on jobs desired by white men. Southern congressmen early in 1946 successfully opposed the enactment of

[20] The Atlantic Monthly, CLXXI, 94–100 (January, 1943).
[21] Gunnar Myrdal, An American Dilemma, I, 540.
[22] Herbert R. Northrup in The Annals of the American Academy of Political and Social Science, CCXLIV, 42 (March, 1946).

Roosevelt's Fair Employment policy into permanent statute. They did so with a unanimity comparable to that with which their predecessors fifty-six years earlier had resisted federal intervention in elections.

There was a Solid South in economic matters as well as in political affairs. The possibility that certain profitable war contracts might have gone to Negroes was not generally exploited by those interested in the race's economic advancement. Evidently the Negroes themselves were resigned to remain at the bottom of America's economic ladder. The majority of them squandered their high wages and did not take advantage of opportunities to improve their living standards to the same extent as the whites.

It was too optimistic for Northern Negro leadership to expect the United States Army to use World War II as an opportunity to abolish the color line. Early in the conflict the War Department maintained that to make changes in the time-tested policy of segregating colored and white soldiers "would produce situations destructive to morale and detrimental to the preparation for national defense." [23] In deference to this principle Negroes generally were not allowed to play more conspicuous roles in World War II than in World War I. Colored troops trained in the South had to conform to local segregation customs and laws. Superior posts in Negro military outfits were given to white officers; the one Negro general did not command any troops. The Army, cautious of American public opinion, assigned most colored soldiers to labor battalions, where their services were useful but not arresting. Although officers were generous in praising Negroes for brave acts, the American public as a whole did not acclaim colored heroes. Negro troops went into combat with prophecies of cowardice and stupidity echoing in their ears. Their white officers were often incompetents who regarded the command of Negro troops as an unpleasant chore and held exaggerated notions of the ignorance of their men. The Ninety-Third Division performed only mopping-up work in the wake of conquests by white troops. So poor was the training of the Second Cavalry Division, and so low the high command's faith in its ability, that this famous old Negro organization was disbanded as a combat unit once it arrived overseas, out of range of the criticisms of Negro politicians and press. The men of the Ninety-Second Division, the only large colored unit to experience hard fighting, were generally ineffective. "By ineffective, I mean," wrote an observer,[24] "that they were unable to undertake determined offensive action, that they failed to hold ground in the face of enemy counteroffensive sometimes conducted with very limited

[23] Cited in *The Negro Handbook*, 1942, p. 64.
[24] Warman Welliver, "Report on the Negro Soldier," *Harper's Magazine*, CXCII, 336 (April, 1946). Cf. Bell I. Wiley in *The Journal of Southern History*, XIV, 265 (May, 1948).

forces, that their patrolling was listless, and that there were no colored infantry units of any size on which a commander could rely to carry out an assigned task involving contact with the enemy." This failure can be explained by insufficient education and social experience of a caste-bound race along with a preconceived lack of confidence in its ability. Another factor was America's absurd position of fighting an enemy at least partly on racial grounds when similar prejudices were endured at home. There was, too, the exaggerated sense of grievance on the part of Negro leaders that forced the employment of colored troops for political reasons rather than for sound military policy.

The swing away from Roosevelt's leadership in domestic affairs by Southern members of Congress continued uninterruptedly during the war years. They bolted White House leadership on practically every domestic issue dear to Roosevelt and his New Dealers. During the Congressional session that convened in January, 1943, Senator Harry F. Byrd of Virginia acted as the spearhead of a movement to cut to the bone the appropriations for reform agencies. Senator John H. Bankhead of Alabama led the farm bloc's fight against the administration's consumer-food subsidy. Senator Walter F. George of Georgia spiked ambitious tax increases proposed by the Treasury and had much to do with overriding the President's veto of the 1944 revenue measure. Senator Tom Connally of Texas and Representative Howard W. Smith of Virginia sponsored the antistrike bill which became law over Roosevelt's veto in 1943. Representative John E. Rankin of Mississippi opposed the simplified federal ballot for servicemen, and Representative Martin Dies of Texas, as chairman of the House Committee on Un-American Activities, carried on an energetic campaign against radical members of the Roosevelt bureaucracy.

Goaded by the assertion that there was an "unholy alliance" between the Republicans and the Southern Democrats, Senator Josiah W. Bailey of North Carolina cried in December, 1943: "They [the liberal Democrats] can drive us out [of the Democratic party]. . . . There can be an end of insults, there can be an end of toleration." Southern congressmen knew that they were capable of paralyzing the Roosevelt administration. They held half the Democratic seats in Congress, 16 of the 36 chairmanships of standing committees of the Senate, and 22 of 46 committee heads in the House. They were backed by a rural-minded constituency to whom a centralized and paternal government was instinctively repugnant. The Southern people continued to receive the generous economic and social gifts of the Roosevelt administration, "not with docile gratitude but in a spirit of resentful criticism." [25]

[25] Vance Johnson, "The Old Deal Democrats," *The American Mercury*, LIX, 53 (July, 1944); and William Haynes, *Southern Horizons*, p. 6.

The possibility of Roosevelt's re-election in 1944 caused talk of a third party. Governor Sam H. Jones of Louisiana asked the South to bolt because dominant New Dealers had abandoned states' rights and low tariffs and were attempting "to use the war as an instrument for forcing social 'equality' of the Negro upon the South." The Mississippi Democratic convention put a slate of uninstructed presidential electors on the ballot. In Texas, where it was believed that if Roosevelt were re-elected "it would mean that the Mexicans and the niggers will take us over," a group of Regulars representing the big business wing of the party, after a furious fight for the control of the state Democratic party, entered the election as a third party. A movement to nominate Harry F. Byrd for President received the support of many businessmen.

Despite these manifestations, however, those who understood Southern politics could predict with a high degree of certainty that the section would support Roosevelt. Its admiration for his statesmanlike conduct of the war was unstinted. Conservative leaders feared that the creation of two Southern parties of nearly equal strength would lead to competition for the Negro vote, as had recently occurred in New York, Pennsylvania, and Ohio. Roosevelt himself pursued a policy calculated to prevent a recurrence of the Al Smith debacle of 1928. He did not press to a conclusion his allegedly radical ideas on racism, and the speeches of Mrs. Roosevelt appeared to be curbed.

In deference to the South and to the political bosses of big Northern cities, the Chief Executive made what his liberal friends described as the most costly sacrifice of his entire political career. He allowed Vice-President Wallace to be shelved in favor of Harry S. Truman, a member of the Kansas City political machine. The South was pleased by Roosevelt's selection of a running mate. Henry A. Wallace, according to Senator Bankhead, "advocated a total and complete abolition of racial segregation in the South." Governor Chauncey Sparks of Alabama stated that Truman had told him he was "the son of an unreconstructed rebel mother." Governor Jones's agitation collapsed. The Byrd-for-President movement failed without receiving the endorsement of the cautious Virginia boss. Theodore G. Bilbo had a hand in squelching the independent movement in Mississippi. The Texas Regulars were overwhelmed by Roosevelt's great vote. The South solidly supported Roosevelt and Truman.[26]

Although the South made concessions to wartime liberalism it frankly let the nation know that it did not intend to make significant changes in the practice of white supremacy. This attitude was most apparent when the United States Supreme Court in 1944 decided against the exclusion of Negroes from party primaries conducted under statu-

[26] V. O. Key, Jr., op. cit., pp. 256 and 243-4.

tory authority. While the states with small Negro populations applauded, the states of the lower South tried to circumvent this decree by bold stratagems.[27] In 1944 South Carolina's House of Representatives passed a violently worded resolution demanding "that henceforth the damned agitators of the North leave the South alone." [28]

Offers of Negro support of political leaders were spurned. "The Democratic party in Arkansas," declared Governor Homer M. Adkins of that state, "is a white man's party. I have never solicited the Negro vote." And an Alabamian leader asserted: "Men of character and ability, loyal to the social order that has produced the highest civilization are not going to kow-tow to Negroes to get elected to office." A liberal Atlanta journalist, in advocating obedience to the suffrage decrees of the United States Supreme Court, used as his principal argument the premise that nothing untoward would arise. "There have been," he declared in December, 1945, "no racial upsets in Louisiana and Texas since their Democratic primaries were adjusted to the Supreme Court's ruling. There have been no disturbances or perils to the established social order in Tennessee, Kentucky, and North Carolina, where duly qualified Negro voters have long since been admitted to the Democratic primaries." [29]

A Negro who announced for Congress in Mississippi against a veteran Democrat in 1942 was promptly run out of the state. According to an observing journalist, had this Negro remained in the contest, "lethal and devastating clashes would have been probable." [30] When the sheriff of the Southern city which tolerated the largest number of Negro voters heard of pro-Negro political agitations in his midst in 1944, he stated: "Had I known the Negro Randolph and those he brought with him were speaking ill of Mr. Hale and Mr. Crump, I would have pulled them out of the pulpit." [31]

Sectional contentions not directly concerned with the race problem seemed to fade into the historic background before the great outpouring of national patriotism precipitated by World War II. Northern soldiers by the thousands learned to know the South with thoroughness unequaled since Frederick L. Olmsted made his journey eighty years earlier. While on maneuvers they explored the remotest areas of the countryside, and their families were lodged in Southern homes. Despite these wartime contacts between Southerners and Northerners their es-

[27] See below, p. 608.
[28] Cited in *Time*, XLIII, 13 (March 13, 1944).
[29] Cited in *Christian Century*, LXI, 1060 (September 13, 1944); LXII, 1389 (December 14, 1945); and LXIII, 1046 (September 12, 1946).
[30] Virginius Dabney in *The Atlantic Monthly*, CLXXI, 96 (January, 1943).
[31] Oliver H. Perry of Memphis, cited in *Christian Century*, LXI, 572 (May 3, 1944).

teem for each other did not increase. As already cited, the distinction the average Southerner made between devotion to his specific section and to his entire country allowed him to be a good American while evincing a profound disdain for the customs and concepts typical of Northerners.

This scorn was confirmed and accentuated by association with the teeming masses of Northerners who crowded into every Southern center and peered into every corner of the land. In place of the selected tourists and businessmen Southerners were accustomed to see, there were the polyglot people of Northern cities, factories, and farms. The uneducated came with the educated; the Jew, the Italian, and the Slav with those who conformed to standards of accent and appearance nearer the Southern conception of an American. The manner in which properties were abused, local customs ridiculed, and public services criticized almost convinced Southerners that their beloved land was undergoing a second Yankee invasion. The risks of marrying strangers found expression in rumors that the offsprings of such unions were colored in some cases. Even if such painful disillusionments were not experienced by Southern mothers, there were marital conflicts growing out of differences in religion, politics, and domestic habits. The usual price of a happy intersectional marriage was for the Northern husband to allow himself to become a Southerner.

The suspicions and aversions of Southerners were amply reciprocated by the strangers in their midst. Those naïve Northerners who had been fed on the romantic legend of the South observed the unvarnished actuality and were disappointed, even disgusted. They beheld the dilapidated dwellings and vast wastelands around the army camps and wondered if they were still within the limits of the world's richest country. The discriminating character of Southern hospitality made many a soldier from above the Potomac feel that he was stranded in a land hostile toward lonesome Americans. Failing to receive a cordial reception, these boys railed against the abysmal restaurants and meager entertainment facilities of cities and towns unequipped for so many visitors at one time. They retaliated against exorbitant rents by pilfering and defacing rooming houses and hotels. The fact that Northern soldiers did not flaunt racial conventions kept these irritations from getting out of hand.

The expansion of Southern industry during wartime did not alter the relative position of the section in the national economy. In the 1940's, as in the 1880's and 1920's, the South enthusiastically accepted technological advances without experiencing the necessity of changing its social and cultural customs. The Northern-owned units of its expanding economy adapted themselves to its ways as readily as in earlier decades. Despite the fact that during the war years the average per capita income of Southerners increased more rapidly than the national average, in all Southern states this figure in 1945 remained well below the national average of $1,150. In Mississippi, for example, it was $556, and in only four non-Southern states was it lower than in the highest Southern states.

War contracts were distributed among the states of the Union approximately in proportion to the existence of prewar industry. This meant that the great industrial states of the East and the Middle West, not those of the relatively backward South, carried off the lion's share of war production agreements. The $7,043,109,000 supply and facility contracts negotiated in Alabama, Florida, Georgia, Mississippi, South Carolina, and Tennessee by December, 1943, represented only 4.3 per cent of the national total. Thirteen Southern states received 27 billions in government contracts, or only 12 per cent of the national total of 228 billions. Texas led the list with 8 billions, followed by Virginia with 2.5 billions, Georgia and Louisiana with 2 billions apiece, and North Carolina and Tennessee with 1.8 billions respectively. On the other hand, the more productive states of New York and Michigan each received 23 billions in war supply and facility contracts, while California was awarded an even 20, and Pennsylvania and New Jersey emerged with 14 billions apiece. The federal government, however appreciative it may have been of the need of a more equitable distribution of industry, was primarily dedicated to the task of achieving maximum war production and placed its contracts where skills and factories were most available.

The complaints of Walter P. Webb and others against the hold of Easterners on Southern industry were as valid in the forties as they had been in the thirties. It was the task of outside capital to direct Southern manpower and resources toward performing their share in the war effort. The purchase by Northern interests of Southern-owned textile mills for $19,000,000 in 1946 indicated that absentee ownership was still very much in the picture. Texas—the Southern state which enjoyed the greatest industrial expansion—could still be called "New York's most valuable foreign possession." "Monopoly during the war," wrote an economist traveling through the South in the fall of 1946,[32] "strengthened its hold everywhere, including the South. So the South will continue to ship out huge sums, in interest and profits."

The South was not identified in any special way with any one of the great heroes of World War II. But the region below the Potomac for two reasons got much satisfaction out of its participation in this struggle. It shared in the American paradox of being able to enjoy more of

[32] Avahm G. Mezerik in *The Nation*, CLXIII, 524 (November 9, 1946).

the material comforts and profits of life than ever before while engaged in the waste and destruction of war. It shared fully in the patriotic emotions of the times. In its faith was room for the sacrifices of battle and hopes for a better world when God visited retribution upon a wicked enemy. The physical aspect of the section was altered by the construction—not destruction—of war. But it was a South that was still able to indulge in its particular paradox. It embraced with zeal the techniques and enthusiasms of a united country without surrendering its own sectional distinctiveness.

CHAPTER XXXIII

Southern Economy Since the War

>>>->>>

THOSE who planned the South's future were apprehensive over peace-time adjustments when World War II ended in August, 1945. The section's unprecedented prosperity depended heavily upon businesses created by the war effort. Did not, commented informed economists, "the industries which had more sound reconversion possibilities and those which would aid particularly in further industrialization" account "for a relatively small part of the industrial expansion program of the South?" Less than one per cent of the war manufacturing awards in the South were in plants manufacturing vehicles; barely one per cent in machinery and electrical equipment plants, and only 4 per cent in iron and steel facilities. On the other hand, 20 and 31 per cent of the section's war awards were respectively in munitions and chemicals, plants believed to have major reconversion handicaps.[1] There was apprehension over what would be the result when restaurants, lunch counters, rooming houses, beer parlors, jewelry stores, and dance halls became deserted with the abandonment of military and naval training centers. As early as November, 1946, some predicted that "in the South, the home of the poorest American poor relations," the day was "just around the corner" when scarcities and high prices would give way to glutted markets and people without money to make necessary purchases.[2]

[1] Frederick L. Deming and Weldon A. Stein, cited in Calvin B. Hoover and B. U. Ratchford, *Economic Resources and Policies of the South*, p. 124.
[2] Avahm G. Mezerik in *The Nation*, CLXIII, 525 (November 9, 1946).

Such gloomy forebodings, however, were not prevalent among Southerners generally in the months after fighting ceased. The section contemplated its assets and anticipated a continuation of wartime prosperity. It knew that from its resources of climate, soil, and manpower had grown many war plants and a backlog of skilled and semiskilled craftsmen; these could be converted to peacetime needs. Southern economists sought to direct both local and imported capital into channels of production; industrial researchers and engineers were prepared to apply mechanical and chemical discoveries to all available resources. Public opinion demanded that Southern congressmen sustain the postwar boom by voting for the removal of wartime controls on industrial production and consumer prices, for the continuation of price supports on farm commodities, for heavy subsidies to foreign nations under the Marshall Plan, and for huge armies and fabulous armament appropriations to meet the Communist menace in Europe and Asia.

Construction contracts for the first nine months of 1946 totaled $1,348,234,000, as compared with $788,795,000 for the corresponding months of 1945. Although shipyards and army camps were almost deserted, other war centers had been converted to plants with orders for goods which in many cases would require two years to fill. Chattanooga, to cite an example of what was occurring in a Southern city late in 1946, had reconverted its 169 war plants to peacetime purposes and was producing goods at high speed. In this Tennessee city, Du Pont was erecting a $20,000,000 nylon-fiber plant; Borg-Warner had bought the Air Products plant to manufacture compressors for refrigerators; the Wheland Company, which previously made 90-millimeter guns, was contracting to make automobile parts for General Motors. In Birmingham a huge aircraft modification center, possessing 2 million square feet of floor space, now turned out bus bodies, aluminum window screens, flame cultivators, and lightweight automobiles. A former shipbuilding concern began to produce Diesel locomotives, and a manufacturer of shells started to make consumer goods ranging from furniture to attic fans. In Jackson within a few weeks of the surrender of Japan eleven new industries began to build plants, and sixteen existing factories initiated expansion programs.

By the end of 1947—more than two years after the surrender of Japan—the confidence of the South in the permanence of its wartime gains was justified. In that year expenditures in the section for new plants and equipment was well over a billion dollars. This was a larger investment in proportion to investments previously made than the national average.[3] Employment, wages and incomes were not far below wartime peaks. The autumn crops of 1947 secured almost unprece-

[3] Hoover and Ratchford, *op. cit.*, pp. 130-1.

dented prices: tobacco veered toward 50 cents a pound, and cotton reached a twenty-seven-year high of 41 cents a pound. The streets of Southern cities and towns milled with crowds eager to empty well-filled pockets. Merchants smiled while upper-class conservatives complained over purchases of unaccustomed luxuries by Negroes and poor whites. The number of students on college campuses swelled to twice that of prewar days.

Visitors brought up on the legend of a poverty-stricken region found in the appearance of the landscape evidence galore to sustain the thesis, "The South Has Changed." They noted that gardens and grass had replaced run-down yards; that houses, barns and fences had been painted; that flashy new store fronts faced courthouse squares; that there were consolidated schools, swank drive-in theatres, streamlined mills, and landscaped tourist camps with more baths and inside toilets than whole communities possessed in 1940. The average individual was better dressed and better nourished. In front of rickety Negro school houses in Mississippi were shiny bicycles; the children coming out of the new Church of God Tabernacle looked almost as straight-legged and as well dressed as the businessmen's children coming out of the Presbyterian church on the other side of the railroad tracks; and the daughters of cotton pickers, after a stroll during the noon recess by the display windows of the synthetic textile factories in which they worked, were able to buy dresses as chic as those of the daughters of cotton planters.[4]

"And the statistics are there if you want them," wrote the chroniclers of the South's most recent prosperity. In the 1940's the per capita annual income of the average Southerner rose from less than 50 per cent to 65 per cent of the national average. This meant an increase in the average annual wage of those engaged in manufacturing from less than $800 to more than $2,000; hourly wages in the textile industry rose from an average of 23 cents to an average of 87 cents. Adjustments made for changes in the price level showed that the increase in real wages averaged only 55 per cent, but this figure compared so favorably with national increase of 38 per cent that some economists predicted the closing of the North-South wage gap. Higher wages were accompanied by the creation of 1.25 million new jobs and an increase in the "spendable income" of the South of 375 per cent. The standards of living and wealth of the region, said a Southern industrialist in 1951,[5] "have increased to make the South no longer a so-called backward area, but a leading area in many of the branches of the process industries."

[4] Mary H. Vorse, "The South Has Changed," Harper's Magazine, CXCIX, 23 (July, 1949); George C. Stoney, "New Opportunities in the South," Survey, LXXXVII, 149 (April, 1951).

[5] Edwin Cox in the New York Times, June 17, 1951.

Between 1940 and 1950 the rural states of Oklahoma, Arkansas, and Mississippi lost population, as did the predominantly rural regions of all Southern states. This was caused almost entirely by the migration of one third of the rural Negroes. More than 2 million Negroes moved out of the South to join other millions of their race who had previously settled in the North. Despite this loss, the Far West was the only region of the United States which exceeded the South in percentage of population growth during the decade. The South as a whole gained 13 per cent. Florida led with an increase of 46 per cent, and Texas was a second with a gain of 20 per cent.

A sensational growth of towns and cities was responsible for a more populous South. Once-stagnant towns like Charleston, Wilmington, Alexandria, and Augusta nearly doubled in size and throbbed with trade, industry and preparations for war. Baton Rouge catapulted from an obscure river port of 35,000 inhabitants into an industrial giant of 124,000. The number of Southern cities with 100,000 or more inhabitants increased from twenty-one in 1940 to thirty in 1950. Atlanta, the third smallest in percentage of growth, was so "alive with a welter of activities" that it gave "the impression of breathing in all its pores." [6] Memphis, with 100,000 persons added to its population, had doubled the number of its factories in ten years. Texas had seven cities on the 100,000 list. Dallas with its 614,799 residents was trying to make itself into a style center like Paris or New York; actually it was the commercial and cultural capital of Texas. Houston, with 594,321 persons, had forged ahead of New Orleans as the largest city of the South. It was a raw and rollicking place still enjoying a hundred-year boom and expecting to have 3 million people by 1980. It spent half a billion dollars annually in new constructions and possessed downtown lands which sold for $2,000 a front inch. Among its many multimillionaires was one who lavished his wealth on a municipal university and another who built the South's most luxurious hotel as a monument to his fame.

The expansion and improvement of Southern industry characteristic of the World War II period went on in the years that followed at an accelerated pace. An increasing proportion of towns and villages became the sites of small industries. There was a garment factory in one town, a shoe factory in another, a shop for the making of electric appliances in a third, and one for automobile seat covers in a fourth. The section in 1951 showed a greater percentage increase in values added to manufactures than the United States as a whole. The most noted industrial development was the processing of the section's forest products. In 1951 these products created an income of $1,300,000,000, and the wood pulp and paper branch of the industry was planning a program

[6] Mary H. Vorse, *loc. cit.,* p. 27.

of expansion costing $100,000,000. The industrial economy of the section was becoming more diversified. Its heavy industries were expanding; the area was producing a third of the country's inorganic chemicals; its petroleum industry had grown into a gaint as valuable as all of its industries fifty years earlier; and it was experiencing the strange sensation of possessing at Oak Ridge the only laboratory in the world devoted to the development and use of radioisotopes.

In the meantime the South's oldest factories showed no signs of senility. Its cotton textile industry was a vigorous adult spending $1,000-000,000 on improvements in the five years after World War II. These improvements took the form of increased use of synthetic fibers as additions to the basic cotton; the consolidation of mills into Northern-owned chains in which all the processes of manufacturing and marketing were under the same control; the adoption of new policies of branding and advertising; increased emphasis on managerial and research skills; trade agreements that lessened the perils of overproduction; and a general overhauling of buildings and machinery that gave the mills a new look.

Industrial expansion was not made at the expense of agriculture. The section in 1950 possessed 52 per cent of the country's farm population. Its growing towns, its textile mills, and its chemical industries created bigger markets for its vegetables, fruits, and the materials out of which the new synthetics were made. The most novel advance in this direction were the so-called tree crops by which thousands of Southern farmers supplemented the traditional types of agriculture. Tree-planting was feasible because of the rapid growth of Southern pines and because of the demands of the mills for them; it was encouraged by bank loans, by the reforestation and fire-prevention policies of state government, and by the educational policies of the wood-consuming industries.

Paradoxically it was southern agriculture rather than Southern industry that underwent the greater transformation. The tractor was replacing the mule as the performer of the heavier tasks of the farm. Between 1945 and 1950 the number of tractors more than doubled. Rural electrification developed at such a pace that Georgia, Virginia, North Carolina, Texas, and Alabama had a higher percentage of their farms wired than the national average.

Surprising is the fact that cotton, conventionally accepted as a mill-stone around the neck of Southern progress, showed an expansive energy comparable to that of the new crops that progressives wished to see usurp the throne of the old king. The curse of overproduction of cotton gave way in 1950 to a scarcity that prompted curbs on exports, threats of rationing, and the dissipation of the so-called cotton surpluses in federal warehouses. The 1950 crop amounted to only 10 million bales.

The price soared to 45 cents a pound. The farmers applauded when the Department of Agriculture in 1951 removed restrictions on production and set 16 million bales as the national goal. The year's harvest amounted to 15,144,000 bales. The 1952 harvest was almost as great as that of 1951. Full use was made of the twentieth-century strategies by which handicaps to cotton-growing were overcome. The possibility of having to pay Negro choppers as much as $8 a day was partly met by the application of a vigorous research program designed to mechanize cotton culture from seeding to harvesting. In 1952 Allis-Chalmers was advertising a successful cotton-picking machine. The problem of insect infestation was met by shifting the center of cultivation westward. Sixty per cent of the crop was grown west of the Mississippi; California moved to third place among the states in production. The depressing effect of increased production on prices was largely neutralized by federal guarantees of high minimum prices and by the fact that despite the competition of synthetics the average American in 1951 consumed 33 pounds of cotton as compared with 24 pounds in 1920 The much-heralded day when satisfactory substitutes could be found for the South's great contribution to the clothing of mankind had not dawned.

The South profited from the development of peanuts and soybeans into major sources of fat in the American diet. Soybean production in the section increased from 3 million to 18 million bushels between 1929 and 1948; the total cash returns, from $2,000,000 to $36,000,000. Peanut production during the same period increased from less than a billion pounds to over 2 billion pounds; the total cash returns, from $32,000,000 to $221,000,000.

The growth of the cattle and dairy industries was sensational. As the traveler rode north from New Orleans to Virginia he noted an almost endless expansion of green fields with grazing cattle where ten years before had been cotton fields and pine barrens. Between 1929 and 1948 livestock receipts increased 257 per cent. This revolution was caused by the increased milk and beef demands of the American people. The advantages of the long pasturage seasons of a warm climate were supplemented by the importation from India of Brahma cattle which sweat like horses and are therefore more able to stand the heat of the Southern lowlands than cattle of European origin. By crossing the Brahma with the European-type dairy cow, a sweating cow was developed with unimpaired milk capacity. The result was that in 1950 five Southern states earned more money from animal industries than from all other agricultural sources. The dominance of Northern and Northwestern commercial dairying was threatened by the region where dairy herds could feed in open fields for most of the year.

The Southern farmer took full advantage of the near monopoly he enjoyed over the nation's most ancient staple. In 1951 he produced 90 per cent of the nation's tobacco and got 50 cents a pound for it. The dizzy price was caused by the increasing quality of the commodity, the increasing demand of the whole earth for it, and particularly to the perfection of the controls and the price supports that the federal government imposed. This condition of monopoly was also true of rice and peanuts.

The current prosperity of the South is less likely to resolve itself in a cycle of boom and bust than that of the period after World War I. The shift to industry, to a more diversified agriculture, and to crop controls was a means of preventing overproduction and a disastrous fall in farm prices. A decline in the export of cotton from 58 per cent in the twenties to 37 per cent in the forties betokened a declining dependence on uncertain foreign markets. Southern industry was prepared to prevent the perils of overproduction through private output controls. This was especially true of the highly integrated textile industry. The fear that the ironing out of wage differentials between the sections would make Southern industry less attractive to investors proved unfounded. A startling fact is that the steady increase in the Southern wage scale in the forties was accompanied by a steady increase in industrial investment. The lessening of the advantages of cheap labor was more than counteracted by the expansion of Southern markets, the availability of Southern raw materials, and the quality of Southern labor. It was discovered that this labor was still abundant in quantity and was "more efficient than other labor, more eager to learn and—of particular importance—more willing to work third shifts." [7]

Evidence of supreme faith in the future of Southern industry was the increased willingness of Northern capital to invest in it. New England cotton mills continued to move South, the steel industry entered Texas, and there were few Southern towns too unpromising to attract at least one garment factory. The giant among the great Northern concerns expanding in the South was E. I. du Pont de Nemours and Company, which by 1951 had placed nearly half of its investment below the Potomac. Its Southern holdings consisted of twenty plants in nine states. These included an orlon plant at Camden, South Carolina, a nylon yarn plant at Chattanooga, a neoprene rubber plant at Louisville, an agricultural chemicals plant at La Porte, Texas, and the great new hydrogen-bomb plant which in 1952 was transforming the remote village of Ellenton, South Carolina, into a city of fantastic promises.

Despite great gains there had been by the fifties no radical alteration in the relative position of the South in the national economy. The South had grown richer; so had the rest of the United States. The Negro re-

[7] Stoney, loc. cit., p. 150.

BLAST FURNACES AT FAIRFIELD, ALABAMA. *These mammoth installations of the Southern division of the United States Steel Corporation typify the fruitful combination of the North's capital and mechanical skill with the South's abundance of natural resources and black and white labor.*

RAILROAD YARDS AT NORFOLK, VIRGINIA. *This scene at the greatest port of the South Atlantic coast gives proof of the significant part the outward movement of raw materials plays in Southern industry.*

HOUSTON SKYLINE. *This cluster of office buildings is the headquarters of the oil, cattle, and cotton businesses through which a Texas town became by 1950 the largest city in the South.*

ceived better wages; so did other Southerners. The income of the average Southerner was only two thirds of the national average at the end of the forties. The difference in dollars between these two averages had actually increased $200 during the decade. The much-heralded expansion of Southern industry did not override the fact that the region possessed only a limited share of the national total; this share in 1947 was 17.7 per cent as compared with 16.4 per cent for the year before World War II.[8]

Certain lasting realities accounted for the continuation of the economic differentials between the sections. The South's soil, its basic resource, remained "mediocre in quality, highly erosive under intensive cultivation, and badly damaged by past experience." The movement of thousands of the region's more energetic adults to the more prosperous regions of the country continued. The abundance of its labor supply, despite the counteracting influences already mentioned, inevitably checked wage increases to a degree not evident in regions where labor was scarcer. At an ever-growing pace, both old and new Southern industries were falling into the hands of non-Southerners. This development increased wages and salaries paid Southerners but decreased their share of incomes from investments. The region offered little opportunity for the development of research and managerial skills through which home-owned industries might have been developed. There was a tendency for large Southern industries, such as the tobacco companies, to move their financial headquarters to New York City. Thereby the region lost employment opportunities in management and the high commissions paid traders in securities.

If one should like to know, wrote a Negro journalist in 1951,[9] how "rigidly and shamefully Negroes in the United States are treated economically," he should "take a look at his community and see the kind of low-paying jobs, comparatively, Negroes are permitted to have." It was affirmed that the white masters of the business world still restricted Negroes "to the most menial and the most arduous work." This gloomy conclusion is supported by the assertion of agents of the federal census that the median white income of $3,000 in 1950 was almost twice as great as that of colored persons. The average income of Negroes on farms was $942 as compared with $2,235 for whites. Only 0.2 per cent of Negro families were prosperous enough to earn $10,000 or more annually; the corresponding figures for white families was 2.4 per cent. The few well-to-do Negroes got their earnings from serving segregated communities in funerals, medical care, and insurance. The business opportunities for Negroes continued to be less in the South than else-

[8] Hoover and Ratchford, op. cit., pp. 46–8.
[9] P. L. Prattis in the Pittsburgh Courier, June 23, 1951.

where. "The color occupational system," reported a Negro economist in 1949,[10] "remains entrenched and unchallenged in the region save in a few outstanding instances."

The comparatively low economic standards of the Negro are revealed by the presence in every city and town of slum areas to which Negroes are restricted by immutable custom. Such areas often deteriorated more rapidly than the federal housing projects could create substitutes. One such slum was so close to the center of federal activities in Washington that United States senators in 1950 experienced its smells and unsightliness from their office windows.

Social commentators hopefully predicted that lags in social and economic opportunities for Negroes were survivals of the past which would vanish with the prosperity of the mid-century. They noted that the urban Negro worker was able to command a wage two thirds as large as his white brother and that there was a radical falling off in the number of colored persons who were willing to stay in the lowly paid occupation of farm hand and domestic servant. Yet certain factors worked against the closing of the economic gap between whites and Negroes this side of a revolutionary millennium. In 1950, at a time Negroes were said to be ready to compete effectively with whites in business enterprises, the American economy because of consolidations was less receptive than ever to new talent either from the white or the black race. The Negro's chance of joining the business elite had grown more remote.

The thousand or more industries that Northern capital had established since 1945 in the South almost universally gave preference to white labor. This means that few Negroes were employed, because white labor was plentiful enough to supply most demands. That this shutting off of employment to blacks was beyond immediate remedy is attested by the conduct of the Atomic Energy Commission, an agency that has always acted with a great regard for the advance of human welfare. It accepted Southern employment practices at its Oak Ridge and Ellenton installations. At the Tennessee center only 1,200 of its 37,000 inhabitants were Negroes, and the Negroes were employed as common laborers. In 1952 there were reports of similar employment curbs thrown around Negroes at the South Carolina center.

After 1940 the South lost more than 2 million of its colored inhabitants. Its proportion of Negroes in the national total was thereby reduced from 74 per cent to 63 per cent. This emigration was partly the result of an enclosure movement as far reaching in its effect on humble laborers as was the notorious development under the same name which

[10] Robert C. Weaver in *The Journal of Negro Education*, XIX, 24 (Spring, 1950).

in the eighteenth century turned England into a sheepwalk. Southern landlords, angered by the increased wages their black tenants were able to command, turned them off the land, allowed tenants' cabins to decay, and adopted a type of land use that required the minimum manpower: they became cattle raisers. Many cotton cultivators reduced their dependence on Negro labor through mechanization.

That this uprooting of blacks from cotton-growing did not cause a major tragedy was due to the compensating employments which America has usually managed to offer the dispossessed. Negroes were able to improve their economic status by moving to the cities. This escape from the farm in a sense was progress in the Negro's struggle for a fairer share of the good things of American life; but it was not indicative of a generous spirit that the rural South, in its decade of greatest prosperity, narrowed the employment opportunities of its largest laboring class. And by a turn of irony it was the agricultural scientists, the most effective group of Southern educators, who taught the planters the devices through which they could gain greater prosperity by ridding themselves of their tenants.

Organized labor after World War II made attempts to add to the substantial gains it had made in the South before 1940. Both the American Federation of Labor and the Congress of Industrial Organizations became busy. But their progress was no greater in the South than in the rest of the country. The result was that the South in 1952 remained relatively backward in the field of collective bargaining.

The most significant attempt to break an important segment of Southern labor from the Southerner's habit of identifying his welfare with that of his employer was made by the CIO in 1947. That group, fresh from triumphs in the North, launched Operation Dixie for the purpose of unionizing the textile industry. The young Northerners who directed this drive believed that they would have success. The Southern textile worker had already demonstrated enough class consciousness to vote for Cole L. Blease and to participate in the bloody Gastonia riots of the twenties and in strikes enforced by flying squadrons in the thirties. Under the protection of the National Labor Relations Board there seemed to be a way of getting recognition of collective bargaining without provoking the violence with which the South was in the habit of getting rid of outside agitators. The federal laws provided for elections under which the workers could decide for themselves by the peaceful processes of democracy whether or not they wanted unions. The union organizers avoided violence in the faith that Southern public opinion, Southern mill managers, and Southern officers of the law would accept labor organizations if the mill workers voted for them.

The unions won some elections and were able, under the law, to demand contracts calling for wages and working conditions like those prevailing in the North.

Yet reports in 1951 proved that textile unions had lost 10 per cent of their membership and that in twenty-seven of the forty elections held in that and the previous year on the question of organization the unions lost. A keen observer told how "fifteen years of prosperity had made vast changes" in the status of textile workers without, however, altering the class distinctions which "show themselves clearly in the textile worker's attitude toward himself and his fellows—his lack of self-confidence, his mistrust of his own leaders in dealing with such a superior being as his boss, his dependence on outside leadership." [11] He enjoyed too well his war-born prosperity, the new personnel policies of the larger mills, and the minimum wage laws to feel the need of paying union dues to strange labor leaders.

Veteran labor chieftains scoffed at the faith of the textile organizers in the judicial process. A local union often disintegrated within the year or two which elapsed between the time the union won the right to negotiate and the day the National Labor Relations Board and the federal courts applied enforcement orders. Unlike such persons in many Northern communities, the Southern people and their police and politicians believed that unions were a menace to the section's industrial expansion and its accepted class distinctions. The mill management felt that its duty was to protect employees from dues extortions. They did this by supplementing acts of autocratic benevolence by acts less principled. They threatened to close mills, told stories of the foreign birth and the non-Anglo Saxon lineage of union leaders, exhibited pictures of CIO executives dining with Negroes, resorted to endless litigation, and aroused the antiunion sentiments of whole communities by sponsoring letters, speeches, and advertisements purporting to prove that the unions were against the American and the Southern way of life.

[11] George C. Stoney, loc. cit., p. 152.

CHAPTER XXXIV

The South Retains Its Past

>>>->>>

STARK YOUNG'S assertion in 1930 that the changing South was still the South applied with equal force twenty years later. There had been, as we have seen, a great increase in the section's wealth without any great alteration in its relative economic position in the nation. There had been no social or political revolution. The South was set off from the rest of the United States by issues not much different from what they had been for the past generation or two.

Religion in the fifties perhaps to a greater degree than in previous decades, was a potent conservator of the Southern way of life. Church membership continued the long-established trend of growing faster than the whole population. The new prosperity and the new means of communication caused no turning away from God. Church edifices dotted the newer suburbs, and the radio resounded with hymns, sermons and prayers. "A definite resurgence of religion is to be noted in this city," ran a report in 1950 typical of the larger centers of population.[1] "People are joining the church in numbers that indicate an all-time high for membership. . . . Church building programs are also of unprecedented magnitude."

General assemblies of clergymen urged the churches to abandon segregation on lines of class and race as undemocratic. But the actual emphasis was on the old-time religion. This meant absorption in other-worldliness with little or no concern over the social problems which worried a few progressive pastors. A study made in 1948 demonstrated that only one tenth of one per cent of American Negro Protestant

---

[1] From Richmond, in *Christian Century*, LXVII, 570 (May 3, 1950).

Christians attended church along with whites.[2] Confusion and misunderstanding were created at Little Rock in 1951 when a Negro tried to take a seat outside the section reserved for his race at an evangelistic meeting. The body blow given the Biblical affirmation concerning the origin of man at Dayton in 1925 was answered in 1950 by a renewed faith in Biblical guides concerning the destiny of man. Prophecy, more satisfying to the Southern masses than teaching about the past, was used effectively to proclaim the imminence of the Second Coming.

A glance at current items from the press proves that the trend in Southern religion was conservative in the late forties and early fifties. The year 1945 marked the birth at Greenville, South Carolina, of the Speckled Bird Church of God, a growing primitivist sect. Two years later the headlines proclaimed that holiness sectarians in Virginia, Kentucky, Tennessee, and Alabama were testing Bibical promises by going through the ritual of allowing poisonous snakes to bite them. In 1948 religious instruction in public schools was reported as uninterrupted by the ban of the United States Supreme Court. In 1949 the conservative church forces were strong enough to prevent the repeal of prohibition in Oklahoma; to foster the appearance before Youth of Christ assemblies of a procession of Fundamentalist preachers; and to make the Church of Christ "the most rapidly growing denominational group in the South." The secret of this denomination's strength was its evangelistic enthusiasm and its literal interpretation of Biblical texts.

That the old-time religion was able to adjust itself to the realities of the contemporary world was proved by four events of 1950. Billy Graham, a flaming-eyed evangelist of thirty-two, jammed the football stadium of Columbia, South Carolina, with 40,000 persons to hear him berate "sex, sin and communism." Waco, Texas, was able to boast that it had "the largest Baptist school in the world," in which was held "the world's largest prayer meeting." The harmony which had developed between religion and football was signified by the establishment in Texas of prayer before each kickoff. The Green Pastures legend of the reduction of religion to the consistencies of everyday life was demonstrated when 20,000 Negroes enjoyed in the Mason Temple of the Church of God in Christ at Memphis an all-night fish fry and religious pageant entitled "Two Fish and Five Loaves."

The most powerful demonstration in the middle of the twentieth century of Southern religious ambitions was the conduct of the Southern Baptist church. This most distinctly Southern of the great religious bodies grew to 6,700,000 members by 1950 and thereby remained the second largest Protestant denomination in the United States. Its phenomenal growth was caused by the intensification of its evangelical ef-

[2] Frank S. Loescher, *The Protestant Church and the Negro, passim.*

forts and its spread into regions wherever Southerners settled. In 1949 Illinois had 586 Southern Baptist churches and the states of Washington and Oregon had 24. In 1950 there were as many Southern Baptist state conventions outside the states of the former Confederacy as there were within that area. Symbolic of this territorial aggressiveness was the holding of the general conventions of the church in Chicago in 1950 and in San Francisco in 1951. When the Northern Baptist church expressed resentment against this invasion of its territory by changing its name to the American Baptist church, the Southern Baptists removed all territorial restrictions on the work of their boards and agencies.

The strength of the Southern Baptist church stemmed from the same cause as that of the Roman Catholic church: its utter refusal to compromise with liberal tendencies of other churches. Its pure congregationalism or "spiritual democracy" tended to become a fiction through the creation of centralizing agencies. Yet conservative influence of the local congregations remained strong enough to deter Baptist ministers from following other Protestant clergymen into compromises with modernism. The Southern Baptist remained as adamant as the Church of Rome in rejecting overtures from other religious bodies. Its general convention of 1951 decreed, "Churches which accept alien immersion, practice open communion or affiliate with Federal Council of Churches or any other similar unionizing organization shall be considered unsound in faith and practice."

The South, as has been its habit since it acquiesced in the abolition of slavery, voluntarily accepted in the years after World War II some reforms suggested from the outside. This trend was most evident in the field of race relations. South Carolina and Tennessee repealed their laws requiring the payment of a poll tax as a prerequisite for voting, and in 1951 Georgia joined numerous other Southern states and communities in outlawing the wearing of disguises. Public opinion had grown so intolerant of Ku Klux outrages that wholesale convictions of those guilty of masked violence took place in North Carolina in the summer of 1952. In 1949, 232 Negro police officers were on duty in thirty-seven Southern cities; in 1950 Richmond returned to the long-abandoned practice of having a unit of Negro fire fighters. There were scattered cases of the conviction of whites for raping Negro girls and of police officers for cruelty to Negro prisoners. The region accepted without violence an increase in Negro voting, the abolition of segregation in army organizations, the showing of "Pinky," "Lost Boundaries," and other moving pictures attacking Southern race concepts, and the entrance of a few Negroes in its universities.

The region below the Potomac, despite the Jeffersonian pronouncements of its statesmen, continued to be as eager as other sections of the

United States to accept aspects of the welfare state. Its people and its politicians demanded federal subsidies and controls which raised prices for its farmers and merchants. State governments seemed intent upon drowning out the inherited sins of the section in a welter of expenditures which made the financial orgies of Reconstruction look puny. A multitude of contractors, bureaucrats, and common people demanded newer and better roads, health services, and schools. The eight Southern states having legislative sessions in 1951 authorized expenditure of $2,500,000,000 within the following two years. This was an increase of $400,000,000 over the expenditure of the two previous years. It was made possible by the imposition of tougher sales taxes.

The most strenuous endeavors to wipe out cultural deficiencies of the section was in public education. The most specific stimulus to action in this field was the race against the day when Jim Crow states would be held in judgment before the federal courts for inequalities in school opportunities for Negro children. There was a more fundamental reason for action. It was the complete acceptance by the South of the American system of universal education as the best cure for social ills short of divine intervention. A society that in all other respects held on tenaciously to class distinctions accepted the idea that all classes (within the white race) should attend the same schools; the Southern rich and well-born showed less inclination than the rich and well-born of other sections of the civilized world to segregate their children in private schools. There were complaints against "a triumphant 'progressive' education which progresses even faster than in the North and which has been rushing school systems off into a life of sin as fast as they are born," and against school management by "gentlemen of such spectacular mediocrity that their antics give the impression of watching parvenu poor whites on a gaudy holiday." [3] More reasonable were the complaints of teachers against the insistence of tyrannical supervisors on fitting children into stereotypes, against the watering down of curricula to the level of the lowest talent, and against the system of "pressure promotion" under which all children were advanced to higher grades. [4]

But the directors of the Southern school systems were too secure in the pride of their accomplishments to be worried by such criticisms. Against the charge of lowered standards they pointed to the ever-increasing enrollments of the schools as proof of approach to the ideal of serving all the people. They saw wisdom in the abandonment of the classical curriculum in favor of a course of study illustrative of the

[3] Robert S. Heilman in Allen Tate, ed., *A Southern Vanguard*, pp. 127–9.
[4] *Christian Century*, LXVI, 1467 (December 6, 1949).

problems of everyday life. The remedy for the failure of Southern schools to measure up to the achievements of other sections of the country was always the same: there must be more appropriations, more school buildings, and more teachers. The Southern legislatures patiently responded with greater subsidies and hopefully looked forward to the better society they believed the schools were creating.

That this better society had not come about by 1952 was evidenced by the numerous tales of interracial crimes that darkened the record of that and previous years. Neither whites nor Negroes had become saints. Some Negroes continued to rape, steal, and kill. In 1951 shocking revelations came out of their sections of the cities of juvenile drug addiction and crime, of the harboring of vice, of political leaders angling in rackets, and of gangsters accepted in respectable social circles.

The whites, on the other hand, continued to give the perennial Northern critic cause for complaints. Although lynching almost vanished, Virginia and Mississippi sent Negroes to the electric chair for rape. Municipal ordinances to the contrary notwithstanding, the Ku Klux Klan engaged in demonstrations ranging from cross-burning parades and mountaintop ceremonies to shooting sprees and the whipping of roistering Negroes. In 1947 an interracial group assisting in the construction work of the Lights of Tyrrel Credit Union in North Carolina was forced to decamp by a mob of 200 whites. The next year a group of Northern white girls in an American Friends Service camp at a Negro college were forced by whites to leave. In 1949 and 1950 there were interracial swimming-pool brawls in Washington and St. Louis. Attala County, Mississippi, was in 1950 still a place where three drunken white men could invade a Negro cabin and wantonly shoot to death four of its occupants and yet before a local court get off with their necks and assorted terms in prison.

Attempts to break down residential segregation met with as much violence during 1951 and 1952 as during any two years within more than a decade. Bombs were tossed in Miami and Birmingham, whites in a suburb of Chicago rioted against a Negro family moving into their midst, and on Christmas day the Negro leader Harry T. Moore and his wife were killed by an assassin's bomb in their home at Mims, Florida.

Such happenings were the seamy side of the determination of the South to preserve its ways. It was felt that the Negro still had to be "kept in his place"—by harsh methods among the hoodlum element of the population, by benevolent methods among the responsible element. Representative of the responsible element was the declaration in 1948 of the section's most distinguished historian. "The South," Douglas S. Freeman warned the nation, "is going to keep the line drawn between civil rights and social privilege. Civil rights should be recognized; social privilege is a matter of individuals. The South is going to keep that line drawn and that's all there is to it."

The millions spent on education had worked no revolution. So indurated was ignorance among the masses that 38.7 per cent of the section's men called for military service in 1951 could not pass the mental tests necessary for induction into the army. The people of the South were described as "different," partly because of their comparative lack of the sort of communications which bring innovation and progress. An investigator[5] demonstrated that the South had only 14.9 telephones per hundred persons compared with the national average of 24.2; that Southerners listened to radios less than other Americans, and that their radio program preferences were in favor of sentimental music, old-time religion, and serial stories; that their newspaper-reading was only from 60–75 per cent of the national average; and that they ranked lowest in the purchase of books and the patronage of libraries. The Southerner's lack of effective schooling was still the subject of accurate caricature: through the bumptious provincialism of Colonel Claghorn of the radio and through Walt Kelly's good-humored demonstration in the Pogo Possum comic strips of the ignorance of the inhabitants of the Southern swamps.

The refusal of the South to follow the world-shaking events of World War II by important modifications of its attitudes led to a grand assault upon its folkways bolder than that of the Franklin D. Roosevelt administration and almost as comprehensive as that of Charles Sumner and Thaddeus Stevens. The nineteenth-century formula that stateways do not make folkways was changed into the conviction that the federal government could and should use its greatly expanded powers to destroy the whole Jim Crow structure. Some advocated the elimination of race distinctions to the extent of lifting the ban on interracial marriages.

Urgency was given to these agitations by the belief that racial intolerance was the dark spot on the American escutcheon which gave greatest encouragement to Communist enemies of the United States. Race distinctions were said to threaten the loss of the friendship of a billion and a half nonwhite people in the death struggle with Russia. "We must," declared in 1951 the son of a famous agitator for world democracy,[6] "push civil-rights measures strictly in the selfish interest of all Americans. It means, in fact, the lives of American boys." As a hundred years earlier with the case of slavery, race prejudice was held

[5] Harry E. Moore, "Mass Communications in the South," *Social Forces*, XIX, 365–76 (May, 1951).
[6] Philip Willkie in the *New York Times*, June 28, 1951.

to be the cause of a multitude of moral and social delinquencies that afflicted the American body politic. It was ironically suggested that General Douglas MacArthur, who had imposed American democracy upon a dark region of the Far East, should be appointed to extend his good work into the benighted region of his own country.

All sorts of persons joined in the mid-century assault upon the Southern way of treating the Negro. In this motley phalanx were American and European Communists, capitalistic newspapers and philanthropies, Northern industrialists, labor chieftains, a few Southern liberals, and many editors, professors, public officials, and lawyers of the Jewish, Negro, and other races.

The leadership in the assault was taken by the Truman administration, which inherited from Franklin D. Roosevelt the conviction that a duty of the Democratic party was to advance the rights of the lowly Negro. This attitude had paid Roosevelt dividends in the votes of the Negroes who had settled in the North in the wake of World War I. It was destined to pay Truman greater dividends because of the increased northward movement of Negroes during World War II. Furthermore, Truman was more than a political opportunist. In the name of democracy he was willing to imperil his standing in the South by a franker championship of Negro rights than that undertaken by the more politic Roosevelt. The more sanguine Northern Democrats thought that the President could win national elections by an indifferent attitude toward the Southern minority, like that of Lincoln in 1860.

The issue was met by the publication on October 29, 1947, of the report of President Truman's Committee on Civil Rights. It was signed by two Southerners and thirteen Northerners prominent in law, labor, education, or industry. This document forthrightly urged the immediate abolition of all governmental and some private sanctions of race discrimination or segregation. Among its thirty-five recommendations were laws abolishing segregation in the armed services, in public conveyances, in public schools, in housing, and in places of public accommodation; a federal antilynching law carrying drastic penalties; a federal law establishing a permanent Fair Employment Practice Commission that could penalize employers refusing to employ Negroes on every job on the same basis as white persons; a federal anti-poll tax law if the states themselves refused to repeal their poll-tax requirement for voting; and a federal statute protecting the right of all qualified persons to participate in all so-called federal primaries and elections against interference by public officers or private persons.

The belief that equality of services was possible without abolishing segregation was repudiated. "No argument or rationalization," the Civil Rights Committee asserted, "can alter this basic fact: a law which forbids a group of American citizens to associate with other citizens in the ordinary course of daily living creates inequality by imposing a caste status on the minority group." The coercion of the South was justified as follows: "It is a sound policy to use the idealism and prestige of our whole people to check the wayward tendencies of a part of them." To implement its objective the authors of the report asked for the denial of federal financial aid to any public or private agency permitting race discriminations and for the creation of elaborate staffs within the federal government to ferret out persons guilty of violating civil rights.

The report of the President's Committee on Civil Rights might have become one of the many admonitions for social reform which the American people have long been in the habit of receiving indifferently from its nonpolitical leaders but for one circumstance. President Truman called it "an American Charter of human freedom," and in 1948 asked Congress to implement some of its provisions. This son of a Confederate soldier demanded a federal Fair Employment Practice Commission, federal anti-poll tax and antilynching statutes, and prohibition of the enforcement of segregation in interstate carriers by the carriers themselves. These measures had the support of Northern Democrats and of the Republican majority in Congress. The Southern minority in Congress answered this attack by asserting that the Truman proposals sounded "like the program of the Communists," and that the Northern wing of the Democratic party was controlled by "an organized mongrel minority." There were signs of a Southern revolt like that of 1928. "The people of the South," declared Senator John J. Sparkman of Alabama, "are so bitter that they will never accept Truman as a candidate."

The issue between the Southerners and those who would reform the social practices of their section reached a climax at the National Democratic convention of 1948. "Give us the right to govern our own fundamental affairs," declared a Tennessee delegate in support of a proposal for the protection of the states against interference in civil and social relations. This measure was defeated by vote of 925 to 309, and a platform expressing the radical views of the North and the West was adopted. It commended Truman "for his courageous stand on the issue of civil rights" and urged Congress to repeal the poll tax, make lynchings a federal offense, end segregation in the armed services, and create a Fair Employment Practice Commission. "The South" said a journalist, "has been kicked in the pants, turned around and kicked in the stomach." Immediately the Mississippi and half the Alabama delegates stalked out of the convention hall. The rest of the Southerners remained to contest vainly the sentiment of the convention in favor of Truman as its presidential candidate and to sit in sullen wrath during the demonstration in favor of the nominee.

Three days after the Philadelphia fiasco the dissenters met in convention at Birmingham to organize the States' Rights or Dixiecrat party. The assembled company waved the Confederate flag, snake-danced under the portrait of Robert E. Lee, and condemned as "infamous and iniquitous" the suggestion of equal rights for Negroes. Governors J. Strom Thurmond of South Carolina and Fielding Wright of Mississippi were respectively nominated for President and Vice-President.

The Dixiecrats conducted their canvass under heavy handicaps. The most conservative Southerners had turned "radical" in one of the few meanings of that word their constituents were able to understand. They were affronting the established prejudice of their section in favor of party regularity under all conditions. Embarrassed by this fact, Governor Wright evasively declared. "This is not a bolt. It is not a fourth party. . . . We are the true Democrats of the Southland and of the United States." The ruling politicians of all the Southern states except those of Alabama and Mississippi had stayed away from Birmingham. They remembered the fate of Furnifold M. Simmons and the other bigwigs who bolted in 1928; they did not wish to sacrifice the Truman patronage; and they joined the Southern liberals in not wishing to bring upon their section the odium of a movement easily stigmatized as reactionary.

Thurmond got the nomination because he was eager and ambitious rather than because of his personal or political strength. He suffered from the stigma of anti-Negroism and from the accusation that his declarations were a front to cover the selfish ambitions of millowners, oil magnates, bankers, and other members of the Southern upper class and their corporation allies in New York City. Yet the South Carolina governor and his fellow Dixiecrats carried on a gallant campaign. They cried out against the "mongrel minority who had captured the Democratic party in order to destroy the liberties of the states and lead the country into a totalitarianism comparable to that of Russia or Germany." "The South," said a clerical supporter of the movement,[7] "will no longer be impaled on the barbed rack of loyalty to a party whose leadership in many cities and states has passed into the hands of racketeers and venal experts."

During the months in which the South was pondering over the wisdom of the Dixiecrat movement it gave unmistakable evidence that it stood with Thurmond and Wright in their championship of the section's race distinctions. Henry Wallace and Glenn Taylor, the candidates of the Progressive party, came to the South to proclaim and to practice race equality. Taylor was arrested because he violated a Birmingham ordinance requiring race segregation at public meetings. The

[7] G. Stanley Frazer in *Christian Century*, LXV, 1210 (November 10, 1948).

Virginia authorities tactfully ignored Wallace's violation of their segregation laws; but this brave radical's example of riding through the streets with his Negro secretary and of sleeping in Negro houses was too much for the vaunted liberals of North Carolina. Crowds drowned his words and pelted him with rotten eggs and tomatoes. Truman probably would have received the same treatment had he implemented his liberal talk by appointing Negroes to office in the South or by fraternizing with members of the inferior caste.

The voters of the South refused in 1948 to execute a political revolution. Thurmond and Wright carried only South Carolina, Alabama, Mississippi, and Louisiana. Their thirty-nine electoral votes were not sufficient to deny Truman a majority in the electoral college. The voters had taken orders from their party bosses; they had voted for Thurmond and Wright only in the states where the two Dixiecrats had been officially declared the candidates of the Democratic party. Thereby was avoided the bugbear of Southern politics: the opportunity for the Negroes to hold the balance of power through divisions among the whites. Such directors of political behavior as Harry Byrd, James F. Byrnes, and Herman Talmadge were noncommittal. The political bosses of Arkansas, Texas, Tennessee, and North Carolina supported Truman and thereby prevented the Dixiecrat vote in their states reaching formidable proportions.

With a mandate from the American people to press for his principles, Truman once more in 1949 put his civil rights program before Congress. This time he was administered blows as stunning as those he had imposed upon the Southern bolters of the previous year. A group of elderly senators from the Deep South used what a political scientist [8] mockingly calls the third and fourth houses of Congress. One was the seniority rule, which gave them the advantages of long service. The other was the right of unlimited debate which they boldly used to give practical effect to John C. Calhoun's doctrine of Concurrent Majorities. With the aid of younger colleagues with lustier lungs, they engaged in endless talk against the civil rights program. The Truman forces tried to curb them by calling for a stricter cloture rule. The Southerners then adroitly turned the debate from a struggle over Negro rights into a defense of freedom of speech. When the administration leaders foolishly requested the limitation of debate by simple rather than by two-thirds majority, the Southern opposition was joined by the Republican senators. The latter, more interested in maintaining their minority rights and in frustrating the Truman program of domestic reform than in Negro rights, helped defeat the proposal by a vote of 46 to 41. The rule

[8] James B. Shannon in *Annals of the American Academy of Political and Social Science,* CCLXXV, 58 (May, 1951).

finally adopted made cloture more difficult than ever by requiring the approval of two thirds of the whole Senate. The struggle for civil rights had ended in defeat.

That Southerners approved the 1949 stand of their senators was indicated by the outcome of subsequent elections. Only in Arkansas did they show sympathy for policies of the Truman administration by electing Sid McMath to the governorship. Virginia once more demonstrated its faith in Byrd, the Democratic senator who scored highest in opposing Truman's measures. In 1949 that conservative commonwealth elected a member of the Byrd machine to the governorship. South Carolinians in 1950 made James F. Byrnes their governor. That veteran statesman, after serving the New Deal in Washington in offices as high as that of Secretary of State, returned to his native hearth convinced that the South Carolina way was best.

In the year of Byrnes's election sensational defeats were visited upon Senators Claude Pepper of Florida and Frank Graham of North Carolina, Southern liberals possessing records of almost complete loyalty to the Truman administration. Pepper voted for social legislation and had given utterance to racial sentiments before New York audiences not in harmony with the views of his Florida constituents.

Graham during his nineteen years' presidency of the University of North Carolina won fame as the champion of liberal or radical causes. He fought for organized labor, for academic freedom, and against race discrimination; he was active in organizations later designated as Communist fronts; and he signed enough liberal manifestoes to put the South in the reformer's paradise. He was one of the two Southerners who served on Truman's Committee on Civil Rights. When after a short term in the Senate he stood for re-election, his liberalism was used against him. Yet he led in the first primary of May 27 by 53,000 votes. His simple manners and deep human sympathies made him immensely popular. It was realized that a disarming generosity rather than a rational understanding had made him into a radical, and that despite his utterances he was a member of an old family with friends among the rich and the politically powerful. He lost in the second primary because of unfair emphasis upon his pro-Negro declarations and because pro-Negro decisions of the United States Supreme Court came just before the primary.

The conservative trend in 1950 did not mean a general endorsement of the third partyism of 1948. Thurmond in the former year was defeated for a United States senatorship by Olin D. Johnston, a politician who was acrobatic enough to be both a party regular and an enemy of Trumanism. At the same time Herman Talmadge, who was more blatant than Thurmond in his anti-Negroism, was re-elected governor of

Georgia. He had failed to bolt the party in 1948. In Alabama the regulars won control of the party machinery from the Dixiecrats and a much-admired naval hero made little headway as an independent candidate for the United States Senate. The Republicans made no gains in the general election, and the multitude of newly enfranchised Negroes meekly accepted the leadership of the elders of the Democratic party.

These elders held that party regularity was too strong a Southern tradition to be disturbed safely. They believed that without sacrificing Southern principles there were ways of doing business with Truman. They wanted their shares of the federal patronage, and their constituents wanted defense contracts and farm subsidies. The stronger grip on Congressional committees that the Southerners won because of the elections of 1950 made the President see the necessity of coming to terms with them. Thereby he won their undivided support of his foreign policy and their partial support of his domestic program.

During the time in which the South was able to protect itself against hostile acts of Congress and against revolution through the ballot box, its social and political traditions were challenged by an arm of the federal government as powerful as a Senate filibuster. The federal courts, for many years after Reconstruction protectors of capitalistic and racial privilege, had in the time of Franklin D. Roosevelt turned their activities in the opposite direction. Under the inspiration of the Truman victory of 1948 they applied with renewed zeal the original meanings of the Fourteenth and Fifteenth amendments. The American habit of allowing laws, however benevolent, to fall into abeyance when these laws affronted local custom gave way to a revival of the belief of the radical reconstructionists that undemocratic practices could be eradicated through central authority. There was no device short of mob violence through which the federal courts could be stayed in their desires to alter or abolish state laws.

The Democratic organizations of several Southern states met the court decision of 1944 invalidating white primaries by repealing state laws regulating them. This was on the theory that the placing of these agencies outside the structure of government made them immune to judicial interference. The federal courts struck back by invalidating this move. When the South Carolina Democratic authorities countered with the requirement that prospective voters take an oath repudiating Truman's civil rights program, United States District Judge Waties Waring was furious. This South Carolina aristocrat turned radical ordered the enrollment of Negroes as party members without taking humiliating oaths. He told the Negroes who jammed his court room: "It is a disgrace when you have to come . . . and ask a judge to tell you how to be an American." He did what no white resident of his state had ever done before: entertained Negroes in his home on a basis of social equality.

The South Carolina Democrats were helpless. They could not drive from their midst a man who was both a native aristocrat and a federal judge. They were forced to allow 20,000 Negroes to participate in their 1948 primary. In the South as a whole some 700,000 voted in the presidential election of that year, and by 1950 there was a 300 per cent increase in the Negro vote over that of 1940.[9] Negro leaders in the summer of 1952 hoped that the race's vote in the presidential election of that fall would total one million.

Before the end of World War II state educational authorities, under pressure from the federal courts, had accepted as ultimate goals equal facilities for Negro children and equal pay for Negro teachers. They showed little ill-will when the courts compelled compliance with this principle in specific instances. But they were confounded by the idea that the federal courts should be used by radical non-Southern agencies as the means of breaking the Southern pattern of school segregation. They feared that the white South might be provoked into stark reaction that would undo all constructive advances made in Negro schools and other Negro welfare agencies.

The chief lawyer of the National Association for the Advancement of Colored People declared, "We are going to insist on nonsegregation in American public education from top to bottom . . . from law school to kindergarten." In conformity with the American practice of beginning educational reform at the top, segregation practices were first attacked in the professional and graduate schools. Here Negro education was weakest. The Southern states had done practically nothing for the training of Negroes in the fields of law, engineering, dentistry and medicine. This was because there was not sufficient demand within each state to make such education practical and because the Negro state colleges were so inherently weak that they were incapable of expanding into graduate and professional schools comparable to those of the whites.

The advocates of nonsegregated schools blocked the efforts of the school authorities to comply with a 1896 decision of the United States Supreme Court tolerating separation in public facilities provided these facilities were equal. When certain states tried to equalize professional education by paying Negro students the difference between the cost of education at home and in the North, the enemies of segregation got the courts to declare against this scheme. When the plan of a regional university for Negroes supported by all Southern states was hit upon as a practical means of securing equality, its execution was blocked by the

[9] *The Journal of Negro Education*, XX, 324–50, 490 (Summer, 1951).

friends of racial integration. They persuaded Congress to refuse the sanctions necessary for a treaty among states. The Southern states' only recourse was to establish at their Negro state colleges facilities for advanced instruction. The few Negroes who presented themselves for such schooling were mostly in the field of law. These law schools were absurd affairs because they had so few students. "In a class by himself," said an observer in 1949, "Kentucky's only Negro law student is not suffering from lack of instructors." Seven state university professors made a weekly journey of twenty-five miles to meet his needs!

It was easy now to secure the admission of Negroes into graduate and professional schools of state institutions by proving that the separate schools provided for Negroes were not equal. This was done in all states except a few of the Deep South. Beginning in 1947 colored students trickled into white universities. In 1950 two hundred or more such persons enrolled in twenty-one graduate and professional schools in eleven of the seventeen states in which separate schools had previously been maintained by law. Kentucky modified its law against interracial schools to the extent of allowing the admission of Negroes to undergraduate work in those institutions of higher learning whose trustees so elected. As a consequence several colleges, including Berea and the Southern Baptist Theological Seminary, opened their doors to Negroes. The University of Louisville applied this principle to the extent of abolishing its Negro branch.

These triumphs encouraged the National Association for the Advancement of Colored People to enter suits against biracial public schools. The issue came to a head when a federal tribunal consisting of Judge Waring and two Southern conservatives heard in May, 1951, a plea for the abolition of segregation in the lower schools of Clarendon county in the South Carolina black belt. In the following February the petition of the Negro high school students of Prince Edward county in the Virginia black belt to enter a white school was heard by another panel of federal judges. Proof that both the South Carolina and Virginia schools in question gave Negroes second-rate privileges was supplemented by the assertion that legal separation created among the Negro children "psychological roadblocks" which prevented them from "fully absorbing" the educational process. The South Carolina authorities answered by promising amends through a $75,000,000 school equalization program, and the Prince Edward authorities promised that county's Negro children a luxurious high school. The courts in both cases allowed the continuation of segregation with the proviso that the school authorities give proof that they were fulfilling their promises. The National Association for the Advancement of Colored People appealed the cases to the United States Supreme Court. This appeal was heard in

December, 1952, with the promise of a decision in the spring of 1953.

Will the placing of the members of the two races in the same class-rooms be an opening wedge to the ultimate abolition of the Southern caste system? Contrary to predictions, there was no violence against the entrance of Negroes into white universities like that which kept Negroes out of white residential areas. But no fundamental alteration in race relations is likely to result immediately. The Georgia legislature in 1951 provided for the withholding of state financial aid from public schools and units of the state university if any court should order the admission of Negroes to a white educational institution; Governor Byrnes threatened the abolition of the public schools of South Carolina as an alternative to mixed schools, and the voters of South Carolina in November, 1952, approved by a great majority the removal of the constitutional obligation to maintain public schools. Influential political leaders in other Southern states mapped for their legislatures programs similar to those threatened in Georgia and South Carolina.

The legal authorities of most Southern states have fought against the abandonment of segregation case by case and school by school. The federal courts have enunciated no broad doctrine on the issue, contenting themselves with deciding constitutional questions in the context of particular cases. Although universities were enjoined against setting apart their Negro students through statute or regulation, the courts have nothing to say against the refusal of individual whites to commingle with Negro students. There has been little or no such commingling.[10] It is therefore likely that the average Negro, for the same reasons that he goes to a separate church, will for the indefinite future prefer the school of his own race.

The approach of the presidential election of 1952 found the defenders of the Southern position in politics as strong as they were in 1950. They had respected leaders in Byrd, Byrnes, and a Georgia group headed by Governor Herman Talmadge and Senator Richard Russell. They won the gratitude of those interested in national security by keeping the controversy over the dismissal of General Douglas MacArthur within reasonable bounds and by protecting Truman against the enemies of his foreign policy. At the same time they continued a largely successful opposition to the President's domestic policies. This opposition came to a head when Senator Byrd at Atlanta on June 25, 1951, called on the South to contest Truman's policies at the Democratic national convention of 1952.

"The South is not impotent," warned the Virginian. "True, it is a minority in the Democratic party, but no Democratic President can be

[10] See Horace Mann Bond's emphatic confirmation of this assertion in *The Journal of Negro Education*, XXI, 242-4 (Summer, 1952).

elected without the vote of the Southern states." He demanded the restoration of the two-thirds rule for the nomination of presidential candidates and the adoption of a platform opposing the heavy costs of the federal establishment and the President's social and economic program. A few months later this champion of conservatism at Selma, Alabama, denounced "fiscal irresponsibility," "civil rights," "tin-horn political incompetents," and "socialistic do-gooders."

These ominous words were supplemented by provisions being made for the reassembling of Democratic state conventions in Virginia, South Carolina, Georgia, Mississippi, Louisiana, and Texas if the national party nominated a candidate and adopted a platform odious to the South. That such a candidate would be nominated and such a program adopted was made clear by Truman and the Northern majority. But what the Byrd-Byrnes leadership would do was not clear when the national convention assembled in July, 1952. Would Byrd and Byrnes attempt to do what they refused to do in 1948: lead a sufficient number of the states of the former Confederacy in a revolt which might deprive Truman's candidate of a majority in the electoral college?

No bolt of Southern delegates took place like that of 1948. An attempt was made by a group of Northern liberals to deny seats in the convention to those who refused to obligate themselves to be loyal to the nominee and platform of the national party. These liberals felt that they could win, as Roosevelt and Truman had done, without the support of the Solid South. But the older heads of the party feared to take this risk and evolved a loyalty oath which meant different things to different men. Most of the Southern delegates signed with their fingers crossed. Not so the Virginians, the South Carolinians, and the Louisianians. They rejected such a pledge as "unnecessary, unprecedented and insulting." A motion to seat the Virginia delegation was carried by the narrow margin of 615 to 529 only after the Illinois delegation shifted its vote in favor of the Virginians. This concession was the sugar-coating of the bitter pill the South was expected to swallow: the nomination of Adlai Stevenson, the pro-Truman governor of Illinois.

In the meantime a platform was adopted endorsing the social welfare and the civil rights program of the Truman administration and calling on the United States Senate to adopt a more effective cloture rule. But the platform lost its sting because it was adopted without debate and did not carry a specific endorsement of compulsory Fair Employment practices.

A majority of Southern politicians remained loyal to the party. This included Talmadge and Russell of Georgia, the Longs of Louisiana, the dominant elements in the former Dixiecrat states of Alabama and Mississippi, the party bosses of North Carolina, Tennessee, Kentucky, and

Arkansas, and at least 90 per cent of the Southern members of Congress. There was much at stake in the way of political patronage and Congressional power. There was much in the party platform that appealed to the interests of the farmers and common people of both races of the poorest section of the United States. The Presidential nominee appealed to the South's genteel tradition. Governor Stevenson was a cultivated member of a distinguished family with Virginia and North Carolina forebears.

There were, on the other hand, forces at work threatening a party break like that of 1928. President Truman and his administration was suspected and even hated by most white Southerners. This was because of the civil rights program, the alleged extravagance and corruption of the federal services, and the almost instinctive aversion of a strongly traditional people for government interference in social and economic matters. The cry of the Southern upper classes against high income taxes and business regulations was echoed by a people accustomed to accept the advice of their betters. There was a tendency to cling to Stevenson as long as there was hope that he might promise to temper the Truman policies. But when the Presidential candidate forthrightly endorsed the civil rights and the social welfare programs, and the plan for federal ownership of the offshore oil reserves of Louisiana and Texas, the hope of maintaining the Solid South went glimmering. Byrnes and Byrd repudiated Stevenson and rededicated the South to white supremacy and capitalistic freedom.

The result was that Virginia, Florida, and Texas by large majorities, and Tennessee by a small majority, gave their votes to Dwight Eisenhower, the victorious Republican candidate. The rest of the South remained in the Democratic column. But in South Carolina, Louisiana, and Kentucky the Republican candidate almost won, and in every other Southern state except Alabama and Mississippi, Eisenhower polled more than 40 per cent of the votes.

The Presidential election of 1952 showed that the patience of Southern Democrats could be exhausted through the pro-Negro and radical policies of the national party. It may mean the emergence of a genuine two-party system, with Republican leadership in the hands of the wealthy and with the existing coalition between the Republicans and Southern congressmen made into something formal and permanent. Because of narrow majorities the Republican Congress of 1953 must curry favor with the Southerners to carry out the Eisenhower program. On the other hand, the defeat of 1952 may mean that the Northern wing will return to its pre-Roosevelt tradition of pleasing the South and thereby bring about the intersectional unity that has often brought success to the party. Certainly thousands of those who voted for Eisenhower still thought of themselves as Democrats. There was little tendency to join the Republican party or to repudiate any Democratic leaders except Truman and Stevenson.

* * *

The South in the 1950's accepted with its accustomed eagerness everything in machines and investments Northerners offered. Provincial behavior did not vanish with imported material innovations. Economic carpetbaggers were accepted only on condition that they not become social or political carpetbaggers. The inhabitants of Northern-style houses behind well-clipped lawns were no more receptive to alien ideas than were the inhabitants of old mansions behind bushy lawns. Restaurants bright with bakelite facings and neon lights served food as greasy and as overcooked as cabins in the backwoods. The people continued to show little class consciousness; the masses continued to imitate their betters. The traditional type of political leadership was more universally accepted than in the days of Ben Tillman and Theodore G. Bilbo. The Negro showed little more inclination to use his newly won political privileges along lines of non-Southern radicalism than he had used the religious freedom he had won eighty years earlier. Most prophets believed that the region below the Potomac would ultimately incorporate the Negro in the main stream of its social, economic, and political life; yet in 1952 there were few signs of this expected revolution. The South had learned largely because of outside pressures to be more generous in bestowing governmental benefits upon its lower caste; it showed no inclination to share important elements of power with its Negroes.

The South in 1952 was almost as complacent as when it was attacked by the abolitionists or the Reconstruction radicals. This was symbolized by the appearance in 1951 of Confederate flags in many places—on the windshields of automobiles, on desks, on neckties. This was pure sentiment, not an effort to revive the Confederate States; but it was a sentiment based on the conviction that the traditions stemming from it should have a part in protecting America from forms of outrageous modernism. The section's many surviving virtues still appealed to its people of both sexes and both races. These people had the advantage of a traditional society in which, as Donald Davidson says, family, kinship, folkways, and custom supplied needs that in a progressive society must be supplied at great cost by artificial devices like schools and government agencies. True Southerners were warmed by what Norman Foerster describes as "a land of varied forests and varied contour, from mountain to sea, a land of exceptional natural beauty" inhabited by a people who "impress one at once with their different voices, different accent, their sense of manners, the courtesy that appears in all classes, their organic folksiness (as if of one family), their awareness of the past as a force both hampering and helping." [11]

[11] "Iowa, North Carolina and the Humanities," *The North Carolina Historical Review*, XXIII, 222 (April, 1946).

Bibliography

⋙-⋙

CHAPTER I

THE LOUISIANA State University Press promises the publication of a ten-volume series, "History of the South," under the editorship of Wendell H. Stephenson and E. Merton Coulter, of which the following have appeared: Wesley F. Craven: *The Southern Colonies in the Seventeenth Century, 1607–1689* (Baton Rouge, 1949); Charles S. Sydnor: *The Development of Southern Sectionalism, 1819–1848* (Baton Rouge, 1948); E. Merton Coulter: *The Confederate States of America, 1861–1865* (Baton Rouge, 1950), and *The South during Reconstruction, 1865–1877* (Baton Rouge, 1947); and C. Vann Woodward: *Origins of the New South, 1877–1913* (Baton Rouge, 1951). Pending the completion of this scholarly series the most satisfactory substitute is Julian A. C. Chandler and others: *The South in the Building of the Nation* (13 vols., Richmond, 1909–13). This example of the best scholarship of the New South movement has excellent sections on agricultural and industrial history. Clement Eaton: *A History of the Old South* (New York, 1949), is both comprehensive and sprightly. Robert S. Cotterill: *The Old South* (Glendale, California, 1936), is a series of challenging essays that emphasize western expansion. William B. Hesseltine: *The South in American History* (rev. ed., New York, 1943), stresses the ante-bellum period. Benjamin B. Kendrick and Alex M. Arnett: *The South Looks at Its Past* (Chapel Hill, 1935), is a brief but comprehensible statement of regional problems. William G. Brown: *The Lower South in American History* (New York, 1902); James W. Garner, ed.: *Studies in Southern History and Politics* (New York, 1914); and David K. Jackson, ed.: *American Studies in Honor of William Kenneth Boyd* (Durham, 1940), present essays on important phases of Southern history.

Numerous aspects of institutional life are appraised by thirty-one authors in William T. Couch, ed.: *Culture in the South* (Chapel Hill, 1934). Rupert B. Vance: *Human Geography of the South* (Chapel Hill, 1932), and

Almon E. Parkins: *The South, Its Economic-Geographic Development* (New York, 1938), ably discuss the relation of physical environment to the life of the people. Histories of the states and their people are imaginatively described in the "American Guide Series" of the Writers' Program of Work Projects Administration. Pertinent volumes are *Mississippi* (New York, 1938); *New Orleans* (Boston, 1938); *North Carolina* (Chapel Hill, 1939); *Florida* (New York, 1939); *Tennessee* (New York, 1939); *Kentucky* (New York, 1939); *Texas* (New York, 1940); *Georgia* (Athens, 1940); *Virginia* (New York, 1940); *South Carolina* (New York, 1941); *Alabama* (New York, 1941); *Arkansas* (New York, 1941); *Louisiana* (New York, 1941); *Oklahoma* (Norman, 1941); and *Atlanta* (New York, 1942).

Among recent one-volume state histories are John G. Fletcher: *Arkansas* (Chapel Hill, 1947); David D. Wallace: *South Carolina, a Short History* (Chapel Hill, 1951); E. Merton Coulter: *Georgia, a Short History* (Chapel Hill, 1947); Kathryn T. Abbey Hanna: *Florida, Land of Change* (Chapel Hill, 1948); Matthew Page Andrews: *Virginia, the Old Dominion* (New York, 1937); Rupert N. Richardson: *Texas, the Lone Star State* (New York, 1943); and Thomas D. Clark: *A History of Kentucky* (New York, 1937). The most interesting general history of Virginia is William C. Bruce: *The Virginia Plutarch* (2 vols., Chapel Hill, 1929). The most attractive history of Tennessee is Donald Davidson: *The Tennessee* [River] (2 vols. New York, 1946 and 1948). The following state histories have much that is valuable hidden among bulky biographical data: David D. Wallace: *History of South Carolina* (4 vols., New York, 1934); David Y. Thomas, ed.: *Arkansas and Its People* (4 vols., New York, 1930); Philip M. Hamer, ed.: *Tennessee, a History, 1673–1932* (4 vols., New York, 1933); Dunbar Rowland: *History of Mississippi* (2 vols., Jackson, 1925); Albert B. Moore: *Alabama and Her People* (Chicago, 1925); Robert D. W. Connor, William K. Boyd, and J. G. de Roulhac Hamilton: *History of North Carolina* (6 vols., Chicago, 1919).

A wealth of magazine material on Southern history can be found in *The Journal of Southern History* (Baton Rouge, 1935–44; Nashville, 1945–48; Lexington, Kentucky, 1949—); *Southwestern Historical Quarterly* (Austin, 1897—); *Southwestern Social Science Quarterly* (Norman, 1920—). *The American Historical Review* (Richmond, 1895—); *The Mississippi Valley Historical Review* (Lincoln, 1914—); *Agricultural History* (Washington, 1927—); *Social Forces* (Baltimore, 1922—); *Southern Economic Journal* (Chapel Hill, 1933—); and *American Literature* (Durham, 1929—), contain many articles on the South. The least antiquarian local historical reviews are *The William and Mary Quarterly, a Magazine of Early American History* (3 series, Williamsburg, 1943—); *The Georgia Historical Quarterly* (Savannah, 1917—); *The North Carolina Historical Review* (Raleigh, 1924—); and *Louisiana Historical Quarterly* (New Orleans, 1917—). *The Sewanee Review* (Sewanee, 1892—), first edited by William P. Trent; *The South Atlantic Quarterly* (Durham, 1902—), first edited by John S. Bassett; *The Southwest Review* (Dallas, 1915—); *The Virginia Quarterly Review* (Charlottesville, 1925—), first edited by James Southall Wilson; *Southern Review* (Baton Rouge, 1935–42); and *The Georgia Review* (Athens, 1947—), present many articles of interest to the historian.

Among helpful general works on American history are Allen Johnson and Dumas Malone, eds.: *Dictionary of American Biography* (21 vols., New York, 1928–1944); James T. Adams, ed.: *Dictionary of American History*

(5 vols., New York, 1940); Edward Channing: *A History of the United States* (6 vols., New York, 1905–25); James Ford Rhodes: *History of the United States from the Compromise of 1850* (7 vols., New York, 1893–1906); Harold U. Faulkner: *American Political and Social History* (4th ed., New York, 1946); Oliver P. Chitwood and Frank L. Owsley: *A Short History of the American People* (New York, 1945); and Samuel E. Morison and Henry S. Commager: *The Growth of the American Republic* (2 vols., New York, 1942); and Harry J. Carman and Harold C. Syrett: *A History of the American People* (2 vols., New York, 1952).

Attempts to define the South are made by James G. Randall: *The Civil War and Reconstruction* (Boston, 1937), pp. 3–6; Ulrich B. Phillips: *The Course of the South to Secession* (New York, 1939); Avery O. Craven: *The Repressible Conflict, 1830–1861* (Baton Rouge, 1939), pp. 1–30; William E. Dodd: "The Emergence of the First Social Order in the United States," *American Historical Review*, XL, 217–31 (January, 1933); John C. Ransom: "The South Defends Its Heritage," *Harper's Magazine*, CLIX, 108–18 (June, 1929); Count Hermann Keyserling: "The South—America's Hope," *The Atlantic Monthly*, CXLIV, 605–08 (November, 1929); Francis B. Simkins: "The South," in Merrill Jensen, ed.: *Regionalism in America* (Madison, 1951); and the essays by Herbert M. McLuhan, Robert B. Heilman, William Van O'Conner and Louis B. Wright in Allen Tate, ed.: *A Southern Vanguard* (New York, 1947).

CHAPTER II

THE COLONIAL South is comprehensively treated in Thomas J. Wertenbaker: *The Old South: the Founding of American Civilization* (New York, 1942). John Fiske: *Old Virginia and Her Neighbors* (2 vols., Boston, 1900), is still the most interesting narrative. Handy yet comprehensive is Curtis P. Nettels: *The Roots of American Civilization* (New York, 1938). Older treatments of seventeenth-century foundations are Lyon G. Tyler: *England in America* (New York, 1904), and Mary Johnston: *Pioneers of the Old South* (New Haven, 1921). The latest and most just appraisal is Wesley F. Craven: *The Southern Colonies in the Seventeenth Century*. Exhaustive and refreshingly tolerant of aristocratic concepts are the three works of Philip A. Bruce: *Economic History of Virginia in the Seventeenth Century* (2 vols., New York, 1896); *Institutional History of Virginia in the Seventeenth Century* (2 vols., New York, 1910); and *Social Life of Virginia in the Seventeenth Century* (2nd edition, Lynchburg, 1927).

Problems of early Virginia are explained in George B. Parks: *Richard Hakluyt and the English Voyages* (New York, 1928); Edward Arber and Arthur G. Bradley, eds.: *Travels and Works of Captain John Smith* (2 vols., Edinburgh, 1910); Thomas J. Wertenbaker: *The First Americans, 1607–1690* (New York, 1929); John G. Fletcher: *John Smith—also Pocahontas* (New York, 1928); and E. Keble Chatterton: *Captain John Smith* (New York, 1927).

The activities of the non-English in the early South are set forth in Herbert E. Bolton: *The Spanish Borderlands* (New Haven, 1921); Herbert I. Priestley: *The Coming of the White Man, 1492–1848* (New York, 1929); J. Bartlet Brebner: *The Explorers of North America* (New York,

1933); Woodbury Lowery: *The Spanish Settlements within the Present Limits of the United States, 1513–1561* (New York, 1901); John T. Lanning: *The Spanish Missions of Georgia* (Chapel Hill, 1935); Albert Phelps: *Louisiana* (Boston, 1905); and Henry E. Chambers: *Mississippi Valley Beginnings* (New York, 1922). The Indian problem is explained in Clark Wissler: *The American Indian* (New York, 1922); Chapman J. Milling: *Red Carolinians* (Chapel Hill, 1940); and Samuel C. Williams, ed.: *Adair's History of the American Indians* (Johnson City, 1930).

CHAPTER III

THE EARLY history of Maryland is set forth in Matthew P. Andrews: *The Founding of Maryland* (New York, 1933); Bernard C. Steiner: *Beginnings of Maryland, 1631–1639* (Baltimore, 1903); and Newton D. Mereness: *Maryland as a Proprietary Province* (New York, 1901). The founding of Carolina is treated in Alexander S. Salley, ed.: *Narratives of Early Carolina, 1650–1708* (New York, 1911); Edward McCrady: *History of South Carolina under the Proprietary Government, 1670–1719* (New York, 1897); W. Roy Smith: *South Carolina as a Royal Province* (New York, 1903); Arthur H. Hirsch: *The Hugenots of Colonial South Carolina* (Durham, 1928); David D. Wallace: *South Carolina, A Short History*; Robert D. W. Connor: *North Carolina, Rebuilding an Ancient Commonwealth*, Vol. I; Charles L. Raper: *North Carolina: A Royal Province, 1729–1775* (Chapel Hill, 1901); John Lawson: *The History of North Carolina* (Richmond, 1937); and Louise F. Brown: *The First Earl of Shaftesbury* (New York, 1933). The settlement of Georgia is in Amos A. Ettinger: *James Edward Oglethorpe* (Oxford, 1936); James R. McCain: *Georgia as a Proprietary Province* (Boston, 1917); and Lawrence H. Gipson: *The British Empire before the American Revolution* (New York, 1939), Vol. II, chap. vi.

The settlement of the back country is set forth in Charles A. Hanna: *The Scotch-Irish* (2 vols., New York, 1902); Henry J. Ford: *The Scotch-Irish in America* (Princeton, 1903); Albert B. Faust: *The German Element in the United States* (2 vols., Boston, 1909); Verner W. Crane: *The Southern Frontier, 1670–1732* (Durham, 1928); Arthur P. Whitaker: *Spanish-American Frontier, 1783–1795* (Boston, 1927); Constance L. Skinner: *Pioneers of the Old Southwest* (New Haven, 1919); Archibald Henderson: *Conquest of the Old Southwest* (New York, 1920); Everett Dick: *The Dixie Frontier, a Social History* (New York, 1948); Thomas P. Abernethy: *Three Virginia Frontiers* (Baton Rouge, 1940), and *From Frontier to Plantation in Tennessee* (Chapel Hill, 1932); Archer B. Hulbert: *Boone's Wilderness Road* (Cleveland, 1903); John E. Bakeless: *Daniel Boone* (New York, 1939); Carl S. Driver: *John Sevier* (Chapel Hill, 1932); and Katheryn H. Mason: *James Harrod* (Baton Rouge, 1951).

CHAPTER IV

THE GENERAL histories by Nettels, Wesley F. Craven, Charles M. Andrews, Philip A. Bruce, and David D. Wallace have much to say about the development of the provincial governments. They are supplemented by Herbert L.

Osgood: *The American Colonies in the Eighteenth Century* (2 vols., New York, 1924); Lawrence H. Gipson: *The British Empire before the American Revolution*, Vol. II; and Beverley W. Bond, Jr.: *The Quit-Rent System in the American Colonies* (New Haven, 1919). The governmental development of individual colonies is explained in Percy S. Flippen: *The Royal Government of Virginia* (New York, 1919); Julian A. C. Chandler: *History of the Suffrage in Virginia* (Baltimore, 1901); Robert Beverley: *The History and Present State of Virginia* (Chapel Hill, 1944); Leonidas Dodson: *Alexander Spotswood* (Philadelphia, 1932); Louis K. Koontz: *Robert Dinwiddie* (Glendale, 1941); Coralie Parker: *The History of Taxation in North Carolina, 1663-1776* (New York, 1928); John S. Bassett: *The Constitutional Beginnings of North Carolina* (Baltimore, 1894); Edson L. Whitney: *The Government of the Colony of South Carolina* (Baltimore, 1895); Edward McCrady: *South Carolina under the Royal Government, 1719-1776* (New York, 1899); and James Glen: *A Description of South Carolina* (London, 1761). The role of the governing gentry is brilliantly set forth in Carl Bridenbaugh: *Seat of Empire* (Williamsburg, 1950) and Charles S. Sydnor: *Gentleman Freeholders* (Chapel Hill, 1952). Intraprovincial sectionalism is explained in Thomas J. Wertenbaker: *Torchbearer of the Revolution: the Story of Bacon's Rebellion and Its Leader* (Princeton, 1940); John S. Bassett: "The Regulators of North Carolina," American Historical Association, *Annual Report* (Washington, 1894); and William A. Schaper: "Sectionalism and Representation in South Carolina," American Historical Association, *Annual Report*, Vol. I (Washington, 1900).

CHAPTER V

THE ORIGINS of Colonial agriculture and labor are set forth in the works of Ulrich B. Phillips and Lewis C. Gray listed in the bibliography of Chapter VIII. White labor is explained by Abbot E. Smith: *Colonists in Bondage, White Servitude and Convict Labor in America, 1607-1776* (Chapel Hill, 1947); Eugene I. McCormac: *White Servitude in Maryland* (Baltimore, 1904); James C. Ballagh: *White Servitude in the Colony of Virginia* (Baltimore, 1895); and Julia C. Spruill: *Women's Life and Work in the Southern Colonies* (Chapel Hill, 1938). Studies of Negro labor in the several colonies are Jeffrey R. Brackett: *The Negro in Maryland* (Baltimore, 1889); James C. Ballagh: *A History of Slavery in Virginia* (Baltimore, 1902); Virginia Writers' Project: *The Negro in Virginia* (New York, 1940); Edward McCrady: "Slavery in South Carolina, 1670-1770," American Historical Association, *Annual Report* (Washington, 1896); Frank J. Klingberg, *An Appraisal of the Negro in Colonial South Carolina* (Washington, 1941); and John S. Bassett: *Slavery and Servitude in North Carolina* (Baltimore, 1896). The role of the staple crops is explained in Joseph C. Robert: *The Story of Tobacco in America* (New York, 1949); Duncan C. Heyward: *Seeds from Madagascar* (Chapel Hill, 1937); and Harriott H. Ravenel: *Eliza [Lucas] Pinckney* (New York, 1909).

Colonial architecture is discussed in Fiske Kimball: *Domestic Architecture of the American Colonies and Early Republic* (New York, 1922); Rexford Newcomb: *The Colonial and Federal House* (Philadelphia, 1933); Henry C. Foreman: *The Architecture of the Old South, Medieval Style,*

1585–1850 (Cambridge, Mass., 1948); Thomas T. Waterman: *The Mansions of Virginia, 1706–1776* (Chapel Hill, 1946); and Harold R. Shurtleff: *The Log Cabin Myth* (Cambridge, Mass., 1939). Social life in the colonies is described in Arthur W. Calhoun: *A Social History of the American Family from Colonial Times to the Present* (3 vols., Cleveland, 1917–19); Thomas J. Wertenbaker: *The Old South: the Founding of American Civilization* (New York, 1942); Charles M. Andrews: *Colonial Folkways* (New Haven, 1921); Alice M. Earle: *Colonial Dames and Good Wives* (Boston, 1895); William K. Boyd, ed.: *William Byrd's Histories of the Dividing Line Betwixt Virginia and North Carolina* (Raleigh, 1929); Andrew Burnaby: *Travels through North America* (new ed., New York, 1904); Hunter D. Farish, ed.: *Journal and Letters of Philip Vickers Fithian, 1773–1774* (Williamsburg, 1943); and Carl Bridenbaugh: *Cities in the Wilderness: The First Century of Urban Life in America, 1625–1742* (New York, 1938).

Educational history is explained by Edgar W. Knight: *Public Education in the South* (Boston, 1922), and Knight, ed.: *Documentary History of Education in the South before 1860* (3 vols., Chapel Hill, 1949, 1950, and 1952). Cultural history is brilliantly set forth in Frederick P. Bowes: *The Culture of Early Charleston* (Chapel Hill, 1942); Vernon L. Parrington: *Main Currents of American Thought: The Colonial Mind, 1620–1800* (New York, 1927), Vol. I; and Louis B. Wright: *The First Gentlemen of Virginia: Intellectual Qualities of the Early Colonial Ruling Class* (San Marino, 1940). Most comprehensive and stimulating is John M. Mecklin: *The Story of American Dissent* (New York, 1934). Effective defenses of the Anglican establishment are Edward L. Goodwin: *The Colonial Church in Virginia* (Milwaukee, 1927), and George M. Brydon: *Virginia's Mother Church* (2 vols., Richmond and Philadelphia, 1947 and 1952), and *The Established Church and the Revolution* (Richmond, 1930). Overcritical of the Virginia church are Francis L. Hawks: *Contributions to American Church History* (2 vols., New York, 1836–39); and Bishop William Meade: *Old Churches, Ministers and Families of Virginia* (2 vols., Philadelphia, 1857). An able exposition from the viewpoint of the dissenters is Wesley M. Gewehr: *The Great Awakening in Virginia* (Durham, 1930). Revealing if naïve is Robert B. Semple, *A History of the Rise and Progress of the Baptists in Virginia* (Philadelphia, 1894). Scholarly treatments are to be found in Albert W. Werline: *Church and State in Maryland* (South Lancaster, Massachusetts, 1948), Reba C. Strickland: *Religion and the State in Georgia in the Eighteenth Century* (New York, 1939).

CHAPTER VI

THE GENERAL state, sectional, and national histories previously mentioned do not neglect the American Revolution. Special treatments are John C. Miller: *Origins of the American Revolution* (Boston, 1943); Carl L. Becker: *The Eve of the Revolution* (New Haven, 1918); and Claude H. Van Tyne: *War of Independence* (Boston, 1929). Social aspects of the movement are emphasized in Evarts B. Greene: *The Revolutionary Generation, 1763–1790* (New York, 1943); Allan Nevins: *The American States during and after the Revolution* (New York, 1924); Thomas P. Abernethy: *Western Lands and the American Revolution* (New York, 1937); and J. Franklin Jameson: *The*

American Revolution Considered as a Social Movement (Princeton, 1926). Intellectual aspects of the movement are considered by Carl L. Becker: *The Declaration of Independence* (New York, 1942); Randolph G. Adams: *The Political Ideas of the American Revolution* (Durham, 1922); Charles E. Merriam: *A History of American Political Theories* (New York, 1928); Adrienne Koch: *The Philosophy of Thomas Jefferson* (New York, 1943); and Parrington: *The Colonial Mind.* State histories of the revolutionary period are Hamilton J. Eckenrode: *The Revolution in Virginia* (New York, 1916); Eckenrode: *Separation of Church and State in Virginia* (Richmond, 1910); Charles R. Lingley: *Transition in Virginia from Colony to Commonwealth* (New York, 1910); Enoch W. Sikes: *Transition of North Carolina from Colony to Commonwealth* (Baltimore, 1898); Leila Sellers: *Charleston Business on the Eve of the Revolution* (Chapel Hill, 1934); Edward McCrady: *South Carolina in the Revolution* (2 vols., New York, 1902); Isaac S. Harrell: *Loyalism in Virginia* (Durham, 1926); and Robert O. DeMond: *The Loyalists in North Carolina during the Revolution* (Durham, 1940).

Post-Revolutionary developments in the South are treated in Andrew C. McLaughlin: *The Confederation and the Constitution* (New York, 1905); Merrill Jensen: *New Nation* (New York, 1950); Carl Van Doren: *The Great Rehearsal, the Story of the Making and the Ratification of the Constitution of the United States* (New York, 1948); Hugh B. Grisby: *The History of the Virginia Federal Convention of 1788* (2 vols., Richmond, 1891); Charles G. Singer: *South Carolina in the Confederation* (Philadelphia, 1941); Louise I. Trenholme: *Ratification of the Federal Constitution in North Carolina* (New York, 1932); and John H. Wolfe: *Jeffersonian Democracy in South Carolina* (Chapel Hill, 1940).

Pre-eminent among the many biographies of Southerners of the Revolutionary generation are Douglas S. Freeman: *George Washington, a Biography* (5 vols. to date, New York, 1948–1952); David May: *Edmund Pendleton* (2 vols., Cambridge, Massachusetts, 1952); Dumas Malone: *Jefferson the Virginian,* and *Jefferson and the Rights of Man* (2 vols. to date, Boston, 1948 and 1951); Irving Brant: *James Madison* (3 vols. to date, Indianapolis, 1941, 1948, and 1950); Helen D. Hill: *George Mason, Constitutionalist* (Cambridge, Mass., 1938); George Morgan: *The True Patrick Henry* (Philadelphia, 1907); Griffith J. McRee: *James Iredell* (2 vols., New York, 1857); Ross F. Lockridge: *George Rogers Clark* (Chicago, 1927); David D. Wallace: *Henry Laurens* (New York, 1915); and Burton J. Hendrick: *The Lees of Virginia* (New York, 1935). Richard Hofstadter: *The American Tradition and the Men Who Made It* (New York, 1948), contains a brilliant characterization of the Revolutionary leaders.

CHAPTER VII

SECTIONAL controversy is discussed in the general histories by William G. Brown, Cotterill, Eaton, Hesseltine, Randall, Carman and Syrett, and Morison and Commager. Charles S. Sydnor: *The Development of Southern Sectionalism, 1819–1848* is a reappraisal based on the sources. Other intensive period studies are Frederick J. Turner: *Rise of the New West* (New York, 1906); William MacDonald: *Jacksonian Democracy* (New York, 1906); Frederic A. Ogg: *Reign of Andrew Jackson* (New Haven, 1919); George P.

Garrison: *Westward Extension* (New York, 1906); Nathaniel W. Stephenson: *Texas and the Mexican War* (New Haven, 1919). Fresh treatments of the subject are provided by Carl R. Fish: *The Rise of the Common Man, 1830–50* (New York, 1927), and Avery O. Craven: *The Coming of the Civil War* (New York, 1942). Abolitionism is covered by Albert B. Hart: *Slavery and Abolition* (New York, 1906), and Gilbert H. Barnes: *The Anti-Slavery Impulse, 1830–1844* (New York, 1933). Among defenses of slavery by contemporaries are Thomas R. Dew: *Review of the Debates of the Virginia Legislature of 1831 and 1832* (Richmond, 1832); Albert T. Bledsoe: *An Essay on Liberty and Slavery* (Philadelphia, 1857); and E. N. Elliott, ed.: *Pro-Slavery Argument* (Augusta, 1852). William S. Jenkins: *Pro-Slavery Thought of the Old South* (Chapel Hill, 1935), gives a comprehensive estimate. This may be supplemented by Joseph C. Robert: *The Road from Monticello: A Study of the Virginia Slavery Debate of 1832* (Durham, 1941), and Wilfred Carsel: "The Slaveholders' Indictment of Northern Wage Slavery," *The Journal of Southern History*, VI, 504–20 (November, 1940). The history of the political ideas of the Old South is ably presented in Charles E. Merriam: *History of American Political Theories* (2nd ed., New York, 1922); Vernon C. Parrington: *The Romantic Revolution in America, 1800–1860* (New York, 1927); Jesse T. Carpenter: *The South as a Conscious Minority, 1789–1861* (New York, 1930); Clement Eaton: *Freedom of Thought in the Old South* (Durham, 1940); William E. Dodd: *The Cotton Kingdom* (New Haven, 1919).

Internal politics of the Old South are discussed by Fletcher M. Green: *Constitutional Development in the South Atlantic States, 1776–1860* (Chapel Hill, 1930), and "Democracy in the Old South," *The Journal of Southern History*, XII, 2–23 (February, 1946); Gus W. Dyer: *Democracy in the South before the Civil War* (Nashville, 1905); Arthur C. Cole: *The Whig Party in the South* (Washington, 1913); Ulrich B. Phillips: "The Southern Whigs, 1834–54," in *Essays in American History Dedicated to Frederick Jackson Turner* (New York, 1910); Robert R. Russel: *Economic Aspects of Southern Sectionalism* (Urbana, 1924). Nullification is treated by David F. Houston: *Critical Study of Nullification in South Carolina* (Cambridge, Mass., 1896); Frederic Bancroft: *Calhoun and the South Carolina Nullification Movement* (Baltimore, 1928); Chauncey S. Boucher: *Nullification Controversy in South Carolina* (Chicago, 1916). Political problems of individual states are analyzed by Theodore H. Jack: *Sectionalism and Party Politics in Alabama 1819–1842* (Menasha, 1919); Ulrich B. Phillips: "Georgia and State Rights," American Historical Association, *Annual Report*, II (Washington, 1901); Horace Montgomery: *Cracker Parties* (Baton Rouge, 1951); Richard H. Shryock: *Georgia and the Union in 1850* (Durham, 1926); Henry McG. Wagstaff: *States Rights and Political Parties in North Carolina, 1776–1861* (Baltimore, 1906); Charles H. Ambler: *Sectionalism in Virginia from 1776 to 1861* (Chicago, 1910); William A. Schaper: "Sectionalism and Representation in South Carolina," American Historical Association, *Annual Report* (Washington, 1901), I, 237–463; John G. Van Deusen: *Economic Basis of Disunion in South Carolina* (New York, 1928); Thomas P. Abernethy: *From Frontier to Plantation in Tennessee* (Chapel Hill, 1932). An interesting phase of politics is explained by W. Darrell Overdyke: *The Know-Nothing Party in the South* (Baton Rouge, 1950). Division of the churches is treated in William W. Sweet: *Story of Religion in America* (rev. ed., New York, 1939); Mary B. Putnam: *The Baptists and Slavery, 1840–1845* (Ann Arbor, 1913); John N. Norwood: *The Schism in the Methodist Episcopal Church, 1844* (New York, 1923).

Among older biographies of Calhoun are Galliard Hunt: *John C. Calhoun* (New York, 1908), and William M. Meigs: *Life of John Caldwell Calhoun* (2 vols., New York, 1925). Margaret L. Coit: *John C. Calhoun, American Portrait* (Boston, 1950), is brilliantly human; Charles M. Wiltse: *John C. Calhoun* (3 vols., Indianapolis, 1944–51), exhibits careful scholarship. Biographies of Clay include Carl Schurz: *Henry Clay* (2 vols., Boston, 1909); Bernard Mayo: *Henry Clay, Spokesman of the New West* (Boston, 1937); and Glyndon G. Van Deusen: *Life of Henry Clay* (Boston, 1937). Andrew Jackson is portrayed by John S. Bassett: *Life of Andrew Jackson* (2 vols., New York, 1925); and by Marquis James: *Life of Andrew Jackson* (2 vols., Indianapolis, 1938). Competent biographies have been written of other political leaders of the Old South. Among them are William C. Bruce: *John Randolph of Roanoke, 1773–1833* (2 vols., New York, 1922); Charles H. Ambler: *Thomas Ritchie* (Richmond, 1913); Laura White: *Robert Barnwell Rhett* (New York, 1931); Elizabeth Merritt: *James Henry Hammond, 1807–1864* (Baltimore, 1923); Oliver P. Chitwood: *John Tyler, Champion of the Old South* (New York, 1939); Dumas Malone: *The Public Life of Thomas Cooper, 1783–1839* (New Haven, 1926); Theodore D. Jervey: *Robert Y. Hayne and His Times* (New York, 1909).

CHAPTER VIII

THE CLASSIC description of the slave system from the Southern viewpoint is presented in Ulrich B. Phillips: *American Negro Slavery* (New York, 1918), *Life and Labor in the Old South* (Boston, 1929), and *Plantation and Frontier Documents, 1649–1863* (2 vols., Cleveland, 1909). The first two works are scholarly and interesting; the introduction of the third offers an excellent brief survey. Other compact treatments of slavery appear in such general histories of the United States as James F. Rhodes: *History of the United States*, I, chap. iv, 302–83; John B. McMaster: *History of the People of the United States* (New York, 1883–1903), Vol. VII, chap. lxxvi; Edward Channing: *History of the United States*, Vol. V, chap. v; Albert B. Hart: *Slavery and Abolition*. William E. Dodd: *The Cotton Kingdom* (New Haven, 1917) is an engaging picture of plantation life. The South's peculiar institution is accorded space in the general histories mentioned for Chapter I —the works by Cotterill, Eaton, Carman and Syrett, Morison and Commager, Faulkner, and Chitwood and Owsley. William Johnson: *Diary of a Free Negro* (Baton Rouge, 1951), and William D. Postell: *The Health of Slaves on Southern Plantations* (Baton Rouge, 1951), present neglected aspects of slave life. Kenneth M. Stampp: "The Historian and Southern Negro Slavery," *The American Historical Review*, LVII, 613–24 (April, 1952), presents revisionist views of the slave system. Conventional views of the defects of the slave economy are effectively challenged in the monumental study by Lewis C. Gray: *History of Agriculture in the Southern United States to 1860* (2 vols., Washington, 1933). His findings are supplemented by Robert W. Smith: "Was Slavery Unprofitable in the Ante-Bellum South?" *Agricultural History*, XX, 62–4 (January, 1946). Slavery is presented with intelligent sympathy by James G. Randall: *The Civil War and Reconstruction,* chap. ii; also Avery O. Craven: *The Coming of the Civil War,* pp. 67–166. A standard work is that by Matthew B. Hammond: *The Cotton Industry* (New York, 1897). A brilliant correlation of American slavery with other industrial systems is made by Edgar T. Thompson: "The Natural History of Agricultural Labor in the South," in David K. Jackson, ed.: *American Studies in Honor of William Kenneth Boyd.*

Frank L. Owsley and his students through an analysis of census manuscripts refute the contention that the Old South had a one-sided economy in which yeoman farmers were unimportant. Their studies are contained in Frank L. and Harriet C. Owsley: "The Economic Basis of Society in the Late Ante-Bellum South," *The Journal of Southern History,* VI, 24–45 (February, 1940), and "The Economic Structure of Rural Tennessee, 1850–1860," *ibid.,* VIII, 161–82 (May, 1942); Harry L. Coles, Jr.: "Some Notes on Slaveownership and Landownership in Louisiana, 1850–1860," *ibid.,* IX, 381–94 (August, 1943); Blanche H. Clark: *The Tennessee Yeoman, 1840–1860* (Nashville, 1942); Herbert Weaver: *Mississippi Farmers, 1850–1860* (Nashville, 1945). These writers are challenged by Fabian Linden: "Economic Democracy in the Slave South: An Appraisal of Some Recent Views," *The Journal of Negro History,* XXXI, 140–89 (April, 1946).

The foreign slave trade is treated in W. E. Burghardt Du Bois: *The Suppression of the African Slave-Trade* (New York, 1896). Domestic traffic is described by Winfield H. Collins: *The Domestic Slave Trade of the Southern United States* (New York, 1904), and by Frederic Bancroft: *Slave-Trading in the Old South* (Baltimore, 1931). Among scholarly appraisals of slavery in the individual states are James C. Ballagh: *A History of Slavery in Virginia* (Baltimore, 1902); Rosser H. Taylor: *Slaveholding in North Carolina* (Chapel Hill, 1926); Charles S. Sydnor: *Slavery in Mississippi* (New York, 1933); Ralph B. Flanders: *Plantation Slavery in Georgia* (Chapel Hill, 1933); Charles S. Davis: *The Cotton Kingdom in Alabama* (Montgomery, 1939); J. Winston Coleman: *Slavery Times in Kentucky* (Chapel Hill, 1940); Harrison A. Trexler; *Slavery in Missouri* (Baltimore, 1914). Special phases of the slave regions are handled by Avery O. Craven: *Soil Exhaustion as a Factor in the Agricultural History of Virginia and Maryland* (Urbana, 1926); John S. Bassett: *Southern Plantation Overseer as Revealed in His Letters* (Northampton, 1925); James C. Bonner: "Genesis of Agricultural Reform in the Cotton Belt," *The Journal of Southern History,* IX, 475–500 (November, 1943); Avery O. Craven: "The Agricultural Reformers of the Ante-Bellum South," *The American Historical Review,* XXXIII, 302–14 (January, 1928); Charles S. Sydnor: "Pursuing Fugitive Slaves," *South Atlantic Quarterly,* XXVIII, 152–64 (April, 1929); John C. Hurd: *The Law of Freedom and Bondage* (2 vols., Boston, 1858–62); Howell M. Henry: *The Police Control of Slavery in South Carolina* (Emory, Virginia, 1914). Among contemporaries defending the economy of the Old South are James D. B. De Bow, ed.: *The Industrial Resources of the Southern and Western States* (3 vols., New Orleans, 1852–53), and Thomas P. Kettell: *Southern Wealth and Northern Profits* (New York, 1860). Attacks by contemporary Southerners include Daniel R. Goodloe: *An Inquiry into the Causes Which Retard the Southern States* (Washington, 1846), and Hinton R. Helper: *The Impending Crisis of the South* (New York, 1857). Among biographies revealing Southern plantation methods are Susan D. Smedes: *Memorials of a Southern Planter* (New York, 1887);

Broadus Mitchell: *Frederick Law Olmsted* (Baltimore, 1924); Avery O. Craven: *Edmund Ruffin, Southerner* (New York, 1932); E. Merton Coulter: *Thomas Spalding of Sapelo* (Baton Rouge, 1940); Charles S. Sydnor: *A Gentleman of Old Natchez: Benjamin L. C. Wailes* (Durham, 1938); Wendell H. Stephenson: *Isaac Franklin, Slave Trader and Planter of the Old South* (Baton Rouge, 1938); Edwin A. Davis: "Bennett H. Barrow, Ante-Bellum Planter of the Felicianas," *The Journal of Southern History*, V, 431–46 (November, 1939); J. Harold Easterby, ed.: *The South Carolina Rice Plantation as Revealed in the Papers of Robert F. W. Allston* (Chicago, 1945).

Of the many travelers who recorded their impressions of the Old South, the most indefatigable and critically intelligent was the New York landscape architect Frederick Law Olmsted, who wrote *A Journey in the Seaboard Slave States* (New York, 1856); *A Journey through Texas* (New York, 1857); and *A Journey in the Back Country* (New York, 1860). Others included the English scientists George W. Featherstonhaugh: *Excursion through the Slave States* (London, 1844), and Sir Charles Lyell: *A Second Visit to the United States* (2 vols., New York, 1849). Hostile but brilliant was the English actress Frances A. Kemble: *Journal of a Residence on a Georgia Plantation in 1838–1839* (New York, 1863); more kindly was the actor Tyrone Power: *Impressions of America* (2 vols., Philadelphia, 1836). Other Britishers who came principally to criticize were James S. Buckingham: *The Slave States of America* (2 vols., London, 1842); Basil Hall: *Travels in North America* (3 vols., Edinburgh, 1829); Harriet Martineau: *Society in America* (3 vols., London, 1837), and *Retrospect of Western Travel* (3 vols., London, 1838); James Stirling: *Letters from the Slave States* (London, 1857); William Chambers: *American Slavery and Colour* (London, 1857). The Swedish feminist and novelist Fredrika Bremer left a lively record of her travels in *Homes of the New World* (2 vols., New York, 1853).

CHAPTER IX

CLASSIC descriptions of society in the Old South are contained in William E. Dodd: *The Cotton Kingdom*, and Ulrich B. Phillips: *Life and Labor in the Old South, and American Negro Slavery*. The social psychology of various classes is presented with unconventional brilliance in the first chapters of Wilbur J. Cash: *The Mind of the South* (New York, 1941). Class differences are set forth discerningly by Lewis C. Gray: *History of Agriculture in the Southern States to 1860*, chapters xxi and xxii, and Roger W. Shugg: *Origins of Class Struggle in Louisiana* (Baton Rouge, 1939). The problem of the plain whites is explained graphically in Paul H. Buck: "The Poor Whites of the South," *The American Historical Review*, XXXI, 41–55 (October, 1925); A. N. J. Den Hollander: "The Tradition of 'Poor Whites,'" in William T. Couch, ed.: *Culture in the South;* Shields McIlwaine, *The Southern Poor-White: From Lubberland to Tobacco Road* (Norman, 1939); and Frank L. Owsley: *The Plain People of the Old South* (Baton Rouge, 1950). Rollin G. Osterweis: *Romanticism and Nationalism in the Old South* (New Haven, 1949), exploits Southern ideals.

The life of the free Negro is explained with scholarly precision by John H. Russell: *The Free Negro in Virginia, 1619–1865* (Baltimore, 1913);

Luther P. Jackson: *Free Negro Labor and Property Holding in Virginia, 1830–1860* (New York, 1942); James W. Wright: *The Free Negro in Maryland, 1634–1860* (New York, 1921); Rosser H. Taylor: *The Free Negro in North Carolina* (Chapel Hill, 1920); John H. Franklin: *The Free Negro in North Carolina, 1790–1860* (Chapel Hill, 1943); E. Horace Fitchett: "The Traditions of the Free Negro in Charleston, South Carolina," *The Journal of Negro History*, XXV, 139–52 (April, 1940), and "The Origin and Growth of the Free Negro Population of Charleston," *ibid.*, XXVI, 421–37 (October, 1941). A vivid description of Southern conditions by a contemporary Southerner is offered in Daniel R. Hundley: *Social Relations in Our Southern States* (New York, 1860). Local society is set forth in the following scholarly monographs: Minnie C. Boyd: *Alabama in the Fifties* (New York, 1931); Rosser H. Taylor: *Ante-Bellum South Carolina* (Chapel Hill, 1942); F. Garvin Davenport: *Ante-Bellum Kentucky: A Social History* (Oxford, Ohio, 1943), and *Cultural Life in Nashville on the Eve of the Civil War* (Chapel Hill, 1941); Guion G. Johnson: *Ante-Bellum North Carolina, a Social History* (Chapel Hill, 1937), and *A Social History of the Sea Islands* (Chapel Hill, 1930); Clanton W. Williams: "Early Ante-Bellum Montgomery," *The Journal of Southern History*, VII, 495–525 (November, 1941).

Kindly pictures of the Old South are offered by Edward Ingle: *Southern Sidelights* (New York, 1896); Thomas Nelson Page: *Social Life in Old Virginia before the War* (New York, 1897); Mildred Cram: *Old Seaboard Towns of the South* (New York, 1917); Robert Q. Mallard: *Plantation Life before Emancipation* (Richmond, 1892). The legend of the Old South is sharply attacked by Thomas J. Wertenbaker: *The Planters of Colonial Virginia* (Princeton, 1912), and by Francis P. Gaines: *The Southern Plantation: A Study in the Development and Accuracy of a Tradition* (New York, 1925). Attention is given to ante-bellum society by the general histories of the United States cited for Chapter VIII, especially those by Randall, Craven, Hart, Rhodes, McMaster, and Morison and Commager; and by the travel books mentioned there, particularly those by Olmsted, Featherstonhaugh, Kemble, Martineau, Hall, Buckingham, and Bremer.

Other observations of social conditions are presented by La Rochefoucauld-Liancourt: *Travels through the United States* (2 vols., London, 1799); Brissot de Warville: *New Travels in the United States* (2 vols., Dublin, 1792); Francois Jean Chastellux: *Travels in North America* (2 vols., London, 1787); A. de Puy Van Buren: *Jottings of a Year's Sojourn in the South* (Battle Creek, 1859); Nehemiah Adams: *A South-Side View of Slavery* (Boston, 1854); Catherine C. Hopley: *Life in the South* (2 vols., London, 1863); Joseph H. Ingraham: *South West, by a Yankee* (2 vols., New York, 1835); William H. Russell: *My Diary North and South* (Boston, 1863). In addition to the biographies by Craven, Smedes, Coulter, Sydnor, and Stephenson listed for Chapter VIII, the following works emphasize social conditions: John W. DuBose: *The Life and Times of William Lowndes Yancey*; John L. Wade: *Augustus Baldwin Longstreet* (New York, 1924); and William P. Trent: *William Gilmore Simms* (Boston, 1892).

CHAPTER X

THE INTELLECTUAL outlook of the Old South is comprehensively treated in Clement Eaton: *Freedom of Thought in the Old South*, and Charles S.

Sydnor: *The Development of Southern Sectionalism, 1819–1848.* The following are genuinely stimulating: Chapters i and ii of Wilbur J. Cash: *The Mind of the South;* Chapter I of Benjamin B. Kendrick and Alex M. Arnett: *The South Looks at Its Past;* Merle Curti: *The Growth of American Thought* (New York, 1943), chap. xvii, Virginius Dabney: *Liberalism in the South* (Chapel Hill, 1932); Richard H. Shryock: "Cultural Factors in the History of the South," *The Journal of Southern History,* V, 332–47 (August, 1939).

Most general histories neglect the religious life of the Old South; exceptions are those by William E. Dodd: *The Cotton Kingdom;* Ulrich B. Phillips: *American Negro Slavery* and *Life and Labor in the Old South;* Carl R. Fish: *The Rise of the Common Man;* Arthur C. Cole: *The Irrepressible Conflict* (New York, 1927). The establishment of a religiously solid South is best explained in William W. Sweet: *The Story of Religion in America* (New York, 1930), and *Revivalism in America* (New York, 1944); and Catherine C. Cleveland: *The Great Revival in the West, 1797–1805* (Chicago, 1916). The origin and progress of different sects are described in detail by Philip Schaff and others, eds.: *The American Church Series* (13 vols., New York, 1893–97); and in *The Census of Religious Bodies, 1936.* Many of the travel books cited in the bibliographies for Chapters VIII and IX treat religious practices. These can be supplemented by Andrew Reed and James Matheson: *Narrative of the Visit to the American Churches* (London, 1835), and Lester B. Shippee, ed.: *Bishop Whipple's Southern Diary, 1843–1844* (Minneapolis, 1937).

Slave religion is explained in Charles C. Jones: *Religious Instruction of the Negro* (Savannah, 1842); Benjamin H. Mayes: *The Negro's God* (Boston, 1938); Haven P. Perkins: "Religion for Slaves," *Church History,* Vol. X (September, 1941); and Carter G. Woodson, *The History of the Negro Church* (Washington, 1921). Problems of religious dissent are explained by Dumas Malone: *The Public Life of Thomas Cooper;* Moncure D. Conway: *Autobiography* (2 vols., Boston, 1904); Clarence Gohdes: "Some Notes on the Unitarian Church in the Ante-bellum South," in David K. Jackson, ed.: *American Studies in Honor of William Kenneth Boyd.*

Details of the temperance movement are presented by John A. Krout: *The Origins of Prohibition* (New York, 1925). The best biography of a Southern religious leader is by John D. Wade: *Augustus Baldwin Longstreet.* Older biographies with revealing documents are Benjamin M. Palmer: *The Life and Letters of James H. Thornwell* (Richmond, 1875); Thomas Cary Johnson: *The Life and Letters of Benjamin M. Palmer* (Richmond, 1906), and *The Life and Letters of Thomas L. Dabney* (Richmond, 1903); William M. Polk: *Leonidas Polk* (2 vols., New York, 1894). Walter B. Posey: *Development of Methodism in the Old Southwest, 1783–1824* (Tuscaloosa, 1933), and "The Early Baptist Church in the Lower Southwest," *The Journal of Southern History,* X, 161–73 (May, 1944), are among the few treatments of local church history handled objectively.

CHAPTER XI

THERE is no critical history of education in the South; all the literature on this subject is inspired by official interest. Outstanding works of this type are furnished by Edgar W. Knight: *Public Education in the South;* Amory D. Mayo: "The Organization and Development of the American Common School in the Atlantic and Central States of the South," United States Commissioner of Education, *Report for 1899–1900,* I, 427–561; "The Common School in the Southern States beyond the Mississippi from 1830 to 1860." *ibid.,* 1900–01, I, 357–401; articles by George H. Denny, James H. Kirkland, and others in *The South in the Building of the Nation,* X, 184–425; and Charles W. Dabney: *Universal Education in the South* (2 vols., Chapel Hill, 1936).

Conventional summaries of educational progress are given in many of the histories of the states cited for Chapter I. Details are thoroughly presented in the histories of education in individual states cited for Chapter XXIII. This plethora of official digests is supplemented by Richard M. Johnston: *Early Educational Life in Middle Georgia* (Washington, 1895); William E. Dodd: "Religion and Education," in *The Cotton Kingdom;* John Gould Fletcher, "Education Past and Present," in Twelve Southerners: *I'll Take My Stand; the South and the Agrarian Tradition* (New York, 1930).

Special aspects of education are explained by Carter G. Woodson: *Education of the Negro Prior to 1861* (New York, 1915); Thomas Woody: *A History of Woman's Education in the United States* (2 vols., Lancaster, Pennsylvania, 1929); William A. Maddox: *The Free School Idea in Virginia before the Civil War* (New York, 1918); William H. Weathersby: *A History of Educational Legislation in Mississippi from 1798 to 1860* (Chicago, 1921). Jefferson's educational ideas are analyzed by Herbert B. Adams: *Thomas Jefferson and the University of Virginia* (Washington, 1888), and Roy J. Honeywell: *The Educational Work of Thomas Jefferson* (Cambridge, 1931). Education and culture are integrated in Clement Eaton: *Freedom of Thought in the Old South;* E. Merton Coulter: *College Life in the Old South* (New York, 1928); Allen P. Tankersley: *College Life in Old Oglethorpe* (Athens, 1951); F. Garvin Davenport: *Cultural Life in Nashville on the Eve of the Civil War.* The problem of the tutor is presented by A. de Puy Van Buren: *Jottings of a Year's Sojourn in the South,* and Joseph H. Ingraham, ed.: *The Sunny South* (Philadelphia, 1860). The academy movement is the subject of Edgar W. Knight: *The Academy Movement in the South* (Chapel Hill, 1919), and Ralph M. Lyon: "Moses Waddel and the Willington Academy," *The North Carolina Historical Review,* VII, 284–99 (July, 1931). Among the few biographies of ante-bellum educators may be mentioned John D. Wade: *Augustus Baldwin Longstreet;* Dumas Malone: *The Public Life of Thomas Cooper;* Henry D. Capers: *Life and Times of C. G. Memminger* (Richmond, 1893); Stephen B. Weeks: "Calvin H. Wiley and the Organization of the Common Schools of North Carolina," United States Commissioner of Education, *Report for 1896–97,* II, 379–471.

The finest introductions to the history of college education are in the previously cited works by E. Merton Coulter; Donald G. Tewksbury: *Founding of American Colleges and Universities before the Civil War* (New York, 1932); and Albea Godbold: *The Church College of the Old South* (Durham, 1944). College education in individual states is treated by Lucius S. Merriam: *Higher Education in Tennessee* (Washington, 1893); Alvin F. Lewis: *History of Higher Education in Kentucky* (Washington,

1899); and Colyer Meriwether: *History of Higher Education in South Carolina* (Washington, 1899). Broader treatments of the subject are Kemp P. Battle: *History of the University of North Carolina* (2 vols., Raleigh, 1907, 1912); Philip A. Bruce: *Centennial History of the University of Virginia, 1819–1919* (5 vols., New York, 1920–1922); David D. Wallace: *History of Wofford College* (Nashville, 1951); and Daniel W. Hollis: *University of South Carolina* (Columbia, 1951), Vol. I.

CHAPTER XII

THE MOST notable appraisal of ante-bellum Southern letters is by Vernon C. Parrington: *The Romantic Revolution in America, 1800–1860* (New York, 1927). Energetic criticisms are offered by C. Alphonso Smith: *Southern Literary Studies* (Chapel Hill, 1927); Edd W. Parks: *Segments of Southern Thought* (Athens, 1938); and Shields McIlwaine: *The Southern Poor-White.* Johnson and Malone: *Dictionary of American Biography*, contains authentic articles on every Southern author. More detailed if less critical is the comprehensive work of Edwin A. Alderman and Joel Chandler Harris, eds.: *Library of Southern Literature* (17 vols., Atlanta, 1907–23). A wealth of Southern data, especially articles by Edwin Mims, William K. Boyd, William B. Cairnes, and Will D. Howe, is included in William P. Trent and others, eds.: *The Cambridge History of American Literature* (4 vols., New York, 1917–21). There are useful articles on "Literature" in the fifteen volumes of the Federal Writers' Program of the Work Projects Administration, "American Guide Series," which are cited for Chapter I. See also under Chapter XXVI the list of histories of Southern literature by Samuel A. Link, Carl Holliday, and Montrose J. Moses; and of Southern anthologies by Louise Manly, William P. Trent, Alma Kate Orgain, Edwin Mims and Bruce R. Payne, Maurice G. Fulton, William T. Wynn, and C. Addison Hibbard.

The significance of Southern magazines is advanced by Edwin Mims: "Southern Magazines," in *The South in the Building of the Nation*, VII, 457–69; Frank L. Mott: *A History of American Magazines* (3 vols., Cambridge, 1938–39); Bertram H. Flanders: *Early Georgia Magazines* (Athens, 1944); David K. Jackson: *Poe and the Southern Literary Messenger* (Richmond, 1934). Among historians of national literature who recognize Southern contributions are Walter F. Taylor: *A History of American Letters* (Boston, 1936); Lorenzo Sears: *American Literature in the Colonial and National Periods* (Boston, 1902); Leonidas W. Payne: *History of American Literature* (New York, 1919).

Distinguished biographies of writers of the Old South include William P. Trent: *William Gilmore Simms;* John D. Wade: *Augustus Baldwin Longstreet;* Hervey Allen: *Israfel: the Life and Times of Edgar Allan Poe* (2 vols., New York, 1934). Other biographies are those of Edward M. Gwathmey: *John Pendleton Kennedy* (New York, 1931); Linda Rhea: *Hugh S. Legaré* (Chapel Hill, 1934); Henry T. Thompson: *Henry Timrod* (Columbia, 1928); Constance Rourke: *Davy Crockett* (New York, 1934); Elizabeth P. Allan: *Margaret Junkin Preston* (Boston, 1903); Damon S. Foster: *Thomas Holley Chivers, Friend of Poe* (New York, 1930). Abram J. Ryan: *Poems* (New York, 1896), contains a memoir by John Moran.

Mary C. Simms Oliphant and others, ed.: *The Letters of William Gilmore Simms* (Columbia, 1952—), Vol. I, contains a brilliant defense by Donald Davidson. When completed in five projected volumes this work will be a monument of literary history.

CHAPTERS XIII–XIV

THE COURSE to secession is extensively set forth in James Rhodes: *History of the United States from the Compromise of 1850,* Vols. I and II. Ample space is also given to the sectional issues in other standard works—Edward Channing: *History of the United States,* Vol. VI; John B. McMaster: *A History of the People of the United States,* Vol. VI; and James G. Randall: *The Civil War and Reconstruction,* chaps. v–x. The general histories cited in Chapter I do not neglect this period—Cotterill, Hesseltine, Chitwood and Owsley, Morison and Commager, and Faulkner. Among the many books covering the 1850 decade are Henry H. Simms: *A Decade of Sectional Controversy, 1851–1861* (Chapel Hill, 1942); Theodore C. Smith: *Parties and Slavery* (New York, 1906); Dwight L. Dumond: *Anti-Slavery Origins of the Civil War* (London, 1939); Ulrich B. Phillips: *The Course of the South to Secession* (New York, 1939); Arthur Y. Lloyd: *The Slavery Controversy* (Chapel Hill, 1939). Opposing viewpoints are set forth in Arthur C. Cole: *The Irrepressible Conflict;* Avery O. Craven: *The Coming of the Civil War,* and *The Repressible Conflict, 1830–1861*

Biographies of statesmen of the period include Laura A. White: *Robert Barnwell Rhett;* Avery O. Craven: *Edmund Ruffin;* Harvey Wish: *George Fitzhugh* (Baton Rouge, 1943); Percy S. Flippen: *Herschel V. Johnson* (Richmond, 1931); Ulrich B. Phillips: *Robert Toombs* (New York, 1913); John W. DuBose: *William Lowndes Yancey* (Birmingham, 1892); Henry H. Simms: *Robert M. T. Hunter* (Richmond, 1935); Louis Pendleton: *Alexander H. Stephens* (Philadelphia, 1908); Rudolph von Abele: *Alexander H. Stephens* (New York, 1946); Robert McElroy: *Jefferson Davis, the Real and the Unreal* (2 vols., New York, 1937); William E. Dodd: *Jefferson Davis* (New York, 1907); George F. Milton: *The Eve of Conflict: Stephen A. Douglas and the Needless War* (Boston, 1934); also the studies of Robert E. Lee, Judah P. Benjamin, and others, cited for the next chapter.

Controversial literature of the times includes Hinton R. Helper: *The Impending Crisis of the South;* Thomas P. Kettell: *Southern Wealth and Northern Profits;* George Fitzhugh: *Sociology for the South* (Richmond, 1854); Daniel R. Hundley: *Social Relations in Our Southern States.*

The background of secession is presented by John G. Van Deusen: *Economic Bases of Disunion in South Carolina* (New York, 1928); Robert R. Russel: *Economic Aspects of Southern Sectionalism;* Henry S. Schultz: *Nationalism and Sectionalism in South Carolina* (Durham, 1950); and Jesse T. Carpenter: *The South as a Conscious Minority.* General studies of secession are made by Dwight L. Dumond: *The Secession Movement, 1860–1861* (New York, 1931), and *Southern Editorials on Secession* (New York, 1931); French E. Chadwick: *Causes of the Civil War, 1859–1861* (New York, 1908); Nathaniel W. Stephenson: *Abraham Lincoln and the Union* (New Haven, 1921). The Fort Sumter incident is described in detail by Samuel W. Crawford: *The Genesis of the Civil War* (New York, 1887), and John S. Tilley: *Lincoln Takes Command* (Chapel Hill, 1941). Lincoln's responsibility for the beginning of violence is presented in Charles W. Ramsdell: "Lincoln and Fort Sumter," *The Journal of Southern History*, III, 259–88 (August, 1937); and Kenneth M. Stampp: "Lincoln and the Strategy of Defense in the Crisis of 1861," *ibid.*, XI, 297–323 (August, 1945), and *And War Came* (Baton Rouge, 1951). "Lincoln's Election an Immediate Menace to Slavery in the States?" is the subject of a scholarly debate between Arthur C. Cole and J. G. de Roulhac Hamilton in *American Historical Review*, XXXVI, 740–67 (July, 1931), and XXXVII, 700–11 (July, 1932).

Secession in the individual states is treated in J. Carlyle Sitterson: *The Secession Movement in North Carolina* (Chapel Hill, 1939); Henry T. Shanks: *The Secession Movement in Virginia, 1847–1861* (Richmond, 1934); Percy L. Rainwater: *Mississippi, Storm Center of Secession, 1856–1861* (Baton Rouge, 1938); Clarence P. Denman: *The Secession Movement in Alabama* (Montgomery, 1933); E. Merton Coulter: *The Civil War and Readjustment in Kentucky* (Chapel Hill, 1926).

CHAPTER XV

A CONVENIENT general history of the Civil War is to be found in Robert S. Henry: *The Story of the Confederacy* (Indianapolis, 1931). Classic Northern expositions include James Ford Rhodes: *History of the United States*, Vols. III, IV, and V; Edward Channing: *History of the United States*, Vol. VI; and John B. McMaster: *A History of the People of the United States during Lincoln's Administration* (New York, 1927). A Northern scholar, James G. Randall, bends backward to be fair to the South in *The Civil War and Reconstruction*. Other general appraisals of the war are made by James K. Hosmer: *The Appeal to Arms, 1861–1863* (New York, 1907), and *The Outcome of the War, 1863–1865* (New York, 1907); Nathaniel W. Stephenson: *Abraham Lincoln and the Union* (New Haven, 1920); Clifford Dowdy: *Experiment in Rebellion* (New York, 1946); and William Wood: *Captains of the Civil War* (New Haven, 1921). Among the briefer histories of the United States with a grasp of Confederate problems are those of Morison and Commager, Chitwood and Owsley, Faulkner, and Carman and Syrett, previously cited.

Pre-eminent in the vast literature on military phases of the South's struggle is the admirable work of Douglas S. Freeman: *R. E. Lee: A Biography* (4 vols., New York, 1934–35), and its supplement, *Lee's Lieutenants* (3 vols., New York, 1942–44). Other notable biographies are those by George F. R. Henderson: *Stonewall Jackson and the American Civil War* (new ed., 2 vols., London and New York, 1936); John F. C. Fuller: *Grant and Lee* (London, 1929); John P. Dyer: *"Fightin' Joe" Wheeler* (Baton Rouge, 1941); Andrew Lytle: *Bedford Forrest and His Critter Company* (New York, 1931); John W. Thomason: *Jeb Stuart* (New York, 1930); Hamilton Basso: *Beauregard, the Great Creole* (New York, 1933); Donald B. Sanger and Thomas R. Hay: *James Longstreet* (Baton Rouge, 1952); and Vernon C. Jones: *Ranger Mosby* (Chapel Hill, 1944). Naval activities are treated by John T. Scharf: *History of the Confederate States Navy* (New York, 1887); William M. Robinson, Jr.: *Confederate Privateers* (New

Haven, 1928); Francis B. C. Bradlee: *Blockade Running during the Civil War* (Salem, Massachusetts, 1925).

The internal history of the Confederacy is for the first time comprehensively appraised by E. Merton Coulter: *The Confederate States of America, 1861–1865*. Briefer appraisals are by Nathaniel W. Stephenson: *The Day of the Confederacy* (New Haven, 1920), and by Charles W. Ramsdell: *Behind the Lines in the Southern Confederacy* (Baton Rouge, 1944). The former writes brilliantly and imaginatively; the latter from the vantage of a lifetime of research on the subject. Details of Confederate history have been set forth in many special studies. Among these are personal accounts, of which the following are notable: Mary B. Chesnut: *Diary from Dixie* (new ed., Boston, 1942); Julia Le Grande: *Journal: New Orleans, 1862–1863* (Richmond, 1911); Eliza F. Andrews: *The War-Time Journal of a Georgia Girl, 1864–1865* (New York, 1908); Kate Cumming: *Journal of Hospital Life in the Confederate Army* (Louisville, 1866); Judith W. McGuire: *Diary of a Southern Refugee* (Richmond, 1889); John B. Jones: *A Rebel War Clerk's Diary* (2 vols., Philadelphia, 1866); Thomas C. DeLeon, *Four Years in Rebel Capitals* (Mobile, 1892); Catherine C. Hopley: *Life in the South* (London, 1863); and William H. Russell: *My Diary North and South* (2 vols., London, 1862).

Important biographies of civil leaders are Robert D. Meade: *Judah P. Benjamin* (New York, 1944); Louis M. Sears: *John Slidell* (Durham, 1925); Ulrich B. Phillips; *Robert Toombs* (New York, 1913); Haywood J. Pearce, Jr.: *Benjamin H. Hill* (Chicago, 1928); Louise B. Hill: *Joseph E. Brown* (Chapel Hill, 1939); Wirt A. Cate: *Lucius Q. C. Lamar* (Chapel Hill, 1935); Frank E. Vandiver: *Josiah Gorgas* (Austin, 1952); Clement Dowd: *Zebulon B. Vance* (Charlotte, 1897); Henry H. Simms: *Robert M. T. Hunter* (Richmond, 1935); Eron Rowland: *Varina Howell, Wife of Jefferson Davis* (2 vols., New York, 1927); Gamaliel Bradford: *Confederate Portraits* (Boston, 1914); and the lives of Davis, Stephens, and others, cited in the bibliography of the preceding chapter. Bell I. Wiley: *The Life of Johnny Reb* (Indianapolis, 1952), treats the common soldier.

The problems of civil administration are explained by Rembert W. Patrick: *Jefferson Davis and His Cabinet* (Baton Rouge, 1944); Burton J. Hendrick: *Statesmen of the Lost Cause* (New York, 1939); William M. Robinson: *Justice in Grey* (Cambridge, Mass., 1941); and John C. Schwab: *A Financial and Industrial History of the South during the Civil War* (New York, 1901). Social and political difficulties are treated by Frank L. Owsley: *State Rights in the Confederacy* (new ed., Chicago, 1931); Albert B. Moore: *Conscription and Conflict in the Confederacy* (New York, 1924); Georgia L. Tatum: *Disloyalty in the Confederacy* (Chapel Hill, 1934); Ella Lonn: *Desertion during the Civil War* (New York, 1928); and Charles H. Wesley: *The Collapse of the Confederacy* (Washington, 1937). Behind-the-lines problems are discussed by Ella Lonn: *Salt as a Factor in the Confederacy* (New York, 1933); William B. Hesseltine: *Civil War Prisons* (Columbus, 1930); Bell I. Wiley: *The Plain People of the Confederacy* (Baton Rouge, 1943); Francis B. Simkins and James W. Patton, *The Women of the Confederacy* (Richmond, 1936); Alfred H. Bill: *The Beleaguered City: Richmond, 1861–1865* (New York, 1946); Mary E. Massey: *Ersatz in the Confederacy* (Columbia, 1952); and Robert C. Black, III: *Railroads of the Confederacy* (Chapel Hill, 1952).

Confederate foreign relations are treated in Frank L. Owsley: *King Cotton Diplomacy* (Chicago, 1931), and in Samuel B. Thompson: *Confederate Purchasing Operations Abroad* (Chapel Hill, 1935). Problems of individual states are analyzed in James W. Patton: *Unionism and Reconstruction in Tennessee, 1860–1869* (Chapel Hill, 1934); E. Merton Coulter: *The Civil War and Readjustment in Kentucky;* John K. Bettersworth: *Confederate Mississippi* (Baton Rouge, 1943); Jefferson D. Bragg: *Louisiana in the Confederacy* (Baton Rouge, 1941); Walter L. Fleming: *Civil War and Reconstruction in Alabama* (New York, 1905); William W. Davis: *The Civil War and Reconstruction in Florida* (New York, 1913); and David Y. Thomas: *Arkansas in War and Reconstruction* (Little Rock, 1926).

CHAPTER XVI

THERE is no entirely satisfactory account of Reconstruction, free of race and sectional prejudices, that fuses political, economic, and social forces. Yet, within certain limitations, the period is competently treated by a number of writers. Most comprehensive are the works of E. Merton Coulter: *The South during Reconstruction, 1865–1877,* and Walter L. Fleming: *The Sequel of Appomattox* (New Haven, 1919), and *Documentary History of Reconstruction* (2 vols., Cleveland, 1906–7). Peter J. Hamilton: *The Reconstruction Period* (Philadelphia, 1905), and Myra L. Avary: *Dixie after the War* (New York, 1906), are as varied in their interests as Fleming, without being so objective.

Earlier works of William A. Dunning: *Reconstruction, Political and Economic* (New York, 1907), and of James F. Rhodes, *The History of the United States from the Compromise of 1850,* of which Volumes V and VII are concerned with Reconstruction, remain the most scholarly political treatments of the period. James G. Randall: *Civil War and Reconstruction,* supplements Rhodes with the discoveries of more recent research. Robert S. Henry: *The Story of Reconstruction* (Indianapolis, 1938) is encyclopedic but uninspiring, while Claude G. Bowers: *The Tragic Era, the Revolution after Lincoln* (Boston, 1929) presents the period brilliantly as seen by a Democratic partisan. W. E. Burghardt Du Bois: *Black Reconstruction* (New York, 1935) is partly successful in correcting the anti-Negro bias of Fleming, Rhodes, and Dunning, but is narrowly political and marred by irrelevancies. Entirely successful in this respect is Vernon L. Wharton: *The Negro in Mississippi, 1865–1890* (Chapel Hill, 1947).

Plans for a fairer appraisal of the whole era are suggested by Du Bois: "Reconstruction and Its Benefits," *The American Historical Review,* XV, 781–99 (July, 1910); Howard K. Beale: "On Rewriting Reconstruction History," *ibid.,* XLV, 807–27 (July, 1940); Alrutheus A. Taylor: "Historians of Reconstruction," *The Journal of Negro History,* XXIII, 16–34 (January, 1938); and Francis B. Simkins, "New Viewpoints of Southern Reconstruction," *The Journal of Southern History,* V, 49–61 (February, 1939).

One or more studies have been made of each of the states during Reconstruction, partly under the direction of Professor William A. Dunning and his students. Scholarly but ultraconservative and political are John S. Reynolds: *Reconstruction in South Carolina, 1865–1877* (Columbia, 1905);

J. G. de Roulhac Hamilton: *Reconstruction in North Carolina* (New York, 1914); William W. Davis: *Civil War and Reconstruction in Florida* (New York, 1913); Hamilton J. Eckenrode: *The Political History of Virginia during the Reconstruction* (Baltimore, 1904); Edwin C. Woolley: *The Reconstruction of Georgia* (New York, 1901); Thomas S. Staples: *Reconstruction in Arkansas* (New York, 1923); John R. Ficklin: *History of Reconstruction in Louisiana through 1868* (Baltimore, 1910); and Charles W. Ramsdell: *Reconstruction in Texas* (New York, 1910).

Not so limited to politics are Walter L. Fleming: *Civil War and Reconstruction in Alabama* (New York, 1905); James W. Garner: *Reconstruction in Mississippi* (New York, 1901); C. Mildred Thompson: *Reconstruction in Georgia, Economic, Political, 1865–1872* (New York, 1915); and Francis B. Simkins and Robert H. Woody: *South Carolina during Reconstruction* (Chapel Hill, 1932).

Scholarly works include E. Merton Coulter: *Civil War and Readjustment in Kentucky* (Chapel Hill, 1926); James W. Patton: *Unionism and Reconstruction in Tennessee, 1860–1869* (Chapel Hill, 1934); Ella Lonn: *Reconstruction in Louisiana after 1868* (New York, 1918); and Thomas B. Alexander: *Political Reconstruction in Tennessee* (Nashville, 1950). Attempts by Negroes and carpetbaggers to answer white scholars are carefully presented by Alrutheus A. Taylor: *The Negro in South Carolina during Reconstruction* (Washington, 1914), and *The Negro in the Reconstruction of Virginia* (Washington, 1926); Horace M. Bond: *Negro Education in Alabama: A Study in Cotton and Steel* (Chicago, 1937); Henry C. Warmoth: *War, Politics and Reconstruction: Stormy Days in Louisiana* (New York, 1930); and John Wallace: *Carpetbag Rule in Florida* (Jacksonville, 1888).

Descriptions of conditions after the surrender may be found in Sidney Andrews: *The South since the War* (Boston, 1866); Whitelaw Reid: *After the War: A Southern Tour* (Cincinnati, 1866); Robert Somers: *The Southern States since the War* (London, 1871); John T. Trowbridge: *The South* (Hartford, 1866); Carl Schurz: *Reminiscences* (3 vols., New York, 1907–08); and James L. Sellers: "Economic Incidence of the Civil War in the South," *The Mississippi Valley Historical Review*, XIV, 179–91 (September, 1927).

CHAPTER XVII

SINCE state and general histories listed for Chapter XVI deal at length with the establishment of Reconstruction governments, only special authorities on the subject are cited here. Constitutional problems are ably presented by John W. Burgess: *Reconstruction and the Constitution, 1866–1876* (New York, 1902); William A. Dunning: *Essays on the Civil War and Reconstruction* (New York, 1904); and James G. Randall: *Constitutional Problems under Lincoln* (New York, 1926). George F. Milton: *The Age of Hate: Andrew Johnson and the Radicals*, and Howard K. Beale: *The Critical Year: A Study of Andrew Johnson and Reconstruction* (New York, 1930), introduce other factors besides the constitutional in explaining Reconstruction problems.

Lincoln's actions are described by Charles H. McCarthy: *Lincoln's Plan of Reconstruction* (New York, 1901), and by Eben G. Scott: *Reconstruction during the Civil War* (Boston, 1895). President Johnson is redeemed from his detractors by William A. Dunning: "More Light on Andrew Johnson," *American Historical Review*, XI, 574–94 (April, 1906); Robert W. Winston: *Andrew Johnson, Plebeian and Patriot* (New York, 1928); and Lloyd P. Stryker: *Andrew Johnson, A Study in Courage* (New York, 1929).

The plans of the radicals are revealed by Benjamin B. Kendrick: *Journal of the Joint Committee on Reconstruction* (New York, 1903); Charles E. Chadsey: *Struggle Between President Johnson and Congress over Reconstruction* (New York, 1897); and in biographies of Charles Sumner by Moorfield Storey, Edward L. Pierce, and George H. Haynes; of Thaddeus Stevens by Samuel W. McCall and James A. Woodburn; of Carl Schurz by Frederic Bancroft, Claude M. Fuess, and Joseph Shafer; of Zachariah Chandler by Wilmer C. Harris; of Salmon P. Chase by Albert B. Hart; of James G. Blaine by Edward Stanwood and David S. Muzzey; of James A. Garfield by Theodore C. Smith.

Special phases of the beginning of Reconstruction are treated by Jonathan T. Dorris: "Pardoning the Leaders of the Confederacy," *Mississippi Valley Historical Review*, XV, 3–21 (June, 1928), and "Pardon Seekers and Brokers: A Sequel of Appomattox," *Journal of Southern History*, I, 276–92 (August, 1935); J. G. de Roulhac Hamilton: "Freedmen's Bureau in North Carolina," *South Atlantic Quarterly*, VIII, 53–67, 154–63 (January–April, 1909), and "Southern Legislation in Regard to Freedmen," in James W. Garner, ed.: *Studies in Southern History and Politics* (New York, 1914); Paul S. Peirce: *The Freedmen's Bureau, A Chapter in the History of Reconstruction* (Iowa City, 1904); and Walter L. Fleming: "The Formation of the Union League in Alabama," *Gulf States Historical Magazine*, II, 73–89 (1903).

CHAPTER XVIII

RECONSTRUCTION histories cited for Chapter XVII fully describe the radical governments and their overthrow. The following works are devoted to descriptions of these governments: James S. Pike: *The Prostrate State: South Carolina under Negro Government* (new ed., New York, 1935); Charles Nordhoff: *The Cotton States in 1875* (New York, 1876); Edward King: *The Southern States of North America* (Hartford, 1875); William G. Brown: *The Lower South in American History;* Powell Clayton: *The Aftermath of the Civil War in Arkansas* (New York, 1915); Walter Allen: *Governor Chamberlain's Administration in South Carolina* (New York, 1888); John Wallace: *Carpetbag Rule in Florida* (Jacksonville, 1888); Charles H. Coleman: *The Election of 1868* (New York, 1933); William W. Davis: "The Federal Enforcement Acts" in James W. Garner, ed.: *Studies in Southern History and Politics;* and Samuel D. Smith: *The Negro in Congress* (Chapel Hill, 1940).

The following biographies throw light on the radical governments: William B. Hesseltine: *Ulysses S. Grant, Politician* (New York, 1935); Lillian A. Kibler: *Benjamin F. Perry* (Durham, 1946); E. Merton Coulter: *Parson Brownlow, Fighting Parson of the Southern Highlands* (Chapel Hill,

1937); Hayward J. Pearce, Jr.: *Benjamin H. Hill, Secession and Reconstruction* (Chicago, 1928); Edward Wells: *Hampton and Reconstruction* (Columbia, 1907); Wirt A. Cate: *Lucius Q. C. Lamar* (Chapel Hill, 1935); Nelson M. Blake: *William Mahone of Virginia, Soldier and Political Insurgent* (Richmond, 1935); Charles H. Ambler: *Francis H. Pierpont* (Chapel Hill, 1937); and E. Ramsey Richardson: *Little Aleck: a Life of Alexander H. Stephens* (Indianapolis, 1932).

There is no satisfactory history of the Ku Klux Klan. Stanley F. Horn: *Invisible Empire, the Story of the Ku Klux Klan, 1866–1871* (Boston, 1939), is disappointing. The older work of J. C. Lester and D. L. Wilson: *The Ku Klux Klan, Its Origin, Growth and Disbandment* (New York, 1905), is better. See also Francis B. Simkins: "The Ku Klux Klan in South Carolina, 1868–1871," *Journal of Negro History*, XII, 606–47 (October, 1927). The rapprochement between North and South is brilliantly appraised by Paul H. Buck: *The Road to Reunion, 1865–1900* (Boston, 1937). Special attention is given to the overthrow of the radical regimes in C. Vann Woodward: *Reunion and Reaction: The Compromise of 1877 and the End of Reconstruction* (Boston, 1951); Hamilton J. Eckenrode: *Rutherford B. Hayes, Statesman of Reunion* (New York 1930); Paul L. Haworth: *The Hayes-Tilden Disputed Presidential Election of 1876* (Cleveland, 1906); William B. Hesseltine: "Economic Factors in the Abandonment of Reconstruction," *The Mississippi Valley Historical Review*, XXII, 191–210 (September, 1935); J. S. McNeilly: "Climax and Collapse of Reconstruction in Mississippi," *Publications of the Mississippi Historical Society*, XII, 283 ff. (1902); Henry T. Thompson: *Ousting the Carpetbagger from South Carolina* (Columbia, 1926); and Hilary A. Herbert, ed.: *Why the Solid South? Or Reconstruction and Its Results* (Baltimore, 1890).

CHAPTER XIX

THE MOST comprehensive treatment of the nonpolitical aspects of Reconstruction is Coulter: *The South during Reconstruction* and Julian A. C. Chandler and others: *The South in the Building of the Nation*, Vol. VI. The books cited above by Avary, Nevins, Fleming, C. Mildred Thompson, Garner, and Simkins and Woody also stress the nonpolitical phases. Among observers of the social and economic scene are Hope S. Chamberlain: *Old Days in Chapel Hill* (New York, 1926); Marietta M. Andrews: *Memoirs of a Poor Relation* (New York, 1927); Susan D. Smedes: *Memorials of a Southern Planter* (New York, 1889); William H. Dixon: *White Conquest* (2 vols., London, 1875); Henry Latham: *White and Black: A Journal of Three Months Tour* (London, 1867); Stephen Powers: *Afoot and Alone: a Walk from Sea to Sea by the Southern Route* (Hartford, 1872); George Rose: *The Great Country, or Impressions of America* (London, 1868); Robert Somers: *The Southern States since the War, 1870–1871* (London and New York, 1871); Sir George Campbell: *White and Black: the Outcome of a Visit to the United States* (London and New York, 1879); and Edward King: *The Great South* (New York, 1875).

Agricultural problems are presented by Matthew B. Hammond: *The Cotton Industry* (New York, 1897); Robert P. Brooks: *Agrarian Revolution in Georgia, 1865–1912* (Madison, 1914); Eugene W. Hilgard, ed.: "Report on Cotton Production in the United States," Volumes V and VI of *Census of the United States, 1880* (Washington, 1884). Transportation difficulties are discussed by Carl R. Fish: *Restoration of Southern Railroads* (Madison, 1919); Albert B. Moore: "Railroad Building in Alabama during the Reconstruction Period," *The Journal of Southern History*, I, 421–41 (November, 1935); and Ulrich B. Philips: "Railway Transportation in the South," *The South in the Building of the Nation*, VI, 304–16.

Educational achievements are described by Edgar W. Knight: *The Influence of Reconstruction on Education in the South* (New York, 1913), and "Reconstruction and Education in Virginia," *South Atlantic Quarterly*, XV, 25–40, 157–74 (January–April, 1916), and Charles W. Dabney: *Universal Education in the South*. More satisfactory are the articles by Amory D. Mayo scattered through the United States Commissioner of Education, *Annual Report* for the years following 1900, especially "The Work of Certain Northern Churches in the Education of the Freedmen, 1861–1900," *Report for 1901–02*, I, 295–314, and "The Final Establishment of the American Common School System in North Carolina, South Carolina and Georgia, 1863–1900," *Report for 1904*, I, 999–1090.

There is no general history of the reconstruction of Southern churches. Their problems are touched upon by William W. Sweet: *The Story of Religion in America;* and Carter G. Woodson: *The History of the Negro Church* (Washington, 1921). Hunter D. Farish, *The Circuit Rider Dismounts: A Social History of Southern Methodism, 1865–1900* (Richmond, 1938), is the most elaborate single treatment. Brief but satisfactory histories of numerous Southern sects are given in *Census of Religious Bodies, 1916* (Washington, 1919). Special aspects of Southern religious life and organization are seen in William J. Allen and others, eds.: *Slave Songs of the United States* (New York, 1867); Daniel A. Payne: *Recollections of Seventy Years* (Nashville, 1888); Mark Mohler: "The Episcopal Church and National Reconciliation," *The Political Science Quarterly*, XLI, 567–95 (December, 1926), and Francis B. Simkins: "White Methodism in South Carolina during Reconstruction," *The North Carolina Historical Review*, V, 35–64 (January, 1928).

CHAPTER XX

A THOROUGHLY original interpretation of the period after Reconstruction is C. Vann Woodward: *Origins of the New South, 1877–1913*. Holland Thompson: *The New South, a Chronicle of Social and Industrial Evolution* (New Haven, 1919), though brief, is comprehensive and fair. Paul H. Buck: *The Road to Reunion*, is a brilliant presentation of the thesis of the growing amity between the sections. A comprehensive discussion is "The Past Does Not Come Back" in Benjamin B. Kendrick and Alex M. Arnett: *The South Looks at the Past*. Older works have a limited usefulness. Chief among them are Philip A. Bruce: *The New South* (Philadelphia, 1907); Julian A. C. Chandler and others, eds.: *The South in the Building of the Nation*, especially Vols. VI and X; papers on "The New South" in *Annals of the American Academy of Political and Social Science*, Vol. XXXV (1910); Edgar G. Murphy: *Problems of the Present South*. Other books of less historical value are William D. Kelley: *The Old South and the New* (New York, 1888);

William G. Brown: *The Lower South in American History* (New York, 1902); Hilary A. Herbert, ed.: *Why the Solid South?* (Baltimore, 1890). William B. Hesseltine: *Confederate Leaders in the New South* (Baton Rouge, 1951), is whimsical and informing. Forgotten chapters in Negro history are brought to light in Wharton: *The Negro in Mississippi, 1865–1890*, and George B. Tindall: *South Carolina Negroes, 1877–1900* (Columbia, 1952).

Staunch defenses of the Bourbon position are advanced by William W. Ball: *The State That Forgot: South Carolina's Surrender to Democracy* (Indianapolis, 1932); Susan D. Smedes: *Memorials of a Southern Planter* (Baltimore, 1887); Henry Watterson: *Marse Henry: an Autobiography* (New York, 1919); William A. Percy: *Lanterns on the Levee: Recollections of a Planter's Son* (New York, 1941). The biographies of William Mahone, L. Q. C. Lamar, and D. H. Hill, cited for Chapter IX, should be supplemented by Rebecca L. Felton: *My Memoirs of Georgia Politics* (Atlanta, 1911); Edwin A. Alderman and Armistead C. Gordon: *J. L. M. Curry, a Biography* (New York, 1901); Robert D. W. Connor and Clarence Poe: *Charles Brantley Aycock* (Garden City, 1912); James A. Barnes: *John G. Carlisle, Financial Statesman* (New York, 1931); Raymond B. Nixon: *Henry W. Grady, Spokesman of the New South* (New York, 1943); C. Vann Woodward: *Tom Watson, Agrarian Rebel* (New York, 1938); John P. Dyer: *"Fightin' Joe" Wheeler*; George C. Osborn: *John Sharp Williams, Planter-Statesman of the Deep South* (Baton Rouge, 1943); Sam A. Acheson: *Joe Bailey, the Last Democrat* (New York, 1932). Claude Gentry: *Private John Allen: Gentleman—Sage—Prophet* (no place, 1951) and Isaac F. Marcosson: *"Marse Henry": A Biography of Henry Watterson* (New York, 1951), do not live up to their subjects. See also Charles C. Pearson: *The Readjuster Movement in Virginia* (New Haven, 1917); W. A. Scott: *The Repudiation of State Debts* (New York, 1893); and Willie D. Halsell: "The Bourbon Period in Mississippi Politics, 1875–1890," *The Journal of Southern History*, XI, 519–37 (November, 1945).

CHAPTER XXI

THE MATERIAL progress of the New South is adequately explained in the books of C. Vann Woodward, Holland Thompson, Philip A. Bruce, Edgar G. Murphy, and William D. Kelley, cited immediately above. The spirit animating the movement is revealed by Sidney Lanier: *Retrospects and Prospects* (New York, 1899); Walter H. Page: *The Rebuilding of Old Commonwealths: Being Essays toward the Training of the Forgotten Man in the Southern States* (New York, 1902); Edwin Mims: *The Advancing South* (Garden City, 1926); Robert D. W. Connor: "Rehabilitation of a Rural Commonwealth," *The American Historical Review*, XXXVI, 44–62 (October, 1930); and the previously cited works of Paul H. Buck and Raymond B. Nixon.

The best general histories of the textile industry are those by Broadus Mitchell: *The Rise of the Cotton Mills in the South* (Baltimore, 1921), and Broadus and George S. Mitchell: *The Industrial Revolution in the South* (Baltimore, 1930). Illuminating studies are made by Holland Thompson:

From Cotton Field to Cotton Mill (New York, 1906); Marjorie A. Potwin: *Cotton Mill People of the Piedmont* (New York, 1927); and George T. Winston: *A Builder of the New South: D. A. Tompkins* (New York, 1920). The rise of cities is described by William K. Boyd: *The Story of Durham* (Durham, 1927); Gerald M. Capers: *Biography of a River Town: Memphis, Its Heroic Age* (Chapel Hill, 1939); and Thomas J. Wertenbaker: *Norfolk, Historic Southern Port* (Durham, 1931).

Other phases of industrial development are treated by Meyer Jacobstein: *The Tobacco Industry in the United States* (New York, 1907); Milton Whitney and Marcus L. Floyd: "Growth of the Tobacco Industry," *Yearbook of Agriculture, 1899* (Washington, 1900), pp. 429–40; John W. Jenkins: *James B. Duke, Master Builder* (New York, 1927); John K. Winkler: *Tobacco Tycoon: Story of James Buchanan Duke* (New York, 1942); Ethel Armes: *The Story of Coal and Iron in Alabama* (Birmingham, 1910); see also *The South in the Building of the Nation*, Vol. VI, which has a lively appreciation of Southern agricultural progress, as do previously mentioned works by C. Vann Woodward, Holland Thompson, and Philip A. Bruce. Details are supplied by Matthew B. Hammond: *The Cotton Industry* (Ithaca, 1897); J. C. Sitterson, *Sugar Country: the South's Cane Sugar Industry, 1753–1950* (Lexington, 1953); George K. Holmes: "Three Centuries of Tobacco," in *Yearbook of Agriculture, 1919* (Washington, 1920), pp. 151–75; Enoch M. Banks: *The Economics of Land Tenure in Georgia* (New York, 1905); Robert P. Brooks: *The Agrarian Revolution in Georgia, 1865–1912* (Madison, 1914); Rupert B. Vance: *Human Factors in Cotton Culture* (Chapel Hill, 1929); and Edgar T. Thompson: "The Natural History of Agricultural Labor in the South," in David K. Jackson, ed.: *American Studies in Honor of William Kenneth Boyd.*

Labor problems are treated by Alfred H. Stone: *Studies in the American Race Problem* (New York, 1908); Philip A. Bruce: *The Plantation Negro as a Freedman* (New York, 1889); Carl Kelsey: *The Negro Farmer* (Chicago, 1903); Clarence Heer: *Income and Wages in the South* (Chapel Hill, 1931); and George K. Holmes: "The Peons of the South," *Annals of the American Academy of Political and Social Science*, IV, 265–74 (September, 1893).

CHAPTER XXII

NATIONAL historians of agrarian discontent do not neglect the South. They include Solon J. Buck: *The Granger Movement* (Cambridge, 1913), and *The Agrarian Crusade: a Chronicle of the Farmer in Politics* (New Haven, 1921), and John D. Hicks: *The Populist Revolt* (Minneapolis, 1931). Charles H. Otken: *The Ills of the South* (New York, 1894), is a competent statement of farm grievances by a contemporary. Significant if brief interpretations are made by Benjamin B. Kendrick: "Agrarian Discontent in the South, 1880–1900," American Historical Association, *Annual Report, 1920*, pp. 267–72; John D. Wade: "Old Wine in New Bottles," *Virginia Quarterly Review*, XI, 239–52 (April, 1935); Leonidas L. Polk: "The Farmer's Discontent," *North American Review*, CLIII, 5–12 (July, 1891); Frederick W. Moore: "The Condition of the Southern Farmer," *Yale Re-*

view, III, 56–67 (May, 1894); and chapters in Holland Thompson: *The New South*, Benjamin B. Kendrick and Alex M. Arnett: *The South Looks at Its Past;* and C. Vann Woodward: *Origins of the New South.*

Special topics are treated in John D. Hicks: "The Sub-Treasury: A Forgotten Plan for the Relief of Agriculture," *Mississippi Valley Historical Review*, XV, 355–73 (December, 1928), and Joseph C. Manning: *The Fadeout of Populism* (New York, 1928). Among studies of the agrarian movement in the several states, as intelligent if not as profound as similar works on Reconstruction, are Alex M. Arnett: *Populist Movement in Georgia* (New York, 1922); Helen G. Edmonds: *The Negro and Fusion Politics in North Carolina* (Chapel Hill, 1951); William W. Ball: *The State That Forgot;* John Bunyan Clark: *Populism in Alabama* (Auburn, 1927); Roscoe C. Martin: *The People's Party in Texas* (Austin, 1933); Daniel M. Robison: *Bob Taylor and the Agrarian Revolt in Tennessee* (Chapel Hill, 1935); William D. Sheldon: *Populism in the Old Dominion* (Princeton, 1935); Simeon A. Delap: *The Populist Party in North Carolina* (Durham, 1922); John D. Hicks: "The Farmer's Alliance in North Carolina," *The North Carolina Historical Review*, II, 162–87 (April, 1925), and Melvin J. White: "Populism in Louisiana during the Nineties," *The Mississippi Valley Historical Review*, V, 3–19 (January, 1918). Biographical studies of agrarian leaders are C. Vann Woodward: *Tom Watson, Agrarian Rebel;* Francis B. Simkins: *Pitchfork Ben Tillman, South Carolinian* (Baton Rouge, 1944); and Stuart Noblin: *Leonidas L. Polk, Agrarian Crusader* (Chapel Hill, 1949).

The prohibition movement is treated in Leonard S. Blakey: *The Sale of Liquor in the South* (New York, 1912); Ernest H. Cherrington and others, eds.: *Standard Encyclopedia of the Alcohol Problem* (6 vols., Westerville, Ohio, 1925–30); James B. Sellers: *The Prohibition Movement in Alabama, 1702–1943* (Chapel Hill, 1943); and Daniel G. Whitener: *Prohibition in North Carolina, 1715–1945* (Chapel Hill, 1946). Adequate discussions of suffrage and other legal aspects of the Negro question are advanced by Paul Lewinson: *Race, Class, and Party: A History of Negro Suffrage and White Politics in the South* (New York, 1932); Charles S. Mangum, Jr.: *The Legal Status of the Negro* (Chapel Hill, 1940); Stephen B. Weeks: "History of Negro Suffrage," *The Political Science Quarterly*, IX, 671–703 (December, 1894); and Francis G. Caffey: "Suffrage Limitations in the South," *ibid.*, XX, 53–67 (March, 1905). Primary elections are discussed by C. A. Merriam and Louise Overrecker: *Primary Elections* (Chicago, 1928); J. T. Salter, ed.: "The Direct Primary," *Annals of the American Academy of Political and Social Science*, CVI, 1–273 (March, 1923); and O. Douglas Weeks: "The Texas Direct Primary System," *Southwestern Social Science Quarterly*, XIII, 95–120 (January, 1932–33).

CHAPTER XXIII

EDGAR W. KNIGHT: *Public Education in the South* (Boston, 1922); Charles W. Dabney: *Universal Education in the South* (2 vols., Chapel Hill, 1936); Amory D. Mayo's articles in United States Commissioner of Education, *Report for 1903*, I, 391–462, and *Report for 1904*, I, 999–1090, supplemented by Knight: "Recent Progress and Problems of Education," in William T. Couch, ed.: *Culture in the South* comprise valuable appraisals of the South's educational system and reaffirm the faith of its leaders in education as a panacea for Southern problems. More critical analyses of the actual accomplishments and failures of Southern schools are available in H. Clarence Nixon: "Colleges and Universities," in Couch, ed.: *ibid.;* John Gould Fletcher: "Education, Past and Present," in Twelve Southerners: *I'll Take My Stand;* Holland Thompson: *The New South;* Kendrick and Arnett: *The South Looks at Its Past;* and Howard K. Beale: *Are the American Teachers Free?* (New York, 1936).

The following state histories of education, compiled under the authority of the United States Bureau of Education, are old but useful: Charles E. Jones: *Education in Georgia* (Washington, 1889); Willis G. Clark: *History of Education in Alabama* (Washington, 1889); Edwin W. Fay: *History of Education in Louisiana* (Washington, 1898); Edward Mayes: *History of Education in Mississippi* (Washington, 1899); and Josiah H. Shinn: *History of Education in Arkansas* (Washington, 1900). Among more recent state histories are: Barksdale Hamlett: *History of Education in Kentucky* (Frankfort, 1914); Cornelius J. Heatwole: *A History of Education in Virginia* (New York, 1916); Thomas H. Harris: *The Story of Public Education in Louisiana* (New Orleans, 1924); Frederick Eby: *The Development of Education in Texas* (New York, 1925); Henry T. Thompson: *The Establishment of the Public School System in South Carolina* (Columbia, 1927); Oscar W. Harris: *Development of Secondary Education in Alabama Prior to 1920* (Nashville, 1933); Edgar W. Knight: *Public School Education in North Carolina* (Boston, 1916); and Marcus C. S. Noble: *History of the Public Schools of North Carolina* (Chapel Hill, 1930). Problems of higher education are explained by John H. Reynolds and David Y. Thomas: *History of the University of Arkansas* (Fayetteville, 1910); Philip A. Bruce: *History of the University of Virginia, 1819-1919;* and Edwin Mims: *History of Vanderbilt University* (Nashville, 1946).

Important older works on Negro education include articles by Amory D. Mayo and Kelly Miller in United States Commissioner of Education: *Report, 1894-95* and *1901-02;* Jabez L. M. Curry: *Education of the Negro since 1866* (New York, 1894); and W. E. Burghardt Du Bois: *The Negro Common School* (Atlanta, 1901). Important later works on this subject are those by Horace M. Bond: *Negro Education in the South* (Washington, 1939); Carter G. Woodson: *Mis-Education of the Negro* (Washington, 1933); Buell G. Gallagher: *American Caste and the Negro College* (New York, 1933); and Edwin R. Embree: *Brown America* (New York, 1938). The most noted book of a Southern educator is that of Booker T. Washington: *Up From Slavery* (New York, 1901). Other biographies, competent and intelligent if laudatory, are Emmett J. Scott and Lyman B. Stowe: *Booker T. Washington* (New York, 1916); Dumas Malone: *Edwin A. Alderman* (New York, 1940); Edwin Mims: *Chancellor Kirkland of Vanderbilt* (Nashville, 1940); Marcus M. Wilkerson: *Thomas Duckett Boyd* (Baton Rouge, 1935); Catherine O. Peare: *Mary McLeod Bethune* (New York, 1951); and Louise Ware: *George Foster Peabody* (Athens, 1951).

CHAPTER XXIV

RECENT Southern social history is most completely revealed by the volumes of the Writers' Program of the Work Projects Administration: "American

Guide Series," listed for Chapter I. These volumes contain essays on folk-lore, religion, the theater, sports, foods, festivals, and domestic customs. Social life is not neglected in the general appraisals of C. Vann Woodward: *Origins of the New South;* Holland Thompson: *The New South;* Benjamin B. Kendrick and Alex M. Arnett: *The South Looks at Its Past;* Rupert B. Vance: *Human Geography of the South;* Howard W. Odum: *An American Epoch* (New York, 1930), and *Southern Regions of the United States* (Chapel Hill, 1936); and William T. Couch, ed.: *Culture in the South.* The interplay of mind and social behavior is profoundly explored in Wilbur J. Cash: *The Mind of the South.* Arthur F. Raper and Ira DeA. Reid: *Sharecroppers All* (Chapel Hill, 1941), emphasizes class and race struggles. Belton O'Neall Townsend: "South Carolina Morals" and "South Carolina Society," *The Atlantic Monthly,* XXXIX, 467–75, 670–84 (April, June, 1877); Nathaniel S. Shaler: "Peculiarities of the South," *North American Review,* CLI, 477–88 (October, 1890); and Richard Malcolm Johnston: "Middle Georgia Rural Life," *Century Magazine,* XLIII, 737–43 (March, 1892), describe society in the decade after Reconstruction. High life is treated by Perceval Reniers: *The Springs of Virginia* (Chapel Hill, 1941); humble life is the subject of Shields McIlwaine: *The Southern Poor-White;* and Erskine Caldwell and Margaret Bourke-White: *You Have Seen Their Faces* (New York, 1937).

Prominent residents describe their respective states in Ernest Gruening, ed.: *These United States* (New York, 1932). A large group of writers have left unforgettable impressions of society in their memoirs or books of travel. Among early social commentators are Sir George Campbell: *Black and White* (New York, 1879); Samuel Clemens (Mark Twain): *Life on the Mississippi* (New York, 1884); Nicholas Worth [pseud. for Walter H. Page]: *The Southerner* (New York, 1909); Peter M. Wilson: *Southern Exposure* (Chapel Hill, 1927); Ludwig Lewisohn: *Up Stream* (New York, 1923); and John Galsworthy: "That Old-Time Place," *Scribner's Magazine,* LII, 191–2 (August, 1912). Later social commentators include Marietta M. Andrews: *Memoirs of a Poor Relation* (New York, 1927); Maury Maverick: *A Maverick American* (New York, 1931); Carl L. Carmer: *Stars Fell on Alabama* (New York, 1934); Clarence Cason: *90° in the Shade* (Chapel Hill, 1935); Julian R. Meade: *I Live in Virginia* (New York, 1935); Virginia Moore: *Virginia Is a State of Mind* (New York, 1942); John A. Rice: *I Came Out of the Eighteenth Century* (New York, 1942); Herman C. Nixon: *Possum Trot, Rural Community South* (Norman, 1941); William A. Percy: *Lanterns on the Levee;* Jonathan Daniels: *A Southerner Discovers the South* (New York, 1938); Katherine D. Lumpkin: *The Making of a Southerner* (New York, 1947); Hal Steed: *Georgia, Unfinished State* (New York, 1942); David L. Cohn: *Where I Was Born and Raised* (Boston, 1948); Hodding Carter: *Southern Legacy* (Baton Rouge, 1949); Viola G. Liddell: *With a Southern Accent* (Norman, 1948); and Stark Young: *The Pavilion* (New York, 1951).

A few biographies catch the flavor of the Southern community, especially Walter R. Bowie: *Sunrise in the South: the Life of Mary-Cooke Branch Munford* (Richmond, 1942); Raymond B. Nixon: *Henry W. Grady;* Robert W. Winston: *Horace Williams, Gadfly of Chapel Hill* (Chapel Hill, 1942); and Edward L. Tinker: *Lafcadio Hearn's American Days* (New York, 1924). Life in individual communities is described by

Mary N. Stanard: *Richmond, Its People and Its Story* (Philadelphia, 1923); Henry Boley: *Lexington in Old Virginia* (Richmond, 1936); Grace E. King: *New Orleans, the Place and the People* (New York, 1896); Lyle Saxon: *Fabulous New Orleans* (New York, 1928); Herbert Asbury: *The French Quarter* (New York, 1936); Harnett T. Kane: *The Bayous of Louisiana* (New York, 1936); J. Frank Dobie: *The Flavor of Texas* (Dallas, 1936); William B. Bissell: *Rural Texas* (New York, 1924); Samuel H. Hobbs: *North Carolina, Economic and Social* (Chapel Hill, 1930); Marjorie Potwin: *Cotton Mill People of the Piedmont* (New York, 1927); and John Dollard: *Caste and Class in a Southern Town* (New Haven, 1937). Life among the mountaineers is portrayed by Horace Kephart: *Our Southern Highlanders* (New York, 1922); Muriel Sheppard: *Cabins in the Laurel* (Chapel Hill, 1935); Vance Randolph: *The Ozarks* (New York, 1931); and Charles M. Wilson: *Backwoods America* (Chapel Hill, 1934). Special phases of social life are revealed by George P. Jackson: *White Spirituals in the Southern Uplands* (Chapel Hill, 1933); and Hortense Powdermaker: *After Freedom: A Cultural Study in the Deep South* (New York, 1939).

Many novelists treat social life elaborately. Chapter XXI of this book is partly devoted to this theme as developed by Ellen Glasgow, Thomas S. Stribling, William Faulkner, Erskine Caldwell, Dorothy Scarborough, and others. The following is a partial list of other social novels: Robert Rylee: *Deep Dark River* (New York, 1935); Stark Young: *River House* (New York, 1929); Ruth Cross: *The Big Road* (New York, 1931); Donald Joseph: *October's Child* (New York, 1929); Irvin S. Cobb: *Old Judge Priest* (New York, 1915); *Kentucky* (New York, 1924), and *Red Likker* (New York, 1929); Marian Sims: *The City on the Hill* (Philadelphia, 1940); Corra W. Harris: *Recording Angel* (New York, 1912), *In Search of a Husband* (New York, 1913), and *A Circuit Rider's Wife* (New York, 1910); Morris Markey: *The Band Plays Dixie* (New York, 1927); and John Trotwood Moore: *The Bishop of Cottontown* (Philadelphia, 1906). The dark involvements of Southern life are extended in the following works of fiction: Carlyle Tillery: *Red Bone Woman* (New York, 1950); Worth T. Hedden: *The Other Room* (New York, 1947); Truman Capote: *Other Voices, Other Rooms* (New York, 1947); Elizabeth B. Coker: *Daughter of Strangers* (New York, 1950); Caroline Gordon: *Strange Children* (New York, 1951); William Styron: *Lie Down in Darkness* (New York, 1951); and Clifford Dowdey: *Jasmine Street* (New York, 1951).

CHAPTER XXV

Bureau of the Census: *Religious Bodies, 1926* (2 vols., Washington, 1930) and *1936* (3 vols., Washington, 1941), is the chief source for the statistical and narrative history of the South's religious denominations. Each of the fifteen volumes of the Federal Writers' Program of the Works Projects Administration: "American Guide Series" listed for Chapter I has a chapter on religion. Edwin McN. Poteat, Jr.: "Religion in the South," in William T. Couch, ed.: *Culture in the South*, and Richard M. Weaver: "The Older Religiousness of the South," *Sewanee Review*, LI, 237–49 (Spring, 1943), are enlightened interpretations of Southern religious attitudes. Church people in action are portrayed by Hunter D. Farish: *The Circuit Rider Dis-*

mounts: A Social History of Southern Methodism, 1865–1900; Archie Robertson; *That Old-Time Religion* (Boston, 1950); George P. Jackson: *White Spirituals in the Southern Uplands;* Elmer T. Clark: *The Small Sects in America* (Nashville, 1937); Howard Taylor: "How Firm a Foundation," *Virginia Quarterly Review,* VII, 562–72 (October, 1931); Owen P. White: "Reminiscences of Texas Divines," *American Mercury,* IV, 95–100 (September, 1926); and Jesse M. Ormond: *The Country Church in North Carolina* (Durham, 1931).

Social commentators tend to ignore religion, but notable exceptions may be found in Howard W. Odum: *An American Epoch* (New York, 1930), and *Southern Regions of the United States* (Chapel Hill, 1936). Wilbur J. Cash: *The Mind of the South,* and Liston Pope: *Mill Hands and Preachers* (New Haven, 1942), recognize religion as a determining factor of Southern culture. John A. Rice: *I Came Out of the Eighteenth Century* presents an inside view of Methodism. Edwin Mims: *The Advancing South,* and Virginius Dabney: *Liberalism in the South* (Chapel Hill, 1932), and *Below the Potomac* (New York, 1942), provide conventional liberal views of church controversies. They should be supplemented by Maynard Shipley: *The War on Modern Science* (New York, 1927), and by Stewart C. Cole: *History of Fundamentalism* (New York, 1929). Paul N. Garber: *The Methodists Are One People* (Nashville, 1939), tells the story of Methodist unification. Among biographies of church leaders are Thomas C. Johnson: *The Life and Letters of Robert L. Dabney,* and *The Life and Letters of Benjamin M. Palmer;* Henry A. White: *Southern Presbyterian Leaders* (New York, 1912); William M. Polk: *Leonidas Polk;* Paul N. Garber: *John Carlisle Kilgo* (Durham, 1937); and Edwin Mims: *Chancellor Kirkland of Vanderbilt.* The few recent general historians who discuss Southern religion include Arthur M. Schlesinger: *The Rise of the City, 1878–1898* (New York, 1927); and Charles A. and Mary R. Beard: *The Rise of American Civilization* (2 vols., revised ed., New York, 1930).

General historians of American religion tend to neglect the recent South, as becomes evident in William W. Sweet: *The Story of Religion in America;* Henry K. Rowe: *History of Religion in the United States* (New York, 1928); and A. B. Bass: *Protestantism in the United States* (New York, 1929). Negro religious problems are analyzed by Wesley J. Gaines: *African Methodism in the South* (Atlanta, 1890), and Carter G. Woodson: *The History of the Negro Church.* There are state and sectional histories of each of the important denominations, but these books stress origins and offer disjointed facts at the expense of contemporary manifestations and organized sequences. Religion is inadequately exploited by the social novelists. Exceptions are Corra W. Harris: *A Circuit Rider's Wife* and *From Sunup to Sundown;* Ellen Glasgow: *Vein of Iron;* William Faulkner: *Light in August;* James Street: *The Gauntlet* (New York, 1945); and Gael Tucker: *Lament for Four Virgins* (New York, 1952).

CHAPTER XXVI

MORE critical and factual information is available on literature than on any other phase of Southern history since Reconstruction. The most intelligent appraisals are those of Donald Davidson: "The Trend of Literature," in William T. Couch, ed.: *Culture in the South;* Shields McIlwaine: *The Southern Poor-White;* Edd W. Parks: *Segments of Southern Thought;* and the article "Literature" in each volume of the Federal Writers' Program of the Work Projects Administration: "American Guide Series," cited earlier. Problems of the post-bellum author are explained by Charles R. Anderson: "Charles Gayarré and Paul Hayne: the Last Literary Cavaliers," in David K. Jackson, ed.: *American Studies in Honor of William Kenneth Boyd.* A pioneer work in post-bellum analysis is that of William M. Baskervill and others: *Southern Writers: Biographical and Critical Studies* (Nashville, 1897 and 1903). Early works of lesser importance include Samuel A. Link: *Pioneers of Southern Literature* (2 vols., Nashville, 1903); Carl Holliday: *A History of Southern Literature* (New York, 1906); and C. Alphonso Smith: *Southern Literary Studies* (Chapel Hill, 1927). Edwin A. Alderman and Joel Chandler Harris, eds.: *Library of Southern Literature,* contains profuse biographies and quotations. Johnson and Malone, eds.: *Dictionary of American Biography,* presents sketches of important Southern writers who died before December 31, 1935. A history of a Southern magazine is William B. Hamilton: *Fifty Years of the South Atlantic Quarterly* (Durham, 1952).

Among significant articles describing the course of post-bellum literature are Albion W. Tourgée: "The South as a Field for Fiction," *Forum,* VI, 404–13 (December, 1888); Charles C. Coleman: "The Recent Movement in Southern Literature," *Harper's Magazine,* LXXIV, 837–55 (May, 1887); George E. Woodberry: "The South in American Letters," *ibid.,* CVII, 735–41 (October, 1903); C. Alphonso Smith: "The Possibilities of Southern Literature," *Sewanee Review,* VI, 298–305 (July, 1898); John B. Henneman: "The National Element in Southern Literature," *ibid.,* XI, 345–66 (July, 1903); and Maurice Thompson: "A Literary Journey," *Independent,* CII, 2794–8 (November 22, 1900). Anthologies include Louise Manly: *Southern Literature* (Richmond, 1895); William P. Trent: *Southern Writers* (New York, 1905); Edwin Mims and Bruce R. Payne: *Southern Prose and Poetry* (New York, 1910); C. Addison Hibbard: *The Lyric South* (New York, 1928), and *Stories of the South, Old and New* (Chapel Hill, 1931); William T. Wynn: *Southern Literature* (New York, 1932); Hilton R. Greer: *New Voices of the Southwest* (Dallas, 1934); and Robert P. Warren: *A Southern Harvest: Short Stories by Southern Writers* (Boston, 1937).

Among biographical or critical studies of Southern authors are Aubrey H. Starke: *Sidney Lanier* (Chapel Hill, 1932); Julia Harris: *The Life and Letters of Joel Chandler Harris* (Boston, 1918); Lucy L. C. Bikle: *George W. Cable* (New York, 1928); Grant C. Knight: *James Lane Allen* (Chapel Hill, 1935); Rosewell Page: *Thomas Nelson Page* (New York, 1923); Joseph L. King; *Dr. George W. Bagby, a Study of Virginia Literature, 1850–1880* (New York, 1927); Daniel S. Rankin: *Kate Chopin and Her Creole Stories* (Philadelphia, 1932); Edward L. Tinker: *Lafcadio Hearn's American Days;* Carl C. Van Doren: *James Branch Cabell* (New York, 1925); Louise M. Field: *Ellen Glasgow: Novelist of the Old and the New South* (Garden City, 1923); Stuart P. Sherman, Sara Haardt, and Emily Clark: *Ellen Glasgow: Critical Essays* (Garden City, 1929); James S. Wilson: "Ellen Glasgow's Novels," *Virginia Quarterly Review,* IX, 593–600 (October, 1933), Carl C. Van Doren: "Made in America: Erskine Caldwell,"

The Nation, CXXXVII, 443–4 (October 18, 1933), John D. Wade: "Sweet Are the Uses of Degeneracy," *The Southern Review,* I, 449–66 (Winter, 1936); Malcolm Cowley: "William Faulkner's Legend of the South," in Allen Tate, ed.: *A Southern Vanguard,* pp. 13–27; and Irving Howe: *William Faulkner, a Critical Study* (New York, 1952). William P. Trent and others: *The Cambridge History of American Literature,* pioneered in recognizing the South's contributions to national letters.

Other national histories follow its example: Grant Overton: *The Women Who Make Our Novels* (New York, 1922); Charles C. Baldwin: *The Men Who Make Our Novels* (New York, 1924); Fred L. Pattee: *The New American Literature* (New York, 1930); Carl C. Van Doren: *The American Novel* (rev. ed., New York, 1940); Person Boydton: *America in Contemporary Fiction* (Chicago, 1940); Joseph W. Beach: *American Fiction, 1920–1940* (New York, 1941); Oscar Cargill: *Intellectual America: Ideas on the March* (New York, 1941); and Alfred Kazin: *On Native Ground, an Interpretation of Modern American Prose Literature* (New York, 1942). *Book Review Digest* (New York, 1905—) is generous in its appraisals of Southern books.

CHAPTER XXVII

THE MOST useful work on the nonliterary arts of the twentieth-century South is that of Ula M. Gregory: "The Fine Arts," in William T. Couch, ed.: *Culture in the South.* The volumes of the Federal Writers' Program of the Work Projects Administration: "American Guide Series," cited previously, are the most complete source for this subject. Their varied and detailed information is supplemented by other volumes in the same collection: *Tulsa* (Tulsa, 1938); *San Antonio* (San Antonio, 1938); and *Beaumont* (San Antonio, 1939). Some descriptive books do not neglect the arts; for example, Hal Steed: *Georgia: Unfinished State* (1942); Annie H. Howard: *Georgia Homes and Landmarks* (Atlanta), Edward T. H. Shaffer: *Carolina Gardens* (New York, 1937); Augustine T. Smythe, T. Herbert Sass, and others: *The Carolina Low Country* (New York, 1931); George W. Lee: *Beale Street, Where the Blues Begin* (New York, 1934); Nathaniel C. Curtis: *New Orleans, Its Old Houses, Shops and Public Buildings* (Philadelphia, 1933); Lyle Saxon: *Fabulous New Orleans* (New York, 1928); and Carl L. Carmer: *Stars Fell on Alabama.* Outlines of architecture are set forth by S. Fiske Kimball: *American Architecture* (Indianapolis, 1928); its application is treated by Benjamin F. Wilson, III: *The Parthenon of Pericles and Its Reproduction in America* (Nashville, 1936); Architectural Record: *The Restoration of Colonial Williamsburg* (New York, 1935); Russel F. Whitehead: "The Old and the New South," *Architectural Record,* XXX, 1–56 (January, 1911).

What the painters have done is described in Esse Forrester-O'Brien: *Art and Artists of Texas* (Dallas, 1935); Contey V. Sutton, ed.: *History of Art in Mississippi* (Jackson, 1929); Ben E. Looney: "Historical Sketch of Art in Louisiana," *Louisiana Historical Quarterly,* XVIII, 382–96 (April, 1935); and Isaac N. Cline: *Art and Artists in New Orleans during the Last Century* (New Orleans, 1922). The life of the South's greatest resident sculptor is recounted by Jan I. Fortune and Jean Burton: *Elisabet Ney* (New York,

1943). Denham Wooten's interesting "History of the Theatre in Arkansas" appeared in Sunday editions of the *Arkansas Gazette*, November 17—December 22, 1935. Local musical compositions are described in Gladys P. Bumstead: *Louisiana Composers* (New Orleans, 1935); and in Margaret F. Thomas: *Musical Alabama* (2 vols., Montgomery, 1925, and Tuscaloosa, 1936). Folk music is treated by George P. Jackson: *White Spirituals in the Southern Uplands;* Ella P. Richardson, comp.: *American Mountain Songs* (New York, 1927); and Arthur P. Hudson: *Folk Songs of Mississippi* (Chapel Hill, 1936). The contribution of the Negro to music is revealed by John J. Daly: *A Song in His Heart* [Life of James A. Bland] (Philadelphia, 1951); Maud C. Hare: *Negro Musicians and Their Music* (New York, 1936); Louis Armstrong: *Swing That Music* (New York, 1936); Frederic Ramsey, Jr. and Charles E. Smith, eds.: *Jazzmen* (New York, 1939); and William C. Handy: *Father of the Blues, an Autobiography* (New York, 1941). The Little Theater in Texas is described by John Rosenfield: *Three Southwest Plays* (Dallas, 1942). See also Philip Graham: *Showboats: The History of an American Institution* (Austin, 1951).

CHAPTER XXVIII

THE PROBLEMS and realities of Southern economy in the twentieth century are satisfactorily presented by Howard W. Odum: *Southern Regions of the United States.* A convenient summary of the extensive data on this subject is made by Gerald W. Johnson: *The Wasted Land* (Chapel Hill, 1937). *The Annals of the American Academy of Political and Social Science*, CLIII (January, 1931), contain papers by W. J. Carson, J. B. Andrews, Mercer G. Evans, O. E. Kiesling, Thorndike Saville, and others on many phases of Southern emonomy, including electric power and the chemical industries. Less encyclopedic and more general are Almon E. Parkins: *The South, Its Economic-Geographic Development;* Katherine D. Lumpkin: *The South in Progress* (New York, 1940); John V. Van Sickle: *Planning for the South* (Nashville, 1943); William Haynes: *Southern Horizons* (New York, 1946); and E. W. Zimmermann: "Resources of the South," *South Atlantic Quarterly*, XXXII, 213-26 (July, 1933). The Manufacturers' Record: *Blue Book of Southern Progress* (Baltimore, 1909—), provides an annual appraisal of industrial advance.

The problem of alien ownership of Southern industry is forcibly put by National Emergency Council (Lowell Mellett, Executive Secretary): *Report on Economic Conditions of the South* (Washington, 1938); Walter P. Webb: *Divided We Stand* (rev. ed., Austin, 1944); Ellis G. Arnall: *The Shore Dimly Seen* (Philadelphia, 1946); David C. Coyle: "The South's Unbalanced Budget," *The Virginia Quarterly Review*, XIII, 192-208 (Spring, 1937); Maury Maverick: "Let's Join the United States," *ibid.*, XV, 64-7 (Winter, 1929); and Claude Pepper: "A New Deal in Reconstruction," *ibid.*, XV, 551-60 (Autumn, 1939). Industrial and agricultural developments of several states are treated in the volumes of the Federal Writers' Program of the Work Projects Administration: "American Guide Series," cited earlier. Other discussions of state problems are Clarence W. Newman, ed.: *Virginia, Economic and Social* (Richmond, 1933); Samuel H. Hobbs: *North Carolina, Economic and Social* (Chapel Hill, 1930); Wendell M. Adamson: *Industrial*

Activity in Alabama, 1913–1932 (University, Alabama, 1932); Harry Y. Benedict and John A. Lomax: *The Book of Texas* (Garden City, 1916); Malcolm H. Bryan and Thomas J. Askew, comp.: *Readings to Accompany a Course in Contemporary Georgia* (Athens, 1935); and Wilfred H. Callcott. ed.: *South Carolina, Economic and Social* (Columbia, 1945).

A controversial question is discussed in William F. Ogburn: "Does It Cost Less to Live in the South?" *Social Forces*, XIV, 211–14 (December, 1935). Twentieth-century developments in industry are emphasized by Stanley F. Horn: *This Fascinating Lumber Business* (Indianapolis, 1943); Max W. Ball: *This Fascinating Oil Business* (Indianapolis, 1940); Charles A. Warner: *Texas Oil and Gas Since 1543* (Houston, 1939); Ralph Arnold and William J. Kemnitzer: *Petroleum in the United States and Possessions* (New York, 1931); Carl B. Glasscock: *Then Came Oil* (Indianapolis, 1938); Walter H. Voskuil: *Economics of Water Power Development* (New York, 1928); and Nelson C. Brown: *Timber Products and Industries* (New York, 1937). Supplementing items cited for Chapter XVI are detailed discussions of labor conditions, as presented by Abraham Berglund, George T. Starnes, and Frank T. De Vyver: *Labor in the Industrial South* (New York, 1930); Elizabeth H. Davidson: *Child Labor Legislation in the Southern Textile States* (Chapel Hill, 1939); Lois McDonald: *Southern Mill Hills* (New York, 1928); Dorothy Myra Page: *Southern Cotton Mills and Labor* (New York, 1929); Jennings J. Rhyne: *Some Southern Cotton Mill Workers and Their Villages* (Chapel Hill, 1939); and Herbert J. Lahne: *The Cotton Mill Worker* (New York, 1944). Twentieth-century agricultural problems are treated by Clarence Poe: "The Farmer and His Future," in William T. Couch, ed.: *Culture in the South;* Paul B. Sears: *Deserts on the March* (Norman, 1935); Charles S. Johnson, Edwin R. Embree, and Will W. Alexander: *The Collapse of Cotton Tenancy* (Chapel Hill, 1935); and Arthur F. Raper: *Tenants of the Almighty* (New York, 1943), and *Preface to Peasantry* (Chapel Hill, 1939). Harriet L. Herring: *Passing of the Mill Village* (Chapel Hill, 1950).

The Southern phases of the New Deal are depicted in the previously mentioned book by Miss Lumpkin, and in articles by Coyle, Maverick, and Pepper. The TVA experiment is treated by David E. Lilienthal: *TVA: Democracy on the March* (New York, 1944); Robert L. Duffus: *The Valley and Its People, a Portrait of TVA* (New York, 1944); and C. Herman Pritchett: *The Tennessee Valley Authority, a Study in Public Administration* (Chapel Hill, 1943). Skepticism concerning this sociological paradise is expressed by Donald Davidson: *The Tennessee*, Vol. II, and by Calvin B. Hoover and Benjamin U. Ratchford: *Economic Resources and Policies of the South* (New York, 1951).

CHAPTER XXIX

CRITICALLY detached as well as an encyclopedic study of the Negro's place in American life is the work of Gunnar Myrdal, with the assistance of Richard Sterner and Arnold Rose: *An American Dilemma* (2 vols., New York, 1944). Other general studies are those by Willis D. Weatherford: *The Negro from Africa to America* (New York, 1924); Jerome Dowd: *The Negro in American Life* (New York, 1926); Sir Harry S. Johnson: *The*

Negro in the New World (New York, 1910); Edwin R. Embree: *Brown America* (New York, 1931); James S. Allen: *The Negro Question in the United States* (New York, 1936); Abram L. Harris and Sterling D. Spero: "Negro Problem," *Encyclopedia of the Social Sciences*, XI, 335-55; Charles S. Johnson: *The Negro in American Civilization* (New York, 1930); and Edward B. Reuter: *The American Race Problem* (New York, 1927). A comprehensive study of American Negroes, including those in Canada and Central and South America, is John Hope Franklin: *From Slavery to Freedom* (New York, 1947). The most critical of American Negro historians is E. Franklin Frazier: *The Negro in the United States* (New York, 1949).

Pre-eminent among objective fact-finders is Charles S. Mangum, Jr.: *The Legal Status of the Negro* (Chapel Hill, 1940). Similar studies are furnished by Paul Lewinson: *Race, Class, and Party* (New York, 1932); Charles H. Wesley: *Negro Labor in the United States* (New York, 1927); Abram L. Harris: *The Negro as Capitalist* (Philadelphia, 1936); Sterling D. Spero and Abram L. Harris: *The Black Worker: The Negro and the Labor Movement* (New York, 1931); Harold F. Gosnell: *Negro Politicians* (Chicago, 1935); and Jesse F. Steiner and Roy M. Brown: *The North Carolina Chain Gang* (Chapel Hill, 1927). An outstanding social study is provided by E. Franklin Frazier: *The Negro Family in the United States* (Chicago, 1939). Other significant observations of social behavior are presented by Bertram W. Doyle: *The Etiquette of Race Relations in the South* (Chicago, 1937); John Dollard: *Caste and Class in a Southern Town* (New Haven, 1937); Hortense Powdermaker: *After Freedom: a Cultural Study of the Deep South;* and Allison Davis, Burleigh B. and Mary R. Gardner: *Deep South, a Social Anthropological Study of Caste and Class* (Chicago, 1941). William A. Nolan: *Communism versus the Negro* (Chicago, 1951), puts an over-emphasized issue in its proper prospective.

Observations of the following English travelers are wise and moderate: Sir George Campbell: *White and Black;* Sir William L. Clowes: *Black America* (London, 1891); William Archer: *Through Afro-America* (London, 1910); and Maurice S. Evans: *Black and White in the Southern States* (London, 1915). Two informative Northern writers are Ray Stannard Baker: *Following the Color Line* (New York, 1908), and Albert B. Hart: *The Southern South* (New York, 1910). Relief from the liberal optimism of most writers is furnished by Frederick L. Hoffman: *Race Traits and Tendencies of the American Negro* (New York, 1896); William Hannibal Thomas: *The American Negro* (New York, 1901); Alfred H. Stone: *Studies in the American Race Problem* (New York, 1908). Prominent among the older generation of Southern whites who have written on the subject are George W. Cable: *The Silent South* (New York, 1885); Thomas Nelson Page: *The Negro, the Southerner's Problem* (New York, 1904); Edgar G. Murphy: *Problems of the Present South* (New York, 1909), and *The Basis of Ascendency* (New York, 1909).

Most revealing for racial attitudes is the work of Wilbur J. Cash: *The Mind of the South.* A classic among American autobiographies is Booker T. Washington: *Up from Slavery.* Other autobiographical books are James Weldon Johnson: *Along This Way* (New York, 1933); W. E. Burghardt Du Bois: *Dusk of Dawn* (New York, 1940); J. Saunders Redding: *No Day of Triumph* (New York, 1942); Kelly Miller: *Out of the House of Bondage* (New York: 1914); and Richard Wright; *Black Boy* (New York, 1945).

Noteworthy among Negro descriptions of Negro life is W. E. Burghardt Du Bois: *The Souls of Black Folk* (Chicago, 1903). Other books in this category include Robert R. Moton: *What the Negro Thinks* (New York, 1929); Alain L. Locke, ed.: *The New Negro* (New York, 1925); Walter White; *Rope and Faggot* (New York, 1925); Horace M. Bond: *The Education of the Negro in the American Social Order* (New York, 1934); and Roi Ottley: *"New World A-Coming"* (Boston, 1943).

CHAPTER XXX

V. O. KEY, JR.: *Southern Politics in State and Nation* (New York, 1949), is an encyclopedic survey of highest merit. It is featured by an array of graphs and by an intolerance of Southern behavior. Allan A. Michie and Frank Rhylick: *Dixie Demagogues* (New York, 1939), is less comprehensive and more extreme in its anti-Southern bias, but is more colorful. Charles W. Collins: *Whither Solid South?* (New Orleans, 1947), effectively states the case for Southern conservatives. Judicious appraisals are Arthur S. Link: "The Progressive Movement in the South, 1870–1914," *The North Carolina Historical Review*, XXIII, 171–95 (April, 1946); Vincent P. De Santis: "Republican Efforts to 'Crack' the Democratic South," *The Review of Politics*, XIV, 244–64 (April, 1952); Daniel M. Robison: "From Tillman to Huey Long: Some Striking Leaders of the Rural South," *The Journal of Southern History*, III, 288–310 (August, 1937); James W. Garner: "Southern Politics since the Civil War," *Studies in Southern History and Politics* (New York, 1914). Gunnar Myrdal: *An American Dilemma*, especially chapters XX–XXIII, strikes at the roots of Southern politics. Paul Lewinson: *Race, Class, and Party* (New York, 1932), and Howard W. Odum: *Southern Regions of the United States*, utilize detailed researches for enlightening comparisons. C. Vann Woodward: *Origins of the New South*, pp. 369 ff., bring the narrative up to the Woodrow Wilson period. Arthur S. Link: *The Road to the White House* (Princeton, 1947), emphasizes Wilson's Southern support.

Books of travel and observation which dwell upon politics include Ray Stannard Baker: *Following the Color Line;* Albert B. Hart: *The Southern South;* Maurice S. Evans: *Black and White in the Southern States;* William Archer: *Through Afro-America;* William J. Robertson: *The Changing South* (New York, 1927); Jonathan Daniels: *A Southerner Discovers the South;* Virginius Dabney: *Below the Potomac;* and John A. Rice: *I Came Out of the Eighteenth Century.*

Stirring defenses of Southern practices are made by Thomas Nelson Page: *The Negro: the Southerner's Problem* (New York, 1904); William W. Ball: *The State That Forgot: South Carolina's Surrender to Democracy;* and William A. Percy: *Lanterns on the Levee.* State histories cited for Chapter I, especially those by Thomas D. Clark, Kathryn A. Hanna, Rupert N. Richardson, and David D. Wallace, throw light on recent state politics. Pre-eminent for frankness among political reminiscences is the work of Nathaniel E. Harris: *Autobiography* (Macon, 1925). See also Josephus Daniels: *Tar Heel Editor* (Chapel Hill, 1939), and *The Editor in Politics* (Chapel Hill, 1941); Robert W. Winston: *It's a Far Cry* (New York, 1937);

Henry W. Watterson: *Marse Henry;* Champ Clark: *My Quarter Century of American Politics* (New York, 1920); and Oscar W. Underwood: *Drifting Sands of Party Politics* (2nd ed., New York, 1931), with a sketch by Claude G. Bowers.

Treatments of specific political problems are presented by John M. Mecklin: *The Ku Klux Klan: a Study in the American Mind* (New York, 1924); Benjamin B. Kendrick: "The Colonial Status of the South," *The Journal of Southern History,* VIII, 3–22 (February, 1942); Allen W. Moger: "The Origin of the Democratic Machine in Virginia," *ibid.,* VIII, 183–209 (May, 1942); Jennings Perry: *Democracy Begins at Home: The Tennessee Fight on the Poll Tax* (New York, 1944); and John Dollard: *Caste and Class in a Southern Town* (New Haven, 1937). Albert D. Kirwan: *The Revolt of the Rednecks* (Lexington, 1951), is a revealing study of Mississippi politics. Studies of Southern administrative problems include Charles M. Merriam: *Primary Elections* (Chicago, 1928); Elizabeth H. Davidson: *Child Labor Legislation in Southern Textile States* (Chapel Hill, 1939); Charles W. Pipkin: *Social Legislation in the South* (Chapel Hill, 1936); Melvin Evans: *A Study in the State Government of Louisiana* (Baton Rouge, 1931); Roderick L. Carleton: *Local Government and Administration in Louisiana* (Baton Rouge, 1935); Cullen B. Gosnell: *Government and Politics in Georgia* (New York, 1936); Caleb P. Patterson and others: *State and Local Government in Texas* (New York, 1940); and Simeon E. Leland: *Taxation in Kentucky* (Lexington, 1920).

There are seven critical biographies of twentieth-century Southern political leaders: C. Vann Woodward: *Tom Watson: Agrarian Rebel;* Sam H. Acheson: *Joe Bailey, the Last Democrat* (New York, 1932); Francis B. Simkins: *Pitchfork Ben Tillman: South Carolinian;* George C. Osborn: *John Sharp Williams, Planter-Statesman of the Deep South;* Virginius Dabney: *Dry Messiah: the Life of Bishop James Cannon, Jr.* (New York, 1949); Samuel Proctor: *Napoleon Bonaparte Broward* (Gainesville, 1951); John J. Mathews: *The Life and Death of an Oilman: The Career of E. W. Marland* (Norman, 1951). Hendrick: *The Life and Letters of Walter Hines Page,* Vol. I, sheds light on Southern politics. Less restrained are the books of Harold B. Hinton: *Cordell Hull* (Garden City, 1924); Rixey Smith and Norman Beasley: *Carter Glass* (New York, 1939); Charles Jacobson: *Life Story of Jeff Davis* (Little Rock, 1925); Archibald S. Coody: *Biographical Sketch of James Kimble Vardaman* (Jackson, 1922); Carlton Beals: *Story of Huey P. Long* (Philadelphia, 1935); and Harnett T. Kane: *Louisiana Hayride* (New York, 1941). Brief treatments are presented by Hamilton Basso: "Huey Long and His Background," *Harper's Magazine,* CLXX, 663–73 (May, 1935), and Osta L. Warr: "Mr. Blease of South Carolina," *American Mercury,* XVI, 25–32 (January, 1929). Every important figure in Southern politics before 1936 is critically sketched in *The Dictionary of American Biography.* More inclusive but less critical are *The National Cyclopedia of American Biography, Current Biography* (6 vols., New York, 1930–1942); *Current Biography: Who's News and Why* (New York, 1940—); and *Who's Who in America* (Chicago, 1899—). Southern politicians are treated in Adria L. Langley: *A Lion Is in the Streets* (New York, 1945); Berry Fleming: *Colonel Effingham's Raid* (New York, 1943); Robert P. Warren: *All the King's Men;* and T. S. Stribling: *The Sound Wagon.*

CHAPTER XXXI

HOOVER AND RATCHFORD: *Economic Resources and Policies of the South;*
John Temple Graves: *The Fighting South* (New York, 1943); Howard W.
Odum: *Race and Rumors of Race* (Chapel Hill, 1943); Avahm G. Mezerik:
Revolt of the South and the West (New York, 1946); Stetson Kennedy:
Southern Exposure (Garden City, 1946); and Ellis G. Arnall: *The Shore
Dimly Seen* (New York, 1946) present special aspects of the World War II
period. The interaction of war and race is treated by several authors in
Gordon W. Allport, ed.: "Controlling Group Prejudices," *The Annals of
the American Academy of Political and Social Science*, CCXLIV (Phila-
delphia, 1946). Marvin W. Schlegel: *Conscripted City: Norfolk in World
War II* (Norfolk, 1951), is a lively description of a much-alive city.

The war issues are explained by Julian Boyd: "The South and the Fight,"
The Atlantic Monthly, CLXXIII, 53–9 (February, 1944); John Dos Passos:
"The People at War," *Harper's Magazine*, CLXXXVII, 260–6 (August,
1943); and Benjamin B. Kendrick: "The Colonial Status of the South," *The
Journal of Southern History*, VIII, 3–22 (February, 1942). The relation of
the Negro to the war is set forth in Charles S. Johnson: "Race Relations in
the South," *Social Forces*, XXIII, 27–32 (October, 1944); Warman Welliver:
"Report on the Negro Soldier," *Harper's Magazine*, CXCII, 333–9 (April,
1946); several articles in *Survey Graphic*, XXXI, 449–508 (November,
1942); articles by a large group of writers in Charles H. Thompson, ed.:
"The American Negro in World Wars I and II," *The Journal of Negro
Education*, XII (Summer, 1943); and John Temple Graves: "The Southern
Negro and the War Crisis," *The Virginia Quarterly Review*, XVIII, 501–17
(Autumn, 1942). Industrial problems are presented by Donald M. Nelson:
"The South's Economic Opportunity," *American Mercury*, LIX, 422–7
(October, 1944); Dillard B. Lasseter: "The Impact of the War on the
South," *Social Forces*, XXIII, 20–6 (October, 1944); "Deep South Looks
Up," *Fortune*, XXVIII, 95–100 (July, 1943); and Larston D. Farrar: "Dixie-
land Goes to Town," *The Nation's Business*, XXXI, 23–4 (September, 1943).
Wartime politics are judiciously appraised by Vance Johnson: "The Old
Deal Democrats," *American Mercury*, LIX, 50–7 (July, 1944). General dis-
cussions are available in H. Clarence Nixon: "The South After the War,"
The Virginia Quarterly Review, XX, 321–34 (Summer, 1944); David L.
Cohn: "How the South Feels," *The Atlantic Monthly*, CLXXIII, 47–51
(January, 1944); and Virginius Dabney: "Nearer and Nearer the Precipice,"
ibid., CLXXI, 94–100 (January, 1943).

CHAPTERS XXXII–XXXIV

SOUTHERN politics in the very recent past are comprehensively discussed in
Key: *Southern Politics in State and Nation*, and in this book's supplement,
Alexander Heard: *Two-Party South* (Chapel Hill, 1952). Jasper B. Shannon: *Toward a New Politics in the South* (Knoxville, 1949); Taylor Cole
and J. D. Hallowell, eds.: *Southern Political Scene, 1938–1948* (Gainesville,
1948); and S. M. Lemmon: "Ideology of the Dixiecrat Movement," *Social
Forces*, XXX, 162–71 (December, 1951), present many provoking ideas. The

economics of the contemporary scene are presented in Hoover and Ratchford: *Economic Resources and Policies of the South*, and Glenn E. McLaughlin and Stephan Roback: *Why Industry Moves South* (Washington, 1949). E. Franklin Frazier: *The Negro in the United States*, is recent enough to contain mid-century data. Radical verdicts in the controversy over Negro rights are the President's Committee on Civil Rights: *To Secure These Rights* (New York, 1947); Robert K. Carr, ed.: "Civil Rights in America," *The Annals of the American Academy of Political and Social Science*, CCLXXV, 1–233 (May, 1951); "The American Negro and Civil Rights in 1950," *The Journal of Negro Education*, XX (Summer, 1951); "The Courts and Racial Integration in Education," *ibid.*, XXI (Summer, 1952).

The contemporary South is best revealed through periodicals and newspapers. Among the annuals are *The New International Year Book*, *Britannica Book of the Year*, *The Americana Annual*, and *The Negro Handbook*. Keen awareness of the regional problems is revealed by the *New York Times* and by Southern newspapers such as the *Richmond Times-Dispatch*, the *Arkansas Gazette*, the *Atlanta Journal*, and the *Dallas News*. Current events from different angles are summarized in *Time*, *The Journal of Negro Education*, and *Christian Century*. Thought-provoking articles in semipopular magazines are Mary H. Vorse: "The South Has Changed," *Harper's Magazine*, CXCIX, 27–33 (July, 1949); Eric Larrabee: "The Gulf South at Mid-Mourning," *ibid.*, CCIII, 35–42 (September, 1951); and Hodding Carter, "Southern Towns and Northern Industry," *The Atlantic Monthly*, CLXXXIV, 48–51 (November, 1949). More informative are George C. Stoney: "New Opportunities—in the New South," *Survey*, LXXXVII, 148–54 (April, 1951); James J. Parsons: "Recent Industrial Development in the Gulf South," *Geographical Review*, XL, 67–83 (January, 1950); Solomon Barking: "The Regional Significance of the Integration Movement in the Southern Textile Industry," *Southern Economic Journal*, XV, 395–41: (April, 1949); Frank T. De Vyver: "Labor Factors in the Industrial Development of the South," *ibid.*, XVIII, 189–205 (October, 1951); R. C. Weaver: "Negro Labor since 1929," *The Journal of Negro Education*, XIX, 20–28 (January, 1950); Harry E. Moore: "Mass Communications in the New South," *Social Forces*, XXIX, 365–76 (May, 1951); Carlton Ogburn: "Economic Trends in the South," *Georgia Review*, II, 399–405 (Winter, 1948); and Luther P. Jackson: "Race and Suffrage in the South since 1940," *The New South*, III (June–July, 1948).

Index

Index

A NOTE ON THE TYPE

This book was set on the Linotype in Janson, a recutting made direct from type cast in matrices made by Anton Janson some time between 1660 and 1687. This type is an excellent example of the influential and singularly sturdy Dutch types that prevailed in England prior to Caslon. It was from the Dutch types that Caslon developed his own incomparable designs.

The book was composed, printed, and bound by Kingsport Press, Inc., Kingsport, Tennessee.